I0643575

ON TO VICTORY

THE CANADIAN LIBERATION OF

THE NETHERLANDS,

MARCH 23—MAY 5, 1945

MARK ZUEHLKE

ON TO VICTORY

Douglas & McIntyre
VANCOUVER/TORONTO/BERKELEY

Douglas & McIntyre
An imprint of D&M Publishers Inc.
2323 Quebec Street, Suite 201
Vancouver BC Canada V5T 4S7
www.douglas-mcintyre.com

Cataloguing data available from Library and Archives Canada
ISBN 978-1-55365-430-8 (cloth)
ISBN 978-1-55365-619-7 (ebook)

Editing by Kathy Vanderlinden
Jacket and text design by Heather Pringle
Jacket photographs by Lieut. Dan Guravich/Canada Dept.
of National Defence/LAC/PA-137470 (top); Alexander M. Stirton/Canada Dept.
of National Defence/LAC/PA-134377 (bottom)
Maps by C. Stuart Daniel/Starshell Maps
Printed and bound in Canada by Friesens
Text printed on acid-free, FSC-certified, 100% post-consumer paper
Distributed in the U.S. by Publishers Group West

We gratefully acknowledge the financial support of the Canada Council
for the Arts, the British Columbia Arts Council, the Province of British Columbia through
the Book Publishing Tax Credit, and the Government of Canada

Mixed Sources
Cert no. SW-COC-001271
© 1996 FSC
FSC

My dear General, the German is whipped. We've got him. He is all through.

  —*Prime Minister Churchill to General Eisenhower, March 24, 1945*

You kept getting this news from home . . . And they'd say, it was practically over—sporadic fighting and . . . only pockets to be cleaned up. Some of them goddamn pockets were pretty tough.

  —*Don Fowle, Signaller, Lincoln and Welland Regiment*

A lot of Canadian soldiers have stories about liberating the Dutch. We were in Germany for all that time and never liberated anybody.

  —*4th Canadian Armoured Division Veteran*

Near the end of the war, nobody wanted to get killed.

  —*Lance Corporal Stuart Johns, Canadian Grenadier Guards*

[CONTENTS]

W HEN I EXPLAINED the time frame that *On to Victory* encompassed, Dr. Steve Harris at the Directorate of Heritage and History, Department of National Defence, in Ottawa commented that this would be a very different book from the others in the Canadian Battle Series. "No real major battles," he said, "just lots of minor, small actions." It was an opinion repeated often by other historians and even agreed to by some of the veterans involved in those battles. In his book tracing First Canadian Army's march across Northwest Europe from Normandy to victory, Terry Copp correctly pointed out that the events of April and May 1945 have been paid "slight attention" by Canadian historians. Perhaps, he speculated, the great battles of the preceding February and March in the Rhineland had exhausted historians and their assigned word counts just as they had badly worn down the Canadian soldiers who fought there. Whatever the reason, the last weeks of the war have been relegated almost to the status of endnotes in many histories.

On to Victory is the first major account detailing the experiences of First Canadian Army from the moment it joined in Operation Plunder—the forced crossing of the Rhine—through to war's end. Those last short weeks where each day's fighting brought the finish closer, and every death seemed crueller because so little war remained, proved to contain a story of far greater complexity than I had anticipated. Yes, there were many minor actions. But there were also battles of fierce and prolonged intensity. Repeatedly the Germans defended towns both small and large with grim determination. Most canals and river crossings also met strong resistance from an enemy that seemed unwilling to admit that their cause was lost, the ultimate defeat of their nation inevitable and close.

Often when historical events have been scantily told, part of the reason is a shortage of contemporary accounts. Hardly the case here, for in those last days First Canadian Army seemed to be stacking up accounts of its actions as quickly as it spent shells. I was blessed to find hundreds upon hundreds of pages of material, including war diaries, after-action reports, detailed summaries compiled shortly after the armistice, and regimental histories written in the months spent awaiting repatriation. Added to this, of course, were the many veteran accounts. From all these sources it was possible to put together an account of most military operations in which First Canadian Army was involved in the Netherlands and western Germany with remarkable detail and accuracy.

As before, I was struck by how veteran recollections of events accorded closely to the official accounts—each serving to inform the other in ways that assured clarity and fullness. Where a gap existed in the official records, veterans provided stories that added depth and continuity. When veterans were unsure of where or when a certain event occurred, the details could usually be ferreted out from the documented records.

Unfortunately, time is taking its toll on the men and women who fought in World War II. Each year the number passing on grows exponentially. There is little time left to gather the stories of those still able to tell them. If you know a veteran, either a friend or relative, please consider trying to record their experiences in one form or another. Then donate the material to an archive, museum, or other depository where it will be preserved for future researchers and generations.

The Canadian Battle Series is first and foremost a work of remembrance, intended to honour the experiences of a nation's soldiers during the most catastrophic war of modern history. By presenting the many battles they fought in a deeply detailed "you are there" style, I hope to enable readers of all ages to comprehend the reality of what those who are now old endured when they were young soldiers, wanting desperately to live and again see a world at peace.

ACKNOWLEDGEMENTS

THE RESEARCHING OF each Canadian Battle Series book results in new acquaintances and the renewing of relationships developed during work on titles past. In the latter category, I wish to thank veteran Charles Goodman, who again shared his experiences as a young signaller in the South Saskatchewan Regiment. A veteran in the former group is Gordie Bannerman, who provided much information on the Battle of Otterloo and also connected me to a Vancouver Island group of veterans who meet monthly for lunch. Other veterans also provided interviews or correspondence and are mentioned in the bibliography.

Ken MacLeod spent a great deal of time sorting through his taped interviews and transcripts to provide a wealth of personal stories. Rosalie Hartigan kindly provided her late husband's written account of 1st Parachute Battalion in Operation Varsity and granted me permission to quote from it.

A number of people played important roles during my research trip to the Netherlands. In Groesbeek, the charming and knowledgeable Marco Cillessen took time away from work and family to spend several days showing me in detail the Rhineland, Operation Plunder, and Operation Varsity battlegrounds. For the latter part of my travels in Holland, I acted as historian for Marilyn Minnes's

2009 Legacy Battlefield Tour of the Scheldt Estuary and Liberation campaigns. Two tour participants deserve special mention. Bernard Diepman was a young boy during the liberation, and he shared many memories of his experiences, as well as commenting on various aspects of the battles and the influence on events of Dutch geography, topography, and climate. Another Dutch-Canadian, Bert Perey, also helped shape my understanding of the influences of Dutch countryside and culture on the liberation story. Both were also just a lot of fun to be around. Tour driver and retired Canadian armoured regiment officer Mike Charrier was always happy to provide extensive briefings on the pluses and minuses of Canadian and German armour. Fortunately, there are countless Canadian Shermans serving as monuments throughout Holland to provide opportunities for hands-on examination. Mike also always had his hotel room open for Bernard, Bert, and me to drop in and continue discussions started during the day.

Nobody in Holland or elsewhere has contributed more to the research and writing of this book than my friend Johan van Doorn. We spent about three weeks retracing virtually the entire route that First Canadian Army took through the Netherlands and Germany during those last forty-eight days of the war. His knowledge of the campaign from the Canadian, Dutch, and German perspectives is encyclopedic, and thanks to his assistance I was able to see many areas of the battlefield I would otherwise never have visited. As anyone who has researched military campaigns knows, understanding why a battle played out as it did is greatly enhanced by being able to see the ground over which it was fought. Johan shared much material from his extensive archival collection. A dab hand at Excel spreadsheets, he also kept me on track during a frenetic Ottawa research trip where the hundreds of documents requiring consultation threatened to short-circuit this researcher's brain. Johan also carefully read the manuscript with an eye to making sure that the Dutch side of the story was correctly informed by the Dutch documentary record. Relationships like this are particularly special. Thanks, too, to Anneke, for letting him go off on a long trek and for opening their house to me for a considerable stretch of days.

Speaking of Ottawa, once again Dr. Steve Harris at the Directorate of Heritage and History, Department of National Defence smoothed the way for me to consult records there and came through on short notice with a vital and missing part of one of the AHQ histories. At the Canadian War Museum, Carol Reid was her enthusiastic and thorough self, providing me with various documents I otherwise would have missed. Special thanks must go to Paul Marsden at Library and Archives Canada for digging out and providing copies of documents missed in my visit there. Once again the Reginald Roy oral history project archive at the University of Victoria Special Collections was invaluable for yielding up more accounts by veterans, most of whom are no longer with us.

I would be remiss in not thanking Scott McIntyre of D&M Publishers for his continued support of the Canadian Battle Series. The publishing world in Canada is a difficult one, and his dedication to keeping the entire series in print and available to Canadians while supporting its continuation through publication of new titles is commendable. Kathy Vanderlinden stepped up to the plate again to undertake the tough job of editing the book on a very tight deadline. C. Stuart Daniel of Starshell Maps returned to make it cartographically possible to follow the movement of an army across a vast and complex landscape. My agent, Carolyn Swayze, continues to be a great advocate for my work and for keeping the financial and other business sides of things on track.

Finally, most special and sincere thanks to my partner, Frances Backhouse, who was endlessly supportive through the difficult and exhausting process of getting this book written. Every book is its own long campaign and this one proved more so than ever. Thanks again, love.

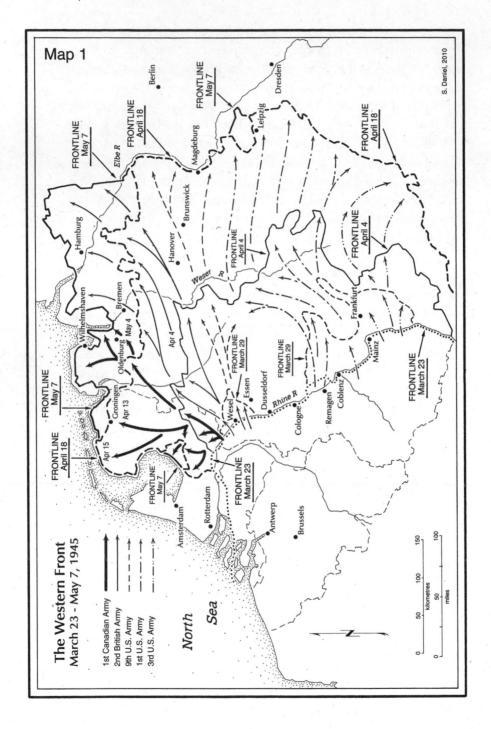

Map 1

The Western Front
March 23 - May 7, 1945

1st Canadian Army
2nd British Army
9th U.S. Army
1st U.S. Army
3rd U.S. Army

S. Daniel, 2010

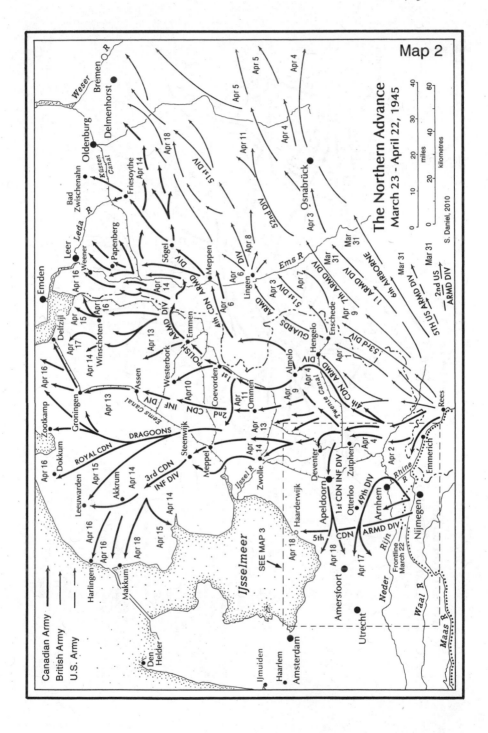

Map 2

The Northern Advance
March 23 - April 22, 1945

S. Daniel, 2010

Canadian Army
British Army
U.S. Army

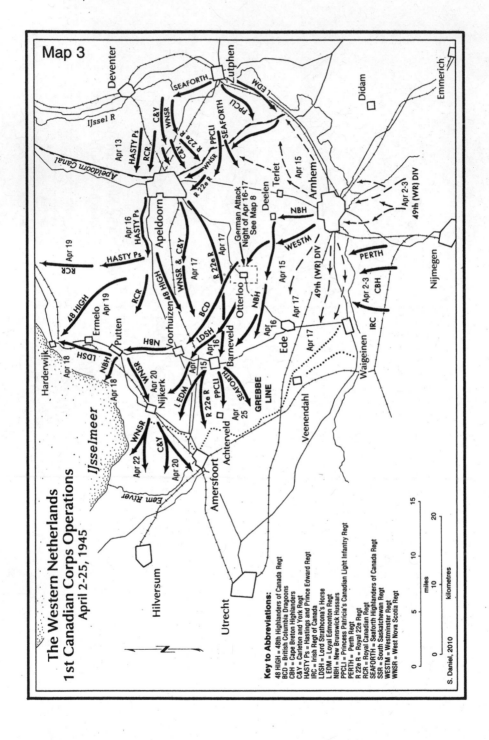

Map 3

The Western Netherlands
1st Canadian Corps Operations
April 2-25, 1945

Key to Abbreviations:

48 HIGH = 48th Highlanders of Canada Regt
BCD = British Columbia Dragoons
CBH = Cape Breton Highlanders
C&Y = Carleton and York Regt
HASTY Ps = Hastings and Prince Edward Regt
IRC = Irish Regt of Canada
LDSH = Lord Strathcona's Horse
L EDM = Loyal Edmonton Regt
NBH = New Brunswick Hussars
PPCLI = Princess Patricia's Canadian Light Infantry Regt
PERTH = Perth Regt
R 22e R = Royal 22e Regt
RCR = Royal Canadian Regt
SEAFORTH = Seaforth Highlanders of Canada Regt
SSR = South Saskatchewan Regt
WESTM = Westminster Regt
WNSR = West Nova Scotia Regt

S. Daniel, 2010

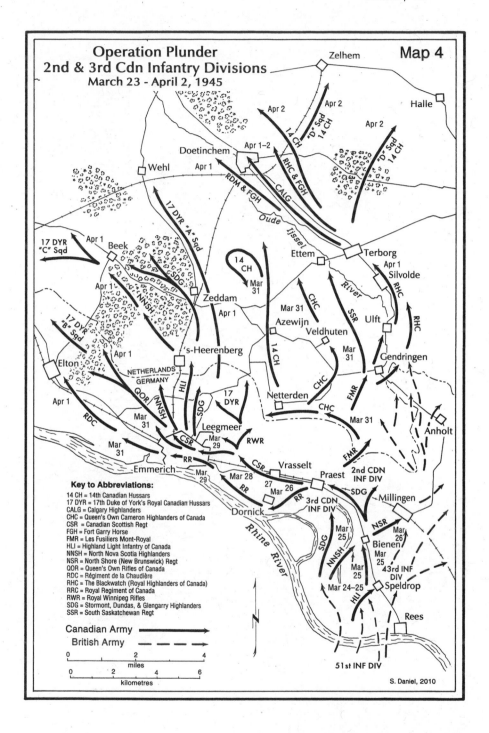

**Operation Plunder
2nd & 3rd Cdn Infantry Divisions**
March 23 - April 2, 1945

Map 4

Key to Abbreviations:
14 CH = 14th Canadian Hussars
17 DYR = 17th Duke of York's Royal Canadian Hussars
CALG = Calgary Highlanders
CHC = Queen's Own Cameron Highlanders of Canada
CSR = Canadian Scottish Regt
FGH = Fort Garry Horse
FMR = Les Fusiliers Mont-Royal
HLI = Highland Light Infantry of Canada
NNSH = North Nova Scotia Highlanders
NSR = North Shore (New Brunswick) Regt
QOR = Queen's Own Rifles of Canada
RDC = Régiment de la Chaudière
RHC = The Blackwatch (Royal Highlanders of Canada)
RRC = Royal Regiment of Canada
RWR = Royal Winnipeg Rifles
SDG = Stormont, Dundas, & Glengarry Highlanders
SSR = South Saskatchewan Regt

Canadian Army
British Army

0   2   4
miles
0   2   4   6
kilometres

S. Daniel, 2010

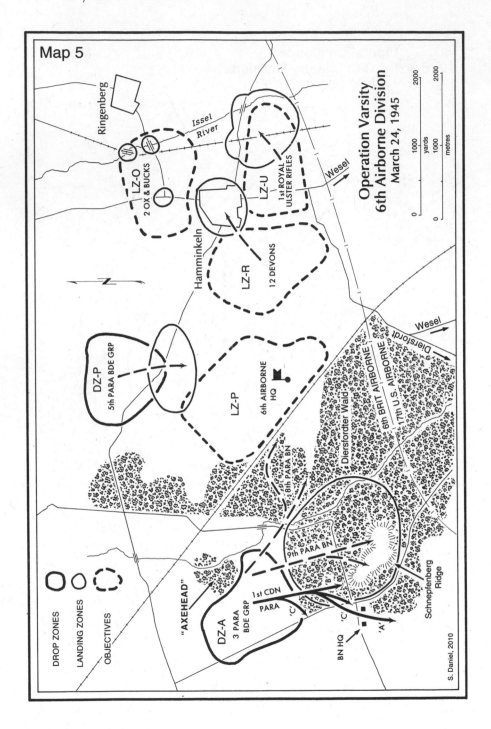

Map 5

Operation Varsity
6th Airborne Division
March 24, 1945

S. Daniel, 2010

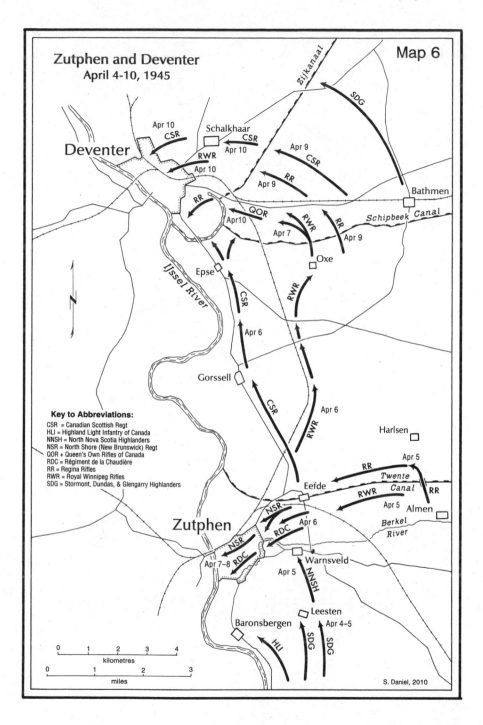

Zutphen and Deventer
April 4-10, 1945

Map 6

Key to Abbreviations:
CSR = Canadian Scottish Regt
HLI = Highland Light Infantry of Canada
NNSH = North Nova Scotia Highlanders
NSR + North Shore (New Brunswick) Regt
QOR = Queen's Own Rifles of Canada
RDC = Régiment de la Chaudière
RR = Regina Rifles
RWR = Royal Winnipeg Rifles
SDG = Stormont, Dundas, & Glengarry Highlanders

Deventer

Schalkhaar

Bathmen

Zijkanaal

Schipbeek Canal

Oxe

Epse

Ijssel River

Gorssell

Harlsen

Eefde

Twente Canal

Almen

Zutphen

Berkel River

Warnsveld

Baronsbergen

Leesten

kilometres
0 1 2 3 4

miles
0 1 2 3

S. Daniel, 2010

Apr 10 CSR
Apr 10 CSR
Apr 10 RWR
Apr 10 RR
Apr10 QOR
Apr 9 CSR
Apr 9 RR
SDG
Apr 7 RWR
Apr 9 RR
CSR Apr 6
RWR Apr 6
CSR Apr 6
RWR
Apr 5 RR
RWR Apr 5
RR
NSR
RDC Apr 6
NSR Apr 7–8 RDC
Apr 5
NNSH
Apr 4–5
HLI SDG SDG

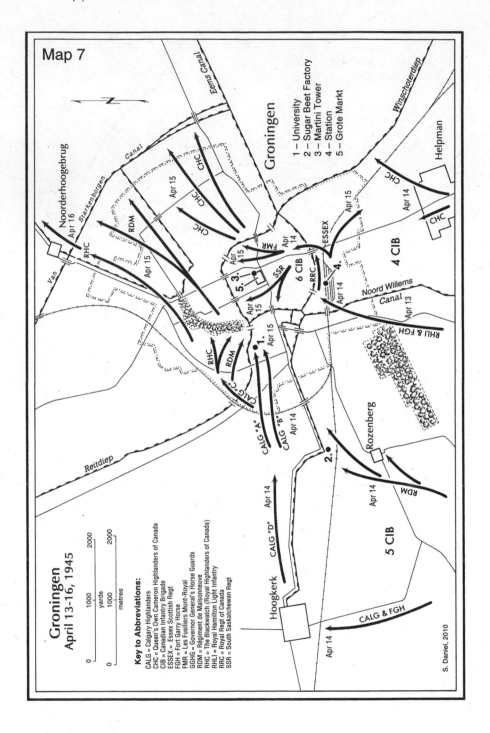

Map 7

Groningen
April 13-16, 1945

1 – University
2 – Sugar Beet Factory
3 – Martini Tower
4 – Station
5 – Grote Markt

Key to Abbreviations:

CALG = Calgary Highlanders
CHC = Queen's Own Cameron Highlanders of Canada
CIB = Canadian Infantry Brigade
ESSEX = Essex Scottish Regt
FGH = Fort Garry Horse
FMR = Les Fusiliers Mont-Royal
GGHG = Governor General's Horse Guards
RDM = Régiment de Maisonneuve
RHC = The Blackwatch (Royal Highlanders of Canada)
RHLI = Royal Hamilton Light Infantry
RRC = Royal Regt of Canada
SSR = South Saskatchewan Regt

S. Daniel, 2010

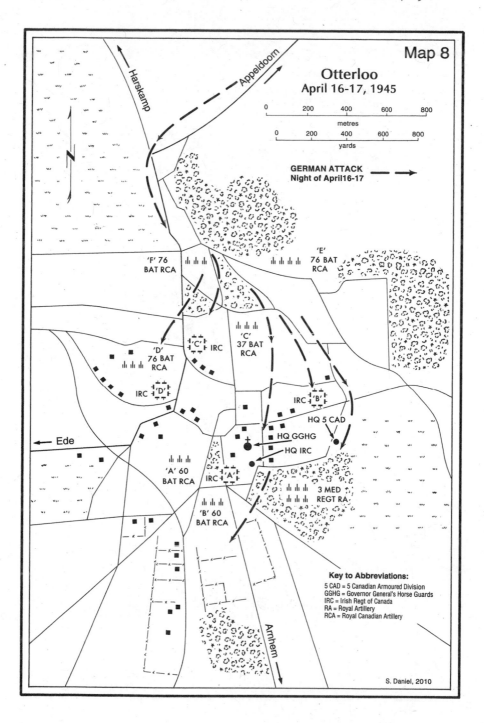

Map 8

Otterloo
April 16-17, 1945

GERMAN ATTACK
Night of April16-17

'F' 76 BAT RCA

'E' 76 BAT RCA

'C' IRC

'C' 37 BAT RCA

'D' 76 BAT RCA

IRC 'D'

IRC 'B'

HQ 5 CAD

HQ GGHG

HQ IRC

'A' 60 BAT RCA

IRC 'A'

3 MED REGT RA

'B' 60 BAT RCA

Harskamp

Appeldoorn

Ede

Arnhem

Key to Abbreviations:
5 CAD = 5 Canadian Armoured Division
GGHG = Governor General's Horse Guards
IRC = Irish Regt of Canada
RA = Royal Artillery
RCA = Royal Canadian Artillery

S. Daniel, 2010

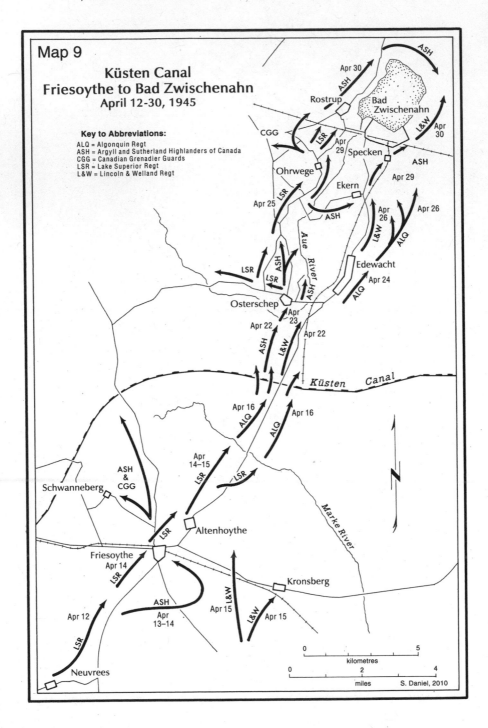

Map 9

Küsten Canal
Friesoythe to Bad Zwischenahn
April 12-30, 1945

Key to Abbreviations:
ALQ = Algonquin Regt
ASH = Argyll and Sutherland Highlanders of Canada
CGG = Canadian Grenadier Guards
LSR = Lake Superior Regt
L&W = Lincoln & Welland Regt

0   kilometres   5
0   2   miles   4
S. Daniel, 2010

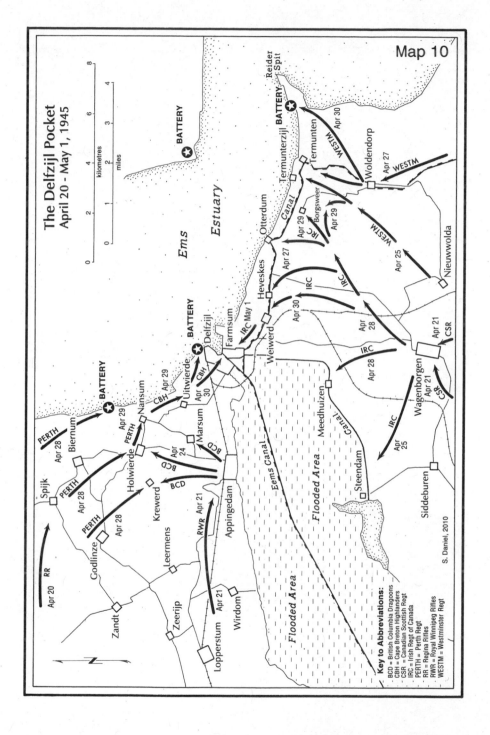

Map 10

The Delfzijl Pocket
April 20 - May 1, 1945

kilometres
miles

Ems   Estuary

BATTERY

BATTERY

Reider Spit

Termunterzijl BATTERY   Apr 30

Termunten

WESTM

Woldendorp   Apr 27

WESTM

Otterdum

Termunterzijl Canal

Borgsweer   Apr 29

IRC   Apr 29

Nieuwwolda

Apr 25

Heveskes

Apr 27

IRC

IRC

Apr 28

CSR   Apr 21

BATTERY

Delfzijl

Farmsum

IRC May 1

Weiwerd

Apr 30

IRC   Apr 28

Wagenborgen   Apr 21

CSR

Uitwierde   Apr 30   CBH

Nansum   CBH   Apr 29

BATTERY

Marsum   Apr 24

BCD

BCD

BCD

Biernum   Apr 29

PERTH   Apr 28

PERTH

PERTH

Holwierde

Krewerd

Meedhuizen

Steendam   Apr 25

IRC

Siddeburen

Spijk

PERTH   Apr 28

PERTH   Apr 28

Godlinze

Leermens

Krewerd

RWR   Apr 21

Appingedam

Eems Canal

Eems Canal

Flooded Area

Flooded Area

RR   Apr 20

Zandt

Zeerijp

Wirdom   Apr 21

Lopperstum

N

S. Daniel, 2010

Key to Abbreviations:
BCD = British Columbia Dragoons
CBH = Cape Breton Highlanders
CSR = Canadian Scottish Regt
IRC = Irish Regt of Canada
PERTH = Perth Regt
RR = Regina Rifles
RWR = Royal Winnipeg Rifles
WESTM = Westminster Regt

The Sweetest of Springs

AMSTERDAM, MAY 7, 1945

LESS THAN FORTY-EIGHT hours after the German surrender in the Netherlands and northwest Germany, the Princess Patricia's Canadian Light Infantry crammed aboard trucks, Bren carriers, and jeeps to roll out of Amersfoort at 0805 hours. The battalion was under orders to speed to Haarlem, and specifically the small village of Bloemendaal on its outskirts, to secure a large ammunition dump and weapons cache. The war was over, administrating the peace a pressing necessity.

Lieutenant Colonel R.P. "Slug" Clark had raced ahead at dawn to contact the German commander at Haarlem and arrange an orderly takeover. With only two companions, Clark approached a roadblock manned by "fully armed" Germans, who "seemed . . . extremely surprised to see an Allied vehicle passing through their fortification." Clark was relieved that the Germans had kept their arms shouldered.

As the jeep passed through Amsterdam "early in the morning, the city appeared to be deserted," until a couple of people appeared and "suddenly recognized an Allied vehicle. There were a few shouts, then heads began to pop out of windows. Before we got to the end of this long main street it seemed as though the whole population of the city was blocking our path . . . From all appearances no Allied soldiers had been along this main road from the south until my small party arrived." Clark would thereafter claim the PPCLI "was the first Allied force to enter Amsterdam."[1]

Amsterdam was ready and waiting when the PPCLI's main body arrived a couple of hours later. "The reception . . . was overwhelming," the battalion war diarist wrote. "Vehicles were completely covered with flowers—thousands of people lined the streets, screaming welcomes, throwing flowers, confetti and streamers, waving flags and orange pennants, and boarding vehicles. Never have so many happy people been seen at one time."[2]

All over Holland the same story was playing out, but nowhere more ecstatically than in the large cities of the Randstad region, which encompassed Amsterdam, Rotterdam, The Hague, Leiden, Haarlem, Hilversum, and Utrecht. This was the liberation. This was the time the Dutch would forever remember as the "sweetest of springs."

"Every village, street and house was bedecked with the red, white and blue Dutch flags and orange streamers, which in the brilliant sunlight made a gay scene," one PPCLI officer wrote. "The Dutch people lined the roads and streets in thousands to give us a great welcome. Wherever the convoy had to slow up for a road block or a bridge, hundreds of people waved, shouted and even fondled the vehicles. When the convoy reached the outskirts of Amsterdam it lost all semblance of a military column. A vehicle would be unable to move because of civilians surrounding it, climbing on it, throwing flowers, bestowing handshakes, hugs and kisses. One could not see the vehicle or trailer for legs, arms, heads and bodies draped all over it . . . Boy scouts as well as civilian police and resistance fighters had turned out in large numbers to attempt to control the crowds and to guide the vehicles to their destinations.

"The Dutch people whom we saw looked healthier than we expected to find them but most of them had sunken eyes betraying months of insufficient food. It was said that there were many thousands in Amsterdam not out to welcome us because they were too feeble from hunger to move into the streets."[3]

Late that Monday morning, a second column of Canadian troops wended its way through Amsterdam's crowds. These were the Seaforth Highlanders of Canada with a squadron of armoured cars driven by the Princess Louise's Dragoon Guards in support. All told, they numbered a thousand men, and their task was to garrison the capital city with its 800,000 people. Lieutenant Colonel Henry "Budge" Bell-Irving thought, "There must have been half a million people throwing beautiful flowers at us. An old lady, handing me a bunch of roses, said from the very bottom of her soul, 'Thank God, at last you've come.'"[4]

"Thousands upon thousands line the streets for four miles," Seaforth padre Roy Durnford scribbled in his diary. "Flowers—roses, tulips & every sort. Crowds load every vehicle including our RAP [Regimental Aid Post] jeep. I stand on running board. *Terrific welcome.* They tell in broken English with tears & unbridled joy how thankful they are to us. Children are lovely. Terrible shortage of food, 1/2 loaf bread, handful of potatoes per week. No fats, no tea, sugar, cocoa, firewood. Thousands of old people die. We camp in park... I rejoice today with the free."[5]

Vondelspark was soon fortified with barricades to keep the surging crowds at bay. The city's heart was an ideal spot for a small army camp. The Canadians hunkered down behind their barricades, knowing they had little or no control over the city. Even the still-armed Germans outnumbered them.

Their encampment was easily infiltrated. The garden gate of young Margriet Blaisse's family home connected the backyard to the park. Looking out the windows, the family watched the soldiers. Turning to Margriet, her father said, "Look, dear, I think the Canadians are in the park. Go over and see if you can talk to one of them." As Margriet dashed out, her father called to her, "Whatever you do, don't fall in love with any of them. They're all going back to Canada and you're staying right here in Amsterdam!"

The first Canadian Margriet set eyes on was tall and slender. She approached boldly. "My parents would be thrilled if you could come to the house, so we can thank you for the liberation. We live right here in the park."

Lieutenant Wilf Gildersleeve smiled, introduced himself, and then called to his platoon. "Hey, fellas, we're going to have a drink or something."

"I came back with twenty Canadians. My parents couldn't believe it. They were all sitting on the balcony laughing, crying, and talking, and the whole bit. Then they left again. In the evening, we still had no electricity, no light, no bell. We heard knocking on the front door. So my mother said to me, 'Go and see who's knocking.'

"I went downstairs, opened the door, and there was Wilf with a friend. Wilf was dressed in a kilt with his arms full of bread and butter and cheese and ham, and I yelled to my mother, 'Two men in skirts,' because I had never seen a fellow in a kilt before. They came in and watched us eat. Oh, my gosh, we ate so much that evening."[6]

ROTTERDAM, MAY 7, 1945

IN THEIR BEST clothes, hair as neatly styled as possible, twenty-one-year-old Wilhelmina Klaverdijk and her nineteen-year-old sister walked downtown. Rumour held that the Canadians had come. In the parking lot of the sprawling Lever Brothers factory, hundreds of soldiers were piling out of large military trucks and milling about in ragged groups. Wilhelmina had only seen German soldiers, who all wore fine uniforms and were well built. In their rumpled and stained khaki, the Canadians looked shabby by comparison. But they were the liberators, the men who had brought freedom to Rotterdam. "See all those soldiers there," Wilhelmina told her sister, "I'm going to kiss all these guys." Striding into their midst without a backward glance, she threw her arms around a soldier. "Thank you for liberating me," she said, before giving him a big kiss.

Wilhelmina was not alone. Hundreds of young women thronged the Canadians with the same mission in mind. "We kissed so many soldiers that day. We did it all that day and the next."[7]

NIJMEGEN, MAY 7, 1945

AT 1ST CANADIAN General Hospital in Nijmegen, Acting Principal Matron Lieutenant Evelyn Pepper at first found it difficult to believe the ceasefire announcement issued on the evening of May 4. "Exultation among the nursing staff was slightly delayed," Pepper remembered, and they were bemused when the "people in Nijmegen flooded into the streets, dancing and singing, and making huge bonfires. They were burning the blackout windows they didn't need anymore. Their doors were opened wide for Canadians to come in and join the celebration. Some of our boys certainly enjoyed the invitation."

But the nurses "could not believe that the message was true. Casualties were still coming to the hospital. Our hospital was well filled. We were all very busy. In retrospect, we were probably in a mild shock. Our thinking cleared, however, on May 7 when a Cease Fire affecting all troops in Europe was issued and VE-Day announced, on May 8, 1945, by Prime Minister Winston Churchill. The long stream of battle casualties had finally ended. As we celebrated that night, a deep sense of relief and quiet thankfulness stirred in our hearts. The war in Europe was over."[8]

NORTH OF OLDENBURG, GERMANY, MAY 7, 1945

"THERE ARE NO boisterous victory celebrations on this north German plain. It is enough to relish the deep relief and gratitude that the fighting is over and that you have survived," Captain George Blackburn of the 4th Canadian Field Regiment wrote. "There is an unreal, aimless quality to these first few days.[9]

Before the ceasefire announcement came at 2200 hours on May 4 with its accompanying order for the Canadians in Germany to stand down, they had been bracing for another day's fighting. Major George Cassidy, commanding 'D' Company of the Algonquin Regiment, was teeing up an attack on a nearby wood, although rumours had been flying about an imminent armistice and Cassidy dreaded committing his men to a last battle. A signaller in the company Bren carrier handed him a message flimsy. By "the dim dash bulb light of the carrier" Cassidy glanced at the paper and "the words seemed to dance" before his eyes: 'Stand down. All offensive action will cease until further notice.'

"Down the road, the tanks, motors rumbling throatily, were crowded with men waiting to ride up to a battle that was not to come off. How appropriate to walk down the column in the gathering darkness and to give, with more meaning than it ever had before the old 'washout' signal. 'Climb down, lads. It's all over. All over.'

"Cheers? None. Emotion? Not visible, at any rate. In a few moments the tanks were churning off the road into a laager, the men were digging in in a soggy field of rich, black earth. In the distance the guns of our artillery were still growling away. Here there was no sound but the clink of the shovels, the soft murmurs of voices. Stealthily, gently, the rain began to fall."[10]

That same morning, in a cold drizzle, 3rd Canadian Infantry Division's Highland Light Infantry had forced a crossing over a German canal southwest of Timmel in assault boats. Meeting only token resistance, the battalion headed for West Grosse. They encountered few Germans, and these happily surrendered their arms. At 1720 hours, they entered West Grosse unopposed and received a wireless signal. "Firm up your present area, accept no casualties, and do not engage in any unnecessary action. Do not use artillery if it can be avoided."[11]

BBC radio soon broadcast that "all German forces in North West Germany, Holland, and Denmark would capitulate at 0800 hours" the next morning. From that moment on, "a strange atmosphere prevailed, everybody appeared happy and relieved but no mood for rejoicing developed," the HLI's war diarist recorded. Morale, he added, was "good and rising."[12]

This was not, however, the unqualified "100%" morale rating he had remarked on that early morning of March 23, 1945, when the men of the HLI had been the first Canadians to cross the Rhine River as part of Twenty-First Army Group's great assault into the heart of Germany. Operation Plunder, as the battle for a bridgehead across the Rhine had been code-named, had initiated an Allied advance that had continued without pause until the ceasefire of May 4.[13]

Forty-three days, start to end. In between, each day had dawned with the soldiers knowing there was a chance this could be the last. It might also be the day they fell wounded or dying. The odds of surviving unscathed grew more remote with every added day of battle. When Brigadier John "Rocky" Rockingham had attempted to rally the ranks of the HLI and other two battalions under his command with the declaration that being first to cross the Rhine would "add further glory to [9th Canadian Infantry Brigade's] name," the words had rung hollow. Glory mattered little now. The men approached war instead with the workmanlike professionalism of veterans who had seen too many battles and knew more must follow, until finally Germany surrendered. Those under its heel—particularly the millions of Dutch in the occupied Netherlands—would only then be free.

PART ONE

OVER THE RHINE, THEN, LET US GO

1

No Possibility of Doubt

"**T**HOSE ARE THE kinds of things that make you an old man," Brigadier Stanley Todd thought, as he meticulously worked through the minutiae of his current artillery fire plan. So many variables, so many possibilities for error, for an overlooked detail to cost Allied lives.[1] On Todd's shoulders lay much of the responsibility for the largest and most complex artillery program the western Allies had ever fired. As II Canadian Corps's artillery commander, Todd was responsible for half of the 3,500 field, medium, and heavy guns supporting Operation Plunder.[2]

The artillery-firing plan was just one piece of an intricate puzzle that included devising a scheme to sneak all the gun regiments assigned to II Canadian Corps's sector into position unseen by the German observers on the Rhine's opposite bank.[3] There were "so many guns," Todd thought at first, "that we didn't have enough real estate to put them on." Methodically, he and his staff had sketched positions on the maps from Kleve eastward to just short of Wissel, checked the ground, and determined where each and every gun could be sited and hidden.[4]

II Canadian Corps and the XXX British Corps to its right held a stretch of the Rhine overlooked by higher ground on the German side. Hoch Elten—a 270-foot wooded ridge to the west of Emmerich and almost opposite Kleve—provided the Germans with a bird's-eye view while concealing them within the trees. The forest rendered their own guns invisible to the British 2nd Tactical Air Force fighter-bombers hunting them.

To blind the observers on the heights, First Canadian Army used smoke generators to cloak the river shore and ground behind throughout the buildup to Operation Plunder. Gradually, as Second British Army had come up alongside the Canadians, this screen had been widened. Newspaper reporters declared it a "man-made sixty-six mile long fog." Knowing that a sudden lift of the smokescreen on the day of the attack to enable the Allied artillery to find their targets would alert the Germans, the Canadians had the smoke generators roar and spew their clouds on some days and on others lie silent. During these "no-smoke" days, preparations for the offensive lessened, so that the front looked idle.[5] When the generators fired up again, men and machines moved at a furious pace.

The gunners particularly depended on the smoke. Lieutenant Colonel Roland Humphreys Webb first saw 12th Canadian Field Regiment's assigned position immediately east of Wissel on March 11.[6] "Scarcely any cover," he grumbled.[7] The "position would have been impossible had there been no smoke screen along the length of the Rhine," he wrote, and only if it was maintained until the guns went into action could "the area be considered suitable."[8] Captain Thomas Bell was less sure of its suitability. "Our proposed gun position was within small arms and mortar range of the enemy. The future did not look too promising!"[9]

Because of the no-smoke days, gun pits could not be dug, since the disturbed earth would be a telltale sign. Instead, when the guns were brought up under cover of smoke, they were carefully scattered "behind buildings and hedges." Even with the cover, men visited their gun areas only on foot to prevent leaving any vehicle tracks in the soft earth.[10]

The 7th Canadian Medium Regiment's position was about a mile back from Wissel and next to the hamlet of Till. Captain A.M. Lockwood considered the smokescreen "a very remarkable thing. Thousands of canisters were kept burning." Behind it, the regiment moved into place two hundred shells for each of its sixteen 5.5-inch guns. There was nothing discreet about a medium gun. Each weighed 5.5 tons, had to be towed by a six-ton tractor, and required a ten-man crew. Its shells weighed seventy-nine pounds each and could range out 11.25 miles, with the gunners capable of firing two rounds a minute.

All the artillery regiments stowed their ammunition and vehicles in barns or carefully camouflaged under netting in farmyards. They worked in a land devoid of civilian life, for the Germans had been forcibly evacuated from the farms, villages, and towns. Military police maintained an exclusion area that stretched back two miles from the river shore.[11]

Through the long, lingering winter, the gunners had been mired in mud—first on the Maas and then during the Rhineland Campaign, which had won the ground where they now worked. Suddenly on March 21, the first day of spring, the muck disappeared, and they returned to "the dust-choking days of Caen and Falaise."[12] Towing the medium guns to their final hiding positions, Lockwood saw other reminders of those dry summer days in Normandy after the invasion. Provost officers directing traffic at each road intersection looked the same as then, "caked in muddy sweat, with black bushy eyebrows and a rim of dust around their goggles." Again smoke saved the day, concealing the great dust clouds that billowed up behind the hundreds of vehicles plying the roads, laden with everything that had to be brought up to the river before the start of the great offensive—one that transcended any in size and complexity that Twenty-First Army Group had carried out since the D-Day invasion itself.[13]

EVEN BEFORE THE Rhineland Battle had ended on March 11, with First Canadian Army's southward advance meeting the northeasterly drive of Ninth U.S. Army's xvi Corps at Wesel, the Allied command had been planning to cross the Rhine. Fed by alpine glaciers in eastern Switzerland, the 820-mile-long Rhine descends between Austria and Liechtenstein, serves as the border between much of Germany and France, and enters German territory before splitting west of

Emmerich into several branches in the Netherlands and draining into the sea. This latter stretch is a study in confusion, with the various arms undergoing rapid name changes and running off in different directions in their seaward quest.

On September 17, 1944, Field Marshal Bernard Law Montgomery had learned the hard way how this maze of rivers west of Emmerich could defeat grand military ambitions. Seeking to bring the war to a rapid end with a deep penetration into the German industrial heartland, Montgomery's Operation Market Garden had dropped three airborne divisions to capture a series of strategically vital bridges across these rivers, while the British xxx Corps carried out a sixty-mile-long dash up a narrow highway to relieve each in turn.

An intricate plan in which every phase had to succeed with clockwork precision, Market Garden began to unravel almost immediately as one setback followed another. Out on the tip of the spear at Arnhem, the 1st British Airborne Division had dropped to seize the rail and road bridges over the Neder Rijn, as this stretch of the Rhine was known. These crossings were Market Garden's ultimate prize, the bridges enabling Second British Army to plunge deep into Germany's heart. Despite heroic attempts, the British paratroops failed to capture the bridges and were instead surrounded by a superior German force within the city. Lacking the bridges, xxx Corps was unable to reach the embattled paratroops. On September 25, Montgomery accepted failure and ordered the paratroops to evacuate their position. By this time, only about 2,500 of the 10,000 dropped remained in the fight. A total of 2,163 were successfully evacuated by engineers manning a flotilla of small boats in the darkness. Many of these engineers had been Canadians, men of the 10th, 20th, and 23rd Field Companies, Royal Canadian Engineers—involved because their large motorized storm boats had greater capacity than anything the British possessed.

With Market Garden's failure, Montgomery had realized—as did Supreme Headquarters Allied Expeditionary Force (SHAEF) commander General Dwight G. Eisenhower—that the best place to cross the Rhine was north of the Ruhr, between Emmerich and Wesel. Montgomery argued that there should be only one Allied attempt on the Rhine and that it must be his to command. Eisenhower, however, favoured establishing a second bridgehead more than a hundred miles upstream between Mainz and Karlsruhe, because having two crossings would render the Ruhr industrial zone vulnerable on two flanks and also position the Allies well for armoured breakouts into Germany's heart.

The British objected, fearing that the dispersion of resources and manpower would jeopardize success. By this stage of the war, the difference of opinion was tiresomely predictable. Repeatedly the British had advocated concentration of strength while the Americans favoured overwhelming the Germans with operations across a broad front. Eisenhower's temperament and training inclined him to favour the American position so ardently presented by both Twelfth U.S. Army Group's General Omar Bradley and his Third Army's General George S. Patton. But the Supreme Commander could not simply dismiss the British, particularly as Montgomery was backed by the Chief of the Imperial General Staff, General Sir Alexander Brooke, and Prime Minister Winston Churchill. Consequently, Eisenhower sought compromise. With the Americans still closing on the Rhine, he agreed that Montgomery could proceed first with Plunder and promised the resources to enable its launching "with maximum strength and complete determination."[14]

Scheduled for March 31, Plunder was advanced by a week. On March 9, Montgomery convened a meeting of his army commanders—First Canadian Army's General Harry Crerar, Second British Army's General Miles Dempsey, and the U.S. Ninth Army's Lieutenant General William H. Simpson—at his headquarters in Venlo, Holland. The Ninth Army had been seconded from Bradley's command to Montgomery's during the February Rhineland Campaign. For Plunder, it was reinforced by stripping Patton of his 95th Infantry Division and five artillery battalions.

It is unlikely that any other American general was better suited to serve under Montgomery than Simpson. A tall man, who shaved his hair to the skull, Simpson possessed a self-deprecating wit that fit well with the British temperament. The fifty-six-year-old sought at every turn to mesh seamlessly into the British command structure, despite the fact that most Americans found both Montgomery and his staff arrogant and idiosyncratic.[15]

Montgomery came to the meeting with a well-devised plan courtesy of Dempsey and his Second Army staff. While the Canadians and Americans had been winning the Rhine's west bank, Dempsey had worked out how to "isolate the northern and eastern faces of the Ruhr from the rest of Germany." At forty-eight, Dempsey was a highly experienced soldier who had entered the army in 1915 after graduating from Sandhurst Military Academy and won a Military Cross while serving with the Royal Berkshire Regiment in the Great War. In 1940, he had led the 13th Infantry Brigade through to its evacuation at Dunkirk, garnering a Distinguished Service Order. Dempsey first served under Montgomery in North Africa, commanding the Eighth Army's XIII Corps, and subsequently played a key role in planning the July 1943 invasion of Sicily. In January 1944, Dempsey returned to Britain to command Second British Army. Montgomery considered him a "first class" army commander, whose loyalty to the field marshal and his opinions was beyond question.[16]

Montgomery's relationship with his third army general had always been more fractious. Harry Crerar had served Montgomery briefly as commander of I Canadian Corps in Italy before assuming command of First Canadian Army. Each man's personal style and temperament grated on the other. Fifty-six-year-old Crerar was fussy about proper dress, a stickler for detailed and extensively written operational plans, and a prickly Canadian nationalist. He was also shy and retiring. Montgomery dressed casually, preferred terse and often orally delivered operating instructions, and was an outspoken, shameless self-promoter. In Italy, Montgomery had concluded that Crerar had no idea how to fight a corps and appeared to think the same of the man's handling of an army, even after his most capable performance during the Rhineland Campaign. Eisenhower had taken note, however, extending personal "admiration" for how Crerar "conducted the attack."[17]

Lieutenant General Sir Brian Horrocks, who had served under Crerar as commander of the British XXX Corps, thought the Canadian "much underrated, largely because he was the exact opposite to

Montgomery. He hated publicity, but was full of common sense and always prepared to listen to the views of his subordinate commanders . . . I grew to like him very much, though, I am afraid I must have been a terrible pain in his neck, for during part of this long-drawn-out battle I was feeling unwell . . . The outward and visible sign was that I became extremely irritable and bad-tempered, yet Crerar bore with me very patiently."[18]

Command was taking its toll on Crerar. He had visibly aged during the Rhineland Campaign. Always a heavy smoker, he was now smoking more cigarettes than ever. The resulting hacking cough was so bad his batman moved out of the general's caravan.[19]

At least one of his subordinates emerged from the Rhineland Campaign convinced that Crerar should no longer command the army. Major General Dan Spry thought Crerar "too old for it and [that] a lot of his thinking was back in 1917–1918. He didn't get along with Monty . . . My own feeling was that, although I liked the man and never had any difficulty with him . . . at his age, and compared to Guy [Simonds]—who was really on top of the situation—[we] might have been better served with Guy in command."[20]

Spry liked the forty-one-year-old 11 Canadian Corps commander despite acknowledging that he could be "icy cold." When angered, Simonds would not shout or become agitated. Instead, his jaw set, his eyes glinted, and his words and manner left "no doubt what he wanted. [He was] very straightforward, determined. He ranked with Monty, way above most." Although Spry found Crerar an able enough manager, it was Simonds, he thought, who really commanded. "Lots of corps and [divisional] plans were Guy's. [He then] got Crerar's okay."[21]

Simonds's meteoric rise from major to lieutenant general in just three and a half years had led many to think he would replace Crerar. Indeed, Crerar's evacuation to England in September 1944 with jaundice had resulted in Simonds leading the army through the Scheldt Estuary Campaign and raised expectations that he would retain command. Certainly Montgomery had lobbied for this. However, Crerar had returned in November and been promoted to the rank of full general.[22]

BY THE TIME Montgomery convened his March 9 meeting, the Rhine assault plan was well massaged. The general intention, Montgomery told his three army commanders, was to "cross the Rhine north of the Ruhr and secure a firm bridgehead, with a view to developing operations to isolate the Ruhr and to penetrate deeper into Germany." Two armies—the Second British and U.S. Ninth—would force the crossing between Rees and Rheinberg. On the left, Second Army would cross with its XXX Corps in the area of Rees, while XII Corps struck near Wesel. Right of Wesel, the Ninth would protect Second Army's flank with crossings at two points along its six-mile frontage from Wesel to Rheinberg.

The primary thrust would be delivered by Second Army's XII Corps at Wesel because this town, with a pre-war population of about 24,000, was a vital rail and road communication hub. Once a lodgement here was secure, XXX Corps would expand the bridgehead northward, so the Rhine could be bridged at Emmerich. The Americans would meanwhile widen the bridgehead southward.[23]

To hasten the expansion, there would be a massive drop by airborne troops. Code-named Operation Varsity, this airborne phase would see XVIII U.S. Airborne Corps—comprising the 6th British and 17th U.S. Airborne Divisions—land about five miles north of Wesel to seize various heights, crossroads, and bridges over the Issel River, a tributary flowing from the east into the IJssel River. These actions by the paratroops would deny the Germans excellent artillery observation points and also block the movement of reinforcements along the main routes running to Wesel from the east.[24]

This would be the third major airborne operation of the Northwest Europe campaign, but it differed greatly from those before it. For D-Day and Market Garden, the paratroops had dropped before the sea landings or ground assault. This time they would jump after the Rhine was crossed. Market Garden, particularly the disaster of Arnhem, had shown that paratroops should not be deployed too far from their objectives or from the ground forces that were to relieve them. Nor should they be landed in packets at widely spaced time intervals. For Varsity, the paratroops and glider-borne troops would land in rapid succession and within close striking distance of their objectives. As it had during the D-Day landings, 1st Canadian Parachute Battalion would land as part of the British division's 3rd Parachute Brigade.

The Canadian paratroops would not, however, be the first Canadians across the Rhine. This honour would go to 3rd Canadian Infantry Division's 9th Brigade, which was attached to xxx Corps. Due to the narrow frontage for Plunder, rather than to Montgomery's lack of confidence in Crerar, First Canadian Army would play no immediate role.

Organizationally, Twenty-First Army Group was highly flexible. During the Rhineland Campaign, xxx Corps was under First Canadian Army command. Now, 11 Canadian Corps shifted to Second Army, with its 3rd Division being directly under xxx Corps command. Moreover, this division's 9th Brigade was placed under the control of Major General Thomas Rennie's 51st Highland Division, and its Highland Light Infantry battalion further assigned to go into the attack under command of that unit's 154th Brigade. The intention was to ensure that 9 CIB would pass quickly over the Rhine and spearhead a "rapid build-up of Canadian forces east of the Rhine, initially under British command." Once the brigade was all inside the bridgehead, it would thrust towards Emmerich, followed by the rest of 3rd Division and ultimately as much of 11 Canadian Corps as might be required to clear the area there—particularly the high, overlooking Hoch Elten feature. When this area was secure, First Canadian Army would commence bridging operations in front of Emmerich. Upon completion, 11 Corps would revert to its command and the Canadians would advance towards the IJssel River, slipping into Holland through the back door, rather than attacking the German defences guarding its southern approaches.

Crerar and his staff remained responsible for holding a long defensive line that stretched from Emmerich to the sea and included a threatened bridgehead over the Waal at Nijmegen.[25] They also had a major administrative role in overseeing "the build-up of ammunition and engineer stores . . . for the only way into the area between the rivers was over First [Canadian] Army's heavily laden and already sagging road system."[26] 11 Canadian Corps staff was also deeply engaged in teeing up the provision of supporting artillery and engineers to XXX Corps.

Another challenge facing First Canadian Army was to integrate a new corps into its midst. In 1943, in a phased movement that began with 1st Canadian Infantry Division's attachment to Eighth Army for the Sicily invasion, 1 Canadian Corps had been transferred from Great Britain to Italy. By early 1944, the corps was complete in Italy with two divisions under command, the 1st Division and 5th Canadian Armoured Division.

There had been a general understanding that the Canadian deployment to Italy was temporary—intended to give the army needed combat experience before its commitment to the Normandy invasion and simultaneously assuage public demands at home that the nation's soldiers should be blooded, as had been its airmen and sailors. But once in Italy, the British high command had been disinclined to bring 1 Canadian Corps back to Britain. Such a movement would have necessitated replacing the corps with a British one. It would have also required vital shipping at a time when all such resources were required for the buildup to the Normandy invasion and subsequent support of operations on the continent. So the Canadians had been left in place, marching with Eighth Army slowly up the Italian boot.

There they would likely have remained had it not been for a Combined Chiefs of Staff decision at the Malta Conference of January 30–February 2, 1945. Much discussion had focused on strategic priorities, and of key import to the Canadians was the decision that "the right course of action was to reinforce the decisive western front at the expense of the Mediterranean Theatre." Suddenly, Italy became a backwater from which it was possible to remove "up to five" Canadian and British divisions.

1 Canadian Corps received immediate instructions to prepare for a transfer, with 5th Division and corps headquarters shipping out in February from Leghorn to Marseilles and then travelling overland to Belgium. By mid-March, 1st Canadian Armoured Brigade completed the journey. As First Canadian Army readied for its role in Plunder, 1st Division was en route and scheduled for operational deployment on April 3.

Crerar welcomed the new corps at the end of March, citing his farewell address in Italy when he had predicted that "we, Canadians, would all meet again, somewhere in Europe, when the Armies of the United Nations converged, and the job we came over here to do was about to be accomplished. Well, the prophecy has come true—and no soldier in the First Canadian Army can be more elated at this situation than I, myself, am. The 1 Canadian Corps returns to the Canadian Army, with a magnificent fighting record, first established in Sicily by the 1 Canadian Division and fully maintained by other formations of the Corps as all, later, fought their way through Italy. We are all very proud of what you have accomplished and it is simply great to get together again. And, now that we are all together, let us all speed to the victory in no uncertain manner."[27]

AS THE CANADIANS regrouped, the behemoth that was Plunder lumbered towards its launch. Between Emmerich and Wesel, the fast-flowing Rhine stretched to a width of 1,500 feet—a formidable obstacle to bridge even in peacetime. To undertake the task, likely under German observed artillery and mortar fire, XXX Corps alone was assigned 8,000 engineers. These were supplied with 22,000 tons of assault bridging that included 25,000 wooden pontoons, 2,000 assault boats, 650 larger storm boats, and 120 river tugs. Eighty miles of balloon cable and 260 miles of steel wire were trucked to the Rhine's banks.[28]

To avoid gridlock on the fragile and limited road system, a complex schedule was developed that ensured that the hundreds of trucks groaning under the weight of bridging supplies "lined up in correct order and plans were all made so that the right material would arrive at the right point at the right time," observed 6th Field Company, Royal Canadian Engineers, Company Quartermaster Sergeant Samuel Alexander Flatt. "The usual Hollywood words, such as *colossal, stupendous* and *unbelievable,* would be of little use in describing the situation as seen here. Nothing had been left to chance and a timetable had been worked out that reminded us of the detailed planning for the 'D' Day assault."[29]

No less colossal and far more destructive in the lead-up to Plunder was the air support, which a Canadian Army historical officer described as "gigantic." Bombing operations by the Royal Air Force and U.S. Army Air Force started in early February to gradually isolate the Ruhr by destroying eighteen bridges on the most important routes leading to the area from central Germany. By the time Plunder's commencement was imminent, only three or four of these bridges still stood, and those that did had suffered damage. In early March, Bomber command had begun "going all out" to cripple the German transportation network to the rear of the battle area with attacks on targets in Germany and Holland.[30] Over three weeks, Allied bombers dumped 31,635 tons of explosives into the area.[31]

A third phase of bombing immediately before Plunder aimed to "reduce the enemy's will to fight, to hinder his defensive preparations, and to disrupt his communications. To this end, key crossroad towns of Haldern, Isselburg, Anholt, and Praest—each little more than ten miles back of the river from Rees and Wesel—were slated for destruction. Haldern and Praest were targeted on D minus 1, the other two to be struck at first light on D-Day.

The fourth phase of aerial operations aimed to seize and maintain air superiority over the assault area and the airborne force's drop and landing zones. Allied air commanders worried that the Luftwaffe would challenge Allied mastery of the skies with the new jet-propelled fighter and fighter-bombers the Germans had recently brought into action. Consequently, beginning on D minus 3 and running through to D-Day, Eighth U.S. Army Air Force pounded airfields within range of the assault area with fourteen hundred planes. At the same time, 2nd Tactical Air Force's Spitfires and Typhoons and planes of the U.S. Eighth Fighter Command cast a thick carpet over the area to interdict any German jets that might sneak in. Inside the assault area, fighter-bombers also struck at known German anti-aircraft gun positions and other identified targets that could threaten the landings. Once Plunder began and Allied forces were across the Rhine, air support was to be constantly available to engage any targets identified by air or artillery forward observation officers operating with the advancing troops.[32]

Added to all the explosives being dropped on the Germans from the skies would be those hurled by the artillery once Plunder began on March 23. Besides the almost 3,500 guns supporting the Second British Army, Ninth U.S. Army had 2,070 guns ready. Both armies had complex fire plans that "included counter-battery preparation, to prevent the enemy shelling our forming-up areas and crossing places, counter-mortar tasks, a preliminary bombardment to lower the defenders' morale...harassing fire and a smoke screen." xxx Corps had the direct support of the divisional artillery regiments of the Guards and 11th Armoured Divisions, the 3rd British, 3rd Canadian, 43rd (Wessex), and 51st (Highland) Infantry Divisions, as well as three Army Groups of Royal Artillery (including the 2nd Canadian Group) and the xxx Corps Troops Royal Artillery. All 11 Canadian Corps artillery not directly supporting the crossing would fire diversionary plans on their flanks to create confusion about whether other assaults might be coming in those sectors.[33]

The complete assault plan, combining aerial and artillery bombardments, multiple crossings along an extended front, and airborne landings behind the Germans dug into the bank of the Rhine, was— as Chester Wilmot, a thirty-three-year-old Australian correspondent for the BBC, understatedly put it—"elaborate."[34]

On the Friday morning of May 23, Montgomery issued a message to all the troops of Twenty-First Army Group. Referring to his earlier message at the beginning of the Rhineland Campaign, he said: "On the 7th February I told you we were going into the ring for the final and last round; there would be no time limit; we would continue fighting until our opponent was knocked out."

Now, he said, "the enemy has lost the Rhineland, and with it the flower of at least four armies—the Parachute Army, Fifth Panzer Army, Fifteenth Army, and Seventh Army; the First Army, further to the South is now being added to the list. In the Rhineland battles, the enemy has lost about 150,000 prisoners, and there are many more to come: his total casualties amount to about 250,000 since 8th February.

"In the East, the enemy has lost all of Pomerania east of the Oder, an area as large as the Rhineland; and three more German armies have been routed. The Russian armies are within about 35 miles of Berlin.

"Overhead, the Allied Air Forces are pounding Germany day and night. It will be interesting to see how much longer the Germans can stand it.

"The enemy has been driven into a corner, and he cannot escape. Events are moving rapidly. The complete and decisive defeat of the Germans is certain; there is no possibility of doubt on this matter.

"21 ARMY GROUP WILL NOW CROSS THE RHINE. The enemy possibly thinks he is safe behind this great river obstacle. We all agree that it is a great obstacle; but we will show the enemy that he is far from safe behind it. This great Allied fighting machine, composed of integrated land and air forces, will deal with the problem in no uncertain manner.

"And having crossed the Rhine, we will crack about in the plains of Northern Germany, chasing the enemy from pillar to post. The swifter and the more energetic our action the sooner the war will be over, and that is what we all desire; to get on with the job and finish off the German war as soon as possible.

"Over the Rhine, then, let us go. And good hunting to you on the other side.

"May 'the lord mighty in battle' give us the victory in this our latest undertaking, as he has done in all our battles since we landed in Normandy on D-Day."[35]

2

Never to Be Forgotten

AS TWENTY-FIRST ARMY Group put the finishing touches on preparations for Plunder, the Germans braced to meet the onslaught. The defenders were General der Fallschirmtruppen Alfred Schlemm's First Fallschirmjäger (Paratroop) Army—badly mauled during its blood-soaked attempt to deny the opposite bank to First Canadian Army. Schlemm had withdrawn the last of his men on March 10, crossing the river at Wesel on the region's remaining bridges. When the last soldier passed over, the bridges were blown. Left behind were fifty thousand men captured, along with all the dead included in the final count of about forty thousand killed or wounded. Exhausted and dispirited, Schlemm wondered if Hitler's insistence on defending the Rhine's west bank had been madness, the heavy loss in veteran troops impossible to replace.

The day after the withdrawal, Schlemm met his new superior at the army's headquarters near Wesel. Generalfeldmarschall Albert Kesselring had taken over from Generalfeldmarschall Gerd von Rundstedt, who had been fired for the second time from his post as Oberbefehlshaber (Commander-in-Chief) West.[1] Kesselring, just arrived from commanding German forces in Italy, was anxious to hear first-hand Schlemm's plans for defending the Rhine. Nick-named "Smiling Albert," Kesselring was noted for unfading optimism at even the direst of moments. He was also masterful at using terrain to defensive advantage. In Italy, Kesselring had routinely brought the Allies to a standstill for weeks, even months, by fighting from behind a major river or from the heights of mountain ranges. Kesselring was also a shrewd judge of morale.[2]

Kesselring was accompanied by Army Group H's commander, Generaloberst Johannes Blaskowitz. The sixty-one-year-old Blaskowitz was a professional soldier of the old pre-Nazi school, who had nonetheless risen rapidly under Hitler. The mastermind behind the German blitzkrieg across Poland, he had accepted Warsaw's surrender on October 22, 1939, and been crowned as the conquered country's military commander. But Blaskowitz soon fell from grace, writing two detailed memoranda that documented and criticized the persecution and murder of Polish Jews. Citing many instances of looting of Jewish homes and shops, countless rapes, and scores of common murders, Blaskowitz warned that the ss "might later turn against their own people in the same way." Incensed by Blaskowitz's "childish attitude," Hitler sacked him. When good generals quickly proved in short supply, he was returned to various commands and ultimately assumed control of Army Group G prior to the Normandy invasion. Cashiered again by Hitler after the Lorraine fell, Blaskowitz was brought back in January 1945 to head Army Group H.[3] This made him the titular German military commander of the Netherlands and one of the most important officers facing the western Allies.

Schlemm told Kesselring and Blaskowitz that if his army was "allowed at least another eight or ten days to re-equip, prepare positions, bring up supplies, and rest," it should be able to defeat the attack. He pointed optimistically to the fact that the army had "succeeded in withdrawing all its supply elements in orderly fashion, saving almost all its artillery, and withdrawing enough troops so that a new defensive front [could] be built up on the east bank." The fifty evacuated artillery batteries could provide protective cover for the new defensive line. Schlemm predicted that the assault crossing would most likely fall between Emmerich and Wesel and that the Allies would support it with an airborne attack. Against that prospect he was feverishly strengthening anti-aircraft defences around the obvious drop zones near Wesel. Total heavy and light anti-aircraft guns in this area would soon number 814.

Farmhouses and summer cottages along the river were being transformed into fortifications. What appeared in aerial photographs as animal shelters or machine-storage sheds attached to the sides of many houses facing the river were often actually new bunkers with heavily reinforced concrete roofs, two-foot-thick walls, and firing apertures for machine guns facing the water. Elsewhere, deep trenches were dug behind the river dykes. Covering the suspected airborne drop zones were specially trained and highly mobile reaction forces.

Given enough time, Schlemm could be as ready as possible. But if Twenty-First Army Group decided to bounce the Rhine with a hurried attack, the odds of holding would be slimmer. Schlemm hoped for ten days and was pleased when Montgomery gave him twelve.[4]

With each passing day, the fifty-year-old veteran of intense fighting on both the Russian Front and Monte Cassino in Italy grew more confident. His defences were steadily being strengthened, and the terrain already worked to his advantage. Before him stood the Rhine, which was running in March at five miles an hour and had a minimum depth of nine feet. On his side of the river, several heights provided commanding positions, while the Allies opposite stood on level ground that was largely unwooded. Containing the river on his east bank was a sixty-foot-wide, thirteen-foot-high dyke paralleled by a railroad embankment. Both provided excellent defensive positions.[5]

Schlemm arrayed his troops along a front that stretched from Emmerich to just south of and opposite Krefeld—a distance of some fifty miles. His best troops, those of the II Fallschirmjäger Corps, held the ground where he expected the strike to fall—between Emmerich and Wesel. The 6th Fallschirmjäger Division manned a front extending from Emmerich to the outskirts of Rees. Here, the 8th Fallschirmjäger Division took over to a position opposite Xanten, and the 7th Fallschirmjäger Division held the line to Wesel. The ground south of this point was LXXXVI Corps's responsibility. Serving as a fire brigade to respond wherever needed, the XLVII Panzer Corps was held back of the front.

11 Fallschirmjäger Corps was much stronger than the other corps in arms, men, and leadership. It also had Schlemm, considered by Allied intelligence as a "fighting man of undoubted military ability," headquartered close by so that he could directly influence the battle.

General der Flieger Eugen Meindl, highly praised by superiors and subordinates alike for his abilities, commanded the corps. A little red-faced man who had originally been an army artillery officer before being seconded to the Luftwaffe's paratroops, the fifty-two-year-old was a veteran of campaigns in Crete, Russia, and Normandy. In the last two operations, he had proved highly capable of extracting divisions from disastrous encirclements. Most of his twelve thousand "tough parachutists" were seasoned veterans. He also possessed about eighty field and medium guns, as well as sixty 88-millimetre anti-aircraft guns adaptable for ground fire. Meindl agreed with Schlemm that the Allies would carry out an airborne drop, but he thought it would come behind Rees rather than Wesel.

The three divisions under Meindl also had capable officers. Generalleutnant Hermann Plocher, whose forceful professionalism was considered by Allied intelligence officers to be a "clue to [understanding] the fierce, skilful fighting [ability] of his parachutists," was typical. After serving in Spain for fourteen months as the German Condor Legion's chief of staff during that country's civil war, he had since 1939 held a mix of Luftwaffe staff and divisional headquarters postings before taking over the 6th Division on October 1, 1944. In March 1945, he was forty-four and had under his command about seven thousand paratroops dug in along a line running from east of Emmerich to just north of Rees. Plocher doubted that the Allied crossings would come in his sector, because the roads leading out of Emmerich were poor. He sided with Meindl in thinking the main assault would be at Rees.

While much of the German army might have fallen into the "depths of dejection," Twenty-First Army Group intelligence staff believed the paratroops "still intended to fight to the end . . . They are proud of belonging to an elite branch . . . They are, as a rule, younger and physically better qualified than other troops. Their relations to the Army are without a stigma, in contrast to the notorious ss gang.

They like to consider themselves the successors of the crack troops which invaded Holland in 1940, Crete in 1941, and made a last-ditch stand in Cassino. Actually, only a handful have survived those 'memorable' days and, considering the quality and length of Para training now given, only very few would equal those accomplishments.

"Practically all of them have been made to believe that Hitler has restored law and order, greatness and equality to the German people. The Hitler myth has taken so strong a hold on them that many refuse to consider even the possibility of a German defeat. Hitler's promise of a victory and of secret weapons to achieve it with is accepted by many like a guarantee from a higher being. Others think that Nazi Germany was a good thing until the War but that Hitler should never have challenged the entire world as he did."[6]

High morale aside, the paratroops were severely handicapped. Intercepts through Ultra—the top secret intelligence unit that had broken the German encryption system and was reading many of their wireless signals—had given Montgomery and his staff details of the German full order of battle from Emmerich to Duisberg. They were also aware of the First Fallschirmjäger Army's serious supply problems. Fuel was reportedly "so short that the supplying of troops is jeopardized" and ammunition so meagre that "150 tons of certain specified calibres was deemed essential."[7]

LXXXVI Corps was in terrible condition. Its 180th Infantry Division, tasked with holding a twelve-and-a-half-mile frontage from Wesel to Duisberg, fielded only 2,500 men and could muster just fifteen light artillery batteries, seven medium batteries, and three heavy-calibre batteries.[8] The corps commander, General der Infanterie Erich von Straube, was held in contempt by his fellow generals, and the 180th's Generalmajor Heinz Fiebig struck many as "a charming fellow to have at a party; the last man to lead a division in the field."[9]

If LXXXVI Corps was weak, XLVII Panzer Corps was barely recognizable as the heavily armoured force it had once been. General der Panzertruppen Heinrich Freiherr von Lüttwitz's two divisions were at 30 per cent of normal strength when he escaped across the Rhine. Although reinforcements had brought his manpower strength up to

50 per cent, he still had only thirty-five tanks. And these were all the Germans had to meet Twenty-First Army Group.[10]

Despite such grim realities, hope seemed to spring eternal among the senior German officers holding the Rhine. On March 20, Kesselring relayed the welcome news that the Führer had ordered 205 tanks and 1,125 armoured fighting vehicles sent their way. Schlemm was to receive 325 of these over the next three weeks and should prepare crews to man them.[11] "My orders are categorical," Kesselring added: "Hang on!"[12]

Certainly Schlemm was prepared to do just that. At 0600 hours that morning of March 21, Schlemm was at his desk in a little cottage tucked well away in a forest near Dorsten. Somewhere in the clear blue sky overhead, planes could be heard.[13] Then someone shouted in alarm, *"Jabos, Jabos."* Fighter-bombers! Everyone scrambled for cover as the scream of the diving planes filled the air, followed by the whistling of falling bombs. A terrific explosion and clouds of black smoke filled the cottage, shards of wood and glass flew, ceiling beams and plaster crashed down. Schlemm was dragged unconscious and severely wounded from the wreckage. He did not regain consciousness until the following day. Although temporarily blinded and barely capable of movement, the general refused to relinquish command. From a bed, he attempted throughout that day and the next to finalize preparations to meet the attack.[14]

Unlike Schlemm, Meindl was under no illusion that his paratroops could fend off an Allied attack. Although he had been reinforced with Luftwaffe ground-service personnel re-equipped to fight as infantry, Meindl considered these a mixed blessing. "They're more a hindrance than a benefit," he grumbled to his staff in a farmhouse near Bocholt, a village about ten miles northeast of the river behind Rees.

Meindl knew he had done all he could to meet the juggernaut massing across the river. "With his huge quantities of ammunition and matériel," he said, "Montgomery can succeed in crossing the river. We need no longer worry as to where and when the crossing will take place, for we know that the enemy can do it wherever he pleases, if he but uses his matériel in a proper way." Meindl told an aide: "It won't be long now."[15]

THE THOUSANDS OF Canadian, British, and American gunners on the Allied side of the Rhine swarmed into their assigned gun areas at noon on March 23. It was a clear, warm day. Visibility was unlimited. It seemed to Lieutenant William W. Barrett of 13th Canadian Field Regiment that simultaneously, throughout the whole area, the men "began digging slit trenches and weapon pits. In the small fields flanked by the houses of Wissel the dirt started to fly as everyone worked feverishly to be ready to fire ahead of the others."[16]

Such activity was bound to attract notice, and in the mid-afternoon, German artillery and mortars began dropping rounds, ranging in from a distance of just twelve hundred yards. Because of the smokescreen, the German gunners were firing blindly, but still one round landed in the midst of 'A' Troop's area. Sergeant Moffat and Gunner Manning were both wounded. A few minutes later, Gunner Pankoski of 'C' Troop also fell.[17]

To avoid detection, 4th Canadian Armoured Divison's 15th Field Regiment was not allowed to roll its trucks and gun-towing tractors towards the river until March 21. Late that evening, the column arrived at its firing position on the river flats immediately south of the village of Huisberden. Guns "were quickly rolled into the waiting pits, command posts were established in dugouts and farmhouse cellars, and by 1400 hours the regiment had reported ready to HQ RCA. Because of the amount of artillery massed to cover the crossing, the regimental area was not large, but there was sufficient room to have the guns well dispersed. The position, under water a couple of weeks before, was open, flat, and almost devoid of cover. The 95th and 110th batteries were dug in on the reverse slope of a dyke which was just forward of the regimental area, and the 17th Battery was in the fields and orchards slightly to the rear. Digging and camouflage parties had done an excellent job. Dugouts, where the gunners lived, and the gun pits were deep and well built. Sod was carefully placed on the upturned soil, and camouflage nets covered each pit. RHQ [Regimental Headquarters] occupied the cellar of a large well built house just on the edge of the dyke. 'A' Echelon... occupied an area to the south of the regimental position; its vehicles were carefully camouflaged, not an easy task in an open field. Behind the guns, on the high wooded ground south of the [Kleve-Kalkar] road, were the wagon lines and ammunition echelons. No vehicles whatever were allowed to remain on the gun position."

Meanwhile, "from dawn to dusk huge billows of smoke [drifted] from the large generators [that] screened the area from observation from the north. Once the screen backfired sending volumes of dirty choking smoke over the gun position, causing a number to wear respirators for the first and only time in action."[18]

Sometimes the smokescreen lifted, whether intentionally or not, the moment that gunners began digging pits and towing guns into position. At 1430 hours, the 7th Medium Regiment's war diarist recorded, most batteries were still preparing to move the large guns into the pits to be ready when "the smoke screen lifted, affording us a perfectly clear view of the eastern bank... Doubtless the Germans had an equally good view of us. Digging continued, and we were not troubled by shellfire. At 1630 hours both batteries reported ready with guns in their pits and camouflage completed." They had finished the job with just thirty minutes to spare until the first rounds were to be fired.[19]

During the early afternoon, the gunners in each regiment's "wagon lines, gun pits, and command posts" had the "outline of the operation... explained." They understood where the crossings were to be made, by which units of Second British Army, and when. They understood their gunnery role. The 15th, as was true of most of the Canadian artillery regiments, would pass briefly under command of the xxx British Corps and join "the formidable force of artillery massed to support the crossing."[20]

AT 1700 HOURS on March 23, the Rhine erupted in a cataclysm of fire. "It sounded as if the gates of hell had suddenly been opened," recorded 7th Canadian Infantry Brigade's war diarist.[21] For Captain Thomas Bell of the 12th Field Regiment, "there seemed to be a solid row of guns firing from our side of the Rhine from Nijmegen... stretching miles to the south... The din was really terrific! Aside from the hundreds of guns firing, there were tracers everywhere and it was a sight never to be forgotten."[22]

Highland Light Infantry's Private Glen Tomlin was up close to the riverbank. The twenty-one-year-old from Clinton, Ontario, had known the vast bombardment was coming. Still, this was like nothing he had witnessed during his march from Normandy to the Rhine. "It was an awful noise, the ground just shook, everything shook . . . The guns started off and then you heard the shells come over, and they whistle different sounds for different shells." The 25-pounders were easy to pick out, passing overhead "in a slow whistle." But as the guns increased their tempo, the sound became "just a continuous roar." Tomlin "could feel them going over, there was an air motion."[23]

With each passing minute more guns weighed in according to a precise schedule. At 1900 hours, to the right of the 12th Field Regiment's guns, positioned almost on the riverbank, the 100th and 32nd Batteries of the 4th Light Anti-Aircraft Regiment started blazing away with twenty-two 40-millimetre Bofors guns. The two batteries were firing a Pepperpot—a technique in which the anti-aircraft guns are lowered and aimed at pre-designated ground targets—to rake German bunkers stationed close to the riverbank with a rapid rate of fire. "Every calibre gun we had in the Army was firing," the 4th's regimental historian wrote. "Over our heads, as we fired, flashed white streaks of fire as more 40-mm behind us . . . turned into red balls of tracers as they passed."[24]

Pepperpots were not the exclusive domain of the anti-aircraft regiments. Adding to the rain of steel were the heavy 17-pounder tank destroyers of several anti-tank regiments. The 4.5-inch mortars and 50-calibre Vickers machine guns of support regiments, such as the Cameron Highlanders of Ottawa (MG) Regiment, also weighed in.

The 4th LAA had earlier dumped eighteen thousand rounds of ammunition next to the two batteries' gun positions. By sighting along aiming posts set out ahead of their position, each gun crew now ranged on sixteen designated targets near Rees that varied from 3,450 to 4,700 yards distant. The gunners were to continue firing until 2055 hours, ceasing just five minutes before the first wave of British infantry started crossing in Buffalo amphibious landing vehicles. Each gun would burn through 750 rounds at rates ranging from eight to ten per minute, maintaining an intensity of fire that the Bofors were not designed to take. The regiment fired 13,896 rounds.[25]

"Jerry took an active interest in us after we had been firing about half an hour, when he realized something big was coming off," the regimental historian wrote. "It was only during a lull, when changing barrels or the break given between targets that we could realize how much mortaring and shelling was coming our way. We had no time to worry about enemy action. Every man had his work cut out to do his own job. The noise was terrific, airbursts above us, mortar shells landing either side of the gun passed nearly unnoticed. We hardly realized they were there. The ammunition numbers worked like slaves, wringing wet, as they handed up clip after clip of shells, layers hung grimly on to their laying hand-wheels as the gun bucked and shook, firers and loaders kept stamping away in well practiced rhythm. Some of the guns had stoppages. A 40-mm is designed for rapid fire in short bursts at infrequent intervals and maintaining [a] rapid rate of fire over a two-hour period gave us a great deal of trouble. Many of the guns were old, being used constantly since February 44. As darkness fell shelling and mortaring increased."[26]

The 100th Battery's 'F' Troop narrowly missed acquiring heavy casualties when mortar salvoes erupted just thirty yards short of their guns. Although the air sang with flying shrapnel, no casualties resulted. Over in the 32nd Battery's area, twenty-six-year-old Bombardier Frank McKay of Steep Creek, Saskatchewan, died under an airburst, and another man was wounded.

In the last forty-five minutes of the fire program, guns started to suffer mechanical breakdowns. Five were soon out of action and several others stayed on line only because the crews scavenged replacement parts from the disabled weapons. When a round jammed in the breech of his gun, Sergeant "Yank" Androlice pried the top cover plate open to take it out. As he reached for it, the round exploded in his face. Androlice was blinded, and his hands and face badly burned.[27] The same exploding round seared Bombardier Kinnear's hands and arms and also singed Gunner Carey's hands. A call was issued for immediate evacuation. Responding, stretcher bearers Gunner R.W. Grey and Gunner B.H. Eaton from 'E' Troop rushed to the scene and carried Androlice back the Regimental Aid Post through drenching enemy fire all along the route.

Major J.M. Cousins, commanding 32nd Battery, was terrifically impressed by the dedication of his gun crews. "All ranks of the four troops engaged in the shoot had excellent fire discipline and showed utmost courage and initiative during difficult moments. In many cases, repairs were made on guns under heavy enemy fire, thus enabling them to go back in action."

In the final five minutes, a single 100th Battery gun fixed aim on a new coordinate. It belched out twenty rounds of tracer per minute on a rigid line to mark the left boundary that the Buffaloes carrying the leading battalions of the 51st (Highland) Division were not to stray beyond during their passage over the Rhine.[28] As the other anti-aircraft guns fell silent and the heavier artillery also lifted fire, the Buffaloes loaded with troops of the 153rd and 154th Brigades lurched over the dyke and wallowed through the muddy ground between it and the Rhine. Radial aircraft engines whining loudly, the lightly armoured tracked vehicles hit the water with a great splash at their top ground speed of twenty miles an hour. Once in the water, they found the current was too strong to allow them to maintain the full water speed of seven and a half miles per hour. The British troops, all wearing lifejackets, felt very exposed in the open-top vessels. The spearhead battalions for 153rd Brigade were the 5th/7th Gordon Highlanders and 5th Black Watch, while the 154th first advanced the 7th Argyll and Sutherland Highlanders and 7th Black Watch. Entering the water close behind the first infantry flights were amphibious duplex-drive tanks manned by the Staffordshire Yeomanry (Queen's Own Royal Regiment). Plunder was underway.[29]

SIX MINUTES LATER, the Buffaloes churned up onto the opposite bank. Troops dashed down the rear ramps or, if they were riding a model lacking these, spilled over the sides. Waiting tensely for word at xxx Corps headquarters, Lieutenant General Brian Horrocks almost shouted with relief when the wireless crackled and a voice said simply, "The Black Watch has landed safely on the far bank."[30]

At Montgomery's tactical headquarters near Venlo, about twenty-six miles from the front lines, the news was equally well received by his distinguished guest, Winston Churchill. The prime minister had flown in to be present for the historic attack. The two men had dined at 1900 hours and "an hour later . . . repaired with strict punc-tuality to Montgomery's map wagon. Here were displayed all the maps kept from hour to hour by a select group of officers. The whole plan of our deployment and attack was easily comprehended," Churchill saw. "We were to force a passage over the River at ten points on a twenty-mile front."

Churchill had expected Plunder to succeed, for everything he had "seen or studied in war" made him doubt that a river could stop the advance of superior powers. "I was therefore in good hopes of the battle even before the Field-Marshal explained his plans to me. More-over, we had now the measureless advantage of mastery in the air. The episode which the Commander-in-Chief particularly wished me to see was the drop next morning of the two airborne divisions, com-prising 14,000 men, with artillery and much other offensive equipment, behind enemy lines."[31]

More immediately, the benefit of controlling the air was proven at 2130 hours when 201 RAF Bomber Command aircraft appeared over battered Wesel and pulverized it further with eleven hundred tons of explosive. This destruction was intended to break the backbone of German defensive positions and open the way for the assault by 1st Commando Brigade that kicked off XII Corps's river crossing.[32]

Wearing their trademark green berets, No. 46 Royal Marine Commando jumped off thirty minutes later as the first wave. Like the 51st Division's Black Watch, they rode across the Rhine aboard Buffaloes and reached the far shore in three and a half minutes. Despite the bombing, their crossing met opposition. A phosphorous mortar round scored a direct hit on one of the amphibious vehicles, sending flames shooting fifteen feet into the air. Nine men aboard died, while most of the others were plunged into the icy river, wounded and burning. But the commandos soon gained the muddy flat of their landing site, and by midnight the entire brigade had crossed over and fought its way into Wesel.

The 13th-century historic town was devastated. Streets were unrecognizable, badly cratered and filled with the rubble of shattered buildings. Water and sewage from shattered pipes gushed into the craters and gurgled around the rubble. Flames from severed natural gas lines roared and hissed. In the midst of this chaos, the commandos and an ad-hoc German division clashed in a costly yard-by-yard melee.[33]

South of Rees, the 15th (Scottish) Infantry Division started crossing at 0200 hours on March 24 under a starry sky. The leading battalions quickly gained their first objectives, and the division began ferrying more troops into the bridgehead. At the same time that 15th Division had launched its Buffaloes, the lead company of the U.S. Ninth Army's 30th Division boarded motorized assault boats to the south of Wesel. The division quickly crossed under cover of raging fire from 1,250 guns and every available American tank and tank destroyer. The troops were met by hundreds of Germans eager to surrender. Coated in brick dust, with ears, noses, and eyes bleeding, these men had been incapacitated by the fury of the bombardment, which had concentrated 65,261 shells in the vicinity of the landing site. Two hours later, all three of the division's regiments had two battalions over the Rhine, along with supporting tanks. Casualties were remarkably light.

At 0300 hours, the Ninth Army's 79th Infantry Division crossed at the army's second landing site. Despite much confusion due to thick blankets of fog and smoke shrouding the Rhine, which caused some boats to turn about so the troops aboard invaded the wrong riverbank, the bridgehead was quickly established.

Neither Ninth Army division could claim to be the first Americans across the Rhine. That honour went to the men of the U.S. First Army, who had pulled off a coup by seizing a bridge at Remagen, about twenty miles south of Wesel. Having won this bridge on March 7, they had since been steadily expanding their bridgehead. And, true to a vow that he would not let Montgomery beat him to the Rhine, General George Patton's Third U.S. Army bounced the Rhine with a surprise attack on the night of March 22–23. Not bothering with a preliminary artillery bombardment, Patton's men had gone over in boats at Oppenheim, south of Mainz. Catching the Germans entirely by surprise, Patton had about fifteen thousand men across by the time Montgomery began delivering his massed artillery bombardment. Neither the fact that the German troops on his front were scarcer and of poorer quality than those Montgomery faced, nor that the river was about half the width at Oppenheim, detracted from Patton's self-congratulation. In an afternoon phone call he urged General Omar Bradley to "for God's sake tell the world we're across. I want the world to know Third Army made it before Monty starts across!"[34]

If Montgomery was piqued that Patton had not only beaten him but done so without the elaborate buildup of Plunder, he gave no indication. As per his long-standing and rigidly adhered to habit, the field marshal retired to bed at precisely 2200 hours on March 23. After sending a telegram to Joseph Stalin in Moscow, Churchill followed suit. "It is hoped to pass the river tonight and tomorrow," he had written, "and to establish bridgeheads. Once the river has been crossed a very large reserve of armour is ready to exploit the assault."[35]

3

Go for the Goddamn Woods

THE FIRST CANADIANS over the Rhine were nine men led by Acting Captain Donald Albert Pearce of the Highland Light Infantry's carrier platoon. Crossing with the first British Argyll and Sutherland Highlanders' wave on March 23, their job was to guide the rifle companies to pre-designated assembly areas. At 0345 hours, the rest of the battalion followed. As their Buffaloes launched, the Germans were recovering enough from the artillery battering and surprise of the first landings to engage in sporadic shelling. This threw up great waterspouts as the Allied vehicles chugged towards the eastern bank. Rumbling up onto a grassy mud flat two and a half miles west of Rees, the little flotilla was met by Pearce's party.[1]

Racing on foot across the mud flat to secure the dyke, 'C' Company came face to face with thirty Volkssturm (People's Militia) "sitting along" it. "Using their 1913 style rifles apparently did not appeal to the Volkssturm and they were pleased [to be] sent along to the PW [prisoner of war] cage."[2]

The Volkssturm performance lived up to Allied expectation. A Hitler invention, the Volkssturm dragooned men aged forty to sixty and boys of sixteen or younger. Untrained, poorly armed, and badly led, Volkssturm were supposed to be inspired by their Nazi conviction. Generally, they just surrendered.

Resistance had collapsed along the riverbank when Lieutenant Colonel Phil Strickland and his command group dismounted from Buffaloes at 0545 hours. But 154th Brigade was facing heavy resistance in Speldrop.[3] Rather than striking out for previously assigned objectives, Strickland was told to hold the HLI where it was, in case the 1st Black Watch—"wholly involved in the attack on Speldrop"—needed reinforcement.[4]

The XXX Corps landing site close to Rees suffered a crippling deficiency—any northward movement was channelled into a narrow choke point created by large water bodies. Running hard by Bienan's western flank was the eastern arm of the Alter Rhine—a remnant of the originally winding Rhine River before it was straightened. The Alter Rhine remained as two horseshoe-shaped arms that followed tight arcs before joining to spill into the Rhine's new course immediately south of Dornick. Both arms still held water, serving to drain the low ground immediately behind the Rhine's new channel. A mile to the east of Bienan, the north–south trending Millinger Meer (Lake) closed that flank. Between the most easterly arm of the Alter Rhine and Millinger Meer, Bienan sat in the middle of a gap barely half a mile wide. Speldrop was less than two miles due south of Bienan. To expand the bridgehead northward, both places had to be taken. The British had counted on 154th Brigade to quickly overrun the towns and then dig in across the choke point to meet the inevitable counterattack that was a standard German defensive tactic. They would meet this with a storm of machine-gun, mortar, rifle, artillery, and even air power that would slaughter the advancing Germans.

But General der Fallschirmtruppen Alfred Schlemm had anticipated this and garrisoned both communities with paratroops from the 8th Fallschirmjäger Division, heavily armed with self-propelled guns and medium machine guns. Buildings had been fortified and the paratroops ordered to hold at all costs.[5]

Regaining his eyesight on the morning of March 24, Schlemm had risen painfully from bed and been driven to a viewpoint overlooking the British bridgehead. Schlemm satisfied himself that Rees was the British offensive's focal point.[6] He could see his troops in Speldrop and Bienan resisting with ferocity. For the moment, the British were blocked.

He ordered the 15th Panzer Grenadier Division to reinforce the two paratroop regiments with 115th Regiment and directed its 104th Panzer Grenadier Regiment to break through to Rees on a line immediately south of Millinger Meer. The sudden arrival of these forces left the Anglo-Canadian forces in the bridgehead outnumbered.[7]

Adding to the developing crisis, 51st Division's commander was killed. Major General Thomas Rennie had expressed grave reservations about Plunder, telling Horrocks that "he hated everything about it." Baffled, Horrocks had wondered if Rennie, like "so many Highlanders" was "fey." When Rennie crossed the river in the morning to congratulate 7th Black Watch on being first over the Rhine, his jeep took a direct mortar round as he was dismounting. Rennie died almost immediately.[8]

As news of Rennie's death pulsed through 51st Division's ranks, the 1st Black Watch was forced out of Speldrop by repeated counterattacks. Losses were heavy, but the Black Watch soon fought its way back into the streets. A confused melee erupted, with fighting at close quarters. By late morning, the situation deadlocked, and the Highland Light Infantry was told to relieve the Black Watch and take over the fight. This operation was to be heavily supported by artillery and would not begin until after Operation Varsity—the airborne drops—had been carried out.[9]

AS TWENTY-FIRST ARMY Group was crossing the Rhine, in Britain and France 13,750 paratroops of the 6th British Airborne and 17th U.S. Airborne divisions comprising the XVIII U.S. Airborne Corps mustered on twenty-three airfields for the largest air armada in history.[10] Clogging these airfields—eleven in Britain and twelve in France—were 1,696 troop transports and 1,050 tug transports with their 1,348 gliders in tow.[11] The American paratroops assembled at airfields in France, the British and Canadians in Britain.

By any measure, Operation Varsity was daunting. Its aim was to seize the Diersfordter Wald and other ridges that overlooked the Rhine from about three to five miles east and north of Wesel and also gain control of the five-by-six-mile forest blanketing most of this high ground. The ground and Issel bridges east of Diersfordter village were assigned to the Americans, while 6th Division would "seize, clear and hold the Schnep[f]enberg feature and the village of Hamminkeln, together with designated bridges over R[iver] Issel." There were three such bridges, which were to be wired with explosives for demolition but not blown unless German recapture "became certain."

The British 3rd Brigade, of which the Canadian battalion was part, would lead the divisional drop and seize the woods on the 150-foot-high Schnepfenberg ridge on the division's left flank. Within the brigade, the British 8th Battalion would seize the eastern part, the 9th the centre, and the Canadians the extreme western flank.[12] The drop zone lay less than one thousand yards north of these objectives—a relatively open area of dry ground bordered on the south by the Diersfordter forest and on the north by some farm buildings set among patchy woods. On the western flank, the Wesel–Rees road and a small farm alongside it provided the boundary marker. Several farm buildings stood almost in the drop zone's centre, and three hundred yards east of these a raised double-tracked railway cut obliquely across it. A seventy-five-yard-square cluster of tall spruce trees, code-named the Axehead, jutted out of the Diersfordter forest towards the centre of the landing site. This tree cluster fell into 8th Battalion's zone of operation.

On the Canadian's southernmost operational area, a clutch of houses had been designated as the battalion's main objective. 'C' Company would advance one platoon to seize an intersection on the Wesel–Rees road, while its other two swept the western corner of the woods. 'A' Company would then pass through 'C' Company's positions to clear and hold the houses, which would become battalion headquarters. 'B' Company would support 'A' Company and protect its eastern flank. Once the objectives were in hand, the battalion's task was to aggressively patrol beyond this perimeter to guard against counterattacks and establish contact with XII British Corps as it advanced out of Wesel.

It was a bold plan, as the paratroops would drop right into the midst of the Germans defending the Rhine. All sides of the brigade's drop zone provided ideal defensive ground from which the Germans could sweep its entirety. "In the imaginations of the paratroops concentrating to memorize the features of their detailed briefings," Sergeant Dan Hartigan wrote, "it was not difficult to visualize the prime targets the enemy would behold. There would be nearly thirty slow flying c-47s sliding slowly across their gun sights every minute-and-a-half, for five consecutive times. When the gliders would begin to land, a few minutes after the paratroops, the targets would be even larger and slower, but hopefully by that time, although a lot of enemy machineguns would remain, there would be nowhere near the number which would have begun the fight less than ten minutes earlier."[13]

Success rested with the first troops on the ground, including the Canadians. Lieutenant Colonel Jim Nicklin—the thirty-two-year-old former Winnipeg Blue Bomber football player turned elite solider—emphasized that "SPEED and INITIATIVE on [the] part of all ranks is the order of the day. RISKS will be taken. The ENEMY will be attacked and destroyed wherever he is found."[14] Speed, initiative, risk, attack, and destroy were watchwords for paratroops everywhere, and the Canadians had carved out a reputation for daring and toughness in previous campaigns. They had jumped at D-Day, 50 per cent being killed, wounded, or taken prisoner in the ensuing days. They next fought in the Battle of the Bulge—the German attempt in December 1944 to break through to Antwerp out of the Ardennes forest. When not fighting they trained hard and relentlessly under Nicklin's demanding hand. At six-foot-three, he was a big, powerful man with a strict demeanour, zero tolerance for slacking, and endowed—in the words of his second-in-command, Major Fraser Eadie—with "bags of guts."

Preparing for Varsity, Eadie later said, the Canadians were drilled to understand "that when they were thrown into the middle . . . they were on their own hook. It would all be confusion. To cope with the things that could happen to them—like dropping in the middle of a woods alone, perhaps being wounded—and then find their positions as fast as possible, physical fitness and discipline were the two things that were going to get them there."[15]

Reveille on March 23 came at 0400 hours and 3rd Brigade was trucked to Chipping Onger, an airfield outside of London. The soldiers carried full battle kit. Upon arrival, parachutes were fitted, kit bags and weapons stowed aboard assigned airplanes, and then, at noon, the men were trucked back to camp for final briefings and a church parade.[16] Brigadier James Hill was feeling upbeat. "Gentlemen," he said, "the artillery and air support is fantastic! And if you are worried about the kind of reception you'll get, just put yourself in the place of the enemy. Beaten and demoralized, pounded by our artillery and bombers, what would you think, gentlemen, if you saw a horde of ferocious, bloodthirsty paratroopers, bristling with weapons, cascading down upon you from the skies?" The Germans, he declared, "you will treat . . . with extreme disfavour."[17]

At 0445 on that Saturday morning, the men, having had "a good breakfast," headed back to Chipping Onger. By 0615, they were donning gear.[18] Over his standard battle dress, each man wore a parachute smock whose many pockets were crammed with personal effects. The webbing belt fastened on over the smock, an entrenching tool hooked to one side of the rump, and a small pack with ammunition pouches on either side was strapped across the chest. A toggle rope—useful for lowering oneself down from a tree—was wrapped around the waist. Ammunition bandoleers for personal weapons and the unit Bren guns were draped around the neck. Over all this went the jump jacket, which was sleeveless and fitted with a belt that passed under the crotch to prevent it becoming entangled in the equipment and clothing it covered. A kit bag equipped with a quick-release mechanism was hooked to one leg. When the release was triggered, the kit bag fell away and dangled from a twelve-foot length of rope tied to one end of the parachute harness. Some soldiers put their rifle into the kit bag, but most kept it on their person for easy and immediate access upon landing or even during the descent. So burdened, the paratroops shuffled, rather than strode, to the planes.[19]

Dawn yielded precisely the weather forecasted. "Unlimited visibility existed over our bases in the United Kingdom, on the continent and over the target area, although a considerable smoke haze persisted over the latter throughout the operation," one observer noted.[20]

The 6th British Airborne Division's parachute element began lifting off aboard 240 c-47s manned by the U.S. IX Troop Carrier Command at 0730 hours. Following close behind the parachutists

were 429 British c-47, Stirling, and Halifax aircraft towing 429 gliders—381 Horsas and 48 Hamilcars. Simultaneously, 17th U.S.
Airborne Division took off from twelve airfields in the Paris area
aboard 903 c-46 and c-47 aircraft. Some carried paratroops, but
about half were, for the first time in a combat operation, towing two
gliders apiece rather than just one.[21]

Soon the great armada was airborne, blocks of aircraft circling
into formations. Closing around the transports were 213 Royal Air
Force fighters tasked with shepherding them to the drop zone and
home again. Over France, 676 U.S. 9th Air Force fighters similarly
protected the American formation. Another 1,253 U.S. 8th Air Force
fighters were already aloft and isolating the Rhine area from interference by German fighters or accompanying a diversionary raid by
U.S. 15th Air Force bombers on Berlin.[22]

The Canadians had never worked with American pilots. They were
scruffier than the British pilots, with a penchant for wearing baseball
hats and smoking cigars. But they exuded an easy confidence that the
Canadians liked. Brigadier James Hill was also impressed. Hill's trust
in the skills of these Americans had convinced him that the plan to
drop 2,200 paratroops in an area measuring little more than 800 by
1,000 yards in just six minutes was sound.[23]

Aboard his plane, Private A.H. "Sid" Carrignan of 'A' Company's
No. 1 Platoon found the flight to the Rhine "smooth and uneventful.
Old Sweats from Normandy were more serious and thoughtful than
the 'Greenhorns' like me." He saw "nothing unusual except that
there were a lot of aircraft in a long stream. Surprised at how green
the landscape was and the sudden rise or drop of aircraft beside ours.
One moment 30 yards higher, the next 30 yards lower. What
impressed me was the way Non-Commissioned Officers checked
and rechecked every man's gear, and went over the allotted tasks.
Their calm confident behaviour was very reassuring."[24]

The 6th Division formation gained the European coast near Cal-
ais and swung northward to rendezvous with the American division
south of Brussels, forming into a long, wide column with the planes
bearing the British and Canadians on the left and the Americans on
the right.[25] Sitting close to an open cargo door, Sergeant Hartigan

could see not only the hundreds of transports carrying the parachutists, but Stirlings and Halifaxes towing gliders or stocked with bomb-shaped parachute containers packed with equipment and supplies that were to be dropped to resupply the paratroops. The parachutes for these containers were much larger than those used by the men and brilliantly coloured according to a system that identified load content. Reaching in through the open bomb-bay doors, the slipstream had jerked some of these parachutes free of their pouches and torn them to shreds. "Brilliant orange, scarlet, blue, yellow, and emerald trailers... held by suspension lines" fluttered gaily from the bomb bays and "gave the whole scene, so serious, dangerous, powerful and crammed with portent, a slightly carnival atmosphere."

Hartigan was particularly impressed by the big Horsa and Hamilcar gliders. Many were loaded with glider troops, but others carried 17-pounder anti-tank guns, extra Vickers and Bren guns, ammunition carriers, jeeps, jeep-trailers, light artillery howitzers, heavy mortars, additional small arms, rations, vast quantities of ammunition, medical supplies, typewriters, paper and copy flimsies for the clerical staff at various headquarters, and drinking water loaded into tank-trailers—everything necessary to enable paratroops to fight and survive in isolation until reached by the regular infantry and armoured formations.

The armada's sheer size stunned Alex Pakulak, a Canadian medic. Later he learned that it took two hours for all the planes to pass over a specific spot. "It was very impressive, the numbers of airplanes were so large. I sat opposite the open door—all one could see was blue sky and airplanes... it was fantastic. I could imagine how the enemy was going to feel."

Less awed, Sergeant R.F. "Andy" Anderson of 'B' Company found the routine the "same as always... bucket seats are hard as hell. Some feign sleep, some really sleep. Others tell stories and try a few jokes that don't go down too well."[26]

A GROWLING HUM that grew to a deafening thunder signalled the armada's approach for both the Allies and Germans on the Rhine. "It was full daylight before the... intense roar and rumbling of swarms of aircraft stole upon us," a delighted Winston Churchill recorded.[27] "Never in this war had there been such a spectacle as we witnessed that morning," Canadian Press correspondent Ross Munro wrote. "From the banks of the Rhine we watched it spellbound."[28]

Overhead, the paratroops gazed out at an awesome scene as well. Hartigan looked on "highways and the fields beside them . . . jammed with Army traffic and stores of every kind. Flights of bombers going for softening up can be seen flying eastward. Fighters and Typhoons are in evidence everywhere, going in and coming back, a sign that the front is near. Soon a dusty haze becomes evident, and below is the unmistakable Rhine River. It is slow moving with a slick surface. Already Engineers have built pontoon bridges a good way out from the western bank."[29]

The twenty 'C' Company men in Hartigan's plane were commanded by No. 7 Platoon's Lieutenant Eric Burdon. The lieutenant would jump first, followed by the rest of the "stick" with Hartigan being last to exit. As the plane suddenly slowed for the approach, the flight engineer asked, "You guys are going to land right on top of them today, aren't you?" Without waiting for a reply, he added, "The whole crew wants to wish you good luck, and they want you to know how much they respect you guys." Hartigan shook the offered hand. "Thanks. We'll be okay. We're trained for it."

Turning to look down the line formed up in a single-file stick that stretched the length of plane, Hartigan bellowed, "Listen clear now! Pay attention! Don't forget now! As soon as you hit the bloody deck, and you're out of your parachutes, fix bayonets and go for the goddamn woods!"

Beside him, the red light still glowed. Just up the line a new nineteen-year-old trooper made the sign of the cross and whispered a prayer. Someone else shouted, "What the hell's wrong with our pilots; they're letting the red light stay on too long." Burdon was in the door, hands braced either side of the cowling, head out, looking for the drop zone. The plane shuddered as flak burst close and the air was crisscrossed by machine-gun tracers streaming up from the ground. Suddenly, the light went green and Hartigan yelled for the stick to go.

"Lieutenant Burdon, a strong, stocky man, jumps straight out. It's as though he's trying to jump all the way to the forest." Hartigan saw some nearby C-47s with engines burning, while others rocked and pitched as flak shells and machine-gun rounds ripped them.[30]

The stick piled out—one man hard on the heels of the other. But the plane kept rocking and rolling, causing a fraction of delay for each jumper. Then they were all gone and it was Hartigan's turn. He took to the silk and immediately saw the raised railway embankment about two hundred yards ahead. That meant he was badly off course, far to the east. Directly below, German soldiers dashed across a field towards the embankment. On the raised rail bed, several enemy machine-gun positions were visible. Hartigan frantically climbed his parachute risers, twisting to redirect the descent towards a nearby wood. Tracers slashed holes in the chute. As the chute rushed towards the forest canopy, he dropped back into the parachute seat. With a jerk the chute snagged a tree and his descent was arrested. Ready for it, Hartigan slipped free of the chute to drop a few feet into the bushy understory, just as a machine-gun burst tore chunks out of the tree trunk and showered him with bits of splintered branches. The moment the gun ceased shooting, Hartigan slithered away— heading low and fast through the woods towards the Canadian battalion's objectives. Hartigan figured he had landed a mile off course and could see nobody else from his stick.[31]

The first planes had reached the Rhine on schedule at precisely 0955. In a plane carrying 'C' Company's second-in-command, Captain John Clancy, Private Lawrence Dyck was No. 18 in the stick. Private Norman Rimmer stood directly ahead. Suddenly, just short of the drop zone, the plane "began to rock and smoke billowed up everywhere," Clancy later reported. "We surely had been hit . . . there was a delay up front caused by the pitching of the C-47 . . . Norm Rimmer went out with me close behind. So close that when my chute opened up I found myself enveloped in Rimmer's parachute. I managed to kick free just before we hit the ground, uninjured."[32]

Vickers Platoon's Private Len Hellerud's plane was hit just as it crossed the Rhine, and one engine started burning. Then the American jumpmaster was killed by a bullet or shrapnel that tore through the plane's skin. The green light came on just then and the Canadians piled out in a desperate rush to escape the crippled plane. Hellerud was second to last out the door. By then the plane was only about 250 feet off the ground. He caught a brief glimpse of the c-47 exploding in a ball of flame before he struck earth. Hellerud was square in the designated drop zone. Shrugging off his parachute, he began jogging towards the headquarters company's rendezvous area. Other paratroops were already there, digging slit trenches.[33]

ALL OF 3RD Brigade had dropped directly into a firefight with men from the 7th Fallschirmjäger Brigade, paratroops whom Company Sergeant Major John Kemp later declared "as good as us." Opposition was fierce. From machine-gun positions dug into the tree lines, buildings, and any embankments, the Germans slashed the open fields. Enemy artillery and mortars pounded the area at point-blank range. Dead and wounded men lay tangled in the shroud lines of parachutes. Others were cut down as they struggled free. Realizing he was two hundred yards from the rendezvous point on the edge of the woods, Major Fraser Eadie crouched low and ran "like hell." Around him bullets sang through the air and he saw several men lying motionless—presumably dead—in the middle of the drop zone.[34]

"Go for the goddamn woods," Hartigan had shouted. In the midst of chaos, such clear orders made duty simple. "Some men put down smoke with two-inch mortars. Others plop where they are on the open fields and pump Bren machine-gun fire into the enemy positions. The majority rush the enemy [in the woods], firing as they charge. The officers and platoon sergeants, together with their section leaders, shout directions, trying to guide men they could recognize into some form of organized assault pattern. Most often, however, the confusion is too much, and everyone races for the Diersfordter, firing from the hip as they charge. Among those who land close to the forest some throw smoke grenades, trying to spoil the enemy's aim, and then charge through the smoke, repeating the process until they overrun the enemy paratroops dug in on the forest's edge."[35]

Typical of paratroops, especially the Canadians, leadership came from all ranks. Private James Oliver Quigley landed in a field raked by "fierce fire from mortars, light automatics and rifles [positioned] at two corners of the area." Seeing that a number of men were confused about where the rendezvous point (RV) was, Quigley "by his . . . contempt for the hail of bullets inspired them to follow him." The group had just arrived at the RV when Major Eadie ordered the remnants of 'B' Company to go for its objective—clearing the woods east of the main building cluster. Quigley set off with the lead 'B' Company platoon, everyone firing on the run right into the teeth of the German fire. That was the last straw for many of the Germans, who dropped their weapons and stood with arms raised and shouted, "*Kamerad, Kamerad.*"

As the Canadians started gathering in the Germans, a nearby enemy machine gun opened fire. Quigley spun and grabbed a Bren gun from a comrade and, "firing as he ran, dashed into the midst of the post and destroyed the whole enemy section." This was the kind of "raw courage and intense determination to destroy the enemy," his Military Medal citation later acknowledged, that "inspired his platoon and company."[36]

Heroism was in no short supply during those "two hours of real killing," as one Canadian officer later described them.[37] Company Sergeant Major George Green had no sooner collected many of 'A' Company's men at their RV when their commander, Major Peter Griffin, ordered an immediate attack on the buildings because the fire from them was only intensifying. Clearly, a "strong and determined force" had transformed the buildings on the edge of the cluster into a highly fortified position that was getting stronger by the second as the Germans recovered from their surprise. Thirty minutes had passed since the landings and the company was at about 70 per cent strength when it started towards the buildings, only to be checked by heavy fire. "Success hung in the balance," Green's Distinguished Conduct Medal citation read. "In this emergency, under heavy fire, CSM Green led a PIAT [Projector Infantry Anti-Tank Gun] detachment up to the first house. Having organized covering fire, he led the assault . . . on the house. After capturing it, he then cleared all the remaining houses in quick succession. The enemy was full of fight but was worsted by the vigour of CSM Green's attacks." Green's "quick and determined action" had provided the "greatest value in clearing a dangerous obstacle and restoring the impetus of the advance."[38]

Everywhere, the Canadians imposed order on confusion and carried the day. But nowhere had the battle developed according to the detailed battalion, brigade, divisional, and corps plans. Casualties on the drop zone had been heavy, and some men had been dropped far afield. A few were taken prisoner; others were covertly evading German patrols and strongpoints while persistently attempting to rejoin the battalion. Among the missing was Lieutenant Colonel Nicklin. 'C' Company's Major John Hanson, noted for his courage in combat throughout the Normandy campaign, had suffered a broken collarbone on landing and was unable to function because of excruciating pain. He was tagged for immediate evacuation at the first opportunity. Further complicating 'C' Company's situation was the fact that the second-in-command, Captain John Clancy, was also missing. (He had dropped in the middle of a group of Germans and been taken prisoner.) 'A' Company's Captain Sam McGowan, another Normandy veteran, strode into its RV bleeding heavily from a scalp wound. A bullet had punched into the front of his helmet, buzzed around the inside rim, and then spiked a hole out the back.[39] Twenty-one-year-old Lieutenant J.J. "Jack" Brunette of Sarnia, Ontario, died on the drop zone.

In Nicklin's absence, Eadie assumed command. He had joined the battalion in the last days of the Normandy fighting, then temporarily commanded it during the advance to the Seine, and was now again in charge. "His brilliant handling and inspiring leadership" that day enabled the battalion, "in spite of heavy opposition and considerable casualties," to capture all its objectives. Eadie's actions earned the Distinguished Service Order.[40]

Lacking both senior officers, 'C' Company organized itself loosely by platoons and within five minutes of landing had gained the intersection and the stretch of Wesel–Rees highway that formed the drop zone's western boundary. They quickly became embroiled in a battle to clear several heavily manned bunkers and many slit trenches that connected them. The bunkers were dug deep and had log roofs reinforced with piles of earth to harden them against artillery fire. One eight-man team, led by Sergeant "Maxi" Maxwell, rushed the first bunker with guns blazing, causing the Germans inside to promptly surrender. Maxwell leapt straight up on the roof and paused, looking "angry, like a fighter in a boxing ring with his fists up, only instead in the reality of war [he was] bracing himself against the recoil of the Bren machinegun he was firing at the next dug-out."

Another team, meanwhile, rooted out Germans manning the slit trenches to the east, killing some and accepting the surrender of more. At the same time, left of Maxwell's group, another team closed on a bunker. The section leaders had just started divvying up the men for an organized attack when Sergeant Myles Saunders told them to give him a moment. He had a Gammon bomb—an explosive charge paratroops used as an anti-tank weapon—with two sticks of dynamite taped to it for additional effect. Unscrewing the cap that ignited the bomb's detonator, he chucked it up against the bunker's entrance. When the dust from the blast settled, fifteen to twenty Germans staggered out with raised arms. Resistance was beginning to crumble.[41]

In fact, the flow of prisoners coming into battalion headquarters— established inside the cluster of houses—quickly proved problematic "because they numbered almost the strength of the battalion. It was fortunate that Germans were killed by the hundreds, otherwise it would have been impossible to corral and guard them in the early hours of the operation," the battalion war diarist recorded. This was an overstatement. When the fighting ebbed at about 1400 hours, there were five hundred Germans under guard and approximately another one hundred counted as killed by the Canadian troops.[42]

Relative to the ferocity of the fight, Canadian casualties were considered light: two officers dead, one missing, and one wounded, as well as twenty-six other ranks killed, three missing, and thirty-four wounded.[43] Initially the missing count had been higher, but as the day progressed, many of the paratroops, such as Sergeant Dan Hartigan, turned up. Others stole through German lines to enter the XII Corps bridgehead. Lieutenant Colonel Jim Nicklin was among those later discovered to have been killed. Thirty-six hours after the jump, a patrol found his bullet-riddled body dangling from his tree-entangled parachute in a small wood.[44]

Many units were harder hit. On March 27, the casualty figures for 17th U.S. Division were calculated at 1,584, including 223 killed with 666 missing and largely presumed captured, as their planes had dropped them far from their drop zones. The 6th British Airborne Division counted only 370 men missing, but 238 dead and 736 wounded, exceeding the American figure of 695. These British figures incorporated 1st Canadian Parachute Battalion losses.[45]

Had it not been for one man's heroism, more Canadians would surely have died. Medical orderly Corporal Frederick Topham was a twenty-seven-year-old blond giant of a man, who had been a Kirkland Lake miner before enlisting. "Toppy" was quiet and reserved, never seeking the limelight but considered steady in a crisis. Topham had no sooner struck earth than he heard a man crying for help out in the bald open. Two other medical orderlies rushed forward only to be killed as they knelt at the man's side. Ignoring the murderous fire sweeping the drop zone, Topham dashed out and started dressing the man's wounds. A bullet pierced Topham's nose. With blood spewing and in terrific pain, he gathered up the soldier, draped him over a shoulder, and at a slow, steady pace "through continuous fire [carried him] to the shelter of the woods."

Refusing treatment, Topham spent the next two hours carrying in other wounded, "showing complete disregard for the heavy and accurate enemy fire. It was only when all casualties had been cleared that he consented to his own wound being treated." Weakened by blood loss, his face extremely swollen, Topham was ordered by the medical officer to stay in the battalion aid post. Instead, he pleaded "so earnestly on his own behalf that he was . . . allowed to return to duty."

Heading out, Topham saw a mortar platoon Bren carrier explode into flames from a direct hit. Incapacitated by their wounds, the three men aboard were trapped in the burning vehicle. Knowing its ammunition load would soon start detonating, an officer warned everyone to stay clear and leave the men to their fate. Ignoring the order, Topham lumbered to the carrier. With mortar rounds erupting inside it and German bullets cracking off the armour, Topham pulled each man free of his seat and gently lowered him to the ground. One of the men died, but Topham saw the other two safely evacuated to the cover of the woods.[46] Topham's selfless heroism garnered the Commonwealth's highest gallantry award, the Victoria Cross. "I only did what every last man in my outfit would do," he explained later.[47]

About the time Topham was rescuing the men in the carrier, the paratroops guarding the western flank of the perimeter heard tracked vehicles approaching from the river. A column of Bren carriers and British tanks arrived moments later at 1500 hours. This reconnaissance patrol by the 15th (Scottish) Division was "warmly welcomed."[48]

[4]

Rugged Resistance

AS THE SUN set on March 24, the Allies declared Operation Varsity a success, the two airborne divisions now joining those that had crossed the Rhine to play a traditional ground operation role until relieved. Collectively, the task now was to extend the bridgehead.[1] The 9th Canadian Infantry Brigade's Highland Light Infantry was already in the midst of doing this, having assaulted Speldrop in the late afternoon as part of 51st (Highland) Division's ongoing effort to break through the "Bienan gap"—a narrow piece of ground between the Alter Rhine and Millinger Meer. The British 1st Black Watch had been so badly mauled that it was ordered to pull out and make room for the artillery to smash the German defenders. Under a covering smokescreen, "the battered members of the Black Watch [withdrew,] leaving their wounded sheltered in cellars. One platoon which could not be extricated was advised by wireless to take what cover they could from our artillery fire," stated one report.[2]

A long-time HLI officer, Lieutenant Colonel Phil Strickland had risen to its command during the blood-soaked Scheldt Estuary campaign. Brigadier "Rocky" Rockingham considered him "terribly clever, full of courage and ability. I admired him most in the world." He was a good tactician, meticulous and methodical.[3]

Strickland's plan to win Speldrop "relied strongly on artillery support to cover the troops into the town. All approaches were covered
by the enemy with [self-propelled] guns, making it impossible to use
tanks during the initial stages."[4] The ground was billiard-table level
for the twelve-hundred-yard approach and absent any ground cover.
Strickland secured generous artillery support in the form of the
guns of six field regiments, two medium regiments, and two 7.2-
inch heavy batteries.[5]

One of these was 14th Canadian Field Regiment, which had
entered the bridgehead and set up only a short distance behind the
HLI's start line for the attack. His Canadian gunners, Lieutenant
Colonel Gordon Browne declared, were the first artillerymen to cross
the Rhine. They "lost no time in digging in . . . as shelling and mortaring were considerable. Presently airburst commenced coming in
on the beach head so I decided to run the carrier over the slit trench
which had been dug sufficiently large to accommodate the entire
crew of four. This plan did not prove possible as the trench, which
had been dug in rather sandy soil, caved in, thereby necessitating
some extra labour, but driving home the lesson that in soft soil the
narrower the slit trench the better."

Browne drafted Strickland's fire plan. Realizing the advancing
infantry would be naked to heavy machine-gun fire from the high
ground on the left flank, Browne ordered one regiment to screen it
with smoke. Two field regiments would provide a creeping barrage in
two-hundred-yard lifts to the village, while the remaining field regiments, medium regiments, and heavy regiments slammed designated
defensive targets "in and beyond the town. One gun per regiment
would fire smoke rounds against these targets to create a 'fog of war.'"[6]

Strickland opted to send his men in tight, rather than across a
broad front, to lessen their exposure to fire from Speldrop. 'B' Company would lead. Given chronic shortages of infantry manpower,
that meant only eighty to ninety men. They were to establish a firm
base, securing a group of buildings along the hamlet's northern
fringe. Typical of many rural German buildings, these were large
structures with living quarters in the front occupying both the first
and second storeys, and an attached barn at the rear for animals,

tools, and equipment. Once these buildings were secured, 'B' Company would cover the advance by first 'A' and then 'C' Companies. 'D' Company would remain in reserve.

At 1730 hours, Major Joseph Charles King and 'B' Company went into the attack. Only by "hugging" the artillery barrage were they able to cross the open ground, which was "still swept by [machine-gun] fire and enemy [artillery] and mortar fire" despite the shelling of Speldrop.[7] Gaining the building cluster, the company fought at close quarters, and casualties mounted.[8] All three platoon leaders were struck down. Lieutenants Bruce Frederick Zimmerman and Donald Arthur Isner, both twenty-four, were killed and the third officer incapacitated. Non-commissioned officers took over. King ran from one farm building to the other, directing the actions of each platoon despite exposing himself to raking heavy machine-gun and mortar fire. From somewhere inside Speldrop, three self-propelled guns bowled shells up the lanes, while German paratroops in fortified buildings facing 'B' Company's objective lashed out with machine guns and hand-held Panzerfausts.

King realized that if 'A' Company passed through as planned, it would be cut to pieces. He sent an urgent call for the HLI's anti-tank platoon and its troop of three Wasp Mk II Bren carriers.[9]

Bren carriers were retrofitted into flame-throwers by hitching an eighty-gallon fuel tank on the rear and running a hose to a large spray nozzle that projected from a hole cut in the thin frontal armour plate. As the fuel gushed down the line, it was pressurized with carbon dioxide and then passed through a heat exchanger attached to the carrier's engine. When the gunner fired the trigger, it sparked a small dribble of gasoline, and a second later fuel gushed through the main valve, passed over the flame, and burst into fire, which was projected from a nozzle to a maximum range of about 150 yards.[10] This "golden rain" of burning fuel broke into millions of ignited blobs of gasoline that showered widely and set alight any vegetation or wood it struck. A few tiny blobs of burning fuel attached to a man could be quickly smothered, but larger adhesions were impossible to quell, "and in this case the fats in the human body were literally burned up," one Wasp specialist recorded.[11]

'B' Company was unable to wait for King to get this support going. Instead, No. 12 Platoon had punched in among the buildings and immediately come under withering fire from several 20-millimetre anti-aircraft guns used in a ground-fire role and several heavy machine guns positioned in a nearby orchard. The platoon's commander fell, and Lance Sergeant Cornelius Jerome Reidel "immediately took command of the platoon, ordered the men to fix bayonets, and taking a Bren gun, led the platoon into the orchard in the face of heavy small-arms fire. The platoon captured the orchard, and cleared the buildings beyond, killing ten Germans and capturing fifteen prisoners and three 7.5-centimetre infantry guns . . . The success of the platoon action enabled the battalion to gain a foothold in the town," Reidel's Military Medal citation read.[12]

Responding to King's plea, Major John Alexander Ferguson had led out a column of the battalion's Wasps and carriers towing the four 6-pounder anti-tank guns. Ferguson, who won a Military Cross for this action, rode in a jeep, the sacrificial lamb on roads "unchecked for mines." Luckily, the column reached King's position unscathed.

Directed to set his guns to the right of 'B' Company's position to protect its flank, Sergeant Wilfred Francis Bunda faced the same predicament that Ferguson had—leading troops down a road that might be mined. Bunda headed out "on foot ahead of his guns to lead them into position." The anti-tank gunners arrived safely but found the position subjected to "constant enemy mortar and small-arms fire." Knowing that German SPGs lurked in Speldrop, Bunda calmly sited each gun and urged the gunners to dig in quickly. When several men were wounded, Bunda ensured that they were placed under cover. Once the guns were in action, he oversaw evacuation of the wounded.[13]

With the supporting weapons up, King led one 'B' Company platoon forward and quickly cleared the fortified buildings. The way was now open for the other two HLI companies to close on Speldrop and begin house-by-house clearing of the paratroops, who were fighting "fanatically."[14]

When 'A' Company pushed into the hamlet's eastern flank, it met a blast of German machine-gun fire from three fortified buildings and was forced to ground. The company commander ordered Lieutenant George Oxley MacDonald's No. 8 Platoon to lead an attack across a two-hundred-yard stretch of open ground to take the first building. With the carrier platoon throwing out covering machine-gun fire, MacDonald rushed forward, only to come under "withering fire" from two machine guns on the platoon's flank. All his section leaders were quickly struck down, but MacDonald was able to maintain control of the platoon and establish a fighting position inside a house. From here his men laid down such heavy suppressive fire that another section was able to clear the houses. MacDonald's "courageous and brilliant action" was recognized with a Military Cross.[15]

This kind of gallantry on the part of the Highland Light Infantry's officers and men squeezed the German paratroops into ever-smaller pockets of the village. When the dreaded Wasps prowled into the streets to sear buildings with gouts of flame, resistance cracked. Not that the Germans stayed around to be immolated. Despite attending the sites of innumerable Wasp actions over many months, flame-thrower specialist Lieutenant George Bannerman never found a single immolated or even badly burned German. There was even a medical officer at First Canadian Army headquarters who had issued a standing order that any dead or even seared Germans should be delivered for examination. "If we ever found one we were to alert him at Army HQ, but we never found one . . . As soon as the gunner pressed that trigger, everyone on the other side quit." Bannerman believed that this horrific weapon saved lives because the Germans were so afraid of it they usually surrendered at its mere appearance.[16]

As darkness fell upon the shattered village, Wasps growled and flamed through the streets, anti-tank guns blasted enemy positions at close range, and the rifle companies relentlessly fought from one building to the next. The paratroops lost ground steadily. Buildings burned, while others were reduced to piles of rubble by shellfire directed against them by artillery forward observation officers working alongside the HLI. Most fortified houses had been close to the edge of the village. When these were taken, the "backbone of the resistance was . . . broken."[17]

Soon after midnight, 'C' Company slipped into the southern end of Speldrop and rescued the platoon of 1st Black Watch that had been trapped for hours in cellars. It was a potentially deadly moment for both sides. Private Glen Tomlin spotted movement in a basement and loosed a burst with his Sten before realizing he was firing at a British soldier. Struck in the shoulder by four of Tomlin's bullets, the man thanked him "for his trip back to England." One of Tomlin's buddies accidentally felled another Black Watch soldier with five slugs to the body. "Careful there, mate, I'm British," the man cried. "Screw me, chum. I'm sorry," the gunner stammered and then shouted, "These guys are British in here!"[18]

Still the Germans fought on. "Houses had to be cleared at the point of the bayonet and single Germans made suicidal attempts to break up our attacks. Wasp flame throwers were used to good effect. It was necessary to push right through the town and drive the enemy out into the fields where they could be dealt with." In the morning, 'D' Company "sent a strong patrol out . . . and captured several MG crews who were asleep at their guns. What they had been through in the past 24 hours of almost continual attack had apparently rendered them completely exhausted."[19]

By dawn on March 25, resistance had collapsed to a few lingering snipers attempting to cover a withdrawal back towards Bienan. When these were eliminated, the HLI declared the hamlet secured. Relieved by the British 7th Black Watch, the weary Canadians walked back to the river for a bit of sleep and a meal. They were to go back into the maw shortly, as 9th Canadian Infantry Brigade would assume primary responsibility for pushing through the Bienan gap. If the brigade's other two battalions bogged down, the HLI must fight again, despite counting two platoon lieutenants and eleven other ranks dead, with another three officers and twenty-one men wounded.[20]

BY LATE AFTERNOON on March 24, 9 CIB had finished crossing into the bridgehead at Rees. Brigadier Rocky Rockingham established his tactical headquarters in the same building used by the British 154th Brigade, so the Canadian relief could be as seamless as possible. At 1405, Rockingham briefed his battalion commanders. The

Stormont, Dundas and Glengarry Highlanders would take over the 51st Division's left flank from the 7th Black Watch.[21] British attempts to gain Bienan so far had proved futile; the 7th Argyll and Sutherland Highlanders stopped cold at a farm 150 yards short. After dark, the North Nova Scotia Highlanders would relieve the Argylls.

Rockingham planned to commit the Glens and North Novas to an early morning two-pronged advance. On the far left, the Glens would clear the ground bordered on either side by the Alter Rhine's horseshoe-shaped arms. Their first objective—the farm complex of Grietherbusch—lay smack in the horseshoe's middle and 2,500 yards from the start line. From Grietherbusch, the Glens would move on a smaller farm called Tillhaus to finish ejecting the Germans from the horseshoe.

The North Novas, meanwhile, would move up the right bank of the Alter Rhine's eastern arm, relieve the Argyll remnants still holding the farm code-named in their honour, and then attack Bienan. With the HLI still tied up at Speldrop, 3rd Canadian Infantry Division agreed to send 8th Canadian Infantry Brigade's North Shore (New Brunswick) Regiment across the Rhine early to provide Rockingham with a reserve that would be operational just after sunrise.[22]

At 1930 hours, the Glens started relieving the 7th Black Watch. While the switchover of rifle companies would not occur until after dark because the forward lines were too close to the Germans, the swap of battalion headquarters and medical personnel happened at dusk. When medical officer Captain Phil Rance arrived at the new Regimental Aid Post (RAP), he saw "many dead Germans in the field outside caught by our mortars when they counter-attacked the Black Watch."[23]

"It is a bright moonlit night, and a very noisy one," the Glens' war diarist, Lieutenant J.C. Kirby, wrote. "Our art[iller]y is putting up a terrific barrage and Jerry is putting over the odd shell, some of which land uncomfortably close to this HQ. We lend a cynical ear to the commentators who babble about the light resistance offered by the Jerries to our landings across the Rhine, and who talk about our great advances. From where we sit it looks rugged . . . The SDG [Stormont, Dundas and Glengarry Highlanders] have the unique position of being on the left of the whole Allied push."[24]

In a muddy slit trench dug into the ditch alongside a road leading from the river to Bienan, North Novas' Lieutenant Donald
Pearce observed that the "horizon all the way around was faintly
glowing, more a murky glow than a definite light, the reflection of
burning farms and towns in the distance; and occasionally there
were angry, pulsing flashes low down along the horizon directly to
our front."[25]

At 0630 hours on March 25, the artillery supporting the Glens
opened fire, and the infantry advanced. Despite the prevailing fine
spring weather, the Glens slogged their way forward across ground
still sodden from winter rains. Standing pools of water and mud-
holes confined the rifle companies to a road that ran due north to
just short of Grietherbusch before doglegging into it. Confined to
the road, the Glens advanced with just 'D' Company out front until it
reached a small farm that proved undefended. 'C' Company passed
to the front for the next leg to another small farm, where two stragglers wanted only to surrender. Not until Major Jack Peterson took
the lead at 0800 hours for the next five-hundred-yard push did the
Germans suddenly awake to the approaching attack.[26]

Artillery and mortar fire bracketed the road. One shell landed on
the roadside next to a Bren carrier from the battalion carrier platoon
that was providing close machine-gun support and knocked it out.[27]
Nearby, despatch rider Private Larry McKay fell off his motorcycle
with shrapnel wounds to his right shoulder and back. A second despatch rider, Private Carmen Piercy, suffered a right leg wound that
required amputation. All this damage, McKay lamented, "from the
same shell!" He was evacuated on the same Buffalo that had brought
him across the Rhine less than twenty-four hours before.[28]

Closing on Grietherbusch at 0900, 'B' Company was forced to
ground by heavy machine-gun fire. "'B' [Company] have really hit a
snag," Lieutenant Kirby reported. "They have been pinned down by
MG fire and have sent for flame."[29] A number of men had been
wounded. Major Peterson had been shot through "the upper end of
his right femur."[30]

Losing men with each lurch forward, 'B' Company crept towards
Grietherbusch. The fire was so intense that platoon commanders
were unable to coordinate each section's actions. When the lead pla-

toon's lieutenant and sergeants were all wounded in a matter of seconds, Corporal John Handley took charge. After reorganizing the survivors to keep them in the fight, he ran back to the company's headquarters section and arranged for the Wasp flame-throwers to come forward before going back to carry on running the platoon. Handley received a Military Medal.[31]

Despite withering German fire, the battalion's No. 2 section of Wasps under Lance Sergeant Alvin Clifford Dolan rushed forward. "Without any covering fire, [Dolan] led his carriers forward to the strongpoint, flushing the enemy fortifications with flame and chasing the defenders screaming from their hide-outs," read his Military Medal citation.[32]

Contrary to their reputation, the mere appearance of Wasps was often not enough to break the paratroops in Grietherbusch. Private James Allan William Whitacre's No. 10 Platoon was pinned down trying to close on a fortified house surrounded by trenches and machine-gun emplacements on the outskirts. Loopholes punched through the exterior walls of the house allowed snipers and machine-gunners to shoot without fear of being struck by return fire. With just two men, Whitacre led a gun-blazing charge through the trenches and emplacements. As they broke into the house, the paratroops scattered. Another Military Medal went to a Glen.[33]

Despite such acts of bravery, 'B' Company and the Wasps were still fighting to get inside Grietherbusch at noon. Ordering them to stand fast, sDG commander Lieutenant Colonel Neil Gemmel had 14th Field Regiment smother the farm with shells and then advanced 'D' Company, under Captain John Alexander Dure, to renew the attack. Despite the artillery pounding, Dure "launched his attack in the face of intense fire from the enemy dug-in positions." The lead platoon faltered, as had the one at the head of 'B' Company, but this time Dure ran out into the open ground and shouted for the men to cover him. With two sections following on his heels, Dure charged into the left-hand side of the farm complex and the rest of the company was soon forging through the buildings. Once the shooting ceased, 'D' Company counted fourteen Germans killed or wounded and another twenty-two taken prisoner. Grietherbusch was theirs, and Dure had earned a Military Cross.[34]

Pressing on quickly to Tillhaus, the Glens were able to drive the paratroops out before they could organize a defence. The Glens not only took the horseshoe but reported capturing a 6th Fallschirm-jäger Battalion colonel and his adjutant to boot.[35]

5

The Enemy Fought Like Madmen

THE PRIMARY PURPOSE of clearing the Alter Rhine horseshoe had been to secure the left flank of the route that the North Nova Scotia Highlanders used to approach Bienan. Grietherbusch, parallel to Bienan, was expected to be taken before their attack went in. The North Novas also understood that the ground between Rosau—where the battalion headquarters had been established close to the windmill of a large farm—and Argyll Farm was free of Germans. Hence, Argyll Farm had been designated as their start line, and the approach to it was a simple matter of marching. An artillery bombardment, including covering smoke, was to begin at 0845 and the attack to start at 0900 hours. Further fire support came from the battalion's 3-inch mortar platoon and the 4.2-inch tubes of the Cameron Highlanders of Ottawa (MG), which were both set up behind buildings in Rosau. A single troop of tanks from the British 8th Armoured Brigade's Staffordshire Yeomanry (Queen's Own Royal Regiment) would advance alongside the leading 'A' Company.[1]

A ten-foot-high dyke next to the Alter Rhine offered the only cover, so Lieutenant Colonel Don Forbes decided to advance two companies—one behind the other—alongside it to Argyll Farm. If the infantry hugged close to the western side of the dyke, its thick earthen wall would protect their right flank while the horseshoe to the left would be clear.

Delaying the move to Argyll Farm until 0815 hours, to allow the Glens time to secure the horseshoe, 'A' Company led off in single file beside the dyke. 'B' Company was in trail. Major Don Learment commanded 'A' Company, and Captain Jack Fairweather had 'B' Company. Ten minutes later, a few hundred yards short of Argyll Farm, Learment's men came under intense mortar and machine-gun fire from Grietherbusch. Several men in No. 7 Platoon fell. Learment yelled for the company to flee to the other side of the dyke, but as the first men came up on top, they were met by sniper and machine-gun fire from positions to the south and east. Spotting a network of German slit trenches dug into the top, of the dyke, Company 'A' plunged into their cover just as mortar rounds showered around them.[2] Learment reported that his men were pinned down.[3]

'B' Company fared no better. The leading No. 11 Platoon had been struck by fire from all the same points. Lieutenant W.G. Tulloch got his men under cover without anyone being hit, but there was no way they could advance. Fairweather ordered his company headquarters section and the other two platoons to dig into the side of the dyke for shelter and signalled Forbes that the advance was stalled.[4]

At 0845, the artillery bombardment started.[5] The shells exploding in Bienan were of no use, but the smokescreen gave Learment a chance to lead 'A' Company in a full-tilt sprint towards Argyll Farm. Lieutenant E.J. Smith's platoon led, racing in a line along a ditch. As the platoon started dashing across a dugout large enough to have hidden a tank, a machine gun to the east fired through its entrance. Smith and one section were out front and lunged for cover on that side, while the other two sections ducked back to get out of the line of fire. Regaining their breath, the following two sections dodged past the gap in clutches timed to the rhythm of the Germans changing ammunition belts. Reunited, the platoon soon took refuge in Argyll Farm, finding it held by just a few exhausted Argylls.

The rest of 'A' Company safely navigated the same hazardous course. Looking back from Argyll Farm, Learment saw that one of the British tanks was bogged down in mud by the dyke, the second had been knocked out by an anti-tank round, and the third was retreating. Directing one platoon into the house where Smith was located, he sent the third, under Lieutenant Bob Hart, towards another building on the left-hand side of the farm. As they closed on the building, Germans inside it opened up with rifles and light machine guns. Private P.A. Sidney immediately rushed the position with his Bren gun barking out rounds so accurately that the German gunners were forced to ground. Ramming home a fresh magazine, he dashed into the house. Nineteen paratroops surrendered. 'A' Company now had a toehold in supposedly secure Argyll Farm, but going for Bienan was impossible. Every time Smith ventured forth with his platoon, the fire from the village immediately drove them back. Several men were killed or wounded before Smith quit trying.

Captain Fairweather reached the farm with just twenty-five of his men, mostly from No. 12 Platoon. The rest of 'B' Company was stuck on the dyke.[6] Back at battalion headquarters, the wireless reports coming in led the war diarist to accurately conclude that the North Novas "had quite definitely lost the initiative." At 1030 hours, Brigadier Rockingham came up to look at the situation first-hand. He and Forbes walked from Rosau to where they could see Bienan in the distance. "Start from scratch and do the attack over again with the two remaining companies," Rockingham said.[7] As the two officers were looking towards Bienan, Rosau behind them was being shelled and mortared from the Germans on Hoch Elten's commanding heights. Movement anywhere in xxx Corps's bridgehead invited fire. The guns were relentless, preventing construction of bridges over the Rhine and equally harassing the assault on Bienan. Rockingham told Forbes that until he pushed through the gap so Hoch Elten could be dealt with, the entire bridgehead was in jeopardy.

Near the town of Millingen on a slight rise to the east of Bienan, more German gun batteries were bearing on the North Novas. A line of machine-gun positions were also dug in along the gentle slope running down to Bienan. Several self-propelled guns could be seen prowling in Bienan's streets, and there were anti-tank guns dug in on its right flank. The entire southern edge of the village had obviously been heavily fortified, and these positions were too close to Argyll Farm for artillery to fire without risk of hitting the men there.[8]

Unable to walk the North Novas into Bienan, 14th Field Regiment pounded suspected and known German gun and mortar positions. When the attack went in, the gunners would create a screen of red smoke from Millingen west to Hoch Elten to blind the German artillery observers.[9] A flight of Typhoon fighter-bombers would bomb and rocket Millingen. Rockingham scrounged a new troop of tanks from the 4th/7th Royal Dragoon Guards.[10] The 3rd Canadian Anti-Tank Regiment's 94th Battery was also called upon. The battery consisted of three troops. One was equipped with three self-propelled 17-pounders mounted on the turretless chassis of obsolete Valentine tanks, the second fielded four towed 17-pounders, and the third used Bren carriers to tow four 6-pounders. As the last two troops were too vulnerable to artillery, the North Novas would be supported by the Valentines.[11]

Rockingham and Forbes knew that the North Novas were going into action with a paucity of support compared to the firepower the Germans in Bienan could call upon. The paratroops also outnumbered the battalion and fought from fortified positions, while the North Novas must assault across open ground. The only improvement since the mauling of the first two companies was that the Glens had since won the horseshoe.

Forbes was still working up a plan when the XXX Corps commander, Lieutenant General Brian Horrocks, arrived and told him "that the advance should be hastened with all possible speed."[12] As if to emphasize the point, both Horrocks and Rockingham sat in on his briefing of 'C' Company's Major Lloyd Winhold and 'D' Company's Major Dave Dickson at 1315 hours. Another frontal assault would only fail, Forbes told them, so Dickson was to creep along the western edge of the Alter Rhine dyke and come up opposite Bienan just before the attack started. When the artillery opened up with its shells and smoke, it would also lay down a smokescreen in front of the village, so that the Germans would think a frontal attack was coming. Instead, Winhold's 'C' Company with Wasp carriers in support would make a wide arc to the south and back towards the village inside the screen covering Millingen. Both companies should manage to cross the open ground before them and establish toeholds on opposite sides of the village before the paratroops realized they had been duped. Neither Rockingham nor Horrocks offered comment, and zero hour was set for 1430 hours.

WITH THE GLENS controlling the horseshoe, the two companies were able to gain their start lines unmolested and were ready when the supporting fire opened up at 1415. The artillery cast smoke in front of Bienan and hammered the village from its centre back to the northern outskirts.[13] Across the river, 13th Field Regiment weighed in to help create the red smokescreen from Millingen to Hoch Elten.[14] From positions inside Argyll Farm, 'A' and 'B' Companies fired everything they had at Bienan to create the appearance of a frontal attack. The 4th/7th Royal Dragoon Guards tanks also shot directly through the smoke, screening the village.

Obscured by smoke, 'C' Company struck out on its wide arc, while 'D' Company headed single file along the western side of the dyke. Once the latter drew abreast of Bienan, two platoons would go over the top in line. Both platoons would make for specified clusters of houses on the village's western flank—Lieutenant G.L. Monkley's No. 17 Platoon on the right and Lieutenant Donald Pearce's No. 16 Platoon on the left. Pearce's main objective was a large three-storey fortified building. Once both platoons secured their objectives, Dickson would follow with his company headquarters, an artillery forward observation team, and Lieutenant Ron Boyce's No. 18 Platoon. The work of clearing Bienan house by house would then begin.

Company Sergeant Major Harry Bishop thought the scheme so perilous that he convinced Dickson to leave fifteen men, who either showed signs of battle exhaustion or were recent reinforcements, back at the dyke. Neither could be considered reliable in a jam, he said. In a pinch, they could serve as a reserve.[15]

Lieutenant Pearce and his men, meanwhile, were lying on the edge of the dyke "in a long crouching, extended line opposite our objective," watching the artillery hitting Bienan. "Only a few minutes and the town was smoking like a pile of autumn leaves." Thirty yards away, the houses looked still and quiet.

Dickson waved an arm and the two platoons, together only fifty strong, scrambled onto the dyke, only to run headlong into a wall of fire. Ten of Pearce's men fell dead or wounded, while the rest slithered down into a six-inch-deep ditch at the dyke's base and flattened into its cover. The platoon's two Bren gunners rose above the lip of the ditch with guns shouldered and were shot dead. Pearce saw paratroops firing machine guns out of the overlooking windows and others hurling stick grenades down from the top storey of the large building. "We've got to make a dash for it. We've got to get that house," Pearce shouted to his corporal, who slumped over, wounded. The infantryman next to Pearce tried to sight in on a German machine-gun position but cried out and collapsed on the lieutenant's arm. "Take it easy," Pearce told the man, even as his face turned greenish. Paratroops stationed north of Bienan had spotted the Canadians moving along the other side of the dyke and had alerted troops within the village. 'D' Company was ambushed.

Pearce feared they were all going to die, until Private Gordon Philip Cameron stood up in the midst of the massacre and "walked deliberately over to two of the German weapon-pits as if he were an invisible man." Casually, the twenty-one-year-old from Springhill, Nova Scotia, dropped a grenade into each position, turned around, and started back to the company, before being fatally shot in the back. The exploding grenades killed four Germans and wounded three others, causing a sudden slackening in the drenching machine-gun fire. Knowing the respite would be brief, Pearce shouted at his men to follow him in a hasty retreat behind the dyke. Only one man did so; the others were all either immobilized by wounds or dead.[16]

While No. 16 Platoon had been shredded, Monkley's No. 17 managed to dash to its assigned houses despite losing several men on the way. Those who made it chucked grenades through the doors and windows and then burst in with Bren guns, Sten submachine guns, and rifles blazing. Several paratroops fell dead and eleven others surrendered. Then about ninety Germans, who had only just arrived and were still preparing positions in adjacent houses, poured out with hands raised.

Monkley did not keep the initiative of surprise for long, as other paratroops directed their fire against the houses from three sides. Dozens of machine guns ripped away, and mortars zeroed in. Roofs were torn open by exploding rounds, while bullets ripped splinters out of wood siding or crumbled brick walls to dust. Ceilings collapsed, plaster walls erupted, the air filled with choking dust, bullets, and shrapnel, glass shattered, and furniture splintered into slivers that cut to the bone. More North Novas fell dying or wounded.

Dickson decided to reinforce Monkley's limited success with the rest of 'D' Company. Gathering Lieutenant Ron Boyce's No. 18 Platoon and the fifteen men the CSM had insisted be left behind, Dickson clawed his way to the top of the dyke. Rising to his full six-foot-three height and turning to encourage the others forward, he presented a perfect target to the sniper who punched a round through the pipe-tobacco tin Dickson carried inside his battle dress. It caused the slug that would likely have severed his spine to sheer away and exit cleanly. Blood spilling from the entry and exit wounds, Dickson collapsed. As Sergeant Edison Alexander Smith came up alongside the fallen major, a mortar round exploded on the dyke and his torn corpse was thrown upon Dickson. Slowly the body rolled free and slid down the slope.[17]

Bombardier Robert Muir saw Dickson's fall from a spot on the dyke's west bank, where he had been waiting with a wireless set for his officer to show up. Muir dragged the major to safety. He and two North Novas sporting arm wounds carried Dickson to where Private Daniel Isaac Shanks was shuttling casualties back to Rosau with a jeep via a narrow track on the west side of the dyke. Fourteen times Shanks made this trip with the wounded packed in any which way. He then drove over the top of the dyke "in direct view of the enemy" to pick up wounded on that side. Realizing the jeep would bog down before it could reach most of No. 16 Platoon's wounded, Shanks jumped out, ran to the men, and carried the most badly injured one by one to the jeep. Roaring back to Rosau, he delivered this load to the RAP and then gathered up volunteers from Support Company personnel. This party went in and recovered the rest of the wounded. Shanks received a Military Medal for saving "very many of his comrades' lives."[18]

'D' Company was so badly mauled that its survivors were barely hanging on to the couple of buildings won by No. 17 Platoon.

Lieutenant Boyce had been wounded, ten men were dead, and another twenty-three were wounded. CSM Bishop, who would earn a Military Medal, dashed repeatedly from the houses to the other side of the dyke to send messages back to battalion headquarters and evacuate the wounded. Struck in the shoulder by shrapnel, he refused to leave for the next six hours, his iron hand helping keep the shrinking garrison fighting.[19]

While 'D' Company had been fighting for survival west of Bienan, 'C' Company had struck out from behind Argyll Farm on its wide sweep towards the eastern flank of the village, along with the Wasps, Valentines, and British tanks. At first the smokescreen kept them invisible as planned. But as the force closed on Bienan, its men saw the fuzzy lines of the buildings through the thinning smoke and realized the Germans would spot them at any moment. Major Winhold shouted for his men to charge and yelled into the wireless for the battalion mortars to fire more smoke in front of Bienan. As the screech of machine guns began opening up from within the village, 'C' Company sprinted forward.

The supporting mortars responded instantly, drenching the edge of Bienan with two hundred smoke rounds in a four-minute continuous volley that left the crews sweating and panting. Winhold, meanwhile, climbed onto the tank commander's Sherman and told the officer to fire everything he had over the heads of his men.[20]

'C' Company was being cut apart and was beginning to waver when No. 13 Platoon's Sergeant George Stewart broke off with a section and overran a concentration of machine guns firing from a dugout to its left. This eased the German firing just enough to allow the leading No. 15 Platoon to reach the Bienan–Speldrop road and head for the nearest building in the village. Only eight of the men still followed Lieutenant Bill Myers. As they dashed across the road, a German officer stepped out of the building's front door and shot Myers, just as the Canadian unleashed a burst of fire that killed the man. Myers, who received a Military Cross, was paralyzed for life.[21]

Seven men remained to seize the building. This they did while No. 13 Platoon was also breaking into the village. Fifteen minutes was all it had taken for 'C' Company to journey from Argyll Farm to

Bienan, but half of its men never got there. Eight lay dead on the ground and another twenty-four had fallen wounded.[22]

Inside Bienan the fight was at close quarters, with the paratroops determined to regain the couple of buildings lost. Back in the open, the wounded were drawing German fire as well. No. 14 Platoon's Sergeant Joseph Prokopchuk had been cut down by two bullets through his legs as he came up on the road. Despite his wounds, Prokopchuk dragged twelve other wounded men to safety. Turning back for another trip into the open field, he collapsed. Prokopchuk would recover and was decorated with a Military Medal.[23]

Inside Bienan, 'C' Company was withering so fast that Winhold combined two platoons into one and put it under command of the courageous Sergeant Smith, while he led the third. All the other officers were wounded. Despite these losses, Winhold decided to take the offensive. He led the men deeper into the village. They went alone, the tanks and other vehicles too vulnerable in the narrow streets to anti-tank guns and Panzerfausts. The Wasps could have helped, but all three had either broken down or been knocked out.[24]

The company moved through fire that came from all points of the compass. Twenty-five-year-old Private Hugh Patterson Christie of English Town, Nova Scotia, charged one machine-gun nest with his four-man section. He and his men were all killed. Christie was discovered later with one hand gripping the barrel of the MG-42 that had mortally wounded him even as he killed the entire crew.[25]

NOTIFIED THAT 'C' AND 'D' Companies had a tenuous hold inside the village, Lieutenant Colonel Forbes ordered Major Don Learment and Captain Jack Fairweather to bull their way into Bienan from Argyll Farm, where they had been reorganizing the survivors of 'A' and 'B' Companies respectively. What each had left was an oversized platoon, but both men immediately complied, with 'A' Company heading for the houses immediately in front of Argyll Farm and 'B' Company attempting to reach 'D' Company. The Dragoon Guards tanks growled over to support 'A' Company's advance across the open ground by setting the village's outlying buildings ablaze with phosphorous shells.

Fairweather's 'B' Company headed for the large three-storey fortress house, which was being used to pound 'D' Company. Seeing the Canadians coming, the Germans inside swung their weapons towards them, only to have to duck the British tank fire directed against the upper-storey windows. No. 10 Platoon reached the house first and broke into the main floor behind a shower of grenades, killing or capturing the few paratroops there.

Most of the Germans were upstairs, which became immediately evident when the ceiling erupted with bullets shot by the paratroops firing blindly downward. Fairweather responded by having No. 12 Platoon and the tanks hammer the upper storeys from outside, while the North Novas inside chucked grenades up the staircases and fired their guns through the ceiling. Men from No. 12 Platoon closed in to chuck grenade after grenade through the upper windows as they dodged grenades being flicked down at them. After a few minutes of this, the paratroops shouted their surrender. The Canadians took two officers and forty men prisoner and counted about fifty dead or dying scattered through the building. With the fortress taken, the German defence of Bienan began to crack.[26]

'B' Company found 'D' Company under command of the wounded Sergeant Bishop. A strange quiet settled over the village, both sides standing back like punch-drunk boxers to ready for the next round. Then, at 1500 hours, the Canadians advanced through the streets with the British tanks and Valentines in support. 'C' Company moved its two platoons along parallel streets and managed to reach the village's centre. Then, just after sunset, three SPGs and "a strong body of infantry" lunged out from several streets all at once. Two British tanks were knocked out, and the rest of the armour fled. Winhold could only follow, withdrawing to join 'A' Company in order to combine their fire. Having dashed after the surviving tank and talked its commander into returning, Winhold guided it back into position as the German SPGs and paratroops approached the fragile Canadian line. Winhold directed the tank's fire onto the SPGs and one was knocked out with the opening shot, causing the other two to retreat. Having lost their armour, the paratroops melted into the darkness. For his inspired leadership, Winhold received a Distinguished Service Order.[27]

The North Novas went back on the offensive, cautiously probing towards the northern edge. Each house had to be won in turn, so the pace was excruciatingly slow. But the gains now came at little loss of Canadian blood, indicating that the paratroops hoped only to delay and no longer stop the advance. At 2200 hours, Learment's 'A' Company reported reaching a large creamery close to Bienan's north-eastern corner.

If the Germans in Bienan were nearing the end of their endurance, the same was true for the North Novas. The companies were so badly shot up and the men so exhausted that the battalion was ready to collapse. Recognizing this, Brigadier Rockingham ordered a halt. As the Highland Light Infantry had finished winning Speldrop several hours earlier, giving it the briefest of rests, he directed Lieutenant Colonel Phil Strickland to relieve the North Novas at 2300 hours.

After the hand-off, the surviving North Novas trudged out of Bienan. "It was a long, hard bitter fight against excellent troops who were determined to fight to the end," their war diarist wrote. "Over 200 prisoners were taken and many killed." But the North Novas had paid a brutal price. Thirty-five other ranks dead, seven officers and seventy-two other ranks wounded, and a further four men evacuated with battle exhaustion, for a total of 118 casualties.[28] Bienan was its second-most-costly battle of the war. And still the Germans in Bienan continued to resist.

THE HIGHLAND LIGHT Infantry, its ranks badly depleted at Speldrop, moved into a nighttime battle in which every building turned out to be heavily fortified and once again fanatically defended. The three Valentine tank destroyers proved immediately welcome when a German self-propelled gun drove one HLI platoon to ground with machine-gun fire. Warned by the burning wreck of a Royal Dragoon Guard tank, the Valentine troop was in hunting mode when the SPG opened fire. Troop commander Lieutenant John Anderson jumped out of his own Valentine and guided the one ahead along a street in search of an angle of fire on the SPG. When the gun suddenly ceased firing, they heard it start growling off towards a new location.[29] Deciding to force the SPG's hand, Anderson removed the Bren gun from its mount and slipped off to one side. He then fired a magazine in the SPG's general direction. "This fire brought back heavy retaliatory fire," Anderson's Military Cross citation noted.[30] The Valentine immediately fired. "There was a metallic sound of the round striking the target," and the SPG started to burn.[31]

The HLI fought on from one building to another with grenades and bayonets. "Progress was very slow, as the enemy fought like madmen," the regiment's war diarist wrote. "Isolated houses had to be cleared and [this] proved most difficult. The enemy arty and mortars poured shells into our [troops] continually. Again single paratroopers made suicidal charges . . . They were consistently chopped down but sometimes not before they had inflicted casualties on our sections."[32]

The HLI divided Bienan up, with 'C' Company responsible for the northeastern portion. No. 13 Platoon headed for some buildings set off from the rest of the village. As the platoon moved out from the shelter of some houses, it was struck by machine-gun and rifle fire coming from their objective. Several men were cut down. Acting Sergeant Frederick James Jarman, who was commanding, suffered head and arm wounds but led his men into the buildings as the Germans retreated. Taking advantage of the lull, Jarman accompanied the wounded back to the RAP and had his own wounds dressed. When the medical officer told him he was to be immediately evacuated over the Rhine, Jarman refused, as the platoon had nobody else to lead it. Instead, Jarman returned and led it in an attack on the next group of buildings, which were gained easily. The men no sooner entered than the Germans opened fire at close range. Only after this attack was driven off and the company's reserve platoon had passed through No. 13 Platoon's position did Jarman agree to evacuation. He was awarded an immediate Military Medal.[33]

When the sun rose behind a mask of chalk-grey clouds, the German paratroops still fighting in Bienan no longer offered a unified defence, their resistance consisting instead of isolated groups or individual snipers "who refused to quit." Soon these were all killed or captured. 'D' Company pushed out from the village about one thousand yards to where a deep anti-tank ditch cut across the breadth of the Bienan gap.[34] Lieutenant Colonel Phil Strickland instructed Sergeant Wilfred Francis Bunda to reinforce the company with his anti-tank-gun section.

Bunda faced a repeat of his experience in Speldrop, with the guns needing to be pulled forward across ground that was under German observation and swept by machine-gun fire from the right flank. The road was also laced with mines. Dismounting from his carrier, Bunda walked forward at the head of the column, guiding the vehicles around suspected mines as bullets zipped all around him. Just short of the designated gun position, the men met a roadblock, and from either flank paratroops opened up with machine guns and mortars.

Yelling at his men to unhook the 6-pounders from the carriers, Bunda had them manhandled up a narrow track towards their assigned firing position. Crouching low behind the gun shields as they shoved the weapons forward, the men had some scant protection from the fire. But Bunda, who constantly dodged from one gun to the other to help position them, was dangerously exposed. He was also charmed, and came through unscathed to accept a Military Medal.[35] The anti-tank guns secured the HLI hold on the anti-tank ditch, and Bienan was finally taken.

From the anti-tank ditch, the North Shore (New Brunswick) Regiment attacked Millingen. Only after this battalion moved forward in the early afternoon of May 26 were the exhausted Highlanders withdrawn to a rest area. Given the intensity of the fighting during the long night, it was surprising that only four men had been killed. But among the dead was Lieutenant George Oxley MacDonald, who had shown such gallantry at the head of 'A' Company's No. 8 Platoon in Speldrop. Twenty-eight other ranks had been wounded. A draft of reinforcements soon arrived that made good these other-rank losses but did not replace those who had fallen in Speldrop. Also there was only one officer. The regiment was terribly weak, which was true of all three 9 CIB battalions.[36]

6

More Than Battered About

HROUGHOUT 9TH CANADIAN Infantry Brigade's struggle to
uncork the Bienan gap, it had been hamstrung by limited
access to artillery and armour. The latter had consisted of just one
British tank troop per battalion, with the 3rd Canadian Anti-Tank
Regiment's 94th Battery's Valentine troop dashing to wherever the
need was greatest. Artillery support had been confined to the field
regiments of 3rd Canadian Infantry Division. With two of these firing obliquely from across the Rhine and the fighting taking place at
such close quarters, the gunners had often had to shell only positions well back or provide smoke cover. While these supporting arms
undoubtedly helped the infantry carry the day, the price paid in casualties would have been less if support had been closer to normal
levels.

Brigadier Rocky Rockingham, who the brigade's war diarist
thought looked "a bit tired after not having any sleep since landing
and being constantly engaged with a stubborn enemy during that
time," was consequently relieved to learn on the morning of March
26 that he would be reinforced by 3rd Division's Canadian Scottish
Regiment.[1] Also his brigade was to come under the newly arrived
British 43rd (Wessex) Division, which would commit its 130th Brigade to attack north from Rees through the village of Androp to

Millingen simultaneously with the North Shore Regiment's assault from Bienan.[2]

The NSR would also enjoy a bounty of support from a complete squadron of the British 4/7th Royal Dragoon Guards. Rockingham had priority call on the corps artillery as well.[3] Timing of the attack was continuously revised as this support was geared up and the HLI laboured to secure the anti-tank ditch start line north of Bienan.

Sensing a buffet of support at his beck and call, Lieutenant Colonel John Rowley requested and was promised a strike by Typhoon fighter-bombers on Millingen before the attack. Rockingham provided seven field regiments and two medium regiments firing "a continuous barrage" that would advance two-hundred-yard lifts when the lead rifle companies requested the guns to advance. The tank squadron was to be out front "taking on everything they can." Even Crocodiles—flame-thrower-equipped tanks—were available.

Rowley planned to advance three companies in train while sending 'B' Company to clear the Germans out of a group of houses on the left flank. The main body would see 'A' Company leapfrogged by 'C' Company, with 'D' Company delivering the final assault into Millingen. After some delay, zero hour was set for noon.[4]

Rowley walked among the ranks, exchanging brief words with officers and men. Thirty-three-year-old Rowley had been commissioned in 1933 as a reserve officer in Ottawa's Cameron Highlanders along with his older brother, Roger. When war came, the two became the city's best-known officers. As the campaign in Northwest Europe advanced, both Rowleys had risen to command battalions—Roger, the Glens in Normandy; John, the North Shores in December 1944. Both quickly overcame their regimental status as outsiders. Roger cemented a reputation for daring impetuosity that won him a Distinguished Service Order in the fighting at Boulogne and a bar to the DSO during Operation Switchback in the Breskens Pocket. Less flamboyant than his brother and more inclined to detailed planning before entering a battle, John had also proved a competent battalion commander and earned a DSO during the Rhineland Campaign. Because of their battlefield exploits, with their battalions often fighting in close proximity, the Rowleys became known as the "brother act." On March 1, however, the act had closed with Roger's transfer to 3rd Division Training School.

Precisely at noon on March 26, the remaining Rowley still in action ordered the North Shores to advance alongside a road that led from the anti-tank ditch eastward to the small village of Am Stevert, immediately northwest of Millingen. 'A' Company's Major L.S. Murray had two platoons out front with one following in reserve. Am Stevert lay just under a mile away across wide-open ground, and the company was to lead for six hundred yards to a straggle of farmhouses and then let 'C' Company through. This company would advance to Am Stevert, and then 'D' Company would hook from the village into Millingen. 'B' Company should have come up by then on its path to enter the town in line with 'D' Company.[5]

Under a barrage that Lieutenant M.H. Rogers described as "tremendous," 'A' Company hugged it all the way to the houses. Murray reported at 1240 hours that the farm was secure and he had prisoners. "Opposition was not heavy," he added.

Five minutes later, battalion headquarters learned that Rowley had been killed by a shell while walking back to the HLI headquarters. Major Neil Gordon roared forward in a jeep to take command, and there was no pause in the operation.[6]

Out on the left flank, 'B' Company headed towards the suspected fortified houses, came under machine-gun fire from them, and was forced to ground. From where he kissed the dirt, Acting Corporal Reginald Alastar Shepherd realized they were going to be slaughtered. Signalling his six-man section, Shepherd led them in a crouched dash across the open ground to strike the buildings from a blind side. He and another man kicked in a door on the closest building and were tangled in a fierce fight. But after several Germans were killed, the remaining twenty-three in the building surrendered, and four machine guns were silenced. This weakened the overall German defences sufficiently to enable 'B' Company to carry the other buildings. Shepherd's dash was recognized with a Military Medal.[7]

Meanwhile, Major Blake Oulton's 'C' Company had just been moving off the start line when one platoon was smothered by artillery fire. Several men were killed or wounded, and it took the leadership of Sergeant Joseph Lawrence Hennigar to get the survivors moving again. They rejoined the company just in time to move through 'A' Company and discover that fifteen hundred yards of level ground, absent any cover, stretched between them and Am Stevert. Oulton, though, had the support of artillery and British tanks. "We walked in under the barrage and the guns of the tanks and in very short order the Germans came flooding out of the houses and trenches, about 200 of them. The defences were good and the guns were there but the platoons were on them before the Germans could lift their heads. For those who couldn't be dealt with at once, I called up the tanks, and soon we were solid."[8]

The major's account downplayed the intensity of the battle. Some Germans in Am Stevert sought a fight and were well positioned and equipped for it. Hennigar's platoon had easily seized its objective but had come under heavy fire from houses to the front, which forced the men into a trench they had just cleared. Unable to see the source of the shooting, Hennigar stepped out into the open so that he could direct his men's fire. They had gained the upper hand when a German tank rumbled out from behind a building and tore into them with its 75-millimetre main gun and machine guns. Grabbing a PIAT gun, Hennigar dropped to the ground, shouldered the awkward weapon, and discharged a bomb that damaged one of the tank's tracks. This convinced its commander to reverse back the way he had come. Hennigar then turned the PIAT against the buildings and pummelled them with two bombs. The resulting holes in the walls and scattering of shrapnel inside decided the issue, and ten surviving Germans stumbled out. Hennigar's Military Medal recognized his leadership both at the start line and throughout the fight at Am Stevert.[9]

Lieutenant Phil Chiasson and his platoon were approaching a house when a German appeared, waving a white flag out one of the windows. The Canadians had seen this ruse before, so Chiasson held his men in place rather than moving into the open to accept the surrender. Sure enough, the Germans suddenly let loose a Panzerfaust round that narrowly missed the lieutenant, who returned fire with a long burst from his Sten gun. That convinced the Germans to surrender for real.

Captain Bob Albert led 'D' Company into Millingen and bagged a good number of prisoners. He was just setting up a headquarters in a house when two Germans came "ambling down the street as nonchalant as could be. I assumed they were prisoners sent along by the platoon and yelled at them to get the hell along . . . One got down on his knees, pointed a bazooka [Panzerfaust] at me and let go. I just had time to dive into the door of a house when about half the wall came down on me. That was the lesson I needed. There was no further trouble from that pair, then or afterward, and my rule in the next scrap was 'shoot first and ask questions afterward.'"

'D' Company advanced through Millingen towards an "old-world castle. It was heavily constructed and was thought to be well fortified." Albert called artillery and even tactical air on assigned targets. The castle was designated for both, and the artillery marked its position for the Typhoon fighter-bombers by striking it with several red smoke shells. The Typhoons screamed down and fired rockets. "The noise was deafening. Then came the big explosions. Our ringside seats were a bit too near and we had two casualties." The moment the explosions ceased, 'D' Company rushed the castle. "We expected things to be really tough, but all we found was 25 Volkssturm with not much fight left." The castle had served as a military hospital, hastily abandoned. In the cellars, civilian refugees huddled.[10] At 1700 hours, the NSR linked up with British troops from the 130th Brigade, and the Bienan bottleneck was uncorked.

AN HOUR AFTER Millingen was secured, the Glens stepped out from the anti-tank ditch and walked north into what remained of the Bienan gap. Their goal was the village of Praest, on a sharp angle west of the Alter Rhine. This was the start of the 11 Canadian Corps advance on Emmerich, about five miles west of 9 CIB's new front. The purpose was to create enough elbow room inside the bridgehead to allow 3rd Canadian Infantry Division to establish itself in its entirety as the XXX Corps's left flank anchor.

The Glens advanced warily, fearing another ambush. Praest lay one and a half miles from the start line, and the ground was the usual open field with a few small, scattered farms that could be German forts. 'A' Company's Major James Wallace Braden was surprised to encounter no resistance at all en route to its first objective. One after the other, the companies passed through each other, meeting barely any opposition. Building clusters whose names had more letters in them than there were houses were quickly cleared. Grevenshof, Hueth, and Phalenhof fell without a shot fired. On one occasion, Braden's men discovered three German soldiers sleeping soundly and had to shake them awake to take their surrender.

'A' Company was beginning to lark along a thousand yards ahead of the rest of the battalion and was closing on Praest. It was beginning to look like a pleasant evening stroll until just before Praest, when the Germans suddenly counterattacked from the village with infantry supported by Tiger tanks. Weighing almost seventy tons and mounting an 88-millimetre gun, these behemoths were a nightmare vision for both Allied infantrymen and tankers. In a shootout, the more lightly armoured and under-gunned Shermans stood little chance. Most infantrymen tended to think all German tanks were Tigers, but whether they were Tigers or not, the approaching armour was more than capable of overrunning Braden's company.

In the opening moments of the action the artillery forward observation officer (FOO) accompanying the Glens had been killed, so Braden and his second-in-command, Captain Blair Gilmour—who had initially been trained as an artilleryman—got on the wireless set. With Gilmour helping him work out the firing coordinates, Braden called in artillery against the German tanks crunching up against the hasty perimeter 'A' Company had thrown together to meet the attack. While Braden directed artillery against the tanks, he concentrated most of the fire on the closing infantry and broke their attack. As the infantry withdrew in disorder, leaving many dead and wounded on the field, the tanks began milling about uncertainly. Braden and Gilmour immediately turned all the artillery on the tanks, which caused them to scatter and flee back to Praest.[11]

Counterattack beaten off, the Glens marched on, and by first light on March 27 were positioned in four strongpoints extending back from a clutch of houses identified as Berg, about one thousand yards east of Praest, to the anti-tank ditch by Bienan. Intensive patrolling followed, and throughout the day patrols returned with no prisoners and no reports of sighting Germans. Finally, at 1445 hours, one patrol picked up thirty Germans all wearing civilian clothes but looking very much like soldiers. An increasing number of legitimate civilians were reporting Praest clear of paratroops. The Glens soon set up on the outskirts, securing the start line for an advance by the Canadian Scottish Regiment on Emmerich, from which the civilians claimed the Germans had withdrawn.

It was hard to know what to make of German civilians. The Glens found them "moderately friendly and almost obeisant... If they hate us they choose to dissemble their hatred. As is to be expected though, their sympathies are aligned with the German soldier. Upon our arrival here we buried three dead Jerrys found on the premises and the mistress of the house, a reserved, dignified German matron, quietly asked us for the identification of the dead in order that she might, we supposed, mark the graves and communicate with the surviving families."[12]

With German opposition limited to the incessant artillery and mortar fire emanating from the woods on the heights of Hoch Elten, the Canadians were able to rapidly expand their presence across the Rhine on March 27. Rockingham and his 9 CIB were clearly worn out, so the advance to Emmerich fell to 7th Canadian Infantry Brigade, with the Can Scots entering the bridgehead at 1300 hours, followed soon after by the Regina Rifles and Royal Winnipeg Rifles. All these battalions crossed on bridges rather than Buffaloes.

Until that morning, most movement of men, vehicles, and supplies had been restricted to a massive amphibious operation that employed hundreds of sappers, pioneers, and Royal Naval personnel equipped with Buffaloes, amphibious trucks (DUKWs), boat ferries, and large rafts capable of transporting tanks and other heavy equipment over the Rhine.[13] Although the engineers had erected the first bridge at Rees as early as 0100 hours on March 26, "Waterloo Bridge" was a Class 9 folding boat bridge with limited capacity. This was followed by "Lambeth Bridge," a Class 15 pontoon bridge, which opened at 0835 hours, and "London Bridge," a Class 40 Bailey pontoon bridge at 2345 hours. The same day, Canadian engineers from the

29th, 30th, and 31st Field Companies started working west of Rees on a second Class 40 bridge that would be "the longest Bailey Bridge in the world," at 1,814 feet.[14]

Following a gruelling round-the-clock schedule, the Canadian sappers and pioneers working on "Blackfriars Bridge" used artificial moonlight provided by searchlight beams bounced off low clouds for night illumination. When the all-too-common fog settled in, search-lights were pointed directly at the structure. Despite the punishing pace, completion was not expected until March 30.[15] Hampering all bridging work was the harassing fire from Hoch Elten.

This constant barrage made 7 CIB's forthcoming advance on Emmerich all the more urgent, as it would allow 11 Canadian Corps to begin bridge construction in front of the city and would lead to opera-tions against these heights. Crossing on foot over wobbly Waterloo Bridge on the late afternoon of March 26, the Can Scots found "the whole area . . . under shellfire from . . . enemy guns. The Bridgehead was shrouded in a smokescreen; and this, added to the weird flashes of guns, made a ghostly scene as we traversed this last barrier to For-tress Germany."[16] Their regiment's pipers led the way, the drone of the bagpipes almost a supernatural sound in the false mist.[17]

WHILE THE CAN Scots formed for their attack, Brigadier Stanley Todd, the 11 Canadian Corps chief artilleryman, directed a massive artillery program against the city and Hoch Elten that would attain its height on March 28. Once the Rhine bridgehead had been estab-lished, Todd had turned the fury of the Canadian artillery against these two targets. Todd knew how artillery weakened the soldiers under its fire: land a shell within fifty to sixty yards of a man and he generally cowered. So in the four days leading up to the attack on Emmerich, Todd decided to make sure every German there would be cowering. Dividing Emmerich and Hoch Elten into hundred-yard squares on a map, he assigned at least one gun to each square. By this strategy, "it wouldn't be possible for anybody to be outside the range of 50 yards of an individual shell. By firing about four rounds to the hour, at irregular intervals, left to the discretion of the individ-ual gun sergeant, not a German soldier on that hill could go more than 15–20 minutes without having a shell within 50 yards of him. With the technical variances applicable to each shell, none would fall in the same place a second time."

Todd sought to pin the enemy "to the ground, unable to sleep, crawl to the latrine safely, unable to get meals, unable to get together and unable to give orders."[18] How many shells were ultimately directed against Emmerich and Hoch Elten during these days was never officially recorded, but the 13th Canadian Field Regiment's historian estimated four million shells were fired at Hoch Elten alone. "So heavy was the shelling that in some places the contour of the feature had been noticeably changed, and little remained but stumps and shattered trunks of the heavy growth of trees which had covered the hill."[19]

Despite the massive destruction wrought on Hoch Elten, the German artillery and mortars on its heights slackened their fire only marginally. Their guns and bunkers were dug so deep they remained relatively unscathed. They were also protected by the distance across the Rhine. It was impossible for artillery to gain the correct angle for the fall of shot to be directed on specific targets. Mostly the Canadians fired blind, and that meant the odds of a direct hit were poor.

Like Hoch Elten, Emmerich—a city with a normal population of sixteen thousand—had been all but destroyed by previous bombing and shelling, the former over a long period preceding Plunder. "Emmerich had been more than battered about," the Canadian Scottish regimental historian wrote. "It had been blasted time and again even before the Rhine had been crossed, and was continually hammered afterwards. Instead of bricks knocked into the street by shellfire, whole walls had crumbled down under attack from the air and land bombardment to block the thoroughfares, and buildings, burning without hindrance, sent tons of masonry, wooden beams and steel girders crashing down into the streets."[20]

Deciding he still lacked sufficient firepower to root the Germans out of their formidable fortifications, Todd brought up 4th Canadian Armoured Division's 4th Canadian Armoured Brigade and strung its three tank regiments in one unbroken line alongside the river. A total of seventeen thousand shells had been stored in pits next to the Shermans for firing at Hoch Elten and Emmerich.[21]

At 1700 hours, 7th Brigade's Brigadier Graeme Gibson tersely ordered Lieutenant Colonel Larry Henderson to "move along and . . . take over the advance" from the Glens. Forty-five minutes later, Henderson told the Can Scot company commanders that they would simply advance up the Rees–Emmerich road until they either ran into trouble or walked unmolested into Emmerich. Along the way, they would clear Praest and Vrasselt. 'A' and 'B' Companies would lead, moving along opposite sides of the road. 'C' and 'D' Companies would follow, with the headquarters support platoon and its vehicles strung out on the road farther back. Unlike some Canadian battalions, the Can Scots were in good shape with 801 men and 39 officers. They were rested and ready to go, which they did at 1830 hours.[22]

The lead companies swept rapidly through Praest, where "all the houses in the town and along the road display[ed] white sheets, pillowcases or shirts to indicate the surrender of the sullen civilian population in their wrecked villages and homes." Anticipating "that there would be no major opposition before we reached the outskirts of Emmerich," Henderson decided to keep the 'A' and 'B' Companies out front.[23]

By midnight the battalion closed, still unopposed, on Vrasselt, encouraged "to see all the white flags hanging from the houses as the men probed on." Vrasselt was thoroughly searched for enemy by 0115 hours, and the battalion sent patrols towards a long row of brickyards and kilns that lined the road to the west of the village. 'A' Company soon sent back the first prisoners—a "motley crowd [that] included 3 Italians, 6 Frenchmen, 1 Pole, 1 Belgian, 1 Dutchman, and 3 Germans. There was no way of telling which was enemy and which was friend so they were all treated as suspicious and sent to the [POW] 'Cage.'"[24]

The Can Scots were still probing for German defences in front of Emmerich when Gibson issued new orders. Although he had only taken over 7 CIB on February 27, Gibson was a seasoned brigade commander, having led 3rd Brigade from October 1943 to April 1944 and then 2nd Brigade until the conclusion of the Gothic Line battle that October. During his time in Italy, Gibson's leadership ability had been found lacking, and he had been packed off to administrative postings

in England. Then, due to a growing shortage of experienced brigadiers, he was returned to combat duty just as the Rhineland
Campaign concluded. This current operation was the first opportunity for his battalion commanders to see their new leader in action
during combat. Gibson quickly made it clear that he expected rapid
results, even if it cost lives. Expressing impatience with Henderson's
cautious patrolling, he insisted at 0400 hours that the Can Scots
"not . . . await the return of their patrol but . . . push [forward] until
they gained contact."

At 0430 hours, Henderson renewed the advance, with 'C' and 'D'
Companies at the battalion's head. Despite Gibson's demand for haste,
the Can Scots were slowed to a crawl by mines sown across the road
and along its verges.[25] Still, they met no opposition. At sunrise, 'C'
Company's Major H.F. Bailey and his 'D' Company counterpart, Captain Kenneth Stuart Douglas Corsan, saw a narrow stream about a
hundred yards ahead that cut across their front. This was the Landwehr, which the two companies were to cross, establishing a
bridgehead through which the other two companies would pass. The
stream was only a few yards wide, but they could see that the bridges
over it had been blown. Beyond the stream, an open field sloped up
from the Rhine to the railway line that ran from Rees through Emmerich. Along the tracks was an industrial area—a cluster of oil
refineries, slaughterhouses, and several factories. Smashed up by
artillery and bombing, its buildings were mostly now piles of rubble.

In the ruins of a nearby brickyard, a patrol encountered several
Dutch refugees, who claimed the Germans had withdrawn into
Emmerich.[26] So encouraged, Bailey and Corsan signalled to battalion headquarters their intent to cross the stream "per syllabus" and
establish a foothold inside the industrial area.[27] They advanced
through icy showers and under heavy cloud cover that cast the day in
a quasi-twilight. The Landwehr might be narrow, but it had cut a
deep channel that could not be crossed by tanks or other vehicles
without a bridge. 'C' Company scrounged planks from the wreckage
of one bridge and created a catwalk, which they crossed in single file
at 0800 hours. Fanning out by platoons in the field beyond, the men
started up the slope towards the industrial area. Everyone was on

edge, expecting fire from the rubble at any moment. Just as 'C' Company came up onto the Rees–Emmerich road, machine guns started flashing amid the rubble. The men broke into the cover of several large pits that had been dug into the side of the road to conceal German vehicles from the artillery across the Rhine. Adjacent pits were being used by the paratroops as firing positions, and the Can Scots were immediately engaged in a shootout at close range. Grenades were chucked back and forth and automatic weapons crackled.[28]

WELL BEFORE THE Can Scots came to this impasse, Gibson had been stepping up the pace of the entire brigade. Having in the late evening ordered the Regina Rifles to move up to the anti-tank ditch in order to follow behind the Can Scot advance, within an hour he had issued counter-instructions to instead move immediately towards Dornick—a town on the edge of the Rhine parallel to Vrasselt.[29] Twenty minutes later, Gibson demanded, "Are you on the move yet?" Lieutenant Colonel Al Gregory quickly responded, "No, in about fifteen minutes." Gibson came back in just ten minutes, at 0115 hours on March 28, and received Gregory's assurance that the Reginas were moving.[30]

An hour later, they controlled undefended Dornick and had moved out to the immediate west and dug in. Patrols started pushing towards Emmerich, two miles distant. 'D' Company's No. 16 Platoon lucked out by finding German slit trenches that spared them any spadework. The platoon had a new commander, Lieutenant J. Walter Keith, who had joined the Reginas on March 6 and taken over the platoon two days later. The regiment had been badly mauled in the Moyland Wood just before and its ranks still remained thin, with No. 16 Platoon fielding only thirty-two men. These NCOS and riflemen impressed Kieth with their professionalism.

To help individualize each man in his memory, Keith kept detailed notes in his platoon roll book. Their ages ranged from nineteen to thirty-five, but twenty-eight were under twenty-six years—five being only nineteen. Just one man was thirty-five. Nineteen hailed from Saskatchewan and seven from other western provinces. Only one was married. A mere six of the men, including Platoon Sergeant

R.S. "Tommy" Tomlinson, had been in the assault wave at Juno Beach. Corporal Homer Adams, the platoon's first section leader, was another D-Day veteran. The leader of the second section had joined the regiment on June 15, 1944, and the third had got his combat christening on the Leopold Canal that September. Keith knew he was lucky to have NCOs with such extensive combat experience. At first, he worried that Sergeant Tomlinson—who had commanded the platoon for two weeks before Keith's arrival—might resent "having a new and very green officer put over him." But Tomlinson's first words had been, "Jesus, am I glad to see you, Sir!" When Keith asked why, the sergeant replied that he just liked having an officer around.

While the rest of the platoon settled into the trenches, as per routine, two men set off to forage for food and returned with a "Nazi chicken," which was quickly plucked and tossed into a pot along with vegetables dug from a nearby garden. No sooner did the stew begin to boil, however, than an order to saddle up arrived. Disconsolately, the men shrugged into their gear and slung weapons. As they trudged forward, Keith saw one man gingerly carrying the hot kettle full of still-simmering stew. Things shortly got too busy for the lieutenant to remember whether the meal was ever eaten.[31]

As they advanced, the Reginas could hear the cacophony of the Can Scot's skirmish in front of the industrial area, so a fight was expected. When Gibson barged into Gregory's tactical headquarters and demanded he "push on as quickly as possible," Gregory had already decided to advance the battalion along a dyke bordering the Rhine in order to gain Emmerich left of the embattled Can Scots. By 1000 hours, 'A' Company was moving, with 'D' Company to its left and the other two rifle companies behind.[32]

From across the Rhine, the 120 Shermans of 4th Canadian Armoured Brigade started ranging on designated targets at precisely the same time that the Reginas went forward.[33] Guardsman Stuart Louis Johns was a loader/wireless operator in a tank from No. 2 Troop of No. 2 Squadron of the Canadian Grenadier Guards. His tank was also No. 2 in line within the troop, so the twenty-year-old from Windsor, Ontario, had come to think that two must be his lucky number. On March 28, his tank was just one in a long row of

Shermans. An artillery survey crew had earlier climbed on the back deck, and using transits and other gadgets that meant nothing to Johns, had aligned its main gun to fire on a specific target. Thereafter, all the tankers had to do was respond to orders about how many shells to fire at a given time. "Each unit had a schedule and every tank had a schedule," Johns later recalled. "Sometimes you would fire as a barrage and other times you would fire three rounds. Another time you'd only fire one and then maybe a barrage again."[34]

Also offering support to the Can Scots was 12th Field Regiment, which had only crossed into the bridgehead in the early morning hours of March 28 and set up gun lines next to Grietherbusch. Most of the targets were in the industrial area, but one gun was sighted on a church tower inside the city itself, since it would be an ideal observation post for the Germans.[35] This target "was about four thousand yards away," Captain Thomas Bell observed, "but out of eighty rounds fired over seventy hit the church spire and needless to say very little was left of it."[36]

7

Pretty Sticky

***

ARTILLERY AND TANK fire alone could not subdue Emmerich—
that would take boots on the ground. The Canadian Scottish
Regiment's 'C' and 'D' Companies sought to break the deadlock
along the Rees–Emmerich roadway where they and clusters of paratroops duelled from positions inside the vehicle pits. At 1145 hours
on March 28, 'C' Company's Major H.F. Bailey threw No. 15 Platoon,
under Lieutenant R.F. "Rolie" Campbell, out on the right flank to get
behind the Germans facing his front. Bailey cautioned Campbell to
keep on the south side of the railway embankment because it was
probable that superior numbers of Germans were using the other
side for cover and he wanted to avoid the platoon being caught in an
uneven shootout.

Campbell spotted three large shell craters north of the embankment as the platoon advanced along it. Deciding to ignore Bailey's
instructions, Campbell led his men in a dash over the embankment
and scattered them inside the craters by sections. He was just con-
gratulating himself on acquiring such a solidly defensible position,
when a German soldier began running towards the platoon. "I stood
up to wave him in with the thought that when he came in the rest
of the Germans would come in too. In fact, I could visualize head-
lines, 'Rolie Campbell captures Emmerich single handed!' The

soldier kept running towards us until he was within a hundred yards, and then he decided we were not his own troops and proceeded to turn back but on showing we wanted to talk and throwing down our weapons, he stayed.

"Corporal Oldenburger went out and held a conversation with the German soldier and asked him to give up and bring his friends with him. The German soldier said he wanted to do so but feared for his life as the others would not give in and would shoot him if he [did]." Both men returned to their lines, and the Germans started shooting at the platoon. Remembering his orders to get behind the German position, Campbell jumped out of a crater, shouted for the platoon to follow him, and then was punched back by a bullet in the chest. Seriously wounded, he collapsed into the crater, and his men went to ground.

Major Bailey learned of No. 15 Platoon's plight just as an artillery officer arrived at his tactical headquarters. Bailey asked for a smoke-screen in thirty minutes to cover the platoon's withdrawal. As the artillery officer began teeing up this mission, paratroops struck the entire company front. Fluent in German, Lieutenant S.F. Lettner told Bailey he could hear an officer exhorting his men to push on, saying they outnumbered the Canadians five to one. 'C' Company was engulfed in "about as mixed up a fight as I ever saw," Bailey later wrote. "As it got pretty sticky, and since we could not get back, I ordered the forward platoons to pull into a tight group and have it out. About this time the smoke screen came down and the German officer, probably suspecting an attack on his flank, ordered his men to pull back . . . with the result that the Germans and Canadians were going in opposite directions." With paratroops withdrawing past them on both flanks, No. 15 Platoon was unable to escape and remained pinned in the craters on the north side of the railway embankment.[1]

When the Germans pulled back at 1440 hours, Lieutenant Colonel Larry Henderson sent 'B' Company into the fray, even as he received the disheartening news that the engineers trying to bridge the Landwehr had withdrawn because of heavy German artillery fire.[2] The Can Scots would have to win this fight alone.

Early in their advance along the rail embankment, Major Earl English's 'B' Company was able to cover No. 15 Platoon's retreat from the craters. But as the platoon broke cover to get clear, a German shell landed in its midst, killing an entire section.

As night fell on March 28, the three Can Scot rifle companies dug in still short of Emmerich proper. Henderson called his officers back to discuss the next day's operations.[3] It had been a costly day for the Can Scots, who counted one officer and ten other ranks killed and another officer (Campbell) and twenty-two men wounded.[4]

While the Can Scots had been fighting to gain a foothold inside Emmerich, the Regina Rifles had come up alongside their left flank by advancing next to the dyke bordering the Rhine. While encountering no German troops, they were dogged the entire way by heavy mortar and artillery fire, which caused "negligible" casualties.[5]

As these two battalions regrouped, Brigadier Graeme Gibson ordered his third battalion—the Royal Winnipeg Rifles—out of reserve for a night attack. The objective was a house cluster, called Kleine Netterden, about a mile north of the Emmerich–Rees highway and the same distance northeast of Emmerich. The attack was to go in at 2300 hours.[6]

"WE HAVE WON the Battle of the Rhine," Field Marshal Montgomery declared on March 28, even as the fighting in the Rhine bridgeheads continued at fevered pitch. Montgomery was already looking towards the Elbe River and the ultimate prize of Berlin.[7] If he could gain the capital ahead of the Russians, Montgomery and Prime Minister Churchill believed the peace would protect Western Europe from Soviet ambitions to impose communism throughout its occupied territory.[8]

Because of their anchor position in Hoch Elten, the Germans were still able to offer stiff resistance on the extreme left flank of the bridgehead but were stretched like a rubber band across the rest of its thirty-five-mile width. The average penetration from the Rhine between Rees and Wesel had reached twenty miles. On the night of the 28th, the overstretched German defences hemming in the bridgehead snapped when a column of paratroops from the 17th U.S. Airborne Division, supported by a British tank regiment, busted out of Diersfordter forest and easily sortied thirty-five miles up the Lippe River valley. By dawn, this advance had turned the German flank to the east and left the enemy incapable of stopping an armoured break-out onto the Westphalian Plain. The tanks were hindered less by the Germans than by the ruined cities and towns they had to pick their way through. Digging into this rubble, German rearguard troops managed to slow the Allied advance, but they could not stop it. Montgomery had twenty divisions equipped with fifteen hundred tanks at his disposal that were ready to punch through this weakly held centre gap between Holland and the more heavily defended Ruhr Valley.

On the western flank, the Germans and Canadians continued to fight a bitter battle. His wound-induced fever spiking over 40 degrees Celsius, General der Fallschirmtruppen Alfred Schlemm ceded command on March 28 to General der Infanterie Günther Blumentritt. Despite the new commander's assessment that General der Flieger Eugen Meindl's 11 Fallschirmjäger Corps provided "the only useful" divisions "capable of carrying on any real resistance," those alone gave him a potent force. Even Meindl's brutally rationalist conclusion that "once the Allied bridgeheads were secured . . . Germany was finished" failed to lead to an admission of tactical defeat. Instead, Meindl told Blumentritt he would delay the breakout through his front for as long as possible and then begin a slow fighting withdrawal northeastward to protect Germany's North Sea ports.[9]

But Meindl's proposed strategy, however logical, was at odds with Hitler's plans. Despite the Russian advance on the Oder River—which marked the boundary between Poland and Germany—and the breaching of the Rhine, Hitler insisted there be no retreats. As a result, thousands of German troops that could have been brought home to defend the Fatherland remained in such inactive regions as Denmark and Norway, and even greater numbers were left to fight on such distant and doomed fronts as Italy, Hungary, and Yugoslavia. In the Netherlands, about 150,000 Germans prepared to meet First Canadian Army.[10]

Allied intelligence had given little credence to reports that the Germans in Holland would stay to fight there. After meeting with Montgomery in Venlo on March 27, Crerar wrote that "recent intelligence indicated that the enemy might be intending to evacuate the western Netherlands, a likelihood that would be increased as [11] Canadian Corps pursued its northward advance." On the other hand, Montgomery had warned him, "if the enemy did not withdraw and for high political reasons it became necessary to carry out military operations against him in that part of the country," these would be under Crerar's command. "Field Marshal Montgomery... [was] inclined to believe, however, that such a diversion of forces would not be necessary as it would tend to detract from the effort to achieve the main object—which was the complete defeat of the main German armies in northwest Europe."[11]

Montgomery wanted First Canadian Army's operations in the Netherlands initially dedicated to opening up a supply route through Arnhem, which could be used to feed supplies to Twenty-First Army Group during its northward advance to the Elbe. Once this route was secure, the Canadians would "operate to clear Northeast Holland, the coast belt [of Germany] eastwards to the Elbe, and West Holland [if necessary]." Meanwhile, once the British Second Army gained the Elbe, it would cease advancing and swing whatever forces to the west were required to "assist Canadian Army in its task of clearing the coastal belt."

In order to establish the supply route, the Canadians were to force a crossing over the IJssel River to open a route through Arnhem north to Zutphen. But before they could begin this task, they still had to win the battle for Emmerich and Hoch Elten.[12]

On March 28, the Canadian move into the bridgehead was greatly accelerated by the remarkable noon opening of Blackfriars Bridge. At 1,814 feet, this was the longest Bailey bridge built in Northwest Europe. Yet the Canadian engineers constructing it had beat their scheduled clock by a full forty-eight hours in an incredible example of physical endurance. Linking together thirty-eight buoyant sections, called bays, that varied in length and were anchored to piers set into the river, the engineers had spent 9,492 man-hours positioning them.[13]

Lieutenant William Fernley Brundrit of 30th Canadian Field Company, RCE had dictated the pace. Assigned as officer-in-charge on March 15, he had spent the ensuing days before construction started completing "an enormous amount of work on the technical and organizational planning of the operation." On March 24, he meticulously examined the crossing site in person—dodging German artillery and hoping not to step on a hidden mine—to match plans to reality. When construction began on March 26, Brundrit "worked unceasingly without regard for shelling, eating and sleeping; aiding in construction and in arranging for the large quantities of stores and equipment to arrive at the job, at the right time and place. When the bridge was completed . . . he fell asleep in his vehicle, completely exhausted." The lieutenant's remarkable achievement earned a Military Cross.[14]

When the bridge opened at noon, one of the first Canadians across was Lieutenant General Guy Simonds, who, along with his staff, established a forward command post near Bienan. This enabled Lieutenant General Sir Brian Horrocks to hand responsibility for the bridgehead's left flank to 11 Canadian Corps, and 3rd Canadian Infantry Division reverted to its command. With Blackfriars exclusively dedicated to moving his troops, Simonds quickly moved this division's last brigade—the 8th Canadian Infantry—into the bridgehead and set it up behind 7 CIB. Simonds warned its commanders to be ready either to take over the assault on Emmerich or, if 7 CIB managed to clear the city, to attack Hoch Elten.

The 2nd Canadian Infantry Division also began moving in on March 28—its 6th Brigade relieving 9 CIB, which "had largely 'carried the ball' for the [3rd] division since the crossing." The Sherbrooke Fusiliers armoured regiment, less a squadron already across and moving to help 7 CIB at Emmerich, set up alongside 6 CIB.[15]

Despite the thousands of Canadians cramming into the narrow patch of real estate inside the bridgehead, First Canadian Army could not unleash its great might until engineers could put bridges across the Rhine in front of Emmerich. The toehold across the Rhine was still too narrow for more bridges to be built east of the city, so Blackfriars Bridge would remain the only one available to serve the Canadians until Emmerich fell and work in front of it could begin.[16]

As March 28 closed, the Can Scots regrouped amid the ruins of Emmerich's industrial area. East of Emmerich, the Regina Rifles' 'D' Company set up for the night in a brick factory after advancing two miles from Dornick, and the rest of the battalion camped in nearby positions to the left. Lieutenant Walter Keith was just having a comfortable latrine squat when German artillery opened with a fury on the entire brigade front. Immediately abandoning his mission, he "ran like a scalded cat for the brick ovens." Most of 'D' Company crowded into these, "while the German guns landed shell after shell on top of the building. We tried to sleep but were kept awake by the shelling and watching the cracks in the oven tops grow wider each time a shell landed."[17]

AT 2300 HOURS that night, the Royal Winnipeg Rifles' 'A' and 'B' Companies moved towards Kleine Netterden, which overlooked Emmerich from the high ground to the northeast. At first there was little resistance, but when 'A' Company closed on a large cement factory at the entrance to the village, it came alive with paratroops madly firing automatic weapons. A prolonged firefight broke out around the factory and soon the entire battalion was engaged. It took until 0300 hours to quell the resistance. Eighty Germans, evenly divided between the 346th Infantry Division and 16th Fallschirmjäger Regiment, surrendered.[18] Some reported that their officers had warned them that if they surrendered, the Allies would shoot them, and if they ran, their superiors would do it.[19]

The RWR was instructed to hold the village until relieved by the division's reconnaissance regiment, the 17th Duke of York's Royal Canadian Hussars. Once the hussars reached the scene with their armoured cars, the battalion was to assault Leegmeer, a suburb on Emmerich's northern flank, and then clear some woods on the edge of the city that sheltered enemy artillery and mortar positions.[20]

While this attack was being geared up, the Can Scots slowly pushed through the ruins of the industrial sector. It was a terrible night that "saw what was probably the most vicious fighting of the battle for Emmerich."[21] Periods of "stealthy approaches" were interspersed with "sharp, savage fire fights."[22]

'A' Company was preparing to hook into the city from the north by swinging through the hamlet of Groendahl when it was struck by "cunningly concealed mortars." With several men hit, the company scattered. While the company commander tried to regroup them to put in the attack, his wireless operator, Lance Corporal Albin James Kellerman, crept into the darkness and located the mortars. Amidst "the storm of mortar fire, and despite the efforts of German snipers to knock him out," Kellerman fed the mortar position's coordinates over the wireless to the Can Scots' mortar platoon. His directions were so accurate that the first rounds wiped out the German position, a feat for which he received a Military Medal.[23]

With the mortars silenced, 'A' Company quickly cleared Groendahl. It then joined 'C' Company in pushing into Emmerich's northeastern outskirts, which outflanked the Germans holding the industrial area and caused them to slow down the fight there. These gains freed the Landwehr from German observation, enabling the engineers to start bridge construction under the cover of darkness. Using the footings of a demolished sluice gate, the engineers—despite continual harassing fire—opened a crossing for tanks at 0630 hours on March 29.[24]

Shortly after dawn, the Can Scots—with the Reginas' 'D' Company moving just off to the left to link the two battalions—punched into the city proper. The rest of the Reginas, supported by a troop of tanks from the Sherbrooke Fusiliers' 'C' Squadron and a troop of the Fife and Forfar Yeomanry, equipped with Crocodiles took up station somewhat farther to the left. To the right, the Winnipegs—also supported by tanks and Crocodiles—advanced into Leegmeer.

Lieutenant Walter Keith's No. 16 Platoon had the objective of two factory buildings separated by a narrow lane. Keith decided that the platoon section commanded by Corporal Homer Adams would lead, with the other two following in an arrowhead pattern. Thinking a leader should be out front, he told Major Dick Roberts he would go forward with Adams's section. "You'll stay behind that section," Roberts growled. As the men started forward, a Sherbrooke 17-pounder Firefly Sherman rumbled up behind and fired several rounds over their heads towards the factories. This unexpected and deafening support set Adams and his men "yelling and firing across the street" as they ran. From the nearest factory a German opened up with a Schmeisser, and the section dived for cover behind a stub of rubble that had once been a perimeter wall. Keith and the rest of the platoon slid in beside them. Quickly fanning out along this minimal cover, the men started shooting their rifles and Bren guns at the building. After a pause to reload, No. 16 Platoon charged through a gaping hole in the factory wall. The same German popped up from behind a low wall and ripped off a burst that ricocheted bullets off a steel column supporting the factory roof. As the Reginas advanced, the man fell back, firing as he gave ground, and then fled out the back door.

Keith and his men emerged warily from behind the cover of a small brick shed. Rifleman Milo Thorson dodged to one side and assumed a prone position behind a mound of shattered bricks in order to cover the platoon's forward move with his Bren gun. As he braced the gun into his shoulder, a sniper round struck him in the forehead. Keith saw "his chest heave with his last breath." Sergeant Tommy Tomlinson dashed out and dragged him back to the shed without a thought for the risk taken. Platoon stretcher bearer T.J. Swalwell, a Torontonian, dusted yellow sulpha powder into the hole in Thorson's forehead and then bandaged the wound. It was a futile effort. The twenty-year-old, who hailed from a farm south of Dollard, Saskatchewan, was already dead.[25]

Meanwhile, the Regina's 'B' and 'C' Companies were advancing on Emmerich to the left.[26] 'B' Company was supported by the Crocodiles, and 'C' had the Sherbrooke Shermans. The two companies pushed through the ruins in a rain of heavy mortar, machine-gun, and Panzerfaust fire from German paratroops. Piles of rubble blocked the streets, hampering movement of the supporting armour. One Crocodile was knocked out by a well-concealed self-propelled gun. At 1300 hours, 'A' Company joined the other two Regina companies and met the same dogged resistance. Several men were wounded by mines.[27]

The farther the Reginas advanced, the harder the paratroops fought, using a simple but effective tactic. Armed with large numbers of automatic weapons, a small group sprayed bursts towards the Reginas, forcing a deployment for an assault. Once the Canadians were spread out and ready, the Germans would slip back and repeat the process from another position. Because of roadblocks and increasingly narrow streets, the supporting armour had trouble keeping pace. Railway cars had been wedged crosswise throughout the streets and then filled to bursting with rubble, creating road-blocks weighing many tons. The tanks were unable to push them aside and so would have to seek an alternative route in the maze of streets and destroyed buildings. Finally, the armour was completely stymied, and "the operation became a straight infantry fight . . . For the next six hours the slugging match continued, the troops fighting their way from house to house. All this time the entire town was sub-jected to heavy enemy shelling, but by 1900 hours about half the town had been cleared against decreasing opposition."[28]

'D' Company remained in the thick of things, tying together the Reginas and Can Scots. As No. 16 Platoon braced to dash across the lane and into the second large factory, a pile of rubble to Lieutenant Keith's left shot up in the air several times as if of its own accord. Keith suddenly realized the pile was being struck by armour-piercing rounds, but he was unable to spot the tank.

Sergeant Joe Moran from another 'D' Company platoon, mean-while, saw the tank but mistook it for a Sherman and walked towards it. "When the big gun started moving around toward him, he waved at it, and then realized it was too long to be one of ours! He got down behind a low wall and leaped along with the German shells follow-ing just behind him."

As the tank chased Moran, Keith's men dashed across the lane. They burst into the factory, yelling and firing from the hip. Seeing that one of his men had stopped shooting, Corporal Adams yelled at him to do so. "Why? There's nothing to shoot at," the man snapped back. He was right; the factory had been abandoned. No. 16 Platoon scoured several deep bomb shelters dug under the factory floor. Looking back from the factory, Keith saw what looked to be a Sher-man burning (actually, the knocked-out Crocodile), and soon "a German armoured assault gun came backwards down the railway track, its horribly long gun facing backward. It passed close to us."[29]

During their advance, the Can Scots had called for supporting mortars to deliberately set a massive cement plant on fire with phos-phorous rounds to avoid having to secure the sprawling facility. This action seemed to so unsettle the paratroops that they quickly began giving ground.[30] By 1600 hours, the Can Scots had two companies—

along with the Regina's 'D' Company—in control of the entire factory area, and the battalion's other two companies were well inside the town and advancing alongside the main body of Reginas.[31]

THE ROYAL WINNIPEG Rifles advanced into Leegmeer at 1800 hours on March 29. 'A' Company led, with 'D' Company close behind. Resistance was "fairly heavy," but "the attack went well." As the advance progressed, 'B' Company leapfrogged 'A' Company, and 'C' Company passed through 'D' Company. 'C' Company continued in this role through difficult fighting until 'D' Company returned to the lead at 2200 hours and led the way out of the built-up area to gain the woods, which was the final objective.[32]

An hour later, "though tired from continuous marching and fighting," the Regina Rifles "regrouped and continued the advance to clear whatever opposition remained in the southwest corner of Emmerich." Three rifle companies, 'D,' 'C,' and 'A,' advanced in a ragged line.[33] No. 16 Platoon headed for a liqueur distillery and adjacent machine shop. The men figured the first would be worth a fight, but both were undefended and the distillery was "smashed like everything else in Emmerich." They scoured the ruins for Germans and hoped for bottles, but came up empty on both counts. Dashing about to check on his three sections, Keith took a nasty fall that resulted in a painful groin injury. Setting his platoon headquarters in the distillery's basement, he fell asleep, only to be jolted awake by the sound of shells being lobbed at the building's skeletal upper structure from a German tank on the railway embankment. It was 0300 hours on March 30, and all of 'D' Company was on its final objectives and bracing for a possible counterattack.

Fearing the tank might presage one, Keith called on Corporal Blacky Turner to set up the PIAT and said he would serve as the loader. Turner's nerves were so shot that he "shook all night," but Keith figured the corporal would perform well if he had to engage the tank. Everyone was exhausted, their nerves increasingly frayed. Sergeant Tomlinson slumped next to Keith and said, "Geez, sir, you were great! I thought you'd been in action a lot before." The comment made Keith's night.[34]

Although 'D' Company's advance had gone off without significant incident, the other two companies faced stiffer fighting through
a long night and into the following morning. 'C' Company played
hide and seek with paratroops moving from house to house, until
they were finally surrounded and forced to surrender. Grenade
exchanges were frequent, and during one of these the company commander, Major John Gordon Baird, was wounded. Moments later the
Germans involved in this duel gave up. The company was on its
objective at 0330 hours.[35]

'A' Company had the hardest time, coming up against the last
major resistance point, a heavily fortified and manned strongpoint
in some shattered buildings on the southwestern edge of the city.
Unable to gain ground frontally, the company called for assistance.
Striking from the right at 0400, a 'C' Company platoon fought its
way into the strongpoint but was immediately ejected when paratroops heavily armed with Panzerfausts and machine guns
counterattacked.

At the same time, the rest of 'C' Company tried to close on its
final objective but was repelled by heavy machine-gun fire from
some devastated oil plants off to one flank and a tank firing from the
front. Regrouping, the company tried again and finally took its objective at 1610 hours.[36]

That left only the formidable strongpoint, which "baffled the
riflemen throughout the morning." A proliferation of roadblocks
fanning out along the streets and lanes approaching it bedevilled
attempts to bring up armour. Finally, at dawn, a route was opened
and three Wasp carriers came up to support a new attack.[37]

One rifle platoon advanced alongside the Wasps, which bathed
the buildings with fire, until they ran out of fuel and the attack
crumbled. As they withdrew, however, the riflemen were informed
that the ruins of the two buildings in which the strongpoint was
anchored were connected by a series of basement passages heavily
fortified for use as firing positions and to provide sheltered lines of
communication throughout the bastion.

Deciding that more firepower was required, the Reginas refu-
elled the first Wasps and brought up another three. Divvying up the

six Wasps so that each building would be subjected to an equal number of flame showers, 'A' Company attacked. Both buildings were set ablaze, but still the Germans in the underground passages fought on. It was only when the riflemen got on top of several entrances and "plenty of grenades had been thrown down the cellars that some 50 odd enemy decided that the war for them was over and gave up."[38]

As the Reginas had been finishing this fight, the Winnipegs were counterattacked by paratroops supported by two self-propelled guns and six tanks.[39] Rifleman George "Bunker" Hill was part of a crew from the anti-tank platoon manning a 6-pounder set up beside a small house. Hill had just fallen asleep when the men on watch shouted that Germans were coming their way. Dashing to a window, Hill stuck his head out and found himself staring point-blank at a Tiger's 88-millimetre gun. "How can he fire that thing without killing all of us?" Hill thought, as he stepped away from the window. Fortunately, the tank rumbled off a short distance and then paused, apparently unaware of the men in the house.

Armed with a Gammon anti-tank grenade, which was filled with nitroglycerine and could be attached to a tank's armour, Hill snuck out to attack the Tiger from behind. Unable to close on it, he suddenly remembered he was an anti-tank gunner and, wisely forgetting about the solo mission, returned to the gun by the side of the house. Realizing the sight the gun still mounted was intended for day use rather than night, Hill decided to fire by dead reckoning. "I lowered the barrel to where I was pointing right at the tank. I looked over the gun two or three times to try and make sure. I finally let go and hit him dead on. When I hit him it lit the street right up just like day. He sure knew where I was and fired right back and hit me and threw me and my gun up against the house. I thought I had had it but I rolled around and got up and shook myself when I got to my feet. It was a miracle that I hadn't been wounded. When I got moving around, I found out that the rest of the fellows were gone. They thought I had got it. I could not hear much for a few days, but did eventually get back to normal. Lucky for me the machine-gunner in the tank had to put in a new belt of ammo and so there was just enough time for me to make my getaway."[40]

Confusion reigned in the Winnipeg lines as the counterattack struck 'B' and 'D' Companies. Major Latimer Hugh Denison of 'D' Company was killed, and casualties within the ranks mounted rapidly. 'B' Company lost contact with two of its platoons. Cut into three parts, they each fought separate, desperate battles.[41]

Finally, the counterattack was beaten off with help from 'L' Troop of the 3rd Canadian Anti-Tank Regiment's 105th Battery. Seeing 'D' Company pinned down by the fire of several tanks and SPGs about two hundred yards away, Sergeant D. Gomez manoeuvred his Valentine tank destroyer to where he could fire at the rear of an SPG positioned behind a ruined house. Gomez's crew fired five rounds of armour-piercing shot and scored three direct hits. Then they fired two high-explosive rounds into a cellar sheltering paratroops. An hour later, Gomez spotted another SPG firing on 'D' Company's headquarters. He moved into the open and engaged it in a shootout that silenced his opponent with one round. Subsequent investigation determined that Gomez's single shot had punched through the armoured side protecting one track and burned out the inside of the SPG's hull. Gomez's actions yielded a well-earned Distinguished Conduct Medal.[42]

Well south of this action, a counterattack fell on the Reginas' 'D' Company. Lieutenant Jim Koester was shot and killed. Just before the assault on Emmerich, Koester had told Keith, "After the war I want to sit by the side of the road and be a friend to man." Keith thought sadly of the man's recently acquired English wife, so soon widowed.[43]

The paratroops putting in the counterattack seized two large buildings on 'D' Company's left flank and started harassing the entire perimeter with sniper fire. Major Roberts told Keith to take them with a bayonet attack. As the company's 2-inch mortar crew fired smoke and explosive rounds, Keith lined up No. 16 Platoon and then "we went running flat out, yelling and screaming, and firing our rifles from the hip. We could see the mortar bombs landing directly on the German position, dead on time. They stopped just before we charged up and we hit the trenches to find the Germans gone! Don't know whether it was the mortar bombs or our noisy charge that scared them off!"

Keith climbed a high earth embankment and spotted a German machine-gun position just as it snapped off a burst to his left. Someone shouted, "Blacky's hit." The short burst had instantly killed the twenty-three-year-old Turner, who hailed from Hamilton, Ontario. "I have a strong feeling Blacky knew the night before that he was going to be killed. He had that distinctive look of someone who was soon to die; apparently it was quite common. It was still a tragedy. Blacky had landed on D-Day and had, as far I knew, not been wounded. I regret not having him evacuated as a battle exhaustion case. He certainly was." It took an air strike by Typhoon bombers firing rockets to finally dislodge these last diehard paratroops.[44]

In the late afternoon, the Can Scots moved to finish the job of clearing Emmerich. Each company worked alone. Because of the profusion of roadblocks, they were seldom supported by armour or Wasps. By 1702 hours, both 'A' and 'C' Companies reported "the 'going' was not difficult." They were picking up prisoners and at 2100 all companies reported they were on their objectives.[45]

"And so on Good Friday, 1945," Regina Major Eric Luxton wrote, "Emmerich was declared, 'kaput.'" His battalion commander, Lieutenant Colonel Al Gregory, summed up the bitter battle for the city as one "for control. The heavily bombed town with [road]blocks and rubble presented difficulty in keeping direction and in denying the use of close supporting arms . . . It was in a sense guerilla fighting, each house had to be cleared as [infantry] advanced, no telling which could hold snipers. The number of automatic weapons was out of all proportion to what would normally be encountered in fighting regular German infantry. Every enemy carried an automatic of some type. Mines proved a bugbear." The Reginas reported 150 prisoners and had no idea how many paratroops they had killed or wounded. In exchange, their casualties numbered seven officers and sixty other ranks.[46] The Can Scots reported thirteen killed and forty-six wounded.[47] Winnipeg Rifle casualties were not recorded, but the other two battalions suffered a total loss of 126 men and officers, and 7 CIB's overall casualties were reported as thirteen officers and 156 men. Undoubtedly, the Winnipeg Rifles accounted for most of the unidentified forty-three additional casualties.[48]

Brigadier Graeme Gibson wrote in his war diary entry for March 31: "The battalions did a splendid job under the most trying conditions. The Germans fought hard and fanatically to prevent our occupying the town—but due to the persistence and courage of all our [troops] the town was taken."[49]

8

Utmost Tenacity

E VEN AS EMMERICH fell, 3rd Canadian Infantry Division threw
its last brigade at Hoch Elten on March 31 from start lines
west of the city. The Régiment de la Chaudière was on the left and
the Queen's Own Rifles on the right, with the North Shore (New
Brunswick) Regiment in reserve. Just after midnight, the QOR
moved with almost reverential care "through the shattered tomb that
once was a town . . . in darkness that was crowded with hushed
voices and scuffling boots." At 0200 hours, 'C' Company led off,
with each company passing through another in turn until the
battalion reached the hamlet of Ingenhof halfway to the heights.
There was no opposition.[1]

When the Chauds' 'A' Company bumped scattered opposition
from inside a group of houses two hundred yards short of its objective, 'B' Company swung in from the right flank and dislodged the
Germans with heavy gunfire. 'A' Company took fourteen prisoners,
but counted two other ranks killed and one wounded, while an
unscathed 'B' Company rounded up four prisoners. Passing through,
the other two companies advanced along the road from Emmerich
that led to the heights. Although sporadic, the French Canadians
were dogged by Panzerfaust, machine-gun, and sniper fire while
having to constantly watch for mines. Four men from 'D' Company

were wounded in exchange for twenty-five Germans captured. One Chaudière officer decided that the Germans, now "clinging at the end of their rope . . . are to inflict the most casualties they possibly can, and then give themselves up."[2]

Both battalions ran into small shootouts as they pushed on through the early afternoon. Each time the Germans offered a stand, 'A' Squadron of the Sherbrooke Fusiliers weighed in with its Shermans. The defenders immediately "fled into the woods" and were usually quickly rounded up as prisoners. Given the rapidity of the advance at little cost, Brigadier J.A. "Jim" Roberts decided against rotating his reserve to the front. The QOR was ordered to continue the attack "non-stop."[3] Opposition across the Chaudière front collapsed as they approached the base of the heights and the occupation was made without any difficulty, except for a few bombs that fell sporadically onto their positions. By 1430 hours, the battalion reported itself solid before the heights, within shattered woods laced with innumerable abandoned gun pits.[4]

As the QOR closed on the foot of Hoch Elten, however, it came under heavy machine-gun, mortar, and artillery fire from its heights and suffered several casualties. Some disarray followed, and it was not until 1600 hours that 'B' Company led the way towards some buildings hugging the slope next to a road that cut across the feature. As the men moved in among the buildings, they were caught by heavy artillery fire, and several men were killed and wounded. Snipers also started potting away from the woods to the right, but the tanks quickly silenced them. At 1700 hours, 'D' Company passed through to "scramble" another two hundred yards up the slope, even as shellfire struck down several more men.

The advance continued at a crawl up the steep, exposed slopes that had been stripped clear of their natural foliage by Allied shelling. At midnight, 'C' Company passed to the front. Moving "silently in the darkness and encountering no opposition," the battalion consolidated on the summit and at dawn advanced to the northwestern flank. Below, on the left, was the village of Elten and beyond, an unimpeded view deep into Holland. "The enemy had withdrawn and the area was quiet," a QOR officer subsequently wrote.[5] Reduced to a wasteland of shattered stumps intermingled with countless bomb and shell craters, Hoch Elten resembled a Great War landscape. The troops scattered across it made it clear they were anxious to move on and leave this terrible place behind. The brigade's casualty toll for winning the feature was far lighter than expected—one officer and sixty-four other ranks killed or wounded.[6]

A wireless message sent to First Canadian Army headquarters reported that "at least one company of infantry [was] now on top of Hoch Elten feature," and the staff officers broke into cheers.[7] The news came in the nick of time, for at 1030 hours that April 1 morning, the Canadian engineers had been ordered to start bridging operations opposite Emmerich regardless of whether the heights were taken. Unimpeded by artillery and mortars on Hoch Elten, the men finished the approaches for a Bailey bridge stretching 1,348 feet from shore to shore by noon. Melville Bridge was scheduled to open early the next day. Meanwhile, more engineers started work on a 1,757-foot bridge, slated to open in three days' time.[8]

The 17th Duke of York's Royal Canadian Hussars had eagerly awaited Hoch Elten's fall, for it "finally started unclogging the holes of the salt cellar they had been in for the last few months and all that was necessary was for someone to 'tip it' and the fast Recce patrols, shaking the last few bits of mud from their wheels, would begin pouring all over the country." This morning, 3rd Division's Major General R.H. "Holly" Keefler "tipped that salt and out poured the regiment," wrote the 17th's official historian.

On the day before, March 31, 9th Canadian Infantry Brigade had secured a start line for the armoured car regiment about three miles north of Emmerich at the village of s'Heerenberg, which stood on the edge of the Stokkummer Bosch—a large forested area northeast of Hoch Elten. Striking out of the village early on the morning of April 1, the 17th's 'A' Squadron, under Captain J.O. MacArthur, headed for a road that ran north into Holland to Wehl, about five miles distant.[9]

All went smoothly until the advance patrol's commander, Lieutenant R.K. Smith—just returned to the regiment after being wounded in the opening days of the Normandy invasion—"found himself in a rather precarious position." Smith's party consisted of a pair of Daimler Mk I armoured cars mounting 2-pounder guns for main armament and crewed by three men. Smith "was feeling his way down the long slope into the crossroads at Kilder, when suddenly the loud crash of an '88' came from the high woods [of Stokkummer Bosch] to his left. He looked around and saw that the second car, commanded by Sgt. W. Duggan, had been knocked out. As two more shots narrowly missed his Daimler, Smith hastened for cover amongst the buildings clustered around the crossroads. This was a very tight spot, as he could not advance without support from another armoured car. He had also bypassed the Germans who had knocked out Duggan's car, so retreat was not an option." Getting on the wireless, Smith summoned artillery down in the general area of the German gun to make its crew duck and kept the fire raining in until some Stormont, Dundas and Glengarry Highlanders arrived and silenced the "lone weapon. Lt. Smith and his crew breathed a deep sigh of relief and rejoined their troop, who now had to get along without one of their finest NCOS, Sgt. Duggan and his Gunner-operator, Tpr. Pullen."[10] Both Sergeant William Francis Duggan and Corporal Earl Joseph Pullen had died when the 88-millimetre round pierced the Daimler's thin armour.

While 'A' Squadron advanced into the open country east of s'Heerenberg, 'C' Squadron had followed a due-westerly course along a country road running through Stokkummer Bosch. Emerging from the dense woods unopposed, the squadron swept through the hamlet of Beek and on towards the town of Diadem, some two miles due west. No. 9 Troop was motoring along a stretch of road bordered on either side by inundated farm fields when it came to a "huge crater, which was covered by MG and rifle fire." Hooking out from behind, No. 10 Troop swung south and gained the other side of a boggy stream, only to be driven back by heavy Panzerfaust and machine-gun fire. The thin armour of the cars was easily penetrated by the Panzerfaust bombs, so the squadron pulled back from the roadblock and set up a defensive perimeter to await the arrival of 9 CIB infantry battalions.

'B' Squadron also punched due west on April 1 from a start line inside Hoch Elten earlier secured by 8 CIB's Queen's Own and the Chauds. The armoured cars followed a railway that hugged the

Rhine from Emmerich to Arnhem. Cutting past the southern face of Hoch Elten, the armoured cars rumbled through Elten and then along a northwesterly course for four miles to Zevenaar. Midway between the two communities, the squadron crossed the Dutch–German border, rounding up twenty to thirty German prisoners en route. A mile short of Zevenaar, resistance stiffened, and the squadron also formed a perimeter and waited on the infantry.[11]

APRIL 1 CLOSED the curtains on 3rd Canadian Infantry Division's role in Operation Plunder. Along with the rest of 11 Canadian Corps, this division began to conform to First Canadian Army's directions from Montgomery to advance into the Netherlands and westernmost Germany. Having crossed into the bridgehead on March 28, 2nd Canadian Infantry Division had already embarked on this operation by having 6th Canadian Infantry Brigade establish a footing for a northwestward advance through Netterden, Wieken, and Gendringen—three small communities lying at the base of a narrow Dutch salient that thrust southeastward into Germany. Once these communities were in hand, the brigade would advance six and a half miles northwest to gain Doetinchem.

The Queen's Own Cameron Highlanders of Canada had played the first hand late on March 29 with aggressive patrols towards Netterden that bagged sixty-four prisoners.[12] Most of them had surrendered personally to Sergeant John Ruczak when he led a 'B' Company patrol towards Gendringen. Approaching a farm complex, the platoon encountered three guards and took them prisoner. Hot on the heels of a fleeing German, Ruczak dashed into a building, only to be confronted by about forty soldiers preparing to defend it. Loosing several bursts from his Sten that drove the Germans to cover, Ruczak then gestured threateningly at them with his weapon while shouting in a mixture of English and crude German that they could surrender or die. The bluff worked, the Germans meekly surrendered, and Ruczak netted a Military Medal.[13]

The Camerons' easy advance encouraged Lieutenant Colonel A.A. "Bert" Kennedy to advance 'D' Company towards Netterden and have 'C' Company loop behind the village to cut off any line of retreat.

Major Dennis Dickens Sweeting approached the village warily after a patrol reported Germans dug in on the outskirts. Rather than blundering about the village streets, Sweeting decided to wait for first light. As his men attacked at 0400, 'C' Company also came in from behind. Sandwiched, the Germans decided to fight to the end, and "bitter fighting ensued on the streets."[14]

With casualties mounting rapidly on both sides, Sweeting realized the Camerons risked being wiped out unless the two companies could marry up. Dashing across three hundred yards of bullet-swept ground, Sweeting reached 'C' Company and guided it back to his men. Having created a unified front, the two companies advanced against the most heavily defended group of buildings.[15] When all the Germans here were either killed or wounded, a momentary lull followed, during which the two sides carried out a shouted and suspicious negotiation. The result was an agreement to allow each side to evacuate its wounded. While this was going on, Sweeting approached a German officer and gave him thirty minutes to surrender or "be totally destroyed."[16] Before the deadline expired, two officers and twenty-two men surrendered, and Netterden was taken.[17] At a cost of four Camerons killed and ten wounded, the battalion had taken 130 prisoners.

The advance moved into open farm country, with 2nd Division's 8th Reconnaissance Regiment (14th Canadian Hussars) armoured cars rolling directly towards Doetinchem and the Camerons moving on a northerly line towards Veldhunten. While the armoured-car squadrons were there to protect the Cameron's left flank, they were also seeking to contact 3rd Division's 17th Duke of York Royal Canadian Hussars, believed to be operating to the west.

By the early morning of March 31, the 14th Hussars and all three of 6 CIB's battalions were meeting stiffening resistance. Soon the two leading Cameron companies were pinned by machine-gun fire just short of Veldhunten.[18] To the left, the Hussars were hampered more by impassable inundated fields than by Germans. Unable to locate their Duke of York colleagues, the regiment spent a frustrating day wallowing through country more suited to infantry.[19] At day's end, divisional command agreed and directed the regiment to swing around to the extreme right flank to support an advance by 5 CIB the following morning across the Oude River IJssel and then along a highway leading to Doetinchem. Right of the Camerons, meanwhile, 6 CIB's Les Fusiliers Mont-Royal had advanced on Gendringen, harassed every step of the way by mortar and shellfire.[20] Finally gaining the town at day's end, they were met by Dutch civilians, "as usual cheering like mad." While such exuberance was normally welcome, in the midst of an ongoing firefight, the Fusiliers found that the Dutch were "becoming a nuisance with their grateful demonstration."[21]

Brigadier Jean Allard quickly passed the South Saskatchewan Regiment through Gendringen with instructions to push on a farther three and a half miles north to Etten "if the front should suddenly go soft."[22] Suffering only three men killed and another fifteen wounded, the SSR was soon firmly ensconced within Etten. On April 1, while 6 CIB was advancing rapidly along the river's eastern bank, 5th Brigade's Canadian Black Watch had passed 'A' company across the river at 0100 hours to lead the advance on Doetinchem. Under a clear night sky, the company made steady progress until it closed on the outskirts of Terborg.[23] From positions around several windmills, the Germans opened fire, and a close-quarters firefight ensued. Rushing to the rescue, the Fort Garry Horse's 'A' Squadron quickly quelled German resistance. Ten prisoners, including an officer, were brought in.

When the Black Watch's Danish-born acting commander, Major Eric Motzfeldt, interrogated the man, he said his twenty-five-man force had been ordered to guard Terborg's approaches at any cost. Those men not taken prisoner were either killed or had deserted. Motzfeldt distrusted this intelligence, as 'A' Company was repeatedly bouncing into resistance pockets firing from well-placed machinegun positions. Each had to be taken in turn, with the Germans yielding only when the fight moved to close quarters. During one such dust-up, two 'A' Company men crawled up on a hidden slit trench and a German inside clubbed one of them with his rifle butt. The other man shot the German dead. The battered Canadian reported only feeling groggy and suffering a headache.[24]

Shortly after this action, 'B' Company moved through and made its way along a section of the highway bordered by tightly spaced houses on either side. Each house had to be cleared in turn, so progress slowed to a crawl. Growing increasingly impatient and also plagued by poor wireless communication back to battalion headquarters, Motzfeldt went forward at 0422 hours to personally assess the situation. After being reamed out, the company commander "decided to go right in on his objective without any more searching . . . so the [company] walked the remaining 500 yards [down the street] to their area around the church . . . having not a shot fired at them en route." The only casualty was a stretcher bearer who almost had his entire ear bitten off when he tried to treat a wounded German. Soon 'C' Company arrived, and the two companies swept through Terborg without meeting significant resistance. By 0620 hours, the village was sufficiently cleared to allow the Calgary Highlanders to head for Doetinchem.

South of Terborg, the Black Watch's 'D' Company had been busy clearing woods threatening the battalion's left flank. As the men moved up a gentle wood-shrouded slope, they came under "intense fire from rifles, machine-guns, and rifle grenades. One platoon disengaged and made its way round to the northern end of the woods. Some prisoners were taken as they endeavoured to escape across to the belt of wood on the left of 'D' [Company's] line of advance and as the squeeze play began to work more prisoners were taken and more attempted to escape to the wood on the left."[25]

Behind the squeeze play was Lance Corporal Raymond Eaton Stacey, who had taken control of No. 17 Platoon when its commander fell wounded. Initially intending only to draw fire away from the rest of the company, Stacey realized his move had panicked the Germans in the woods and they were breaking contact. Stacey's men raced after them, but were able to overtake only twenty-eight of the fleet-footed Germans. Stacey was awarded a Military Medal.[26] The Black Watch's total prisoner count around Terborg numbered sixty-one, and an unknown but large number of Germans had been killed. In return, the battalion suffered eleven casualties. Moving just beyond Terborg, the Black Watch settled in the open fields on either side of the highway for a well-deserved rest. However, the battalion was on notice that the rest would be short-lived. Once the Calgary Highlanders gained a toehold inside Doetinchem, the Black Watch would go around the city on the right flank in order to threaten the German rear.[27]

CIVILIAN REPORTS LED Lieutenant Colonel Ross Ellis to believe that the Germans had run back to Doetinchem, so he made for the city without assuming a battle formation. Leading the way at 0800 hours on what resembled a peacetime manoeuvre was Captain I.J. Coady in a jeep. Coady was navigating, with Ellis right behind him in a Bren carrier. Following these two vehicles was the rest of tactical headquarters in trail, then the support companies' assorted collection of Wasps, towed anti-tank guns, and miscellaneous carriers. Coming up behind at a route-march pace were the battalion's rifle companies.

Within an hour, this extenuated column had advanced two miles—tactical headquarters gaining two of the battalion's intermediary objectives unopposed. Proceeding along the main road, Ellis and his headquarters section approached a crossing about halfway to Doetinchem, "only to have the bridge . . . blown up in their faces." The pioneer platoon set off in carriers to check for nearby bridges, but these were also destroyed by explosions, and five Germans—presumed responsible for the demolitions—were spotted taking flight. Abandoning the vehicles to find a suitable crossing, the rifle companies waded across the stream and headed for the city, with 'D' and 'C' Companies following the road while the other two companies followed a paralleling railway track. By the time the battalion's scouts and pioneers unearthed a still-standing bridge, the rifle companies were far ahead and 'D' Company had had "a stiff fight" that yielded twenty-two prisoners.[28]

After months in hospital recovering from a serious wound he got in the Scheldt Estuary campaign, 'D' Company's Captain Mark Tennant had just recently returned to duty. He had refused to be shipped back to Canada and mustered out of the service. "I talked myself back into the war," Tennant said later. "I volunteered to fight a war,

Canadian Grenadier Guards stack 75-millimetre shells near their Sherman tanks on March 28. The regiment's 120 tanks participated in a massive barrage fired across the Rhine against the German strongholds in Emmerich and the heights of Hoch Elten. J. Smith, LAC PA-134433.

top left · Infantrymen of 4th Canadian Armoured Division march past burning buildings after helping to repel a German counterattack on Sögel on April 10. Alexander M. Stirton, LAC PA-129754.

bottom left · A South Saskatchewan Regiment platoon engages snipers during the crossing assault on the Oranjekanaal. Visible in the middle distance is the top of the lift on the bridge over the canal. Dan Guravich, LAC PA-113909.

above · Buffaloes carry infantry across the IJssel River during Operation Cannonshot. The tower visible in the background is the church in Wilp. Jack M. Smith, LAC PA-132607.

above · The Fort Garry Horse Sherman commanded by Sergeant Walter Chaulk slammed into Paterswoldseweg No. 188, on the outskirts of Groningen, after the tank was knocked out by a Panzerfaust on Friday, April 13. Trooper Fred Butterworth died instantly. Flames from the Sherman spread to the houses, causing the damage shown in this photograph. Dan Guravich, LAC PA-130947.

top right · Essex Scottish stand guard at the end of the Paterswoldseweg, the major thoroughfare in Groningen, to intercept any Germans that might try retreating from positions to the west. Rejoicing civilians move about, apparently oblivious to the battle still underway. Dan Guravich, LAC PA-130951.

bottom right · Les Fusiliers Mont-Royal soldiers flush a sniper from a building on the Radesingel in Groningen. Dan Guravich, LAC PA-130964.

On April 14, vehicles of 4th Canadian Armoured Division roll through the battered streets of Friesoythe before the fires were started. Alexander M. Stirton, LAC PA-113712.

not a portion of a war. They were my men and I figured I could prob-
ably look after my men better than anybody else. I loved my men."
With Major George Stott on leave, Ellis had been happy to give 'D'
Company to this experienced veteran.[29]

On the edge of Doetinchem, Captain Bill Lyster passed his 'C'
Company through Tennant's men and moved along the main street.
Out front, No. 13 Platoon had just passed several buildings when a
machine gun fired up the street and mortar rounds started falling
around it. Everyone dived into a roadside trench, which proved too
shallow for proper cover. Knowing he had to silence the machine
gun quickly, Lyster threw No. 14 Platoon out to the right. Corporal
William John Henry Sherring turned the corner of a building at the
head of the leading section and was fired on by a machine gun dug
into an orchard about three hundred yards distant. Dismissing this
fire as irrelevant to the main task at hand, Sherring led his men in
clearing several buildings from which No. 13 Platoon was taking fire.
Gaining a crossroads, Sherring sprinted across it alone and seized a
building on the other side. No sooner had he set his men up inside
than the building came under intense fire from Germans in a building about one hundred yards away. Taking one man with him,
Sherring charged the building and drove the Germans off. He then
returned to the rest of the platoon and guided them to fire positions
that could take on the Germans in the orchard. Once they started
laying down fire, Sherring flanked the orchard from the left with his
section and eliminated the Germans there. Sherring's actions
renewed 'C' Company's advance. Although unrecognized by the
Canadian Army, his courageous action was rewarded with a Dutch
Bronze Lion medal.[30]

By 1700 hours, 'A' Company was on its objective and receiving a
typical Dutch liberator's welcome. But Tennant's 'D' Company had
struck "a stone wall at the entrance to the town square."[31] A large
group of diehard Germans had transformed the square into a seemingly impregnable fortress by blocking all the entrances with
cement-laden railway cars and covering these approaches with inter-
locking machine-gun and mortar positions. Every building
overlooking the square contained snipers armed with light machine

guns. Several artillery pieces stationed outside the city had zeroed in on the square, their fire badly hampering any movement on the streets. Hoping to break the enemy's resolve, Tennant slipped one platoon behind them to capture a bridge and cut their line of retreat. Secure within their bastion, the Germans refused to yield and fought on "with the utmost tenacity."[32]

During sporadic lulls in the gunfire, the men in 'D' Company could hear the Dutch elsewhere cheering the rest of the battalion. Then a mortar chugged out a round. They tensed, listened to the whir of flight, and calculated its trajectory. A few minutes after the round exploded, the sounds of cheering again carried on the gentle breeze blowing that fair Easter Sunday.

Private Lloyd Daniel and several other men worked up a street towards the square, hopscotching from doorway to doorway in small groups, with two or three other men providing covering fire from behind. About fifteen feet ahead of Daniel, Lance Corporal John Heinrichs was sprinting along a high metal fence when machine-gun tracers started sparking up its length. Ahead he spotted a pillbox standing in the centre of the street. The two men turned about and fled, Daniel diving through the door of a bicycle shop. Turning, he saw Heinrichs fall from a bullet shot through one leg. When he tried to stand, another round punctured his chest just below the heart and Heinrichs went down hard. Nobody could reach him until a Fort Garry Horse tank rumbled up and offered its armoured hide as shelter for some of the men to go forward behind it. The men retrieved Heinrichs, who survived his severe wound.

Throughout the day, the battle for the square raged. Because of the railway cars, the tanks and other supporting vehicles were of little use, and the infantry was not strong enough to win on its own. Dutch civilians, overwhelmed by the prospect of liberation, kept mixing in among the Canadians even as they were shooting and taking fire. Sitting on the floor inside a house, Private H.J.E. MacDonald had just cracked a joke to a couple of buddies when a salvo of German shells fell around their position. MacDonald jumped to his feet, and suddenly two Canadians, each with a Dutch girl in tow, "came dashing through the door and down the basement stairs to safety. As

they started down, another shell burst right outside one of the basement windows, flinging fragments of gravel and concrete, along
with the blast, through the window. This panicked the girls and they
tried to struggle back upstairs. Before we could force them back
again, a devil's tattoo of shell crashes rocked the building, filling the
place with dust and fumes. I felt a numbing burn in my left hip and
upper leg and in a trice was flung down the stairs . . . [Joe] Segal, who
had been manning one of the basement windows, was trying to
cram a mattress into it to stop the blast and fragments . . . Salvo after
salvo rocked the house. Then, as suddenly as it began, it quit. I was a
bit numb but could stand and walk. Everyone else in the basement
seemed to be O.K., so I crawled up the stairs and there was my best
friend 'Brownie' [Private Walter B. Brown] flat on his back, dead."[33]

As evening fell, the four Calgary companies finished surrounding the square. Still the Germans remained defiant. On either side
of Doetinchem, 5 CIB's other two battalions were bypassing the city
and pushing on. The Black Watch had passed to the right aboard
Fort Garry Horse tanks while Le Régiment de Maisonneuve did likewise on the left.

Ellis decided that continuing the city fight in darkness would only
cause needless casualties, so he had the men rest as well as they
could while he worked up a new plan. Ellis figured that using crews
of engineers to demolish the railway cars with mighty explosives
would allow the battalion's Wasps and 6-pounders to gain the square.
'D' Company was also equipped with several man-carried flame-
throwers called Lifebuoys.[34] Weighing almost fifty pounds and
loaded with four gallons of fuel ignited by detonating a .303 cartridge,
the Lifebuoy could shoot a two-second jet of flame up to 150 feet.
After ten jets, the flame-thrower was empty.[35] Lifebuoys were terribly
unpopular with the infantry, who considered them as dangerous to
the operator as they were to the enemy.

On April 2, however, several 'D' Company men used them to
good effect by working around behind the railway cars and flaming
the immediate defenders out of their positions. This enabled the
engineers to safely blow gaps through the roadblocks, and the Wasps
and several Fort Garry Horse Shermans surged through. With the

Lifebuoy operators flaming buildings and the Wasps splashing flame about with abandon, the German resolve cracked. Soon, sixty-three men surrendered. Many corpses were strewn about on the square and inside the surrounding buildings.[36] In one building seventeen bodies were counted. At 1800 hours, the Calgary Highlanders finally won Doetinchem at a cost of nine dead and thirty-two wounded.[37]

All across the Canadian front, April 2 had been a day of steady advance for both 2nd and 3rd Divisions. At First Canadian Army headquarters, General Harry Crerar and his staff took stock of the losses suffered since Operation Plunder had opened on March 23. Canadian casualties numbered 51 officers and 692 other ranks.[38]

Opposing Plunder had cost the Germans far more and left Allied intelligence staff scratching their heads as to the purpose of the fanatical resistance. "It is difficult to explain why Hitler's High Command imagined that it could carry on the fight," one Canadian concluded. "The German losses had been enormous and the signs of complete defeat were all too clear. Moreover, it is certain that the most seasoned of his professional soldiers, those high-booted and self-exalted members of the Officers Corps, realized that disaster was imminent and were ready to accept defeat quite unconditionally ... The answer to the enemy's unwillingness to give in must be looked for among the fanatical principles of the Nazi-cult which decreed that according to the intuitions of one man, The [Führer], an entire people must triumph or fall. With speed and violence our attack had driven the enemy into a corner; escape was impossible. Hitler's army was on its knees, the knock-out blow was about to be delivered."[39]

Nobody thought this final blow would be easy. From General Crerar to the lowliest Canadian private, each man knew it would often be necessary to wrest the ground from Germans willing to fight to the last. By April 1, Regina Rifles 'D' Company commander, Major Gordon Brown, had gained a new nickname: "I-can't-understand-why-they-don't-quit Brown." The men made a joke of it, but most pondered the same question, fearing that the German doggedness would end in their own death in some field or cobbled street, ultimately forgotten when the fighting ceased.

PART TWO

DELIGHTED WITH
THIS ENTIRE SHOW

9

All Together Again

AT PRECISELY ONE minute to midnight on April 1, the command of 11 Canadian Corps reverted from the Second British Army back to First Canadian Army.[1] This was a historic moment for Canada's army in World War 11, marking the end of a twenty-one-month separation. Beginning in July 1943, elements of 1 Canadian Corps had rapidly been deployed to the Mediterranean Theatre for operations first in Sicily and then on the Italian mainland. Now the army was formally reunited at last.

Denied one of its inherent corps, First Canadian Army had gone into the Normandy invasion bulked up by units drawn from other nations. British I Corps had been substituted for the missing Canadian corps. At various times and for differing durations, Polish, Belgian, Czech, Dutch, and American forces had also served under the army's banner. By April 2, the British corps consisted only of its headquarters units and the 49th (West Riding) Infantry Division, its other formations gradually being stripped away for service elsewhere. While the former assumed administrative and logistical control of Antwerp's ports, the latter division came under 1 Canadian Corps's command. The previous day, 1st Polish Armoured Division had been transferred from the British corps to the Netherlands District.[2]

Originally formed in February to develop an Allied plan for delivering humanitarian relief to the starving Dutch in the western Netherlands, this command was now also responsible for overseeing the guarding of the long front running along the south bank of the Maas to the North Sea. Despite the improbability of German attack anywhere along its length, this frontage still had to be guarded, and the Poles had been performing this function under First Canadian Army direction through the British corps. Handing off the defence of this area to Netherlands District freed the Canadians to concentrate all their attention on developing offensive operations. Although the front was largely passive, German forces still lurked, and the Poles were harassed nightly by shelling, searching machine-gun and rifle fire, and the occasional patrol crossing in boats to conduct raids or collect intelligence. The Poles responded in kind, so a combat footing was necessary.[3]

Although 1 Canadian Corps was now reunited with the army, it was not yet ready to join the fighting. The last of its formations had arrived from the Mediterranean only in mid-March, and most were only just completing a hectic two-week period of refitting and reorganizing. British Eighth Army in Italy had utilized much equipment and operated in ways that were alien to British–Canadian forces in Northwest Europe. Infantry in Italy, for example, had been equipped with American Thompson submachine guns because early-version Sten guns had proven hazardously unreliable. Forced to surrender their beloved Tommy guns during departure from Italy, the troops were now given Stens and an assurance that the weapons were greatly improved.[4] The Seaforth Highlanders of Canada's regimental historian summed up the general feeling that the Sten still "seemed a poor substitute and looked like a piece of plumbing." He conceded, however, that "it was lighter to carry and its small calibre rounds [9-millimetre versus .45-calibre] meant one could pack more magazines in less space."

Nobody took issue with swapping the bulky, inaccurate .38-calibre revolvers for 9-millimetre Browning pistols. The officers carrying them agreed almost to a man that the latter were superior.[5]

Artillerymen received a mixed bag. On one hand, the 8th Canadian Field Regiment (Self-Propelled) happily exchanged its worn guns for Sextons mounting a 25-pounder gun on the chassis of old Ram tanks. On the other, the 98th Field Regiment (Self-Propelled), which was attached to 1st Canadian Armoured Brigade, had to surrender its 105-millimetre Priests for Sextons that its men found to be "in much poorer condition" than the tanks that 1 CAB's armoured regiments received.[6]

Tankers all profited. Since the early days in Normandy, when the 75-millimetre Shermans had been routinely outclassed by the heavier-gunned and armour-plated German Panthers and Tigers, the Allies had sought to create a more even playing field. As a result, 1 CAB's regiments were reconfigured so that their three squadrons were each comprised of four troops with four tanks apiece. Two of the tanks in a troop were the deadlier 17-pounder Firefly Shermans, while the other two were standard 75-millimetre Shermans. Two Shermans in each squadron headquarters section mounted 105-millimetre guns and the third, a 75-millimetre. This gave the regiments thirty-one Shermans mounted with 75-millimetre guns, twenty-four with 17-pounders, and eight with 105-millimetre guns. The regimental reconnaissance squadron was also made stronger with eleven Stuart VI (Cadillac) class light tanks that mounted a 37-millimetre main gun to replace the Honey—a Stuart tank that lacked a turret. Honeys had been powered by an incredibly noisy aircraft engine that made a joke of any attempt to conduct an unobtrusive reconnaissance. The Stuart VI's 220-horsepower gasoline engine was quiet and yielded more speed, making in an instant hit. While its top road speed was officially set at forty miles per hour, Sergeant Gwilym Jones of the Three Rivers Regiment's reconnaissance troop claimed his driver could hit sixty-five on a straight stretch.[7]

The allotment to 5th Canadian Armoured Division tank brigades was slightly different. Each regiment received the following number and class of tanks: twenty-four Firefly 17-pounders, thirty Sherman 75-millimetres, six Sherman 105-millimetres, eleven Stuart VI light tanks, and three even lighter reconnaissance tanks. This yielded a total strength of seventy-five tanks per regiment.[8]

Most of the men took organizational and equipment changes in stride. More of a challenge was marrying into First Canadian Army itself. The army imposed various training schemes to teach the veterans of the Italian campaigns its way of war, but Captain Farley Mowat noticed that his Hastings and Prince Edward Regiment did not take it "very seriously, for with the constantly optimistic battle news they knew that the war was almost at an end. Many believed they would not again see battle. And in any case *they* were the veterans. Their fellow Canadians wearing the shoulder patches of the Second, Third and Fourth Divisions were treated with some condescension. The names of Carpiquet, Falaise and the Scheldt meant as little to the men of the Regiment as the names of Cassino, Ortona and Ravenna mean to those Canadians who had fought their war in Northern Europe. But the soldiers of First Division knew that they had been in action almost a year longer than their fellows. They had nothing to learn."[9]

Instead, knowing the opportunity was surely fleeting, they embraced the luxuries afforded them. Most were billeted in private homes or above taverns in Belgian villages and towns for the duration of the refit. In Terhagen, 3rd Canadian Field Regiment was welcomed "by the gay and friendly population in their comfortable and scrupulously clean houses. There were plenty of pubs, everyone loved dancing and parties, and leave to England and Continental cities was started immediately. It was unanimously agreed that it was the 'best go' of the war."[10]

Scattered by companies through three villages, the 48th Highlanders of Canada could hardly believe their luck. Drink was plentiful, but so too were other pleasures. Major Jim Counsell savoured the first buttermilk he had tasted in years. "The countryside seemed immaculate, and the contrast of the Flemish way of life was sharp to the filth, flies and primitive hovels of the Italian peasant. The Highlanders had almost forgotten such things as white curtains, and rugs on the floor. Life was sheer pleasure."[11]

Not far out of view, however, the war ground on, and Princess Patricia's Canadian Light Infantry's Captain Syd Frost soon realized his men were ready to return to combat. With each day the men in his company seemed increasingly weary of the training, the luxuriousness of their billets, and the chickenshit spit and polish that First Canadian Army insisted of men when they were not in the fighting lines. He thought his men were "ready and anxious to rejoin our old comrades in the Canadian Army and show them how to fight. This may seem strange to someone who has not served with the fighting troops, but it is a fact. It is the eternal dilemma of a soldier—he is never completely happy for long. After a short rest he becomes bored and itches to get back into the fight. But when he has been in action for a prolonged period, gone days without proper sleep, food or shelter, endured constant shelling, narrowly escaped death or injury a hundred times and seen his comrades blown to bits—after these and other discomforts, he can't wait to get back to the rest area. As P[rivate] Norton succinctly puts it: 'Why the hell did I ever join the goddamn army in the first place!'"[12]

THE CANADIANS FROM Italy would not have long to wait for a return to action, for even as they settled into this new theatre, their corps commander and his staff had already, on March 15, started work in the town of Wijchen, about seven miles southwest of Nijmegen. At first, however, Lieutenant General Charles Foulkes found himself in the unusual circumstance of commanding no Canadians. Instead, his sole unit was the 49th (West Riding) Division, which had been engaged for weeks in planning the clearing of the so-called Nijmegen Island as a preparatory requirement to assaulting Arnhem.

Operation Market Garden had left the Allies in possession of a bridgehead on the north bank of the Waal immediately opposite Nijmegen that extended about five miles towards the Neder Rijn and stretched about ten miles from east to west. One of the Rhine River's diversions, the Neder Rijn had been subjected to a series of canalization projects started in the 1700s and continued into the early 1900s that enhanced its usability for shipping and reduced flooding of the adjacent flood plain to create farm and pasture lands. The resulting approximately five-and-a-half-mile-long waterway was named the Pannerdensch Canal and extended to where the IJssel broke off from the Neder Rijn to meander on a northwesterly course into the IJsselmeer. The Pannerdensch was about four miles east of the bridgehead's boundary and ten miles west of Emmerich. The Neder Rijn, with Arnhem standing on the northern bank, was five miles from the bridgehead's apex. To the west, the bridgehead stretched to a point just south of the town of Randwijk—which stood close to the south bank of the Neder Rijn opposite the larger city of Wageningen.

The ground enclosed on three sides by the Waal, the Neder Rijn, and the Pannerdensch Canal comprised the Island. It was so named because the Waal and the Neder Rijn come within about three miles of joining each other at the Island's western extremity close to the town of Opheusden. Crisscrossed with ditches, the low clay country of the Island had been transformed into a quagmire by the Germans, who disabled or destroyed drainage systems and breached dykes to inundate it. All main roads were confined to the tops of dykes, so any vehicle movement was extremely vulnerable to enemy fire. Before the 49th Division's changeover to 1 Canadian Corps control, several plans had been devised to clear the Germans out of the Island, but they were abandoned when winter conditions made such operations either too difficult or too vulnerable to counterattack.

With the improving weather and the success of Operation Plunder, Foulkes and Major General G.H.A. MacMillan agreed the time was now ripe. Once Emmerich and Hoch Elten fell, the British Division would lead the operation. To enable MacMillan to concentrate his division's operations to the east opposite Arnhem, Foulkes planned to deploy 5th Canadian Armoured Division's 11th Infantry Brigade against the western portion of the Island. The 1st Canadian Armoured Brigade's Ontario Regiment would provide tank support to the British division.[13]

1 Canadian Corps's chief of staff, Brigadier George Kitching, worked closely with Foulkes on the overall plan. This late in the war, the thirty-five-year-old Kitching was one of the Canadian Army's most experienced chiefs of staff—and one who had also commanded both a brigade and division in battle. From December 14, 1942, to October 30, 1943, he had served as 1st Division's chief of staff before being given command of 5th Division's 11th Infantry Brigade for a short three months. On January 30, 1944, Kitching was promoted to acting major general and commander of 4th Armoured Division. Just thirty-four at the time, Kitching had been Canada's youngest general officer. Kitching's stellar rise proved short-lived. A combina-

tion of bad luck, faulty communications, and possibly poor judgement resulted in the division performing poorly in the Normandy fighting from August 7 to August 21, 1944. Kitching had been sacked, demoted, and returned to Italy as the 1 Canadian Corps chief of staff on November 12, 1944. Shortly thereafter, Foulkes had arrived as the new corps commander, and the two had overseen the last months of Canadian operations in Italy and the subsequent movement to Northwest Europe in February and March of 1945.

In Italy, Kitching had been "impressed with Charles Foulkes' military decisions." Now, working through an ever-changing panoply of schemes rendered down from Montgomery's headquarters—which seemed unable to make up its mind about how to put this new corps to best use—Kitching saw Foulkes quickly exert a controlling hand over each potential task. The "many plans we worked on were all based on sound common sense and I think his eventual orders to the commanders of our 1st and 5th Divisions and the British 49th Division were as well thought out and as well executed as any other battle plans of World War II."[14]

Foulkes had always been something of an enigma within the Canadian officer corps. English-born but educated in London, Ontario, he had entered the army in 1926. Starting off as a major, he had been rapidly promoted during the early war years. By 1942, he was a brigadier and soon received a posting to the army's general staff. Here he caught the eye of Crerar, who considered Foulkes both a skilled administrator and a knowledgeable tactician. Crerar smoothed the way for his promotion to major general and command of 2nd Division in January 1944. Foulkes had led this division through the fighting in Normandy and in the process attracted the ire of Lieutenant General Guy Simonds. The II Canadian Corps commander would have axed Foulkes for what he considered incompetence had it not been for the man's closeness to Crerar. Since then, Foulkes's career had continued to prosper.

Although Crerar's patronage helped advance Foulker's career, his patron's unpopularity within the officer corps tarnished Foulkes's reputation as well. Physically, he was a short, rather dumpy man, which denied him the command presence and sharp appearance so prized within the Permanent Force. Like Crerar, he was also dour and aloof, attributes fed by an introverted personality. Foulkes mixed with his peers only when necessary. Fishing was his sport and he cast his lines alone. While many senior officers were known for their standoffishness—Crerar, Simonds, and Lieutenant General Tommy Burns were all considered cold fish—Foulkes's brand was often interpreted as concealing a cunning, wily, and ruthless nature, which meant he was not to be trusted.[15]

When his performance was questioned, as it had been by Simonds after the Normandy campaign, Foulkes seemed able to evade any negative consequence, not only by relying on Crerar's patronage but also by passing blame downwards. If 2nd Division had performed poorly in Normandy, Foulkes attested that the cause was the inferiority of the soldiers and not the quality of command. Upon assuming command, Foulkes later said, he had considered the division "about as perfect a fighting machine as we could get. When we went into battle at Falaise and Caen we found that when we bumped into battle-experienced German troops we were no match for them."[16] This simple analysis enabled Foulkes to hide within the ranks of the division's other eighteen thousand soldiers—appearing no more responsible for its failures than any private.

CLEARING THE NIJMEGEN Island was critical to Crerar's larger plan for future First Canadian Army operations, which he explained to Foulkes and Simonds in an April 2 directive that coincided with 49th Division opening its offensive. Crerar's immediate concern was to secure the route for rapid movement of supplies from Antwerp's vast port to meet Second British Army's requirements as it swept into the heart of Germany. Montgomery repeatedly reminded Crerar that such a route was "essential to his broader intentions." Accordingly, Crerar told Foulkes to first concentrate on clearing the Island, then seizing Arnhem, and finally clearing a transportation lane between this city and Zutphen. At the same time, Crerar directed that Simonds should secure "the line of country between Almelo and Deventer [and subsequently] advance to clear the enemy from the northeast Netherlands . . . providing that . . . this [could be done] without detriment to the rapid conclusion of his responsibilities for forcing the crossing of the IJssel and clearing an area sufficiently far westwards to enable [Crerar] to develop the very important road and railway communications between Nijmegen, Arnhem and Zutphen; and which run thence through Hengelo into north-western Germany."[17]

Crerar was pleased with the situation as it stood on April 2. 11 Canadian Corps had finally won Emmerich and Hoch Elten, and its northwestward advance along the east bank of the Rhine was proceeding well. So well, in fact, that the First Fallschirmjäger (Paratroop) Army, "our stubborn adversary," had been split in two, with its 11 Fallschirmjäger Corps "reeling backwards [to] the north," having "lost contact with the [LXXXVI] Corps in the south."[18]

One factor that remained in flux and bedevilled Crerar's plans for the new Canadian corps was that SHAEF and Twenty-First Army Group remained undecided about how best to approach the plight of the Dutch in western Netherlands. That a growing humanitarian crisis existed was clearly recognized, but no consensus had been reached on how to alleviate it. Any diversion of First Canadian Army forces to the west would necessarily dilute its strength for the drive through northeastern Netherlands and into Germany as part of Twenty-First Army Group's main offensive. Montgomery had assumed that he would lead the main advance into Germany with three armies under command—the British Second, First Canadian, and U.S. Ninth—and hoped to gain Berlin ahead of the Russians. The full strength of the Canadians would protect his left flank, the Americans of the Ninth his right, and the British would lead the charge in the middle. But Montgomery's dream was scuttled on March 28 by General Eisenhower. Instead of the main thrust being made on the Allied left flank, it would come in the middle and be an American show. Consequently, Ninth Army reverted to command of General Omar Bradley's Twelfth U.S. Army Group. Montgomery's task was now to guard Bradley's northern flank in an advance to the Elbe River. Along the way, his forces would secure the vital German northern ports and liberate Denmark.

Relegated to a supporting role, Montgomery was horrified to also learn there would be no western Allied drive on Berlin. With the

Russians just thirty miles east of the German capital and the western Allies three hundred miles distant, the Americans—in Europe and Washington both—had decided the race was unwinnable. Further, they discounted the political and post-war ramifications of ceding Berlin to the Russians. Eisenhower felt Berlin had ceased to be an important objective. What mattered more was to advance his forces by the quickest route to "join hands" with the Russians and cut Germany in half. This would enable him to direct forces to break up any German attempt to withdraw into the Austrian Alps, where it was feared a "National Redoubt" might be established and defended to the last man.[19]

Even after these decisions were made, Montgomery still expected that all First Canadian Army would march at his side towards Germany—that was just militarily sensible. Would not the best way to bring relief to the Dutch be to defeat the Germans and bring the war to a speedy conclusion? Yet Montgomery was too politically astute not to recognize that military logic might well be overruled by political exigencies. So he warned Crerar to be ready at any moment to direct some of his army towards western Holland. By April 2, Crerar assumed this course of action likely and made his plans accordingly. Like Montgomery, he still hoped military logic would prevail and consequently directed his corps commanders that "should it be decided that the clearing of West Holland by 1 Canadian Corps is not to be undertaken, then First Canadian Army will regroup on a two Corps front, and advance into Germany between the inter-Army boundary on its Right [with Second British Army], and the sea on its Left. Destroying, or capturing, all enemy forces as it proceeds."[20]

Crerar's desire to avoid trying to directly liberate western Holland had been inspired by a Twenty-First Army Group planning staff analysis, released on March 28, of the challenges of such an operation. It was a grim read. Before the operation could even begin, 1 Canadian Corps must first secure a twenty-two-mile line running from Hilversum next to the IJsselmeer, south through Utrecht, and down to Vianen. This meant that the Grebbe Line—a fortified barrier dating back to 1745—would first have to be broken. With its northern flank butted against the IJsselmeer, the Grebbe Line ran along the crest of a modest and heavily forested series of hills and ridges that bordered the Eem and Grebbe rivers to Rhenen on the Neder Rijn. In 1940, the Dutch had laced this main defensive work with pillboxes linked by trench systems to meet a German invasion. When the invasion happened, the poorly equipped but hard-fighting Dutch defenders checked the German advance here for three days, despite knowing their cause was doomed. In the ensuing five years, German engineers had strengthened, modernized, and expanded these defences. The Grebbe Line was deemed a tough nut to crack, especially as the Germans could be expected to make a tenacious stand.

Assuming that the Canadians persevered and gained the Hilversum–Utrecht start line, actual operations in northwest Netherlands would be a nightmare. The majority of the country's largest cities were here, and the British planners foresaw Amsterdam, Rotterdam, The Hague, and IJmuiden being "turned into fortresses, thus forcing us to expend time and lives on street fighting, quite apart from destroying the towns concerned and causing numerous casualties to civilians." Outside the cities, the countryside was "a vast expanse of polder intersected by numerous water obstacles, ranging from large ditches to widespread deliberate inundations." The flooding of huge areas of this polder country—billiard-table-flat land reclaimed from the sea by draining and erecting dykes around each new section—would channel the Canadians onto raised roads. To deny free movement on these roads topping the dykes, the Germans had constructed clusters of mutually supporting pillboxes that could smother each approach with machine-gun and artillery fire.

The planners considered four possible strategies and found each fraught with difficulty. A general advance across the whole front was deemed "impracticable" due to the extensive inundations and a lack of sufficient roads. Concentrating on Amsterdam, which was closest to the existing Allied line, was rejected because the Germans had already "wrecked the port" and "demolished the locks and harbour installations at Ijmuiden." Amsterdam could not therefore be used to ship food and other supplies into the western region, which was the sole purpose of the advance. Making for just Rotterdam, or alternatively The Hague and Leiden, would allow the Germans to concentrate their substantial forces to meet the Canadians head on. Recognizing this, the planners suggested as their fourth and final proposal that these last two courses be somehow combined, so that the Canadians advanced on The Hague and Leiden while also driving towards Rotterdam. Such an approach would liberate the national capital and secure the great port of Rotterdam, which "although heavily demolished [was] still likely to prove of value." The hitch was that these three cities were all strongly defended by excellent fortified lines or lay behind extensive areas of inundation.

Because of the lack of good roads and already widespread flooding, the planners envisioned there being operational room for only two brigades at a time. Therefore, rather than suggest that 1 Canadian Corps commit both its divisions, they foresaw the offensive being carried out by a single infantry division supported by just one armoured regiment (tanks being entirely confined to the roads topping the dykes) and a complement of artillery.

"Operations in Western Holland will be fraught with difficulty and will be very slow," the planners concluded. They also feared that the Germans might stalemate the operation by flooding virtually the entire region. Except for a line of hills 250 to 300 feet high that ran through the area and a coastal belt of dunes, everything lay below sea level. "Flooding may be caused by the breaching of dykes or by stopping pumps," the planners warned. "As the pumping stations throughout Holland have recently very largely been converted to electric power, interference with power stations can easily and rapidly have a wide and disastrous effect." Assuming that the operation would occur only because "political pressure has forced us" into it, the planners concluded that such an advance would likely only escalate the existing humanitarian crisis.[21]

Although the Twenty-First Army Group's planning section report was a chilling document, neither Crerar nor Montgomery used it to argue for abandoning the operation. For his part, Crerar continued to refer to its prospect as something that might or might not be demanded of the army. Ultimately, both men knew that the decision on whether to proceed would, just as the planners had foreseen, be made by their political masters.

A Lion and a Tiger

G ENERAL HARRY CRERAR could afford to set aside the western
Holland operation because 1 Canadian Corps would be well
positioned to advance in that direction once it cleared the Nijmegen
Island opposite Arnhem to begin opening the transportation corridor from this city through to Deventer. Meanwhile, he could direct
the more robust 11 Canadian Corps towards operations that fit Montgomery's preferred strategy by having it drive the Germans back
across the IJssel on the bridgehead's western flank and the Twente
Canal to the north. Thereafter, the corps could clear the northern
part of Montgomery's supply route running from Deventer to
Zutphen.

Mindful of Montgomery's desires, Crerar gave 11 Canadian Corps
priority call on all the army's resources and No. 84 Fighter Group,
RAF, which was to provide tactical air support.[1] Lieutenant General
Charles Foulkes got the meagre leftovers.

Foulkes even lost his tough 1st Canadian Infantry Division,
which had earned a reputation in Italy as Eighth Army's elite shock
troops. Crerar considered the frontage over which Lieutenant General Guy Simonds must operate so wide and heavily defended that he
provided him with what he understatedly described as "a very strong

corps." Adding the Red Patch Devils increased II Canadian Corps's complement to three. Simonds also retained his inherent armoured division and 2nd Canadian Armoured Brigade. Additionally, to add "extra fast moving firepower," Crerar stripped Foulkes of his 1st Armoured Car Regiment (Royal Canadian Dragoons). Foulkes kept only 5th Canadian Armoured Division, 1st Armoured Brigade, and the British 49th (West Riding) Infantry Division.

Simonds decided to punch a hole through the German lines on a narrow front. On his right, 4th Armoured Division would advance northeastward to cross the Twente Canal at Lochem. In the centre, 2nd Infantry Division would strike towards Zutphen, with 3rd Infantry Division following a closely paralleling track through Wehl to the left and focused on the same objective. To offer Foulkes some measure of support and prevent the two corps losing contact with each other, 3rd Division's 7th Canadian Infantry Brigade would divert westward from Wehl to Zevenaar and Didam—about midway between Emmerich and Arnhem.[2] Here it might marry up with 49th Division—assuming the British managed to bounce the Neder Rijn and create a bridgehead on the north side of the river immediately east of Arnhem upon clearing the Nijmegen Island's eastern sector. With all his riches, Simonds could afford to place 1st Division in reserve until Zutphen fell. He would then leapfrog it past his other two infantry divisions to strike westward towards Apeldoorn. This advance would protect his left flank, freeing Simonds to direct the entire weight of his normal corps towards northeastern Holland and northwestern Germany without concern for protecting his rear.

Using 1st Division this way would also serve Crerar well if it developed that an advance towards western Holland was ordered. As it closed on Apeldoorn, Crerar planned to return the division to I Canadian Corps should it need to advance westward.

Both Simonds and Foulkes launched their new attacks on April 2. Anticipating a breakout into open country suited to armour, Simonds divided 4th Armoured Division into two highly mobile battle groups that would allow each to fight independently. Canadian armoured divisions fielded just two brigades rather than the three common to infantry divisions. One brigade was exclusively armoured and the other was infantry. Original doctrine had foreseen the armoured brigade making lightning runs across open ground with its preponderance of tanks outgunning anything in its path. Travelling with the brigade would be the division's one battalion of motorized infantry, equipped with armoured personnel carriers that could keep pace with the armour. The infantry brigade would follow behind to mop up bypassed resistance pockets. In reality, European terrain and German defensive tactics seldom allowed such strategies. The profusion of water courses and extensive inundation in Holland and western Germany limited tank mobility while providing the Germans with multiple defensive lines that must be overcome in endless succession. To meet this situation, the Canadians had taken to mixing the two brigades into hybrid battle groups, where tanks and infantry could mutually support each other.

Leading the division's advance, Battle Group Lion was to advance to the Twente Canal. Commanded by 10th Infantry Brigade's Brigadier Jim Jefferson, Lion's armoured strength came from 4th Armoured Brigade's Governor General's Foot Guards and the division's reconnaissance unit, the South Alberta Regiment. Jefferson retained his Algonquin and Argyll and Sutherland Highlander regiments for infantry. He also had the heavy machine guns of the New Brunswick Rangers, the 14th Canadian Anti-Tank Battery, 15th Canadian Field Ambulance, and the engineers of 9th Canadian Field Squadron. Simonds viewed the task as relatively simple because the British 43rd (Wessex) Infantry Division's 129th Infantry Brigade had almost gained Lochem, a village close to the canal.

Once Lion established a bridgehead over the Twente, Battle Group Tiger—under the armoured brigade's commander, Brigadier Robert Moncel—would pass through and lunge eastward to Delden and Borne. After that, Simonds planned to let the division run as far as it could. Moncel had retained two of his armoured regiments, the Canadian Grenadier Guards and British Columbia Regiment, while receiving a boost in infantry from the Lincoln and Welland Regiment. He also had the Lake Superior Regiment (Motor), which normally supported the armoured brigade. Travelling in Tiger's van was the self-propelled artillery of the 23rd Canadian Field Regiment, the 96th Canadian Anti-Tank Battery, and 12th Canadian Light Field Ambulance.[3]

Lion closed rapidly on Lochem, only to be delayed in reaching the canal beyond until 1630 hours by a painfully slow British handover. Predictably, Lochem's bridges were down, so Jefferson ordered the South Alberta's reconnaissance squadron—equipped with Stuart VI light tanks rather than the Shermans used by the rest of the regiment—to search outward on either flank. With two Stuarts, Sergeant Tom Patterson headed west of Lochem for a mile and a half. Here, he turned north on a road that bridged the Twente. En route was a little creek called the Berkel, whose bridge was intact but blocked by "mines on the road and verges." The Stuart crews all dismounted and started digging up the mines. They were nearly done when a German despatch rider roared towards the bridge from the north, spotted the Canadians, and cut a sharp U-turn before anyone could lay hand on a gun. Continuing up the narrow paved road, Patterson's men soon saw that the bridge over the Twente still stood and floored their Stuarts forward.[4]

As Corporal Jimmy Simpson's Stuart accelerated up the incline of the dyke to gain the bridge, an anti-tank gun on the opposite shore fired. Trooper John Lakes, the Stuart's gunner, saw a bright flash as the shell dealt the turret a hard blow. Simpson yelled for the crew to bail out. Making sure the 37-millimetre gun barrel was centred and not blocking either the driver or co-driver hatches, Lakes started to rise from his seat and discovered that his left foot was "turned completely backwards, with the heel to the front, and the toes to the back. My left leg had been shattered and was just hanging by some sinews." Blood gushed from the leg. Despite his wound, Lakes dragged himself to the top of the turret to find the Germans on the other side of the canal firing at the Stuarts with small arms. With his injury, Lakes realized he would be unable to scramble off the turret quickly enough. Nor was jumping down an option. So Lakes launched off the turret in a bellyflop, chin up to avoid knocking himself out on landing. For several seconds he lay on his stomach, wrenching for breath, then crawled to a shallow ditch, where Simpson stopped the bleeding with a tourniquet.

Some of Patterson's men helped Simpson's shaken crew back to their Stuart. As Trooper Clarence Lorenson was helping settle Lakes and other wounded men on the outside hull, he was killed by a sniper round to the head. Patterson rolled the Stuart back to the cover of a thicket, issued an urgent call for Simpson's crew to be evacuated, and awaited reinforcement.[5]

When Lieutenant Colonel Gordon "Swatty" Witherspoon received Patterson's report, he sent the South Alberta's 'C' Squadron racing to the rescue. Lieutenant Bill Luton's No. 1 Troop formed the fire brigade, while the other two troops held back long enough to board infantry. Luton saw himself bound for glory, picturing his tanks grinding unscathed over the bridge. This vision evaporated when he came to the narrow road approaching the canal. His tanks would have to advance single file, and the ground on either side was too boggy for use. He might have waited for the rest of the squadron and the infantry had Witherspoon not made it clear that the bridge was vital. Luton re-evaluated the scene and realized there were in fact two dykes on that side of the canal, a high dyke to hold back winter floodwater, which would screen the Shermans from the Germans on the other side, and a lower dyke that supported the bridge. Luton advanced to the high dyke. Now came the tricky part. He either just barrelled up onto the dyke and dashed for the bridge or took a more cautious approach. Opting for caution, Luton inched his Sherman up just enough to expose the top of the turret. If that failed to draw fire, he would rise to a hull-down posture to enable firing the main gun across the canal. Should this manoeuvre go unchallenged, Luton would go for the bridge.

The moment the turret's top poked above the dyke, "a tremendous explosion shook the ground and a spectacular mass of debris shot far up into the air."[6] Luton stared miserably at the fragments of steel and concrete spattering down upon the canal.

Realizing there were no more bridges in the area to win, Brigadier Jefferson dispersed Lion Force so that the Argyll and Sutherland Highlanders along with the South Albertas were in Lochem, and the Algonquin Regiment was on some high ground immediately south of the town. The Dutch populace turned out to enthusiastically greet the Canadian liberators, even though the Germans were still ensconced across the canal immediately opposite and subjecting the area to sporadic machine-gun and artillery fire. The Argyll's war diarist thought Lochem "the largest and most attractive town [they] had liberated in Holland, and it was regretted we were unable to fraternize with the jubilant population, as our role was strictly an operational one." They also discovered that the Germans had used Lochem as a rear area headquarters and had established several clubs, various recreational facilities, a military hospital, and "countless military offices filled with files, correspondence and in some cases ammunition."[7]

Patrols estimated German opposition at three hundred paratroops.[8] Given the intensity of fire aimed at the Argylls behind the dyke, they seemed determined to fight and were more than adequately armed with 75-millimetre and 88-millimetre artillery.[9]

Given the enemy strength, the mood was sombre when at 1500 hours the Algonquin Regiment's company commanders convened to consider next steps in a "wonderful observation post" inside a "huge leather factory" on the edge of the canal.[10] The entire divisional plan rested on forcing the Twente at Lochem, and the Algonquins had been selected to win a bridgehead with an attack in assault boats if no bridge was won. Such an attack promised to be a bloody affair.

FORTUNATELY, 4TH DIVISION'S Major General Chris Vokes had already abandoned the original plan by diverting Tiger Force to Diepenheim—a town about six miles northeast of Lochem and a mile short of the Twente Canal. Here Brigadier Moncel was to wait until the British 43rd Division advanced to the canal and established a bridgehead within a two-mile front anchored by Delden to the west and Hengelo the east. Once on the other side of the Twente, the British would advance to Borne and guard Tiger's flank as it advanced on Almelo to cross yet another canal—the Almelo–Nordhorn.[11]

Instead of moving quickly as Vokes had expected, the British crawled forward at a snail's pace. Deciding the Canadians might have to take matters into their own hands, Vokes signalled Moncel at 2325 hours on April 2 that if the British were still "not proceeding quickly enough," he "would be responsible for forcing a crossing and establishing his own bridgehead." He was already sending thirty-six assault boats that the Lincoln and Welland Regiment would use for the attack.[12] Deciding a few hours later to proceed with this plan, Vokes told Moncel to send the Lincs across at 2100 hours that evening adjacent to a destroyed bridge opposite Delden.

Moncel had already put things in motion at 0400 hours, instructing the Lake Superior's Lieutenant Colonel Robert Angus Keane to send a patrol out to check an electrically controlled lock one and a half miles west of Delden. If the patrol was able to cross the canal on the lock, it was to set up a bridgehead that he would strengthen with a company before dawn. Moncel thought the lock offered the best chance for an immediately usable structure, because his engineers had warned that even if the Lincs succeeded in their assault, it would require fourteen hours to construct a functional bridge at the Delden site. Moncel wanted armour pushing out beyond the Twente sooner.

Keane assigned the patrol to Lieutenant Bruce Wright's No. 13 Platoon from 'C' Company, whose men had acquired a reputation for being the battalion's best scouts. With Wright providing regular updates by wireless, the patrol crept forward, trying to hide inside the heavy mist that cloaked the low flat ground south of the canal. Detected just short of the lock, the patrol came under heavy small-arms and mortar fire. Wright was ordered to "withdraw slightly but to keep the area under observation."[13]

Recognizing that a crossing would have to be won the hard way, Moncel held a meeting at 1100 hours. Among those present were Keane, the Lincs' Lieutenant Colonel R.C. "Rowan" Coleman, and Lieutenant Colonel R.E. Hogarth from 23rd Canadian Field Regiment (Self-Propelled). The Lincs would assault with a company on either side of the blown Delden bridge, while the Superiors carried out a diversionary attack on the locks. Moncel had learned the locks were partially demolished but hoped they might provide a temporary bridge. Despite Moncel's desire to delay the attack to first light on April 4, Vokes ordered the timetable advanced instead to 1900 hours on the 3rd.[14]

Vokes's decision shocked Coleman. He had just seven and a half hours to get everything ready. Yet his men took to the task without complaint, and he later said, "Everything just got together beautifully, like a jigsaw puzzle."[15] Once Coleman provided an estimated time for the assaulting companies to reach the northern shore, the artillery teed up a fire plan to kick in thirty minutes beforehand. Most of the shells would be high explosive, but a smokescreen would also blanket the front and flanks to hide the boats.

Major Jim Swayze's 'A' Company would cross on the right and Major John Dunlop's 'C' Company the left. Each company had seven assault boats. Once they established a bridgehead, Captain T.F.G. Lawson's 'D' Company would pass through Swayze's men to a railway line that paralleled the canal at a distance of about two hundred yards, while Major John Martin's 'B' Company advanced from 'C' Company's position.[16] At 1646 hours, the attack started.[17]

By now the Lincs had a well-tested routine for boat assaults. First, men armed with machine guns slipped down the side of the dyke facing the canal to ensure control of the launch site. Then the reserve companies sent carrying parties to put the boats into the water. Once the boats were ready, the assaulters tumbled over the dyke, piled in, and launched. With the barrage still pounding the opposite shore and smoke blanketing everything, the men paddled hard. Over their heads the machine-gunners back on the dyke blazed away to keep the Germans' heads down, while in the front of the boat another man also plied a Bren gun.

The assaulting companies reached the opposite shore in minutes, but 'C' Company lost four men in the crossing. Leaping out of the boats, the men clawed their way up the steep dyke. Dunlop led his men about forty yards from the dyke to some farmhouses. They were taking heavy fire, so he spread the company among the buildings.[18] Ahead lay woods, the edge of which had been their first objective. It was 1938 hours.[19]

To the right, Swayze's company met only light resistance and gained the edge of the woods by 1950 hours. Coleman sent Lawson through Swayze's position to start clearing the woods.

On the left, however, Dunlop's men were fighting for their lives in a vicious close-quarters shootout. Each platoon had set up in a farmhouse that the Germans had isolated from the others. Dunlop and his headquarters section with one platoon were in a large barn-shaped house in the centre. The platoon led by Lance Sergeant J.M. "Johnny" McEachern was in a small farmhouse to the right. One of his Bren gunners, Private Clifford Challice, saw a group of Germans concentrating for an assault on Dunlop's position. Followed by his loader, Challice sprinted across a bullet-swept pasture and scattered the enemy with bursts of close-range fire. Returning to the platoon, Challice was just stepping through the doorway when a potato-masher grenade went off at his side. The blast broke his left arm.[20]

Despite intense pain, Challice slung the Bren support strap over the shoulder of his useless left arm and operated the gun single-handed. From a window facing a pasture swept by repeated enemy assaults, Challice let loose a steady fire. Each time a magazine went dry, one of the other wounded men replaced it with a fresh one loaded by other injured soldiers.[21] "I wasn't brave," Challice later stated. "I was mad. A soldier should never get mad, but I don't fight good unless I get mad." Anything that moved outside, he shot.[22] One particularly determined attack brought the Germans to within fifty feet of the house. Bullets were ripping splinters out of the window frame and whickering past either side of his body, but Challice never budged. He killed five more paratroops, wounded many others, and drove off the attack—saving the platoon and garnering a Distinguished Conduct Medal.[23]

Seeing his company being butchered, Dunlop called for artillery directly onto its position. Most of the men were in buildings while the Germans were stuck in the open, and Dunlop figured that gave his men an edge. If he did nothing, they died anyway.

A terrific barrage of shells and mortar rounds hammered down. Rounds exploded all around Challice's house, and the roof suddenly blew apart. Sergeant McEachern had been outside when the barrage fell and suffered a terrible wound. He lay screaming in agony forty yards from the building, but Challice and the rest knew they would be killed if they attempted a rescue. With all the non-commissioned officers wounded or dead, Challice was organizing the platoon's defence and still working the Bren.

Once the artillery lifted, the Canadians saw that the open ground around the houses was littered with German corpses. "We were inside, they were outside," Dunlop said. "Blew the Germans all to rat shit." Although the enemy kept probing and sniping, they made no further attempts to overrun 'C' Company.

Two hours later, at 0200 on April 4, Major John Martin led 'B' Company through Dunlop's battered position, and the Germans withdrew. 'D' Company had meanwhile reached the railway, and patrols were probing Delden. By dawn, the Lincs had the town and thirty-four prisoners.

Challice's war was over. After helping evacuate the more badly wounded, he collapsed from exhaustion and shock. Challice was one of sixty-seven Lincs wounded or killed. Most were from 'C' Company. He would spend the rest of 1945 in hospital. His friend Sergeant McEachern miraculously survived, although he lost both legs.[24]

WEST OF THE Lincs, the Lake Superior Regiment had decided against a direct attack on the lock. Instead, Major R.A. Colquhoun's 'A' Company was directed to cross in assault boats five hundred yards to the west and catch the Germans defending the lock from the rear. Due to the fortuitous appearance of a British artillery officer from the 8th Armoured Brigade, the attack was to be lavishly supported by two XXX British Corps field regiments and four searchlights to create artificial moonlight. Lieutenant Colonel Faire promised that his gunners would plaster the woods that lay behind both the lock and the proposed landing site to ensure that the Canadians got across with little interference.[25] Also lashing the woods would be the New Brunswick Rangers' medium machine guns, the Superior's own mortar platoon, its three Wasp flame-thrower carriers, and one squadron of Canadian Grenadier Guards tanks.

Problems manhandling the assault boats cross-country and then down the steep dyke to the water's edge delayed the assault to 2300 hours. Once underway, however, things proceeded smoothly. Although the leading platoon was fired on by several Germans armed with Panzerfausts, it suffered only one casualty. Surging up the dyke, the men formed a line and silenced the enemy fire with their rifles and machine guns. The other two platoons quickly moved through their position and fanned out towards the lock.

Despite encountering more Panzerfaust fire, which killed Sergeant Martin Hellsten, the lock was soon secured. Hellsten and the man wounded during the landing were the only casualties. Ten Germans were taken prisoner.[26]

Within minutes of the lock being secured, 8th Canadian Field Squadron engineers started work on a bridge. Finding the lock in surprisingly good condition despite German efforts to demolish it, the engineers had only to create a span over a ten-foot gap and widen the decking on the rest of it to ready it for vehicles. At first light, the Superiors' armoured personnel carriers and other vehicles rolled across and started running northward, facing only light opposition.

Lieutenant Bruce Wright and his No. 13 Platoon scouts were again on point and making straight for Almelo with 'B' and 'C' Companies in trail. Wright took the column through Delden, where the Lincs were being overwhelmed by the deliriously happy townspeople. The Superiors waved off the crowds, including the town Burgomaster, still dressed in his nightshirt, and headed up the highway. On one side lay Holland and on the other, Germany. The weather was sunny, the faces of the civilians gathered in clutches alongside the road likewise. "This was warfare such as the Lake Sups had known it earlier, as it had been in France and Belgium; not like that grim, gruesome battling four weeks before in the devastated Rhineland. No longer was there that depressing sense of desolation and destruction. Again the troops enjoyed the heady elation of being looked upon as 'liberators.' And if there were glum countenances and little white flags hanging out of the windows of the German houses, they were forgotten in the profusion of orange bunting that always seemed to hang from those in Holland."[27]

The Superiors moved so quickly they kept overrunning German troops. About a third of the way from Delden to Almelo, Wright's band caught the paratroops in the midst of preparing to blow a bridge. They killed three and took the other five, including an officer, prisoner. Racing on, the platoon won an even larger bridge intact.[28]

Behind the Superiors, the rest of 4th Armoured Division mustered—a great straggling snake of tanks, trucks, carriers, and artillery. At 1300 hours, the British Columbia Regiment nursed its

Shermans gently over the lock bridge. At Delden, engineers were still erecting a large Bailey bridge that could handle the vehicles more quickly than the lock bridge, but by the time it opened at 1600 hours, 4th Canadian Armoured Brigade had all passed over the narrower bridge and was pushing north. By last light on April 4, the Superiors and tanks of the Canadian Grenadier Guards entered Almelo—a city of about 35,000 people—unopposed. Behind, most of the division was across the Twente.[29] From Almelo, Vokes planned a thirty-mile thrust by 4th Canadian Armoured Brigade on April 5 into Germany, to Meppen on the east bank of the Ems River.

"Thus commenced one of the most successful armoured dashes . . . the brigade has ever made," 4 CAB's war diarist recorded on April 5. "Original objectives were overrun in a matter of a few hours and plans were changed on the move." The Germans seemed in complete disorder, either taking to their heels in a desperate attempt to escape the juggernaut or giving up at the first sight of the Canadians.[30]

By mid-morning of that day, the leading Superiors had covered fifteen miles and occupied Emlichheim. From here, the battalion split, with the main body turning east towards Meppen, while 'A' Company headed northwest to test the defences of the Dutch fortress town of Coevorden, which lay just across the border behind the defensive barrier of the OverIJsselsch Canal. As the company approached Coevorden, the bridges over the canal exploded, and a force estimated at about three hundred Germans opened fire with Panzerfausts and machine guns. One of the rounds struck a Bren carrier and it burst into flame. Private Mervin Brampton and Private Montgomery Cliff died, and two other men were wounded. With dusk gathering, 'A' Company pulled out of range and dug in for the night. During the short action, three more men had been wounded.[31]

Last light found 4th Brigade's main column "well into Germany and probably the most northerly tip of the spearhead of Allied armies in Western Europe moving toward the North Sea. Another highlight of the day and another first in the [brigade's] history . . . was that . . . for the first time our [troops] met the Volkstrum and armed [civilians]. These warriors primed as they were to fight to the last man and the last round met our oncoming [troops] with NOT one but both arms raised in a Nazi salute and their weapons piled neatly at their feet ready for the inventory." The brigade also liberated its first prisoner of war camp at Bathorn, and over the ensuing two days 4th Brigade would free more than seventeen thousand Allied POWs from an assortment of camps.

As night fell, the Superiors were still bound for Meppen and far ahead of the brigade's main body. Deciding that the rest of the brigade was moving too slowly, Lieutenant Colonel Keane warned Moncel that if the main column didn't pick up the pace, it would soon be "bloody well . . . out of contact" with the Superiors.[32] Gaining the outskirts of Meppen in the middle of the night, Keane decided to await the dawn before testing its defences.

Far back, Brigadier Jim Jefferson's 10th Infantry Brigade had already lost contact with the rest of 4th Division. Instead of joining the race to Meppen, most of Jefferson's brigade had been left behind to consolidate the Canadian grip on the Twente Canal about Delden and the stretch of the Almelo–Nordhorn Canal that extended from the Twente to the west of Delden up to Almelo. The Germans were trying to retain control of the west side of this canal to keep an escape route open for their forces being pushed north from the Twente by the 2nd and 3rd Canadian divisions. Jefferson's brigade found itself fighting "a sort of private war miles behind the racing armoured group . . . It was an odd situation for 4 Brigade was miles away . . . as was divisional Headquarters and the (10th) Brigade was left so far behind that any wireless or line communications was out of the question."[33]

Mopping up German resistance was tougher than anticipated, a fact the Algonquin Regiment discovered on the night of April 5–6 when it tried to seize the suburban community of Wierden, immediately west of Almelo. Major George Cassidy thought the plan "rather weird," because it divided his 'D' Company into three separate bodies that were to work independent of each other. One platoon crossed the canal at Almelo and advanced along its western bank, while a second paralleled it on the opposite shore. Company headquarters and the third platoon, meanwhile, moved from Almelo along the highway leading to a crossing into Wierden with a bulldozer in tow, which was to start cutting approaches for a bridge once the two leading platoons had secured the area. Lacking radios, all communication between the three groups depended on runners.

When runners informed Cassidy that the two platoons had both reached the crossing site unopposed and were digging in, the major rushed his group up the road towards the canal, only to be met by a "terrific hail of small arms fire spraying the length of the road." Moments later, another runner reported that in the dark, the two platoons had turned north rather than west and belatedly realized they were dug in eight hundred yards away.[34]

A second crossing attempt next to the destroyed highway bridge was made in broad daylight at 1330 hours on April 6. Carrying two assault boats, the two wayward platoons of the previous night were caught in withering machine-gun and mortar fire.[35] The lead platoon suffered fourteen casualties, three-quarters of its strength, and the following one lost three men wounded. Lieutenant Robert Louis Richard died, and the other platoon leader was injured. 'D' Company secured a toehold on the edge of the canal across from Wierden, but otherwise its operation was an "utter fiasco."

For the next three days, the Algonquins remained engaged in "this queer sort of sideshow battle," until a patrol entered Wierden on April 9 and discovered that the Germans had slipped away into the darkness during the night.[36] Within hours, 10 CIB was racing north to catch up to the rest of the division.

11

Fierce Rearguard Actions

<hr />

THE BREAKOUT BY 4th Canadian Armoured Division conformed with similar advances by xxx British Corps's Guards Armoured Division, which had gained the Ems on April 3 and disrupted German work on a defensive line along the river's eastern bank. Left of 4th Division, meanwhile, 11 Canadian Corps's two committed infantry divisions had been equally busy liberating Dutch real estate between April 2 and 5. The 2nd Division's 4th Canadian Infantry Brigade had gained the most ground on April 2 when Major General A.B. "Bruce" Matthews formed it into a flying column of infantry mounted on carriers and tanks sent towards the Twente Canal. An artilleryman by training, the thirty-six-year-old had been promoted to divisional command in November 1944 and proved as capable an infantryman as gunner. Sensing that the front had gone mushy, Matthews decided on bold action, instructing Brigadier Fred Cabeldu to load the Royal Regiment of Canada onto its carriers and the hulls of the Fort Garry Horse's 'B' Squadron. To protect the vulnerable infantry, the division's reconnaissance regiment, the 14th Canadian Hussars, led the advance. This Easter Monday had dawned heavily overcast with a strong wind that lashed the men with sporadic icy rain.[1]

At the column's head, 14th Hussars' Lieutenant Lorne MacKenzie and No. 1 Troop made nineteen miles unopposed. Emerging from a patch of thick woods, MacKenzie was relieved to see the bridge over a small brook called the Berkel still standing and about a mile beyond the Twente's high dyke. Next to the bridge, a German soldier stood talking to a Dutch civilian. One of the gunners snapped off a burst that hit the Dutchman instead of the German. As the civilian fell dead, the soldier raised his hands. Spotting more Germans in a nearby thicket, the armoured cars riddled the area with fire. Several surrendered while the rest fled.

The bridge's approaches were strewn with mines and its deck had been wired with explosives. Dismounting, MacKenzie and his men threw the mines and explosives into the brook. As the last mine sunk from sight, a Dutch ss soldier stepped out of the thicket with a shouldered Panzerfaust but was cut down before he could fire.

As soon as the other Hussars arrived, No. 1 Troop made for the Twente, only to see the bridge crossing it explode while they were still three hundred yards short of its ramparts. "As it sank to the bottom of the canal," MacKenzie's "soaring spirits went with it. In sheer anger we shot up everything we could see on the other side and then moved back . . . and . . . took up positions guarding the approaches." As they sullenly watched the canal, doodling along the dyke came six Germans on bicycles. "We were still boiling with anger [and] at 75 yards 6 MGs and 3 Brens made quite a mess of them. We felt better after that."[2]

When the Hussars' 'A' and 'B' Squadrons caught up, patrols searching along the dyke found only destroyed crossings. By early afternoon, the tanks and Royal Regiment arrived, the latter bringing up eighteen assault boats. Taking to the boats at 1730 hours, 'A' Company gained the opposite shore unopposed. Scrambling up the dyke, the Royals surprised some German engineers digging fighting pits for a company of infantry just approaching from the left to take up its positions. The Royals opened fire, scattering the Germans into a cluster of nearby houses.

The moment it crossed the canal, 'D' Company advanced across a wide expanse of pastureland, riven with drainage ditches, towards the German-occupied houses. Sergeant Garnet William Eldridge's No. 18 Platoon drew immediate machine-gun and Panzerfaust fire. A hard driver—who would win a Distinguished Conduct Medal that day—Eldridge had never shirked a firefight since first seeing action in Normandy and was out front as usual, replying to the fire with his Sten gun while running right into "the very muzzles of the enemy machineguns and bazookas." Raw recruits, the Germans made the common mistake of the inexperienced and fired so high that their rounds passed harmlessly overhead.[3] As Eldridge approached one house, a German stepped out of the door with a Panzerfaust shouldered. Grabbing a PIAT from its operator, Eldridge did the same with it, despite the weapon being intended for prone firing. Eldridge's 2.5-pound hollow charge struck the German squarely in the chest before he could fire, and he disappeared in a shower of gore. The remaining Germans among the houses fled.[4]

Lieutenant Colonel R.M. "Richard" Lendrum spread his Royals along the canal, with 'D' and 'A' Companies in the centre and the other two companies on either side. Without a bridge, there were no means yet for getting the battalion's support carriers or any armoured cars or tanks into the bridgehead. A party of engineers started work on a ferry at midnight and had it ready to carry one vehicle at a time across at 1000 hours on April 3. Other engineers had been working on a bridge, but it was not scheduled for completion until the end of the day.[5] The ferry service had just finished shuttling the battalion's support troops, half of the Hussars' 'B' Squadron, and half the armoured cars across by 1400 hours when the Germans started heavily shelling the entire bridgehead—forcing the bridging effort to shut down at 1730 hours. German infantry also counterattacked 'A' and 'C' Companies, but were thrown back with heavy losses. At 2100 hours, the Germans scored several direct hits on the ferry, smashing it to pieces. Artillery and tank fire soon silenced the German guns, and a last-gasp counterattack at 2230 hours was easily driven off. As night fell, the Royals counted three men dead, four missing, and twenty-three wounded.[6]

Brigadier Cabeldu suspected that the veteran paratroops had been used up and only inferior units remained, noting that the "enemy tactics appear almost juvenile at times—he is doing every-thing the book says as usual, but his training here shows that the calibre of troops opposing us is not what it used to be. Each enemy attack suffered very heavy casualties and usually a number of PW [were] taken—grubby, dirty, slender youths, boys and old men."[7]

On the morning of April 4, shelling of the bridgehead "rather mysteriously ceased," and the engineers launched a newly con-structed ferry. Repeated German counterattacks directed at the bridge site were easily driven off but still delayed the work. Toiling through the night, 2nd Field Company's engineers were able to com-plete the bridge and open it for traffic at 0900 hours. By noon, the battalions of 5th Canadian Infantry Brigade crossed the Twente and headed for Laren, a village immediately north of the bridgehead.

Also using the bridge were the Regina Rifles of 3rd Division's 7th Infantry Brigade. By passing through 2nd Division's lines across the Twente, this battalion was able to move westward along the bank of the canal towards Zutphen—3rd Division's main objective.[8]

OPERATION PLUNDER HAD seriously depleted 3rd Division's infan-try brigades. The troops were worn out, but there was to be no letup, as the division was ordered to advance simultaneously due north via Wehl towards Zutphen and westward in the direction of Zevenaar on the Emmerich–Arnhem highway. This latter move was to keep the two Canadian corps connected.

Before either advance could proceed, Wehl had to be secured, and it was this task that led to the Reginas crossing the bridge on the eve-ning of April 1. Dutch civilians estimated that four hundred Germans were dug in behind the raised single-track railway that marked Wehl's southern boundary.[9] Doubting they would make a stand, Brigadier Graeme Gibson ordered the Reginas to "march to contact."[10]

Through the afternoon, the rifle companies paced towards Wehl in a long strung-out line, with the armoured cars of the 17th Duke of York's Royal Canadian Hussars' 'A' Squadron out front and the Sher-brooke Fusiliers' 'C' Squadron clanking along to the rear in their Shermans. Lieutenant Colonel Al Gregory suspected the civilians overestimated German strength but agreed that the railway "would provide a logical [defensive position] for a [rearguard] action."

By 1800 hours, his men were practically staggering beneath their weapons and other gear. Gregory decided that "tired, marching [troops] could not either gain contact, nor fight, and the entire [battalion should be] made mobile." Mounting 'B' and 'C' Companies on the Sherbrookes' tanks and the others on support company vehicles sped the advance to Kilder. Here the battalion halted for the night.

Gregory tested Wehl's defences with three fighting patrols, which all drew fire from the railroad. Suspicions confirmed, Gregory teed up a heavy artillery and 4.2-inch mortar concentration on the railway to coincide with the Regina attack at 0400 hours. The attack was to advance up either side of the main road with 'A' Company left and 'B' Company right. A section of Wasps would support each company. Gregory asked the tanks to do likewise, but "they refused to play," invoking armoured doctrine that Shermans were too vulnerable during night actions. Once the leading companies had forced the railway and cleared the southern half of Wehl, the other two companies would pass through and carry the rest. As the sun would be up, the Sherbrookes promised to assist that phase.[11]

Shortly before 0400 hours, 'C' Company's No. 14 Platoon mustered inside a barn, and the quartermaster sergeant gave each man a rum ration while Lieutenant Regan explained the attack. Rifleman Doug Dobie looked at his comrades and felt that "great feeling of comradeship that exists in a front line fighting battalion. Each one knew there was a chance he would not come out alive but that worried no one. Good soldiers are all fatalists and so it was with this bunch of boys."[12]

Outside, 'C' Company formed behind 'B' Company and the column trudged through the darkness to the start line. At 0400 hours, the artillery began pounding the railway and the men advanced. The Reginas were surprised to meet little resistance on the railway, the hard fight coming instead as they entered the village. Lighting up one building after another with flame, the Wasps prowled streets echoing with the chatter and crack of gunfire. It took two hours for 'A' and 'B' Companies to win the southern portion of Wehl.[13]

'C' and 'D' Companies launched past with two Wasps apiece and a troop of tanks from 'C' Squadron of the Fusiliers. Dobie's platoon "went up the road through the shambles of the battle, houses were burning, lots of dead Jerries lying around but we only saw one dead Canadian." Just as it seemed the fight was won, Dobie heard a mighty metallic bang, and a shell from a German self-propelled gun punched the lead tank's turret.[14] The tank commander, Lance Corporal Norman Adrian Beleval, and Troopers William Charles Anderson and David Frederick England were killed. One other crew member was wounded.[15]

'D' Company's Lieutenant Walter Keith saw a Panzerfaust projectile shriek out of a trench and skim harmlessly over one Wasp, which replied with a jet of flame that brought the Germans spilling out with arms raised. "The flame hadn't burned any of them, but was so frightening they surrendered—a marvelous weapon." One soldier informed Major Gordon Brown where a Panzerfaust was located. Brown told Keith to accompany the man and retrieve it. "Keep your pistol trained on him," Brown cautioned. "The German led me into the trench, pointed out the weapon and went to pick it up. I don't know what he intended to do with it but I jabbed my pistol in his ribs and stopped him." The German then said, "Can I get my eatings." Keith consented, and the man lifted a belt from which dangled "large pieces of sausage and black bread." As the two walked back to where Brown had set up a company headquarters, the German said, "Ve vas alright, ve vas shooting your guys but then whoosh, ve quit."[16]

By 0925 hours, most of the Germans inside Wehl had done likewise, although several snipers were still active and occasional mortar rounds struck the village from firing positions inside a nearby wood. Seventy-nine prisoners were taken in Wehl and another twenty were subsequently flushed from the woods.

Wehl was a small battle but one that Lieutenant Colonel Gregory thought yielded a couple of important lessons. First, the defensive methods employed by the Germans had achieved their intent. "A few average troops with stern N.C.O. leadership," he wrote, "well supported by S.P. guns and mortars meant a serious delay and caused at least one brigade to deploy and one battalion to attack." Another "important lesson to be learned . . . is the absolute necessity for getting infantry on the spot as fast as possible and having the troops fresh to fight. Had the entire distance been marched on foot the attack would have probably been abortive. Also the Wehl garrison would have had time to dig further defences as many partially dug pits were seen later."[17]

At 1240 hours, the Royal Winnipeg Rifles passed through Wehl, headed west for Didam and Zevenaar. Lieutenant Colonel Lochie Fulton put 'C' Company out front, with tanks and 17-pounder anti-tank guns giving the force real teeth. However, the Germans, one army report commented dryly, were "apparently not in any way awed by the sight of this war column. The advancing troops were met with a hail of fire as soon as they left the village, and deployment [for combat] became necessary."

Not until dawn of April 3 did the Can Scots cover the last leg of the four-mile distance between Wehl and Didam. "Considering the opposition encountered," the regiment's historian explained, "the advance had been slow, but the alternative meant greater risk and possibly higher casualties. Admittedly, too, there was a certain amount of over-caution on the part of some . . . a not unnatural feeling immediately following the slugging matches such as the battalion had fought at . . . Emmerich."[18] The RWR passed through the Can Scots in Didam at 0530 hours and took until 0800 to cover the mere mile between Didam and Zevenaar.

ON APRIL 2, Wehl had served 3rd Division like a turnstile. Within an hour of the Winnipeg Rifles passing, 8th Canadian Infantry Brigade's Queen's Own Rifles had marched out on the northward-running road to Laag Keppel, where they were to force a crossing over the Oude IJssel. Again, weariness took its toll. Despite very light resistance, which was brushed aside by the supporting tanks, it took until 0130 hours on April 3 to secure the southern portion of Laag Keppel and come up to the river, only to find the bridge blown. Le Régiment de la Chaudière was shuttled in trucks to Doetinchem, from which it marched back along the river to the part of Laag Keppel that stood on the north bank.[19]

Securing the town opened the way for 9th Canadian Infantry Brigade to take over the advance that afternoon at 1440 hours, with the Stormont, Dundas and Glengarry Highlanders and North Nova

Scotia Highlanders leading and the Highland Light Infantry following in reserve. Within the hour the Glens reached their first
objective—a bridge at the village of Hummelo, which was captured
intact. Finding opposition "non-existent," the North Novas fanned
out across a three-mile-wide front to make contact with 2nd Canadian Division on their right and clear the small hamlet of Bronkhorst
to the left. As this locality was also undefended, 'D' Company carried on a few hundred yards to the east dyke of the IJssel River and
started working northward.[20]

On April 4, once again at the forefront of the advance, the Glens
closed on Leesten, about two miles southeast of Zutphen. A large
windmill, which the locals considered the most beautiful of the
three in their district, dominated the hamlet. Leesten consisted of a
blacksmith shop, a carpenter shop, a bakery, a general store, and a
little cluster of farms fanning out beyond the businesses. It perched
on what had once been a dune bordering a riverbed. All around were
other old dunes, between which streams had formerly flowed before
being drained to create farmland. The riverbeds provided the farmers with meadows, while the slopes and tops of the dunes supported
crops. Most farm buildings were situated on the dunes, as the low
ground was subject to seasonal flooding.

The residents of Leesten had taken to their cellars because Canadian artillery sporadically shelled the Zutphen area. On April 2, the
Dykman family had narrowly escaped disaster when two shells
exploded simultaneously on opposite sides of their farmhouse. Young
Henk Dykman's grandmother had been facing a window and working
at a sewing machine when the glass shattered and she was hurled
under a table. Although bruised, she was otherwise uninjured. The
Dykmans were still cleaning up as the Glens approached.[21]

After the unopposed advance of the previous day, the Glens were
surprised to find themselves entangled in a confused series of skirmishes with paratroops. Having had several days to prepare, the
paratroops had dug a network of trenches and gun pits. They had also
hoisted a dozen heavy machine guns onto platforms mounted high in
trees, from which they could fire down into the fields and dunes.
Carefully sighted anti-tank guns covered the roads and open fields.[22]
Mixed in among the veteran paratroops were many young Germans

recently sent from central Germany. These younger paratroops, many no more than sixteen years old, offered "fanatical resistance."[23]

Throughout the morning, the people of Leesten were caught in the middle. Shellfire set numerous buildings ablaze. The beautiful windmill that had been "the pride of the Leesten landscape" was reduced to a smouldering ruin. To the civilians, the battle seemed pure chaos. Germans ran this way, Canadians another, tanks rumbled forward and fired several rounds and then pulled back, flame-throwing Crocodiles ground up to farm buildings and set them on fire to drive out the paratroops inside.

Guus van der Hoeven, the local minister's son, hid in a farmer's cellar along with his and the farmer's families. A bullet pinged through the single cellar window and grazed Guus's brother's forehead, van der Hoeven later recalled. "Everybody screamed in the pitch black cellar . . . When the commotion stopped we heard cautious, heavy footsteps upstairs and my parents called out. My father was the only one of us who knew some English. Next I remember a . . . soldier stepping down into the cellar with a Tommy gun at the ready and a little wax candle in his other hand. He told us to raise our hands and he looked around very carefully. He said that enemy soldiers had fired into the cellar but that everything was alright now. Then he left us again, giving us the little light. He told us to keep that burning. This man has often been on my mind. Undoubtedly his friends were covering him from outside, but he still had a lot of courage to come into our cellar. He was a stocky guy in battledress, quiet and efficient. I wish I could meet that guy again and thank him."[24]

Dina Vink-Jimmink, her sister, and her parents were also in their farmhouse cellar. Looking out a little window, she saw men in khaki "crouching and running with blackened faces. They came straight toward our house and disappeared into a side door as we got ready to greet them. Then all hell broke loose above our heads. Not just rifle and machine gun fire. No! Heavy explosions as well! We were totally frightened. Thank God it did not last long. But then smoke began to drift across our cellar window.

"'We have to get out,' father said.

"Hand in hand we left the house. Outside, behind the farm building, the pig barn had its doors open and inside we saw them again, the Canadians. They were busy tying up each other's wounds. One of them waved to us.

"We ran a long way into the pasture east of our farm. Then we stopped to take a look. Flames were shooting up high from the thatched roof. We watched the shelter of our family and of our fore-bears burn furiously and listened to the bawling of our dying cows. Then father began to cry. Cry like a baby."[25]

Nearby, German soldiers had burst into the Bruggink family's farmhouse at noon and ordered them out. "We are going to defend this place," they shouted. The family had gone but a few hundred yards when the area came under shellfire. They dived into a dry ditch beside the road. Hanna Bruggink "could see the Canadians advance toward our farm. There was some shooting and a carrier with a flame thrower came up. Soon the place was on fire and the enemy soldiers came out with their hands up. 'They didn't have to make a show of it,' father said bitterly. 'They could have stuck up their hands sooner to save the farm.'

"As the shells kept coming and the bullets kept flying, we stayed where we were, all afternoon. Toward dusk we watched some big tanks arrive and they produced enormous flames, burning up the enemy defences just north of us. Then, as they turned away again, all shooting stopped. We got out of the ditch, wondering what to do, when the farmer . . . [farther] west, waved at us. So we went to that place and stayed there overnight."[26]

The battle for Leesten concluded the following morning, April 5, and cost the Glens eleven dead and nineteen wounded.[27] They took fifty-one prisoners on April 4, 'B' Company alone counting thirty-five dead paratroops in its sector.[28]

MEANWHILE, TO THE south, First Canadian Army's new corps had been heavily engaged in clearing the Nijmegen Island. Operation Destroyer opened at 0630 hours on April 2, with 147th Brigade's 7th Battalion, Duke of Wellington's Regiment (West Riding) advancing eastward alongside the Rhine River towards the town of Doornen-burg. This community stood in the angle formed by the Pannerdensch Canal's northward diversion from the Rhine and about three miles from the start line at Haalderen. Supporting the

British battalion were two Ontario Tank Regiment troops under command of Lieutenants J. Cameron and W.B. Stewart, with Cameron's No. 14 Troop following the leading infantry. Stewart's troop was well back but ready to move up on demand. All went well for the first fifteen hundred yards, until the infantry reached a narrow stream called the Rijn Wetering and came under heavy fire from a row of houses on the opposite bank.

Resistance here had been expected, so a solution was readily at hand. Accompanying Cameron's tanks was a Valentine Bridge-Laying Tank. By replacing a Valentine's turret with a folding metal gangway, British engineers had created a mobile apparatus that could launch a thirty-foot self-supporting bridge in minutes. Quickly negotiating their tanks over a series of small drainage ditches, No. 14 Troop closed up on the houses and pummelled them with 75-millimetre main gunfire, while the bridge tank launched its span into place. "Before many minutes, the troop was pounding across the bridge and in very short order the enemy in the area were entirely subdued," the Ontario Regiment's intelligence officer, Lieutenant J. Black, wrote.[29]

Many Germans surrendered, and those that withdrew were too few to further resist the advancing infantry and tanks. By early afternoon, Doornenburg fell. More than one hundred Germans were captured at a cost to the British of two men killed and four wounded.[30]

At 1530 hours, 146th Infantry Brigade passed through and advanced north alongside the Pannerdensch Canal with the Ontario's 'B' Squadron supporting the 4th Battalion, Lincolnshire Regiment. By nightfall the force won the villages of Angeren and Huissen.[31]

Despite damp and unsettled weather, April 3 proved a fine day for the British division and Ontario tankers. In rapid order, 146th Brigade's battalions—supported by 'A' and 'C' Squadrons—scoured up the last Germans in their sector of the Island, which was bordered on one side by the Pannerdensch Canal and on the other by the Nijmegen–Arnhem highway. More than fifty Germans were taken prisoner on a day when resistance remained light and clearly disorganized.[32] It was so light that throughout the day various tank troops from the two squadrons were released by the infantry battalions as being no longer required.[33]

At 1700 hours, the Lincolnshire Regiment slipped some troops across the Neder Rijn just east of Huissen. Dragooning several landing craft previously deployed on the Rhine for Plunder, a 49th Reconnaissance Regiment squadron was lifted into the small bridgehead and its armoured cars advanced two miles to Westervoort. Finding the village clear, it set up a defensive perimeter on the banks of the IJssel east of Arnhem.

Meanwhile, 3rd Canadian Infantry Division's 7th Infantry Brigade had not yet reached Zevenaar, and this left a gap between the lines of 1 Canadian Corps and 11 Canadian Corps. To close it, a second 49th Reconnaissance squadron crossed the Rhine at Emmerich and moved along the riverbank to join hands with 1st Battalion, Leicestershire Regiment, of 147th Brigade—which had earlier crossed the Pannerdensch Canal and cleared the community of Pannerden. At 1700 hours, the reconnaissance troops and infantry were linked up, and 49th Division reported that it now controlled all the ground west of the Emmerich–Arnhem highway.[34]

April 3 had seen 5th Canadian Armoured Division's 11th Infantry Brigade enjoying similar successes clearing the Island's western portion. The Canadians had kicked off the preceding night with all three infantry battalions. Supporting them were tanks from the Governor General's Horse Guards. Although a reconnaissance unit, the GGHG was equipped with Shermans in a mix identical to that of the division's 5th Armoured Brigade regiments.

On the extreme left, the Irish Regiment of Canada's 'D' and 'C' Companies advanced up either side of a road that led to Randwijk, a village on the Neder Rijn's south bank. The unopposed advance was slowed by mines on the road, and not until the early hours of April 3 did the two companies reach the village outskirts. After taking eight prisoners, 'C' Company was suddenly forced to cover by fire from a pillbox that was only silenced when the battalion's anti-tank gun platoon came forward to shoot it up. 'D' Company also bumped light resistance passing through the right-hand side of Randwijk and took four prisoners. By 1030 hours, both companies reported their sectors of the village taken. 'A' Company then hooked out to the right to meet the Cape Breton Highlanders at Heteren. On the company's return hike, it came under heavy shelling from guns on the other side of the river but managed to dodge through the explosions without loss. The Irish Regiment's war diarist considered April 3 "a very successful day."[35]

The Cape Breton Highlanders also encountered no opposition during its night advance of April 2–3, being delayed only by mines and a blown bridge over a canal, which it took engineers until 2340 hours to replace. Chafing at this delay, Lieutenant Colonel Boyd Somerville ordered the leading 'A' and 'B' Companies to pick up the pace.[36]

'B' Company's Quartermaster Sergeant Ronald Finamore, and his friend Private Alfred James "A.J." MacKeigan had just returned from seven days' leave in England. The furlough had enabled A.J. to visit his recently acquired wife in her Birmingham hometown. As the two men reported for duty, they spotted the two rifle companies marching into the darkness. The company's carrier driver, Mac-Keigan rushed to join his partner, Private James Bertram Cusack, in the vehicle, and at 0030 hours the vehicle sped off after the infantry. Fifteen minutes later, Finamore heard a "big bang and we all ran out to the road to look—then we jumped into my carrier and went up the road. There was A.J.'s carrier cross-ways on the road and two or three fellows were running back from the rear platoon. Cusack had fallen down on the floor of the carrier and A.J. was sitting behind the wheel. A big fellow jumped up on top of the carrier—reached down—grabbed A.J. by the belt and pulled—he had only the ragged belt when he straightened up. Cusack had a big lump on the back of the neck—both men were dead—just two days after A.J. had left his wife back in Birmingham. One contributing factor was that there were no sandbags in the bottom of the carrier." These had been removed for the ship movement from Italy to France, and with MacKeigan on leave they had not been replaced. "The mine came right through the bottom of the carrier—we guessed that the explosion broke Cusack's neck and pieces hit A.J. in the hip and waist." They were the battalion's first men to die in Northwest Europe.[37]

The moment Lieutenant Colonel Somerville learned that 'B' Company's carrier had been destroyed and two men killed, he radioed

'A' Company to warn its leading troops to be extra wary of mines. A few minutes later, the company commander reported being held up by a spot so badly cratered by demolitions that the carrier could not pass. Somerville told him to leave it behind. He then sent the battalion's pioneers and sappers from the supporting engineers to repair the road. By 0520 a GGHG tank troop, a platoon of medium machine guns from the division's Princess Louise Fusiliers support battalion, and two battalion anti-tank guns moved up to shadow 'B' Company.[38]

Despite being continually slowed by mines, the Highlanders secured Heteren by mid-morning and reached the dyke overlooking the Neder Rijn. 'A' Company had just finished digging in behind it at 1100 hours when ten German infantrymen launched a hopeless attack. They "were soon shot up and those who weren't killed, fled in the direction they came from. Later a small fighting patrol went out in search of the enemy but they seemed to have disappeared completely." One Highlander was wounded in the exchange.

At 1400 hours, 'B' Company contacted the Perth Regiment on the right flank. Things remained quiet all along the battalion's front until 1830, when 'A' Company spotted about thirty Germans trying to paddle across the river in boats. Artillery drove them back, but the moment the guns ceased firing the Germans again launched their boats. Renewed artillery convinced them to abandon the venture.[39] Clearing their section of the Island cost the Highlanders three men killed and five wounded.[40]

The Perth Regiment faced stiffer opposition and suffered the most casualties in its advance on Driel. Even as the rifle companies formed up on the evening of April 2, they came under heavy shelling that caused three casualties. Although 'B' and 'C' Companies encountered little resistance during their night advance towards the road leading into Driel, when the other two companies passed through at 0400 hours on April 3, 'A' Company had a rough scrap for control of a cluster of houses around a road junction, and three men were killed or wounded. A single Dutch ss soldier taken prisoner surprised the Perth's war diarist by "willingly giving information about the enemy in Driel. He told us that our artillery fire had considerably lessened their numbers." This made Major P.F. Fisher decide to attack immediately.[41] With Nos. 1 and 2 Troops of the GGHG's 'A' Squadron following, 'A' Company and 'D' Companies went forward.

As the force entered Driel's outskirts, two machine-gun positions east of the village drove the infantry to ground.[42] The tanks quickly silenced the guns, but Driel itself proved defended by diehard Dutch ss snipers. Even after the tankers smashed buildings in which they hid, the survivors continued to plink away with rifles from new hiding spots until either killed or driven to a new location.[43] It took until 1400 hours to silence the last of the snipers. Everyone was settling down for a rest when 'D' Company—set up outside the village—was hit by two heavy counterattacks, which were beaten off "without much trouble." Inside Driel, 'A' Company was attacked by ten Germans, who killed one man before the GGHG tanks drove them off with machine-gun fire. Only in the late afternoon did the enemy concede Driel's loss. Even then, heavy machine-gun and artillery fire from positions on the Arnhem side of the river continued harassing the Perth lines. In the two-day action, the Perths had four men killed and nine wounded.[44]

Although the Island had fallen rather easily, it was not a pleasant spot to be in afterwards—particularly the eight-mile Canadian sector extending west from Driel to Randwijk. Across the river, a low ridge provided excellent observation, and throughout the day any movement drew fire. "The greatest disadvantage of this front is not being able to move around the forward areas in daylight," the Cape Breton Highlander war diarist observed. "The ration vehicles have to go forward before first light in the morning and not again until after last light in the evening, making the day pretty long." On April 5, it was decided to deploy seven generators to mask the corps positions "behind a cloud of noxious smoke."[45]

APRIL 5 WAS a fine, warm day full of the promise of spring. Well back of the soldiers sheltered along the Rhine behind the foul smoke-screen, Crerar welcomed Montgomery into his office at Venlo. Montgomery personally informed the First Canadian Army commander that the politicians had reached their decision. As he left, Montgomery handed Crerar written orders that instructed him to send one corps comprised of "at least two divisions" to "operate westwards to clear up western Holland. This may take some time; it will proceed methodically until completed." Meanwhile, the bulk of the army was to "operate northwards to clear northeast Holland, and [eastward] to clear the coastal belt and all enemy naval establishments up to the line of the Weser.

"In the operations of Canadian Army the available resources in engineers, bridging equipment, etc, may not be sufficient for all purposes. In this case the operations [in northeast Holland] will take priority; the clearing of western Holland will take second priority. Canadian Army will be responsible for establishing civil control in western and northeast Holland as these areas are cleared.

"Canadian Army will have priority for all amphibious resources of 79 [Armoured Division], e.g. buffaloes, etc. These will very probably be necessary in western Holland and may serve to speed up the operations in that area."[46]

Although he would bow to the inevitable, Crerar was not optimistic about his chances of success. It seemed as if the Germans within western Holland had "chosen to fight a separate battle, standing first along the IJssel and then the Grebbe and New Water lines [farther] to the west. For such a contest the Commander of the Twenty-Fifth Army would have the combined resources of the troops still remaining in the country as a garrison, and the formations now falling back across the river as a result of my offensive to the north. It was to be assumed that his total forces would number about 100,000 men. Not all of his formations were experienced in battle, nor all at full strength, but with the varied water obstacles which they were evidently prepared to exploit without regard to the further devastation by flooding of large areas of the country at this stage of the war, they [would] be capable of putting up a strong defence. At the same time, I held only a low priority on the special resources necessary to carry my operations westward to the North Sea." Montgomery had made it clear that an advance into western Holland was secondary to supporting his push through Germany. If, and when, 1 Canadian Corps embarked on this mission, it would do so while standing at the bottom of the supply chain and equally lacking in priority for calls on such supporting arms as tactical air.[47]

12

On the Brink

NOWHERE IN WESTERN Europe did the German occupation go so horribly awry as in the Netherlands. This was a great shock to the Germans. When they invaded on May 10, 1940, they expected an easy victory and on the surface appeared to have won one. Yet, in five days of fighting, the Dutch armed forces had inflicted twelve thousand casualties and destroyed 10 per cent of the Luftwaffe's aircraft. Along with the royal family, about 4,600 Dutch officers, sailors, soldiers, and policemen escaped to England to form the backbone of a government-in-exile.

Hitler should have been warned. The pre-war Dutch fascist party—the Nationaal Socialistische Beweging (NSB)—had been one of Europe's weakest pro-Nazi parties. It had held only four of one hundred seats in the Netherlands Parliament's Lower Chamber and had a reputation for being "vocal but not really influential."[1] Its membership of 3.9 per cent of the population was declining.[2] But despite the country's lukewarm enthusiasm for fascism, Hitler expected to reshape the Netherlands into a National Socialist state.

He believed it was only a matter of time before the Dutch recognized their kinship with Germany. They were Aryan, the majority undiluted by interbreeding with inferior races. Queen Wilhelmina's husband was German, and in 1936 Crown Princess Juliana had married Bernhardt zur Lippe-Biesterfeld. However, immediately adopting the Dutch spelling, Prince Bernhard had proven loyal to the Netherlands. After fleeing to Britain, he refused to accompany Juliana and their two children to safety in Canada. Instead, while they took up residence in Ottawa, he joined the RAF and earned his pilot's wings.* In August 1940, he was also appointed as a Dutch naval captain and army colonel. With each passing year, Bernhard's influence within the government-in-exile and involvement in developing the growing resistance movement within the Netherlands increased.

At first, Hitler extended a velvet glove. There was no looting. No assaults. No rapes. The soldiers told the Dutch they were "cousins." Many people believed there would be none of the atrocities common in countries such as Poland. And, for a while, the policy did seem to be working, partly because of a widespread historical antipathy towards the British going back to the defeat and subsequent perceived mistreatment of the Dutch Boers in the South African War.

Certain conditions following the invasion also encouraged compliance. When most government ministers fled with the Queen to Britain, they left behind a group of bureaucrats with no idea how to respond to the occupation. The Germans stepped in to fill this leadership vacuum. No nascent resistance movement existed yet either, so there was an absence of viable opposition or outlets for dissent to find expression. Instead, to advance their careers or curry political favour, men and women had to win the approval of German authorities. Accordingly, NSB membership increased dramatically. The Dutch ss was born, and twenty thousand Dutchmen—the largest contingent from any western European country—even volunteered for service with the German Waffen-ss.[3]

---

* Bernhard did visit Juliana in Canada, and their third daughter, Margriet, was born there. To ensure that Margriet's citizenship would be solely Dutch, the Canadian government temporarily declared the hospital where Juliana gave birth to her Dutch soil. Juliana left Canada in 1944, but her children remained until the following year. Juliana's modest but determined personality captured the hearts of the country. "My name is Juliana . . . please don't regard me too much as a stranger," she said in her first radio address in Canada. "Do not give me your pity," she added. "Pity is for the weak, and our terrible fate has made us stronger than ever before."

The Dutch majority, however, refused to embrace fascism or col-laborate in any way with the German occupation forces. Remaining loyal to the monarchy, most people attempted to quietly go about their lives, despite the defeat that Holland had suffered. To replace Queen Wilhelmina, Hitler imposed a German head of state invested with all the powers she had enjoyed and more. Reichkommissar Arthur Seyss-Inquart had overseen unification of his Austrian home-land with Germany in 1938, being rewarded with the governorship of the resulting Austrian province. He came to the Netherlands from a posting as Poland's deputy governor. Seyss-Inquart had told his wife, Gertrud, "The Führer wishes me to plant tulips."[4]

Tall and balding, Seyss-Inquart had a studious manner, his thick, horn-rimmed glasses giving him the appearance of a mid-level bureaucrat. A mountain-climbing accident had left him with a pro-nounced limp, which inspired the Dutch to call him *manke poot* (lame paw), although a more common nickname was the Dutch equivalent of "six-and-a-quarter"—a wordplay on his name that demeaned his intelligence. However, Seyss-Inquart was anything but dimwitted. A lawyer, he was intelligent and systematic.[5]

In the beginning, Seyss-Inquart attempted to maintain the illu-sion that the occupation meant little change, even as he introduced measures that dramatically altered Dutch society. All political par-ties other than the NSB were banned. Dutch Nazis filled most of the provincial commissioner and community burgomaster posts. An Allied analysis concluded that the level of German control in the Netherlands was "more direct and rigid than in either France or Bel-gium." Because the provincial and municipal governments were retained, it appeared they were still "nominally controlled by the Netherlanders." Yet even the Dutch Nazis holding government posi-tions were not independent, being supervised by a German commissioner who kept quietly in the background like an unseen puppet master.[6]

At first the Dutch economy thrived under German occupation, with 1941 proving to be one of the most successful in many years because of exportation of goods to Germany. But any illusions about prosperity and the benevolence of the occupation soon began to crumble as the war continued and German fortunes turned for the worse. With British triumphs in North Africa and the decisive defeat at Stalingrad in the winter of 1942–43, Seyss-Inquart introduced increasingly repressive measures to impose control over the Dutch and siphon off agricultural and industrial products to Germany without compensation. By September 1942, many basics such as meat, clothing, and blankets were rationed. Two months later, natural gas and electricity joined the list. Families and individuals were issued ration cards to redeem for such goods, but shortages were endemic and a black market soon emerged. Officials also used ration cards to punish or reward individual behaviour. Without a ration card, necessities could only be acquired through the black market at usurious rates. Even with rationing, major shortages appeared in the major urban centres.[7]

Before the invasion, thousands of German Jews had fled to the Netherlands. Some of these had been among the approximately nine hundred Jewish passengers who escaped Germany on May 13, 1939, aboard the Hamburg–American line ss *St. Louis*. Cuba, Argentina, Uruguay, Paraguay, and Panama all refused the refugees. Appeals to U.S. president Franklin Delano Roosevelt for safe harbour drew no response, and an American gunboat shadowed the ship as it sailed towards Canada. Prime Minister William Lyon Mackenzie King declared the refugees were not a "Canadian problem." ss *St. Louis* finally trailed back to Europe and docked in Holland. As an interim measure, the Dutch settled the passengers in Westerbork camp, established in the northeastern province of Drenthe, near the towns of Westerbork and Assen. When the Germans occupied Holland, they turned Westerbork into a transit camp through which the country's Jewish population was moved eastward to extermination camps.

The 140,000 Dutch Jews had enjoyed the same rights as everyone else before the occupation. But, by 1941, Seyss-Inquart introduced measures barring them from the civil service and requiring mandatory registration of every man, woman, and child. In one of the first real displays of an organized resistance, the Dutch Communist Party called a national strike on February 25, 1941—the only anti-pogrom strike in German-occupied Europe. The Germans and their Dutch police surrogates responded brutally within two days. Nine strikers were shot dead and hundreds others arrested, eighteen being subsequently executed. Hundreds of young Jewish men aged twenty to thirty-five were rounded up and shipped to the "work camps" of Buchenwald and Mauthausen.[8]

After the strike, Seyss-Inquart decided the Dutch were a lost cause and escalated the repression. Over the ensuing months, 165,000 Dutch were forcibly sent to Germany to work in factories and other industries. By 1942, about sixty thousand of these had illegally returned to their homeland—most going into hiding. Called *onderduikers* (under-divers), such people took refuge in cellars, attics, and farm buildings. Some were hidden by relatives, friends, clerics, and perfect strangers. By 1945, the number of *onderduikers* had risen to about 330,000. Among them were students who refused to sign loyalty oaths or those men who ignored call-ups as workers to Germany or to help with construction of coastal fortifications and other defences. About twenty thousand Jews were also hiding. It was a dangerous course for both the hidden and those helping. To be caught meant certain arrest. Jews were automatically sent to Westerbork and immediately deported to death camps. Non-Jews faced imprisonment or assignment as slave labourers for either the German army in the Netherlands or in German industrial operations.[9]

Unlike Anne Frank and her family—the most famous of all *onderduikers*—most hid individually and spent the majority of their time in total isolation, seeing their protectors only briefly to receive food and other assistance. Those hiding them had to also share their meagre rations.

In step with the mounting repression came a rapid growth in the number and size of organized resistance movements. On September 5, 1944, the government-in-exile formed the Interior Forces under Prince Bernhard's command. Although identified as the Binnenlandse Strijdkrachten (NBS), this resistance movement had three official arms that operated relatively independently. These usually were identified by their acronyms—LO, KP, and OD. The Central Government Organizations for Help to People in Hiding (LO) was formed to provide direct aid to the growing multitude of *onderduikers*.

Its members counterfeited ration cards and distributed legitimate cards filched by loyal Dutch employed by the Nazis. LO operatives also broke into government offices to steal cards and attempted to gather advance intelligence on forthcoming police raids on *onderduiker* hideouts. Deliberately maintaining a low profile, LO members did not engage in open defiance or sabotage.

Such operations were the domain of the Central Government Fighting Group (KP), which organized in local cells that operated independently of any national centralized direction. Its fighters destroyed railway tracks, telegraph and telephone lines, and German supply points. Assassinations of German soldiers and officials and Dutch collaborators were occasionally carried out, but retaliatory measures were so brutal that the resistance and government-in-exile largely discouraged these. The Order of Service (OD), meanwhile, represented former Dutch military officers and administrators who had been supplanted by Nazi sympathizers. Its efforts were focused on setting up a covert administration that could maintain civil order and administrative services once the Allies liberated the country.

To provide a layer of coordination to the underground movement, the government appointed a core group of resistance leaders to the College van Vertrouwensmannen (College of Trusted Men). Their primary role was to be ready to fill any power vacuum that might occur when the country was liberated and until the government-in-exile could re-establish its authority.

Several other resistance organizations existed that had no affiliation with the government-in-exile or were even hostile to it. The largest of these was the Communist Party, which carried out active resistance and fomented strikes. It was particularly strong in Amsterdam and the northeastern part of Groningen province, including the port city of Delfzijl. [10]

With the Allied invasion in June 1944 and subsequent breakout from Normandy, the prospect of liberation spurred the government-in-exile and resistance organizations to increase their activities, which the Germans responded to with escalated repression. Deportation of Jews accelerated, as did impressment of Dutch to work in Germany. Dutch soldiers, released from prisoner-of-war camps in 1940, were again ordered imprisoned—prompting another wave of *onderduikers*.

Anticipation of imminent liberation grew to fever pitch in September 1944, when the Allies took Antwerp and launched Market Garden. When British troops reached Antwerp on September 4, Radio Oranje trumpeted the news. Throughout the country, the occupation forces seemed to be panicking and preparing to flee. Seyss-Inquart ordered all German civilians to move east to where they could easily escape into Germany. A car carried his wife across the border to safety. Hundreds of Dutch collaborationists, peddling dilapidated bikes, jockeyed for space on roads clogged with German troops streaming east.[11] To the Dutch, "almost as satisfying as the Allied advance is this spectacle of fear striking into the hearts of the Dutch Nazis and their masters," a Canadian intelligence report observed. "The climax [was] reached on Tuesday the 5th of September. All roads leading to the east of the country are jammed with German military cars loaded down with hastily packed luggage and pilfered goods. Holland is convinced that liberation is only a matter of days."

Many radio news reports of cities being liberated on what would be remembered as Mad Tuesday proved false, but the rumour mill continued to churn. Hearing that Breda had been freed and mistaking the Dutch city in Brabant province for a nearby hamlet just outside of Amsterdam, thousands stood at the city's southern entrance "with bunches of flower hidden under their coats, waiting for the liberators to arrive. Night passes. In the sober light of morning it is only too apparent that wishful thinking has had its fling. Holland is not yet free from the Germans."[12]

The German panic had, in fact, quickly subsided, Seyss-Inquart and the military commanders imposing order on their forces and reasserting authority over the Dutch. A hardening resolve had not been foreseen by Allied intelligence, which had assumed a "complete German withdrawal from the Netherlands by 1 October, 1944."[13] This conclusion had circulated to the Dutch government-in-exile, which, along with Allied intelligence agencies, had passed the message to resistance groups in the Netherlands.

Instead of fleeing, the Germans appeared ready to implement a "scorched-earth policy," using water rather than fire. Between 500,000 and 800,000 acres of polders were deliberately inundated, taking about 10 per cent of the country's farmland out of production and

reducing total food production by 15 to 20 per cent.[14] In Rotterdam
and Amsterdam, a police cordon surrounded the harbours and huge
explosions rocked the cities. "Cranes tumble into the water like
drunken men. Elevators and docks are smashed. The Germans plunder the great warehouses until they stand empty. Train loads of
machinery are taken away. Factories and wharves are reduced to
heaps of ruins. At each explosion a pain goes through the hearts of
the people of both cities. Everyone realizes that this means that
ten thousand hands who once manned this proud port are now rendered idle by one destructive gesture, that liberation is going to mean
that Holland will be a land of destroyed harbours and widespread
poverty."[15]

With the failure of Market Garden and the realization that they
were not to be cut off from their homeland, the Germans in Holland
decreed a "reign of terror." Anyone acting against the occupation
forces, Seyss-Inquart proclaimed, would be executed. For every German soldier killed by the resistance, at least three Dutchmen would
die, Higher ss and Police Leader Hans Albin Rauter promised.[16]

Hoping to weaken the German ability to move troops and war
matériel throughout the Netherlands, the Dutch government in London called for a national railway strike. "The children of Versteeg
should go to bed," Dr. Wilhelm Hupkes, deputy-president of the
nationally owned Netherlands Railway Company, was informed by
clandestine radio on September 17, 1944.[17] Versteeg was his code
name and the children were his workers. Hupkes had previously
resisted such calls and agreed to carry out German transportation
orders to avoid the company being either taken over directly by the
Germans or placed under Dutch-Nazi management. This proved a
controversial accommodation, for during the occupation years, Netherlands Railway transported more than 500,000 Dutch forced
labourers to Germany, 120,000 Jews to the border for transshipment
to extermination camps, and tens of thousands of political prisoners
and prisoners of war out of the country. Hupkes's decision was not
made independently—the Dutch government-in-exile was complicit
in keeping the railways running. Any time the government called for
a strike, Hupkes had promised to comply.

Now the order had come directly from Prime Minister Pieter Sjoerds Gerbrandy in England, who still believed the German occupation was on the verge of collapse. Issuing the call on a Monday, Gerbrandy told Radio Oranje's Louis de Jong: "Don't worry. On Saturday we shall be in Amsterdam."[18]

While Hupkes spread the word quietly through official company channels, Radio Oranje pre-empted him. "On account of a request received from Holland, and after consultation with Supreme Command . . . the Government is of the opinion that the time has come to give instructions for a railway strike, in order to hinder enemy transport and troop concentrations," the announcer read. Implicit and accepted was the fact that while hampering German movement, the strike would also stop food and coal from reaching the major cities.[19]

Before the day was out, the railway was crippled, about 28,000 of the thirty thousand workers vanishing to become *onderduikers*. The following day, Seyss-Inquart requested that the newspapers run an appeal to the strikers to cease their "serious and dangerous game," which could only cause crippling food shortages. To his surprise, the normally compliant publishers refused. On September 22, he tried again with a warning that if the railway workers did not return, many thousands of Dutch would starve to death. Again most papers refused to print his message.[20]

Although the railway was an important carrier of food and coal, at least as much of these staples were shipped via the country's complex system of rivers and canals. Seyss-Inquart ordered these barges and ships halted. Bringing in German railway workers enabled him to get the trains back on line, and he limited them to carrying only supplies for occupation forces. Worsening the situation, prowling Allied aircraft strafed any trucks, boats, barges, or trains encountered. What food reached the cities was usually confiscated by the Germans or NSB police.

As 1944 drew grimly to conclusion, the three southern provinces of Zeeland, Brabant, and Limburg stood liberated by Allied forces— the first two largely by First Canadian Army—but the rest of the country descended into the "Hunger Winter." In October, most towns' gas and electrical systems failed, leaving everyone reliant on coal or wood for fuel. Candles and oil lamps provided the only illumination. "Holland now lives in chilly rooms, without light," one analysis reported. "Fumes from improvised coal stoves hang in the air already redolent of not too tasty potato soup. Streetcars don't run any longer. Some of them have even been dismantled and shipped to Germany. Telephones are out of use. Worst of all, the secret radio receivers are now silent because of the lack of electric power . . . In the towns, prices rise to fantastic heights. Potatoes once 10 cents a kilogram are now 800 cents. Butter rises in price from 1 to 100 guilders a pound."[21]

Until September, rationing had managed to provide an average of seventeen hundred calories per person per day. Although little more than half the pre-war average of three thousand calories, this was sufficient for sustenance and in line with Allied policy that civilians in recently liberated countries should receive a minimum of two thousand calories.[22] With the strike and Seyss-Inquart's resulting food shipment ban, daily caloric intake plummeted. Seyss-Inquart also made it clear that the Dutch should not look for help as long as the strike continued. Indeed, he warned that the Germans would hinder food supply efforts by the Dutch authorities "as much as possible."[23] By mid-December, the American Operation of Strategic Services reported that daily rations in cities of western Holland had declined to 630 calories, the black market had practically no food for sale, and reserves were sufficient for only ten more days. Thereafter, the rationing system ceased to operate, and the people of the big cities were reduced to scavenging.[24]

During the first weeks of 1945, the crisis mounted alarmingly. In January, between 16 and 20 per cent of Dutch civilian deaths were due to starvation. With each passing week the percentage increased; by the week of April 9–14, malnutrition was responsible for 54 per cent of all fatalities. That same month an estimated 3.6 million people in the western provinces were reported by Allied intelligence as "living on the brink of death by starvation."[25]

THE ALLIES HAD been aware of the impending food crisis before it became fact and had recognized that relief would be necessary to "maintain the health and working capacity of the population and to preserve order." Until October 1944, however, they had assumed that the Germans would abandon Holland without a fight. Once this illusion was shattered, SHAEF ordered a new "supply plan for the entire Netherlands with special consideration of the western regions." Completed on October 16, the plan divided Holland into three areas. Area A was the already liberated region south of the Waal River. Few problems were foreseen here, as the area was agriculturally self-supporting. Area B was the region west of the IJssel River, and Area C included everything east of the IJssel. Because Area B encompassed two greatly different regions, it was subdivided into two sectors along a line running from Hilversum through Utrecht to Tiel. B-1, which stretched from this line east to the IJssel, was largely self-sufficient.

It was area B-2—which included all the largest Dutch cities—that posed the "biggest problem yet found in the Theatre" in terms of providing relief to civilian populations. Supplies here would have to come "entirely from imported stocks with no existing stocks or transport facilities." Providing even one pound of food a day to each citizen would "require the daily importation of some 2,026 gross tons."

The problem went far beyond providing food. Coal, liquid fuel, clothing, medical supplies, soap, and water-supply equipment were all needed. Arranging road transport and other transportation was so mired in difficulty that the planners decided B-2 would have to be treated "as an entirely different operation" from all other relief projects in Holland. The report recommended that Twenty-First Army Group establish a special staff, with representatives from SHAEF's Mission to the Netherlands and Dutch authorities attached. This working group would devise a plan for creating a fourteen-day stockpile of food and other supplies that could quickly be dispersed into western Holland the moment it was liberated.[26]

Already a Dutch stopgap proposal had been advanced by the government-in-exile to lift the Allies' strict blockade of German-occupied Europe and permit two Swedish freighters to deliver food to Delfzijl for transshipment into B-2. The International Red Cross added its weight to the appeal in November 1944 by seeking safe passage for a ship carrying supplies from Switzerland to sail from

Lisbon to Delfzijl. Both proposals were approved by the Allies and Germans. The two Swedish ships carrying a 3,200-ton cargo reached Delfzijl on January 28, but it took two weeks for German and Dutch authorities to move these supplies to Amsterdam. Although the IRC ship had departed Lisbon on December 15 with the Swiss supplies, various problems slowed its progress so that it only reached Delfzijl on March 8. It carried approximately 1,600 tons of flour, rice, lentils, and oat flakes, which were distributed under strict control of Dutch government representatives and overseen by IRC officials. About 3.2 million people received two weekly bread rations from this ship's supplies. The Red Cross also oversaw the distribution of 2,657 tons of rye that the Germans agreed to supply the Dutch from stockpiles in Germany.[27]

One IRC official reported: "The physical situation of the western provinces having reduced the inhabitants almost to a primitive state, they are obliged, in the struggle for existence, to engage in the black market, in usury and even in theft; men eat flower bulbs. The bombed houses are pillaged and looted of all combustible material. The trees in the gardens are cut and carried away by night. Horses killed in bombardments are immediately cut up by passers-by. The bread wagons in the cities can only circulate at 4:00 o'clock in the morning because if they go about in broad daylight crowds threaten to attack and plunder them."[28]

SHAEF planners continued developing their massive relief initiative to be implemented the moment B-2 was liberated. In addition to the fourteen-day stockpile to be delivered by Twenty-First Army Group ground transport, it was decided that "extensive use of airplanes for flying in food [should] also be considered." Prime Minister Gerbrandy pressed the point politely in a November 15 letter to General Eisenhower. "In view of the conditions which are expected to prevail immediately after departure of the enemy from the area, I believe that a delay of one or two weeks before supplies will begin to arrive would have most unfortunate circumstances . . . Transport by air of substantial quantities" was the only remedy. Within the week, Eisenhower assured him that plans were underway for a large supply of goods by "such air transport as is not urgently required for military operations."

The Dutch government still believed that the evolving plans would "fail to provide, in practice, anything approaching the relief required" and that without a concrete supply plan, the gap between the liberation and the arrival of supplies might result in a catastrophe within "a fortnight to a month."[29]

By January, the Dutch in London were frantic, and Queen Wilhelmina issued a personal plea to King George, Prime Minister Churchill, and President Roosevelt. The people in B-2, she said, face "hunger, cold, darkness, dirt, disease, and floods" as well as "physical destruction." She urged that the Allied military be ordered to immediately liberate western Holland. Failing that, the Allies should arrange "immediate relief in the form either of mass evacuation or [provision] of food, clothing, and medical supplies."[30]

THE DUTCH WERE under no illusion that the Allies would suddenly shift the mission of its armies, now massing on Germany's border for a spring invasion, to the liberation of western Holland. But Wilhelmina's plea was the first step in a rapidly evolving and breathtakingly daring Dutch initiative to negotiate a ceasefire in the region, under which the Germans would permit Allied relief to proceed even as the war continued elsewhere. However, rather than advance the proposal immediately to the Allies, it was decided to first test the waters with Seyss-Inquart. If he showed interest, the Dutch would choose the moment to raise the idea with the Allies.

Dr. H.M. "Max" Hirschfeld, a government deputy secretary who remained in the Netherlands after the conquest, was asked to open the remarkable discussion that ran counter to every Allied agreement—particularly the sacrosanct requirement that there would be no cessation of hostilities anywhere prior to a full German unconditional surrender. As secretary-general of the Departments of Agriculture and Fisheries, and Commerce, Industry and Shipping, Hirschfeld was the most influential Dutch bureaucrat working inside Seyss-Inquart's administration. His opposition to violent resistance or strikes had earned him a reputation within the underground and even the Dutch government in London as a collaborationist. But Hirschfeld believed the retribution visited on the Dutch populace by open defiance exceeded any value gained.

Having maintained clandestine contact with the government-in-exile, Hirschfeld now raised the idea of relief negotiations with Seyss-Inquart on December 14 during a three-hour meeting. Because of the sensitivity of the issue—Seyss-Inquart warily considering a course Hitler would deem treasonous and the Dutch coyly extending an offer to end hostilities that violated Allied resolutions—no transcript was kept. In general terms the two men discussed the growing crisis in western Holland and possible solutions. At an equally secret meeting in January, they looked more specifically at the possibility of the Germans allowing the Allies to provide relief directly.

Whenever Hirschfeld proposed open negotiations, however, Seyss-Inquart shied away from what he described as treason. The Dutch equally realized they walked a fine line and that the Allied governments and SHAEF were unlikely to approve direct talks.[31]

In February, Seyss-Inquart met Hitler in Germany and was so inspired by the Führer's optimism that he pulled back from further discussion.[32] His spirits soon fell, however, when the Allies bridged the Rhine in late March and First Canadian Army started advancing into eastern Holland. Seyss-Inquart realized the end of the war was near and that Germany was doomed to defeat. When Hitler ordered destruction of key dykes and pumping stations that would inundate much of the Netherlands, Seyss-Inquart ignored him.[33] Instead, he summoned Hirschfeld.[34] This time, Jacob van der Gaag, a secret representative of the commander of the Dutch Forces of the Interior and also a member of the College of Trusted Men, attended. In January 1945, van der Gaag had slipped through the German lines to the Allied side to establish direct contact between the resistance movement and the government-in-exile. He then infiltrated back into occupied Holland with the mission to find "a basis of agreement between the German forces and the Allies so that a 'status quo' could be applied."[35]

Following this meeting, Seyss-Inquart visited Reichminister Albert Speer in Oldenburg, Germany, on April 1. Much like Seyss-Inquart, Speer had been ordered to carry out a scorched-earth policy but on German soil. When Seyss-Inquart confessed that he "did not want to inflict any more damage on Holland," Speer smiled. He admitted to ignoring his own order and also stated his belief that the war would end in three months at the outside because arms production was no longer able to meet demand. Returning from Germany, Seyss-Inquart met Hirschfeld the next evening.[36]

While on the surface these talks were still entirely initiated by the Dutch, Allied high command was privy to them and quietly supportive. Select officers within First Canadian Army and Twenty-First Army Group were kept apprised of their progress, even as they remained one of the war's most closely guarded secrets. Anyone made aware was formally warned that the "negotiations [between] Dutch Forces of Interior and [Seyss-Inquart] will be treated as more, repeat more, secret than BIGOT, and handled by selected [officers] whose names will be recorded."[37] When the stamp bearing the letters BIGOT appeared on Allied military documents, it meant that only personnel possessing the highest security clearance were to have access. Such personnel could attest to their being "bigoted." The highly secret plans and maps setting out Operation Overlord, for example, had born the BIGOT stamp. There had previously been no higher secrecy classification than BIGOT.

Hirschfeld and Van der Gaag had made it clear to Seyss-Inquart that these negotiations assumed an eventual German unconditional surrender. Seyss-Inquart responded that "he had been ordered to hold out under all circumstances, and to carry out the necessary demolitions and inundations for that purpose." However, he acknowledged that such "drastic measures" would "prove catastrophic for western Holland" and suggested that "until Germany ceases to resist—at which date they [the German forces in western Holland] would also surrender unconditionally—the Allied troops [should] not advance beyond the Grebbe Line." This would allow the German forces to continue to hold North Holland, South Holland, and Utrecht. Within these provinces, the Gestapo would cease executions, political prisoners would be decently housed and properly looked after, and the culprits who carried out new attacks on German personnel would be tried by a civilian court and spared the death sentence. There would be no further inundations. The

Germans would also help facilitate the opening of Rotterdam's port to barges bearing food and coal from the south.

Seyss-Inquart emphasized that there would be no official surrender and the occupation would be maintained. It was imperative that his proposal be a closely guarded secret. Outwardly, the Canadian forces closing on the Grebbe Line "would just stop . . . and not attack any further."

If the Allies agreed, Seyss-Inquart said the Germans would abide by the unofficial terms. But if his proposal was rejected, the Germans "would be obliged, and they were still under Hitler's orders, to carry out the demolitions and inundations, in order to stop the Allied advance." Both parties, he added, knew there was only sufficient food in western Holland to last, at most, three more weeks, and a catastrophe was inevitable after that. Millions would certainly perish—either by drowning, starvation, or disease—if the proposal was not carried out.

When Lieutenant Colonel M.L. DeRome—one of the approved officers at First Canadian Army headquarters—read the report of this meeting, he drafted a memorandum favouring acceptance of Seyss-Inquart's terms. Bearing in mind "that we only have a small number of troops available for clearing this part of Holland," he wrote, agreement "that there will be no more large scale shooting" once the Grebbe Line was gained offered "the only possible way of saving these three provinces from complete destruction. Unconditional surrender will still take place, though at a later date."[38]

On April 3, Hirschfeld and four members of the College of Trusted Men met to discuss Seyss-Inquart's proposal. The college members urged him to pass the proposal directly to the government in London. Hirschfeld's message suggested that the Germans in western Holland were willing to disobey orders and cease hostilities once driven back to the Grebbe Line. In exchange, the Allies would halt there and then isolate Fortress Holland—as western Netherlands had been declared by Hitler—by advancing to the north and northeast to cut lines of communication from western Netherlands to other parts of the country and Germany beyond.[39] It was now up to the Allies to either agree to Seyss-Inquart's proposals or risk his carrying out Hitler's orders.

13

Crazy Young Devils

THE PROSPECT OF a ceasefire between Twenty-Fifth Army and First Canadian Army did nothing to lessen the intensity of fighting in early April. The German army was unable to present a unified defence, yet ad-hoc battle groups resisted fiercely wherever terrain or fortifications offered advantage. This continued resistance baffled the western Allies but accorded with Hitler's pronouncement that if "the war is lost, the German nation will also perish. This fate is inevitable. There is no need to take into consideration the basic requirements of the people for continuing even a primitive existence . . . Those who will remain after the battle are those who are inferior; for the good will have fallen."[1]

While some German soldiers embraced Hitler's call to die fighting, others continued to resist out of the naive belief that the longer they resisted, the more likely the western Allies were to agree to a separate peace that excluded the Soviet Union. This scenario reached its ultimate delusory form when Germans imagined the western powers joining with them to destroy the Soviets. Whatever the motivation, the German army fought on with a fatalistic determination.

Where the Twente Canal joined the IJssel River at Zutphen, 3rd Canadian Infantry Division's 9th Brigade met precisely this kind

of "fanatical resistance put up by teenaged youngsters" of the
361st Infantry Division and 3rd Parachute Training Regiment, "who
all seemed to be armed with automatic weapons and had a fair
amount of [artillery] at their command."[2] Major General Holly
Keefler had expected the city to fall quickly to this advance from the
south on April 4. Instead, he was forced to commit his entire division to battle.

That evening, Keefler trucked 7th Brigade through the night to
the Twente bridge crossing at Laren, about five miles east of the city,
so it could advance a battalion along either bank of the canal. Once
7 CIB closed on Zutphen, Keefler would pass his 8th Brigade
through it. The 9th Brigade, meanwhile, would continue advancing
on the city from the south.

The Regina Rifles crossed the bridge and moved along the northern bank, while the Royal Winnipeg Rifles paralleled their course on
the opposite shore. Keefler thought the Germans defending Zutphen were too weak to be able to meet both this attack and 9 CIB's.
As 7 CIB threatened to trap them in Zutphen, he expected the Germans to withdraw rather than be surrounded.

The Reginas' Lieutenant Walter Keith had slept through the
entire truck ride. "Sleep served to drown the worrisome thoughts of
what was to come at the end of the ride. I had experienced by now
the awful mental let down between battles, which was far worse
mentally than the battle itself. Thoughts of what had happened and
dread of what was to come were not good."[3]

At 0540 hours, the Reginas had clambered out of the trucks, and
'B' and 'C' Companies advanced with the other two rifle companies
in trail. Leading 'D' Company's No. 16 Platoon, Keith walked
through light drizzle across the flat fields bordered by the canal and
raised railway embankment to the battalion's right. Sporadic mortar
and artillery fire dogged their steps, but no casualties resulted.

To protect the infantry's exposed right flank, 'C' Squadron of the
17th Duke of York's Royal Canadian Hussars had been ordered to
clear the railway embankment. The Hussars were wary, having
recently encountered groups of Hitler Youth "armed with machine
guns and Panzerfausts." Repeatedly the "armoured cars would sud-

denly be confronted by one of these boy-soldiers, who, standing in the middle of the road a few yards away would open up with a Schmeisser and . . . the gunner-operator, feeling anger, hate and pity all at the same time would take careful aim and 'let go' with a burst of blazing Besa [machine-gun fire]. Had these lads been properly schooled in war-waging, their 'do-or-die' tactics might have done. As it was they died."[4]

When the Reginas gained Eefde—a small suburban village—at about 0830 hours, Major Gordon Brown ordered Keith's platoon to cross over the railway and clear a small cluster of houses to the north. Imagining the Germans hunkered behind the embankment, Keith reluctantly ordered Corporal Chris Vogt to lead the way with his section. "As they went up the incline to the tracks I felt really bad waiting for German machine guns to open on them when they reached the top and wished I had led them up. Chris led them up with no hesitation. Fortunately there were no Germans in the area." The platoon quickly searched the houses and was just about to return when the section on the left spotted some Germans coming in to surrender. As Keith and Corporal Homer Adams hurried over, the lieutenant spotted about a dozen enemy troops between the railway embankment and a house. "They were being harangued by an NCO and seemed reluctant to come any further. We rapidly saw that, rather than coming in to surrender, they were counter attacking us. The NCO was carrying a machine pistol. Adams, fearless and reck-less 21-year-old kid that he was, ran up to the NCO hollering, 'Put it down.' Instead, the German swung the muzzle to fire at Adams, who snapped off a single shot from the hip that dropped the man. Adams ran back toward Keith shouting, 'Get shooting!'

"'I can't,' Keith yelled back, 'you're in the road.'" By the time Adams cleared Keith's field of fire, the Germans had dashed behind some houses. The two Reginas dodged into a house as well and took up position on the second storey, where a bedroom window faced the Germans. They were soon joined by a couple of men from the battal-ion's anti-tank platoon who had a Bren gun. Keith saw that the enemy had gone to ground inside a bunker between two of the houses "and one idiot repeatedly stood up and fired his sub-machine gun in our direction. Each time we opened up with rifles and the anti-tank crew's Bren. We finally winged the German and soon white flags were raised." After rounding up the prisoners and delivering them to company headquarters, Keith and Adams walked back to check the dead NCO. "He was an old gray head, probably a WWI veteran. Adams' unaimed shot had got him right through the heart. We were increasingly running into very old and very young Germans."[5]

While the Reginas had tightened their hold on Eefde, the Royal Winnipeg Rifles had marched unopposed along the Twente's southern bank. The two battalions' clearing of the canal to a point immediately east of Zutphen enabled 6th Canadian Field Company engineers to start erecting a seventy-foot Bailey bridge at 1500 hours. A smoke-generator team concealed the bridge site to good effect until the last bolts were being tightened at 1730 hours. Just then, a sniper in the city outskirts "opened up on the bridge with a Schmeisser and although his aim was bad, it was most unpleasant," one after-action report mildly stated. Thirty minutes later, the bridge was ready for traffic.[6]

With a bridge of his own, Major General Keefler tightened the vice on Zutphen, ordering 8 CIB to renew the advance from the east, while 9 CIB continued its operations to the south. Having managed to drive the Germans back from Leesten on the morning of April 5, the Stormont, Dundas and Glengarry Highlanders provided a firm base for 9 CIB's Highland Light Infantry to execute a leftward hook directed at gaining the village of Baronsbergen and the banks of the IJssel immediately beyond. The North Nova Scotia Highlanders, meanwhile, passed through Leesten to drive north into the suburb community of Warnsveld directly southeast of Zutphen.

On paper, Brigadier Rocky Rockingham's plan seemed to say that the three battalions would be engaged in a coordinated push, but in fact the "numerous streams and rivulets . . . made any large organized advance dangerously impractical." Rockingham soon realized he "could do little else besides harass the enemy's southern outpost defences, leaving the reduction of the canal-bound fortress" of Zutphen to 8 CIB.

Even this limited aim proved costly. Zutphen was ringed by old Dutch fortifications in which the Germans were able to establish "supporting strong points" that had each to be taken in turn.[7] Although the three battalions made steady gains, the HLI reported "heavy going" with the "fanatical young Nazis from [paratroop] training battalions" fighting well and led "by well qualified NCOS." No sooner did the battalion root out the defenders at one resistance point than another was encountered. As April 5 drew to a close, the HLI was still unable to wipe out one group of Germans holding a pocket between them and the Glens on their right.[8] Rockingham ordered the Glens "to ensure" that this pocket was cleared in the morning, but it took until 1427 hours on April 6 for 'D' Company to do so.[9]

The North Novas, meanwhile, had slugged it out with sixteen-year-olds, "who were fighting fanatically and surprisingly well with very little support outside of machine guns and bazookas [Panzer-fausts]." From hides inside the many small and dense woods, the Germans launched repeated ambushes. A profusion of narrow roads cutting this way and that through the trees left the company commanders confused as to their whereabouts. Around every corner, more paratroops seemed always to lie in ambush or be ready to defend a roadblock of interlaced fallen trees.

Leading 'B' Company through one wood, Major J.S. Wright was raked by a burst of machine-gun fire that severely wounded him in both legs, and Lieutenant James Gordon Murray was mortally struck. Captain Jack Fairweather rushed forward to take command, and with support from a troop of Crocodile flame-thrower tanks, the North Novas burned their way through the resistance.[10]

While pushing into one wood, 'A' Company became entangled in a bizarre fight for control of a mental asylum. Although it was clearly marked with red crosses, paratroops were inside and determined to defend it. To one side of the main building stood a small bungalow, and as the Bren gunner leading one section approached it, he called back that there were people in beds inside. When the section leader called for them to come out, there was no response. Kicking in the door, the Bren gunner yanked the bedding off the first bed and stared down at a corpse. The bungalow was the asylum's morgue and each bed held a body, recently washed and readied for burial.

Inside the main building, "Germans ran through the wards and fired from the windows, while the violent patients, fastened to their beds, were laughing and crying and singing and shouting. Every care had to be taken not to wound any of the inmates." Gradually the asylum was cleared. A thorough search of the facility turned up eight paratroops hiding under laundry and in closets.[11]

From the asylum the North Novas advanced into Warnsveld, where snipers and machine-gun crews roamed independently among the buildings. One North Nova was killed and several others wounded before the town was cleared at nightfall. April 5 had cost the battalion two officers killed, another two wounded, and twenty-nine other-rank casualties, of which four were fatal.

The average age of the Germans encountered, the war diarist added, was sixteen or seventeen. "Fanatic, when interviewed they still thought Germany would win and their belief in Hitler and Nazism was still unshaken. However, there were cases among the prisoners of just badly scared boys... Most... had only been in battle a week and the average had only been in the army three months."[12] Warnsveld was as far as the North Novas had to go towards Zutphen, Keefler having decided that the city could now be cleared from the east by 8 CIB.

BECAUSE BRIGADIER JIM Roberts was in England on leave, the Queen's Own Rifles' Lieutenant Colonel S.M. "Steve" Lett temporarily commanded 8 CIB. Lett's plan called for the North Shore (New Brunswick) Regiment to drive through the northern portion of Zutphen parallel to the railway track, while Le Régiment de la Chaudière worked its way into the southern part. The Sherbrooke Fusiliers' 'B' Squadron would support both battalions.[13]

Lett had just two battalions because his own QOR had been detached on April 5 to clear a portion of the IJssel River around the hamlet of Rha, well south of Zutphen. The operation was expected to be simple, the battalion enveloping the hamlet from the east and then advancing a short distance beyond to gain the riverbank. Support was provided by the Duke of York's 'B' Squadron and four Cameron Highlanders of Ottawa heavy machine-gun platoons. Three infantry companies advanced as one, 'D' passing Rha to the north, 'B' to the south, and 'A' moving directly through it.[14]

Major Elliott Dalton—just returned after recovering from wounds suffered in the Juno bridgehead the previous June—commanded.

Kicking off at 1600 hours, 'D' Company had an easy time. Encountering an extensive German trench system "that criss-crossed the area," Major Ben Dunkelman and his men wound through it. "But for the mud and water that half-filled the trenches there was no opposition," a QOR report stated.

For the other two companies, the story was entirely different. Approaching a small outpost south of Rha with two platoons forward and one back, Major W.J. Weir's 'B' Company was greeted with a hail of mortar and small-arms fire. "The situation rapidly became hopeless," and only the following platoon providing covering fire enabled the two forward to extricate themselves. Lieutenant John Gordon Kavanagh was killed and three men wounded before the company escaped.

'A' Company "was even in a worse state of affairs."[15] This company had been in poor shape before the attack. Like the rest of the battalion, it had been badly mauled in the Rhineland battles and recently rebuilt with about thirty reinforcements, which still brought its strength to just seventy men. Its commander, Major D. Hogarth, had previously served in the battalion's anti-tank platoon and only recently been promoted. A tall man, he loomed at least thirteen inches above the veteran Company Sergeant Major Charlie Martin. Only No. 8 Platoon had an officer, a young fresh-faced lad newly arrived from Canada. Sergeant Jackie Bland had No. 9 Platoon, Sergeant A.T. Caverley No. 7. Both platoons had freshly promoted corporals leading the sections.

From the moment Hogarth stated his intentions, Martin disliked the plan. Instead of going straight at Rha with everything the company had, Hogarth was going for its flanks, with No. 8 Platoon sent to the north and No. 7 Platoon the south. Once each platoon had gained the edge of the hamlet, flares would be fired and then the two would push towards the centre in concert. This was all by the textbook, but Martin thought it tactically outdated. Worsening the situation, Hogarth had decided to lead No. 7 Platoon himself, as Caverley was new to his rank. Martin's job was to do what Hogarth should be doing—run the company headquarters section and coordinate with battalion any artillery, mortar, or air support.

Within an hour of the two platoons pushing off, a rifleman from No. 8 Platoon marched in a number of prisoners. He told Martin the lieutenant had led them past the edge of the hamlet without firing the flare or waiting to coordinate the advance with No. 7 Platoon. With the Germans surrendering in droves, the platoon just kept going, rounding up more prisoners until "they became prisoners of the prisoners." No. 8 Platoon kept heading west, and company headquarters lost all contact with it.

On the right flank, No. 7 Platoon had entered a deep trench system full of waist-deep water and mud. As Rha came in sight, Hogarth and Caverley's party came under heavy mortar and machine-gun fire. Sheltered by the trench, the platoon suffered minimal casualties. But advancing through the incoming fire was impossible. One man with a broken arm and chest wound was sent back to company headquarters. He told Martin the platoon was soaking wet and covered in mud, and most weapons were so clogged with filth and water they were useless. Hogarth had also been shot in the shoulder when he tried peeking out of the trench.

As the man finished his account, Martin heard someone from the direction of No. 7 Platoon shout: "Fix swords! Let's take them with our bare hands." This was followed by the long sheet-tearing screams of several German MG-42 machine guns and a deathly silence. Eventually the platoon trailed into company headquarters. It had lost six men wounded and a dozen missing. Hogarth was evacuated with his wounds. No. 8 Platoon still wandered somewhere in No Man's Land, and the survivors from No. 7 Platoon had weapons rendered useless by filth. Martin decided No. 9 Platoon would have to take Rha alone and divided it into two combat sections. He then had the hamlet drenched with mortar and artillery fire followed by rocket-firing Typhoons. While one section provided covering fire, the other dashed to a new firing position through which the other section leapfrogged. In this manner, the little force gained Rha, only to have Dalton order it to pull back to the battalion start line because it was too weak to hold the town.[16]

The QOR remained in place throughout April 6, giving Rha "a good dusting off during the day" with mortars and 6-pounder anti-tank guns. Joining in this fire were the tanks from the Sherbrooke's 'B' Squadron. A new attack plan was worked up for the following day. Just before dusk, however, the battalion was ordered to rejoin 8 CIB.[17] Divisional intelligence had decided that "the sting had been taken out of Rha."[18]

The final casualty count proved less than initially feared. Lieutenant Kavanagh and four other ranks were dead, another man had been lost as a prisoner and later died, and two officers and ten other men had suffered wounds. To Martin, Rha exemplified an action in which men "were too brave . . . took on too much themselves . . . and . . . did not . . . carry the day."[19]

NORTH OF RHA, the battle for Zutphen had also shown that bravery alone was not always sufficient. Regional wisdom held that Nijmegen, with a pre-war population of 25,000, was the oldest local city, Arnhem the gayest, but Zutphen the wealthiest. A picturesque old city wrapped in a network of waterways, it was an ideal fortress.[20] Preliminary reconnaissance by the North Shores determined that the ground they must cross alongside the railway embankment was too soft for tanks but would support their Wasps.[21] In front of the Chauds on their left, the ground was harder, and two troops of Shermans gathered behind the infantry.[22]

Both infantry battalions formed in the dark behind a road about twelve hundred yards from the city. Before them the ground was flat, absent any cover, and marshy. At 0430 hours, Le Chaudière led off and quickly crossed the open ground to gain a row of houses. Behind the houses were a canal and the remains of a blown bridge. While the infantry were able to dash down the steep embankment and splash through the shallow water, the tankers looked for an alternative route.

Sergeant Hubert Atkinson, commanding No. 1 Troop, spotted a likely crossing point to the left. Despite heavy sniper fire, Atkinson and his crew dismounted to create a crude bridge by dumping logs in a row across the water. Three of Atkinson's men were wounded and, just as the job was finished, the twenty-six-year-old Montrealer was shot dead.[23] Atkinson's heroic effort enabled the other tanks in his troop to reach the Chauds and provide badly needed support.

No sooner had the infantry crossed the canal than they had become locked in a deadly fight with a pack of fanatical young paratroops. At the head of his platoon of men from 'D' Company, Lieutenant Paul Piché seemed to be everywhere that trouble erupted. When the company was forced to ground by a German machine-gun post, Piché and four volunteers sprinted across two hundred yards of open ground to kill the crew, the lieutenant personally accounting for five Germans. Seeing a group of civilians trying to find shelter in an area subjected to German artillery fire, Piché guided the twenty-four people to a building with a stout basement. For his gallantry in assisting these people, Piché was awarded the Netherlands Bronze Lion medal.[24]

When the first Sherman across Atkinson's improvised bridge turned its 75-millimetre gun and machine guns onto the paratroops at point-blank range, resistance quickly collapsed. By 1000 hours, 'A' and 'B' Companies had gained the regiment's first objective despite "beaucoup de résistance."[25]

To the right, the North Shores had attacked before dawn, and 'B' Company was now searching for a crossing over the waterway. The company's newly promoted Major Harry Hamley was not surprised to see the bridge blown. Knowing the battalion risked being caught in the open when the sun came up, Hamley began frantically seeking a way over the canal. Already things were bad, the paratroops opposite "thoroughly aroused and fighting back with the desperation of cornered rats. Machine guns and rifles had opened up on the company from both right and left flanks."

At 0625 hours, Hamley reported that he, his signallers, and one platoon were pinned down. Small packs of five or six Germans had separated Hamley's group from the other platoons farther back. They were firing in both directions at the North Shores and chucking stick grenades around with wild abandon. Spotting about twenty Germans forming behind a dyke to overrun his embattled position, Hamley grabbed a Bren gun from its wounded operator. Charging into the face of enemy fire, Hamley burned through a magazine as he ran, shooting eight Germans dead, wounding several others, and scattering the rest.

Despite the breaking up of this attack, the situation kept worsening. Surrounded, Hamley's men were engaged in a constant shootout at point-blank range. Casualties mounted fast. Hamley took a slug in the chest and was forced to relinquish command to the platoon leader, Lieutenant W.J. Kearns, only to see him fall wounded a few minutes later. Having led his platoon through to Hamley's group, Lieutenant N.H. Whiston assumed command.

Off to one side, 'B' Company's remaining platoon worked its way along the dyke towards the others. Repeatedly, two or three men were forced to charge German positions with bayonets while the rest provided covering fire, so the advance was slow and bloody. Lieutenant Dave Doig personally led one assault. As he approached a trench, a teenager popped up and shot him in the head. Although the bullet slashed a furrow clean to his skull, it only staggered Doig. A Bren gunner at his shoulder emptied his magazine into the German.

Doig had just regrouped his team when a group "came over the top of the dyke like devils, but we had our grenades ready and gave them the works, then following in with machine-gun and rifle fire," the lieutenant recounted. "We had a few casualties but wiped out three times our number of those crazy young devils."

BACK AT 'B' Company's main position, Whiston was desperately keeping its shrinking ranks fighting. Company radio signaller Private Ernest Fowlie Watling kept coolly reporting the situation to Lieutenant Colonel Neil Gordon while loosing regular bursts from his Sten gun.

Deciding 'B' Company had to be extricated, Gordon advanced 'D' Company to wipe out the Germans behind it. Major M.W. Carroll's men managed to fight through and then the two companies began slowly withdrawing under fire. Last to leave was Private Watling, who stayed behind to the last moment, covering the withdrawal with Sten-gun bursts. His courage was recognized with a Military Medal.[26]

While this withdrawal was underway, Lieutenant Colonel Lett and the Chaudière commander arrived at Gordon's headquarters.

The three decided that the front facing the North Shores was too favourable to the defence to breach and Gordon's battalion should move to the right of the Chaudière sector, where the advance was proceeding relatively well. Due to a delay in carrying out this realignment, Lett postponed further advance until the following day.[27]

The next morning, the two battalions renewed their attack. On the right, the North Shores were led by 'C' Company. Encountering a blown bridge, Lieutenant Jack McKenna's platoon waded through waist-deep water to the far shore. Because the approaches on either side were mined, Major Blake Oulton held the rest of the company back and sent the pioneers to clear the mines. While this was going on, Oulton crossed to the other side alone. In a building he was considering for a temporary headquarters, the major discovered a rubber boat equipped with an air pump. Oulton inflated the boat, floated it across to the company, and the men paddled over in small groups to land dry-shod.

'A' Company soon joined 'C' Company across the canal and the two pushed hard into the heart of the city, with the Wasps in support under command of Sergeant Ray Savoy. 'C' Company met stiff resistance almost immediately near a railway that crossed in front of it, and Savoy raced to assist. Savoy "came down the exposed street at full speed with his Browning machinegun spewing a steady stream of bullets. His carrier wheeled around the intersection and let fly its flame full upon the enemy position. He then gave covering fire for the other two carriers ... It was something to see those three carriers come up with machineguns chattering and wheel in with flame streaming from their noses and withdraw in a hail of bullets," Oulton recalled. Aboard Savoy's carrier, nineteen-year-old Private Lionel Valley was killed.[28]

To the left of the New Brunswick battalion, the Chaudière had carriers and tanks prowling alongside. Whenever the infantry was pinned down by snipers or machine guns, the armour and carriers soon drove the Germans off. As the day dragged on, divisional intelligence staff was able to conclude that "for the first time there was evidence that the enemy's attitude was gradually changing and although he fought well at times, the old tenacity was lacking."[29]

And yet this grindingly slow process was still underway at dusk on April 7, when the Canadians paused for the night in a large warehouse district. The next morning, Major Oulton's 'C' Company again led the North Shore advance. This time it was accompanied by Wasps and Crocodiles. His company met little resistance. But when 'A' Company struck out on the flank into the main freight-marshalling rail yard, some of its men were shot down crossing a stretch of open ground. Lieutenant Ernie Finley was among those killed. Under a rain of sniper fire, several volunteers ran out and carried the wounded to the safety of a large warehouse, which soon caught fire. Lieutenant M.H. Rogers, Lance Corporal Doug Bevan, and Private John Barry, along with two other men from Rogers' platoon, started hauling the wounded men out of the building. Before it collapsed in flames, they successfully carried all the men to the battalion's Regimental Aid Post.[30]

By nightfall the rail yard had been cleared, and on the morning of April 8, the two battalions pushed deep into the factory area bordering the IJssel River. Within a few hours, most of the surviving paratroops escaped across the river in rubber boats. Those who lingered were either killed while sniping at the Canadians or taken prisoner.[31] The battle for Zutphen had lasted the better part of four days. Neither infantry battalion bothered noting how many men it had lost in the battle, but the North Shores' Padre R. Miles Hickey buried twenty of his men there.[32]

"Canadian soldiers rate the boyish defenders of Zutphen among the most fanatical troops they have encountered," wrote Douglas Amaron, a Canadian Press war correspondent. "The S.S. had some sense but these Hitler youths were absolutely mad . . . Nazis to the core."[33] In the late afternoon, the Chaudière left the city and the North Shores set up a defensive line along the IJssel to prevent German infiltration from the opposite shore.[34] The Queen's Own Rifles came in from their debacle to the south and assumed responsibility for defending and policing the city's southern outskirts, freeing 9 CIB's Stormont, Dundas and Glengarry Highlanders to move with that brigade's other two battalions to support 7 CIB's advance on Deventer. As the tired and muddy Queen's Own trudged into the city, the citizens poured out to give them a "royal welcome," which became a literal one the next day when Prince Bernhard arrived to tour Zutphen.[35]

In the midst of the festivities the war intervened, when both the North Shores and the QOR were ordered to immediately mount trucks for a hurried move northward. The rest of the division was closing on Deventer, and 8 CIB's job was to take over positions held by 7 CIB, so that the latter could attack the city from the south.[36]

AS THE BATTLE in Zutphen had raged, 7 CIB had pushed in a straight line out of the 3rd Division bridgehead across the Twente Canal at Eefde at 0630 hours on April 6. The Canadian Scottish Regiment led with sights set on Gorssel, a small community midway between Zutphen and Deventer. Although one trench and bunker system after another was encountered, none was defended. Resistance was limited to light artillery fire from guns stationed west of the IJssel and small handfuls of seemingly disorganized and demoralized infantry that the battalion's war diarist dismissed as "nuisance resistance."

When a patrol returned five prisoners, battalion headquarters translator Lance Corporal W. Winkleman interrogated them. A corporal said the men had been sent from a strongpoint immediately south of Deventer and on the north side of the Schipbeek Canal. The Germans there had reportedly blown the bridge and were digging in on the canal's north bank. As the enemy apparently intended to make its stand behind the Schipbeek, which ran from the east past Deventer's southern outskirts to spill into the IJssel, Lieutenant Colonel Larry Henderson ordered his rifle companies to make haste for the canal.[37]

By 1010 hours, the Can Scots had marched through their earlier objective of Gorssel without pause. Brigadier Graeme Gibson, meanwhile, had met with Major General Holly Keefler and, on the basis of the new intelligence, been ordered to advance the Royal Winnipeg Rifles up the Zutphen–Deventer railway a mile east of the road the Can Scots were following. The brigade war diary reported that the "advance was quick and unhindered and the [battalions] made the most of the easy going." At 1600 hours, the Can Scots entered Epse and sent patrols a few hundred yards north to the Schipbeek Canal.[38]

On their right flank, the Winnipeg Rifles had set up battalion headquarters in Oxe, a small cluster of buildings that until the previous day had been the area's Gestapo headquarters. Several riflemen poking around in an adjacent "solid brick building" discovered that one of its exterior walls was spattered with blood and bits of flesh. "The earth at the base of the wall was extremely soft and one of the men was curious enough to start digging. In a few minutes time the battered body of a middle-aged man appeared. This was only part of the dismal and gruesome sight for after a few hours ten similar bodies lay on the surface. The bodies were identified the following day by a member of the Dutch underground. He told us that the German Gestapo had held these people as prisoners for they were suspected to be members of the Dutch underground. We were also informed that when the Gestapo heard that we were coming they murdered their prisoners and evacuated the camp," reported the Winnipeg war diarist.[39]

Even as this discovery was being made, the battalion had attempted to force a crossing over the Schipbeek. Although the rail bridge had been blown, the Winnipeg pioneers managed to salvage enough timbers from its wreckage to erect a footbridge, despite heavy small-arms fire from the opposite bank. By 2100 hours, 'D' Company was across. Casualties were light, and when the usual counterattacks failed to materialize, 'A' and 'C' Companies moved into the bridgehead at 0300 hours and, under cover of darkness, pushed it out about a quarter-mile from the canal bank.[40] By dawn, Lieutenant Colonel Lochie Fulton had his headquarters inside the bridgehead and patrols out well beyond. These soon returned with seventeen prisoners and several captured medium machine guns. Most of the prisoners were noted to be "extremely young fighters."[41]

14

Minor Skirmishes

A BRIDGEHEAD OVER THE Schipbeek Canal was vital to 11 Canadian Corps's next operational phase. Looking at his battle map on April 7, Lieutenant General Guy Simonds was presented with an unusual picture. No divisional front stood alongside another. Instead, the front line straggled from 4th Canadian Armoured Division's far advanced position on the Ems River at Meppen south to Almelo and then curled along the Twente Canal before hooking north from Zutphen towards Deventer. South of Zutphen, a small holding force extended along the IJssel to Doesburg and a junction with 1 Canadian Corps.[1]

After its stunning sixty-mile dash in just three days from the Twente Canal to Meppen, 4th Division was badly strung out. Its artillery regiments were particularly far behind the leading armoured regiments and were hampered in their efforts to catch up by poor roads. It was clear this division could not resume its rapid run without some regrouping. Once that was complete, however, Simonds wanted it to force a crossing and advance north up the eastern flank of the Ems.

The corps's 2nd and 3rd divisions, meanwhile, were to advance into northern Holland, their flanks protected by the IJssel River to the west and the OverIJsselch Canal to the east. This left Simonds with an ever-widening gap between 4th Division and his two infantry divisions. To plug this, General Harry Crerar placed 1st Polish Armoured Division under his command.

Meanwhile, Deventer—a vital link in the transportation corridor sought by Twenty-First Armoured Group and also the start line for 1st Canadian Infantry Division's forthcoming advance westward to Apeldoorn—had to be won also. While 3rd Division had been fighting for Zutphen, the Red Patch Devils had concentrated behind it to prepare their planned amphibious assault across the IJssel—codenamed Operation Cannonshot. But until Deventer fell, its crossing sites were too insecure to allow the operation to begin.[2]

Simonds expected Deventer to be as stubbornly defended as Zutphen, since the German Twenty-Fifth Army was obviously determined to hold on to the east bank of the IJssel for as long as possible. The tenacity of this defence surprised First Canadian Army's intelligence staff because it so dramatically differed from the collapse that had taken place in front of 4th Armoured Division's "lightning thrust northward on the right flank[, which had been] the cause of great confusion to the enemy."

From the German perspective, 11 Fallschirmjäger Corps commander General der Flieger Eugen Meindl described that rout as "a period of complete confusion in which each commander acted on his own initiative without reference to higher authority." The Dutch border had formed the boundary for his corps and that of LXXXVIII Corps, but contact between the two had been lost as 4th Division cut into his divisions. Meindl's 6th Division had been in touch with LXXXVIII Corps on the right and had become separated from the rest of the corps, which was being left behind while his other divisions retreated into Germany. Meindl retained only the 7th and 8th Fallschirmjäger Divisions to attempt to stall the Canadian advance at the Ems River.

As the Canadians poured over the Twente Canal, Generalleutnant Hermann Plocher's 6th Division had been forced to escape westward from Germany into Holland. Sorting through the confused, vague, and contradictory orders that reached him, Plocher had decided his job was to move behind the IJssel River and defend its western bank, putting his men close to Deventer.[3]

The German command chain in Holland had been disrupted when the Supreme Commander of the Wehrmacht in the Netherlands, General der Flieger Friedrich Christiansen, had been replaced by Generaloberst Johannes Blaskowitz. Assuming direct command of Twenty-Fifth Army, Blaskowitz's orders were to defend Fortress Holland at all costs. On the night of April 7, he set up headquarters at Hilversum, in the heart of the western Netherlands, and began preparing for a last stand. Always energetic and inclined to aggression, Blaskowitz was not about to rely on Seyss-Inquart's tentative opening of negotiations towards a ceasefire. Instead, he assumed his troops would face 1 Canadian Corps from behind the Grebbe Line and was determined to check its advance there. Breaching the dykes enclosing the Eem and Grebbe rivers, Blaskowitz flooded the country to the east of the line and closed sluices to raise the IJsselmeer so that its waters inundated the weak point in the Grebbe Line defences north of Amersfoort. Should his men be forced back from the Grebbe Line, a second stand would be offered along the old Holland waterline works to the west of Utrecht.[4] In order to buy time for strengthening the Grebbe Line's defences, Blaskowitz ordered Deventer held for as long as possible.

Like Zutphen, Deventer was ideal for defence. Its approaches were well protected by "a maze of waterways," and the Canadians were once again forced by these canals into attacking the city from the east. Although a canal called the Zijkanaal barred the approach from this direction, it was a less formidable obstacle than the Schipbeek Canal on the city's southern outskirts.[5]

The 7th Canadian Infantry Brigade attack on Deventer called for the Regina Rifles to advance out of the bridgehead gained on April 7 by the Royal Winnipeg Rifles and to cross the Zijkanaal directly in front of the city, while the Canadian Scottish on their right seized the village of Schalkhaar on the northeastern outskirts.[6]

At 0040 hours on April 8, the Reginas' 'A' Company led off with an attack to clear a small wood bordering the Schipbeek Canal's north bank and to secure a jumping-off point for crossing the Zijkanaal.[7] By noon, the company had taken thirty-five prisoners and secured the wood for 'C' and 'D' Companies to use for the main attack. Both companies were to advance to a bridge that appeared intact and cross over to establish a bridgehead. Supporting arms were in generous supply—a squadron of Sherbrooke Fusiliers, a troop of British Crocodiles, and good lines of communication to call in tactical air as required. Zero hour was set for 1500 hours.

As the two companies formed on the start line, shells inflicted several casualties, but after that the advance proceeded smoothly. The few pockets of German resistance encountered surrendered the moment the Crocodiles released their "great inducement" of flame. After a two-hour advance that yielded eighty prisoners, the Reginas reached the bridge and found it damaged. To cover the engineers as they made the bridge passable for armour, the Reginas were to establish a small force on the other side.[8]

A sharp counterattack threw back the first attempt at 0235 hours on April 9, but by 0700 hours the next morning, the Reginas had a complete company on the opposite shore. With the Reginas keeping German snipers at bay, the engineers began working on the bridge.[9]

At 2030 hours on April 8, the Canadian Scottish had also launched "a 3,000 yard attack straight north of our position" that was "to be a prologue to the attack on Deventer, as we must be sure our flanks are cleared before this assault," their war diarist explained.[10] 'A' and 'C' Companies advanced across "two miles of fields, woods, and swampland." Travelling with them was a Sherbrooke squadron and a troop of Crocodiles. Searchlights bounced off the clouds and "cast an eerie moonlight effect over the battlefield."[11] 'C' Company was pestered by indirect machine-gun fire from a position on its right flank, which wounded two men. Shortly after midnight, 'B' and 'D' Companies leapfrogged to the front and the push continued. Map inaccuracies caused more delays than the Germans, 'B' Company entering a supposed forest that was really "a first class bog."[12] The morning of April 9 found the Can Scots on their objectives with a bag of thirty-six prisoners.[13]

In the early afternoon, the sporadic sniping in the Reginas' perimeter escalated rapidly and forced the bridging effort to shut down.[14] Brigadier Graeme Gibson decided to try capturing a new bridge to the north and ordered a two-mile advance by the Canadian Scottish, which "meant another sleepless night in store for the men."[15] The brigadier also moved the Royal Winnipeg Rifles up on the left of the Reginas to protect their exposed flank. With all three battalions now committed in front of the Zijkanaal, Major General Holly Keefler passed the Queen's Own Rifles from 8th Brigade to serve as 7 CIB's reserve. The QOR was to secure the Schipbeek Canal, but also to "project one company" across the Zutphen–Deventer railway track and occupy a southern wedge of ground where the Schipbeek and Zijkanaal met.[16]

THE BRIDGE THE Can Scots headed for lay astride the Zijkanaal two miles due east of Schalkhaar. By the time 'C' and 'D' Companies with the troop of Crocodiles were on the move, it was already 1330 hours. Hopes that Deventer would fall quickly had already fizzled for want of a bridge, but Gibson counted on the Can Scots retrieving the situation. The two leading companies soon reached the midway point. 'A' and 'B' Companies passed through and reached the canal at 1950 hours, finding the bridge badly damaged but still usable by infantry. After a quick inspection, the company commanders advised that the engineers would have to put a Bailey bridge across to handle any vehicles. As 'A' Company started feeding its platoons single file across the rickety remains, the Germans opened up with mortar fire.[17] Within ninety minutes, however, the Can Scots had both 'A' and 'B' Companies across the canal and were widening a bridgehead sufficient to protect the engineers from small-arms fire. At 2230 hours, 'C' Company pushed the bridgehead out to the west.[18]

The engineers started constructing the Bailey bridge just before midnight, and Gibson decided to funnel the brigade's main drive on Deventer over it. To make room, he ordered Lieutenant Colonel Larry Henderson to capture Schalkhaar. "This would enable us to push in an attack on the town very rapidly and quite easily." With the brigade establishing itself across the canal, the only obstacle then barring an advance into Deventer would be an anti-tank ditch that surrounded the town.[19]

The Can Scots moved off at 0100 hours on April 10, its "tired platoons" advancing "along the white concrete road, stepping over telephone wires, fallen tree branches and other debris of war." They encountered only one German wandering lost through a wood. Within two hours the battalion gained Schalkhaar. Everything was quiet, but Henderson told his staff he was "extremely suspicious of the enemy's intentions." For his part, Gibson declared himself "delighted with the entire 'show.'"[20]

North of the village, a section from the carrier platoon had established a blocking position alongside a house about a hundred yards from an intersection. The carriers were tucked out of sight behind the house, while the section had set up inside it. Sergeant Alfred Robertson Minnis and his eleven men were opening ration packs for an early breakfast when a couple of shots rang out. The twelve men dashed up to the house's second storey, clutching Bren guns and spare cans of ammunition. Heavy mist cloaked the ground, but Minnis spotted a long line of troops following a hedge about a hundred yards to his right. Although the men moved "as if they didn't have a care in the world," Minnis was not sure if they were Canadians or Germans. Suddenly a ray of sunlight cut through the mist and glistened on the clearly identifiable helmets of a party of heavily armed German paratroops. From the house, three Bren guns started chugging out rounds in unison, and a nearby section from the battalion's mortar platoon joined in. "It wasn't long until the white flag was raised and we got 23 prisoners out of the bunch," Minnis reported.

A quiet hour ensued before Minnis spotted about seventy-five paratroops forming in woods five hundred yards from the house. Lurking among the trees were also three enemy tanks. Undeterred by the presence of German armour—an increasingly rare occurrence—the twelve men opened up on the infantry as they entered a ditch by the road. Obviously caught by surprise, the Germans scrambled back to the woods. Knowing that if the Germans advanced their tanks his men would be seriously outgunned, Minnis was happily surprised to spot four Shermans rumbling up to his right. He dashed out of the house to contact the troop commander.[21]

The tanks were the No. 2 Troop of the Sherbrooke's 'B' Squadron. Minnis pointed out the German armour on the edge of the wood, and the Shermans opened fire. One German tank burst into flame and another took a direct hit that caused it to hurriedly withdraw.[22] The remaining tank struck back with three rounds that smashed into the building sheltering the Can Scots. Most of the men were in a room facing the road, and one of the shells flashed through its window to explode inside. Twenty-one-year-old Corporal Frank Arthur Cherry was instantly killed. Privates J.J. Hards, K.D. Williamson, and D. MacDonald, and Corporal H.M. Edwards were wounded. Minnis and the other eight uninjured men managed to evacuate the wounded out the back door and escape in one of the carriers to a position across the road. The German force also withdrew. Minnis was awarded a Military Medal for his leadership.[23]

At 0400 hours, the Queen's Own Rifles had advanced 'A' Company out of the bridgehead to clear the wedge of ground where the Schipbeek and Zijkanaal met. A bridge here linked the small suburb of Snippeling to Deventer, and the QOR was to try and take it intact. No. 9 Platoon headed straight up the road leading to the bridge with No. 7 Platoon and company headquarters trailing, while No. 8 Platoon advanced to the left. After a brief firefight for possession of Snippeling, the company made for the bridge, only to come under heavy artillery, mortar, and machine-gun fire from positions inside Deventer. Although the bridge had been blown, a small footbridge was discovered still standing next to it.[24]

Suddenly a runner from No. 8 Platoon arrived and reported that it had been heavily counterattacked while moving along a narrow lane in the half-light of dawn. The platoon had been badly cut up by the time its sergeant sent the runner for help. He believed everyone had either been killed or taken prisoner moments after his escape. Lieutenant Colonel Steve Lett immediately sent 'C' Company to No. 8 Platoon's rescue. They soon found the site of the violent encounter. Scattered pieces of equipment and spent shell casings covering the ground attested to a sharp fight, but the bodies of two dead riflemen were all that remained of the platoon.[25] "During the whole war the battalion had one officer and twenty-seven other ranks captured by the enemy. It was rather ironical that twelve of the twenty-seven were taken at this point in a minor skirmish," the regimental historian later wrote.[26]

The battalion dug in facing the bridge and spent most of the next day under heavy mortar fire from positions inside Deventer. Seething with anger at the loss of their comrades, 'A' Company's survivors eyed the footbridge and waited for covering darkness. At midnight they would lead the battalion across and carry the fight to the Germans.[27]

WHILE THESE SMALL, intense skirmishes fought by the Can Scots and QOR had unfolded in the early morning of April 10, Brigadier Gibson had been making final plans for taking Deventer that afternoon. At the same time, Major General Keefler had decided 7 CIB could be left to finish the job with the four battalions and supporting forces on hand. The rest of 3rd Division must start its bold advance, which Simonds expected to punch through all the way to Leeuwarden, the capital city of Friesland, about fifty miles due north—almost on the North Sea coast. To achieve this, 9th Canadian Infantry Brigade and the 17th Duke of York's Royal Canadian Hussars were to carry out a running charge, keeping them apace with 2nd Division's advance to the right towards Groningen, the largest Dutch city outside the western Netherlands. If successful, this advance would liberate virtually all of Holland to the east and north and free Simonds to swing his entire corps into northwestern Germany.

Adding urgency to the northward push was a bold and unusual gamble taken by Twenty-First Army Group on the night of 7–8 April. Since the end of March, plans had been in the works to drop small packets of Special Air Service (SAS) troops well to the front of First Canadian Army. With the many canals and streams offering ideal defensive positions for the Germans, SAS commander Brigadier J.M. Calvert had proposed that parachuting in small groups of these elite troops, equipped with jeeps to provide rapid mobility, could confuse and disrupt enemy operations. Twenty-First Army Group embraced the plan, code-naming it Amherst. Two French SAS units, chafing to see combat before war's end, were selected—the 2nd and 3rd Régiments de Chasseurs Parachutistes. Together they numbered about seven hundred men and would be dropped along with their armoured jeeps into a triangular area formed by Groningen, Coevorden, and Zwolle. Added to the SAS force was 1st Belgian Parachute

Battalion, which would race into the area by jeep rather than be air-dropped. Unlike the French paratroops, the Belgians had seen action with a drop behind the lines in France and in the Ardennes during the Battle of the Bulge.

Once on the ground, the primary French task was to secure two airstrips at Steenwijk. Beyond that, their job was to sow chaos in the German rear—seize bridges to speed the advance by 11 Canadian Corps, harass the enemy, and provide the Canadians with guides and intelligence as each came into contact with the advancing ground forces. Because the Canadians were expected to reach the SAS troops quickly, no arrangements were made for resupply air drops. They would carry sufficient rations, ammunition, and other supplies to last to the linkup.

From the outset, Amherst had encountered problems. Deficiencies in training caused the paratroops to be dropped without any of their jeeps. Although some jeeps were then driven in overland, many of the troops were left reliant on their feet. They were also scattered across a much broader front than intended. While Canadian forces reached a few of the French paratroops and the Poles linked up with the Belgians on April 9, it would take six or seven days for the others to be contacted. The paratroops did succeed in spreading chaos as directed, but the Steenwijk airfields remained in German hands. Ultimately, ninety-one SAS troopers were killed, wounded, or lost as prisoners. Post-war assessments of the value of Amherst could not determine whether the results justified these costs.[28]

ON THE NIGHT of April 8, 9 CIB's battalions had established themselves across the Schipbeek Canal and opened a second bridgehead for 3rd Division to the south of Bathmen. By the morning of April 10, the Stormont, Dundas and Glengarry Highlanders had reached the Zijkanaal to the north of 7 CIB's frontage and gained a crossing, while the North Nova Scotia Highlanders and Highland Light Infantry pushed up the eastern bank of the canal with elements of 2nd Division to their right.

The afternoon found the North Novas closing on Wesepe, a village about five miles to the northeast, astride the Deventer–Raalte road. From Raalte, three miles farther on, the brigade could hook to the right towards Zwolle or bypass this city to the east and follow roads leading directly towards Leeuwarden.[29] During most of this advance, Brigadier Rocky Rockingham was heartened by the absence of resistance and believed "the enemy's line was crumbling fast. If this was the case, then speed in following up was vital."

Also on April 10, several miles farther back, the Canadian Scottish Regiment and Royal Winnipeg Rifles launched a joint assault on Deventer at 1215 hours. The Rifles advanced into the southern part of the town and the Can Scots into the north. Both were supported by the Sherbrooke's 'B' Squadron and each had a troop of Crocodiles. Forward observation officers from the 12th Field Regiment also accompanied the infantry, and the division's three field regiments shelled previously identified enemy positions. Due to an unusual oversight by the Germans, the telephone line between Deventer and Schalkhaar remained intact. Dutch resistance fighters attached to the infantry battalions phoned friends inside the city and acquired details on the enemy defences. They also reported that the Germans were "in a most unhappy state of mind."[30]

The Can Scots advanced fifteen minutes ahead of the Rifles, with 'B' Company on the left and 'D' Company on the right, followed respectively by 'A' and 'C' Companies. Before them lay a five-hundred-yard-wide open field with the wide anti-tank ditch in its centre. As soon as the infantrymen stepped into the open, they came under heavy fire from the front and left flank. Rifle grenades, machine-gun fire, and 20-millimetre rapid fire anti-aircraft guns shooting over open sights tore into the Can Scots. At the anti-tank ditch, the fire thickened. Lieutenant Clayton Leroy Mitchell at the head of 'B' Company's lead platoon was killed and another platoon leader, Lieutenant K.M. Little, fell wounded.

Realizing the attack was crumbling, Major Earl English sent a plea for Lieutenant Colonel Larry Henderson to unleash the Crocodiles, rather than holding them back until the city was gained. This decision proved to be the best possible, English later related, "for when the flame throwers blasted at the 20-mm. guns, the enemy broke and allowed the company to carry through." The Crocodiles

soon burned the Germans out of their fortified bunkers on the edge
of the city, and the Can Scots quickly pushed into Deventer. The two
leading companies kept "hard on the enemy's heels instead of waiting for the other two companies to pass through them as previously
planned. Once the enemy was on the run the best idea was to keep
him running, even though it called upon the last reserves of the men
who were dead tired after two days with almost no sleep."[31]

To the left, the Winnipeg Rifles had gone forward at 1230 hours
with 'A' and 'C' Companies out front. The supporting tanks and
Crocodiles followed close behind, with the other two companies back
of the armour. "The Germans were waiting," the battalion war diarist concluded, "for no sooner had the [troops] entered the open
ground . . . when all hell broke loose. Our [troops] were met by everything the Jerry had. Our [tanks] retaliated, the Crocodiles swept the
area with flame and the mortars and [artillery] blanketed the
approach to the town. The rugged riflemen overran the Hun with
every step and shortly after the first assault almost 200 PWs were
ours." The anti-tank ditch proved so wide and deep that the tanks
and Crocodiles were unable to get across, and "precious minutes
were lost awaiting a bulldozer" to fill it in. The riflemen "dashed on"
without waiting for the armour. "Finally the first buildings were
reached and the tough half of the battle was won. Fresh and eager 'B'
and 'D' [Companies] now entered the fray."[32]

Inside Deventer, the Can Scots had been met by more Dutch
underground fighters—identified by orange armbands—who volunteered as guides. During a pause, 'C' and 'A' Companies took over
the lead. At this point, 'A' Company commander Captain S.L. Chambers wrote, "We had far more difficulty forcing our way through the
jubilant civilians than we had from the enemy. The Underground
men with me kept popping into houses to telephone into the next
block to find out where the Germans were and in this way we eventually reached the railroad embankment. We came under fire from a
small park but No. 8 Platoon, under Sgt. J.H. Diamond returned this
fire with such vigour that most of the Germans fled and the German
officer working around the flank surrendered to Lieutenant Cornish
of No. 7 Platoon."[33]

As the infantry pushed on, 12th Field Regiment's forward observation officer (FOO) established himself in the upper storey of a building. To the east he could see the regiment's gun lines, and on a street between him and the 25-pounders stood several German 88-millimetre guns. Realizing that FOO protocol for directing fire had never anticipated a situation where he would be behind the target rather than facing it, the gunner spent several puzzled minutes working out how to provide coordinates that would make sense back at the regiment. When the shells started to drop, however, he was pleased to see they fell right on target and that two of the six German artillery pieces were destroyed. The crews manning the rest managed to hurriedly drag them into another street and out of sight.[34]

Despite sporadic firefights, incoming German artillery, and the occasional shells called down by the 12th Field Regiment FOOs, the "happy, rejoicing citizens, free for the first time in five years, thronged the streets, singing, dancing, waving flags, rooting out a few collaborators . . . all in a state of intense excitement that the long-awaited moment of liberation had come . . . Now and then shells from German guns would land in the streets, killing or wounding some of the Dutch civilians."

When the underground informed the Canadian Scottish that they had taken control of the telephone exchange but were having trouble staving off German attempts to regain it, Lieutenant Colonel Henderson ordered 'C' Company to hurry two platoons to the building. Lieutenant W.K. Wardroper set off with Nos. 13 and 14 Platoons. In the lead was No. 14 Platoon, and as it moved "along a small lake in a park area to open ground on the [IJssel] River embankment, [it] got itself pinned down in a firefight with some of the enemy who had crossed the river. Before proceeding with clearing the centre of town I had to take No. 13 Platoon to extricate them," Wardroper later wrote. "With the two platoons I turned south-east and with the assistance of the Dutch Resistance Forces seized the telephone exchange which I left in the hands of a Dutch Lieutenant and proceeded to the main square of the city and the City Hall. We went down the main streets while the Dutch soldiers scoured the back alleys catching the Germans as they popped out of back doors. At one point my platoon was mobbed by fifty deliriously happy girls from a nursing school who flung themselves about the necks of my men amidst the odd burst of machine-gun fire and stray shells from across the IJssel. We rounded up about forty or fifty Germans."

Wardroper was taken to city hall, where the council had already convened its first post-liberation meeting. The young lieutenant managed to convince the burgomaster to issue a directive warning all civilians to stay off the streets until the fighting was finished. By this time, however, the German defence was collapsing. At 1700 hours, the Canadian Scottish and Winnipeg Rifles reported Deventer in hand, with only a few isolated pockets remaining to be mopped up.[35] When at midnight the Queen's Own Rifles pushed 'A' Company across the footbridge and into the southern corner of the city, they met no opposition beyond twenty-five Germans eager to surrender and easily passed through to the IJssel River.[36] None of the rifle battalions recorded casualties suffered during the fight for Deventer, but the Can Scots reported that on April 9 they had three men killed and twelve wounded. April 10 was more costly, with twenty-seven casualties, of which five were fatal.[37]

PART THREE

BREAKOUTS

15

Long Way Out Front

WHILE 3RD CANADIAN Infantry Division had been clearing Zutphen and Deventer, 4th Canadian Armoured Division had closed on the Ems River at Meppen in Germany. After its stunning dash from the Twente Canal to the Ems, a pause would normally have followed—enforced either by the Germans digging in behind the river and offering a fight, or by the division outrunning its resources. In this case, neither circumstance arose. Although 4th Division's supporting arms straggled back for miles behind the leading infantry and armoured battalions, Major General Chris Vokes had decided on the afternoon of April 6 to bounce the river with the forces on hand.

Meppen straddled both banks of the Ems. 'C' Company of the Lake Superior Regiment (Motor) had been first to reach the city's western outskirts with orders to bull through to the main bridge. The company's agile wheeled armoured-personnel carriers had pulled far out ahead of the main body of 4th Canadian Armoured Brigade because the cobblestone roads built on compacted sand that led to Meppen had begun breaking up under the relentless weight of hundreds of passing military vehicles. On either side of the roads, heather and peat bogs stretched to the horizon. As the carriers, trucks, and tanks from various regiments ground the road down, "the difficulties of maintaining a mobile force in the midst of a peat bog became all too apparent."[1]

Company Commander Major Leslie Edwin Pope's scout car was out on point when it came under fire from heavy machine guns and 20-millimetre anti-aircraft guns. Rounds from one of the rapid-fire flak guns shredded the car's thin armour. As Pope jumped clear of the wreckage, he was knocked down by a sniper round. Captain G.U. Murray, the company's second-in-command, took over as Pope was evacuated.[2] Despite several more casualties, the company advanced until it could see that the bridge had been demolished and then withdrew from the city.

"It immediately became obvious that the crossing at Meppen would be a considerable task," the 4th Brigade's war diarist reported. Brigadier Robert Moncel ordered the Argyll and Sutherland Highlanders to hasten to join Murray's company and told Lieutenant Colonel Fred Wigle he was to coordinate a planned attack across the Ems. The tanks of British Columbia Regiment's 'A' Squadron also ground forward with instructions to help Murray's company gain control of the city's western section.[3]

Just getting to Meppen was difficult. "The condition of the roads and the thick traffic caused by supplies which were being passed up to forces already at Meppen, made this one of our hardest journeys," one tanker wrote. "Matters were further complicated by some trouble with [xxx] British Corps which was moving on the same centre line. No less a personage than the British Corps Commander . . . descended from his vehicle to order Captain Lungley to remove his tanks at once. As one generally prefers to argue with Corps Commanders as little as possible the tanks were driven off the road, where they bogged down completely and [hours were lost] digging them out."[4]

Despite the delays, 'A' Squadron joined the Superiors in time for a night attack. The presence of the British Columbia Regiment (BCR) tanks proved decisive, and shortly before midnight the combined force gained the riverbank, and western Meppen was reported clear.[5]

The Argylls, meanwhile, had been on the move from where they had only just completed pacifying the area of Coevorden, about twenty-two miles west of Meppen. The road demarcated the Dutch–German border, and the Argylls found it "unusual to see children with orange flags . . . on one side of the road, waving to us, while a mere 50 yards away would be German farmhouses displaying their white flag of surrender."

Wigle, meanwhile, had raced to Meppen ahead of his battalion to begin planning the river assault. Divisional intelligence reported that only a few days earlier a strong garrison consisting of armoured and infantry formations had withdrawn. Left behind were some infantry and paratroop remnants. When a German sergeant—who proved to be Polish—was brought in, he provided "a very detailed account of German defences and positions. The information was as accurate as it was detailed and the positions were engaged with artillery during the late afternoon."[6]

In the Netherlands, artillery bombardments and air strikes were limited in order to reduce civilian casualties. Wigle exercised no such discretion against a German city. At 1430 hours, thirty-two Typhoons appeared overhead, and "although the aircraft ran into a good deal of light anti-aircraft fire, each dived repeatedly to rocket and strafe the offending positions."[7] Completing their "very thorough going over" at 1500 hours, the Typhoons flew home unscathed by the anti-aircraft fire. No sooner had the Typhoons faded from view than the anti-aircraft gunners depressed their 20-millimetre guns and started firing "point blank" at the Argylls now forming on the riverbank. Meppen-defending remnants seemed determined to fight.

Observing the amount of 20-millimetre and small-arms fire thrown across the river convinced Wigle that preparations for an assault would have to occur under cover of darkness but that the attack itself should take place in daylight, with artillery blanketing the river with smoke just before the boats hit the water at 0600 hours.[8] Promoted to battalion command in February, the thirty-one-year-old officer was facing his biggest attack. Prior to taking over the Argylls, Wigle had served on 4th Division's general staff and seen little combat. In short order, however, he had led the battalion through the Rhineland campaign and then Operation Plunder, earning both a Distinguished Service Order and appointment as an

Officer of the Order of the British Empire (OBE). The latter was a sure sign that he had the eye of the army's high command.

Even as Wigle made his plans, Brigadier Moncel and Major General Chris Vokes looked beyond Meppen's fall to their next moves. Previously, they had expected the division to operate on the western shore of the Ems, but with 1st Polish Armoured Division slotting into place there, Vokes was free to range out from the other side of the river on a northeastern axis towards the North Sea. Although this change of direction required major regrouping, Vokes was determined not to lose momentum. The moment the Argylls secured Meppen, Moncel would reprise the Twente Canal breakout with another flying column dashing east from the Ems. The Lake Superiors would lead. Provided with motorized transport, the Lincoln and Welland Regiment would be second in line. Following in order behind would be Moncel's headquarters (protected by 11 Canadian Corps's armoured car regiment, the 12 Manitoba Dragoons), the 12th Canadian Light Field Ambulance, the tanks of the Governor General's Foot Guards and Canadian Grenadier Guards, and finally the self-propelled artillery of the 23rd Field Regiment. The goal was the Küsten Canal and ultimately the city of Oldenburg.

From assembly areas near Coevorden and Emlichheim, the column began rolling towards Meppen at 1500 hours. Like the BCR before it, the column encountered heavily damaged roads that only worsened as each vehicle passed over.[9] The main body of the Lake Superior Regiment, advancing from Emlichheim, followed the exact same route taken by the BCR and encountered ever-worsening conditions, until "finally at about 2000 hours [the road] gave up the ghost completely and the cobble stones disappeared into the peat bog and in places the [road] ceased to exist. Move came to a complete halt and our position was not enviable." Scouts finally located an undamaged "sandy trail." Picking their way carefully through the darkness, the Lake Superiors reached Meppen at 0400 hours and the rest of the column straggled in well before the assault's commencement at 0600 precisely.[10]

Thirty minutes before the attack went in, 23rd Field Regiment (Self-Propelled)—which had hastened to get its guns deployed—

started dropping smoke shells along the riverfront. Smoke blanketed the river as "in the dim light of breaking day the men rose . . . hustled their boats over the dyke with feverish haste, scrambled . . . into the frail craft and were paddled furiously over to the far side, where they lost no time in leaping ashore and making for their objectives . . . Except for two or three ineffective bursts of 20-millimetre fire and a few snipers, the crossing had been unopposed. There was in fact only one fatal casualty, but that one was an irreparable loss to the Battalion, Captain [Malcolm Stewart] Smith, commanding Support Company, who was shot through the heart by a sniper in carrying out his duties as beachmaster during 'A' Company's crossing. This officer had made himself beloved of all ranks by the sheer power of the gaiety, energy and wit of his personality. Known to everyone as 'Smitty,' he had been an invaluable adjutant and had just two days previously arrived from hospital in England to assume command of Support Company."[11]

The Argylls crossed into the centre of Meppen expecting a hard fight, but the Germans proved unwilling to engage in close-quarters combat. As the Canadians closed in, the Germans offered only token resistance and then either fled or surrendered. "Opposition broke quickly and clearing proceeded with little difficulty," the 4th Armoured Brigade war diarist recorded.[12] At 0730 hours, Lieutenant W.J. MacArthur's 'A' Company platoon rushed three 20-millimetre guns, captured two crews, and destroyed all the guns.[13] Despite the weak resistance, the Argylls moved cautiously through this large German city. They were in the home of the enemy, so mopping up was "systematic" and thorough. Although it took the morning and most of the afternoon to complete, the Argylls took about seventy-five prisoners and suffered no casualties other than the unfortunate loss of Captain Smith.[14]

INSTALLATION OF A Bailey bridge by engineers from the 8th and 9th Canadian Field Squadrons, with assistance from the Argyll's forty pioneers, had started at 1130 hours. The 215-foot span opened to traffic at 1930, and Moncel's column immediately started crossing. The Lake Superior Regiment struck a course due eastward from

Meppen towards the village of Lohe about two miles away. At Lohe the column would turn to the north and make for Sögel, about another eight miles beyond.[15]

There was no rapid dash, the Superiors crawling along in inky darkness that even artificial moonlight beaming across the Ems failed to penetrate. What made conditions poor for movement perfectly suited ambush, and after only a few hundred yards several Germans opened fire with Panzerfausts. In the lead, 'B' Company piled out of its vehicles, and a firefight ensued. Fifteen Germans were taken prisoner. Like the dead scattered along the road, they wore civilian clothes, and the Superiors had no idea whether they fought soldiers or guerillas.

A few hundred yards farther on, a large roadblock barred a road junction, and 'B' Company established a cordon to protect the party of engineers called up from Meppen to clear it. The company also sent a patrol on the northward road to Lathen, while 'A' Company did the same along the road to Lohe. The latter company's scout platoon ran into a party of paratroops and, after a rapid gunfire exchange, took two prisoner and sent the others running. They also discovered the road blocked by a network of barriers.

At 0200 hours on April 9, the engineers finished clearing the roadblock, and 'B' Company reported that its patrols up the highway had encountered neither obstacles nor German troops. As the Lathen route was the most direct to the Küsten Canal, Lieutenant Colonel Robert Keane radioed Moncel for permission to change course. Moncel, eager to see real movement, assented.[16]

It was the right decision. Keane put the scouts of 'C' Company's No. 13 Platoon at the column's head, with 'B' Company behind. Despite the continuing impenetrable darkness, the advance rolled smoothly forward. At 0430 hours, Lieutenant Bruce Wright picked up a member of the Volkssturm on the outskirts of Lathen. Wright was preparing to send the man to demand the town's surrender when his carriers came under heavy fire. 'B' and the rest of 'C' Company, which had been following close behind, pushed into the town with support from a Canadian Grenadier Guards tank troop, and by 0800 hours, Lathen was taken. Among the hundred prisoners were a number who confessed they had been caught unprepared by the rapidity of the Canadian advance from Meppen. A further sharp fight to seize the railway station north of the town netted fifty-nine more prisoners.

'A' Company moved to the column's head and was only five hundred yards from the station when it drew fire from several 20-millimetre anti-aircraft guns and a battery of anti-tank guns. They also found a rail bridge and the main highway bridge across a canal north of the station blown. Deciding a fight here was unnecessary, Keane made a quick decision to switch eastward along a road that bore straight from Lathen through to Sögel. Leaving 'A' Company to maintain control of Lathen until relieved by the Lincoln and Welland Regiment, the regiment pushed off with 'C' Company leading. Once more the Germans were caught off guard, and the Superiors met no resistance in the eight-mile run that brought them to Sögel, which was undefended. Turning north, 'C' Company made another five miles before coming under heavy fire. Its commander pulled his men back to some high ground out of enemy range. [17]

Having outrun the rest of the battalion, 'C' Company was far ahead of the flying column's main body, which was also having to shed units to temporarily garrison each German community through which it passed. A squadron of tanks from the Governor General's Foot Guards and a Lincoln and Welland Regiment company held Sögel. Lathen was in Canadian Grenadier Guard hands. The Argylls and British Columbia Regiment were concentrated at Meppen. While the Superiors had been moving on Borge, the 12th Manitoba Dragoons had also taken the original route towards Lohe. Although the armoured cars had to work around roadblocks, mines, and craters, they reached Sögel unopposed and reported a good, intact bridge south of town that would well serve the division's advance northward.

Evening of April 9 saw the column's leading edge twenty-five miles from its starting point. Moncel contemplated pressing on through another night, "but it was apparent that his troops were much too tired; orders were therefore given to half the advance and dig in while artillery harassing fire tasks were laid on to soften up the enemy's positions ahead." Moncel, however, was not prepared to lounge around long. The Lincs were put on notice to move at 0600 hours the next morning towards Werlte, a village about eight miles east of Sögel—expanding the Canadian frontage east of the Ems to make contact with the British xxx Corps on 4th Division's right flank.[18]

AT 0550 HOURS on April 10, the column rolled out of Sögel with six tanks from the Governor General's Foot Guards Reconnaissance Squadron at its head. Two companies of Lincolns followed, with 'B' Company riding on the Shermans of the Guards' No. 1 Squadron and 'D' Company on the battalion's carriers. 'C' Company remained in Sögel, while 'A' Company moved into reserve east of the town.[19] Sögel was bursting with Canadians. In addition to the Lincs, both Brigadier Moncel and the Superior's Lieutenant Colonel Keane had their headquarters there, and the latter's 'D' Company was deployed nearby. The 12th Canadian Light Field Ambulance had opened its advanced dressing station, and the engineers of 8th Canadian Field Squadron had set up shop in buildings near the medical team. In an open field on the town's northeast corner, 23rd Field Regiment's self-propelled guns were dug in—its regimental historian declaring the location an example of how "aggressively" Moncel was deploying artillery in this rapid drive into Germany. The position, the gunners soon realized, was actually in front of the infantry and armour they were to support, resulting in defensive fire plans submitted by the infantry in Sögel being sighted "either right on our gun position or at a range of 500 yards or less! Hardly the kind of thing to engender confidence in the situation!"[20]

April 10 dawned with heavy ground fog shrouding Sögel and the surrounding countryside. Bound for Werlte, a village six miles due east of Sögel, the column moved along a road bordered by invisible woods and the occasional equally obscured field. Sergeant J.G. Kimberley's reconnaissance section of three tanks was well to the front when it entered dense woods about two and a half miles from Sögel and triggered an ambush. Hidden among the trees lining the road, 150 Germans let loose with a storm of fire that included machine guns, mortars, Panzerfausts, 20-millimetre anti-aircraft guns, and 75-millimetre anti-tank guns. A Panzerfaust round slammed into Kimberley's tank, setting it ablaze. Although Corporal S.A. Roberts and Guardsman J. Crawford were badly burned, everyone managed to bail out of the burning wreck. Outside, Lance Corporal R.W. MacKay provided covering fire with his Sten while the other four men escaped. After being severely wounded in the abdomen, MacKay managed to stagger to safety. The remaining two tanks were struck repeatedly by 20-millimetre rounds, and a 75-millimetre shell ripped the bogey wheel off one track.[21]

As soon as the ambush was sprung, Major John Martin's 'B' Company piled off the Shermans and engaged the Germans, while a bombardment from a medium artillery regiment was also called in. The speed and violence of this response broke the enemy force—twelve surrendering and another eighty "seen running down the [road]."[22] This sharp action ended at 0830 hours.[23]

The moment the Germans broke, the unscathed Guards reconnaissance troop commanded by Lieutenant H.H.M. Griffin dashed into the fog towards Werlte.[24] No. 1 Squadron's leading troop under Lieutenant E.J. Canavan also headed into the blue without reloading any Lincolns, and both parties were soon a "long way out front."[25] As Griffin's tanks raced up to Werlte's outskirts, it ran into another ambush and all three tanks were knocked out, their crews escaping into slit trenches alongside the road. Although they tried to fend off the Germans until reinforcements arrived, the others surrendered when Guardsman Lawrence Frederick Bellafontaine was killed.[26]

Canavan's troop arrived to find the tanks burning and concluded from "the equipment on the side of the road [that] . . . the three crews had been searched there after being made prisoner." One of Griffin's crew was found unhurt the following day, and a few days later a divisional casualty-clearing station reported that Griffin and Guardsman E.G. Ross were being treated there for second-degree burns to their faces and necks. The rest of the troop members were assumed lost as prisoners.[27]

The rest of the column reached Werlte at 0930 hours. Lieutenant Colonel R.C. "Rowan" Coleman, figuring the assault was going to be a tough one, ordered Major E.J. Brady's 'D' Company to advance along the north side of the road and Major Martin's 'B' Company the south.[28] The Foot Guards would provide support. The approach was across an open field backed by a row of brush with the town beyond. 'B' Company had just entered the recently ploughed field when the sun suddenly burned off the fog as if someone "had pushed a button and the curtain went up." A machine gun spewed tracer from the woods ahead, and the company hit the dirt.

Brady managed to dash to the rear and tried to get the tankers to come up, but the commander refused to move into the open and expose his Shermans to anti-tank fire. "I was so goddamn mad, I couldn't see," Brady later said.[29]

No. 1 Squadron's Major Allen Smith was no happier. Three tanks had been damaged on the road to Werlte, three more destroyed on its outskirts. The open field was a ploughed-up, muddy morass, and he had every reason to expect there were anti-tank guns and troops with Panzerfausts waiting in the woods. Smith's tanks would provide covering fire from the shelter of the woods bordering the field, but they were not venturing into the open.[30]

The tanks shelling the woods enabled the Lincs to renew the advance. Brady could only watch his men go, for an accidental discharge from the rifle of a recently arrived reinforcement had left him with a leg wound. Sergeant Thomas Staszuk led, until a bullet shot out one of his eyes just as the men entered the woods. Company Sergeant Major C.E. Brown rushed forward and led 'B' Company on to the town. 'D' Company fought its way in at 1100 hours.[31] Coleman, meanwhile, had brought 'A' Company forward from its reserve position back near Sögel and hooked it into the town to the right of 'B' Company.

The Foot Guards quickly ground into the town, and a bitter fight ensued. One machine-gun position after another had to be cleared and snipers were constantly active, but slowly the Lincs pushed forward. At 2030 hours, with darkness closing in, Coleman ordered the advance stopped, and the companies took up defensive positions. Renewing the attack in the morning, by noon the battalion had faced only a few stray snipers, which were "dealt with by the [tanks] and [troops]."[32] Werlte cost the Lincolns forty-six casualties.[33]

THE FOG THAT had slowed the column's advance on Werlte had also covered a strong German force that crept up on Sögel for a counter-attack at 0800 hours.[34] Several hundred troops from 31st Fallschirmjäger Battalion launched a ferocious onslaught out of the woods to the north and east of the town, achieving complete surprise.[35]

The 23rd Field Regiment was "getting packed in anticipation of another move when small arms started to whistle around the area." One truck exploded into flames, as the officers shouted at their men to hold fire because they could see no visible targets and feared esca-lating a possible friendly-fire incident. "Then mortars started dropping into the area and reports of casualties came in. Doubts as to the origin of the firing [were] rapidly dispelled. It was a counter-attack and there didn't appear to be any infantry in front of us." The regi-ment's 36th Battery took heavy casualties, and Lieutenant Doug Denton was fatally wounded while loading an injured man into a half-track for evacuation. Gunner Victor Hubacheck died when struck by a bullet ricochet, and Gunner George Allan Buchanan fell mortally wounded. Another six men were injured by bullets and shrapnel.[36]

Minutes after the counterattack began, the fog lifted and the gun-ners rallied to meet the attack. The battery's 'C' Troop fired its 25-pounders over open sights, while other gunners grabbed up Bren and Browning machine guns and "sprayed . . . every part of the woods." Lieutenant Harry Smith with Lance Bombardier Bruce MacArthur commandeered a tank used by the regiment for forward observation and brought its Browning to clear the enemy threaten-ing the embattled battery. "A number of enemy were killed and half a dozen taken prisoner" before the attack broke.[37]

The counterattack on Sögel lacked coordination. Instead, para-troops popped up randomly throughout the town. Civilian snipers also fired on Canadian troops.

One group of thirty paratroops charged 12th Canadian Light Field Ambulance's dressing station, forcing the medical personnel "to take up arms. Some of the enemy were killed within 10 yards of the . . . entrance. After about one hour a troop of tanks arrived who blasted houses from which the enemy were sniping. When the attackers were finally wiped out, we realized that we had been holding a small portion of the front. If we had not taken up arms we would have been shot up and the enemy would have gained access to the main street of the town. We ha[d] 5 of our personnel wounded, one seriously." Two of the unit's stretcher bearers were also wounded while evacuating injured engineers and members of a Royal Canadian Army Service Corps unit, which had been overrun in the opening moments of the counterattack.[38]

The headquarters of the Lincolns and of the Superiors were both embroiled in the fighting. The counterattack was finally driven off when the companies each battalion had retained in the town managed to come to grips with the Germans. By late morning, the paratroops had withdrawn to the woods northeast of Sögel. The Lake Superiors spent the rest of the day preparing a full set-piece assault with supporting arms in the form of Wasps, tanks, mortars and self-propelled guns, set to begin the following morning. 'A' and 'B' Companies struck at first light behind a deluge of fire, only to find the woods "clear of enemy." The infantry pushed on two miles northeastward to the village of Spahn "and cooked a hot meal."[39]

Back in Sögel, an investigation by divisional intelligence staff confirmed that civilian snipers had been involved in the April 10 counterattack and that some Canadians killed had fallen to this fire. "Accordingly, as a reprisal and a warning, a number of houses in the centre of Sögel were ordered destroyed by the engineers to provide rubble" for road construction.[40]

Throughout the course of April 11, 4th Division concentrated its rear echelons around the town while preparing for the next big push. With 10th Canadian Infantry Brigade having rejoined the division from operations in the Almelo area, a two-pronged thrust to the Küsten Canal was planned. On the right, 4th Armoured Brigade would carry out the main thrust through Friesoythe to gain the canal where it intersected the headwaters of the Leda River about twenty miles to the north. Once across the canal, it would advance on Oldenburg.

To the left, meanwhile, 10 CIB had already started advancing on April 10 from Meppen along the east bank of the Ems River towards the canal. Meeting no opposition, the Algonquin Regiment, which led this column, gained the canal that morning and determined that all bridges had been destroyed and the Germans held the opposite bank "in some strength." A hurried plan to force a crossing in the afternoon was soon cancelled by brigade headquarters.[41]

The 4th Brigade did not move towards the canal until the morning of April 11, when the Canadian Grenadier Guards No. 1 Squadron, with the Argylls' 'D' Company mounted up, pushed out beyond Werlte at 0945 hours—even as the Lincoln and Welland Regiment was still clearing the place. The regiment's reconnaissance troop led the way along a road bordered by farmhouses, which it set on fire with phosphorous shells while passing. Brushing aside roadblocks created by fallen trees, the force made good time and encountered no enemy. Closing on Lorup, after a four-mile advance, the tankers saturated the village with 75-millimetre shells, while a medium artillery regiment to the rear showered heavier ordnance on it. At 1730 hours, the Argylls entered the village and found it had been undefended. Grenadier commander Lieutenant Colonel E.A.C. "Ned" Amy wanted to press on with a night move, but Moncel ordered the force to stand down.[42]

Both brigades had by day's end linked up south of the canal near Börger—a village about five miles north of Sögel. Meanwhile, the Algonquin's 'A' Company with the British Columbia Regiment's 'A' Squadron had bumped into major resistance at about 1000 hours, when it closed on the town of Breddenberg, four miles northeast of Börger. As the lead tanks and mounted infantry closed on the town, they came under heavy machine-gun and Panzerfaust fire.[43] The infantry scattered to either side of the road while the tanks pressed forward, only to have the forward troop leader, Lieutenant Ray Walmsley, killed by a sniper round to the head. He was a regimental old-timer from before the war, and his loss struck the Dukes—as the BCR was nicknamed—hard.[44] Enraged, the tankers opened up on every building and clutch of trees that might harbour enemy, while the Algonquin's Major Robert Stock had the two battalion Wasps flame the hedges bordering the road.[45]

The Wasps and tanks kicked up such a racket that Sergeant George Caya's No. 7 Platoon were unable to hear his shouted orders, so he resorted to signalling them with a waved arm to charge a trench system. Dashing forward, Caya looked back to see his men had gone to ground and he stood alone on the lip of the first trench. Flee or fight, he thought. Deciding he would rather die with his face to the foe, Caya looked into the trench and saw only a single German—visibly shaking with fear—in its depths. Knowing he could not leave the man at his back, Caya killed him with a Sten gun burst. Moving to the next trench, he surprised two more Germans and cut them down with gunfire. At the third trench, Caya emptied his magazine into the single German there. Shaking uncontrollably, nerves shot, Caya reached the fourth trench, and a lone German popped up with hands raised. Had the Sten been loaded, Caya would have shot the man dead. Instead, he jerked the German's bayonet from its scabbard and pointed back towards where his section was still holding. Caya's actions earned a Military Medal.[46]

To the left of Caya's position, Sergeant John Francis Flannery's platoon had kept with him during its charge on another trench system. But as the platoon became increasingly mired in a vicious close-range shootout, Flannery got ahead of his men and his Sten jammed. When a German started to spin towards him with machine pistol raised, Flannery tackled the man and strangled him to death.[47] Snatching up the German's weapon, Flannery went on to kill three more enemy and take eight prisoners. He was awarded a Military Medal.[48]

Caya's and Flannery's decisive leadership won entry into the town, which the Algonquins cleared after a four-hour fight "against fanatical resistance."[49] The company counted three men killed and eight wounded, while the BCRs had lost one man, Lieutenant Walmsley. Fifty-four Germans were taken prisoner and thirty-two killed. Why Breddenberg had been so stoutly defended was soon explained when the Algonquins discovered the farm had housed a German non-commissioned officer training school. These high-calibre troops had been well equipped and, despite being cut off, had "fought with extreme tenacity."[50]

Beyond Breddenberg, 4th Division entered a new, ominous type of terrain on the morning of April 12. Before the Canadians stretched a seemingly endless expanse of peat bogs extending from the Dutch border all the way north to Wilhelmshaven. The Algonquin's Major George Cassidy realized it was country that would profoundly affect the battle to follow. It was "flat as a pancake, soaking wet, and fairly heavily treed. The side roads, suitable for farm traffic, were practically useless for tanks or heavy army vehicles. The main roads had sufficient surfacing to hold traffic for some days at least, and hence it was decided to attack boldly along the main road, trusting to heavy air and artillery support to blast a way through. But in so doing we would lose nine-tenths of the effectiveness of our tanks, our thrust-line would be tied quite closely to the main road, and we would be faced with massed enemy resistance. Further, the country was ideal for an anti-tank and anti-infantry role. The flatness limited the visibility to a matter of only a few hundred yards. Every field was dotted with drying stacks of peat blocks, each one providing a miniature fortress for a sniper or a machine gun."[51]

Smack in the middle of such country sat Friesoythe, through which the main road across the Küsten Canal passed. It was a town eminently suited for defence and reportedly held by at least five hundred Germans. Brigadier Moncel appreciated that going straight up the road towards it would ensure that the column "met with disaster." Instead, he planned to wait and gather his forces. Then, on the night of April 13–14, the Argylls would attack by moving along a series of trails, which would be scouted and mapped first by brigade patrols.[52]

16

On to Groningen

A s 4TH CANADIAN Armoured Division became mired in peat
bogs, the rest of 11 Canadian Corps had broken out across the
northern Netherlands to the North Sea. Intelligence reports had led
General Harry Crerar to conclude that while it was "possible that the
enemy might try to delay my northern advance on Groningen, I did
not expect this part of the Netherlands to be heavily defended, with
the exception of the coastal areas opposite the naval base of Emden."[1]

On April 11, his intelligence staff reported that the Germans here
had four options. They could sideslip to the west to "join the garrison
in Western Holland, surrender on the spot, be driven back into the
sea," or "head eastwards to Germany."

Having secured Deventer and begun advancing north along the
eastern bank of the IJssel River towards Zwolle, 3rd Canadian Infantry Division was rapidly closing the door into the western
Netherlands. As 1st Polish Armoured Division had reached Emmen
on April 10 and thereafter driven an arrowhead north along either
bank of the Ems River to its mouth at Leer, fleeing into Germany
was fast disappearing as an enemy option. Intelligence reports further indicated that the Germans in northern Holland were in
disarray, poorly equipped, and scattered and confused by the French
sas troops dropped into their midst. Given their current state, intel-

ligence staff predicted that many would "decide there was not much point in putting up a fight."[2]

Events on 2nd Canadian Infantry Division's front had supported this assessment. As the division punched northward from the Schipbeek Canal on April 8, opposition had proved slight and lacking any coherency. Even a couple of bridges, apparently "overlooked by German demolition parties," had been taken intact. Accordingly, 5th Canadian Infantry Brigade had enjoyed a two-day free run to Ommen before encountering any resistance.[3]

It was late afternoon on April 10 when the Black Watch spotted German troops dug in along the railway on Ommen's outskirts and saturated the enemy position with mortar and artillery fire. The battalion's commander, Lieutenant Colonel Sydney Thomson, had just taken over four days earlier, and he was demonstrating a penchant for using artillery whenever he could to crack opposition and avoid casualties. Looking beyond the railway positions, Thomson called down "a 'hate' stonk... on the town itself."[4] Although new to the Black Watch, Thomson was no neophyte battalion commander. He had previously commanded the Seaforth Highlanders of Canada in Italy before being posted to an administrative position in England for about five months.

With intelligence reports estimating four or five hundred Germans in the town, Brigadier W.J. "Bill" Megill paused to tee up a set-piece attack for the morning of April 11. Divisional commander Major General Bruce Matthews, meanwhile, decided to try to trap the Germans at Ommen by sending 6th Canadian Infantry Brigade through the Polish Division lines on the right to get behind the town. Provided with the Royal Canadian Dragoon armoured cars of 'D' Squadron, the brigade would hook thirteen miles east to Gramsbergen and then make a twelve-mile return run to Balkbrug, which lay six miles north of Ommen.[5]

At dawn, a Black Watch patrol from 'C' Company checked the bridge crossing the Vechte River into Ommen and discovered that "with little difficulty it could be crossed by infantry, as there was only a four foot gap in the middle. The patrol proceeded farther into town and saw two Germans on bicycles, and fired upon them." Thomson ordered 'C' Company to provide security for a team of engineers while they cleared road obstructions leading to the bridge, and also to push "a strong patrol in[to] the town, but first thing we know, the [company] had reported the town cleared." Thomson funnelled his other three rifle companies across and anchored a jumping-off point for the rest of the brigade to pass through.[6]

Still hoping to overrun the Germans, Brigadier Megill sent the Calgary Highlanders through Ommen with orders to advance to Balkbrug and either relieve 6 CIB—if it had completed its twenty-five-mile right hook through Gramsbergen—or "take the town themselves depending on who gets there first."[7] On point for the Calgary advance were the armoured cars of 14th Canadian Hussars and also those of the Dragoons' 'B' Squadron. These reconnaissance troops were waiting impatiently on the south side of the Vechte for the engineers to repair the bridge. The past couple of days had been hugely fulfilling for the Dragoons with their heritage as Canada's senior cavalry regiment. During its long service in Italy, the regiment had never managed the "classic cavalry task—the mad dash into the enemy's territory to heighten the confusion of the breakthrough."[8] Events of April 9–10 had given the Dragoons a belief that "now or never they would establish their reputation as the truly great Regiment they knew themselves to be and to a man the Regiment hoped and prayed that here at last after the bitter memories of the Liri, Gothic Line, Marrechia, Savio, and all the other rivers and canals where they had fought and crossed, the golden opportunity of a proper armoured car role would present itself."[9]

Nobody felt the moment riper than their commander, Lieutenant Colonel K.D. Lendall. He spent the morning dashing about in a jeep, checking in with one headquarters after another for information on what lay beyond Ommen, while also monitoring the wireless sets packed into the vehicle's back. Everything he learned suggested that a breakout into the German rear was imminent, perhaps already underway. Finally, "an intercepted message plucked out of the air from Divisional Headquarters confirmed this fond hope and, as though to emphasize the fact, a sudden surge of traffic piled up at the bridging site. The electric news was on every lip—'Break Through'—and the tired troops shouting happily to one another pressed forward to the pursuit. Thus, quite suddenly, a completely new aspect was given to the operation and the cry for armoured cars echoed loudly through the earphones as the Dragoons struggled through a mass of traffic to the new battleground." The schmozzle at the bridge soon sorted out, the Dragoons rolled across. Close behind were their support vehicles bearing fuel, ammunition, and reserve rations, which the crews packed into the holds of their armoured cars. Then, at 1300 hours, 'B' Squadron was away, leaving the Calgary Highlanders to trail behind on foot.[10]

The race for Balkbrug was on, two Dragoon squadrons vectoring towards it from opposite directions—both running far ahead of infantry they supported. Also dashing up the main road that led through Hoogeveen, Assen, and on to Groningen from Ommen were 'B' and 'C' Squadrons of the 14th Canadian Hussars, with 'A' Squadron and the headquarters squadron trailing in reserve. The two leading squadrons had already "started to run wild, and we're burning up the miles" when Major J.F. Merner—headquarters' squadron leader—gave "the old familiar command that we had heard so often . . . 'Mount Up, Start Up,' and away we went again."[11]

Approaching Balkbrug from the east, the Royal Canadian Dragoons' 'D' Squadron had enjoyed a one-hour head start on 'B' Squadron. Whichever reached the town first, both were long gone when the Calgary Highlanders arrived at 1530 hours.[12] All of 6 CIB had also previously passed through, at 2300 hours, establishing its brigade headquarters in a wood outside Spier.[13]

The reconnaissance squadrons had already been well north of here, the 14th Hussars' 'B' Squadron arriving at the tiny hamlet of Spier in the early morning in the nick of time to rescue, "in the best manner of the films," the commander of 3rd Régiment de Chasseurs Parachutistes and a small group of his men facing "imminent annihilation by far superior German forces."[14] The paratroops said "they had a tough time, but put up a damn good show, and were almost surrounded, and out of ammunition, when our boys arrived. They lost a couple of men (killed) and some wounded," the war diarist recorded. At 2000 hours, trucks carried the French paratroops to the rear and they "were a happy looking crowd when they left."

The Hussars established their regimental headquarters at Spier in the early afternoon, and several staff officers were led by civilians to a nearby barn where they were shown the corpses of fourteen Dutchmen murdered by the Dutch security police. "Their heads were beaten to a pulp, and some of their wrists were burnt, and it appeared as if they had been shot through the back of the neck, when they had been tortured sufficiently enough to satisfy the low brow bastards that had done it." The men had been executed out of suspicion that they were providing food to the embattled paratroops.

By day's end, the Hussars had travelled forty-five miles, at times ranging twenty miles ahead of the infantry.[15] The Dragoons had put even more miles behind them. At 1700 hours, 'D' Squadron was searching for a crossing over a canal that barred the way into Beilen, a town about twenty-five miles north of Ommen on the road to Groningen. Finding a damaged bridge three miles west of Beilen, one troop used the light bridging materials it carried to get across. Advancing two miles farther, it reached the village of Hijken on the south side of the Oranjekanaal "without incident."[16]

The infantry battalions of 6 CIB, meanwhile, had closed on the canal south of Beilen, and Brigadier Jean Allard, anxious to keep the advance rolling, ordered Les Fusiliers Mont-Royal to force a crossing in the night, despite reports that the town was held by at least one hundred Germans.[17]

LES FUSILIERS MONT-ROYAL'S 'B' Company struck at 0200 hours on April 12. Achieving complete surprise, the lead platoon moved into the houses bordering the canal and captured several prisoners. When 'A' Company came up on 'B' Company's flank, however, it came under fire from a concrete blockhouse. After Major Bob Lucy, a 6th Field Regiment FOO, hammered the blockhouse with shells, a white flag appeared. This opened the way for the battalion to start clearing the streets of Beilen.[18] By 0700 hours, the FMR had its carriers and Wasps across the canal and approaching Beilen from the north to corral the Germans within. As the vehicles approached the houses covering the main street, the first Bren carrier was knocked out by a Panzerfaust. Several machine guns also opened up and

Panzerfaust rounds whistled in to explode around the other carriers. The Wasps immediately pushed to the front and started setting buildings on fire, which caused the Germans to retreat. Fighting in the streets continued for two hours, and when it was over the FMR had taken two hundred prisoners, including one officer. Beilen had a population of about four thousand, and the FMR soon learned that "every family wants at least one or two soldier to be billeted in their house. Our rest here will be most pleasant," the war diarist noted.[19]

While the FMR assaulted Beilen, the brigade's South Saskatchewan Regiment had outflanked the village to the east and headed for a bridge that crossed the Oranjekanaal about three miles to the northeast. The SSR had started this move at 0330 hours, only to have Lieutenant Colonel Vern Stott's carrier throw a track. Then, after transferring the vital wireless sets to another carrier, a fifteen-minute job, the driver ran into a ditch just four hundred yards past the start line. "It looked at this time as if the jinx was on," complained the war diarist, "and, as the old saying goes, there was one more to come. And it came! Shortly after the CO's vehicle had been pulled out of the ditch and the column had started on the move—one of the TCV [troop-carrying vehicles] drivers had fallen asleep and held up the rest of the convoy for another 30 minutes before it was discovered. From then on the convoy proceeded to the debussing point without incident."

Stott set zero hour for 0730. Although the bridges were out, 'B' Company crossed unopposed in assault boats and quickly established a bridgehead sufficiently deep to enable engineers to start on a bridge. By 0900 hours, the situation was stable enough for Stott to order 'D' Company to work westward along the canal to gain control of the road running from Beilen towards Groningen, a little less than three miles distant. 'C' and 'B' Companies, meanwhile, expanded the bridgehead out to about a mile north of the canal.

'D' Company made good progress against thickening opposition until it was within sight of the road and paralleling railway tracks. A large party of Germans could be seen digging in around the objective, so 'D' Company melted into the trees and shrubbery bordering the canal while its commander got on the wireless with Stott, who arranged to have 6th Field Regiment and 4.2-inch mortars of the Toronto Scottish Regiment work the position over.[20] When the bombardment lifted, a sharp fight broke out, and 'D' Company soon issued an urgent call for Wasps or other support. Two Wasps duly rolled to the rescue. After closing to within one hundred yards, and with the wind helping to carry the flame forward, the Wasps "sent enemy machine gunners running and screaming out into the open, and the battle was over. A good number of prisoners were taken and a greater number of dead and burned were counted. The company suffered eleven casualties, including one killed."[21]

For an operation that breached a canal that would normally have been fiercely defended, the Saskatchewan losses were surprisingly light. This mirrored the overall situation, as the Germans—mostly paratroops from 6th Fallschirmjäger Division—proved unable to stem or even delay the division's advancing tide.

Once again, the reconnaissance regiments were running loose. Having left Spier at first light, mid-morning found the 14th Canadian Hussars seven miles north. Its 'B' Squadron was roaming off to the right of the main highway when it stumbled on Westerbork Transit Camp. The guards having fled, the remaining one thousand inmates—primarily Jews—were "delirious with joy."[22] Many were among the camp's first occupants, particularly those from the ill-fated ss *St. Louis*. When the Germans had taken over Westerbork, these inmates were found to be already managing the camp so effectively that they were left in place, while newer arrivals were selected for shipment to the extermination camps.

Closing on the heels of the armoured cars were the rifle battalions of 4th Canadian Infantry Brigade, which had leapfrogged 6 CIB at the Oranjekanaal. The Royal Hamilton Light Infantry (Rileys) relieved the Hussars to enable the armoured cars to continue roaming. Just outside the camp, the Rileys' 'D' Company bumped a pocket of heavy resistance that turned out to be local pro-Nazi paramilitary troops, who feared they would be executed as collaborators if taken prisoner and turned over to the Dutch authorities.

"Then we ran into the concentration camp itself," Lance Corporal John Lisson recalled. "It was a horrible experience. The Jews came

streaming out of the place yelling, 'Tommy, Tommy'" because—
seeing the pisspot-style helmet worn by most Commonwealth
troops—they mistook the Canadians for British soldiers. "Those that
got to us began to throw their arms around our necks and hang on.
We had to shake them off. After all, we were right in the middle of
this set-piece operation, and we had to get moving.

"I had to fire my Sten gun over their heads to scare them away. It
was all pretty horrible. We had to get on the move."[23] The situation in
the camp was so chaotic, however, that 'D' Company's Major Doering sent a message back to Lieutenant Colonel H.C. Arrell that he
had "never seen anything like it before . . . These Jewish women had
apparently been starved in more ways than one and 'D' Coy personnel were heavily taxed in quenching their thirst, the results of five
years of isolation." At 2100 hours, the company was relieved by divisional medical and provost personnel. Doering complained that "the
'D' Coy boys do not like the prospects of leaving the place." In fact, he
experienced "some difficulty" in rounding them up. At 0300 hours
on April 13, however, the recalcitrant company had been separated
from the women and was installed in a battalion bivouac at the
nearby village of Hooghalen.[24]

Within a few days of Westerbork's liberation, First Canadian
Army's Senior Jewish Chaplain Samuel Cass visited. He conducted a
Sabbath service attended by about five hundred inmates. Cass alternated between English for the Dutch Jews and Yiddish for the
German Jews. "For them my presence and my address was the final
evidence of their liberation, and after the service hundreds passed by
to shake my hand and express their gratitude." Cass told his wife the
visit "may be one of the most dramatic memories I shall bring back
from the experiences of this war."[25]

WHILE THE RILEYS had been liberating Westerbork, the rest of
4 CIB had pushed about five miles northward to Assen. Essex Scottish Regiment's 'B' Company led, mounted on Fort Garry Horse 'B'
Squadron Shermans. Not far beyond the Oranjekanaal, the road had
been heavily mined, so one Sherman, commanded by Corporal William James MacDonald, probed cautiously forward with two jeeps

carrying the Essex's pioneer platoon close behind. When mines were detected, the pioneers dismounted to lift or detonate them with explosives. From a cluster of trees far ahead, a German soldier fired a Panzerfaust at MacDonald's tank. Although they saw the round hurtling towards them, the crew was unable to take evasive action before it penetrated the Sherman's turret and killed MacDonald. As the tank began burning, the rest of the crew bailed out. Three of the men were injured.[26]

Burning fuel spilling from the tank spread to the jeeps. Loaded with ammunition and explosives, both jeeps exploded and the pioneers' commander, Lieutenant M. Sheppard, and eight men were wounded. Corporal George Bradshaw was killed. Despite the pioneer platoon being virtually wiped out, the company and tank squadron continued advancing and, after fighting several brief skirmishes, gained Assen's outskirts shortly after nightfall.[27] From a spot near a bridge that spanned a canal in front of Assen, a machine gun opened up and several men in the lead platoon were hit—including its officer and sergeant. Corporal Leo Nahmabin got the survivors under cover. To locate the gun, Nahmabin strode into the middle of the road. Firing his Sten gun and shouting invectives towards the Germans managed to goad them into betraying their position with a long burst of fire. Nahmabin quickly led the platoon in a charge that eliminated the MG42 position, killing all five crew.[28] As usual, the Germans had attempted to demolish the bridge crossing, but the demolitions had failed to drop the span. Under 'B' Company's protective fire, engineers were able to clear away the debris and effect repairs to permit tank traffic. The Essex put a couple of companies across the canal to guard the precious bridge, and 6 CIB awaited the dawn.[29]

Brigadier Fred Cabeldu decided during the night not only to take Assen by frontal assault, but at the same time to cut off the German line of retreat northward to Groningen by having the Royal Regiment of Canada sweep around the city's right flank. In order to get some of the battalion behind Assen quickly, one company was loaded in Kangaroos—M7 Priest self-propelled guns converted into armoured personnel carriers by removing their main weapon and other equipment to accommodate a dozen infantrymen. The battalion headed into the night, leaving Cabeldu fretting at his brigade headquarters because wireless contact was immediately lost. He could only hope the men reached the Assen–Groningen highway in time to achieve their mission.[30]

Friday, April 13, dawned fair and warm. After ensuring that the woods on either side of the road approaching the bridge were clear, the Essex's 'B' Company spearheaded the attack on Assen. Lieutenant Earl Thompson's platoon soon came up against a roadblock flanked on one side by an anti-tank ditch filled with water and on the other by a cement pillbox. The pillbox bristled with machine-gun ports and was protected by wire and slit trenches manned by German paratroops.[31] After a brief artillery barrage, the battalion's Wasps flamed the position.[32] The moment the flames ceased jetting from the carriers, Thompson led his men through an "intense cross-fire" from slit trenches off to the flank, capturing the pillbox and taking twenty prisoners.[33]

The way now open, Lieutenant Colonel K.W. "Ken" MacIntyre sent the entire battalion into the town, supported by the Fort Garry Horse's 'B' Squadron. Resistance was confined to groups of Germans and Dutch paramilitary troops fighting at random from various houses. Although these positions were generally overrun, the sporadic way in which they were manned necessitated checking each building before the infantry and tanks could pass by. The narrow streets were bad for tanks, a fact proven once again that morning when a Panzerfaust round flashed out of an upper-storey window and punched into Sergeant Robert George Finch's Sherman. The thirty-three-year-old long-time regimental veteran and his gunner, Lance Corporal Frederick William Lockinger, were killed.[34] Many Germans chose to surrender rather than fight it out, however, so the Essex were able to work their way through to the city centre with only light casualties.[35]

North of Assen, meanwhile, the Royal Regiment had managed to work its way in behind the town and sever the German line of retreat. The part of the move made in darkness had been particularly hairy for Major R.T. "Bob" Suckling's 'A' Company, which had ridden ahead in the Kangaroos. With six miles to cover, time was of the essence, and Suckling had the vehicles race along at thirty miles an hour despite the constant risk of triggering a mine or being ambushed. Passing through the narrow streets of Loon, a Panzerfaust round flashed past the lead Kangaroo and several unseen enemy opened up with small arms. The Kangaroo drivers slammed the pedals to the floor, each vehicle's Browning machine gun spitting out long bursts of lead as they careened through the village without stopping. It was "quite dark," wrote the regiment's historian, "and the wild drive through unknown territory had quite a gay and cavalier touch to it—*Blitzkrieg* at its colourful best."

When 'D' Company, with the battalion's two anti-tank guns and two 17-pounder guns for support, reached Loon, the enemy had flown. By first light the Royals approached the main road at the small village of Peelo, just outside Assen.[36] A patrol soon moved south, arriving at a bridge just "at the moment enemy [troops] were in the act of attempting to demolish the structure. Dramatic action was taken here, enemy [troops] being killed at the switches they were about to throw. The [bridge] was saved, thus saving considerable time in the [advance] of the [brigade group]."[37]

By the time the Germans decided to quit Assen, the Royals were solidly astride the road, supported by two sections of the Essex's carrier platoon that had hooked tightly around the town's right flank. Unaware that the Royals had been sent to pinch off the German retreat, the carriers were attempting the same task. Some 14th Hussars, prowling for trouble, also showed up.[38] When the Germans appeared, some were gunned down and the others wisely opted to surrender.

Cabeldu was elated. "A further dividend to this action was the bag of some 600 PW . . . taken by the Essex and [Royals] in mopping up the town of Assen," the brigade's war diarist wrote. "The tactics had been simple, but had clearly taken the enemy by surprise and beaten him. Whilst the Essex . . . kept the enemy situation focused on the main axis by its steady pressure, the [Royals] had cut off his line of withdrawal. This bag was complete and, as subsequently proved, many enemy whose task it was to withdraw and fight other delaying actions on the [road] to Groningen, were taken PW at Assen."[39]

A now familiar scene greeted the Canadians the moment they entered Assen. Captain Robert Meanwell noted that the Essex were "accustomed to warm welcomes by liberated Dutch towns, but the tumultuous reception given by the people of Assen outdid everything previously experienced. Even with small arms fire flying dangerously near, the happy citizens could not be restrained from rushing about tossing flowers at our vehicles and serving refreshments to our men. TAC [tactical headquarters] was set up in the sumptuous town hall, which was situated close to the town jail. The latter was the scene of many heart-rending and dramatic episodes. First the moving scene as the gates burst open releasing 300 Dutch prisoners to the waiting arms of friends. Later the same prison was host to the previous jailers as hundreds of German prisoners were temporarily billeted there for questioning. The full cycle of justice was reached when Dutch collaborators and informers were paraded through the crowds to ponder over their treason in the relative security of the very jail to which they had sent many patriotic Dutchmen. No honest Dutchman shed a tear of sympathy that day. No Canadian, participating now as a spectator, could feel anything but pride for the part his country and regiment had played in once more enthroning decency and justice in the fair city of Assen."[40]

The Fort Garry Horse war diarist was equally touched by the reception, but looked ahead to orders instructing 2nd Division and the tankers to rush on to Groningen—"the last important centre below the sea." Looking back over the past few days, "the regiment could scarcely believe that so much had been achieved at so little cost. Home seemed very close indeed."[41]

CAPTAIN MEANWELL WAS more realistic. "But the war was not yet over," he wrote. "Ahead of us lay the largest city in north Holland, Groningen . . . To give the enemy no reprieve or rest, the order of the day was, 'On to Groningen.'" At 1700 hours, the Essex moved out.[42] They no longer led, the Rileys having taken over that duty and going forward mounted in Kangaroos. Running ahead of the Kangaroos to provide protection was 'B' Squadron's No. 3 Troop, commanded by Sergeant Walter Chaulk.[43]

The advancing force met no opposition and saw only a few Germans, who immediately fled into the countryside. Not bothering with these stragglers, the Fort Garry Horsemen and Rileys pushed on unopposed for about fifteen miles. At 1600 hours, a signal reached Cabeldu that the force was approaching the outskirts, and Cabeldu instructed them to seize any major road or railway bridges still standing.[44]

Grabbing a jeep, Cabeldu, his intelligence officer, and the brigade's artillery representative raced forward to contact Lieutenant Colonel H.C. Arrell and urge the Rileys on. But even as they set off, it was becoming clear to the infantry and tankers on the sharp end that Groningen's outskirts were heavily defended. Each forward movement was met by more intense machine-gun and mortar fire. Dozens of roadblocks, largely constructed of logs and boulders, slowed the advance to a crawl—the surrounding area first having to be secured before the infantry battalion's pioneers and engineers from 2nd Field Company could remove them.

Cabeldu arrived to find the column backed up for miles—"an amazing sight to behold." Formed in a long line that the jeep carefully bumped past on the verge were carriers, tanks, Kangaroos, the tractors and guns of 4th Field Regiment—operating well ahead of their normal placement—and anti-tank guns, "all pressing into the city. And down the road going the other direction came the bedraggled, amazed looking Boche." When Cabeldu's party contacted Arrell, the brigadier and lieutenant colonel agreed that the Rileys "would put in a planned attack in the outskirts where a number of enemy were keeping up a constant harassing fire with MGs and rifles. It was felt that if this outer crust could be crushed quickly . . . the [defence] of the rest of the city might collapse quickly and . . . the original plan could be followed through before darkness."[45]

On the very tip of the battle column, Sergeant Chaulk's No. 3 Troop faced a log roadblock that completely barred the highway. It was being heavily defended by Germans armed with a 20-millimetre gun, various small arms, and a number of Panzerfausts. Poorly concealed mines were strewn in front of the roadblock. Spotting the 20-millimetre gun, Chaulk pointed it out to Trooper Fred Butterworth, who snapped off a 75-millimetre round that reduced it to a twisted wreck. Despite the small-arms fire flying around, Chaulk jumped down from the tank. Reeling out a steel cable from the front of the Sherman, Chaulk picked his way through the mines and looped it around the centre log in the roadblock. When the tank backed up, the roadblock collapsed.

No. 3 Troop continued pressing into Groningen's outskirts, shooting up two machine-gun positions, destroying five vehicles, and otherwise spreading mayhem as it went.[46] Groningen was the largest Dutch city Canadian troops had encountered. A medieval university city, it was the country's sixth largest, with a normal population of 124,000—now swollen to more than 150,000 by refugees fleeing the fighting to the south. The city's core was surrounded by a wide ring canal spanned by a dozen bridges—three per geographical side. The inner city's streets were ancient and narrow, its buildings mostly 15th- and 16th-century, three- to five-storey structures. Beyond the canal, Groningen's outskirts were also densely populated. The southern approach was dominated by the city's large railway station and marshalling yard, as well as by an expansive, heavily defended municipal park. Another large park was situated on the western approach. Scattered throughout the city were many churches, water towers, and tall factories providing excellent observation points and firing positions. Cutting across the Canadian line of advance were also numerous canals that had to be crossed before the ring canal could be gained. Groningen was thus ideally suited for defence, and in past weeks its garrison of German troops and Dutch ss had added additional fortifications.[47]

No. 3 Troop had no sooner pierced the outskirts and passed by about eight houses than Chaulk's Sherman took a direct hit from a Panzerfaust. Twenty-three-year-old Trooper Butterworth was killed, and Chaulk severely burned. Despite intense pain, Chaulk shrugged off the efforts of his other three crewmen to evacuate him to the rear until he had pointed out to the infantry where the Panzerfaust round had come from. For his actions throughout the course of April 13, Chaulk was awarded a Military Medal, the citation mentioning that he had maintained the "impetus of the advance" while also killing fifteen Germans and wounding another twelve.[48]

Nightfall found the Rileys and Fort Garry horsemen firmly established in the southwest outskirts with two rifle companies pressing on for the bridges, but facing stiffening resistance from machine guns and snipers. The snipers were particularly "taking a comparatively [heavy] toll of our men and making everyone fighting mad. The fighting continued on into the night—fierce hand-to-hand encounters—with our men having to clear every room of four storey [apartments] and even then the snipers would come back again because our [troops] could not occupy so much space . . . As the battle unfolded . . . it became apparent there would be no easy entry into Groningen." Cabeldu ordered the Royal Regiment up on the right flank of the Rileys because it "was felt the attack should be put in on as many fronts as possible to further confuse the enemy and allow him no time to organize his [defences]."[49]

17

Waited So Long

WHILE 2ND DIVISION had closed on Groningen, to the left 3rd Canadian Infantry Division had likewise dashed towards the North Sea. On the morning of April 12, Major General Holly Keefler had saddled the leading 9th Infantry Brigade on twenty Ram gun-towers borrowed from 6th Canadian Anti-Tank Regiment. Any troops unable to squeeze aboard these ad-hoc armoured personnel carriers piled onto hulls of Sherbrooke Fusiliers tanks or into the gun tractors and trucks of 14th Field Regiment. At 0830 hours, this unusual "cavalcade" rolled north from Raalte towards Zwolle with a screen of 17th Duke of York's Royal Canadian Hussars armoured cars protecting its front and flanks.

Progress was slow at first due to roads heavily cratered by German demolitions and blown bridges that had spanned the many narrow canals and drainage ditches. Three miles north of Raalte, the advance stalled entirely before a wide stream's destroyed bridge. With engineers predicting several hours' delay constructing a crossing, Brigadier Rocky Rockingham set off in a jeep to find an alternative route. To the east he soon discovered a narrow, light bridge. After he and a couple of other men strengthened it with thick planks, a Sherbrooke tanker "very gingerly . . . eased his massive vehicle out on the span, and across the stream." Soon the entire tank squadron was across and advancing alongside the Stormont, Dundas and Glengarry Highlanders rifle companies, who had dismounted from vehicles to "scramble over [the stream] in typical infantry manner."[1]

Closing on Heino, the Glens were approached repeatedly by Dutch civilians offering confused and contradictory reports on German strength within the village. Some said two hundred, others a handful possessing no heavy weapons, while a few declared it abandoned.[2] In the end, Heino proved lightly held. From the village's church steeple, the Germans were able to direct accurate artillery and mortar fire onto the Glens as they approached. A couple of self-propelled guns also weighed in with direct fire. But despite this opposition, 'A' and 'D' Companies cleared the village at a cost of two Glens killed.[3]

By 1510, the remounted column was through Heino and bound for Zwolle. Rather than make directly for the city, Rockingham decided to give it a wide berth for the moment and cross the OverIJsselsch Canal five miles to the east in front of Dalfsen.[4] Two miles past Heino, a smaller canal—Kanaaldijk–Noord—cut across the column's route. Hoping its bridge might still be intact, the column embarked on "a wild ride" and arrived to find it, save one girder, destroyed. As the pioneers began removing explosive charges, 'B' Company "swarmed across at the double and took up position at the crossroads just beyond the Kanaal." To the northeast of the crossroads was a relatively large forest in which a growing number of Germans were mustering. The Glens' Lieutenant Colonel Neil Gemmel positioned 'C' Company in some buildings right of the road and facing the woods, with 'D' Company to the left of the road among some farm buildings positioned on either side of a raised berm. 'A' Company was directed past 'B' Company into a smaller wood, separated from the larger forest by open fields.

While the Glens established the bridgehead across the canal, the tanks and other vehicles waited for the engineers to repair the bridge. As soon as the engineers set to work, however, the Germans started shelling and mortaring the site. The fire was so accurate and disruptive the structure was quickly nicknamed "Salvo Bridge." As night drew in, the only vehicle the Glens had north of the canal was a jeep they had physically manhandled across.[5]

Because neither the Germans nor the local Dutch farmers had anticipated the Canadians using this route, all the farmhouses were still occupied, so families took shelter in the basements. One farm 'D' Company took over was owned by the Diepman family. As the Canadians advanced towards the house, the teenage son Bernard Diepman had glanced out a window and spotted the men coming across the open field. He quickly retreated to the basement. From there, he could hear artillery and mortar rounds exploding nearby.[6]

At 2045 hours, a strong German infantry force supported by several self-propelled guns or tanks—the Glens were unable to tell which in the gathering darkness—and three armoured reconnaissance cars counterattacked out of the forest. A confused battle followed, with German armour swirling across the fields and around farmhouses while infantry tried to overrun the Canadian positions. The Germans appeared to have no sense of the Glens' actual deployment, so the infantry attacked sporadically in small groups, while the armour roamed freely without coordinating with the foot soldiers. At one point the three armoured cars roared straight through 'A' Company's lines and into the farmyard where Gemmel's headquarters was situated. Met by headquarters personnel firing PIAT guns, the armoured cars beat a hasty retreat through 'B' Company's position. Passing by at high speed, one machine-gunner fired a burst that fatally hit Lieutenant George Hunter in the groin.[7]

Several German infantrymen began pitching grenades through the windows of one house, only to have the Glens inside toss them back out. A German tank firing at point-blank range set another farmhouse on fire.[8] The Germans were so close and so mixed in with his own men that Gemmel and his forward observation officer started directing artillery to within fifty yards of each company's position. The FOO directed the artillery fire, while Gemmel controlled the Cameron Highlanders of Ottawa's 4.2-inch mortars and his battalion's 3-inch mortars—the latter firing five hundred rounds alone in front of one company position in just a few minutes.

Realizing artillery and mortar fire was unlikely to stop the German armour, the battalion's second-in-command, Major J.A. Stothart, gathered an ad-hoc collection of "drivers, snipers, cooks, and batmen" and together they manhandled the 6-pounder anti-tank guns across the still unfinished bridge. The carrier crews, meanwhile, stripped the Browning 50-calibre machine guns off their vehicles and carried these over to bolster the defences.

Not until the early morning hours of April 13 did the Germans break off the action and withdraw. By 0600 hours the bridge opened, and the Highland Light Infantry passed through to lead the brigade towards Dalfsen, while the Glens would spend the day reorganizing after their stiff night action. It was soon clear that the Germans had fled. The HLI not only gained the OverIJsselsch Canal unopposed but by 0930 hours had ferried all four rifle companies across in a barge and surrounded Dalfsen. Instead of having to fight Germans, the Highlanders paraded through crowds of cheering civilians with the local brass band leading the way.[9]

Back at the Diepman farm, young Bernard spent the day watching the Canadians with fascination. During the night some soldiers, exhausted by the fighting, had slept on the main floor, while the family remained hidden in the cellar. The men had simply flopped on the floor or stretched out fully clothed atop beds and couches. One even claimed the kitchen table. In the morning, discovering the family was still there, the troops moved into the barn for the following night. On the morning of April 14, the Glens readied to join 9th Brigade's advance.

Bernard had previous experience watching German troops on the march. The occupying soldiers had always been sharply turned out—equipment gleaming, uniforms sharply pressed, boots glistening with polish. Seeing the Canadians mustering, he hurried to catch the triumphal departure of his liberators. By ones and twos the platoon of men straggled out of the barn. Most smoked cigarettes that hung almost as an afterthought from the corner of their mouths. Uniforms were rumpled, stained, and dirty. Boots scuffed, some with laces undone. The helmets of a few were pushed far back on their heads, while some cocked theirs to one side like a beret, and several others appeared to prefer them plunked on square and flat. Men shrugged into web kits and battle packs, then slung rifles onto shoulders with careless nonchalance. One gripped his Bren gun by the barrel and tossed it onto his shoulder, as Bernard's father might a shovel when he walked to the fields.

Bernard looked for an officer, waited for someone to issue a command. The entire grubby group looked the same. He could see no sign of a man with authority. Their expressions were those of labourers heading towards a job rendered routine and dull by the years. The words exchanged were like that, too—muttered curses, a soft quip that solicited laughs or grunts of agreement from the others, a comment on the weather, that this morning was fair and warm. One man sighed, nodded. Might have said "Let's go," but so softly Bernard was unsure. The Glens started walking. A group of men moving as they liked, some together, others off a bit by themselves, a few chatting, more just staring ahead. Their pace was neither hurried nor slow. It was steady. The kind of stride men as hard and lean as these Canadians could maintain all day and that would eat up the miles. Bernard watched them, not a single man looking back, until they went up the road behind a row of trees and were gone.[10]

NOT LONG AFTER the Glens disappeared from Bernard's sight, they met their transport and joined 9 CIB's rapid advance north from Dalfsen. April 14 was to prove a romp, not only for the brigade but for all of 3rd Division. The Germans had flown, and nothing but blown bridges over innumerable canals and ditches delayed the Canadians. An expected fight for Zwolle failed to materialize, 8th Brigade's Le Régiment de la Chaudière entering the city without opposition.[11]

This was in no small part due to the intrepid intervention of Private Leo Major, who had infiltrated Zwolle the previous day on his own initiative after a scout platoon patrol he was part of was shot up at a roadblock well short of the city. Despite the death of the patrol's leader and his close friend, Corporal Wally Arsenault, Major continued alone to Zwolle via a six-hour circuitous trek.[12] Once there, he managed to contact the local Dutch underground and advised its fighters to attack the German garrison from within while the Chauds struck from without. To throw the enemy off-guard, he and several resistance men burned down the Gestapo headquarters. The consequences of this act exceeded expectations, as the entire

German force fled. For his courageous leadership that day, Major was awarded a Distinguished Conduct Medal.[13]

North of Zwolle, 9 CIB led the division forward at a cracking pace. The North Nova Scotia Highlanders were on point and enjoyed a fine day of liberation without spilling blood. They rolled through Meppel, then Steenwijk (securing the air strips that the French SAS units had failed to capture earlier), and went on to Heerenveen without a shot fired. At Heerenveen, a group of Germans fired one burst from the other side of a bridge before fleeing. The bridge was undamaged, and the battalion settled in for a deserved night's rest. It had covered more than forty miles and stood within twenty miles of the division's primary objective of Leeuwarden, the capital of Friesland province. The Fries were a distinct people who, although part of Holland, had their own culture and spoken language. Friesland's NBS was one of the most organized in the country and, as the Canadians closed on the province, it had risen against the Germans—virtually liberating the capital and much of the province. But the Fries were badly outnumbered and desperately needed to be reinforced by the Canadians.

When the Glens reached Heerenveen later that afternoon, Lieutenant Colonel Gemmel was approached by two NBS members, who led him to a power station. Gemmel took the proffered telephone and found Leeuwarden's NBS leader on the line, who provided a detailed report on German dispositions throughout the province, as well as advice on what roads still had intact bridging.[14]

"There was no fighting," the North Nova Scotia Highlanders' war diarist wrote of April 14. "The enemy was retreating from northern Holland in headlong flight and the 9 Canadian Infantry Brigade was rolling through. The Dutch people were going crazy, lining the route and cheering and waving. There was orange bunting everywhere."[15]

The next morning, the brigade rushed towards Leeuwarden with the Highland Light Infantry leading. Hopes of quickly gaining the provincial capital were dashed, however, by a blown bridge just two miles from the start point. With the engineers needing all day to make repairs, Rockingham decided to try another personal reconnaissance. Meeting no opposition en route, he and the two officers who accompanied him travelled fourteen miles to Drachten, where they linked up with the resistance. Learning that the telephone lines were intact through most of the province, Rockingham had the resistance members phone every village on the way to Leeuwarden and determine which routes through the intervening maze of waterways had standing bridges. Soon Rockingham had charted out a zigzagging route, which he ordered the North Novas to follow. Rockingham and the others in his jeep also set off directly for Leeuwarden.[16]

Rockingham's brigade was not alone in trying to reach Leeuwarden on April 15. Nor was it unique in establishing a telephone link with the resistance there. The Royal Canadian Dragoons had also been put in contact by phone with the leader of the city's resistance forces. Lieutenant Colonel K.D. Lendall "was advised that the underground had risen, 5,000 strong, and after several bitter local encounters with the German garrison had assumed control of the city but they . . . asked for assistance to repel an anticipated recapture by the Germans." Lendall sent 'C' Squadron running towards the city, his regimental headquarters squadron close behind. The other squadrons were thrown out to the right with instructions to make the coast if possible.[17]

The Dragoons directed on Leeuwarden arrived at 1100 hours.[18] It was drizzling lightly on this Sunday morning, and the streets "were bare except for isolated groups of armed patriots, but, as the first giant armoured cars thundered into the main square, a suppressed air of excitement, of hope, and of a dream realized, crystallized into a flaming, roaring welcome to the liberators. Miraculously, national flags fluttered from the windows while hysterically cheering crowds thronged the streets. People wept, sang, danced, thumped the Canadian soldiers on the back and pressed upon them quantities of food and drink. Over and over again they repeated, 'We have waited so long, so long.' The armoured cars were piled high with flowers and orange bunting, extemporaneous civic and military receptions were planned and given, while far into the night the happy crowd rejoiced. This then was liberation, sincere and unrestrained and many a Canadian soldier that day, saw in the scene, the fulfillment of that inarticulate sense of right and wrong which had brought him across the seas four and five years before."[19]

Brigadier Rockingham's party arrived not long after the Dragoons and was swept up in the celebrations. But it was not until 0030 hours on the morning of April 16 that the North Novas gained the outskirts and set up guard positions for the night.[20] The Dragoons never mentioned the presence of any 9 CIB units in either its regimental histories or war diaries, and the brigade's various records likewise ignored the Dragoons.

When April 15 closed, the Dragoons had liberated not only Leeuwarden but also Dokkum and Zoutkamp on the northeast coast. In reaching these towns, the Dragoons had fought many running battles with German forces in the process of withdrawing. While their own losses were light, the enemy had suffered severely. Typical of such actions was one in which 'B' Squadron overran a party of thirty-nine Germans escaping on bicycles. When the armoured cars appeared, the Germans dismounted and surrendered. Not long after, however, Lieutenant William Thomas Buddell was shot in the shoulder by a sniper. He died the following day.[21] Buddell was an old original, who had served with the regiment since the 1943 Sicily invasion.[22] During the day, the Dragoons counted fifteen hundred prisoners taken, four hundred Germans killed—although later Dutch estimates put the number at about one hundred—and "an undisclosed number wounded." Most of the captured were handed to the NBS to lock up in local jails so that the Dragoons could keep rolling.[23]

While the Dragoons swept across the open Friesen countryside east of Leeuwarden, 8th Canadian Infantry Brigade had advanced towards the southwestern coast to cut the IJsselmeer causeway that crossed the neck of the 1,250-square-kilometre IJsselmeer. The Dutch had created this lake in 1932 by erecting a thirty-kilometre-long dam that closed the former inland sea known as the Zuider Zee. Running along the top of the dam, the causeway provided a major and more direct transportation link between Friesland and western Holland. It now provided the only remaining connection between the Twenty-Fifth Army in Fortress Holland and German forces in the northern Netherlands.

The 8 CIB battalions had enjoyed a two-day victor's journey from Zwolle, arriving at Heerenveen on the evening of April 15. In every community, cheering civilians had thronged the troops. Heerenveen turned out in force to give the Queen's Own Rifles a hero's welcome, and the "boys spent an enjoyable evening," the battalion's diarist noted. Even as Orders Groups (O Groups) were held to plan the combat operations expected for the morning, it was as if the brigade had moved into a rest area—the Knights of Columbus even arrived to show a movie.[24]

That same evening, Le Régiment de la Chaudière had pushed a patrol out to Sneek, through which the brigade had to advance to gain the causeway area, and found it largely controlled by resistance fighters.[25] When the North Shore (New Brunswick) Regiment led the way through the town in the morning, they were opposed only by cheering throngs and continued on to Bolsward, where "under the bright warm sky, the picturesque town of canals and simple buildings was a pleasant background to crowds of happy citizens."[26]

Bolsward provided a pivot point for the brigade to break up by battalions for its drive to the sea, with the Chauds bound for Woudsend (having left the brigade at Sneek), the North Shores towards the port of Makkum, and the QOR towards Wons and the causeway itself. Artillery support was provided by 13th Field Regiment, which had individual batteries tagging along within gun range of the infantry. Tanks from the Sherbrooke Fusiliers also backed up the infantry with sections of the Cameron Highlanders of Ottawa (MG) providing heavy mortar and machine-gun support.

The Chauds and North Shores encountered nothing more than demoralized pockets of Germans, who either scattered or surrendered when fired upon. Action over the following couple of days remained light and was delayed more by destroyed bridges than by German opposition.

Not the case for the Queen's Own. At first things had looked promising, the carrier platoon almost reaching Wons before encountering a roadblock. When the carriers rolled to a halt to look over the situation, they were raked by fire from behind the roadblock and from the village itself. Two of the carriers were knocked out by a 20-millimetre anti-aircraft gun, and several men were killed or wounded. The platoon might well have been wiped out had not

'B' Company made a timely arrival and separated into platoons for the assault on both the roadblock and Wons. By 1330 hours, both objectives were taken. Six Germans were taken prisoner and the 20-millimetre gun's crew killed.[27]

'A' Company passed to the lead with orders to gain the causeway, two miles beyond. The only protected route forward through the open fields and past small farms was along a raised dyke, which was about thirty feet wide with a road in the centre lined on both sides by mature poplars. The dyke was bordered on either side by a water-filled ditch. The company moved up the road until it was a half-mile from the entrance to the causeway. Ahead was a narrow stone bridge and behind it some buildings, around which German troops were visible. Major J.P. Secord quickly directed No. 9 Platoon down into the ditch left of the dyke and No. 7 Platoon into the one to the right. Using this cover, the leading platoons moved towards the enemy, while one of the battalion's Wasps rushed up and shot flame over the bridge towards the German positions. When its fuel was exhausted, the carrier whirled about and headed to the rear.

For once the Wasp was completely ineffective, only serving to stir up a hornet's nest of enemy fire. Swarms of rounds from machine-gun, small-arms, and several quick-firing 20-millimetre anti-aircraft guns snapped around the advancing infantry, and No. 9 Platoon went to ground among the poplars and in the ditch.

Lieutenant Colonel Steve Lett, meanwhile, had sent the company reinforcements in the form of one of the surviving carriers with six men aboard. The carrier roared towards the bridge with its machine gun blazing, only to be hit by a stream of 20-millimetre gunfire that killed all the men aboard. Corporal Alexander Cockburn, a Juno Beach veteran, had commanded the carrier. Also killed were Privates F.R. Shepherd, W.J. Jackson, H.W. White, B.B. Pennell, and G.W. Ouderkirk.

Moving along the tree line to the left of the road and well ahead of the wrecked carrier, Company Sergeant Major Charlie Martin was aware that Secord had responded to this unexpectedly determined resistance by laying on supporting fire from the artillery and Cameron's mortars. He also mistakenly thought that No. 8 Platoon was down in the ditch right of the dyke and ahead of his position. Martin should have been down in one of the ditches rather than on top of the dyke, but he was dogged by a bad chest cold and wanted to avoid the icy water. For added warmth, he had stuffed a thick piece of red flannel into the front of his tunic. The Germans ahead, Martin figured, were more Hitler Youth, fanatical but also poorly trained. When the artillery came down, he expected 'A' Company to quickly sort them out.

Even as the artillery and mortar fire began working over the German positions behind the bridge, Martin moved to cross it. The only weapon he carried was a .38-calibre revolver, tucked into the front of his belt. He was the CSM, and despite the many firefights he had led since landing on Juno Beach, Martin had planned to stay back this day. But suddenly he was right out there on point, and the 20-millimetre guns were cracking shells all around him that sent shrapnel and bits of brick and stone flying in every direction. Right there to his left was also a young German with a Schmeisser, burning off a burst that ripped up his right leg, shattered the binoculars dangling from his neck onto his chest, and proceeded to chew up his left arm. Grabbing his revolver even as he was falling backwards, Martin fired a single shot from the waist that caught the German cleanly above the bridge of the nose.

He was dimly aware of No. 7 Platoon dashing past just as the artillery lifted and then stretcher bearer Slim Cole leaning over him, crying. Martin's tunic had been shredded, exposing the mass of red flannel that Cole mistook for a bloody, gaping chest wound. Cole started injecting Martin with morphine as the CSM whispered, "Please let me die in peace." When Martin asked for some water, Cole gave him a sip from a canteen containing pure rum. Raising his head, Martin could see white flags waving from the various buildings, around which the smoke from exploding shells still drifted. No. 7 Platoon was rounding up prisoners. Cole was still weeping. Major Secord crouched down and gave Martin a hug. "Thanks, Charlie, for everything," he said in a choked voice, and then was away to oversee the surrender. Martin thought from all the sadness that he must be a goner. It was a feeling reinforced at the Regimental Aid

Post, where the battalion padre also broke into tears as the doctors dressed Martin's wounds with hurried efficiency.

An ambulance soon whisked him to the rear, going so fast it ran into a ditch, and many minutes were lost until it was towed out and on the way again. At the hospital, Martin's leg wounds started to bleed furiously, and he was dragged into emergency surgery. Martin fell unconscious. He would not awaken until May 8.[28]

The Queen's Own, meanwhile, had finally gained the entrance to the causeway at 1030 hours on April 18, when resistance collapsed.[29] This ended 8th Brigade's clearing of Friesland. Along with the rest of 3rd Division, its regiments embarked on a short but welcome period of guarding the ground won.

18

Piece of Cake

WHEN II CANADIAN Corps's divisions had begun their drive through Holland and western Germany, the attached 1st Infantry Division had remained at the IJssel River to prepare for Operation Cannonshot—the precursor to any 1 Canadian Corps advance into western Holland to liberate the great cities there. The selected crossing site was in front of the village of Gorssel, midway between Zutphen and Deventer. Here the river followed a wide westward dog-leg, and Major General Harry Foster planned to gain the opposite shore square in the middle of this natural salient that thrust into Twenty-Fifth Army's front line. Because the launching sites and approaches were exposed to German observation, all sides of the dog-leg would be masked by a giant smokescreen created by a heavy bombardment of smoke shells and deployment of many mobile generators. Crossing in Buffaloes, 2nd Canadian Infantry Brigade would establish the beachhead with the Seaforth Highlanders of Canada on the left, the Princess Patricia's Canadian Light Infantry the right, and the Loyal Edmonton Regiment staying back in reserve. The Shermans of 1st Hussars Regiment's 'A' Squadron would be rafted into the beachhead as soon as possible.[1]

In the next phase, 1st Canadian Infantry Brigade, supported by the rest of the 1st Hussars, would advance on Apeldoorn. The 3rd Canadian Infantry Brigade would come up on the left and make for the Apeldoorn Canal running south from the city. Once Apeldoorn fell, Cannonshot would be concluded, and the division would return to 1 Canadian Corps command for whatever operations westward followed.[2]

"It's a clever, well-thought-out plan," PPCLI Captain Syd Frost concluded. "Whatever harsh words I've had for generals and the staff in the past, I've got to admit they occasionally come up with some bright ideas."[3] Frost was impressed that the plans gave him time to thoroughly reconnoitre the assigned river crossing site and study the battalion plan in detail. "It was such a sensible way to go to war compared to the Italian campaign, where we had been thrown into river crossings so many times with no chance for any recce or planning. The more I saw of the orderly, deliberate way the [First] Canadian Army went about its tasks, the more I liked doing business with them."[4]

What Frost disliked was the selected crossing site, although he admitted it was likely as good as any possible. From a covering wood the battalion's officers spent hours studying the ground. With binoculars, Frost could see his company objective—"a group of houses about 1,000 yards from the crossing place, but they were sheltered by a dyke that could mean real trouble. The river itself seemed about 100 yards wide, muddy and sluggish. From our vantage point to the near bank of the dyke, the area was as flat as a billiard table and no cover was available."

Turning to Major J.M.D. Jones, whose 'C' Company would be on the left of Frost's 'D' Company, he asked, "Does this remind you of anything we've seen before?"

"Christ, it's the Italian plains all over again," Jones responded.

"Yeah, but maybe this will be our last river."

"It sure as hell will be, if we don't have lots of smoke and reach those dykes *molto pronto.*"

"Hell for leather with two platoons to the dyke while the third lay down covering fire," the two officers decided. Then Frost bet Jones a bottle of whisky his company gained the dyke first.

On April 9, 2 CIB moved to its assembly area about two miles directly east of the crossing site and married up with the Buffalo crews from 4th Royal Tank Regiment. Each company was allotted four, one for each rifle platoon and another to carry the company headquarters section. The PPCLI and Seaforths had recently been reinforced and the companies were almost at full strength—a rare occurrence in Italy—with one hundred men each, just short of the normal 110. Frost liked the fact Buffaloes were armoured, unlike the amphibious trucks (DUKWs) they had sometimes used in Italy. When one crewman said they'd put him on the other shore dry-footed, Frost was dubious. "Piece of cake, old chap," the man assured him.[5]

AT 1400 HOURS on April 11, the PPCLI and Seaforths loaded into the Buffaloes. The Seaforth plan mirrored that of the PPCLI, with two companies making the initial crossing. Once ashore, 'D' Company on the left and 'B' Company the right would advance about seven hundred yards from the river. When all the Seaforths were across the IJssel, 'C' would deepen the advance westward while 'B' Company swung north to tie in with the PPCLI. Once this phase was complete, 'C', 'B', and 'D' Companies would advance on the village of Wilp.[6] The PPCLI would also make for Wilp via a road running to it from the river.

The Seaforth Buffaloes began rumbling towards the IJssel at 1500 hours, a journey that struck 'C' Company's diarist as surreal. Here were the Seaforths loaded with weapons and riding in Buffaloes mounting heavy machine guns on the fronts. In the distance, near the river, the sound of artillery shells exploding could be heard. And yet, "we passed neat houses with laundry drying in the bright sunshine. On the east side of the river, it never looked like a war or an attack was in progress. People were sitting in their gardens and everything seemed awfully peaceful."[7]

As a young platoon leader, Frost had suffered a horrific facial wound in southern Italy, undergone months of painful reconstruction, and returned to the PPCLI in time for the finale of the Gothic Line battle. Recovering from the wound had put him behind the promotion curve, so only now was he to lead a company into combat. "The Buffaloes roar into life and fill the woods with their heavy fumes. I run back to my vehicle and hop on the ramp just as it is pulled up... The great beasts snort and lurch toward the river. God, it feels good to be leading my company into action at last!

"I look at my watch—1530 hours. In 30 minutes the smoke screen will start. It's a fine day for smoke, just a light breeze. We meet Charlie Company Buffaloes. I wave at Maj. Jones . . . We exchange V signs but I am not sure whether his gesture is Churchillian or rude.

"Ten minutes to smoke—five minutes. We emerge from the woods. The artillery opens up. Shells whine over our heads and land on the far bank of the river. Smoke drifts across the whole front, completely shielding us from enemy observation . . . Now we are churning along the flats. The river is about 1,000 yards away. The artillery starts to fire HE [high explosive]. We can't see the targets, but the tremendous explosions tell us Jerry is getting a pasting."

At 1630 hours, Frost's Buffalo hit the water "without missing a stroke. The nose dips down and then bobs up. The thing actually floats! More important it also swims.

"In minutes we are across the river. The craft has trouble negotiating the bank. I indicate to the driver to stay in the water. We can jump to the bank. He is happy. The lower the Buffalo, the smaller the target.

"The enemy has hardly reacted to our attack. Only a few scattered shells fall. Once again, he's been faked right out of his drawers . . . We rush over the nose of the vehicle, fan out, and hit the ground. Now the smoke starts to thin out. We have to get our tails up. [Company Sergeant Major M.] Milko charges over . . . and urges the men forward. They don't really need any urging as now we are getting small arms fire from Ness [buildings that are the company's objective]. But sergeant majors are supposed to give men hell— 'Come on, Dog Company, move it, move it!' he yells. 'Now's the time to earn your King's shilling.'"

Leading the charge, Lieutenant Allan McKinnon's No. 17 Platoon reached the dyke and found it unoccupied. But the fire coming from the houses at Ness was thickening. Frost could also see a tank. This was going to be tough after all.[8]

McKinnon's platoon was 150 yards from the houses and pinned down by the infantry's small-arms fire and the tank's raking machine gun. The platoon's PIAT gunner loosed his three 2.5-pound bombs without effect—the launcher only having an effective range of one hundred yards. McKinnon sent a runner back to get more rounds from the other platoons, his men hunkered down to avoid the incoming fire, and the situation seemed stalemated. Not a stitch of cover offered itself for Frost to advance another platoon beyond the dyke to get inside PIAT range. Frost was still looking for a solution when Lance Sergeant Thomas Hanberry grabbed a PIAT and a single round and headed out alone.[9]

Crawling through the short pasture grass from one shallow ditch to another, Hanberry closed undetected to within fifty yards of the tank. To get a clear shot, Hanberry rolled into the open, propped the PIAT on its bipod, braced the butt hard into his shoulder, carefully sighted on the tank, took a long breath, and, with a slow exhalation, steadily depressed the heavy trigger for the one-tenth of a second it took to fire the charge. The bomb whistled across the fifty yards and knocked the tank out of action.

The moment the tank was silenced, No. 17 Platoon charged, and gained the buildings with only one man being wounded. Hanberry's solo assault earned a Military Medal.[10] Frost reported 'D' Company "snug" inside Ness at 1720 hours, thirty-seven minutes behind 'C' Company. Frost had lost the bet. "Guess you're out one bottle of whiskey," his amused wireless signaller allowed.[11]

In the Seaforth's sector, 'B' Company's signaller, Private A.J. McKay, had piled out of a Buffalo into the mud right beside Major John Bassett. "First we stood quite amazed at what to do for machine-gun fire from houses ahead of us was whistling by our heads and I recall seeing turf being ripped with grass roots upturned only a few feet away." The Buffalo crews were burning off bursts of heavy machine-gun fire to cover the Seaforths. "As though we were both hit by the same thought we [sprinted] directly towards the enemy positions. They must have contracted 'buck fever.'" As McKay fired his Sten through a window, "three Germans came out a side door. One kid was in a shed where I sent three rounds for him to think about . . . I took the prisoners aside to the next house, about twenty yards away . . . There I found a few company personnel, one signaller and a larger group of prisoners."[12]

By 1800 hours, both battalions were complete across the IJssel and expanding the beachhead towards Wilp, despite increasingly heavy artillery and mortar fire from positions around the village. At midnight, the two battalions were about a mile west of the river. German prisoners totalled 122, and one tank and an anti-tank gun had been destroyed.[13] Canadian casualties had been surprisingly light and not all the result of enemy fire. The Seaforth's 'C' Company reported Private Bela Terepocki "killed—by our own artillery. He was a new member of our [company] and it was his first battle."[14]

The intensity of fire seriously hampered engineering efforts to bring bridging equipment forward, but by 2115 hours a small bridge was half built and several smaller ferries were operational, with one under construction that would be capable of carrying tanks. But the engineers were paying a price in casualties—seven 1st Field Company sappers, one 3rd Field Company officer and three sappers, and one 4th Field Company sapper. The bridge opened at 2315 hours, but not until 0300 hours of April 12 was the raft capable of ferrying tanks operational.[15]

Early morning in the Seaforth's sector was fairly quiet, although the continuing shellfire claimed the life of the battalion's second-in-command, Major Haworth Glendinning. The popular officer and DSO holder had just returned two days earlier from leave in England and had been married only a week. At dawn, the Seaforths recorded their casualties for the assault as totalling one officer (Glendinning) and four men killed. Two other officers and sixteen other ranks had been wounded.[16]

The PPCLI, meanwhile, had closed on Wilp with 'B' Company assigned the job of clearing it. Captain Egan Chambers and his men moved towards the graceful brick church, which with its tall spire, soaring arched windows, and tall buttresses dominated the village's few other buildings, when "rattles and rumbles were heard in the darkness ahead." Out front, Lieutenant E.R. Berryman led No. 10 Platoon in a mad dash to gain the tree-shrouded churchyard. 'B' Company just managed to wriggle into firing positions around the church before three tanks appeared with a large force of German infantry marching along behind as if on parade. Chambers waited until the column had passed, and then his men cut into its rear at a range of a few yards. Catching most of the infantry in a fierce melee, 'B' Company quickly took eighty prisoners before the rest of the column—seemingly uninterested in the battle to their rear—melted into the darkness and continued along the road leading to the IJssel. 'B' Company "braceleted the road with festoons of 75 [anti-tank] grenades and awaited the return of the raiders."[17]

Directly in front of the German column, Frost's 'D' Company frantically prepared to meet the tanks head on. Lieutenant Harvey Beardmore's No. 18 Platoon had two PIAT gunners lying in ambush. It seemed a pathetically insufficient response, but Frost's attempts to raise battalion headquarters on the wireless failed, and he remembered that it would be hours before any anti-tank guns or armour were over the IJssel. The infantry would have to meet the tanks alone. Frost was in a farmhouse behind Beardmore's position, still hunkered over the No. 18 wireless set and trying to get through to battalion when a runner burst in. "Three tanks coming down the road," he yelled, just as a shell blew the lean-to shed beside the house to bits. Another shell exploded in the front yard. Frost wished he were back in Italy. Houses there could take a beating from artillery and tank fire, but Frost had noticed that Dutch houses tended to disintegrate. Nearby, a PIAT fired, Bren guns chugged out their slow, steady bursts, a shell crashed into the front of the house, and from upstairs a man shouted, "They're coming at us!" Frost drew his pistol and turned from the wireless just as the door burst open and five Germans lunged in. Before Frost could respond, his signaller emptied his Sten gun in their direction and all the men went down "writhing on the floor in agony."

Outside, the tanks and surviving infantry never paused, just shot their way through 'D' Company and continued for the bridgehead— obviously intent on eliminating the bridge and ferry operations. Alerted by the two previous firefights, 'A' Company was waiting, and the night exploded "in a fearful roar of shells, PIAT bombs, Schmeissers, mortars, Brens and Stens."

Suddenly, the tanks reappeared at 'D' Company's position, "firing wildly in all directions." Lieutenant Bert Bolton's No. 16 Platoon's PIAT gunner fired a bomb, and "a great explosion rents the night air and red flames shoot into the sky." The two surviving tanks spun about and fled back the other way, which only returned them to 'A' Company's lines, where they were quickly knocked out by PIAT bombs. After that, the infantry was easily wiped out.[18]

BY DAWN, 1ST Canadian Infantry Brigade began entering the bridgehead, the 48th Highlanders of Canada crossing the IJssel in
Buffaloes, while the 1st Hussars fed the Shermans of 'A' Squadron
over in rafts. Troops from this squadron quickly linked up with
2 CIB's battalions and assisted in mopping up the last remnants of
German resistance, and the bridgehead was declared secure at 0900
hours. The buildup continued throughout the morning until, at 1015
hours, 1 CIB advanced towards Apeldoorn with the 48th Highlanders leading, followed by the Royal Canadian Regiment and then the
Hastings and Prince Edward Regiment. The Highlanders were supported by the 1st Hussars' 'B' Squadron.[19]

Rather than head due west along lesser roads towards Apeldoorn,
Lieutenant Colonel Don Mackenzie directed his battalion northward
on a road leading to the villages of Steenenkamer and de Hoven.
This would put the Highlanders astride the major highway running
from Deventer to Apeldoorn. Mackenzie sent 'A' Company around
the southern side of Wilp and 'B' Company around its northern
flank. Once past the village, the two companies would advance, with
'A' Company about three hundred yards west of the road and 'B' Company the same distance to its east. 'A' Company's objective was a
crossroads about a mile and a half distant and just south of Steenenkamer, while 'B' Company's was to clear a wood next to this junction.
Mackenzie held his other two companies back as a reserve.[20]

More than at any time before, the thirty-year-old Mackenzie felt
burdened by the responsibility of sending men into battle. Unable to
sleep the previous night, he had asked the battalion's intelligence
officer, Lieutenant Jack Pickering, to sit with him. Mackenzie had
seemed deeply disturbed and repeatedly mentioned that this might
be the last battle the Highlanders fought. The inevitability of casualties, "just at the end," haunted him.[21]

The advance followed behind a heavy artillery barrage. Captain
Mike George's 'B' Company was divided, with a platoon either side of
an eight-foot dyke that led straight to the woods. George's third platoon trailed behind a Sherman that lumbered slowly along the top of
the dyke to keep pace with the forward platoons. Completely exposed,
the tank drew the full attention of the Germans in the woods. They
blasted it with machine-gun and mortar rounds, while a self-

propelled gun firing from the woods scored a couple of hits that failed to penetrate the armour. Preoccupied with the tank, the Germans only realized the presence of the infantry when the company stormed into the woods and drove them out.

Major George Beal's 'A' Company had a tougher time, coming under heavy fire just short of the intersection and being pinned down shortly before 1400 hours. Beal counted six machine guns and three self-propelled guns firing on the leading sections as he crawled across two hundred yards of open ground to join them. First pinpointing the SP guns, Beal radioed the coordinates back to 2nd Canadian Field Regiment's FOO, Major Con Harrington, at Mackenzie's tactical headquarters, and a mix of high-explosive and smoke shells smothered their positions. With the armour blinded, 'A' Company rushed forward and silenced the machine guns.[22]

The fact that Beal had been able to communicate with the battalion tactical headquarters made a difference, but generally the wireless link proved "ragged." Mackenzie's frayed nerves noticeably worsened when the companies were out of contact. He paced back and forth across the floor of a house outside Wilp, growing increasingly agitated. Finally, when Beal reported meeting the machine guns and SPGs, Mackenzie decided to get closer to the action. At 1445 hours, Mackenzie and Pickering set out by jeep to find a location near the road intersection for his tactical headquarters.

En route the two officers met a troop of tanks being shelled and found Captain Bill Leadbeater, the 1st Hussars' liaison officer, there. Pickering was in a dither, wanting to get Mackenzie away from the shelling. But Mackenzie asked Leadbeater if he could establish contact with his tanks that were helping the two forward companies. He stood next to the Shermans while the officer worked the wireless inside the troop leader's tank. Mackenzie began consulting his map, ready to situate the companies when Leadbeater provided the tank coordinates. Suddenly, precisely at 1500 hours, a shell exploded next to Mackenzie and Pickering. Stunned by the explosion and badly wounded in his left arm, Pickering rolled onto his hands and knees. Staring through the drifting smoke and bits of earth spattering back to earth, Pickering saw Mackenzie lying motionless. When he crawled over, Mackenzie looked up at him and said, "See where I'm

hit, Jack." Pickering saw no wound, but in seconds Mackenzie died—
the result of massive internal injuries caused by concussive force.[23]

Mackenzie's death might have thrown the 48th's attack into disarray, but fortuitously the battalion second-in-command, Major Jim
Counsell, had arrived at tactical headquarters just before the lieutenant colonel went forward. Counsell immediately assumed command
and ordered 'D' Company to pass through the forward companies to
clear the northwestern part of de Hoven, while 'C' Company swept
the Germans out of Steenenkamer. Both companies were supported
by tanks, which made short work of German machine-gun positions
in the villages. At de Hoven, 'D' Company set up amid some houses
that sheltered it from sporadic shellfire, while Captain Gus Angus and
his platoon commanders studied the open ground between the buildings and the village proper. Angus figured the village's centre lightly
held, while Lieutenant Morley Hunter asserted that it was "loaded."
Rather than throw a lot of men out in the open, the officers decided on
a fighting patrol formed by Lieutenant R.L. "Tubby" Graham and six
volunteers, all armed with Sten guns. A Sherman tank would accompany the men, and the company's Bren gunners would provide
covering fire from the upper floors of the houses. Two of the men
were wounded during the dash across the open field, but within five
minutes the survivors and the tank were advancing along the main
street with the tank having destroyed four machine-gun positions.
The rest of 'D' Company caught up and closed on a last stubborn German outpost near the railway. Again the tank cleared up the
opposition, hammering the position with main-gun fire that killed
three of nine defenders, convinced three others to surrender, and
prompted the last three to take flight. At 1630 hours, both 'C' and 'D'
Companies had gained their objectives.[24]

An hour later, brigade ordered Counsell to push the battalion on
to the village of Twello, about a mile west and on the road leading
from Deventer to Apeldoorn, while the Royal Canadian Regiment
came up alongside the 48th's left flank to widen out the advance.
Counsell passed 'A' and 'B' Companies to the front. Each company
had a troop of tanks in support. While 'A' Company went forward on
the road, 'B' followed a paralleling railway track.[25] The RCR, mean-

while, advanced with 'B' and 'C' Companies forward—moving along local farm roads.

No sooner had the Highlanders set out than both companies met heavy machine-gun fire from emplacements in houses alongside both the tracks and road. The approach to Twello was quite built up, which made the tankers wary. It was also getting near dusk, when things would begin tilting in favour of the defence, so 'B' Company and the troop of Hussars set up a charge, with two platoons each mounted on a tank and the third following behind on the run. Out front, the troop commander's tank remained unencumbered by infantry in order to allow its main gun and machine guns to be fired unhindered.

The tanks lunged forward at top speed, the Highlanders clinging to whatever hand or footholds they could find. Some fell off, rolling desperately to avoid the tracks, then scrambling to join the third platoon as it panted up. Any German pockets of resistance short of the town were bypassed, the fire from these fortunately flying harmlessly over the heads of the completely exposed and helpless Highlanders. In short order the force gained Twello. "The Highlanders disembarked in a scrambling rush, and raced down the main street in belligerent squads. The startled Germans began running as they saw their attackers were backed by tanks." By nightfall, the village was secure.[26]

On the Highlanders' left flank, the RCR encountered only scant resistance during its paralleling advance. 'B' Company came to a fortified house but quickly killed several of its defenders and took a dozen prisoners. Other Germans, hiding in woods or farm buildings, were easily eliminated at the cost of a single casualty. The day's advance, noted the regiment's historian, "had been less war than beating a preserve, with stray birds apt to be flushed anywhere."

The two companies had expected a stop once they reached Twello, but midnight brought orders to keep marching cross-country while the tanks followed by a roundabout road route. "It was heavily cultivated land with a profusion of small streams; 'C' Company forded eleven of them, some with water breast high. Penny packets of prisoners were plentiful, with the reserve companies picking up almost as many as the forward companies. Sometimes small groups elected to fight . . . a particularly obstinate handful of Germans held up 'B' Company and 'C' Company found itself alone, with snipers on three sides. At 0145 hours on April 13, the tanks arrived and eased the situation; they also brought welcome boxes of food. Two hours later the forward companies called it a day . . . [they] were more than four miles beyond the IJssel, or almost halfway to Apeldoorn."[27]

WHILE 1ST DIVISION had been advancing towards Apeldoorn, the 49th (West Riding) Division had attacked Arnhem, at 2240 hours on April 12. Originally, this assault was to have been made by crossing the Neder Rijn out of the Nijmegen Island, but realizing the river was entirely overlooked by high ground on the northern bank, Lieutenant General Foulkes had directed the British division to force a crossing of the IJssel to the city's east. This was not a popular decision with the British divisional staff, which had devised the earlier scheme and thought Foulkes incapable of making up his mind. When this griping reached the ears of Brigadier C.A. Campbell, 1 Canadian Corps's chief engineer, he snapped back tersely that in Italy, the Canadians had crossed "more rivers than they've had hot breakfasts."[28]

Concerns about the change in plan proved baseless. The 49th's 56th Brigade crossed over unmolested in Buffaloes under cover of a shatteringly heavy artillery barrage that had been preceded by almost continuous Typhoon and Spitfire strafing of the city and its approaches from early afternoon to nightfall. By morning, the brigade had penetrated Arnhem's southeastern outskirts, repulsed a half-hearted counterattack, and firmly controlled a bridgehead filling rapidly with troops, armour, and artillery. Supporting the division were Ontario Regiment tanks, whose war diarist observed that the "enemy nowhere showed much willingness to fight."[29]

The threat of machine-gun positions and snipers in the city's badly battered buildings required the infantry to carefully clear each structure. Two 'C' Squadron tank troops ran into a nasty trap when a cleverly situated anti-tank gun covering an intersection near a factory and the main railway opened fire. While one troop kept the gunners preoccupied with counter fire, the other dodged around the corner and knocked the gun out from behind. On the morning of

April 14, a tank troop under Lieutenant J. Cameron accompanied the British in clearing the city centre through to the northern outskirts, "where his troop spent the day taking a reckless toll of the enemy. The Hun was completely confused and in spite of his numbers and equipment, which included unbelievable numbers of [Panzerfausts] and Anti-Tank guns, he was unable to do anything but give up." One troop of tanks in the southeast corner of the city took two hundred prisoners alone. When three German light tanks appeared in front of another troop, they waddled across the Canadian gun sights like ducks in a shooting gallery. "The first was brewed up; the second was knocked out, and the third gave up." By the end of the day, Arnhem was clear.[30]

At 1 Canadian Corps headquarters, meanwhile, April 13 had been a day for celebration due to the transfer of 1st Division back from 11 Canadian Corps control. Foulkes now had three divisions under command—the 49th, 5th Canadian Armoured, and 1st Division.

The last division's advance towards Apeldoorn continued to progress well. A major transportation hub for the area, Apeldoorn lay at the northern tip of an area of high ground that extended up from Arnhem with two good roads running south from it through this area. Foulkes considered these roads of primary importance to clearing these heights. The Apeldoorn Canal, however, barred easy access to the city and provided an ideal defensive position for the Germans.[31]

Major General Harry Foster wanted to avoid a direct assault across the canal into the city. "It was a friendly city [with a normal population of 72,000], filled with refugees, and I was not prepared to use [artillery] on it. The plot was to isolate the city, by having [1 CIB] face up to it and thus keep the enemy garrison there occupied, and by putting [3rd Canadian Infantry Brigade] across the canal south of Apeldoorn, thus coming in from the rear."[32]

Accordingly, on the morning of April 13, the Hastings and Prince Edward Regiment passed through the 48th Highlanders and took over that axis of 1 CIB's advance towards the canal, while the RCR continued pushing forward on the left flank. Farther to the left, 3 CIB advanced at 1050 hours with the Carleton and York Regiment on the right and the West Nova Scotia Regiment the left. The Royal 22e Regiment provided the reserve.

Supported by the 1st Hussars' 'A' Squadron, the Hasty Ps sent a patrol from 'C' Company mounted on carriers to seize a crossroads about a mile west of Twello. After a short fight, the crossroads was secured, and when the rest of 'C' Company and the tanks caught up, the pace of advance quickened. By noon, the battalion had taken a wood just to the east of Teuge and advanced about two miles from Twello. Along the way, sixty prisoners were swept up and the regiment "had put the fear of the Lord into the Hun in this area," wrote the battalion's war diarist.

To the left, the RCR advance had been delayed by German snipers, who had infiltrated the entire battalion front. 'A' Company spent precious time rounding up eleven prisoners, but the infantrymen were almost outdone by the battalion's cooks, who took it upon themselves to go after snipers near the headquarters and brought back nine prisoners. 'A' and 'D' Companies then headed for the canal at 0800 hours. 'D' Company was drawn into a stiff fight for a group of fortified buildings that took two hours to win, five Germans being killed before the remaining thirty-two surrendered. By noon, 'D' Company had caught up to 'A' Company—which had the surprising good fortune to be able to liberate a hospital housing 789 wounded Allied POWs. One of the two Germans guarding the prisoners, however, shot and wounded one Royal Canadian before they were eliminated.[33]

The initial brigade plan had not foreseen driving all the way to the canal, but with both battalions so close, they were ordered at 1545 hours to go nonstop for it. The Hasty Ps mounted 'A' and 'D' Companies on the tanks and rolled forward, "shooting up small packets of enemy as they advanced," but mostly rushing past and leaving the two reserve companies to mop up. "There was a steady stream of prisoners . . . at this time, the total bag for the day was 242." The battalion's advance was not as one-sided as its war diarist made it sound, for one officer and twenty-three men were wounded and five other ranks lost their lives.[34]

The RCR enjoyed a similarly rapid advance, closing up on the canal at 2100 hours.[35] Arriving three hours later, the Hasty Ps spent the pre-dawn hours of April 14 clearing Germans out of housing on its east bank. Learning that a bridge nearby still stood, 'D' Company hurried to the site, only to have it blow up as they were fifty yards away.

When the bridge was blown, Lieutenant Colonel G.E.B. Renison ordered 'D' Company to establish a solid position facing the wreckage and requested that engineers come forward with bridging material. No sooner had an engineering officer come forward to survey for a possible crossing site than he was wounded by enemy fire. Then, late in the afternoon, orders from brigade advised the Hasty Ps to sit tight. Instead, the 48th Highlanders would pass through and make a frontal assault on Apeldoorn with the RCR alongside.[36]

Left of 1 CIB, the easterners of 3 CIB had expected clear sailing to the canal for both the New Brunswick–based Carleton and York Regiment and the West Nova Scotia Regiment. While this proved largely true for the latter, the Carletons met heavy resistance and had to win the ground piece by piece. 'D' Company with the 1st Hussars' No. 2 Squadron in support suffered many casualties among the infantry and considerable damage to the tanks.[37] 'D' Company's No. 17 Platoon had two men wounded and its commander, Lieutenant Richard Savage, killed. Quickly taking over, Sergeant James Scott led the platoon forward to overrun the main enemy position, killing two Germans and taking eight prisoners.

After that, the company slogged through a seemingly endless string of enemy strongpoints until 'B' Company passed to the front in the mid-afternoon and continued the grinding advance. Passing by the village of Achterhoek, the company came under heavy fire from a group of buildings clustered around a solidly built schoolhouse. Realizing the school was the key position, Acting Corporal John Senechal crawled to within a few yards of it and then dashed inside. He soon emerged with twelve prisoners, who surrendered three machine guns and six Panzerfausts. For singlehandedly eliminating this position, Senechal received a Military Medal.[38] Pushing on through the night, the battalion had gained its objective west of Achterhoek by 0700 hours and secured a start line for the Royal 22e Regiment to pass through and continue the advance. 'B' Company had suffered one man killed and eight wounded, Lieutenant Wilfred Brosseau being among the injured.[39]

The West Novas had been hampered more by the large numbers of buildings along their route that had to be searched before being passed by. Still, they met sufficient opposition that the battalion reported one man killed and fourteen wounded during the course of the day. "The enemy had shown no inclination to make a determined stand and during the day 51 prisoners were taken . . . The general tactics of the enemy were a steady withdrawal covered by sniper and Self-Propelled Gun fire whose slowing up progress was very effective." By nightfall, the West Novas were on their objective and awaiting arrival of the Carletons.[40]

19

Jerry Is Running

O N THE EVENING of April 13–14, Lieutenant General Charles Foulkes realized the 49th (West Riding) Division assault on Arnhem had created an opportunity to exploit. If the 49th advanced north along the IJssel River road at the same time as 1st Canadian Infantry Division drove southward, he could clear the ground across from Zutphen. This would provide an ideal bridging site linking the west bank to a network of roads that converged on the city from all points of the compass.

Although Major General Harry Foster agreed that the bridge would serve 1 Canadian Corps well, he disliked adding a southward advance to his agenda. His 1st and 3rd brigades fully committed to seizing Apeldoorn, Foster must assign the task to 2nd Brigade—returning a unit to action that had already "done enough by making the assault crossing and [establishing the bridgehead.]"

The scheme left his division "facing three ways at once." On the right, 1 CIB—with an exposed north flank—stood before Apeldoorn, 3 CIB was closing on the canal with orders to get behind the city, and now 2 CIB must march south.[1] Facing so many equally urgent demands, Foster was heartened by Dutch underground reports that the Germans were withdrawing from the city and partisans controlled a major bridge over the canal. Three Royal Canadian

Regiment scouts and two partisans confirmed that the bridge still stood, but not whether it was in Dutch hands.

Winning the bridge, Foster decided, "necessitated the immediate rushing of the town."[2] A hurried fire program using artillery, 4.2-inch mortars, and heavy machine guns created sufficient racket to cover the sounds of two 1st Hussars troops from 'C' Squadron running towards the bridge. Ten tanks formed for the attack, with the RCR's 'C' Company saddled on eight while the two remaining Shermans were "to cross the [bridge] and disrupt the enemy." Instructions from the RCR's Lieutenant Colonel William Reid cautioned that 'C' Company "was NOT to kick off... until word had been sent back by the two [forward] tanks that the [bridge] was not blown and they were over."[3]

At 0300 hours, the two tanks charged forward at top speed in "a dashing attempt."[4] Smashing through a log roadblock 2,500 feet short of the bridge, the tankers saw that a second roadblock lay ahead. Hoping to smash it like the first, the troop leader slammed into what turned out to be a reinforced concrete construction.[5] The Sherman bounced off like a tennis ball, was hit by several Panzerfaust rounds, and exploded in flames. Spinning around, the second tank tried to flee but was also set alight. Spewing flames, it collided with the first tank bearing infantry, and several men from 'C' Company were badly injured.[6]

Rapid investment of Apeldoorn scotched, April 14 turned into a day "of slow progress." When the RCR convened an O Group at 1730 close to the canal, a self-propelled gun on the river's east side punched a round through the building's wall. Although the shell failed to explode, it "smashed some metal furnishings which flew in all directions."[7] Captain Frederick Sims was killed. Sims had landed in Sicily, survived more than twenty months of combat, and would be the battalion's last fatal casualty.[8]

South of 1st Brigade, 3 CIB had plodded through the same kinds of delaying actions met the previous day. By day's end, the Royal 22e Regiment (Van Doos) and Carleton and York Regiment were well short of the canal and engaging stubborn German outposts—the former in a dense woods and the latter on the Zutphen–Apeldoorn railway.[9]

This railway provided the boundary for 2 CIB's advance along the IJssel's west bank. While the Seaforth Highlanders led the brigade's main thrust, the Edmontons' 'C' Company provided flank protection along the railroad. Setting out from Voorst, about three miles northwest of Zutphen, 'C' Company reported "stubborn" opposition at 0630 hours and then requested artillery on an enemy-occupied house at 0910 hours. Progress was so slow that at noon Lieutenant Colonel Jim Stone reinforced the single company with 'D' Company's No. 18 Platoon. He was preparing to also send the carrier platoon, when 'C' Company's two forward platoons fell back in the face of a counterattack. When No. 18 Platoon reported also giving ground, Stone took over.[10] Stone had enlisted as a sergeant and worked his way up the ranks to battalion command, gaining a reputation for leading from the front.

The Edmonton attack had bogged down in front of a narrow canal spanned by a heavily defended railway bridge. Stone called for the battalion's three Wasps, which, in his words, "shot the flame across the canal . . . and made an awful mess."[11] This enabled the nine men left in Corporal Arthur Robinson's platoon to overrun three mortar positions, take nineteen prisoners, and kill twenty-one others. At the same time, Private Daniel Dodd from No. 18 Platoon charged and seized the bridge with just the three men left in his section.[12]

The Seaforths, meanwhile, had advanced towards Hoven on the west bank of the IJssel across from Zutphen to secure the bridge-crossing site. The battalion had undergone a leadership crisis the night before with the death of its second-in-command and Lieutenant Colonel Henry "Budge" Bell-Irving suffering a relapse of malaria. Major Oliver Herbert Mace took over.[13]

Mace sent 'D' and 'A' Companies in behind an artillery barrage, but as 'A' Company splashed through a brook and started mucking through a marsh, its leading platoon was pinned by intense fire from a trench system that extended to the IJssel River. Left of 'A' Company, 'D' Company won a bridge across the brook, only to become entangled in a barbed-wire obstacle strung along the top of a dyke. Lieutenant Leonard Joseph Bennett led his platoon in a charge to get around the barrier, but as they turned the barrier, a bullet blinded Bennett in one eye. He ran to the rear, not looking for medical assistance but instead returning with the battalion's Wasps. As the Wasps trundled along either side of the trench, dousing it with flame, the Germans broke. Instead of fleeing towards Hoven, however, they made for a house that 'A' Company had partially surrounded.

Seeing this, Mace signalled 'A' Company's Captain W.D.C. Tuck, "Enemy evacuating slit trenches towards you. Give 'em hell. Jerry is running off. Push on. Push on!" By early afternoon the Seaforths entered Hoven, but it was after dark before the engineers were free to start constructing their bridge over the IJssel.[14]

During the Zutphen battle, Hoven had been heavily pummelled and then again this day. The Seaforth's RAP was consequently over-run by injured civilians. "Great suffering of shell-wracked civilians," Padre Roy Durnford confided to his diary. "Children in RAP, torn—bleeding, dying. Women hear their children crying but they too are stretcher cases & knocked about. I watch & pray with one man as his wife slowly passes away on a stretcher whilst another young woman lies behind us on the verge of death. The poor man has two children in 'no man's land' but can't get to them as Germans fire on Red Cross now. Boys of 16 (Gerries) come in as POWs. They are very cruel, so our boys say, & are less likely to obey Geneva Convention re Red Cross than older men. I talk with them. They speak of Russian millions as menace of Europe as a whole & to Germany in partic[ular]."[15]

'C' Company witnessed young paratroops firing on wounded and stretcher parties. "From 13 Platoon we lost little [Private] Arthur Clarke," the company's diarist wrote. "He was shot [through] the head by a sniper's bullet. He was on the dyke for a couple hours before we could get him out. Getting him out we had that experience of having Gerry fire on the First Aid carrier—wounding our first aid man with a machine gun burst in the legs."

On the morning of April 15, a German paratrooper surrendered. "He was an Austrian and a better type. [Corporal A.A.] Staub talked to him for quite some time and his story is as follows. He has been a paratrooper for 6 mon[ths]. He told us the Original Paratroopers are almost unhuman. He said that . . . he has seen things which we would not believe. He told us that he has seen his own wounded shot and killed by his own men if they were at all detrimental. He would have given himself up last night but he figured we might be mad and shoot him, so he thought he would wait until morning."[16]

Once the bridge was in place, 2 CIB was sent six miles south towards Dieren, where the river turns sharply west to spill into the Neder Rijn outside Arnhem. The Edmontons and Princess Patricia's Canadian Light Infantry advanced, the former moving along the river road and the latter on secondary roads to the west.[17] At 0800 hours, Brigadier Pat Bogert issued his instructions. "We are to 'swan' out southward and make contact with . . . 49th Div[ision]."[18]

Lieutenant Colonel Stone first sent 'B' Company's No. 11 Platoon on four carriers to test the Edmontons' route. Lieutenant J.C. Preston returned at 0930 hours to report "the area swept practically clear of enemy." They had encountered and killed two snipers. Stone decided to assemble a small mobile column to precede the battalion's main body. With Preston commanding, it consisted of the carrier platoon's six vehicles, the anti-tank platoon, the battalion's Wasps, No. 11 Platoon (duly distributed among these vehicles), and seven carriers provided by the supporting Saskatoon Light Infantry, which were mounted with heavy machine guns and 4.2-inch mortars.[19]

Underway by 1320 hours, the column embarked on "a pursuit job."[20] Other than stragglers, the Germans were running. At 1630 hours, the battalion entered Brummen, a large town midway between Hoven and Dieren, enjoying their first Dutch liberation fervour—"the wild enthusiasm of some civilians, like the tears which coursed down the gaunt cheeks of others . . . both moving and rewarding."[21]

The Edmontons stayed the night in Brummen with the PPCLI nearby to the west. Morning saw a leisurely start, the Eddies taking two hours for breakfast before setting off at 0800 hours, while the PPCLI dallied until 1000 hours. Stone's mobile column soon reported Dieren clear, and he raced forward in a jeep to be "received by a cheering and grateful populace."[22]

Actual linkup was made with the British south of the town during the afternoon of April 16 by the PPCLI's 'D' Company. Captain Syd Frost had lost contact with his three platoons, which, tiring of marching, had purloined bicycles and pedalled off to seek either Germans or Britons.[23] Lieutenant Harvey Beardmore's platoon cycled along in "carefree fashion into the south [when] out of the ditch beside the road a balaclava-ed head rose and in broad East Anglian shouted 'CLOSE.' As one man the Patricias replied 'SHAVE.' It was the joint codeword and the gap between 1st Canadian and 49th British Division had been closed."[24]

ARNHEM'S FALL HAD cleared a path for 5th Canadian Armoured Division to advance on a northwestward axis to the IJsselmeer and the Grebbe Line. Foulkes gave Major General Bert Hoffmeister four days to carry out this thirty-mile advance because after that, this division would be lost. On April 18, the 5th Division was to transfer to II Canadian Corps and move immediately to northern Holland—freeing divisions there to advance into Germany.[25]

Hoffmeister decided that 5th Canadian Armoured Brigade, comprised of three tank regiments—Lord Strathcona's Horse (LSH), 8th Princess Louise's New Brunswick Hussars (NBH), and British Columbia Dragoons (BCD)—would lead, supported by only the Westminster Regiment (Motor), while his 11th Canadian Infantry Brigade followed. Each armoured regiment would have a single Westminster company attached. The Hussars and Dragoons would lead, while the Strathconas provided the reserve. Each regiment was also supported by two troops from the 79th British Armoured Division, so-called Funnies. One troop was outfitted with Flails—tanks mounting a large rotating cylinder fitted with lengths of chain to pummel the ground and detonate mines—and the other flame-thrower tanks called Badgers.

"Running due north from Arnhem to the [IJsselmeer] is a pine-covered ridge, the highest hill in the northern half of the Netherlands; in places it rises to 300 feet while the flat lands east and west of it are rarely more than a few feet above sea level and in many places below it, with the North Sea held back by dykes. Our Divisional Centre Line was to start out on the main Arnhem–Apeldoorn highway up the steep hill through the forest which extends for the first 8,000 yards; once clear of the forest it would skirt the northern edge of the wide Deelen Airfield, then northwest through about four miles of sand and scrub pine to the village of Otterloo. From this point on, the country is low flat farmland which might, at this sea-son be too soft to permit tanks to move cross-country. Our route was to be the secondary road through Barneveld to Nijkerk, a small town near the coast. There were no water obstacles other than small ditches," the Strathconas' Lieutenant Colonel Jim McAvity wrote.

"Although . . . by no means ideal tank country, it had been decided that the armoured brigade would take the lead, and 11th Infantry Brigade would follow along, mopping up and picketing the route until First Division reached our axis and pushed on further west." The Dragoons would use the highway and the Hussars a paralleling road to the west. Midway to Otterloo, the Strathconas would pass through the Dragoons and take the village. In the final phase, the Strathconas and Dragoons would advance through to the IJsselmeer.[26]

The Dragoons' Lieutenant Colonel Harry Angle was so concerned by the ground represented on the maps that he asked Brigadier Ian Cumberland for permission to personally reconnoitre it before the advance started. "My request was turned down flat, almost rudely by the brig[adier]," he confided to his diary: "This is the most impossible task for an armoured reg[iment]—to break out of a bridgehead and push three miles through a wood to first objective."[27]

Both the Dragoons and Hussars kicked off at 0700 hours on April 15—late enough to assure sufficient light for gunners to see through their tank periscopes. The Dragoons met little resistance, but 'A' Squadron—following a utility track running alongside a row of power pylons—was slowed by undergrowth. There were also unexpected sand dunes, ranging from fifteen to twenty-five feet high, scattered through the woods that offered good firing positions for enemy infantry. As the tanks rolled forward, those in the lead raked the trees ahead and the flanks with machine-gun fire. Several log roadblocks, sometimes reinforced with concrete blocks or boulders, were encountered, but the tanks bulled around through the adjacent woods. Occasionally, a single German rose from the ditch bordering the road and loosed a Panzerfaust round with haphazard aim. Of the two hits, neither caused disabling damage. No second round was fired, as each German immediately fled.

Just before 'B' Squadron burst out of the forest, it came under fire from a concealed anti-tank gun covering a stout roadblock. The gun's first round bounced harmlessly off the leading tank, and the squadron surged into action with practised skill. "The leading tanks were . . . laying down a heavy concentration of Browning fire and the A/T guns' shooting became very erratic. AP shells could be seen hitting trees and looping crazily down the road. The Sqn. crashed around the road block through the trees and broke out into the open. Here the Sqn. shook out into a loose box formation and started moving more quickly over very open country towards the objective which could now be clearly seen.

"'A' Sqn . . . on the right emerged from the forest at the same time and both Sqns. moved quickly, using Browning machine gun fire and flame throwers liberally on the small groups of Germans encountered." As the regiment's war diarist dryly observed, "The use of the flame throwers to scare the enemy from his positions and the machine-gun fire to kill them once they were in the open was a terribly efficient way of reducing opposition."[28]

As the tanks closed on the objective at 0830 hours, another concealed 75-millimetre anti-tank gun hit the turret of a tank in 'A' Squadron's No. 2 Troop. Its commander, Corporal Ernest J. Clue, was killed, and the gunner, Trooper George A. Wardle, wounded. The reconnaissance section stalked the gun and knocked it out, killing two of its crew and capturing the other three.[29]

Left of the Dragoons, the Hussars had got off to a rocky start when both squadrons ran into roadblocks. 'B' Squadron was able to get past, but 'C' Squadron remained stymied until an armoured bulldozer and a section of engineers cleared the obstacle. Delayed an hour, the Hussars set a cracking pace, breaking out of the woods at 0811 hours.[30] As 'B' Squadron rolled into the open, four 88-millimetre anti-tank guns struck from woods to the right, and Lieutenant Bill Spencer's leading troop had shells striking all around.

"A good and gallant officer," the regiment's historian later wrote, "Spencer moved at once to outflank the position even though it exposed him fully to enemy fire. The Germans struck his tank once; it kept on going. [Trooper] Boone, his gunner, got one gun in his sights and took it out. The crew fell around it. The crew of another gun fled. The tank wheeled towards the other two. There was a flash of hurtling explosive against the steel of Spencer's tank, a glare and burst of exploding light. He fell mortally wounded."[31] The other tanks in Spencer's troop destroyed the remaining guns, but a reconnaissance-section Stuart tank was knocked out first.

The Stuart began to burn, and its commander ordered the crew to bail out. As Trooper Edward Wunsch looked into the lower compartment, he saw that the driver was badly injured and unable to escape because the main gun barrel blocked his escape hatch. With flames licking into the turret, Wunsch traversed the gun away, descended into the fiery hell of the lower compartment, and dragged the gunner out of the hatch. Both men were badly burned, but Wunsch had saved the driver's life.

Getting free of the Stuart provided only scant reprieve. As Wunsch lowered the driver to the rest of the crew, two more anti-tank rounds struck the burning hulk and a machine gun started raking the ground around it. Any moment the tank could explode, and there was no safe cover nearby. Wunsch and the others hugged the dirt, expecting to die. That was when Corporal Frank Buchanan, described by the regimental historian as "a lanky wolf from British Columbia," rolled his Stuart between the burning tank and anti-tank gun. Sitting in the open hatch, Buchannan chucked smoke grenades to screen the men's flight to safety.[32]

Having broken free of the woods, the two tank squadrons with accompanying Westminster companies raced into the open. Seeing that Deelen airfield's hangars and other buildings had "been reinforced until they amounted to fortresses," the Hussars swept past on either flank and left the Westminster's 'B' Company to root the Germans out. "We went hell-bent-for-election, all-out," one Hussar recalled. "We were under fire all the way but we didn't stop for anything. We left a lot of Germans on the airport. They were in and around the various buildings. But killing Germans wasn't our primary objective this time; it was to [reach] those hills beyond."[33]

The Westminsters turned to the task of killing in the midmorning and carried on until "darkness fell on a lurid scene of flame and smoke from fires started during the day by flamethrowers." Westminster casualties were considered light. The anti-tank platoon's commander, Lieutenant John A. Cambridge, died, as did

'B' Company's Corporal Angus Arthur St. Cyr and Private Theodore Huth. Two other privates, Alfred Gammer and Stewart Arthur Mackinlay, died later from wounds.[34]

The reason for the fierce defence at Deelen became evident when it developed that the airfield had served as 858 Grenadier Regiment's headquarters. Included among the prisoners were all this headquarters' staff and its commander, Lieutenant Colonel Otto Lais, who "admitted to having been completely taken by surprise, both as to the direction of our attack and its [strength]."[35]

Caught off balance, LXXX Corps broke, only scattered resistance, which barely slowed the tanks, being offered. By noon, the Strathconas passed through the Dragoons and advanced parallel to the Hussars. The Strathconas were virtually unopposed and fully expected to laager beyond Otterloo. But when 'A' Squadron's leading tank troop under Lieutenant Angus MacKinnon descended a slight hill towards the town, his Sherman was struck by an 88-millimetre shell and began to burn. Troopers George Bowman and Clarence David Graham and Corporal Harold Raymond Forde were killed. The surviving crew member saw MacKinnon roll into a ditch alongside the road. He thought the lieutenant was badly wounded.

Meanwhile, 'A' Squadron was trying to shake the ambush. One of MacKinnon's troop knocked out the 88-millimetre gun, but armoured-piercing rounds continued to screech past the tanks— clear proof there were more hidden guns. On either side of the slope, dense foliage provided perfect camouflage for guns and the numerous snipers who plied their trade. Lieutenant J. Cowley was wounded by a bullet to the head, and the artillery FOO, Captain Mel Donnelly, was killed. A slug went through another tank commander's steel helmet and out the side without leaving a scratch. With night falling, the tankers pulled back to await the morning.

Hearing that Lieutenant MacKinnon might have been left for dead in the ditch, the Strathconas' medical officer, Captain A. Verdicchio, jumped into his medical Bren carrier. As he pulled up to the still-burning tank, Verdicchio found himself surrounded "by a large group of gibbering Germans. Using a mixture of English and French, he explained the mission. The Boches pointed to the tank with pride, probably the first they had scored, then told the M.O. that they had evacuated MacKinnon to a Dutch civilian hospital in Ede. As if to confirm their statement, they gave him the wounded officer's identification card." This report was verified three days later when 49th Infantry Division entered Ede and learned from hospital staff that MacKinnon had died of his wounds.[36]

Despite failing to take Otterloo, the brigade had gained ten miles over difficult tank terrain. During the night, Brigadier Ian Cumberland considered the problem of Otterloo. The last thing he wanted was a fight for possession of the town. Instead, he and Lieutenant Colonel McAvity decided that the Strathconas and a company of Westminsters would punch right through shortly before dawn.

Reveille came at 0400 hours, the men eating biscuits with jam and bully beef washed down with cold water. As they climbed into the Shermans, artillery bracketed the town to cover the sounds of the column's approach. 'C' Squadron led, followed by 'B' Squadron, then the regimental headquarters, the Westminster's 'C' Company, and finally 'A' Squadron. Alternated one-by-one, each tank had its turret traversed so the gun was directed either to the right or to the left. The co-axial machine gun would rake the roadside verge bordered by hedges and trees. The immediate objective was an open field two thousand yards beyond Otterloo. Tucked behind the headquarters section were three Flails, two Badgers, and two armoured engineering vehicles called AVRES. At 0500 hours, the long column ground forward at a steady five miles per hour.

As each tank passed MacKinnon's smouldering Sherman, it began raking the verges. Lieutenant A.D. Raisbeck's lead tank easily ducked around a roadblock just outside the town while simultaneously engaging one anti-tank gun after another by firing at their muzzle flashes. With deadly accuracy, Raisbeck's gunner knocked out one 88-millimetre, a 75-millimetre, and a 37-millimetre gun, plus two trucks. He also sprayed German infantry with the machine gun.

Behind, Major J. Smith's Sherman was struck by a Panzerfaust while rounding the first roadblock, which set the personal kit and ammunition strapped on the outside of the hull ablaze. Everyone bailed out, taking cover in the ditch. The kit strapped on the back of

Lieutenant Bill Guest's 'B' Squadron tank was also set ablaze by a Panzerfaust round, but Guest jumped out of the turret hatch and kicked the stuff off. Several other tanks bogged down trying to get around roadblocks. They and their crews were left to fend for themselves, the column stopping for nothing. By 0800 hours, the majority of the regiment's Shermans were circled like chuckwagons in the field outside of Otterloo with guns pointed outward. Westminster patrols were checking the nearby woods. The Strathconas later learned that at least one infantry battalion numbering about four hundred men had been hiding in the woods next to the town, the commander deciding against tackling the tanks. With Canadian troops on either side of Otterloo, it was also decided to give up the town.[37]

The British Columbia Dragoons pushed 'C' Squadron into the town at 0845 hours and soon took prisoner about three dozen Germans. During the rest of the morning, the regiment's other squadrons concentrated in open fields about two miles to the north. When the infantry arrived, 'C' Squadron joined them.[38]

To the left of Otterloo, 8th New Brunswick Hussars had advanced on Lunteren and the heights to its east. It was a slow, difficult operation with tanks moving along poor secondary roads and regularly encountering infantry armed with Panzerfausts and the odd anti-tank gun. Often the tanks eliminated a resistance pocket, only to have its surviving infantry slip back to the position to cut off the armour. This was the situation when the squadrons forward reported having considerable wounded requiring evacuation. Trooper Horace Basil Parker charged up from the Regimental Aid Post aboard a Bren carrier. Driving straight through several strongpoints that showered his carrier with heavy machine-gun, rifle, and mortar fire, Parker reached the tanks and loaded up the wounded. Running the same gauntlet, Parker came to a position that had been significantly strengthened since his first run and had no choice but to stop. A German officer stepped out and directed him to drive to a nearby house where he and his passengers would be taken prisoner. Parker looked at the machine guns covering his carrier and punched the accelerator. As Parker roared down the road towards the Canadian lines, machine gun slugs shrieked over his head and pounded against the carrier's thin armoured sides. But he and his charges carried on unscathed. Parker's courage was recognized with a Military Medal.[39]

By noon, the Hussars gained the ridge east of Lunteren and formed a defensive circle. From some prisoners they learned that about three hundred Dutch ss troops were in a nearby wood. Lieutenant Colonel J.W. Eaton decided against bypassing such a strong force of fanatics. Yet the dense wood was no place for Shermans, and the single company of Westminsters was too small for the job. The afternoon was therefore spent teeing up a more brutally efficient solution.

While the Westminsters covered the wood's southern edge, the Hussar squadrons lined up along the western side. Retreat to the east or north was barred by rough terrain. Eaton called in a "Murder" concentration by 8th Canadian Field Regiment (Self-Propelled) that had every gun firing constantly for three minutes. At the same time, the tanks slugged the wood with high-explosive shells and raked it with their machine guns. "The resulting concentration was tremendous. The entire woods seemed to blow up and as the survivors scattered they were cut down by MG fire. Very few surrendered and almost none escaped. The wood was soon blazing and fire accounted for most of the wounded. It is estimated that approx[imately] 200 were killed." Eighty prisoners were taken.[40]

The Strathconas, meanwhile, had been bound for Barneveld, about eight miles northwest of Otterloo. They reached the town's outskirts at 1300 hours and realized it was held in strength. Brigadier Cumberland ordered the regiment to pass by on the right, leaving a small force to isolate it. Dashing a couple of miles farther, the Strathconas cut the Amersfoort–Apeldoorn highway and paralleling railway tracks.[41]

Right of the Strathconas, the BC Dragoons had advanced from Otterloo to Voorthuizen—a town astride the Amersfoort–Apeldoorn highway. After a long ten-mile run, the Dragoons had encircled the town by mid-afternoon. Again it was Dutch civilians bent on welcoming their liberators, more than the Germans milling about, that caused the most concern, as a sporadic, running fight raged the rest of the day. Everywhere Germans were on the move, trying to escape

westward rather than tangle with the tankers. Lieutenant Colonel
Harry Angle realized that "the BCDS were some miles behind the
German main position which was facing the other Canadian forces
around Apeldoorn." While some were eager to surrender, "other
Germans would be firing mortars and grenades at any groups they
saw regardless as to whether or not the groups also contained their
own countrymen. The BCDS were fighting in all directions and the
Germans obviously became more and more confused as the day progressed. The Canadians actually saw one small column of German
infantry engaged and shot up by their own guns." Angle "told the
brigadier over the wireless that he did not know if the Canadians had
surrounded the Germans or the Germans surrounded the
Canadians."

With the situation in flux at dusk, the regiment halted northeast
of the town and each squadron formed a defensive circle. The Dragoons were within seven miles of the IJsselmeer and blocking the
line of retreat from Apeldoorn.[42]

AS IMPORTANT AS 5th Canadian Armoured Brigade's gains were to
5th Division's operations, they also broke the stubborn defence of
Apeldoorn and the IJssel River line. The brigade's advance on April
16 convinced the Germans defending the southern stretch of the
IJssel to withdraw, ensuring that 1st Division's 2nd Brigade enjoyed
an easy advance to Dieren. When engineers quickly erected a bridge
over the IJssel at Dieren, Major General Harry Foster decided that
rather than continuing to push his 3rd Brigade through the heavily
defended woods south of Apeldoorn, he would send the West Nova
Scotia Regiment to use it for an end run up the river's west bank.
At the same time, Foster directed 1st Brigade's 48th Highlanders of
Canada and the Hastings and Prince Edward Regiment to cross
the Apeldoorn Canal north of the city directly in front of Het Loo,
Queen Wilhelmina's summer palace. Although aware of 5 CAB's
gains, Foster still believed in the early evening of April 16 "that the
enemy force in Apeldoorn was going to continue its stubborn
resistance."[43]

At 0230 hours, the West Novas loaded aboard trucks and an
assortment of tanks, Crocodile flame-thrower tanks, and self-

propelled guns that would support their advance. It took the column ninety-five minutes to reach Dieren. Two hours after setting out, the West Novas were over the bridge and progressing rapidly towards Apeldoorn, having had "almost no contact with the enemy."[44]

As the West Novas had headed for Dieren, the Royal Canadian Regiment—holding all of 1st Brigade's front—reported its companies "engaged in small arms duels across the canal." At 0300 hours, however, the German "firing suddenly ceased." A few minutes later, two partisans approached 'C' Company's lines and reported that the Germans were quitting the city. Brigade instructed the RCR "to ease" one company across the narrow, partially damaged span of a canal lock to confirm the report. By the time these instructions reached 'C' Company, its commander had already slipped over a small patrol, which captured two German soldiers in the process of wiring explosives on the lock to a detonator. The patrol quickly defused the charges and the rest of the company crossed. Advancing into the city, it encountered no opposition. 'A' Company passed through and reached the main square without incident. By 0700 hours, the entire battalion was patrolling the streets of Apeldoorn and, aided by a large force of partisans, was rounding up German stragglers, who ultimately numbered 214.[45]

None of the battalions closing on Apeldoorn from all sides encountered any Germans except those anxious to surrender. They entered an Apeldoorn that had already erupted into joyous celebration. With its normal population almost doubled by 65,000 refugees, severe food shortages had developed—a situation 1 Canadian Corps had anticipated and began alleviating the very next day with delivery of eighty thousand army rations tallying forty tons.[46] The West Novas "found the streets jammed with wildly cheering Dutch, thronging about the troops and vehicles, kissing the soldiers or seizing their hands and shaking them furiously."[47] On the northern flank, mounted on tanks, the Hasty Ps "made straight for Queen Wilhelmina's Royal Palace and got there without firing a shot, except for the CO [Lieutenant Colonel Renison] who fired three shots in the air to clear some of the people away in order to get through."[48] Captain Farley Mowat commented dryly that the palace "was reached only after a prolonged struggle to escape civilians."[49]

Foster's immediate concern was to get cracking westward from the city to regain contact with the retreating Germans.[50] "There was but little time for the troops to gaze at this fantasy of liberation," Mowat wrote, "for there was still war beyond the next row of trees."[51] By 1000 hours, the Hasty Ps rolled away, with the rest of 1st Brigade following soon after. At the southern end of the city, 3rd Brigade similarly headed westward.[52]

PART FOUR

RISKY BUSINESS

A Stern Atonement

IN GERMANY, 4TH Canadian Armoured Division had mired on the night of April 13 before the heavily defended village of Friesoythe. Just a small village, Friesoythe held the keys to the Küsten Canal because bypassing it in the surrounding flat, feature-less peat country was impossible. All roads running from the south converged on the village, and from its centre, two roads ran a few miles northward on opposing angles to bridges over the canal.

Major General Chris Vokes needed a crossing over the canal to advance the division to the spa town of Bad Zwischenahn, which offered better ground for a swing southeastward to Oldenburg than existed south of the waterway. A road and rail hub for the Wilhelm-shaven peninsula, Oldenburg was a vital preliminary objective for any advance against the major naval ports to the north.[1]

Five hundred Germans, amply equipped with anti-tank guns, garrisoned Friesoythe, and Brigadier Robert Moncel convinced Vokes that it was better to try winning the place through stealth than with a head-on assault. While the Lake Superior (Motor) Regiment launched a feint up the main road to draw German attention, the Argyll and Sutherland Highlanders would sneak cross-country and attack from the east. The Argyll's Lieutenant Colonel Fred Wigle liked the idea and decided to advance his troops through the night in one long column along a narrow track that ran through brushy peat country from a starting point two miles east of Friesoythe. At dawn, the Argylls would storm the village.

Before the main body set off, battalion scouts used white tape to mark the route to the village. Although the tape was needed to ensure that the troops stayed on course during the night advance, it was risk of being discovered by the Germans. It would take only a small ambushing party to foil the plan. Wigle was less worried about being detected by the enemy than losing his wireless link back to brigade. The Nos. 18 and 38 wireless sets used by foot troops were unreliable, so he had a vehicle-mounted No. 19 set—weighing over a hundred pounds—strapped to a stretcher, which the signals section would carry.[2]

Before the force set off in trucks to the start line at 2300 hours, Wigle dashed off a note to his parents in Hamilton. "This letter may be my last. I hope not but I am off on a very risky business and there's a possibility. However you know I love you, always have and always shall. God Bless you both."[3]

As the Argylls unloaded from the trucks in the inky darkness, 15th Field Regiment's gunners shelled Friesoythe to harass the Germans and mask any sounds the infantry made moving through the brush.[4] Personally leading the column, Wigle started down the path with his headquarters section behind. Taking turns, the signallers and others in the headquarters party struggled along with the stretcher.[5] As the long, snaking column progressed, Pioneer Platoon commander Lieutenant Alan Earp saw Wigle step out of line, wait for the stretcher, and take a turn carrying it.[6]

The Argylls gained their rally point fifteen hundred yards from the village without incident and broke into battle formation, with 'B' and 'D' Companies forward, Wigle's headquarters in the centre, and 'A' and 'C' Companies behind.[7] Stalking slowly up to the edge of Friesoythe, the battalion lay down to await the dawn. A bitter north wind cut through uniforms damp from heavy dew.[8]

Wigle had timed the approach so that the wait was minimal, and as the glow of a rising sun cast a dim light, he stood and signalled his men forward. The Argylls surged into the town, and at 0635 hours Wigle sent a wireless report back to his battalion headquarters that the "dangerous manoeuvre was succeeding." Fanning through the village, the Argylls encountered scattered resistance from a clearly disorganized and confused garrison.[9]

As the infantry moved into the village, Wigle established his tactical headquarters inside a modest two-storey house on its outskirts. Lieutenant Earp and several pioneers provided security, but were also responsible for guarding twenty prisoners locked in the cellar. With the attack going so well, however, nobody worried that the house might be vulnerable. Two pioneers climbed the steep stairs to the second storey to catch a nap, "because the rifle companies had gone into the town and this was on the outskirts, so everything was alright."[10]

Glancing out a window, Wigle spotted soldiers to the south and assumed they were Lake Superiors. He sent two scouts to confirm this. Signaller Private William Patrick remained at the window, watching as the men approached the soldiers and then suddenly thrust their hands into the air. From another window Earp realized the soldiers were Germans, now heading straight for the house. Inside, men scrambled to grab guns and started shooting out the windows and doors. Privates Ben Bowland and Vic Taylor had only just stretched out upstairs when "all hell broke loose. There was gunfire, so we came running downstairs." Bowland took up a position close to the front door.

One German chucked a grenade through a window, and the explosion killed Privates John Brown and Cecil French. Wigle emerged from another room by the stairs and Bowland saw him pause, as if unsure whether or not to ascend to the next floor. At the same moment, Earp stepped into the foyer and a Schmeisser burst came through the open outer door. One bullet struck Earp in the head and knocked him backwards, but the rest of the burst caught Wigle full in the chest and he landed "right at my feet," Bowland later said. "That was the end of him." Two Argylls cut the German down with their Sten guns.

From a nearby house, 'A' Company Sergeant Major Wilf Stone had gathered a handful of men and they ran down the road. But "by the time we got to where the action was, the Germans had either been killed, or wounded, or escaped. And Colonel Wigle . . . had been killed."

At main battalion headquarters, news of the attack came at 0830 hours. After that the messages had been chaotic and incoherent, until signaller Private Sidney Webb heard someone say, "Sunray has been milked." Webb had no idea how to respond. Turning to Major Pete MacKenzie, the battalion's second-in-command, he reported the signal. MacKenzie went pale. "The Colonel said if he was to be killed, that was the message that would be put over," he told Webb before setting off in a carrier to take command.[11]

The Argylls were in control of Friesoythe by the time MacKenzie arrived at 1030 hours, and by early afternoon the Lincoln and Welland Regiment passed through to advance on the Küsten Canal.

Within the village, rumours swirled through the Argyll ranks. Particularly prevalent was a report that Wigle had been killed by a sniper wearing civilian clothes, who turned out to be a local villager. Men were angry, talking revenge. Soon another rumour surfaced. Division, or maybe brigade, had ordered Friesoythe burned. Moncel's friendship with Wigle was common knowledge, and it was said the grieving brigadier wanted the villagers punished. Vokes's sharp temper was legendary, and some said his exact words had been, "Burn the fucking town!" As the battalion's Wasps arrived, the Argylls lashed out. "I was driving a flamethrower... and we burnt the whole town down," Private Harold Reid said. "Revenge, eh— 'cause they killed our Colonel." Other soldiers stuffed rags in the spouts of Jerry cans, set them alight, and chucked them one after the other "into each little frame house."

'C' Company's Private Donald Stark stood on a back porch watching the church steeple collapse into the flaming structure below. Then he walked into the house, climbed the stairs, and calmly threw a phosphorous grenade into each of three rooms. Flames were spreading as he strolled away.

When the mortar platoon arrived in its carrier, Friesoythe was blazing. Private J.J. Ross saw a corpse lying in the street and realized it was an old man. His clothes were on fire, flames eating away the flesh.[12]

At 1800 hours, while many Argylls were still torching the village, a small group of officers gathered in a field on its southern outskirts.

After a short service, the bodies of Wigle and four other Argylls killed in the fighting were buried in shallow graves. How many German civilians perished in the fires was never determined. The Argylls reported only that they took eighty prisoners and that sixteen of the Germans who attacked Wigle's headquarters were killed.[13]

Not all of Friesoythe was burned, but its centre was destroyed. The Argyll's war diarist made no mention of the incident, noting only that the night of April 14 was spent under occasional, ineffective German shelling of the town, "in which many fires were raging."[14] "When darkness fell," wrote 4th Canadian Armoured Brigade's war diarist, "Friesoythe was a reasonable facsimile of Dante's Inferno."[15]

The tragedy at Friesoythe went unmentioned at divisional, corps, and army headquarters. No investigation followed. The army's official historian, Lieutenant Colonel C.P. Stacey, only confirmed Friesoythe's burning in a personal visit after the war. He concluded that the false report of a civilian sniper had prompted "a mistaken reprisal," but that there was "no record of how this came about."[16]

No evidence of a deliberate cover-up exists. Indeed, several war diarists, such as the 8th Light Anti-Aircraft Regiment's, alluded to it. "There is a definite hardening in the Canadian point of view," he wrote. "Civilians in Friesoythe are finding that treachery does not pay. The [Argylls] were attacked in that town yesterday by German forces assisted by civilians and to-day the whole town is being systematically razed. A stern atonement, but one which the Hun knows himself and understands. It seems folly now to continue to fight, but as long as fanatical Germans continue to accept [battle], the war will go on."[17]

FRIESOYTHE IN FLAMES behind them, the Lake Superiors advanced in a "night push in the hope that we might catch the enemy off balance and seize a crossing [over] the canal intact."[18] 'B' Company was to secure a small bridge spanning a narrow canal a short distance south of the wider waterway, and then the plucky scouts of No. 13 Platoon would "make a run for the [bridge] over the [Küsten] canal" while the rest of the battalion hurried along in column behind. Once the battalion was north of the canal, the enemy's "back would be broken," 4th Armoured Brigade's war diarist predicted.

Finding the bridge over the small canal intact, No. 13 Platoon had passed three carriers over when it suddenly exploded. The three-man demolition party was quickly caught, with one man killed and the other two taken prisoner. Hoping to retrieve the situation, the scouts ranged out and discovered another bridge, rickety but intact, over which the rest of the platoon crossed and then raced to join the others back at the main road.[19] Eight hundred yards farther on, however, they came to "a tremendous demolition [that had] turned the [road] into a morass and further progress...became impossible... It was a noble effort but it failed."[20] Using the shaky bridge found by the scouts, 'B' Company soon passed over and arrived at the seventy-five-foot-wide, twenty-five-foot deep crater, but the bridge collapsed under the weight of 'C' Company's personnel carriers.

When dawn broke on April 15, 'B' Company managed to wiggle four carriers around the crater, but the larger armoured personnel carriers were unable to follow. The rest of the company and those of 'C' Company dismounted and moved out on foot. The Superiors advanced through the "dreary peat bog, with here and there a stack of drying peat providing cover for enemy snipers and anti-tank guns, and along the roadsides, deep ditches filled with water, with the inevitable row of trees and the occasional farm... the enemy had planned the withdrawal well [and] he fought with determination and oftentimes with considerable skill. Not only did he still have a few paratroopers available, but now he was drawing upon marines from the German naval station at Wilhelmshaven; and if the latter had little knowledge of land warfare, they still had plenty of courage."[21]

The Superiors soon saw the canal in the distance. Germans were streaming in large numbers across a bridge, which suddenly exploded into pieces just as 'B' Company closed on it. Digging in near the canal, the Superiors were under constant mortar fire and realized that some Germans remained on the south bank when an anti-tank gun knocked out two of No. 13 Platoon's carriers. Corporal Henry John Beaudry was killed, the only fatal casualty suffered this day.[22]

Learning there would be no easy crossing, Vokes decided the time had come for Moncel's brigade to have a deserved rest. Winning a bridgehead would be 10th Canadian Infantry Brigade's task, a decision Moncel's staff considered "glad news." A contact team quickly briefed Brigadier Jim Jefferson and his people, so that they could "carry on the good work." The Superiors were relieved by the Algonquin Regiment, while the Argylls and Lincoln and Welland Regiment reverted to 10 CIB control. There would be no rest for the infantry, "who had fought so gallantly, since they had joined us at the Meppen crossing," 4 CAB's war diarist acknowledged.[23]

NORTHEAST OF FRIESOYTHE, the Lincoln and Welland Regiment spent April 15 clearing small villages south of the Küsten Canal. The battalion's 'D' Company ranged even farther to the east to link up with the independently operating tankers of the South Alberta Regiment. "There was a lot of petty fighting," the Lincs' Lieutenant Colonel Rowan Coleman noted, "sniping, this type of thing . . . It was costing us people every day. And I think that type of thing [ramped up the tension] more than a mass attack where a lot of people died. This was more a case of losing one here and two there."[24]

Tasked with keeping contact between 4th Division and xxx British Corps, the South Albertas had been operating for several days across a wide front that saw the squadrons gradually vectoring in on the town of Garrel, about ten miles southeast of Friesoythe. "All along the front came reports of craters, mines, and several bombs for demolitions," the war diarist noted.[25] Lieutenant Colonel "Swatty" Witherspoon was stalwartly doing his duty but grieving for Lieutenant Colonel Wigle, who had been his brother-in-law.

Mines and craters had proven the greatest hindrance, but at about 2000 hours on April 15, 'C' Squadron drew fire from two self-propelled guns and a tank as it approached a small airfield south of Garrel. The two SPGs were quickly knocked out, but the tank proved to be a heavy Tiger 11—virtually impervious to the 75-millimetre gun normal Shermans mounted.[26] While some of the Shermans attempted to shoot it out with the Tiger, Sergeant Tom Milner of No. 2 Troop spotted a couple of smaller tanks—one towing a trailer—rolling across the airfield at a range of about twelve hundred yards. Milner's tank was a Firefly, mounting a 17-pounder gun that could take on the Tiger, and these smaller tanks were sitting ducks. The tank's gunner, Trooper Carson Daley, immobilized both with shots through their tracks. He then punched an armour-piercing round through each tank's turret, and suddenly "the whole damned thing went sky high about five hundred feet." It was later determined the spectacular explosion had been caused by the trailer's payload of several five-hundred-pound aerial bombs the Germans had intended to use for mines.[27]

Lieutenant Danny McLeod's No. 2 Troop and Lieutenant Ken Wigg's No. 4 Troop went for the Tiger, aided by the illumination of falling parachute flares. Each troop's Firefly engaged the Tiger head-on, while the other Shermans manoeuvred to attack it from either flank. Shell after shell slammed into the Tiger, which lashed back ineffectively with its mighty 88-millimetre gun. Finally, a round struck the gun's muzzle and "it was bent back about six inches." The Tiger began backing away but in doing so turned itself broadside, and a high-explosive shell set the engine compartment on fire.[28] Flames quickly engulfed the tank, bringing to conclusion what the South Alberta's war diarist termed "a ding dong fight in the failing light."[29]

At dawn on April 16, 'B' Squadron launched the South Alberta's assault on Garrel from the northwest while 'A' Squadron approached from the northeast. 'C' Squadron, meanwhile, sealed the roads leading north from the town to block the garrison's line of retreat. The three squadrons were entering the outskirts when the town's civil authorities offered to surrender it. Witherspoon told them the surrender would be accepted, but if any of his tanks drew fire or struck mines, the attack would be renewed. As the first tank moved up the main street, it was "brewed up" by a Panzerfaust round. Witherspoon angrily ordered that "every [building] which did not show a white flag [be] fired."[30]

Garrel was so strewn with mines, craters, and other obstacles that Witherspoon decided against keeping tanks there through the night. Several snipers were also at work within the built-up area, and the Lincolns of 'D' Company had arrived in such exhausted condition after a long journey that they were in no shape to finish the clearing operation. After giving them the night off, Witherspoon sent the Lincs into Garrel on the morning of April 17, and they soon reported the town clear.

The previous day had been frustrating for Witherspoon, but not because of Garrel. A battalion reconnaissance section had determined that Aue, a stream east of Garrel, was defended for a long stretch by just two German infantry companies. Witherspoon had immediately realized that if his regiment deployed a tank-launched scissors bridge, it could gain a main road leading directly to Oldenburg by the morning of April 17 and take the city in a surprise attack. The nearest such bridge had been deployed five miles south of Garrel, and Witherspoon ordered it rushed to the Aue. As the Valentine tank fitted with the bridge rolled past the airfield south of Garrel, however, it struck a mine and blew up. Witherspoon declared this misfortune "his greatest disappointment of the war."[31]

HAD THE SOUTH Albertas succeeded in taking Oldenburg from the south, 10th Infantry Brigade's Küsten Canal assault crossing might have been unnecessary. Instead, Brigadier Jefferson knew his brigade faced a costly challenge. There was only one possible crossing—at Edewecht, "a hamlet surrounded by marshes and ditches on the Friesoythe–Bad Zwischenahn road about 11 miles southwest of Oldenburg," so achieving surprise was impossible.[32] Across the canal were two battalions of marine fortress troops from Wilhelmshaven. In reserve behind the marines were elements of the 7th Fallschirmjäger Division.[33]

Completed in 1936, Küsten Canal linked the lower reaches of the Ems to the Weser River. About fifty-five miles long, it had a standard hundred-foot width.

The Algonquin's 'A' Company had closed to its edge in the early morning hours of April 16 and established a base for the forthcoming night assault. Sporadic mortar and artillery fire greeted the company's arrival. Major Robert Stock's reports back to battalion offered little encouragement. The peat bogs presented a "practically insuperable" problem, making the deployment of vehicles or guns anywhere but squarely on the narrow road impossible. The dyke on the opposite shore was higher than the southern one, enabling the enemy "to bring his self-propelled guns right up to the canal in virtually hull-down positions." Only the southern bank's steep landward side "allowed any lateral deployment."[34]

Jefferson and Lieutenant Colonel Robert Bradburn mulled over this information as they worked up an attack plan. At the same time, they had the canal shelled heavily, the fire being directed from 'A' Company's lines by 15th Field Regiment's Captain I. Cristall. His work spotting "plentiful" targets "kept the guns busy." April 16 was a warm, sunny day, perfect for air operations.[35] All "day long, Typhoons and Spitfires were busy bombing and strafing enemy positions and gun and mortar areas north of the canal with considerable success," the 10th Brigade's war diarist recorded.[36]

Jefferson decided to have 8th Light Anti-Aircraft Regiment's 'A' and 'D' Troops provide pepper-pot support, as the 20-millimetre guns had done during the Rhine crossing. The gunners were soon slashing "targets along the [canal] and ducking occasionally as hostile missiles returned across the obstacle."[37] Even more in jeopardy due to lack of cover were the New Brunswick Rangers of No. 5 Platoon, under command of Lieutenant J.S. Drury, who could only get in range by digging their medium machine guns into the high canal dyke. Drury's Vickers .303 machine guns would "lay down rapid fire on enemy positions . . . commencing the moment the boats of the assault [troops] were lowered into the water until they [disembarked] on the other side—his fire will then swing right to engage targets east of the [road]," the Rangers' war diarist reported. The Rangers' No. 4 Platoon dug its 4.2-inch mortars into pits a little farther back with instructions to keep up a steady fire program for forty-five minutes once the boats launched.[38] The Algonquin's Major George Cassidy, Left Out of Battle (LOB) for this crossing, thought it an "unorthodox procedure to place the [machine guns] where they could practically shake hands with the enemy."[39]

Major P.A. Mayer's 'B' Company would lead the assault, followed by 'D' Company under Captain J.J.J. Sunstrum, and lastly 'C' Company, led by Captain Les Taylor because Major Clark Robertson, like Cassidy, was LOB. 'B' Company's job was to land next to the blown bridge and advance four hundred yards to seize a cluster of buildings. 'D' Company, meanwhile, would expand the bridgehead east of the road. 'C' Company would pass through Mayer's men and work out to the north.

Nobody underestimated the difficulty 'B' Company faced crossing the canal. As one report put it, "Success depends entirely upon the initiative of the men who paddle across the water, very often under a hail of fire against which their canvas craft offers no protection whatsoever. If caught by small arms fire in mid-stream, the soldier therefore must fire his own weapons from the boat and neutralize the opposition before he can land. Once he has landed, he must plunge into the darkness beyond to seek out and destroy his enemy in close combat. Such is the lot of the infantryman."[40]

As soon as it was dark, the company carried seven canvas assault boats forward and set them down in a line facing the canal from behind a paralleling road short of the dyke. At a signal from Mayer, the boat crews—those who would do the paddling—quietly moved the boats onto the dyke and lay down alongside them to avoid casting a silhouette. The rest of Mayer's men waited behind the dyke. It was 0045 hours on April 17 and the "company was lined up in complete silence . . . The enemy, who could be heard on the far bank, apparently realized that something was afoot and a good deal of rifle and machine-gun fire was directed onto the ground on which we were lying," Mayer wrote. "A tribute to the discipline of the troops here is evident from the fact that although 4 men were hit, not one cried out to give our intention away."

At precisely 0100 hours, the Rangers fired their machine guns— the signal to the Algonquins to go. Mayer saw tracers flashing across the canal, "shells started to pass over, and as one man the company rose, picked up its boats, and having loaded up, pushed off across the darkened waters." The canal "was covered against fairly heavy fire, which some of the enemy, standing on the north bank, poured onto us; but our own Brens in the bows of the boat replied and neutralized· the opposition long enough to allow us to disembark."

'B' Company bellowed the regiment's Indian war cry and charged up the bank. Guns blazed as they burst over the top of the dyke, and twenty minutes "of brisk hand-to-hand fighting and house clearing followed, at the end of which the leading company was on all its objectives and had taken twenty-one prisoners."[41]

In the brief minutes that the Rangers had spent covering the company's assault, they "had taken a terrible beating, but their guts and determination was of the greatest value to the crossing." Most of the Germans dug in along the canal bank had fired at the Rangers rather than the three Algonquin companies, which consequently crossed with minimal casualties.[42] Two of the Rangers' guns were knocked out and four men wounded.[43]

Within minutes of the assault, 9th Canadian Field Squadron engineers began bridging operations. They had several tasks. First, the roadblock in front of the blown bridge had to be cleared and mines along the road lifted to enable the bridging equipment to come forward. As this work was underway, other crews started launching a ferry service, while still more began constructing a bridge. It was hard, dangerous work, for the Germans had the road-block and approaches "pin pointed by mortar, SP 88 mm, and machine-gun fire . . . Eventually, after a very heavy pounding by enemy fire and suffering three casualties, an armoured bulldozer, driven by S[apper George William] Grieve, cleared a passage through the block." The engineers realized the Algonquin bridgehead was too narrow and insufficiently deep to shelter them from German fire while they worked. "None of us were at all satisfied with our bridge-head," one engineer commented, "however, we decided to have a crack at the job."[44] Grieve's work with the bulldozer earned him a Military Medal.

Despite their efforts, it was soon obvious there would be no bridge until the Algonquins managed to push the Germans out of immediate range. Yet, without the bridge, tanks, Wasps, and other supporting armour that might tip the battle could not cross. The Algonquins fought from ground "poorly suited for defence, the cen-tre line being bordered by many trees and crossed at right angles by numerous drainage ditches which were in turn lined by thick hedge-rows. The ground itself was very marshy and slit trenches reaching a depth of more than twelve inches immediately filled with water. In short, it was ideal terrain from the enemy's standpoint. He was soon to make excellent use of it."[45]

STANDING ON THE south bank, Major Cassidy saw German corpses strewn on the ground and realized most of these had been caught standing in the open when the Rangers and artillery had opened fire. "But though many were lying dead in the checkerboard of drainage ditches that crisscrossed the fields, it soon became clear that the enemy had moved in heavy reserves." Intelligence identified these as more marines, paratroops from 32nd Fallschirmjäger Regiment, and Volkssturm from the 22nd Infantry Ersatz Battalion. Except for the paratroops, these were not first-class troops. But "in this country, well-armed (almost every man had a Schmeisser and many had two or three [Panzerfausts]), and well-supplied with ammunition and food, they were a hard force to be reckoned with."

'C' Company's Captain Taylor observed that while the marines "were young and inexperienced, their inexperience seemed to make them foolhardy. They didn't seem to recognize that Death was permanent. Hence they were damned persistent fellows." Normally, the Canadians offset German fanaticism with superior mobility and firepower of tanks and Wasps. Denied these advantages, the infantry could only "accept battle on the enemy's terms."[46]

The Algonquins did have ample artillery and aerial support. Brilliant sunshine provided excellent visibility for the fighter-bombers. But even as the planes and guns hammered targets, snipers infiltrated the bridgehead.[47] German mortars, artillery, and machine guns forced the engineers to cease work entirely after two rafts built to float anti-tank guns across were destroyed at noon. The "galling fire" only grew in volume and accuracy as the day progressed.[48]

At 1400 hours, the Germans counterattacked 'C' Company—which was farthest inland—from three sides, and only the "constant and effective" artillery and "swooping Typhoon rocket-craft broke up many formed attacks."[49] Knowing he had to get more boots on the ground, Brigadier Jefferson ordered the new Argyll commander to put his battalion over. Lieutenant Colonel A.F. "Bert" Coffin had come to the Argylls from being the South Alberta's second-in-command, and the Argylls were uneasy about this stranger—a tanker suddenly turned infantryman. Delays bringing up the twenty necessary boats ensued and the operation was put off until after last light.[50]

In the bridgehead, the Algonquins clung on. Engaged in "a terrific firefight," 'C' Company's headquarters was constantly "under direct small-arms fire."[51] Dodging bullets, Captain Taylor was unable to control his rifle platoons. No runners could move safely within the company perimeter. Taylor had also lost all wireless contact with the battalion tactical headquarters, and telephone lines strung earlier had been cut by German fire. The company signaller, Private James Shields, kept repairing the line—making one "hazardous journey" after another along its length—a largely futile but brave effort that was recognized with a Military Medal.

At last light, the Algonquins sent two platoons from 'A' Company across to reinforce the bridgehead, and these were thrown out on the left-hand flank.[52] About the same time, the Argylls fed 'A' and 'D' Companies over. While 'A' Company dug in on the left side of the road, 'D' Company pushed out a thousand yards along the side of the canal. The Argylls held a position only a hundred yards deep, beyond which "stretched a wide, flat open space swept by enemy fire."[53]

Suddenly, out of the gathering gloom, a self-propelled gun mounting an 88-millimetre gun ground along the road towards 'C' Company—its big gun slamming shells into the buildings on either side that sheltered the infantry. Desperate, Taylor called for artillery right on his front, which transformed the area into "a veritable hell for Canadians and Germans alike."[54] Several Algonquins were wounded. Unscathed, the SPG rolled slowly past 'C' Company, apparently determined to gain the canal. The infantry accompanying the SPG had been driven to ground by the artillery, and Taylor used the lull before the Germans rallied to pull back into 'D' Company's lines to the right of the bridge. Taylor's "surrounded and shattered platoons got back with far fewer casualties than would have otherwise been possible."

The SPG trundled on, everything the Algonquins threw out harmlessly deflected by its armour, until it stopped fifty yards short of the water. From here it fired at houses across the canal and lobbed shells straight down the road towards Friesoythe. Then the SPG turned about and huffed back the way it had come.[55]

Crisis momentarily over, the Canadians began improving their situation and taking stock. Seventy-six German dead lay inside the bridgehead and "many other corpses in field grey of the Wehrmacht and the dark blue of his Marine battalions littered the ditches." Just before dawn on April 18, the Algonquin's 'B' Company regained the ground 'C' Company had lost.[56] The Argylls, meanwhile, were widening the bridgehead to the west with all four of their companies. Despite continuing heavy artillery and mortar fire, the engineers gained enough elbow room to launch rafts capable of carrying desperately needed ammunition and food into the bridgehead.

By morning, the Algonquins had been in action for more than thirty hours and suffered eleven killed, nineteen missing (mostly from 'C' Company), and thirty-nine wounded.[57]

Through the day, the Canadians struggled to deepen the bridgehead, while the Germans remained determined to overrun it. Three counterattacks struck the Argylls, one getting to within a hundred yards of 'C' Company before being driven back with heavy losses. Once again artillery and Typhoon support proved decisive. Slowly the Argylls expanded their grip to the west of the road.[58] The Algonquins were so battered it was enough that they held their ground.

With the bridging effort still incomplete, the only reinforcement that could be offered was more infantry, and at 1700 hours, Major General Chris Vokes summoned Lieutenant Colonel Rowan Coleman of the Lincoln and Welland Regiment to meet him at 10 CIB headquarters. In the distance, Coleman saw the crossing point, and beyond "an extreme scene of desolation . . . the whole place was a mess . . . The typical World War I battlefield." Vokes, whom Coleman knew well from when the two men had served in 1st Division in Italy, grabbed him by the front of his tunic and growled, "You are going to go across . . . If you don't get across, I'll throw you right in the canal."[59]

Coleman was given three hours. Once on the other side, his job was to expand the bridgehead eastward. 'C' Company was to secure a footing on the edge of the canal, then push a thousand yards along the bank to a rail spur. 'A' Company would then advance as far as it could go northward along the spur. 'B' Company would simultaneously punch north another thousand yards along the east side of the main road to where a railway track cut across on a perpendicular line. "The plan was to hold and firm up a very strong [bridgehead] so that a [bridge] could be built," the battalion's war diarist wrote.[60]

'C' Company crossed at 2230 hours. Veering to the right along the dyke, it reached the rail spur at 2340 hours. Schümines had taken their toll, the men stepping on the detonators that exploded the mines under their feet to mangle a foot and lower leg. Seeing one man being carried off with such a wound, the company commander, Major John Dunlop, walked over and said, "Tough luck, soldier." The man replied, "Not as tough as you think. I came up for a fight for you, sir, and I never fired a shot. I'm sorry."[61]

Despite heavy resistance, the Lincs gained their objectives by daylight of April 19. Just as importantly, the engineers had rafted the battalion's anti-tank platoon over the canal under cover of darkness. Food and ammunition also started to flow freely. All three battalions began deepening the bridgehead, and by 0800 hours the engineers—having worked feverishly through the night—opened a bridge to tanks. The British Columbia Regiment inched a Sherman forward, but it was hit by an 88-millimetre round. Luckily, the tank failed to burn and the crew dumped it into the ditch. Artillery immediately began pounding the German lines, and under its cover "the next tanks came across full tilt, firing directly up the road. In a few minutes, the first troop was successfully across and into firing positions . . . among the grateful infantry."[62]

The tanks doomed any thoughts the Germans might have entertained about overcoming 4th Division's grip on the northern bank, but the delay they had imposed revealed a significant weakness that could not be overcome. As Lieutenant Colonel Mac Robinson, the division's general staff officer, duly noted, "We were an armoured [division] fighting in what was properly speaking inf[antry] country and, early in this battle, we began to feel our shortage of inf. Only so much effort could be expected from the inf resources at our com[mand], and for one short period [we] were reduced to fighting on a one or at the most two-[battalion] front. Further the div. was definitely road-bound—a fact of which the enemy was entirely aware, and not only were we road-bound but it was constantly necessary to rebuild the [roads] over which the Div had to [advance] or actually to construct new roads to permit further advances."[63]

Of the Küsten Canal, Major Cassidy wrote, the "crossing was so hotly contested, and was won by such a slim margin, that . . . it opened up a three-week period of hard fighting that continued to the very end of the War itself. While on most other fronts the Allied armies were rolling over fragmentary opposition and wreaking havoc in the back areas, we found ourselves up against such determined resistance as had not been felt since the horrors of the Hochwald. It was ironical in the days to follow to hear of the long advances and sweeping victories of others, measured in tens and twenties of miles, while we crawled up blood-soaked ditches, and measured our advances in yards."[64]

Large-Scale Street Fighting

Increasingly, it was impossible for First Canadian Army to predict the intensity of opposition its divisions would meet from the Germans. On April 13, when 2nd Canadian Infantry Division gained the outskirts of Groningen, expectation had been that the city's liberation would be easily won. In the late afternoon, 4th Brigade's headquarters staff had confidently predicted that the Royal Hamilton Light Infantry and supporting Fort Garry Horse squadron were "going to victory march right into the city."

When opposition stiffened in the modern suburbs surrounding the medieval city centre, Brigadier Fred Cabeldu continued to believe the Rileys were facing a thin defensive crust that would collapse before nightfall. Resistance, however, had only thickened, and as Canadian casualties mounted they became "fighting mad" that the Germans were insisting on drawing them into a stupid and futile battle for a city of little strategic value.[1]

Groningen formed the southern boundary of an extensive belt of anti-aircraft (flak) guns extending northeastward through the Dutch port of Delfzijl to cross the Eems Inlet to the German harbour of Emden opposite. A North Sea island, Borkum, which guarded entrance into the Eems, had been transformed into a fortress bristling with a dozen flak towers and an array of naval batteries. The bulk of the defensive ring's flak towers were concentrated alongside the Eems, only two such batteries being close to Groningen. Their loss would little improve survival odds for the Allied bombers remorselessly pounding Germany's industrial cities.

The city was the centre of northern Holland's extensive rail, water, and road transportation system, but this was of little value to the Germans now that they had lost their grip on the region. Through the years of occupation, the Germans had diligently fortified the city with an extensive network of trenches, anti-tank ditches, bunkers, and weapon pits that covered the canals ringing the city and their bridges.[2] But on April 5 they had also sent home its major garrisoning force, the 480th Infantry Division, leaving behind a grab bag of units that still numbered between 7,000 and 7,500 men. Most were army regulars, Luftwaffe ground personnel, and naval marines. But also included were ss units, both German and Dutch, and some Hitlerjügend volunteers, German railroad workers, and members of the German Security Service (sd). This last group had its northern Netherlands headquarters in Groningen.[3] Morale was decidedly low, but the sd, ss, and Hitlerjügend forces were, as always, fanatically motivated despite the inevitability of defeat. The ss were able to stiffen other units by threatening to kill any caught trying to surrender. Lacking tanks, they were equipped with many 20-millimetre anti-aircraft guns, mg-42 machine guns, Panzerfausts, and Schmeissers.

The Germans in the city were clearly superior in their possession of automatic and shoulder-launched weapons, whereas the Canadians relied on their greater number of heavy weapons—tanks, Wasps, artillery, and other armoured support. In the narrow city streets, however, fighting would be limited to ranges of a hundred feet or less, distances better suited to hand-held weaponry than to heavy weapons.[4]

Bypassing Groningen was not an option. That would require leaving behind Canadian forces to contain the Germans there, and 11 Canadian Corps needed these men for its imminent move to Germany to fulfill its first priority of guarding the left flank of Twenty-First Army Group's advance towards the Elbe River.[5] There was also the fact that 150,000 civilians would then be left at the mercy of the Germans and their Dutch collaborators.

Drawn into an unexpected battle, the Rileys only realized in the early morning hours of April 14 that their attempts to win bridges over the inner canal ringing the city's core would be met by a foe with no intention of withdrawing. The most remarkable news, however, that Lieutenant Colonel H.C. Arrell gave Cabeldu was that both the main bridge and another smaller one to its right still stood.[6] The battalion's 'B' Company had made two successive failed attempts to win the smaller bridge before admitting it was outgunned.[7]

Cabeldu decided to feed the Royal Regiment of Canada in to seize the smaller bridge. "Gentlemen, when we have secured Groningen, we effectively will have severed Holland from Germany," Lieutenant Colonel Richard Lendrum told his officers in a briefing that 4th Canadian Field Regiment FOO Captain George Blackburn heard through a haze of exhaustion. Before Lendrum finished, he nodded off. Waking thirty minutes before the attack, he saw the Royal's company commanders all sprawled about on the floor of the farmhouse in a similar stupor.[8]

By 0415 hours, everyone was awake and the attack got underway with 'C' and 'D' Companies attempting to clear the approaches to the canal and the bridge. Major Jack Stother's 'C' Company was to seize what appeared on the maps and aerial photos as a cluster of warehouses. 'D' Company would then pass through to secure the section of canal bordered on the southern bank by the city's large railway yards and station.[9] Once this section of the canal was secured, Major J.K. Shortreed's 'B' Company would make the crossing. Blackburn was to accompany Shortreed's men.[10]

The attack rapidly unravelled when Stother's company discovered that the warehouses were actually rows of apartment blocks bristling with snipers and machine guns. Several 20-millimetre guns sent volleys of shells screaming down the streets, forcing the men to hug the walls and hide behind corners. Both companies set to clearing each apartment building in turn, a slow process that took until dawn to complete.[11] The clearing was complicated by the presence of civilian snipers, who were later determined to have been Dutch SS and other collaborators who knew that when Groningen fell they would be "in a serious predicament."[12]

From the apartment complex, 'A' and 'B' Companies moved against the railway station. Shortreed's men advanced in single file up a street bordered by the canal on one side and a row of buildings on the other. Small-arms fire started coming from "a row of shaggy bushes stretching across the far end of the street and marking the boundary of railyards containing several tracks, separated by raised passenger-platforms, which . . . constitute[d] a formidable obstacle course on the final dash from the hedgerow to the main station platform." Heavy fire shrieking up the street towards them forced the Royals to crawl along the angled concrete berm at the edge of the canal.

Across the street, Blackburn ducked into a deeply recessed doorway and pushed his back against the door. As he did so, it opened. Whirling around, Blackburn confronted a Dutch youth, who handed him "steaming coffee in a delicate cup, complete with saucer." Blackburn sipped his coffee while the troops across the road shouted abuse. "Leave it to the bloody artillery, they always get the best of everything," one man yelled. The boy asked what they were saying and Blackburn replied that they wanted coffee as well, even as he saluted them with a raised middle finger while taking another delicate sip. The lad disappeared, returning a few minutes later with two more cups, complete with saucers, and ducked across the bullet-swept street. Kneeling on one knee, he waited calmly for a couple of men to empty the cups, retrieved them, and then trotted through the fire back into the house.[13]

Once the Royals pushed past the brush boundary into the rail yard, opposition became desultory, confined primarily to snipers. Many of the Germans began surrendering, but other pockets—especially those manned by ss and sd personnel—fought to the death.[14]

At 0930 hours, Major General Bruce Matthews met Brigadier Cabeldu in a hotel on the city outskirts. They agreed that Groningen was defended in depth and would require more than a single brigade to subdue. Cabeldu's brigade was to complete clearing the southern suburbs through to the canal, and 5th Brigade would come up on the south to widen the front advancing on the canal ringing the city centre. By day's end, Matthews wanted Cabeldu to have secured the southern edge of the canal to create a jumping-off point for 6th Brigade to cross it. At the same time, 5th Brigade would also force its way into the city centre from the west.[15]

EVEN COMPLETING THE more limited task proved a costly challenge. Dozens of snipers fired from rooftops, while machine-gun crews shot out of loopholes cut in the exposed upper walls of building basements. The Rileys' 'A' Company suffered so many casualties closing on the main bridge that Major W.L. Coleman realized it would be shredded before it got there unless he obtained some support. He pleaded for Wasps to burn a path through the buildings, but was rebuffed because Matthews had ordered that artillery, flame, and other destructive heavy weapons be limited to prevent excessive damage to a friendly city.[16]

One of Coleman's platoons managed to wrest a building from a large force of men but was so badly shot up that Lance Corporal Wilf King—one of the few men still standing—knew they would never withstand a counterattack. There were not enough bandages for all the wounded, and King realized some would die unless they were evacuated immediately. Dashing into the street, King sprinted to Coleman's headquarters with bullets ricocheting off the building walls around him. Coleman gathered a relief party and King led it to the platoon's position, an act that earned a Military Medal.[17]

To the left of 'A' Company, 'C' Company was harassed by one sniper, who "controlled the crossroads, firing from approximately 400 [yards] with deadly accurate fire." The anti-tank platoon's Captain J.D. Bell brought up a 6-pound gun, "but because of the sniper's agile movement was unable to score direct hits and stop the fire." Deciding he needed more punch, Bell had the platoon's 17-pounder hauled up. Several rounds punched into the building the sniper was using, and he stopped shooting.

The Rileys were increasingly fed up with losing men while trying to minimize damage. Seeing a large number of Germans milling around a water tower serving as an observation post, Lieutenant Colonel Arrell ordered the position engaged by the Toronto Scottish Regiment's 4.2-inch mortars and the battalion's anti-tank guns. A suspected army barracks nearby was also "shot up."[18]

By noon, the Rileys had rendered their area "somewhat more habitable," and German prisoners were "pouring in." The past twenty-four hours had yielded 225 prisoners and "there were many more to come now that things are softening up." To the right, the Royals had won the railway station and yards, and the Essex Scottish started passing through at 1235 hours. The Royals reported that the main highway bridge over the canal was still intact and enemy troops were streaming over it to escape into the city centre.[19]

Hoping to keep the Germans from destroying the bridge but also to cut off its use as an escape route, the Toronto Scottish's No. 7 Platoon hauled its heavy machine guns up onto the roof of the railway station. From this elevated vantage, the crews were able to bring both the large bridge and the smaller one to the east within their arc of fire, "denying the bridges to the enemy." The machine-gun crews killed thirty-three escaping Germans and wounded many more. Return fire from a 20-millimetre gun forced them to move cautiously and slightly wounded two men.[20]

As the Essex Scottish moved through the Royals, the battalions were reminded that "it was against orders to use artillery and tank fire in the culturally sensitive Old Town." The Canadians were to use only infantry weapons and what support the carrier and anti-tank platoons could offer.[21] Major Doug McIntyre's 'A' Company and the carrier platoon led the way. Dogged by persistent sniper fire, McIntyre's men closed up to the canal at 1640 hours. Before them was a swath of open ground and then the waterway. To the left, the main bridge still stood. Nobody expected this situation to last for long, so despite their task being only to secure a jumping-off point on the south bank for 6 CIB's use, 'A' Company's No. 8 Platoon decided to dash across. Meeting "murderous fire," most of the men went to ground short of the bridge.[22] Lance Corporal Max Wright and Private William "Bud" Tasker, however, ran right over with bullets whipping all around them.[23] Both men were "mowed down before they could find cover" on the other side. These deaths defeated "the daring attempt," but the platoon did learn that "the bridge was not prepared for demolition and was capable of carrying vehicles."[24]

Essex commander Lieutenant Colonel John Pangman decided a "quick plan to storm the bridge with troops mounted in Kangaroos."[25]

Brigade sent three of these armoured personnel carriers, but their drivers "became lost and instead of stopping at the [rendezvous] with [the] Essex made the turning and crossed the [bridge], where they immediately came under heavy [Panzerfaust] fire. Two... got back. The other disappeared up the street and was not seen again."[26]

With the two remaining Kangaroos under wing, the Essex Scottish teed up the assault. 'C' and 'D' Companies established firing positions on either side of the highway. Removing its Bren guns from the vehicles, the carrier section positioned them in windows of a building overlooking the bridge. The Toronto Scottish crews were still providing covering fire from the railway station. A Fort Garry Horse 'B' Squadron troop had also arrived and would fire selectively to avoid smashing historic buildings.[27] Major McIntyre's 'A' Company crowded into the Kangaroos, which "sped across the bridge and the open spaces there and took up firm positions in houses dominating" the span.[28] After a short, hard fight, the Essex controlled the buildings. McIntyre's leadership, both during the fight to gain a foothold in front of the bridge and in winning the bridgehead on the other side, was recognized with a Distinguished Service Order.[29] The Essex Scottish concluded 4 CIB's operation for April 14 feeling "proud of the springboard we supplied to 6 [CIB]."[30]

AS THE ESSEX had been winning the objective, 5th Brigade had worked its way in from the west. Brigadier Bill Megill had initially advanced the Calgary Highlanders towards the village of Hoogkerk on the city's outskirts. Once this job was complete, Le Régiment de Maisonneuve was to come up on the southern flank to seize a variety of road and rail crossings, a rail bridge over an east-west-running canal, and a large sugar-beet factory. If Hoogkerk proved "soft enough," the Calgaries would continue into Groningen. The Black Watch formed the reserve, and Megill intended to deploy it to support whichever of his lead battalions met the most success.[31]

The Calgaries started out at 1300 hours with Major Francis H. "Nobby" Clarke's 'A' Company supported by a troop of Fort Garry Horse tanks. Swinging around Groningen's outskirts from the south, Clarke led the battalion in a two-mile "walk up" to enter Hoogkerk unopposed.[32] Lieutenant Colonel Ross Ellis had fallen ill on April 4 and been confined to bed, so Major Dalt Heyland was acting commander and facing his first battalion-sized operation. Establishing a tactical headquarters in the town hall, Heyland decided to advance Captain Mark Tennant's 'D' Company across the open ground between Hoogkerk and the city's outskirts. 'C' Company would then hook northwestward to capture a railway bridge crossing the main ring canal.[33]

While Heyland was arranging things, the battalion's intelligence officer used the town clerk's phone to call a pharmacy that local maps indicated would be passed during the attack. A "puzzled voice on the other end [said] that while most of the local inhabitants were hiding in cellars waiting for the fighting to end, a strong force of Germans and Dutch Nazis were still holding the city."[34] This, plus the scouts returning from a patrol to the canal with two prisoners and a report that they had killed or wounded six other Germans, confirmed expectations that the Calgaries faced another stiff fight.[35]

At 1630 hours, Tennant led his men forward. As they reached a crossroads close to the canal, a six-barrelled 20-millimetre gun opened fire and pinned 'D' Company down. Ellis had been a commander who led from the front. Similarly inclined, Heyland and artillery officer Major K. Degin rushed forward. While Heyland directed the mortar platoon's fire, Degin called in artillery. The combined barrage destroyed the German gun.[36] Heyland stayed up with Tennant as the company pushed into the city, and by 1800 hours its objective was reached. The company had captured twenty prisoners and suffered not a single casualty. 'A' and 'B' Companies had passed through and, despite heavy small-arms fire, reached their objectives at 2030 hours.[37] About five city blocks away stood Groningen's university—their priority for the morning.

'C' Company, meanwhile, had been pushed to the railway bridge, finding it intact but raised. Discovering a row of interconnected barges that extended across the canal, the company skipped across them and then wound back through streets leading to the bridge. Coming to a large barbed-wire barrier, the men started removing it, only to have the structure collapse with a large crash. Everyone held their breath, waiting for the Germans to open fire. When nothing happened, they carried on to a building that overlooked the bridge and canal. From inside, they were well positioned to cover an expected advance by the Black Watch.[38]

Advancing to the south, the Maisonneuves had faced so many tasks that each company operated quite independently. At noon, Lieutenant Colonel Julien Bibeau had sent 'D' Company to capture a crossroads west of the city, 'A' company a road and railway junction also west of Groningen, 'C' Company the sugar-beet factory, and 'B' Company a railway bridge crossing an east-west-running canal on the outskirts. 'B' Company had a rough time pushing through a string of sniper and machine-gun positions but succeeded in capturing the bridge intact, along with two 20-millimetre guns. 'A' and 'D' Companies had earlier reported they were tight on their objectives.[39]

'C' Company had gained the road opposite the beet factory without serious casualties, but as Private Arthur Doiron led the dash over, a 20-millimetre round tore his head off. Realizing the gruesomeness of the twenty-three-year-old's death could cause the rest of the company to falter, Captain Jean R. Beauchemin charged across without looking back. His men followed, and slowly cleared the sprawling factory. Beyond was the railway bridge, and Beauchemin could see 'B' Company still closing in on it. As he led his men out to assist in the bridge's capture, they came under fire from a pillbox guarding a roadblock. The Germans inside were impervious to gunfire and refused demands to surrender. Finally, the company's PIAT operator fired a lucky shot that passed through a firing slit. Only the officer inside survived the explosion. He signalled his intention to surrender, but as he emerged a gun fired from near the bridge, and the officer fell dying.[40] Spotting five Germans wiring explosive charges to the bridge, Beauchemin's men shot them down. Moments later, 'B' Company surged across the bridge and secured it.[41]

'B' Company had suffered the most casualties, among them Private Roland Hains of Trois-Rivières. He had joined the regiment at Laren on April 7, recording in his diary being assigned to No. 11 Platoon. The next day his company commander, Major G. Brosseau, was wounded. Then, on April 11, Hains had the satisfying duty of guarding a large group of German prisoners. On April 14, he recorded fighting near the sugar-beet factory and then, with sadness, that he was wounded and would be evacuated after just a week with the regiment. It was a common outcome for inexperienced reinforcements.[42]

CARRYING 5TH BRIGADE'S advance into the city centre fell to the Black Watch, and Lieutenant Colonel Syd Thomson ordered Captain E.D. Price's 'B' Company and Major J.F. Bailey's 'C' Company to lead. Deciding to cross the canal in the dark early-morning hours of April 15, the two men went forward to liaise with the Calgaries. The previous day's warm weather had given way to a cold drizzle, which limited visibility and so favoured the attacker. Jumping into a rowboat crewed by a Calgary sergeant, they crossed the river and confirmed that the bridge site was a good place to cross. With the bridge raised and its mechanism damaged, the two noticed a long barge tied to the edge of the canal's west bank. Freeing the lines holding one end made it an easy matter to swing the barge crosswise. This impromptu bridge left a gap to the other bank of just four feet, "which the men were able to jump with comparative ease, heavily-laden though they were."[43]

'B' Company's objective was a railway bridge over an interior canal, which was gained unopposed and found intact. However, the swing-type bridge had been turned on its pivot away from the railroad tracks and with the controlling gears locked in place. 'C' Company worked more to the north. Initially daunted by the task of checking the many houses along their line of advance for Germans, Bailey divided each platoon by sections and sent each party to check an assigned row of houses. While the rest of the section stood guard, one man then rang the front doorbell and asked the civilian who answered for permission to enter. By 0410 hours, 'C' Company had canvassed its way through the assigned sector without encountering a single German.

Just after daylight, Thomson ordered the other two companies to cross the barge and pass through the leading companies. 'A' Company crossed without incident, but after the first two 'D' Company platoons and the headquarters section had crossed, a 20-millimetre gun opened fire from the top of a nearby water tower and drove the rest of the men back. The company was at an impasse, until some Dutch bargemen sailed up at the helm of a barge that offered a much lower profile. With the higher barge blocking the German line of sight, the rest of 'D' Company crossed unimpeded on the lower one. A small ferry was soon impressed to carry over the battalion's jeep, carriers, and Wasps.

The pioneer platoon rushed in its carriers to the railway bridge. Using some explosive to destroy the gear controls, the pioneers ran lines out to the bridge and hooked these to the carriers. Engines screaming, the carriers dragged the span around and restored the crossing.

By mid-morning, the Black Watch was well along in clearing the city's northern sector. Whenever a platoon met heavy fire from a strongpoint, a section slipped through the backyard gardens, climbing over the intervening walls to take the Germans from the rear. This unorthodox tactic usually so rattled the defenders that they immediately surrendered. Those who proved more obstinate were burned out of their positions by the Wasps. [44]

When the battalion came to a large city park, the first men stepping into it came under fire from Germans dug into bunkers and slit trenches who were well endowed with 20-millimetre guns and machine guns. A two-hour pitched battle followed, "with our men using PIATS and Brens, rifles and grenades, as well as [2-inch] mortars . . . against the heaviest opposition so far encountered in this operation." At 1555 hours, the company 2-inch mortars were called in and the Wasps "fired a few bursts." The moment the mortars and flame-throwers let up, the rifle companies rushed forward as one. At first, the enemy "gave ground reluctantly, but upon being convinced that we meant to oust him from his prepared defences fled or capitulated." After advancing beyond the eastern boundary of the park, the battalion received orders to stand down, and the Maisonneuves continued the advance. Most Black Watch casualties were suffered during the park fight, but these were surprisingly light considering the intensity of the resistance. Total losses for the day numbered one man killed and seven wounded. The battalion netted 247 prisoners.[45]

South of the Black Watch's area, the Calgary Highlanders had fought for control of the university grounds and a nearby German naval barracks. Between their starting position and the university was a large block of apartment buildings "each with three stor[eys] and each apartment having about four rooms containing several civilians and many snipers." Captain Sandy Pearson's 'B' Company led the attack on these buildings at 1055 hours.[46]

A routine German tactic was to position a machine gun on the corner of a building or in its basement in order to fire up the length of the street. The supporting Wasps retaliated by trundling into their 120-foot range with men aboard firing Bren guns into the overlooking windows to keep snipers at bay, and then letting loose a stream of flame. Pearson found this manoeuvre "extremely effective and horrifying...as soon as you would start to use them prisoners would just pour out into the streets."[47]

When Pearson's headquarters section set up in one apartment to await the conclusion of a firefight in the street ahead, an elderly woman emerged and began brewing up ersatz coffee. Emptying the pot into her best china cups, the woman served it to the grubby-handed soldiers gathered in the kitchen. While she was serving the coffee, a Bren gunner smacked his weapon onto a small hardwood table and opened the facing bay window. He then proceeded to fire bursts at a German position. Obviously alarmed that the heavy steel bipod would ruin her table, the woman offered him a little cushion, which he obligingly placed under it. After accepting a cup of coffee and taking a sip, the soldier set the china to one side and resumed firing.

At the edge of the university grounds, the battalion's mortars lay down a smokescreen to cover the advance by Captain Mark Tennant's 'D' Company, but the cold wind blew it away while the men were still in the open. As the men started to take cover, Tennant yelled, "Get going, you sons of bitches, or I'll gun-gut you myself." The entire company renewed the charge. The Calgary's padre approached Tennant after. "Very crude, but rather effective, Mark," he said.

'C' Company led the assault on the naval barracks, which were surrounded by a high wall. Private John Shaw's platoon found a gate, which could only be unlatched from inside. Stripping off his equipment and handing his rifle to another man, Shaw scaled the wall and dropped down. As he regained his footing, a naval officer with his staff milling behind approached and announced he would surrender to an officer of matching rank. Weaponless, Shaw feigned ignorance while slipping the gate open to let the rest of the platoon in. The sergeant stepped up, handed Shaw his rifle, pointed at the officer and said, "He is surrendered, and if he gives you any trouble shove your bayonet up his you know what."[48] It was 1728 hours, and the Calgaries had won all their assigned objectives and bagged about four hundred prisoners.[49]

WHILE 5TH BRIGADE had advanced on the city from the west in the early-morning darkness of April 15, 6th Brigade had jumped off from the springboard won earlier by 4 CIB. Les Fusiliers Mont-Royal led with their advance lit "plain as day" by parachute flares. Major Elmo Thibeault's 'B' Company was out front with Major George Bergeron's 'A' Company in trail, and by dawn the rest of the battalion was across the canal and pushing into the old centre.[50] At 0615 hours, the South Saskatchewan Regiment joined the operation and both battalions made "slow, but steady progress." The FMR found "street fighting on such a large scale . . . quite a new task for the unit, but on the whole the job was nicely accomplished." While the regiment's casualties were considered moderate, Major Bergeron was among those killed.[51]

The two battalions advanced towards the Grote Markt (Great Market) with its 318-foot Martini Tower and large attached church dominating one corner, but the narrow streets lined by ancient brick buildings were easily defended. The advance ground on for hours of surreal fighting, as "great crowds of civilians . . . thronged the streets—apparently more excited than frightened by the sound of nearby rifle and machine-gun fire."[52] Adding to the chaos was the fact that "hundreds of the inhabitants were drunk, or partially so, from liquor stolen from a German liquor dump. Looting from stores and depots was out of hand for hours until the civilian controls were established by Military Government officials."[53]

Private Charles "Chic" Goodman was a nineteen-year-old wireless signaller in the South Saskatchewan's carrier platoon, having transferred to it from 'B' Company after being passed over for promotion to corporal. The carriers joined the battle soon after the rifle companies, and it seemed to Goodman that the operation was easy. Most of the Germans simply gave up after a few shots were fired their way. When the leading companies came to a long row of barges tied up to the side of a canal, a couple of riflemen would jump down into one and knock on the cabin door. Out of several barges, five or six Germans emerged with hands up, surrendering to a polite knock.[54]

By late afternoon, the situation on the Saskatchewan front was sufficiently stable that Company Quartermaster Sergeant Mickey Faille loaded a jeep with rations and set off to deliver them to his riflemen. Losing his way in the winding streets, Faille strayed into the FMR's boundary, only to have a German officer step in front of him and declare that he would surrender his command to someone of equal or greater rank. Telling him to stay where he was, Faille hurried back to battalion headquarters and returned with Lieutenant Colonel Vern Stott in the passenger seat. They found a large party of Germans all milling about with arms already stacked. Stott told the officer to line his 181 men into a column three abreast and then turned them over to the Fusiliers. Among the officers taken were five oberstleutnants and eight majors.[55]

The fact that so many senior officers were among the surrendered clearly revealed that organized resistance in Groningen was disintegrating and increasingly the defence consisted of small independent units. Some were only looking for a safe opportunity to surrender, while others fought on even as their grip on the city rapidly loosened.

As April 16 dawned bright and sunny—becoming hot during the afternoon—the battle for Groningen neared its end. The South Saskatchewan Regiment and Les Fusiliers Mont-Royal pushed through the morning towards the Grote Markt with the Fort Garry Horse Shermans of 'B' Squadron following. Despite the divisional orders to minimize damage to the old city, Brigadier Jean Allard was in no mood to shed Canadian blood to save architecture. To keep the German defenders pinned, the Toronto Scottish laid down continuous fire with its 4.2-inch mortars.[56]

When the two regiments gained the square, they met fierce resistance from German machine-gun positions in the buildings on the northern side. Approaching from the south, infantry and tanks faced the enemy positions across the square's wide and open expanse. One Fort Garry Sherman inched into the open and was immediately fired on from a gun positioned behind the corner of a building on the square's northeastern corner. Unable to gain a direct angle of fire on the German position, the gunner ricocheted an armour-piercing round off the town hall's west wall and knocked the enemy weapon out with a remarkably deft shot.[57]

With the infantry unable to cross the square, the order was given for the tankers to pound the buildings with their main guns. Soon the enemy—mostly German or Dutch ss—were forced to withdraw, setting fire to many of the buildings as they went. The damage to this sector of the old city was heavy, but both the cathedral and Martini Tower were largely untouched.

Private Chic Goodman reached the square as the battle ended. Out in the centre a horse's corpse sprawled. The moment the last shots were fired, bells in the cathedral and the city's other churches started to peal and people spilled into the square. "Suddenly they're all out there with knives and meat choppers and within minutes there was nothing left of that horse, but its hooves. That was when I realized how hungry these people all really were."[58]

The square was cleared about noon, and soon two German adjutants from the garrison's headquarters approached the FMR's lines waving a white flag. They were hustled to Lieutenant Colonel Jacques Dextraze's headquarters. Groningen's commander, they reported, still refused to surrender, but "his officers and men were fed up and would gladly give themselves up."[59] Deciding to attempt an audacious coup, Dextraze went with the German officers back to their headquarters. He took with him only his interpreter, Sergeant W.T.H. van Workum, and two privates, Gaby Morly and A. Dumaine. The garrison's commander consented to meet Dextraze and after about ten minutes of discussion, during which the futility of the German position was made clear, agreed to march the troops remaining under his control to the FMR lines so long as no civilians were permitted to stand on the streets and jeer them. Dextraze isolated civilians from a route and then marched the German colonel and some three hundred officers and men into captivity.[60]

Except for a few lingering pockets of ss and other die-hards unwilling to surrender, the city was taken. The southeastern sector extending from the Grote Markt to the Van Starkenborgh Canal, which marked the outer limit of the old city, was still not cleared when the fighting mostly ceased at noon. It fell to the Queen's Own Cameron Highlanders to check the area. Little opposition was met until 'B' Company closed up on a major bridge over the Van Starkenborgh Canal. The bridge's lifting station was located on the German side and had been raised. As Captain J.H. Ross directed mortar fire, two civilians—one of them the bridge tender—volunteered to help lower the span. To do so, however, meant crossing the canal by throwing a long ladder over to create a catwalk. A small section of Camerons and the two men raced across under heavy machine-gun fire. The section leader, Lieutenant W.C. McNeill, and one of the civilians were wounded. Once across, the small party forced its way into the lift station and the two Dutchmen managed to lower the bridge. The moment the rest of the company streamed across the bridge, the twenty-six Germans surrendered—ending the Battle of Groningen.[61]

The battle had cost 2nd Division 209 casualties—all from the infantry battalions. About 2,400 Germans were taken prisoner.[62] German fatalities were later determined by Dutch sources as numbering 160 killed outright and about forty dying of wounds.[63] Those Germans who escaped streamed northward in a bid to reach the pocket developing around Delfzijl.

Even before the battle had been joined, plans were afoot to rush 2nd Division eastward to slot in between 4th Armoured Division and the xxx British Corps for an advance on Oldenburg. This movement was quickly put into motion. Brigadier Cabeldu's 4 CIB was among the first to leave, moving more than two hundred miles on April 18. By the afternoon of the following day, the brigade's regiments were all in Germany and taking over a sector of frontage from British battalions.[64] The men would never forget the heady days of liberation in Holland, but henceforth their war was one of conquest.

[22]

Operation Cleanser

———————

THE POTENTIAL OF a prolonged and bloody battle to liberate even one of the great cities in western Holland haunted First Canadian Army headquarters staff, and Groningen had reinforced those fears. By April 16, Twenty-Fifth Army had no prospect of escape and Generaloberst Johannes Blaskowitz and Reichkommissar Arthur Seyss-Inquart remained under strict orders to fight to the bitter end. Despite the latter's entering into secret ceasefire negotiations, no agreement had been reached. And on April 17, the Germans demonstrated the catastrophe they could unleash at a moment's notice by opening a dyke near Den Helder to inundate the country's newest polder—the seventy-five-square-mile Wieringermeerpolder.[1] Seyss-Inquart then warned that if the Canadians attacked beyond the Grebbe Line, he would blow another dyke between Rotterdam and Gouda, causing massive flooding all the way north to Amsterdam—effectively destroying western Holland.[2]

Preferring, however, to successfully conclude the ceasefire negotiations, Seyss-Inquart agreed on April 13 to provide safe passage for two resistance leaders, Dr. Lambert Neher and Jacob van der Gaag, to Allied lines. Fearful that the Reichkommissar would renege on his assurance of "immunity for everything you have done in the past," the two decided their chances of betrayal would be lessened if they crossed separately. Van der Gaag crossed the River Maas that evening by boat, while the following day two German soldiers rowed Neher across later in the evening. Both men were met by Canadian officers and taken to meet Prince Bernhard and other Dutch government officials in Breda.

The prince then flew to Reims to meet General Eisenhower. Neher was flown to London on Sunday, April 15, where he briefed Prime Minister Pieter Sjoerds Gerbrandy, who met afterwards with Prime Minister Churchill. Churchill was sick in bed and grieving the sudden death of U.S. president Franklin Delano Roosevelt three days earlier, but he received Gerbrandy at Chequers, his official country home. Also attending was South African prime minister Jan Smuts. At first, Churchill considered the ceasefire proposal requiring the Canadians to stop east of the Grebbe Line too great a concession. When Gerbrandy and Smuts finally convinced him that the Grebbe Line formed a logical demarcation point, he agreed to pursue the idea with the Americans.

The Dutch, particularly Queen Wilhelmina and Gerbrandy, were dismayed when the Americans and British appeared reluctant. The flooding of Wieringermeerpolder only heightened their anxiety. Dutch resistance leaders were now meeting openly with Seyss-Inquart and his close associate, Dr. Ernst A. Schwebel. Events of each meeting were filed with London, with the NBS commander, Colonel Henri Koot, cautioning on April 18 that "with progressive conquest, foot by foot, nothing but water would be left." He urged acceptance of the German proposal.

Churchill now concurred, fearing operations "would be marked by fighting and inundations and the destruction of the life of Western Holland."[3] General Eisenhower had also written that "for sheer humanitarian reasons something must be done at once."[4] Further, Eisenhower argued that Seyss-Inquart's proposal benefited the Allies, "as it would allow them to hold the Grebbe Line with minimum forces."[5] First Canadian Army might be free to send far more divisions to Germany.

Not until April 24, however, did the Combined Chiefs of Staff telegram Eisenhower permission to negotiate directly with Seyss-Inquart.

Two days later, Eisenhower cabled Colonel Koot authorization for a German officer to enter Allied lines and begin negotiations in the vicinity of Amersfoort.[6]

Acting on his own initiative, Eisenhower decided that the Canadians should conform to Seyss-Inquart's Grebbe Line boundary and sent orders via Field Marshal Montgomery on April 12 that First Canadian Army "stand fast before the Grebbe Line, a dozen miles east of Utrecht."[7] Lieutenant General Charles Foulkes confirmed this intention on April 15, writing, "I [Canadian Corps] will clear enemy from Western Holland between the IJssel and the Grebbe Line." This completely reversed instructions he had issued three days earlier to "clear the Germans out of Western Holland," with 1st Canadian Division directed towards Amsterdam and the 49th Division towards Rotterdam.[8] Foulkes was already faced with losing 5th Canadian Armoured Division once its April 18 deadline for concluding the Operation Cleanser advance to the IJsselmeer passed. "Jesus, George," he carped to his chief of staff, "I wouldn't be surprised if our next orders will be to vacate Arnhem and come back over the Rhine." Brigadier George Kitching replied that the corps should just go back to Italy "where we could be used to better purpose."[9] It helped little that the two Canadians knew they must still drive the Germans back to the Grebbe Line and could expect a tough fight achieving this purpose.

GERMAN FORCES BETWEEN Apeldoorn and the Grebbe Line had been thrown into disarray by Fifth Canadian Armoured Division's rapid thrust north from Arnhem to the Apeldoorn–Amersfoort highway at Voorthuizen. To the east, 361st Volksgrenadier Division was on the run from Apeldoorn. Despite 5th Canadian Armoured Brigade's tanks and mobile infantry having reached Voorthuizen, no cohesive barrier blocked the Germans' lines of escape through to the Grebbe Line. Even Voorthuizen and nearby Barneveld were in German hands and too strongly defended for the armour to clear alone.

Major General Bert Hoffmeister had established his divisional headquarters about a half-mile southeast of Otterloo on the evening of April 16. Captain D. Wagner, in charge of headquarters' security, realized the rapid advance had left the division "stretched all the way from Arnhem to Barneveld" and lacking protected interior lines. Neither flank to the east or west was secure and divisional headquarters could well face an attack. Wagner posted a guard of fifty-four infantrymen and positioned four Shermans travelling with the headquarters on the corners of the perimeter. The division's three command tanks—stripped of main guns to make room for large radios but still equipped with Browning machine guns—were to cover the approaches from the north and west.[10]

Hoffmeister's headquarters was not isolated. The Irish Regiment of Canada, having cleared the town during the day, remained inside Otterloo while preparing a morning attack on Harskamp—two miles to the north—where a sizeable German force was reported. The division's Governor General's Horse Guards (GGHG) reconnaissance regiment would support the attack, so their regimental headquarters was inside Otterloo's tall-spired church next to the building the Irish commander was using. 'C' Squadron's Shermans were parked on one side of the town.[11]

Close to Hoffmeister's headquarters was a British 3rd Medium Regiment, Royal Artillery battery, while in open fields bordered by a pine forest on the eastern outskirts 17th Field Regiment, Royal Canadian Artillery had deployed its guns to fire on Harskamp. Lieutenant Alex Ross had laid out the gun lines for the regiment's 76th Field Battery and deployed its 'F' Troop on the west side of a street running out of Otterloo that intersected with the road from Apeldoorn in the town's northeast corner. 'E' Troop was on the opposite side of this street. A short distance behind 'F' Troop, the 37th Battery's 'C' Troop was positioned, while 'D' Troop was farther to the west and north of the Apeldoorn road. 'A' and 'B' troops of the 60th Battery were to the south on the western edge of the town. Because all the regiment's flanks were exposed, Lieutenant Colonel G.A. Rankin had ordered the guns not be dug in as usual. Rather, the gun line was set out in the open, so each 25-pounder could be turned to fire in any direction. Lacking protective infantry, Ross arranged "for the Brens, rifles, and small arms ammunition to be brought to the guns of my ['F'] Troop and for the gunners to dig slit trenches sited so as to give us as much defence as possible." The battery's vehicles were hidden in nearby woods or parked next to the town's cemetery, which lay just behind the gun lines. Ross established his gun troop headquarters in a small brick house that had a lean-to on one side, where wireless equipment and the artillery board for directing fire were positioned. Ross took a jeep and drove a couple of miles north without seeing any signs of life. The dirt road was "dusty, unused, and unmarked." Shortly after dark, Ross was relieved to see three Irish infantrymen walk through the gun position and set up a 2-inch mortar and Bren gun. "It was a thin screen but better than none at all."[12]

Immediately to the north of Otterloo, the road from Apeldoorn forked—one branch proceeding southwest to Ede and the other northwest to Barneveld. Another road followed a more northerly track, through Harskamp to join the Apeldoorn–Amersfoort highway east of Voorthuizen. With 361st Volksgrenadier Division on the retreat, a large number of its troops headed this night directly along the Apeldoorn road towards Otterloo. Leading the march were four understrength battalions. These totalled about one thousand men drawn from the 953rd Volksgrenadier Division, 858th Grenadier Regiment, and a hodgepodge of other units—mostly artillerymen fighting as infantry. The best troops in this formation were the grenadiers of the 858th Regiment, which had been in almost constant action since June 6, 1944. Under orders to retain their heavy equipment rather than abandon it, the Germans had two possible routes, the closest being through Harskamp. Four hundred Germans went that way and escaped without incident. The remainder marched straight into Otterloo just after midnight.[13]

First to arrive were about twenty-five Germans led by a single officer. "Yelling like a gang of fanatics and firing their automatic weapons madly," they attacked the Irish headquarters adjacent to the church. A burst shattered the window in the room where Lieutenant Colonel L.H.C. Payne was sleeping, and he was trapped for several minutes, until some headquarters staff came to his rescue. Four Irish were wounded before the attackers were driven off. Several dead Germans were strewn outside the building. As the enemy patrol withdrew southward, it ran into the Irish 'A' Company, which cut it up and wounded the officer.[14]

One prisoner was taken, and the division's interrogator, Lieutenant J. Hobson, reported that the man "was certainly drunk and smelt strongly of schnapps." The patrol had swept the divisional POW cage just before it met 'A' Company. Hobson and the three guards had dived into a ditch because there was "a lot of lead flying about," thanks to the Germans, who "were whooping and shouting in a drunken manner."[15]

No sooner was this infiltration driven off than 76th Battery reported a large German force approaching along the road from Apeldoorn. Suddenly, a mortar round exploded next to the 25-pounder commanded by 'F' Troop's Sergeant Nelson Humble. Grabbing rifles and Bren guns, the sergeant and his men dived into slit trenches. Seeing shadows, Humble yelled, "Hockey." When nobody responded with "Puck," he and his crew opened fire. A couple of shadows started screaming loudly, which so unnerved Humble he dashed out and took the surprised Germans prisoner. Two of the men had been slightly grazed, but otherwise they were unharmed. Humble escorted the four or five Germans back to the battery headquarters, handed them off, and raced back through thickening mortar fire.[16]

A large chunk of shrapnel flew through the open door of the little brick house that served as the battery's headquarters, and there followed the distinct slap of metal striking flesh. "That hit somebody," Sergeant Bill Copithorn announced. "Yes, me," 'F' Troop's Sergeant Major Gordon Bannerman replied. Struck hard in the abdomen, Bannerman retreated to another room to check his injury. Lowering his pants, he saw just a thin bloodstain on his stomach that looked harmless enough.[17]

Throughout Otterloo mortar rounds were exploding, and all telephone lines connecting the artillery batteries to regimental headquarters had been severed, leaving wireless as the only form of communication. Lieutenant Jim Stone was in charge of the 76th Battery's headquarters. With Germans swarming out of the darkness, he reported that the battery "must have some help, but would hang on as long as they could."[18]

Gunner Roland Bouchard's battery was cut off by Germans he could see digging into a ditch next to the street leading into Otterloo.

Deciding the battery would be overrun unless it was reinforced by infantry, the driver-mechanic jumped into his 15-hundredweight truck and mashed the accelerator to the floor. Enemy small-arms fire raked the truck as it hurtled towards the Irish headquarters, which was about twelve hundred yards distant. By the time he pulled up next to the house opposite the church, his truck was burning fiercely. Bouchard, who would be awarded a Military Medal, received the disappointing news that the Irish were too involved themselves to help out the artillerymen.[19]

It was 0130 hours, and the Irish 'B' and 'C' Companies were tangling with seemingly hundreds of Germans trying to overrun the northern part of the town. 'B' Company was guarding the approaches to the regiment's headquarters, while 'C' Company was astride the road from Apeldoorn and in between the gun positions of 37th Battery. The latter company was short a platoon that had been sent to observe German positions at Harskamp.[20] 'D' Company was out to the west and immediately south of the 37th's 'D' Troop. Guarding the southern approaches to the town, 'A' Company had just dispatched one platoon under Lieutenant J. Maltby to reinforce Hoffmeister's divisional headquarters. The Irish Regiment was spread thin.[21]

There were no clear lines; Germans intermingled with Canadians. The tankers were reluctant to operate beyond their harbours for fear of firing on their own, and so kept their guns dry. Recognizing the conundrum, Payne requested that 'C' Squadron send one tank to drive up and down the streets to intimidate the Germans. Sergeant Wood set out in a squadron headquarters tank, moving up the road towards the advancing Germans. Ordered not to fire, he simply drove back and forth, with Germans repeatedly running alongside shouting, "Canadians surrender, Canadians surrender."[22]

Nobody could make sense of the confused situation. The first shots had caught Private Sam Doggert's section from 'B' Company stripped down to their long johns and fast asleep. Doggert and his buddies were out of their sacks and into uniforms in thirty seconds. Jumping out a window, he started gouging out a slit trench with a bayonet. As a great gaggle of Germans ran past, their new platoon commander, Lieutenant C.H. Clawson, yelled, "Surrender, you are surrounded!" All "they did," Doggert recalled, "was shoot him." The wounded officer was carried off the field.[23]

The situation at 37th Battery was desperate. Lieutenant Stone called for another battery to shell a mortar firing from a position just two hundred yards from his command post. Responding, 60th Battery lobbed shells from a range of only 750 to one thousand yards and silenced the mortar.[24] The command post was drawing way too much German attention. Bullets were coming through the walls and windows, shattered glass flew everywhere, and several fires burned inside. Gunners Ken Nicholson and Tom Coll were both wounded. Lieutenant Ross, who had just returned from a fruitless foot foray back to the town in search of reinforcement by a tank or infantry, set off on a second dash across the bullet-swept open ground to try again. "Sergeant Major, can you get me out to an aid post?" Nicholson called to Bannerman from where he was being bandaged by Signaller Vic Bennet. "Hold on, Ken, Lieutenant Ross should be back with help soon and we'll get you out," Bannerman urged. Some time later he asked a man how Nicholson was doing. "Ken is dead," the man replied. By this time everyone had evacuated the command post and was crouched behind an exterior wall or sheltering in nearby slit trenches.

Bannerman saw houses and vehicles burning everywhere he looked. Gunfire crackled and flashed. Shells and mortar bombs exploded throughout the town. Suddenly, a corporal from the Irish appeared beside him. Everyone else had abandoned the command post and withdrawn to either 'E' or 'F' Troop's lines, so Bannerman and the corporal headed for the nearest 'F' Troop gun. They had just started out when eight or ten Germans pulling a Maxim heavy machine gun on wheels came towards them. The two men dived into a slit trench. "Will we take them on?" Bannerman asked. Pointing out that Bannerman had only a revolver while there was just a half-full magazine for his own Sten, the corporal shook his head. He told Bannerman he would get through to 'C' Company and bring help, then dashed off. When the Germans had passed the slit trench, Bannerman ran to 'F' Troop's lines.[25]

Lieutenant Stone and other officers on 17th Regiment's front lines kept sending reports of German strength back to their headquarters.

The general estimate was eight hundred to one thousand, which Major D.L. Gordon believed was an exaggeration, so he was "systematically dividing every report of the number of enemy . . . by 100."[26] This unwarranted reduction caused everyone at headquarters to completely fail to recognize the seriousness of the situation.

On the town's left flank, Hoffmeister suffered no delusions. He estimated that a brigade of Germans had infiltrated the Canadian position. "They were swarming all around the place. I'm sure they didn't expect to find us there. They were in our sentries and outposts before they realized it and it was quite a night, a highly confusing night. People were shooting in all directions and I think it was the one and only time in the war when all the clerks and batmen and so on around divisional headquarters had an opportunity to fire a shot at anything." Hoffmeister was in the open, trying to control things, "until such time as the whole thing started closing in and it looked as though I could have just been nipped off. At that time, I got into the armoured command vehicle, locked the doors and prepared to stay there to fight it out. There were batmen and so on underneath the armoured command vehicle shooting at Germans as they were going past, but I had to maintain contact and communications. This was the only way I could, from inside the vehicle, for which it was intended. We kept it up all night and it was a fascinating battle."[27]

The 17th Field artillerymen described it more as terrifying. Fighting the Germans face to face, 'F' Troop was in particularly bad straits. When several Germans attempted to overrun the gun commanded by thirty-nine-year-old Sergeant Pop Barkwell, he took them on with bare fists, while his crew shot down other men who closed to within a few yards. This saved the gun.[28]

Five hundred yards back, the nine driver-mechanics from 'F' Troop had all been wounded defending their vehicles. They fell back into Otterloo and joined the Irish.[29] Behind them the vehicles were aflame, ammunition exploding. The fires lit up the gun lines. Lieutenant Ross, having made three fruitless trips back to the Irish for support, finally took cover in a slit trench with one of the gun sergeants. At 0330 hours, fifteen or more Germans tripped over the men hunkered in slit trenches next to their guns. "We could see them clearly as they came toward us, no mistaking their identity especially the potato mashers they carried and their close fitting helmets. The gunners waited in silence. When the outlines seemed to tower over us, I gave the word. One burst from our weapons and the outlines changed shape and then faded. Trouble was we didn't kill all of them, and four or five of the wounded couldn't get away. I fear I must carry the cries of one of them to my life's end," Ross wrote. "We could not evacuate them or give them much assistance. That's one of the puzzling things about combat. You can kill a man and forget about him, but wound him badly and you face quite a different circumstance."

Unable to stand the cries of pain, Gunner William Bull left his slit trench to give the wounded water. Wrapping one man in a blanket, he placed him in a nearby slit trench. Even though Bull was disobeying Ross's orders, the lieutenant thought it "the act of a brave, humane man, especially as the field around us was a ragged kaleidoscope of explosives—our own and the enemy's—shrapnel singing off the steel of our guns."[30]

In 37th Battery's area, the Germans were threatening to overrun the position, forcing the gunners "to abandon all pretence of firing the guns except over open sights as we were now defending ourselves."[31] They fired shells fused for airbursts that exploded seconds after leaving the barrel and found "it very effective."

Farther back, 60th Battery was able to direct targeted fire as requested by any of the beleaguered defenders, despite being under constant mortar fire. So were the big British battery's mediums. To engage targets at ranges of 2,700 yards or less, however, this battery's shells "were barely clearing the houses and trees." Somewhere in the darkness the British gunners knew there was a church, but they only saw its spire when a shell tore the top away.[32]

On the 60th Battery gun line, Sergeant Edward "Eddy" Knight and his crew fired their 25-pounder with furious haste, ignoring the mortar shrapnel and machine-gun bullets whipping through the air. Suddenly, a large German rushed the position. Unarmed, Knight tackled the man. Wrestling the Schmeisser from the German's grasp, Knight—a stocky man with muscles hardened in the coal mines—got his hands around the man's throat. Knight was throttling the German when Gunner Jim Cathcart pushed a rifle barrel under one of the sergeant's arms and killed the man with a bullet to the chest.[33] Knight calmly returned to firing the gun. When a report reached the battery that the Germans might be sending tanks into the town, Knight ordered his crew to push the 25-pounder up a street to where it could cover the major crossroads and protect the rest of the battery from attack. Knight won a Distinguished Conduct Medal.[34]

Only a single self-propelled gun actually got into Otterloo and was driven off at 0600 hours by fire from the 37th Battery firing at a range of three hundred yards.[35] Shortly after, six tanks closed on the town and fired four shots, three of which struck the church and the fourth the Irish headquarters. Two Irish were killed and three wounded. When the GGHG's No. 1 Troop moved to engage the tanks, its commander, peering through the smoke and ground mist, thought they looked like Churchills. When the tanks fired once more, he reluctantly knocked the leader out with a high-explosive round and then managed to signal that Otterloo was in friendly hands. Fortunately, none of the British crew was injured "and their officer apologized profusely, announcing that he had mistaken our troops for Germans."[36]

These tanks were manned by British royal engineers, and at least one of the tanks was a Petard mounting a 290-millimetre spigot mortar that fired a 40-pound round with a 28-pound explosive warhead intended to pulverize fortifications from close range instead of a main gun. The Petard started spitting "flying dustbin" rounds out beyond the 76th Battery's position.[37]

At dawn, most of the Germans either fled back towards Apeldoorn or took to the woods on either side of Otterloo to escape westward, but about three hundred dug in along the verges of the narrow road on the edge of the town. Corporal Walter "Red" Asseltine led the Irish Wasp section towards them.[38] Asseltine was in the lead carrier when it "came under intense small arms fire from three sides at point-blank range, in many cases at four or five yards." Despite the German fire, Asseltine formed the Wasps in a row and they proceeded to advance, spraying the ditches on both sides with flame. When a German Panzerfaust team managed to knock out the second Wasp in line, Asseltine spotted their position in some brush. As it was beyond the range of the flame-throwers, he leapt out of the Wasp and charged the Germans with a Bren gun. Asseltine killed them all, then dashed back through a hail of fire to the Wasp and resumed his fiery march for a total of three hundred yards before running out of fuel. Turning the Wasp about, Asseltine trundled back, picking up the crew of the knocked-out flame-thrower and bearing them to safety. His Distinguished Conduct Medal citation credited Asseltine with killing seventy Germans, wounding many more, and leaving the "remainder so demoralized that the tactical picture was completely changed and the town was quickly cleared of the enemy."[39]

In the aftermath, morbid curiosity drew Lieutenant Ross to view the "ghastly spectacle. The Germans died neatly, all facing the same way and nicely spaced . . . I could see no marks on them—just dead men and already swelling up." He stripped a "Gott mit Uns" belt buckle off one corpse and walked away.[40]

Hoffmeister roamed in a jeep to meet with the troops and congratulate them on their all-night stand. When Sergeant Major Gordon Bannerman told him how Ross had gone three times back to try and bring reinforcements up, Hoffmeister asked to meet the officer. Bannerman hurried to get him, but Ross was busy sorting out 'F' Troop and told him, "I don't have time to talk to Generals this morning." Returning to Hoffmeister, Bannerman said Ross was unable to come but offered his thanks for the general's "concern and interest."[41] Both Lieutenants Ross and Stone were decorated with the Military Cross.

The Canadians present considered the battle of Otterloo their strangest. For six and a half hours, artillerymen had directly engaged German infantry at point-blank ranges and with no support from amour or infantry. The Germans had fought with a desperate, but disorganized, ferocity. Canadian casualties had been slight. The 17th Field had three killed and twenty wounded. They claimed killing thirty-one, wounding nine, and taking 127 prisoners.[42] Irish casualties were three other ranks dead, three officers and fourteen other ranks wounded. They estimated two hundred Germans killed in total from a suspected force of about eight hundred and recorded only twenty-one prisoners.[43] The GGHG had four men wounded, two of whom remained on active duty. Later in the morning, however, Corporal Herbert Stitt, who held a Distinguished Conduct Medal, was run over by a truck and killed. The regiment's historian was moved to comment: "It seems paradoxical that one who had come unscathed through the thick of so many engagements should have lost his life in an accident when the last real scrap was over."[44] Later analyses determined that the German force totalled about six hundred men, with ninety killed and 114 captured. The rest scattered, and most were either killed or taken prisoner over the ensuing days.[45]

WHILE THE "FIERCE little skirmish" at Otterloo, as the army's official historian dubbed it, had played out, the British Columbia Dragoons also fell in the direct path of Germans escaping from Apeldoorn.[46] At 0030 hours, fifty Germans charged out of heavy mist to attack 'B' Squadron. Two hours of confused fighting followed before the Germans broke off. At 0537 hours, still dark with mist cloaking the ground, the Germans tried again—this time with a force of mostly "young boys between the ages of 13 and 16," who numbered between 150 and two hundred. Throwing grenades and firing dozens of Panzerfausts, the boy soldiers charged directly into fire from 'B' Squadron's main guns and machine guns. A Badger (a Ram tank mounting a flame-thrower) rushed to where No. 2 Troop was facing a hard time and "flushed the hysterical youths out of their positions," the troop leader related. "I shall never forget the awful picture of them running back up the ditches and roadways with their clothes and bodies covered in burning fuel. Many of them were killed and a good number were taken prisoner."[47] The Dragoons suffered two casualties, one of them, Trooper Leo C. Clyne, killed.[48]

Despite the German attempts to break through its front, April 17 dawned with 5th Division resuming its advance towards the IJsselmeer, Hoffmeister ever mindful of the April 18 deadline for its transfer to 11 Corps. South of the Apeldoorn–Amersfoort highway, Barneveld had been bypassed the day before by the Lord Strathcona's Horse. Patrols from 11th Canadian Infantry Brigade's Cape Breton Highlanders sent patrols to test the defences, which reported "that the garrison was thinning out." Deciding to strike fast, Lieutenant

Colonel Boyd Somerville sent one rifle company, supported by a troop of tanks and the battalion Wasps. "Brushing off slight opposition," 'D' Company entered the town, and when the rest of the battalion arrived at 0500 hours, its men were standing in the town square sipping hot tea provided by the townspeople.[49] Voorthuizen was likewise easily taken by the B.C. Dragoon's 'B' Squadron and a Westminster Regiment company, proving that the Germans were giving up the fight in favour of reaching the Grebbe Line.[50]

There remained one major line of resistance. The Germans fought hard to keep a road running through Putten and Nijkerk immediately south of the IJsselmeer, as it provided the only remaining escape route for 361st Volksgrenadier Division. When the New Brunswick Hussars and Strathconas passed the Dragoons on either side in a race towards the coast, both met costly resistance here.

Yet the most the Germans could do was save remnants of the units east of the Grebbe Line from the closing divisions of 1 Canadian Corps. From the east, 1st Canadian Division and the British 49th (West Riding) Division were overrunning and capturing Germans by the hundreds while fighting through occasional resistance pockets. The British division, supported by 1st Canadian Armoured Brigade's Calgary Regiment, fought a sharp five-hour action on April 17 at the town of Ede, southwest of Otterloo. Hooking out on the flanks of the advancing infantry, the tankers ambushed several anti-tank and artillery positions from the rear. But the Dutch SS defending the town withdrew into a heavily fortified factory complex. Artillery was called in and after a ten-minute barrage, Captain J.W. Rainey's 'C' Squadron "went over the crest, advanced to the factories and punched holes in the brick walls. Wasp flamethrowers followed, sweeping slit trenches and the interior of buildings. In some cases enemy MGs fired to the last. Some attempted to escape, were captured or cut down by an 'A' [Squadron] troop under [Lieutenant R.G.] Maltby, who waited for them in the rear. From this time on resistance rapidly collapsed. 'A' [Squadron] entered the south part of the town, shot up a barracks, took the [rail] station, cleaned out the southern half of the town by 1310 hours."

'C' Squadron then "committed the error of harbouring in the main square, where hundreds of ecstatically happy civilians cheered, climbed on the tanks, made normal work impossible," commented the regiment's war diarist. He added, "These civilians were happy, but their faces were stamped with the mark of malnutrition or downright starvation."[51]

To the north, 1st Division's Royal 22e Régiment enjoyed an unopposed ten-hour advance from Apeldoorn to Barneveld and arrived at midnight, establishing a link with 5th Division and freeing it to concentrate on the escape corridor to the north by the afternoon of April 17. The 8th Hussars advanced on Putten with 'A' Squadron leading on the left and 'C' Squadron the right. Less than five miles from the IJsselmeer, they were confident of bringing things to a quick conclusion despite the poor condition of the sandy tracks bordered by scrubby pine woods. Three hundred yards east of its starting point at Voorthuizen, Major Lloyd Hill's 'A' Squadron came under intense fire from a German position about twelve hundred yards distant that was "bristling" with six anti-tank guns "manned by good troops." Knocking out two of the guns, Hill's tankers were stumped as to the location of the others and were taking fire not only from them but also from about 150 supporting infantry heavily armed with machine guns and Panzerfausts. Although Hill was short-tempered, his men considered him "a dandy fighting leader." Pressed for time, Hill was in no mood to look for ways around the German force. Instead, he threw the squadron's four troops out on line, and the tanks charged with guns and engines "blazing and snarling."

Lieutenant Ivan Harper's troop bored towards a road, the officer intending to hurtle across before the Germans could bring any anti-tank gun to bear. But his driver was new and, confused, yanked hard on the right tiller to set the Sherman grinding right up the road towards an 88-millimetre gun. "I was sure we'd had it ... But the Germans were apparently more astonished than we were," Harper said. "This must have been the last thing they expected. Anyway, they deserted their gun. We could see them running away ... We destroyed the 88." Leading the troop into a gap through the woods, Harper got behind three self-propelled guns and knocked two out. Before anyone could fire at the third, the crew abandoned it and fled. Harper's actions earned a Military Cross.[52]

'A' Squadron emerged victorious at 1550 hours from its wild gun-fight at point-blank range. Seven anti-tank guns had been destroyed, an ammunition dump blown up, and at least fifty Germans killed. In exchange, four tanks were lost and one suffered mechanical breakdown. No Hussars died and a few suffered light injuries. Hill received a Distinguished Service Order.

To the right, 'C' Squadron also bumped anti-tank guns, but these were poorly positioned and all three were knocked out at the cost of one Sherman. The farther the two squadrons advanced, the more Germans appeared. 'A' Squadron rampaged through a small column of "soft-skinned" vehicles, shooting them up with high-explosive shells from a hundred yards off. Then they tangled with "a hornet's nest" of three 88-millimetre guns and four 20-millimetre anti-aircraft guns, destroying them all before the Germans managed to get off a shot. Luck ran out soon after, when two tanks were knocked out by anti-tank guns so well concealed the tankers were unable to bring them under fire. Lieutenant Colonel J.W. Eaton ordered Hill to pull back and let the Westminsters send a company to deal with the guns. When the motorized infantry arrived, the Germans abandoned their guns and ran.

Nine hundred yards farther on, 'A' Squadron ran into another ambush set by a large infantry force supported by two self-propelled guns and a 105-millimetre artillery piece. Armed with at least fifty Panzerfausts, the infantry lit up the tanks with flares that blinded the crews. 'A' Squadron frantically extricated itself from the storm of shells and Panzerfaust bombs, but lost six tanks before breaking free. The squadron might well have been wiped out entirely, a report later concluded, had it not been for the track links welded to the hulls and turrets to increase the armour's density. Every armour-piercing round or Panzerfaust bomb that struck a track was either deflected or failed to penetrate the tank. The first of two Panzerfaust bombs striking one Sherman "hit the track links, and although these were melted and mangled, the explosion did not penetrate the armour. A second round hit the front of the turret, which is the heaviest amour on the tank. This portion was not covered by track links and the explosion penetrated the turret."

At 2030 hours, 'C' Squadron also got stuck in front of a German strongpoint and, as he had with 'A' Squadron, Eaton ordered it to pull back for the night. April 17 was among the hardest fighting days the Hussars had experienced and ended the earlier impression that campaigning in Holland constituted a stroll compared to the Italian slog. 'A' Squadron had only four of seventeen tanks operational. Two 'C' Squadron tanks had also been lost. Amazingly, only Trooper John Burpe Wallace had been killed and nobody else was seriously wounded. The two squadrons accounted for fourteen anti-tank guns, five anti-aircraft guns, four vehicles, two ammunition dumps, about eighty Germans killed, 120 taken prisoner, and "an enormous number of bicycles captured."[53]

To the west, the Strathconas' advance to Nijkerk had been one of frustration. A single narrow dirt track offered the only route, so 'A' Squadron led with the Westminster's 'C' Company riding on the hulls in order to quickly deploy forward of the Shermans to meet infantry ambushes. Shortly after starting out at 1400, they entered what became known as the "battle of the roadblocks."[54] Deep ditches either side of the track constrained the tanks to driving up in single file, so the first roadblock of "heavy green logs securely braced to form a [five-foot] wall" stopped the tanks cold. An armoured bulldozer was required to remove the obstacle. A thousand yards ahead its twin stood, this time defended by infantry supported by artillery fire that hammered the Shermans with shrapnel until the Westminsters cleared the Germans off and the advance could continue.

"At this rate," Lieutenant Colonel Jim McAvity realized, "it would have been impossible to fight our way through to Nijkerk before dark." He told 'A' Squadron's Major R.J. Graham to check whether a paralleling railway shown on the map would serve as an alternative route. Setting out alone, Graham's Sherman was immobilized a few minutes later by a high-velocity shell. The officer was severely wounded in the chest. Situation hopeless, 5th Brigade ordered the advance abandoned, with the Strathconas instructed to hook instead through Putten once the Hussars secured it. Nijkerk would be left to 1st Division, while 5th Division would close to the coast at the small harbour of Harderwijk.[55] The Strathconas had suffered three officers wounded, five other ranks killed, and eight more wounded.

During the night, intelligence reported that Harderwijk was being used by the German Kreigsmarine to evacuate troops by ship to Amsterdam. Brigade ordered the Strathconas to gain the "high ground south of Harderwijk and shell the enemy taking off in small boats."[56]

But first the Hussars had to take Putten, which they set out to do at first light, with the squadrons converging on it along several different routes. It soon became clear that during the previous night, the Germans had withdrawn. Aided by partisans, Putten was cleared by mid-morning, and at 1035 hours, Captain H. Snell reported his reconnaissance troop had gained the IJsselmeer and "cut Holland completely into 2 sections."[57]

Pushing out from Putten, amply assisted by Dutch resistance, the Strathconas reached Harderwijk at 1630 hours "without a shot being fired."[58] The local underground chief jumped onto the lead tank, and waving "aside the masses of joy-crazy people, he led them through the narrow twisting streets of the quaint old port, through ancient masonry arches, to the beaches. There he pointed out several ships, small fishing craft most of them, full of Huns. A few rounds of 17-pounder resulted in one ship sunk, then a white flag appeared above the others. Meanwhile, the tanks covering the fields east of the town got in some good shooting as more tried to escape there.

"Suddenly it was all over; all over but the cheering, as the saying goes. It had been a wonderful day . . . here, in the narrow old-world streets of Harderwijk, we had come to the end of the journey."[59]

The Strathconas had only intercepted the last stage of the Kreigsmarine in Holland's final naval operation. After the failed breakthrough at Otterloo, about a thousand men from 953rd Volksgrenadier Division had turned for Harderwijk. Beginning at 0800 hours on April 18, a small flotilla of naval ships had evacuated most of them before the Strathconas arrived.[60]

Harderwijk's liberation concluded 5th Division's operations in western Holland. After the briefest break to quickly service vehicles and tanks, the division moved towards the Delfzijl region and the Canadians' final battle in the Netherlands.

Sound Tactical Plans

CANADIAN CORPS'S REMAINING 1st Canadian Infantry Division and the British 49th (West Riding) Division continued towards the Grebbe Line. There was little resistance. While the Canadian division's 2nd and 3rd Brigades led the advance, its 1st Brigade mopped up hundreds of stragglers wandering between Apeldoorn and Barneveld.

When 2nd Brigade reached Barneveld, the Loyal Edmonton Regiment remained behind there as the reserve. On April 19, Lieutenant Colonel Jim Stone was approached by Dutch resistance. They reported about five hundred Germans holed up in a forest to the north who wanted to surrender. Taking the surrender personally was too good an opportunity to pass up, but Stone distrusted the Germans enough to take with him a fighting column consisting of 'D' Company, six carriers, a Saskatoon Light Infantry heavy machine-gun platoon, a tank troop, a troop of self-propelled anti-tank guns, and a section of Edmonton pioneers. Brigadier Pat Bogert cautioned, "Don't get engaged. If they want to surrender, fine. But don't get into any big battle. It's not worth it, we're moving through the country anyhow."

The column soon met a roadblock, and the typical deep ditches blocked passage to the tanks. Stone tried to blow it out of the way with the 17-pounder tanks, but the rounds bounced harmlessly off the obstacle's hard concrete. Snipers started taking potshots at the column from the surrounding woods.[1]

Battalion intelligence officer Lieutenant Keith MacGregor stood next to Stone's carrier. Its machine-gunner was blazing away with the Bren, and spent casings bounced off the vehicle's side. "Suddenly I felt a thump in the shoulder and thought I'd been hit by a casing, so moved to get out of the way . . . and realized that my whole left side was strangely numb. Then I did what I said I would never do. I had seen people do this so many times and always thought, 'How foolish.' I grabbed myself on the left side and felt the numbness. Looked astonished at the person next to me and said, 'I've been hit.'"[2] MacGregor's wound proved not to be serious, and he went on to have a post-war military career.

Stone figured a bullet that had whistled past his head was the one that got MacGregor. Damned if he was going to let the snipers get away with shooting one of his men. Stone radioed Bogert. "Get us a squadron of Typhoons to dive bomb this wood," he said. Reminding Stone not to get tangled in a dogfight, Bogert summoned the aircraft. "That was the amount of support we had by this time. Poor old Jerry had nothing, but we could call up Typhoons whenever we liked. So in came these Typhoons and rocketed the wood while I disengaged and pulled back to Barneveld."[3] Stone had overstated the Germans' helplessness. Including MacGregor, snipers had wounded six Eddies.[4]

Avoiding costly fights was increasingly the order of the day. As one Princess Patricia's Canadian Light Infantry officer described it: "The Battalion has been ordered to advance in a slow and stately manner."[5] Rumours were rife down to the battalion command level by April 20 that a deal was being brokered with the Germans. From Barneveld to the Grebbe Line before Amersfoort was barely seven miles, but 2nd Brigade advanced at a snail's pace to give the Germans time to withdraw.

Yet resistance sharpened the closer the Canadians came to the Ems River, which was now identified by divisional headquarters as the line upon which the advance would halt. On April 24, when the Seaforth Highlanders of Canada patrolled close to the canal, the carrier platoon came under deadly sniper fire that killed Lieutenant

Frank Richard Perrett and Corporal Alfred "Frenchy" French. Perrett had joined the regiment in 1939 and French in 1940. The next day, 'C' Company was sent to clear up the resistance, and Corporal John Myles was shot and killed by a sniper. Private George Francis Votary was then killed by mortar fire. Both men were relative newcomers, having joined the regiment in the fall of 1944.[6]

April 24 was also a bad day for the Edmontons' Lieutenant Robert Dudley. He knew the corps's plan was to push the Germans "back . . . gently so they wouldn't retaliate on the Dutch cities where people were dying of starvation. So we were closing No Man's Land slowly, giving the Germans plenty of time to withdraw without fighting." But some Germans in a wood next to a farm refused to cooperate, which resulted in Dudley's No. 14 Platoon leading a 'C' Company attack to clear them out. Dudley was in the centre with a section on either flank, his headquarters group right behind, and then the platoon's last section on the tail end. Standard formation for a job the platoon had carried off countless times before.

In the second-storey window of the farmhouse, Dudley spotted a German geared up for action. "I decided the thing to do was throw a grenade through the upstairs window. And when it blew upstairs, hopefully taking the Germans out, we would come in the bottom of the building. The normal technique for an experienced infantryman is to pull the grenade pin, let the striker lever come off and count to two and throw. Then, if they pick it up to throw it back at you, they're mush. Five second fuse and I heaved the grenade and it went right through the window like Joe DiMaggio throwing one across the plate. As it crashed through the window, I headed for the door with Corporal Hinkley and his section in hot pursuit. I kicked open the door and moved to the far side and started working the place over with my Sten gun, and there bouncing down the staircase is my grenade. They simply kicked it downstairs. And I said to myself, 'Shit, this is nowhere for Mrs. Dudley's little boy, Bob.'

"I started to hit the deck, but it blows up in my face. I got twenty-three holes. Damn thing happened in slow motion. I'm lying on the floor. My Sten gun is long gone. I've been hit in the wrist and both legs. And I'm trying to get my pistol out because there's a German at the top of the staircase and he's got a Schmeisser. I figure he's going to try and write me off. I'm lying on my right side and I'm fumbling around on my left. Probably [would have] shot myself in the foot if I'd managed to get my pistol out. If he'd fired the Schmeisser the way he had been trained to fire, instead of trying to aim it, he'd have got me. But the next guy through the door was Bill Hinkley and it seemed like slow motion. I thought to myself, 'How terribly undignified. I am lying here and I can see Bill Hinkley's khaki clad battle dress on either side of me and he blows this German away at the top of the stairs . . . I can feel hot spent shell casings hitting my ass as Bill shoots this guy. We left three dead in the place and took ten prisoners . . . I got evacuated and sort of ended the war."[7]

April 24 was the last real day of combat for 1 Canadian Corps, which thereafter entered into what its troops would remember as a "phony war"—the troops facing the Grebbe Line from across the Ems River. Strict orders prohibited any firing on the Germans opposite unless directly attacked. "Even if the brigade sector is being fired upon there will be no retaliation," the West Nova Scotia Regiment war diarist complained. Even when the Germans opened up with "spasmodic fire . . . from machineguns, mortars and artillery," the West Novas were forbidden to respond. Like the rest of the division, the battalion was holding a sprawling ten-thousand-yard frontage that had been reduced to a quagmire by deliberate inundation. To keep dry they constructed above-ground shelters from branches, small tree trunks and other heavy vegetation so that their positions "eventually resembled a muskrat colony."

Back of the front lines, a peacetime atmosphere developed. Nijkerk became the battalion's rest centre, "with movies, games, canteen, shower baths, and clean dry clothing available, and daily ten men from each company went back . . . on a 24-hour pass." Barneveld likewise served 2nd Brigade.[8] In this bizarre quasi peace, 1 Canadian Corps awaited word as to whether their war was truly to be soon done or they must once more advance to take western Holland by force.

ON APRIL 22, Field Marshal Montgomery issued his last campaign directive. Twenty-First Army Group was "to capture Emden, Bremen,

Hamburg, and Lübeck, and to clean up all German territory north of this general line." Second British Army would carry Bremen, clear the Cuxhaven peninsula, secure a bridgehead over the lower Elbe, and capture Lübeck to "seal off the Schleswig peninsula." Operating under British command, XVIII U.S. Airborne Corps—including 6th British Airborne Division and its 1st Canadian Parachute Battalion— would guard the army's right flank. Second Army's final operation would be to occupy Hamburg and Kiel in a thrust that would clear "all German territory north to the frontier with Denmark."

First Canadian Army received very specific directives. In western Netherlands, 1 Canadian Corps would "not for the present operate further westward than the general line now held east of Amersfoort. Further instructions will be issued if it should become necessary, later on, to attack the Germans in western Holland and to liberate that area." 11 Canadian Corps, meanwhile, would guard the Second Army's left flank by advancing alongside it into northern Germany.[9] With General Harry Crerar having left the day before for medical treatment of a shoulder complication, Lieutenant General Guy Simonds again temporarily commanded the army.[10] Montgomery told him to assault Oldenburg, while advancing south of it to maintain contact with Second Army's drive on Bremen. The Canadians must also capture the ports of Wilhelmshaven and Emden, clearing the Germans out of the peninsula between the Ems and Weser rivers.[11]

Simonds retained his corps command while also heading the army, because with 1 Canadian Corps largely inactive, he need only concern himself with the divisions fighting in northern Holland and Germany.[12] The corps sprawled across a wide frontage that spanned all northern Holland from the coast to the German border and then seventy miles east of that. Save the Delfzijl Pocket area on the northeastern coast, all of northern Holland was liberated, and the job of collapsing the pocket was to be carried out by 5th Canadian Armoured Division.

As Major General Bert Hoffmeister's division was still en route to the region, 3rd Division was instructed to bring pressure on the Germans inside the pocket until relieved. Once Major General Holly Keefler handed off to Hoffmeister, 3rd Division would move to

Germany, clear the ground west of the Ems River, then force a crossing at Leer, and advance up the river's east bank to Emden. Simonds wanted 3rd Division to get across the Ems River quickly, so that 1st Polish Armoured Division could then sideslip to advance on a northeasterly axis parallel to 4th Canadian Armoured Division's right-hand hook from Bad Zwischenahn east to Oldenburg. Guarding Second Army's left flank, 2nd Division would also approach Oldenburg from the south.[13]

The multiplicity of tasks facing the Canadians presented endless challenges. The Delfzijl Pocket was particularly worrisome. It was heavily fortified and protected from direct attack out of the south by extensive flooding. On April 20, 3rd Division's 7th Infantry Brigade had attempted to push in the outer defences with a pincer attack on either side of the inundations. The Regina Rifles and Royal Winnipeg Rifles advanced on the western flank, while the Canadian Scottish Regiment approached from the southeast.[14]

Hugging the bank of the Ems Estuary, the Reginas slopped through polders riven with ditches and canals over which all bridges were blown. In the distance they could see Germans retreating, but overtaking them was impossible. Periodically, the big guns on Borkum Island in the estuary's mouth fired salvoes that caused no casualties, but the massive explosions put the men on edge. Occasionally, the batteries across the estuary by Emden and those around Delfzijl churned the ground around them with high-calibre shells. As April 21 drew to a close, the Reginas met their first real opposition at Spijk—its defenders subjecting them to heavy mortar fire. Behind the village, the men could see the fortifications surrounding Delfzijl and reported that it "may prove a hard nut to crack if the enemy elects to fight."[15]

South of the Reginas, the Winnipeg Regiment had advanced at dawn on April 21 with the armoured cars of the 17th Duke of York's Royal Canadian Hussars. Lieutenant Colonel Lochie Fulton had developed a careful route for reaching the battalion's objective of Appingedam but found it barred by blown bridges. The companies and supporting Hussars began weaving along narrow lanes and tracks in "a continuous trial and effort against bad conditions of ground and well-sited defences."[16] Still, by nightfall, they closed on the town. Appingedam, with its population of about seven thousand, stood on the opposite side of a canal whose bridge lay collapsed in the water. As the armoured cars closed on the canal, several were knocked out by anti-tank guns. At this point in the war, Fulton was reluctant to lose men over the pocket, so he hoped to find a bridge, cross over, and surprise the Germans in the town into surrendering.

Night patrols turned up a single rickety bridge, which 'A' Company slipped over at dawn with 'C' Company close behind.[17] "Blown bridges, snipers and MGS make the going very difficult. Our [casualties] are becoming very [heavy]," the regiment's war diarist recorded. It took all day to gain Appingedam's outskirts. Facing them was a large brickyard, and 'A' Company counted seventy to a hundred Germans dug in along rail tracks running east from it. How many Germans were in the brickyard was unknown. Fulton deployed searchlights on the canal's western bank and used them to blind the Germans for ninety minutes. At 0500 hours, the lights snapped off, and the rifle companies attacked. A fierce fight developed in and around the brickyard, but as Fulton had hoped, the Germans had been caught by surprise and more than one hundred soon surrendered. By late afternoon, the town was taken.[18]

Six men had died, and among the wounded was the popular 'A' Company officer Major D.B. Robertson.[19] By 2215 hours on the evening of April 23, the battalion, along with the Reginas, was relieved by the Perth Regiment.[20]

South of Delfzijl, the Canadian Scottish had expected their objective of Wagenborgen could easily be taken by a single company. Major Anthony Compton-Lundie's 'D' Company had approached the village in the dark morning hours of April 21. Funnelled by ditches and canals onto a narrow lane, they encountered a series of roadblocks "covered by machine-gun and 20-[millimetre] gun fire as well as plenty of mortar and artillery support."

Lieutenant Colonel Larry Henderson had Compton-Lundie hold on the village's outskirts until he could send the anti-tank, carrier, and mortar platoons forward. When the company advanced behind these platoons' covering fire, they met an enemy that clearly "knew the area like the back of his palm." The leading platoon, under Sergeant J.E. Dodd, used the cover of a deep ditch next to the main road to close on the village. As the platoon gained the first buildings, a Wasp raced forward to assist. Running over a mine, the Wasp's fuel ignited—"burning both occupants to a crisp. Our platoon suffered quite heavy casualties, and upon coming up to about 150 yards of our objective, there were only eight of us left. We went to ground . . . after having two men shot through the head who were operating the Bren gun." At nightfall, the Germans surrounded Dodd and his remaining men, forcing them to surrender. 'D' Company had taken a mauling. Not only was Dodd's platoon lost, but the tactical headquarters set up in an old barn had been pounded by artillery and engulfed in flames. Compton-Lundie was among several other officers and men killed or wounded by the shelling. In all, the Can Scots lost fourteen killed, twenty-one wounded, and fifteen missing and presumed captured.

'D' Company's losses reverberated through the battalion, and the "complacent attitude . . . brought on by the long advances against little opposition . . . quickly transformed into a rock-hard determination to make the enemy regret his action." Sending the shattered company back to form a reserve, Henderson brought the rest of the battalion up to the edge of the village during the night. In the morning, he briefed his officers. The Germans undoubtedly expected an early attack, but Henderson decided to let them fester through the day and then strike behind a mortar and artillery barrage at 2300 hours. 'A' Company would attack from the west, 'B' Company the southwest, and 'C' Company was to come up on the eastern outskirts to cut off the retreat.

As the artillery lifted, 'A' Company struck out across open fields towards the village and was immediately struck by withering fire, proving the Germans were unimpressed by Henderson's plan. Casualties mounted, but the company gained the edge of Wagenborgen. Men were just starting to board up windows and pile furniture behind doors in a couple of houses to fortify them when the Germans counterattacked. Company commander Captain S.L. Chambers saw a "whole platoon of [Germans coming] down the road in single file and the first dozen were mowed down at about a 10-yard range by No. 9 Platoon. Another party of Germans set fire to one of the two houses occupied by No. 7 Platoon, forcing Corporal Barra's section to withdraw to the other house. This party of Germans made the mistake of getting too close to the glow of the burning house and were picked off by No. 8 Platoon."

While 'A' Company was repulsing the counterattack, 'B' Company had gained the village by stealth, and at dawn both companies started putting the squeeze on. Two hundred Germans soon broke out of the village and moved directly towards 'C' Company's ambush site. No. 15 Platoon allowed the Germans to practically close on it before the men opened fire with four Bren guns and fifteen rifles. "The enemy was caught flat-footed and paid for it." Platoon commander Sergeant B.C. Parson advised over the wireless that the area immediately right of the company was a perfect "killing ground" for the battalion's mortars. Moments later, mortar rounds started exploding and the "eastern approaches to Wagenborgen became a death trap to the enemy."

As this slaughter was underway, another large German force moving to the north of the village was brought under artillery fire, creating the unintended effect of driving them into Wagenborgen. 'A' Company was immediately surrounded and fighting "against heavy odds." Henderson told the company commanders in the village that he was sending tanks—surprise news, as divisional headquarters had said there were none on offer. Fortuitously, however, a squadron of 5th Division's Governor General's Horse Guards had arrived earlier than expected to relieve the Can Scots and now sent a troop to help the infantrymen.

As the lead tank closed on the village, however, it was knocked out. Turning left rather than right, the three survivors trundled into a German ambush and two were set on fire by Panzerfausts. The survivor fled, leaving it to the Can Scots to win their battle alone. Wagenborgen was filling with Germans pouring in from the north, so 'A' Company's Captain Chambers and 'B' Company's Major Earl English directed artillery down all around their positions. Thinking the Germans were "too disorganized to be putting in a counterattack, [English] decided to hold fire until they were in an open field on our left flank which they would have to pass through. Five Brens and two

2-inch mortars were set up and as the enemy entered the field at least 90 percent were killed or wounded, the rest being taken prisoner."

Repeatedly, 'A' Company added to the toll by holding fire until the Germans were just yards from their fortified buildings. Then they tore into them with deadly accuracy. Late in the afternoon, the remnants of 'D' Company dashed through enemy fire to deliver badly needed ammunition and food. Soon thereafter the balance tipped, and by nightfall the village was in Canadian hands. In the early morning of April 24, the Irish Regiment of Canada relieved the Can Scots.

Despite the bitterness of the fighting, losses for the three companies engaged on April 23 proved surprisingly light—just five killed and ten wounded. German losses were estimated at two hundred killed, wounded, or taken prisoner. "Battle trained and hardened veterans, even with a good sprinkling of new reinforcements among them, [proved] more than a match for the quality of troops the enemy had at his disposal," the Can Scots' regimental historian concluded.[21]

WHILE 3RD DIVISION'S 7th Brigade had been opening operations against the Delfzijl Pocket, 8th Brigade had embarked upon the task of clearing the west bank of the Ems River. This was a required first step to enable the division to force a river crossing at Leer and free 1st Polish Armoured Division for its move to the northeast. The Rheiderland Peninsula west of the Ems River was typical polder country, "flat farmland with dyke roads, the surrounding ground being impassable to vehicles of any sort. Consequently it [was] necessary to 'plug away' along the available roads. Craters had [to be] filled or bridged under the most unpleasant conditions, for the enemy knew his ground well and most of the passable routes had been fully registered by his heavy coastal guns."[22]

The North Shore (New Brunswick) Regiment had started things off on April 22 at 1400, advancing out of Brual on a short hop to Diele—about one and a half miles distant. The 13th and 14th Field Regiments were shelling suspected German positions and the village, as 'A' Company led with three Crocodile flame-thrower tanks in support. Once 'A' Company reached its assigned objective, 'C' Company would pass through, and in turn 'B' Company would later move to the column's head.[23] Just beyond the start line, a Crocodile hit a "mat of mines. One crew man got out, one was burned to death, and two more were trapped." Despite the flames and exploding ammunition, Sergeant Wes Chambers and Private Arnold Astle dragged the British tankers out of the wreckage, including one man with severely burned legs. After this mishap, the rest of the advance proceeded without incident. By 1700 hours, the battalion was digging in west of Diele.[24]

At 2200 hours, the Queen's Own Rifles moved through and headed out into the darkness. The only opposition met came from artillery, which dogged the companies throughout the advance. There were no casualties until 'C' Company entered the hamlet of Holthusen at 0200 hours the next morning. As the shelling increased, several snipers opened fire. One man was killed before the hamlet was cleared. The battalion started sweeping the surrounding countryside and lost another man to a sniper. Repeatedly, large groups of men rushed the Canadians, arms raised and waving. Rather than German soldiers surrendering, these proved to be French, Russian, and Polish POWs forced to work as labourers for the German farmers. "Some had been in captivity since 1939. All were very happy."[25]

Lieutenant Colonel Steve Lett was anything but, this day. Under orders to take two weeks' leave in England, he reluctantly turned command over to Major Elliott Dalton. Both knew the war would likely be over before Lett returned, and leaving his men to fight through to the end without him seemed wrong.[26]

Left of the QOR's advance, Le Régiment de la Chaudière had advanced through the early morning hours of April 23 to a set of railway tracks five hundred yards east of Bunde at 0830 hours. Both battalions were within two miles of Weener, the French Canadians facing it from due west and the QOR the southwest. At 1100 hours, the North Shores passed the latter battalion and headed in.[27] No. 1 Troop of the Sherbrooke Fusiliers' 'A' Squadron provided support.[28]

During the Orders Group preceding the attack, Major Blake Oulton had pleaded for a planned artillery bombardment to be delayed because his 'C' Company could never reach the start line on schedule. Lieutenant Colonel Neil Gordon had airily dismissed Oulton's concerns.[29]

By the time 'C' Company advanced at 1045 hours, the artillery had been silent for fifteen minutes. Sniper fire plagued the infantry, while the tanks were repeatedly held up by large craters blown into the road. At 1100 hours, a heavy artillery piece opened up from a hidden position, but combined fire from the tanks and supporting field regiment silenced it. Shortly after noon, the force reached Weener's outskirts.[30] Out in front, Lieutenant Jack McKenna's platoon had an entire section killed or wounded by Panzerfaust volleys. The Germans fired the Panzerfausts high so the bombs would strike buildings on either side of the North Shores to shower them with fragments of brick and steel. Seeing McKenna's platoon taking a beating, Oulton ordered it pulled back. As the platoon withdrew, McKenna had to carry Sergeant Joe Hennigar out piggyback style because he had taken shrapnel in the posterior. Once the men were clear, Oulton called down a heavy barrage, which broke the resistance. When the attack began again, more than a hundred Germans surrendered. Most were marines and other naval personnel.[31]

The first days of fighting in the Rheiderland peninsula set the tone for 8th Brigade's operations here. Each day, the battalions pushed farther north. On April 24, the North Shores cleared Bingum, which stood across the river from Leer—3rd Division's gateway to the eastern bank and the launching point for its drive on Emden. After another three days, in which infantry and tanks were repeatedly brought to a near standstill by extensive road cratering and deliberate flooding, the peninsula was finally declared secure. On April 27, the QOR reached the peninsula's north coast, taking the fishing villages of Pogum and Ditzam. While approaching Ditzam, 'D' Company became badly separated and its platoons ended up disorganized. As a single section entered the village, its sergeant was challenged by two German sentries armed with Schmeissers. The section leader raised his pistol and demanded that the Germans surrender, and their machine pistols clattered to the ground. "On being asked if there were more of their comrades in the house, they declared that there were only civilians. The [sergeant] entered and brought out the 'civilians'—15 of them, complete with steel helmets, uniforms, and kit." The rest of the Germans in the two towns surrendered with little fuss, and by day's end the battalion had rounded up five hundred prisoners.[32]

WITH THE PENINSULA clear, the way was open for 9th Brigade to mount an amphibious attack against Leer on April 28. Situated at the confluence of the Ems and Leda rivers, Leer covered the roads running north to Emden. Protected by the rivers on three sides and by marshes on its northern side, the large town was ideally suited for defence. The Germans had added to this by destroying all bridges crossing the two rivers, so Simonds had decided an assault by storm boat would be necessary. Storm boats were small open-hulled craft powered by an outboard motor and operated by Canadian engineers. Brigadier Rocky Rockingham and his staff expected "an opposed landing . . . as air photographs showed weapon slits dug along the dykes surrounding" the town. From across the Ems, Rockingham studied the dykes with binoculars and saw Germans moving about behind the slits.

At Leer, the Ems was a broad 300 to 350 yards wide and was influenced by tides that limited use of the few suitable boat-launching sites to high tide and the slack current that followed. Unable to find reliable tide charts, the Stormont, Dundas and Glengarry intelligence officer spent twenty-four hours huddled beside the river, measuring the tidal rise and fall.

Rockingham's planning was complicated by Simonds's insistence that the bridgehead be firm and secure before night fell, so that engineers could begin bridge building under cover of darkness and without German interference. Accordingly, Rockingham set the assault for 1500 hours. The tide would be at its highest point then, with sufficient time left before nightfall to secure the bridgehead. However, this meant the boats would operate in broad daylight, something usually avoided. The only solution was to lay on an extensive artillery program that included smothering the opposing shore in smoke to blind German observers.[33] In addition to 3rd Division's three field regiments, Major General Holly Keefler secured the army's 11th Canadian Field Regiment and 7th Canadian Medium Regiment. He then reached out to the British and came up with four more medium regiments, two heavy regiments, and one sub-unit of super-heavy 9.2-inch guns. Keefler's chief gunner, Brigadier L.G. Clarke, designated ninety-one specific targets, allotting a set number of guns to each.[34] Also firing in support of the crossing would be 'A' and 'C' Squadrons of the Sherbrooke Fusiliers. In the afternoon hours preceding the attack, Typhoons would intensively strafe targets inside Leer.[35]

The crossings were to be made in three different spots at precisely the same time "to prevent the enemy from concentrating his defence."[36] One North Nova Scotia Highlander company would launch from the south bank of the Leda River—rendered secure the previous day by 7th Canadian Infantry Brigade—and attack the narrow peninsula that guarded the entrance to Leer's harbour. Assembling on the west bank of the Ems about two miles south of Leer, the Highland Light Infantry would load three companies into thirty boats and drift downstream to land at the junction of the two rivers. Assembling at Bingum, the Glens would cross the Ems directly to assault Leer's western outskirts with a first wave of two companies. Also taking to assault boats to support the two battalion-sized attacks would be a heavy machine-gun platoon of the Cameron Highlanders of Ottawa (MG). Once these initial crossings were complete, the rest of the North Novas would be ferried across to assault the town's southern outskirts.[37]

At 1425 hours, the guns opened with a shattering bombardment that artillery observers reported was "excellent, as burst after burst was seen along the dykes where the enemy was entrenched." In front of the North Nova company, however, the opposite bank was too close for the guns to risk firing on it, and a persistent wind made any artillery smokescreen "impractical." To compensate, 'D' Company's Major Kenneth Nelson Webber had the platoon's mortar section fire smoke while a platoon of Cameron Highlanders and all available Bren guns of the nearby Canadian Scottish Regiment raked the opposing bank.[38] At the designated moment, Webber waved a hand and the rifle platoons and engineering crews hauled the boats over the dyke and across thirty yards of marsh before splashing into the river. The engineers raced the boats across at top speed, cutting the engines just in time to skid the craft up against the shore. 'D' Company tumbled out, each platoon sprinting towards its assigned section of dyke. Most of the defenders were "still cowering in their slits." Three machine guns and four 20-millimetre anti-tank guns were overrun before their crews fired a shot. Pushing inland, Webber saw the HLI landing at the mouth of the Leda. When a large number of Germans attempted to withdraw from in front of the Highlanders, the North Novas opened up from the flank "and either killed or captured" them.[39]

The three companies aboard the first wave of the HLI flotilla had swept down the two miles of river and found the artillery fire on its landing site so "effective that the enemy had had enough by the time the boats touched down."[40] A large number of prisoners were taken, and the battalion established its bridgehead "in record time." Entering Leer, the enemy "returned a hail of sniper fire . . . and also made use of his Panzerfaust against the infantry. However, the first phase of the attack was speedily completed and the troops pushed on."[41]

To the north, the Glens met serious trouble, despite the fact that most of the leading two companies reached the opposite shore just four minutes after launching. A couple of boats suffered engine failure and capsized. Three men aboard one of the boats were unable to swim, and Major J.A. Stothart saw them being swept helplessly downstream. Sprinting through a minefield to get alongside the men, Stothart dived into the river and managed to pull two safely to shore. He then swam after the third man and succeeded in rescuing him as well. 'B' Company's Major Jack Forman and his two signallers had been aboard the second capsized boat. All their wireless equipment was lost, and the men were carried by the current back to the west bank. On the opposite shore, Captain Don Stewart took over the company and led it through a sharp fight for control of the dyke. 'A' Company's landing was a fiasco. Unloading in 'B' Company's area, the troops sunk into waist-deep water choked with weeds, which slowed getting ashore.

Quickly sorting order out of chaos, 'A' Company's veteran non-commissioned officers got each platoon headed towards its designated area. Sergeant Fred Haworth's leadership was typical.

Advancing his platoon in section bounds, Haworth put in a rapid assault across the dyke that overwhelmed several machine-gun positions. Instead of shooting one German machine-gunner, Haworth jumped on his back, yanked him from behind the MG42, and chucked him into a deep water-filled ditch.[42]

By the time 'C' and 'D' Companies crossed over, thirty minutes after the first wave, the situation was mostly in hand. But three of their boats were sunk by German fire. While the men in one waded ashore, fifteen men in the other two boats drowned. These two companies led the assault into the town, where fierce street fighting broke out.

Once the HLI and Glens gained Leer, the North Nova companies in reserve began crossing. When one boat was swamped after its motor failed, five more men drowned, but otherwise the crossing was without incident. The battalion quickly passed through the HLI and entered into the raging street battle. By nightfall, 9 CIB had advanced far enough to enable the engineers to start bridging operations without interference. But the river and weather proved formidable foes, with winds, the tide, and waves hampering ferrying attempts. Persistent engine failures also disrupted operations.[43] As a result, plans to hurry the Wasps and carriers of the North Novas across were not carried out.[44]

Night brought "the most confused fighting" for 9 CIB, Rockingham later wrote. "The enemy took advantage of his local knowledge, and at times fought with the greatest dash, and bravery. Our positions were not clearly defined, thus great care had to be taken to avoid shooting friendly troops. A halt was finally called during the night."[45]

Lieutenant Colonel R.D. Hodgins, who had assumed command of the HLI on April 7 when Lieutenant Colonel Phil Strickland was appointed to serve on the division's general staff, set his tactical headquarters in a house while it was still dark. His staff had just finished getting the wireless sets and other gear operational when they "found themselves surrounded by a [group] of enemy. MGS across the street covered all exits and a Panzerfaust proceeded to perforate the house. Aid was forthcoming as detachments from three [companies] stormed down the street and drove off the attackers." Hodgins decided there was no point in the companies fighting further during the night, "as lighting was poor and the task almost impossible."

As the sun came up on April 27, the slow business of clearing Leer began. The HLI advanced through the north part of the town, running into groups of Germans "that pop up from cellars [while] snipers covered most open areas."[46] Unexpectedly, the resistance suddenly softened. By noon, the HLI had consolidated on the eastern edge of the town, and Brigadier Rockingham reported Operation Duck—as the amphibious assault had been named—complete. Except for the Glens, casualties had been light. The HLI had just four men wounded, and the North Novas reported no losses other than the five men drowned. Except for its fifteen men drowned, the Glens had only two others killed and two officers and thirty-one men wounded.[47] The army's official historian largely credited a sound tactical plan "and the determination of the assaulting troops" for the operation's rapid success.[48]

BY LATE AFTERNOON, 7th Brigade had three battalions across the Ems and was expanding the bridgehead eastward. At 2130 hours, the brigade's attack kicked off with the Regina Rifles on the right and the Royal Winnipeg Rifles the left. The Reginas were to sweep the ground between the southern edges of Julianen Park to the Leda River, while the Winnipegs secured the park itself. Both battalions met only scattered resistance from Germans mostly happy to surrender. Advancing through the night, the two battalions gained the outskirts of the village of Loga by dawn. At 0700 hours, the Canadian Scottish passed through "and thrust into the rubble piles of Loga, meeting only scattered opposition but taking quite a number of prisoners."

Once the village was secured, the Reginas pushed out at 0900 hours on April 30 towards a group of buildings dominated by a large barracks complex. 'B' and 'D' Companies led. The battalion had no information on likely enemy strength, "but in view of the light opposition encountered by our [brigade] generally, no one, least of all the [commanders] of either [company] figured on any sort of a fight. This was to be the usual methodical check-up on houses in the area for hidden and scared [Germans]." Each company was supported by a Wasp section, pioneers to clear booby traps and mines, and a single 6-pounder anti-tank gun.[49]

Leading his 'D' Company platoon along "a road across a wide, flat, open, water-sogged meadow toward the river," Lieutenant Walter Keith saw the large naval barracks off to the left. He had just turned his back on it when a bullet whizzed past his right ear with a mighty crack that deafened him for hours. Realizing the sniper must have recognized him for the platoon's leader and tried for a head shot, Keith led his men in a dash to a water-filled ditch, where they all took cover. Captain Dick Roberts was commanding 'D' Company. When he suggested carrying on, Keith argued they should stay put until 'B' Company cleared the barracks. Roberts agreed.[50]

Entering the barracks complex, 'B' Company's leading platoon was attacked by Germans throwing grenades and firing small arms. Everyone scattered safely to cover, and then the Wasps swept up and blasted the building with flame, which convinced twenty-five Germans to surrender. But the remaining defenders decided to make a stand—Captain Ken Sunstrum and his men locked in a drawn-out battle against eighty naval marines, who "decided to fight rather than throw in the sponge. They were not fanatics—they were good well disciplined marine troops," a Regina report later concluded. Lacking artillery support and possessing no mortars, the marines were armed only with Schmeissers, grenades, and some Panzerfausts. "While their defences . . . were organized, this could be described as unorganized resistance, as the enemy fought from behind well fortified positions in the barracks buildings, content to inflict casualties on us, yet reluctant to continue the fight when in danger of suffering casualties themselves. Why they decided to make a stand is somewhat of a mystery, but it does testify to the total lack of information the enemy had of his own or our troops' positions in the closing days of the war. Interrogation revealed that they were carrying out orders and they did not know resistance had completely crumbled in other parts of the area."

After several hours, the marines fell back to a fortified building where they manned "both the basement and upstairs sandbagged windows with machineguns and Panzerfausts. The Wasps were too vulnerable to this overhead fire to be successfully committed . . . nor could a good shot be got at it with the [anti-tank] gun." Sunstrum deployed his PIAT men, who hammered the building with fifteen bombs "fired from almost point blank range (under 50 yards). The PIAT explosions, in addition to blasting the face of the enemy officer responsible for the fight, set fire to the building with the result they capitulated. With this capitulation a few stray stragglers and snipers were rounded up. This one point was manned by 1 officer and 34 other ranks. Our casualties were 3 killed and 4 wounded, all by small arms fire."[51]

From the ditch to the south, Lieutenant Keith and the rest of 'D' Company watched in amazement as the moment the shooting ceased, about two hundred German marines "came streaming out of the barracks and ran as fast as they could to surrender to us! I remember the field being full of Germans waving white flags. I remember looking down at one of our Bren gunners, his finger was on the trigger and his knuckles were white. One word from me and he would have opened up on those stupid idiots. I think I'm glad I said nothing, but I'm not sure."[52]

By day's end, 7 CIB had taken more than five hundred prisoners, and the last resistance in the Leer area ceased. Already 9 CIB was moving towards Emden and the 8th Brigade for Aurich to seize crossings over the Ems-Jade Canal, but 3rd Division had fought its last real battle. The ensuing days would see its brigades moving slowly northward across increasingly difficult ground made harder to navigate by "extensive demolitions." It would still be short of either objective at war's end.[53]

Some of the carnage left in the wake of the Battle of Otterloo. The corpse of the horse that drew the German ammunition wagon lies next to a destroyed anti-tank gun. This was the main road coming into Otterloo from Apeldoorn. Jack M. Smith, LAC PA-134483.

above · Left to right, General Johannes Blaskowitz (wearing leather coat), Lieutenant General Paul Reichelt (Twenty-Fifth Army's chief of staff), Brigadier George Kitching, Lieutenant General Charles Foulkes, interpreter Captain George D. Molnar, and Prince Bernhard (Dutch lion on shoulder patch clearly visible) discuss details of the surrender agreement in the hotel in Wageningen. Alexander M. Stirton, LAC PA-133321.

top right · Wireless operator Private MacKeays announces the news of the war's end on May 5, as several men of the Seaforth Highlanders of Canada throw their balmorals into the air. This obviously staged photo is at odds with the general sense of weary disbelief that most Canadian soldiers reported feeling. Michael M. Dean, LAC PA-134450.

bottom right · As part of Operation Eclipse, thousands of German soldiers streamed across Holland in long columns to return to Germany after the surrender. This column consists of soldiers from the 20th Fallschirmjäger Division. Note how many of them appear to be teenagers. Jack H. Smith, LAC PA-191988.

During April and the first few days of May, jubilant scenes like this played out again and again in small towns and villages across Holland as the Canadian troops passed through, leaving a free people in their wake. On April 17, this Calgary Tank Regiment Sherman—heavily up-armoured with tracks welded onto every surface possible—rolled into Ede after a sharp battle on the outskirts. Possession of author.

Crossroad Ambushes

W HEN APRIL 22 dawned, 4th Canadian Armoured Division was still hemmed up inside the Küsten Canal bridgehead south of Bad Zwischenahn. Although the Germans were mostly inexperienced naval marines, the terrain favoured them. Everywhere north of the canal the countryside consisted of "endless stretches of wet ground, interlaced with countless ditches and streams. The maps were full of treacherous bogs and ponds; movement—particularly armoured movement—was restricted to a few routes; and these were vulnerable to counter-attack. In this country even an inexperienced unit, if determined, could hold up an entire division."

Despite devastating artillery and air support that left the "main road leading north from the canal . . . literally strewn on either side with German dead," 10th Infantry Brigade had only managed to deepen the bridgehead two miles.[1] The Lincoln and Welland Regiment had suffered such heavy casualties achieving its meagre gains the previous night that its rifle companies had to be reinforced by men from the support company. An attempt during the day to outflank the Germans concentrated before the main road running due north bogged down before a heavily defended streambed, and the Lincs fell back to their start line.[2]

To the left, the Argyll and Sutherland Highlanders also suffered casualties for minimal gains. They faced the Aue River and behind it the small town of Ostercheps. Tying several assault boats together to create an ad hoc bridge enabled 'B' Company to cross. By the time 'A' Company was strung out in an extended line on the boats, the Germans zeroed in with mortars. The third platoon in line was savaged, with five men being killed and ten wounded. Captain S.F. Day and the other two platoons, however, gained the opposite shore and managed to win a toehold on the village's outskirts, through which 'C' and 'D' Companies then passed. As night fell, the Argylls were well inside Ostercheps but so cut up that they were unable to prevent Germans from infiltrating buildings behind their forward positions. When 'D' Company faced being cut off, Lieutenant Colonel Bert Coffin ordered it back to the lines of 'A' and 'C' Companies.[3] Major Bill Whiteside was just moving to comply when the company was attacked from all sides. A splinter from a Schmeisser round shattered against a wall, pierced Whiteside's right eye, and blinded him. Refusing evacuation, Whiteside continued to direct the company's defence through a five-hour fight. When the Germans broke off the action, 'D' Company's fifty survivors pulled back. Whiteside lost all sight in his injured eye. For his action that day, he received a Military Cross.[4]

Neither battalion made any gains on April 23, despite intense support by rocket-firing Typhoons. At midnight, the Algonquins moved through the Argyll positions inside Ostercheps, only to have its lead company mauled when a supporting artillery barrage fell short.[5] Fourteen men were killed or wounded, but 'D' Company pushed on to the edge of the village. 'B' Company then moved out into the open country beyond. Supporting artillery again fired short, causing eight casualties, but the advance never wavered. When 'C' Company took the lead, it also lost a man to friendly fire. Subsequent investigation determined that the shells fell short because after each shot fired, the recoil pressed the guns deeper into the soft ground, lowering their range. Major George Cassidy dismissed the incident as an unfortunate cost of war when "weighed against the number-less times we received ace support from the guns." He was more disturbed to see that recently "the men invariably became careless during the consolidation process, and fell victim to snipers. The same thing occurred this night, for in the hazy moonlight, it was quite possible to spot our men, particularly in open fields, and several more casualties, one of them fatal, resulted from this."

Morning dawned sunny and warm, a break from the bone-chilling "rain and icy winds" of the past week. Back at the Küsten Canal, bridges were now in place with tanks and other support vehicles streaming across. Out front, the Algonquins closing on Edewecht, three and a half miles north of the canal, were supported by a couple of tanks from Major Jim Tedlie's depleted British Columbia Regiment squadron.[6] When the tanks "started to blast houses to the front and beaten Germans threw in the towel," Edewecht was taken.[7] The paratroops that the battalion was now fighting showered it with mortar fire. Battalion old-timer Quartermaster Sergeant Joffre Barlow was killed bringing rations to the rifle companies.

The arrival of armoured support on April 24 coincided with a perceptible weakening of resistance when the Germans became disorganized while replacing the marines with paratroops from the 20th and 21st Fallschirmjäger Regiments. Subjected to a "great deal more punishment than had been intended for them in their battle inoculation," the marines had served their purpose by giving the "fanatical parachute units" time to reorganize and absorb reinforcements.[8]

But even as the marines rotated out and the paratroops in, enemy artillery and mortars maintained a rate of fire "out of all proportion to the strength of his infantry on the ground."[9] Major Cassidy realized that as the enemy "fell back on his supply dumps his ammunition became ample, and rather than lose it, he kept up a ceaseless rain of shells and bombs. Mines of a new type made their first appearance, taken from the naval arsenals . . . These mines consisted either of the warhead of torpedoes or of the large-calibre naval shells, deeply buried in the soft shoulders of the roads, and exploded by the customary pressure devices. The same mechanisms were used for cratering roads, and a real crater they made indeed. As we advanced, one noticed that almost every roadside tree had been prepared for demolition, with a deep notch already cut. In some instances the gun-cotton packages were already wired near the notch, ready to explode and bring the trees crashing down over the roadway."[10]

BY MID-AFTERNOON, THE Algonquins finished clearing the major junction point of Edewecht, prompting Major General Chris Vokes to decide that the opening existed for 4th Armoured Brigade to break through the German front. Giving Brigadier Robert Moncel the Argylls and Lincs as infantry, he ordered a rapid advance from Edewecht to Bad Zwischenahn.[11]

The ground was still horribly ill suited to armoured operations, intelligence reporting that the main road between Friesoythe and Bad Zwischenahn "had to be resurfaced every spring to condition it for even normal farm traffic during the summer, and never before had an enemy succeeded in conquering this country of peat bogs and swamps."[12] Two routes led north, and Moncel decided to advance a force along each to Bad Zwischenahn. The narrow roads, bordered on either side by wide marshes, forced the armoured regiments to move in single file. Only the tank troop at the very head was able to fire its guns forward. These conditions made an armoured charge suicidal, so the leading infantry advanced one company in a two-hundred-yard bound with a troop of tanks right behind. A second company and tank troop then bounded through for another two hundred yards. One small advantage the brigade enjoyed was that "neither the enemy nor our own troops were able to deploy in the marshes, [so] the flanks [could be] largely ignored."[13]

More important, however, was implementation of a new means for calling in Typhoons. Riding in a special tank equipped with wireless directly linked to the pilots circling in cab ranks overhead, a Royal Air Force officer was able to direct rocket attacks so accurately that the Typhoons could fire on targets only three hundred yards from the column's head.[14] Each column had one of these RAF teams, as well as a FOO directing artillery support by the 23rd Field Regiment (Self-Propelled).[15]

On April 25, Moncel advanced the Lake Superior Regiment (Motor) north along the more westerly road with tanks from the Canadian Grenadier Guards in support. But it would be another day before the second column was able to set off because the infantry battalions drawn from 10 CIB needed time after the Küsten Canal fighting to reorganize. In the April 17–25 period of the battle, the three battalions had a combined casualty toll of 402. Hardest hit were the Argylls, with forty-one killed and 105 wounded.[16] This battalion was to follow the Superiors up the western route. The Lincolns would lead the advance along the easterly route, with the Governor General's Foot Guards in support and the Algonquins following.[17]

The Superiors set out with 'A' Company dismounted from its vehicles and marching on foot. No. 1 Troop of the Grenadiers' 2nd Squadron provided the forward tank support, its four Shermans arranged so that Lieutenant Lilly's led, followed by Sergeant Dougart, then Lance Corporal Stuart Louis Johns, and finally Corporal Shuttleworth in the 17-pounder. Heavy mortar and small-arms fire forced the infantry to move along within the cover offered by a deep ditch on the right-hand side of the road. The two leading tanks—the only ones with a field of fire—punched out shells at a fierce rate, so much so that Lilly ran out of ammunition three times during the first two hours of the advance.[18]

'A' Company's objective was an intersection with a road crossing its course at right angles. The intersecting road was bordered by a high berm facing an open field to the right of the Canadian line of advance. From behind the berm's cover, paratroops were throwing out a steady stream of small-arms and Panzerfaust fire. To avoid outrunning the infantry, No. 1 Troop crept along at the pace of the men in the ditch, the tankers not particularly worried by the bullets rattling off the hulls and still outside Panzerfaust range. The gunners raked the berm with their machine guns and occasional high-explosive shells. Just short of the intersection, Lilly advised the other tank commanders by wireless that he was going to have to fall out of line because of mechanical problems. Sergeant Dougart came up a moment later with identical news. The two lead tanks fell out and Johns rolled to the front, with only Shuttleworth remaining to guard his back. Coming alongside the infantry's leading platoon—stopped at a point where the ditch appeared to peter out—Johns also halted.

From his elevated position in the turret, Johns could see that a new, shallower ditch started about thirty yards beyond where the infantry was held up. A tall tree grew in the gap, and Johns saw that a notch had been cut in its trunk and packed with explosives. Poking his head out of the turret hatch, Johns shrugged his shoulders in silent enquiry of what the lieutenant standing in the ditch intended. When the man returned the shrug, Johns decided to dismount so they could talk. He also instructed Shuttleworth to radio back for a Badger flame-thrower tank to come forward to help clear the berm. As Johns scrambled out of the tank, bullets pinged off the armour and sizzled through the air around him. Johns threw himself down behind a tree about two feet from the one where the lieutenant was sheltered. "Sir, what's the orders?" Johns called. The lieutenant replied, "Well, with that type of fire, we can't get out of this ditch." Johns reported the ditch beyond and the explosive-wired tree. "I'll have the gunner knock that tree down. Then, if you can get a few men across into that ditch," he suggested, "I'll advance with your guys right to the intersection without stopping."

The officer remarked that the ground ahead was pretty open. "It's no more open than me getting back into that tank," Johns said. "When the flame-thrower comes up and starts to squirt, we'll take that as the signal to move."

Clambering back through another storm of small-arms fire, Johns returned to his tank. His gunner banged the tree with a shell that struck the explosive charge, and the combined detonation dropped it across the road. When the Badger arrived, Johns stationed it between the two Shermans. As the Badger shot a jet of flame towards the berm, the tanks and infantry advanced. The two Shermans ripped the berm with their machine guns, as the infantry lunged into the new ditch and began advancing towards the intersection. When they gained its centre, the tanks swung behind the berm and Johns's gunner cut down the last five paratroops trying to gain the woods on the northern side of the road. Before the advance continued, Lieutenant Lilly and Sergeant Dougart returned to take the lead. The column moved on, with the two lead tanks firing high explosive rounds and the two trailing raking the flanks with machine guns, until their ammunition was exhausted at 1400 hours.[19]

The Superiors then advanced 'B' Company to the front with 2nd Squadron's No. 4 Troop in support.[20] As the tankers of No. 1 Troop climbed out of their Shermans, one of Johns's crewmen pointed to some holes in his uniform. Johns found three bullet holes in the front and three marking where the rounds had exited through the back. "I had not the faintest idea when it happened, but it must have been when I jumped off the tank and then climbed back on it." For his role in the intersection fight, Johns was awarded a Military Medal.[21]

The Superiors' 'A' Company had suffered three men killed and eight wounded during its advance. Company Quartermaster Sergeant Wilfred Alexander Guerard died when struck by a mortar round. Acting Sergeant Ardagh Orval Cadieu was killed when he "accidentally tripped a wire connected to a booby-trapped [Panzerfaust]." Sergeant Richard Lloyd Burrison had died during the assault on the berm.[22]

"THERE WAS NO reason for the enemy to fight now, but they did and the regiment still suffered casualties," wrote the Governor General's Foot Guards of the advance towards Bad Zwischenahn.[23] The division's senior staff officer, Lieutenant Colonel Mac Robinson, observed that the fight "was both long and tedious" with the "reason for the apparent slowness of our advance . . . basically an organic one." An armoured division was forced to fight in "infantry country and, early in this battle, we began to feel our shortage of [infantry]. Only so much effort could be expected from the inf[antry] resources at our command." Equally problematic, the division "was definitely road-bound—a fact of which the enemy was entirely aware, and not only were we road-bound, but it was constantly necessary to rebuild the [roads] over which the Div[ision] had to advance or actually to construct new roads to permit further advances."[24]

The Lincs started up the eastern road at 1100 hours on April 26, with 'B' Company leading towards the village of Ekern, only four miles distant and about two miles short of Bad Zwischenahn. Five and a half hours bucking sharp resistance yielded just a five-hundred-yard gain. When 'A' Company passed through at 2200 hours to continue the advance through the night, it "had to deal with every type of enemy fire, mines, road blocks, and craters." Communication between infantry and tanks was fragmented by the thick hedges farmers used to demarcate their fields, which was reminiscent of Normandy's *bocage* country. At dawn, the company came up against about fifty Germans armed with several heavy machine guns and by 0800 hours was still less than a mile from the start line.[25]

On either road the Germans surrendered ground grudgingly, even as the Canadian advance continued to press forward around the clock. When dense woods closed against the road the Lincs were on, the Algonquins filtered in among the trees to clear them. The Algonquin war diarist noted on the 27th that the "strenuous battles of the past eight or ten days, coupled with the strain of months of responsibility through many trying periods, has at last begun to take its toll among our senior officers. In the past few days, Maj[ors] P.A. Mayer and C.B. [Clark] Robertson, together with Capt[ain] T.L. Peart, have gone out." Major Robert Stock, "also in need of a rest," was posted to a three-month tour commanding a training battalion. "The reg[iment] now finds itself in the position of having to choose successors for these experienced and battle wise warriors."[26]

"We just kept edging and edging and edging without any real push," one Lincoln observed, in the face of "fanatical resistance."[27] There was never any question of the Germans stopping the advance, for the Canadians were too skilled, too well supplied, and too heavily supported to be denied. By 2000 hours on April 29, both columns gained Bad Zwischenahn's outskirts. Desiring the spa town for his headquarters, Lieutenant General Guy Simonds expressed hope "it could be taken in good condition."[28]

Moncel ordered the Argylls and Superiors to surround the town and attack at 1150 hours on the last day of April. Resistance remained stubborn, but the infantry "gained ground steadily. Craters were bypassed, houses were cleared one by one, and the German defenders continually harassed by . . . artillery, mortars, and flamethrowers. Against this combination the enemy could do little but give up—or die where he stood." By evening, Bad Zwischenahn was sealed off. The division's intelligence staff drafted a demand that the town be surrendered within two hours, which was given to a German priest for delivery to the town's mayor at 1930 hours.

Several hours after the deadline passed, the garrison's commander responded. While refusing to surrender, he said his men would evacuate the town, but if the Canadians entered they would be shelled. Moncel returned the threat that for every German shell fired, the Canadians would fire a hundred, but the garrison would be allowed to leave unmolested. At 0730 hours, a delegation from corps headquarters entered the town. They found the soldiers gone and the mayor ready to formally surrender Bad Zwischenahn.[29]

Corps headquarters personnel and provost officers immediately posted signs on the roads leading into the town that read: "Corps HQ—This town out of bounds to all ranks." The Argyll regimental historian lamented, "The troops . . . responsible for the surrender . . . gnashed their teeth at the sight of 'all that lovely loot going to waste,' as they pushed on past the lake resort, the streets of which soon echoed to roaring motorcycle escorts and be-flagged shining limousines. The surrender, however, was significant; for the first time in the experience of the battalion, a sizeable German place, with soldiers present capable of defending it, had thrown in the towel at the first opportunity. It was another indication of the now evident German collapse."[30]

The divisional plan had called for an immediate swing east towards Oldenburg once Bad Zwischenahn fell, but that plan had been rendered moot by more-rapid advances on the city from the south. Simonds, therefore, instructed Vokes to continue north towards Wilhelmshaven. Returning the Argylls and Lincs to 10 CIB command, he advanced this brigade directly north from Bad Zwischenahn. Meanwhile, 4 CAB—with the Algonquins and Superiors still under command—hooked out to the east into a gap that passed through two large swaths of boggy country and closed on Varel, in order to isolate the Wilhelmshaven peninsula from the rest of Germany.

For the Argylls, Lincs, and supporting arms advancing along the 10 CIB axis it was a replay of the slog north from the Küsten Canal— poor roads, impossible country for manoeuvre, and pockets of stubborn resistance. More forests interspersed between the bogs only added to the hazards, as air-burst shells shattered treetops, spewing showers of steel shards and wood splinters upon the troops.

Although hundreds of mines and the "ubiquitous mud" slowed the armoured brigade, the Germans offered little resistance.[31] "At a few points small groups of infantry knotted around a mortar or a self-propelled gun . . . fought well. More often, however, they have been very ready to surrender," one report noted.[32]

SOUTH OF OLDENBURG, 2nd Division had arrived from Groningen on April 19 to shunt into position between 4th Division on its left and the British 43 (Wessex) Division the right, about fifteen miles south of the city. On April 22, it advanced, meeting "no opposition . . . at all—a few stragglers and deserters, but no real contact with the enemy." The division advanced in two battle groups, with 5th Brigade and the 8th Reconnaissance Regiment on the right and 4th and 6th Brigades to the left. Out front for 5th Brigade were the Calgary Highlanders. Their scouts, working well ahead of the main body, returned two prisoners aged fifteen and seventeen. Drafted only three weeks earlier, they had been given vague orders to join a company of infantry north of the Canadian line of advance but were unable to find it. Speculation was that the company had dissolved, for mines and roadblocks posed the only opposition until the evening, when a carrier in which 'C' Company's Captain Bill Lyster was riding ran into an ambush.[33]

Glancing out of the carrier, Lyster saw some Germans lying in the roadside ditch. Automatically reaching for his Sten, Lyster realized he had set it down somewhere and that his holstered pistol was also beyond reach. Seeing the Germans raising their guns, Lyster jumped down onto two of them. He remembered nothing after that. Lyster had been badly wounded in the left arm and was evacuated to England, where he remained hospitalized until the late fall of 1945.[34] The Highlanders' regimental historian reported that the driver managed to take the two Germans prisoner by bowling them over with the carrier.[35]

Les Fusiliers Mont-Royal of 6th Brigade led the left-hand advance and "found the going very difficult; mines lay everywhere and the tanks of 'C' Squadron [Fort Garry Horse] could only crawl along the precarious and narrow lane cleared by sappers [of 11th Canadian Field Company]. There was practically no opposition, but it was almost five hours before the leading battalion finally consolidated on the northern outskirts of Neerstedt."[36]

On the morning of April 23, the FMR continued towards Kirchatten—three miles distant and about ten miles short of Oldenburg—with the South Saskatchewan Regiment paralleling it on a road off to the right. Again there was no real opposition, but the roads were sporadically cratered and the "verges were infested with Teller mines."[37]

In the Saskatchewan column, Private Chic Goodman and another signaller rode in the back of Lieutenant Graham Scott Blake's command vehicle. Reconnoitering ahead of the rest of the battalion, the carrier platoon moved slowly up a dirt road. Goodman had lately been having trouble concentrating, the months of action weighing heavily on the nineteen-year-old, and he was "starting to get very, very tired." He was grateful to not still be lugging a wireless in Major Fraser Lee's 'B' Company and considered that transferring to the carriers had been a wise decision.

The other signaller was monitoring the wireless, so Goodman scanned the flanks. Spotting a figure standing behind a farmhouse, Goodman raised the German semi-automatic rifle he had recently found and took aim while trying to figure out whether it was a civilian or soldier. Suddenly, there was a deafening blast and concussion punched him upward. Goodman was flying, briefly looked down upon treetops, then plunged earthward and into unconsciousness. He awakened to find someone dribbling rum into his mouth. The carrier was a twisted wreck. Lying around were bits and pieces of a body that turned out to be all of Lieutenant Blake that remained. The carrier driver had a mangled left arm and leg. Blood poured from the other signaller's smashed face. He had been struck full on by the wireless set when the explosion hurled it upwards. Someone said the carrier had run over two large mines stacked one upon the other, the focus of the blast penetrating directly under the front seats where the driver and Blake had sat.

Amazingly, the wireless still worked and an ambulance was called. The message also brought the rifle companies on the run, and first to arrive was 'B' Company. Major Lee walked over to where Goodman lay. "Chic, were you in that?"

"Yes, Sir," Goodman croaked, and then pleaded, "Can I come back to 'B' Company?" Lee promised to seek permission and after being declared fit to return to duty by the battalion medical officer, Good-man once more shouldered a wireless set and walked towards battle.[38]

Once the Saskatchewans and Fusiliers closed up on Kirchatten, the Queen's Own Cameron Highlanders passed through. A large expanse of woods on the northern outskirts sheltered German artillery, which hammered the town after the battalion entered it. As the Camerons dug into slit trenches near the edge of the wood at 1500 hours, two hundred German infantrymen suddenly charged 'C' Company's front, while forty more rushed the battalion's tactical headquarters. When an even larger force slammed into 'D' Company's lines, one platoon started withdrawing until supporting tanks helped drive the counterattack back to the woods, inflicting heavy casualties in exchange for none among the Camerons.

It took until mid-morning of April 24 to secure Kirchatten and allow the Camerons to renew the advance. 'D' Company led the way on a road through forest towards a point a thousand yards distant. Major D.D. Sweeting's orders were to "work [forward] if possible but not to bust in too rashly."[39] Sweeting relied on the battalion's mortars and anti-tank guns to break up resistance. Soon 'B' Company came up on the flank to clear the woods. When Captain J.H. Ross was slightly wounded, Lieutenant F.E. Millar took over. Both companies progressed slowly, constantly harassed by airburst shells exploding in the trees. Three Camerons died this day.[40]

Remorselessly, 2nd Division continued towards Oldenburg. While the Camerons had secured their grip on Kirchatten, 4 CIB had slipped around to the right, coming up between 6 CIB and 5 CIB. By day's end on April 24, all three brigades were advancing in one broad line. Brigadier Fred Cabeldu's 4 CIB was to cut the road running from Oldenburg southeast to Delmenhorst and begin the city's isolation. The Royal Hamilton Light Infantry and Royal Regiment of Canada were met by heavy enemy fire, which the 4th Field Regiment's guns quickly subdued. This proved to be the regiment's last day "of intensive firing." There were thirty calls from the battalions for concentrations to break up resistance between 0630 hours and 1600 hours, with six more called in during the night. Most targets consisted of "Germans firing 40-mm and 20-mm ack ack guns at almost point blank range at the infantry moving forward. The effectiveness of the firing was proven when the infantry followed up the successes of that day; the enemy were found to have withdrawn and were not bumped again until just short of Oldenburg."[41]

From inside a Sherman, Captain George Blackburn directed much of the regiment's fire. Blackburn had served in this hazardous occupation since Normandy, and his nerves were close to snapping. Day and night he carried a canteen filled with rum buttoned into the front of his battledress, but even the liquor could not prevent him getting his "wind up." The war was going to end soon; "you've made it this far . . . you've got to make it the rest of the way."

There were no large battles. Instead, the war had "degenerated into crossroads ambushes, with the Germans showing no tendency to form a line." Blackburn thought they sought only delay, buying time to prepare for another major canal fight behind the Ems-Jade Canal in front of Wilhelmshaven. They blew trees across roads to create a "tangled mess" of branches and shattered trunks behind which the ubiquitous MG42s, Panzerfausts, and 20- or 40-millimetre anti-aircraft guns waited. Their fire would knock out a carrier or a tank, injure or kill a few infantrymen. Blackburn would call in shells to quell the opposition. The pioneers would saw the trees into sections, and the tanks and carriers would drag them off the road. Then the advance would continue to the next roadblock and the same scenario would be replayed.[42]

By April 27, the division reached Oldenburg's southern outskirts. A small part of the city lay south of the Küsten Canal, while most of its population of 79,000 lived and worked north of the canal. Dating back to the 12th century, Oldenburg had escaped Allied bombing, and its ancient and attractive heart remained unscathed. Now the Canadians were at the gates, with 4 CIB and 6 CIB driving German forces out of the southern part while 5 CIB closed in from the east.[43]

Fighting in small groups from behind their endless network of roadblocks, the Germans were able to avoid being overrun. But each day, their losses—as men surrendered or were killed or wounded—grew exponentially. With 4th Division outflanking the city to the west, 8th Fallschirmjäger Division withdrew northward to avoid being cut off from Wilhelmshaven. Left behind was a motley collection deemed incapable of maintaining any bastions.

Intelligence staff had also learned that "the civilian element in Oldenburg is unwilling that the town should be defended. Several PW and line-crossers have reported that the Burgomaster has attempted to have the place declared an open city, as it contains at least a dozen medical installations and many wounded [including] some Allied personnel. It is not believed that the military commander will be influenced by civilian pressure but there are some indications that the defence will be half-hearted, and two [captured officers] have stated that the town will not be held."

To emphasize the folly of further resistance, Major General Bruce Matthews had propaganda leaflets printed that warned of dire consequences for the city unless its garrison surrendered. These were stuffed by the thousands into airburst shells and fired towards the city centre—each explosion showering paper rather than shrapnel on its inhabitants.[44]

On the evening of May 1, Canadians on all fronts learned through BBC radio broadcasts that Hitler had died the day before. How the Führer met his demise was rife with speculation. One theory—supported by translations of German announcements—credited a stroke. Others thought he had been assassinated by cronies eager to negotiate an armistice, while still another explanation held that he had fallen victim to a Russian shell or bullet in the ruins of Berlin.[45] The true explanation that Hitler had committed suicide was never considered.

Any thought that an immediate end to hostilities would result was dismissed by news that Grosseadmiral Karl Dönitz now headed the German government and had vowed to "continue fighting." Hearing this news, 1st Canadian Armoured Brigade's commander, Brigadier Bill Murphy, confided to his diary, "We still have our war for awhile."[46]

Around Oldenburg, 2nd Division continued closing in. Brigadier Jean Allard's 6th Brigade had reached the Küsten Canal. Although the main bridge was jammed in a raised position, Lieutenant Colonel Jimmy Dextraze put Les Fusiliers Mont-Royal unopposed across in assault boats. Engineers hurried to inspect the bridge controls but reported they were beyond repair. Deciding to destroy the screws that controlled the lifting mechanism, sappers first cleared the bridge of mines and then wired their own explosives to the screws. Allard was on hand to view the explosion, which when the detonator was pushed proved to be "enormous. There was dust everywhere. When the dust cleared, we saw the bridge fall heavily into place."[47]

The bridge decking had aligned so perfectly with the off-ramps that tanks of the Fort Garry Horse were soon trundling over and reinforcing the Fusiliers. A subsequent report deemed the likelihood of the bridge being rendered usable with explosives as "one chance in a million."[48]

More luck presented itself on the evening of May 2, when the Royal Hamilton Light Infantry Regiment established its headquarters in a building just south of the canal. Major Jack Drewry, the 4th Field Regiment's FOO attached to the Rileys, found an operational telephone. Summoning the Riley's interpreter, Drewry placed a call to the city centre and requested the garrison commander. "After about two hours, the Commandant came on the telephone and he was asked to surrender. He said it was impossible, and the conversation ended abruptly. However, the cause was not given up and the [Burgomaster] . . . was called. [He] was much more encouraging and said it looked to him as if the soldiers might be pulling out of town. Through the interpreter, he was told that the city of Oldenburg must be surrendered intact and that the artillery would drop large numbers of shells all over it and wipe it out if it wasn't done quickly. A deadline was finally set at midnight."

Drewry briefed his commander, Lieutenant Colonel MacGregor Young, and "asked to have the regiment and the rest of the divisional artillery laid on a target in the centre of the town. Actually the target the guns were laid on was the park with the intention of giving it a blast if necessary as a sample and then again asking the [Burgomaster] for his answer.

"At five minutes to midnight, the gunners were sitting ready at their loaded guns waiting for the order to fire, but instead the order, 'Stand Easy,' came down. The [Burgomaster] had phoned back and said that the town would be empty of soldiers by seven a.m. For the remainder of the hours of darkness the regiment fired harassing fire on the roads leading north of the city" to catch the retiring German troops.[49] In a subsequent conversation with the Burgomaster, he agreed to meet the leading company of the Rileys "and deliver the city to them" at 0800.

At 4 CIB's headquarters, Brigadier Fred Cabeldu was elated, but wary. "All night situation very tense, it not yet being certain that there was not to be a fight," the brigade diarist wrote.[50]

Oldenburg's Burgomaster had been busy on other fronts to prevent the city's destruction. At 2130 hours on May 2, he had contacted 6 CIB's South Saskatchewans to discuss "the surrender of the city." Given a slightly more lenient deadline, he had apparently decided to err on the side of caution by surrendering to the Rileys.[51]

At 0700 hours, the Burgomaster approached the Rileys and offered to "take patrols across to occupy the city." Lieutenant Colonel H.C. Arrell was in no mood for cautious probing, so the entire battalion piled by companies into assault boats crewed by Russian and Polish ex-prisoners for the crossing. By 0830 hours, the Rileys marched intact and unopposed into the city centre.

"Fantastic scenes in the city," 4 CIB's war diarist recorded. "One or two [Canadian officers] armed only with pistols marching back with 50 or 60 enemy [troops] armed to the teeth. Most of the citizens kept in doors greatly assisting the checking. The Burgomaster proved very helpful, particularly in organizing the local police to help in the patrolling. In a very short time all houses had been checked and the citizens had posted up their lists of household personnel. The troops had a wonderful haul of enemy pistols and cameras."[52] Oldenburg had fallen without a shot fired, and 2nd Division's war was almost done.

25

Bitterest Battle

IN THE LAST days of the war, only 1 Canadian Corps's 1st Canadian
Infantry Division, 5th Canadian Armoured Division, 1st Canadian Armoured Brigade—all Italian campaign veterans—the British
49th (West Riding) Division, and a few supporting units remained
in the Netherlands. The two infantry divisions and the armoured
brigade stood before the largely inactive Grebbe Line, hemming
Twenty-Fifth Army up inside western Holland. Although the ceasefire negotiations between the Allies and Reichkommissar Arthur
Seyss-Inquart, which were being brokered by representatives of the
Dutch resistance movement, were still underway, both sides had
effectively stood down to await a final outcome.

In northern Holland, however, the war was still very much ongoing, with 5th Division working to collapse the Delfzijl Pocket. While
the divisions fighting in Germany engaged in small but intense skirmishes against slowly retreating forces, the Delfzijl Pocket offered
the last full-scale battle Canadians would fight in World War II.

With a pre-war population of ten thousand, Delfzijl was one of
Holland's largest secondary ports. The defensive pocket surrounding
it was about twelve miles wide west to east and just over a mile deep. A
continuous trench system protected by barbed wire and wide swaths
of heavily mined ground marked the pocket's inland perimeter.

While the Germans were too few to man the trench's entirety, they had established strongpoints at regular intervals along the portions not inundated. The backbone of the defence rested with three naval fortress battalions, Nos. 359, 360, and 368, all lacking experience in open warfare. Remnants of other units driven north into the pocket by the Canadian advance added strength. Canadian intelligence estimated fifteen hundred defenders, but later determined the number to have been about forty-five hundred at the battle's outset.

Although they had only eighteen 75-millimetre guns, field artillery was not important to the defenders. They called instead upon the heavy 28-centimetre coastal batteries on Borkum Island in the estuary's mouth and those surrounding the German port of Emden on the opposite shore. Several coastal batteries were also situated within the pocket itself, including one at Nansum and the other at the base of Reider Spit on the eastern flank. The guns at Nansum Battery were mostly 105-millimetre, while Reider Spit boasted four 128-millimetre anti-aircraft guns that could be lowered to engage ground targets. Every battery's guns were mounted in strong concrete emplacements virtually impervious to the Canadian artillery. Defensive positions bristling with 20-millimetre flak guns and machine guns also ringed the batteries. There were enough MG42s inside the pocket to arm every man in eight German battalions.

Topography favoured the defence—ground flat, lacking natural cover, riven with ditches and canals. Tanks and carriers were confined to existing roads generally running along the tops of dykes. The many small villages were transformed into defensive strongpoints. In the autumn of 1944, the Germans had inundated the ground on either side of the Eems Canal to block a direct approach from the south, forcing any attacker to approach against the narrower flanks to the east and west.[1]

With the war in its twilight days, the pocket's defensive advantages were so apparent that questions would later arise as to why the Canadians did not merely surround and contain it. Major General Bert Hoffmeister understood that the offensive was required to prevent the Germans from destroying the port facilities. "Dutch authorities," he later said, "were most anxious that Delfzijl be damaged as little as possible, because they were desperate for a port into which ships could move immediately and relieve the terrible suffering that was going on in Holland." The Germans were also using the port to ship stores and evacuate troops from Holland to Emden to strengthen the garrison there. To minimize damage to port facilities, Hoffmeister was instructed by Lieutenant General Guy Simonds to "take it on without any air preparation and without guns heavier than 25-pounders," From intelligence reports, Hoffmeister knew the port quays and cranes were already wired with explosives so they could be destroyed at any time. But the port was also the only viable avenue of escape for most of the garrison, so the Germans were expected to delay destroying it until the last moment. If 5th Division could overwhelm the defenders with a rapid attack, the port might be won intact.

Hoffmeister realized this battle would cost lives. "At that stage of the game, I was really worried about that decision."[2] Accordingly, Hoffmeister said he would agree to it only under one condition, which Simonds consented to.[3] Summoning his two brigadiers, Hoffmeister explained "just what the score was, and told them I wanted them to go back to the troops and see what they think about it. I said, 'I think this is something that can't morally be decided by me or by you. I think we have to refer it to the men.' The answer from the men was, 'let's go.' There wasn't the slightest hesitation or any objection raised, they were prepared to lay it on the line for the Dutch people, take Delfzijl without the usual support that we had from medium and heavy artillery, without air support, and so on."[4]

THE 5TH DIVISION relieved 3rd Canadian Infantry Division on April 23 and went directly into combat. Initially, the operation was to be directly overseen by 5th Armoured Brigade's Brigadier Ian Cumberland. Added to his command were 11th Infantry Brigade's Perth Regiment and the Irish Regiment of Canada, which were immediately deployed on opposite flanks. On the western flank, the Perths relieved the Regina Rifles, while to the east the Irish took over from the Canadian Scottish.

At 2300 hours, two platoons of the Perth's 'C' Company advanced towards a position one thousand yards north of the village of

Holwierde. Arriving on its objective without incident at 0315 hours, they sent back fifteen prisoners. As the men started digging in, the area was struck by prolonged artillery fire.[5] The fire was so accurate that it was quickly concluded that the Germans had previously zeroed their battery guns so that any section of the pocket could be targeted on a moment's notice. Minimizing the effectiveness of the gunnery, however, was the fact that many of the large, heavy shells plunged deep into the muddy ground and exploded harmlessly.

When 'A' and 'B' Companies passed through towards Holwierde, they were heavily opposed by Germans positioned on the village's outskirts. At dawn the Perths were still well short of the village, and 'B' Company was under fire from three self-propelled guns shooting at point-blank range. Only the intervention of artillery against the SPGS and the laying of a smokescreen to blind the German gunners at Nansum Battery enabled the advance to continue. At 1015 hours, 'B' Company was tight in the village. Proceeding towards Nansum Battery in daylight was judged impossible, so the Perths dug in to escape the relentless shelling. By day's end, eight men were dead and another twenty-four wounded. Unlike what had happened in weeks past, when prisoners numbered in the hundreds, the Perths had taken just twenty-two.[6]

After the Irish Regiment had taken over Wagenborgen east of Delfzijl on the early morning of April 24, the Germans had used the momentary confusion as the Canadian Scottish handed over positions to counterattack and regain part of the town. Attempts to hold these gains were half-hearted, and by dawn the Germans had been thrown out and had lost nine men as prisoners.[7]

On either flank, the division spent the daytime hours mustering its strength and shaking out for a fight. The Westminster Regiment (Motor) lined up to the right of the Irish, while the British Columbia Dragoons concentrated in Appingedam to the south of the Perth's line of advance. The tankers were irritated by the way the Royal Winnipeg Rifles had handed over Appingedam, an officer simply telling a Dragoon of equal rank, "The Germans are there, we're getting the hell out of here. Goodbye." They soon discovered that parts of the town were still in German hands and were forced to dismount most of their men to fight as infantry. Even deploying ten tank troops to this duty yielded just 120 men—the equivalent of a single infantry company. Lacking portable wireless equipment, the tankers had to string phone lines behind their advance. Grudgingly, they set about sweeping the town and sending patrols out beyond—being continually harassed by snipers and the fiery rain of shells from the coastal batteries. When the Dragoons entered Appingedam, only about a half-dozen houses had suffered shell damage, but by the time they would leave on May 2, German artillery "had completely destroyed one hundred and nineteen buildings and badly damaged two hundred and forty others."[8]

The need for the Dragoons to provide their own infantry spotlighted 5th Division's inherent deficiency in ground troops—despite Hoffmeister having transferred all 11 CIB's regiments to Cumberland, causing Brigadier Ian Johnston to lament on the night of April 24 that "for the first time in its history [the brigade] had no one under [command]." It was a short-lived situation, for at 0900 hours the next day, Hoffmeister reversed the arrangement and put Johnston in charge of collapsing the pocket. Not only were the infantry regiments returned to his control but also 5 CAB's 8th New Brunswick Hussars and BC Dragoons were passed to 11 CIB. The Westminster Regiment was also placed under Johnston's command. For artillery, 8th Field Regiment (Self-Propelled) deployed on the eastern flank and 17th Field Regiment to the west. Engineering requirements would be provided by 10th Field Squadron.

Johnston was displeased with the scope of his task, for the brigade's frontage sprawled across 25,000 yards lacking even a scrap of cover, while the Germans could hide within the many hamlets and villages. Everyone by now was realizing that intelligence projections of German strength were seriously understated, and that in fact aerial photographs of the battery emplacements and surrounding defences showed them to be virtually impregnable. There were also the guns of Borkum in the middle of the estuary and at Emden across from Delfzijl, which could reach anywhere within the pocket while being immune to anything the Allies threw at them.

His infantry was "spread very thinly," while the armour was road-bound. The 25-pounders that Johnston was restricted to because of the prohibition on heavier artillery "were outranged . . . and appeared to have little effect on the concrete positions." Weather also conspired against him—rain and heavy cloud rendering precise tactical air strikes, which could ensure no damage to the harbour, being impossible. The Germans were so numerous and well deployed that Johnston decided it "would be necessary to have at least three battalions deployed throughout the whole period. There was little cover, the weather was miserable and the enemy shelling was taking its toll of casualties. It was accordingly decided to push forward."[9]

Johnston already had three infantry battalions committed, so only the Cape Breton Highlanders remained in reserve. The BC Dragoons continued in their tankers-cum-infantry role at Appingedam. To the west, the Perths were at Holwierde, and on the eastern flank the Irish and Westminster regiments were engaged. Despite the poor weather, the Perths called for an air strike on Nansum Battery, with the artillery marking its position with smoke. When the "planes arrived too early," however, they attacked without guidance from the artillery, and "the bombing was ineffective."[10]

To the east, the Irish were still trying to figure out, with gingerly extended patrols, where the Germans were located and their strength. The Westminsters, meanwhile, had shifted somewhat westward during the night to allow the Irish to concentrate in a narrower area.[11] With the ground lit up by "a brilliant moon," 'A' and 'C' Companies had crept along water-filled ditches and canals from one farm to the other in order to clear the area. "As Wednesday became Thursday, it became increasingly apparent that Jerry had good observation and fire control, since the slightest movement brought down accurate and heavy shelling, much of it airburst from the very heavy guns" at Reider Spit.

In the early morning, a Dutch farmer connected to the resistance appeared at the Westminster's battalion headquarters and told Lieutenant Colonel Gordon Corbould that the spit's guns were 12.8-centimetres. He described "their size, numbers and subsidiary guns and defences in terms difficult to believe, but which were subsequently substantiated."[12]

Morning of April 26 dawned cold, with a heavy mist that initially helped cover 'C' Company's advance "across the flat, open 'polder' toward the sea." The goal was Termunten, which lay fifteen hundred yards due west of the base of the spit. Its capture would isolate the spit from the rest of the pocket.[13] When the mist lifted just after noon, 'C' Company found itself "in such open ground that they were heavily and regularly shelled. Three were killed: P[rivates] C.G. Lelond, J. Petrak, and D.R. Sawyer, and one was wounded during the . . . advance this sunny spring afternoon in the tulip fields of northern Holland."[14]

Deciding to forgo the attempt to approach Termunten directly, Corbould sent the battalion towards Woldendorp, about five thousand yards southwest of the spit. He planned a pincer attack—'A' Company would strike across flats to the right with 'C' Company close behind, while 'B' Company approached from the left. As any movement by day immediately drew accurate shelling, Corbould planned to make his move after midnight.[15] The Irish Regiment conducted one of the division's last daylight operations during this period when it advanced 'A' and 'C' Companies on a wide right hook towards a position three thousand yards northeast of Wagenborgen in the late afternoon of April 26. Shelling inflicted four casualties en route. 'D' Company then passed through and continued a further two thousand yards along the southern dyke of a large polder to close on a canal within fifteen hundred yards of Weiward. Meeting stiff resistance the whole way, the company netted only five prisoners and finally gained its objective at 2300 hours, most of the move being completed under the cloak of darkness.[16]

Divisional intelligence had cautioned that the Germans were under "a 'last round, last man,' order and the obstinacy of the defenders certainly [did] not point towards a hurried evacuation of the area." Although the many ships reported at Emden might "smack of at least preparation for the exodus," it was deemed too early to clearly divine German intent. But it was thought "reasonable to conclude that the pocket will remain active until the defended perimeter of Delfzijl itself is reached, and it is then and not likely before that a choice between evacuation or 'last man' will be made." The April 25 report concluded that the situation favoured the Germans because of their clear fields of observation and fire. "There appears to be no shortage of food or ammunition, not unnatural in a coastal fortress, and this together with the fact that he has a number of guns does not suggest of any hurried need to leave." Declaring the defenders a "hodge-podge" made up mostly of naval land forces, the report also noted that their relatively poor training was "overcome to a degree by the equally apparent determination and efficiency of their commanders."[17]

Ultimately, the German artillery advantage forced the division to grope forward at a crawling pace in the hours of darkness and to lay low during the day. On the western flank, the Perth Regiment moved to clear the Germans out of the coastal area north of Bierum to a point two thousand yards from Nansum Battery. This would provide them with secure lines to the rear when they attacked the battery itself. With the 8th Hussars' 'A' Squadron in support, the attack was scheduled to begin at 2000 hours on April 26. As the leading 'B' and 'C' Companies formed on their start line, they were caught by artillery fire that killed one man and wounded seven others. After a short delay, the advance proceeded and met little opposition until 'D' Company passed into the lead shortly after sunrise. Dogged by increasing small-arms fire, the company came up onto the coastal road running east to Nansum at 0618 hours and its commander called for tank support.[18]

'A' Squadron's No. 2 Troop responded. When "mines and marshy ground necessitated the tanks moving over narrow dirt trails, the troop came under heavy HE [high explosive] fire from the coastal guns. Despite the jinking of one tank it was eventually hit and knocked out, the heavy HE literally caving in the side of the tank. The remainder were successful in reaching the Perth company position."[19] Advancing farther during the day was deemed impossible and the Perths were still discovering German positions behind their front. As the day progressed they rounded up seventy-one prisoners, all of whom turned out to be sailors from a transport flotilla bypassed by the advance.

At 1445 hours, Lieutenant Colonel M.W. Andrew set out his intention to take Nansum that night. 'A' Company would go for the village and the road leading to it from Holwierde, while 'C' Company took the battery itself. Once these two objectives fell, 'D' Company would move a short distance farther south to block any counterattack aimed at regaining the battery. 'B' Company was to remain in Holwierde to protect the battalion's right flank. The attack was scheduled for 0035 hours on the morning of April 28.

'C' Company soon mired in a minefield. The company commander was wounded and six men killed before Andrew ordered a withdrawal to the start line and began working up a new plan for the next night.

While the Perths had been trying to close on Nansum, the Westminsters had been equally engaged in attempting to isolate the battery on Reider Spit. Despite a late start at 0240 hours on April 27, the attack proceeded better than Corbould had expected. 'A' Company's Major William James Neill decided on a bold dash rather than stealth to surprise the Germans in Woldendorp. Putting Lieutenant James Oldfield's carrier platoon out front, Neill's force charged straight up the road behind a sharp barrage by artillery and a troop of tanks from the 8th Hussars' 'B' Squadron. As the carriers roared forward, the mounted machine-gunners shot "up everything in sight." Neill's Company rushed into Woldendorp, seizing the northern sector, capturing thirty prisoners and killing "a large number for no casualties to themselves."[20]

Woldendorp's loss seriously threatened the Germans' ability to defend Reider Spit, and they immediately counterattacked. The battery opened up with a terrific barrage on the Canadian sector, and at first light the Germans struck from three sides. For two hours the battle raged before the Germans began losing steam. Soon 'B' Company moved up on the western side of the village, and 'C' Company moved into Woldendorp to help 'A' Company clear the portions still in German hands.

Brigadier Johnston visited Corbould at noon. "On most sectors of the Delfzijl Pocket," he reported, "the going was still quite sticky. Some of the units were suffering heavy casualties from shelling and advances were neither great nor rapid." Consequently, he urged Corbould "to get on to the sea in order to put the pressure on the remainder of the pocket, take a number of very bothersome guns [Reider Spit Battery], and prevent a very large scale evacuation from the small port of Termunterzijl [next to Termunten]." Corbould cautioned that he first had to gain control of Woldendorp, and the push for the coast was unlikely to begin until Saturday, April 28.

Inside Woldendorp, 'A' and 'C' Companies were not in contact with each other when Neill's men were assaulted by another counter-attacking force that numbered about two hundred men. Other smaller forces attacked the other two Westminster companies. Two troops of Hussars under Captain H.D. Keith tore into the Germans with their machine guns to devastating effect. But inside Wolden-dorp, 'A' Company's situation grew critical as men began to run out of ammunition, many grabbing up German weapons. Neill, who earned a Distinguished Service Order this day, dashed from platoon to platoon, encouraging the men to stand fast. Finally, at 2230 hours, 'C' Company slugged its way through to 'A' Company's lines and the counterattack broke. Skirmishes continued until 0600 hours, when the Germans melted away. Immediately, the guns at Reider started "shelling and air bursting was heavy and many of the flimsy build-ings were soon reduced to rubble and ashes." Despite the intensity of the bombardment and the counterattacks, casualties were surpris-ingly light. With Woldendorp in hand, the Westminsters passed the daylight hours of April 28 as comfortably as possible, those in the vil-lage hunkering down inside cellars to escape the shelling. Corbould was already making plans for the push towards the coast "to con-tinue after last light."[21]

Left of the Westminsters, the Irish Regiment had spent April 27—"a dirty, rainy day"—under continual shelling with no intention of trying to advance until after dark. Five men were wounded. At 0100 hours the following morning, 'C' Company under Major W.H. Mitchell headed for a position five hundred yards short of the village of Heveskes. This would put them on the south bank of a wide canal that branched off the Eems Canal at Farmsum and extended east-ward towards Termunten. Like the Westminsters, the Irish were trying to close up to the coast between Delfzijl and Reider Spit. Despite considerable opposition and seven casualties, by daylight the company reached the canal. Right of Mitchell's men, Captain Fred Whyte's 'A' Company ran into a rat's nest of Germans firing from all sides and was pinned down. Lieutenant B.D. Sandwell's platoon managed to fight its way back to the start line, but dawn found the rest of the company trapped. Whyte decided to stay put through the rest of the day. Lieutenant Colonel L.H.C. Payne also waited for darkness, planning to send 'B' Company to relieve Whyte and then continue to the western edge of a canal trending on a northeasterly axis from Wagenborgen to Termunterzijl, in order to tie in with the Westminsters on the opposite shore. The relief force rescued Whyte and his men at dawn, but two of the company had been killed and another sixteen were missing and presumed captured.[22]

ON APRIL 28, Simonds met with Hoffmeister to discuss how long the operation was taking. Hoffmeister had decided to go straight for Delfzijl's port itself because "three or four more days of mucking about will cost us more in the end."[23] He and Brigadier Johnston agreed that an attack from the northwest once Nansum fell offered the best chance of success and the Cape Breton Highlanders would be brought out of reserve to carry it out. At the same time, the Westminsters and Irish would advance on Delfzijl from the east while continuing to isolate Reider Spit battery.

The Perth's 'D' Company advanced at 1515 hours on April 28 to establish a strongpoint one thousand yards along the coast immediately north of Nansum Battery. When the company met opposition from a cluster of farm buildings, a Wasp was summoned. "Houses in this area were burned down and the enemy driven outside," the Perth war diarist noted. At 1630 hours, 'C' Company came up behind 'D' Company, which was "having a lot of trouble from shellfire" out of the battery. The two companies kept leapfrogging each other, as the battalion's mortars dropped smoke bombs around the battery to blind its gunners and artillery harassed the emplacements with fire.[24] 'D' Company was within a few hundred yards of the battery at 2045 hours. Moving through quickly and still screened by artillery and mortar fire, 'C' Company "took the Germans by surprise, captured the guns, and bagged 177 prisoners, more than twice the strength of the assaulting company. An examination of the position afterwards showed what a feat the assault had been," wrote the regiment's historian. "The area of the guns was heavily armed with

automatic weapons, and the gun emplacements were of heavy concrete, built into the dyke."[25]

Pushing out of Holwierde, 'A' Company headed for the village of
Nansum west of the battery. By 0525 hours on April 29, they were
close to Nansum's outskirts and had taken seventy prisoners, but
were also running out of ammunition. Fifteen minutes later, the company was counterattacked "and had to resort to using enemy weapons
and ammunition for defence." Calling artillery almost onto the company's position broke the German attack. It took the rest of the day,
but at 1650 hours, 'A' Company entered the town and within an hour
reported it clear. An hour later, the Cape Breton Highlanders began
taking over the front in preparation for their attack of Delfzijl.[26]

By 2300 hours this relief was complete, and thirty minutes later
'B' Company attacked towards the village of Uitwerde, which was
separated from the northern corner of Delfzijl by a narrow canal. 'A'
Company advanced ten minutes later. The speed with which the
Canadians had followed up on the fall of Nansum Battery obviously
confounded the Germans, for by 0300 hours Uitwerde was taken
with 240 prisoners. By dawn, the Hussars had tanks inside the
village.[27]

'A' Squadron's No. 3 Troop was firming up alongside 'B' Company
when a previously unseen large pillbox was spotted. The tanks hammered it with armour-piercing shells to no noticeable effect, and the
Germans inside lashed back with machine-gun fire. Finally, a
17-pounder Firefly blasted it with a Sabot round. Developed by the
British in early 1944, the Sabot armour-piercing shell had a piece of
solid shot set inside a plastic casing, which fell away after leaving the
gun barrel. With a much higher kinetic force than a normal AP shell,
it could penetrate thicker armour. When the shell struck the pillbox
it caused concrete inside to break loose into chunks of shrapnel.
Immediately, the Germans inside showed a white flag. The pillbox
was later determined to have seven-foot-thick walls that normal
shells had penetrated only to a depth of five feet. Having eliminated
the pillbox threat, the tankers turned their guns to a coastal battery
on the northern edge of Delfzijl. Tanks and guns duelled throughout
the day, with neither achieving any decisive hits.[28]

Southeast of Delfzijl, the Westminsters were rapidly reshaping the pocket's perimeter. By the morning of April 29, the battalion was within two miles of Termunterzijl and Termunten. Corbould decided 'B' Company would go for the former and 'A' Company the latter, while 'C' Company held firm in Woldendorp. After resting through the day, the two companies advanced behind an artillery barrage. The Hussars' 'B' Squadron was unable to provide much support due to the Shermans becoming mired in the mud. "Again it was a wild rainy night," but the two companies slowly advanced across the polders—wading through ditches, crawling over dykes, and occasionally fighting through pockets of Germans. When dawn broke, 'B' Company was still a thousand yards short of the small port. Realizing they were going to be caught in the open, Major Ian Douglas ordered his men to charge. Staggering through the wide, marshy fields, they managed to gain the port before the Germans could respond. Some tried to mount a defence, but soon the tanks struggled through the mud to join Douglas's men, and by early morning resistance crumbled.

When the company reached the port's quays, they found five hundred Germans waiting to be lifted off by ships to Emden. It was soon evident that the Westminsters had arrived in the middle of a mass evacuation intended to remove the Germans from the eastern part of the pocket. The enemy caught on the quay meekly surrendered.[29] 'A' Company had gained Termunten quite easily, and by noon both the town and the port were declared mopped up. The Westminsters had succeeded in cutting Reider Spit off from the rest of the pocket, but the guns continued to fire. Corbould sent 'C' Company on a wide sweep south of the battery to gain a position on a dyke from which it would be possible to observe the fortifications and plan an attack.

Soon a deserter claiming to be an impressed Russian entered Westminster lines and reported that the battery personnel were to be evacuated off the tip of the spit during the night. Shortly after midnight, the battery suddenly erupted with a massive shelling of the area, and machine guns spewed tracers across the surrounding polders. Then, at 0300 hours on April 30, all firing ceased, and a sullen quiet settled in. 'C' Company slipped a patrol towards the battery, which soon reported it deserted. Despite the heavy fighting encountered, total Westminster casualties in the pocket were only four killed and fifteen wounded. The Westminsters had seen their last fight. Turning the area over to the Governor General's Horse Guards, they headed for a rest area a few miles south of Groningen.[30]

On the night of April 29, operations by the Irish Regiment had yielded further evidence that the pocket was rapidly collapsing. The previous night, the battalion had almost lost a company against fierce resistance, but 'C' Company had pushed through to the coast at Oterdum unopposed. At dawn, 'B' Company closed on Borgsweer near Termunterzijl. They cleared it without difficulty. Although meeting little opposition from within the pocket, the Irish were dogged by coastal guns firing across the Ems from Emden. The battalion's 3-inch mortar officer, Captain Dick Lancaster, and another soldier were wounded. Many Germans were observed fleeing north towards Delfzijl, prompting the Irish war diarist to write that the enemy "is being squeezed into a smaller pocket every hour."[31]

The squeeze was tightened when the Cape Breton Highlanders struck from the north at 2200 hours on April 30. But the Germans were still ready to fight and their defences remained stout, 'C' Company becoming stuck in a minefield just five hundred yards from its start line that took the pioneers an hour to clear a path through. The advance continued, with 'C' Company headed for a battery of coastal guns immediately north of Delfzijl while 'D' Company was to eliminate more guns inside the harbour itself. Once these objectives were in hand, the battalion would continue to the rail station on the town's edge and then begin to clear the centre of Delfzijl.

'C' Company took its battery with little difficulty and reported fifty prisoners. This cleared the way for 'D' Company to pass by and head for the guns in the harbour. Delayed by three hours, the company lost any chance of surprise and had gone only two hundred yards when flares arced into the night sky.[32] Lieutenant Reg Roy, commanding one platoon, realized "they had us cold." Mortars, shells, and small-arms fire tore into the company and pinned it down. Roy, a veteran of many scraps in Italy, later described this one in his diary. "My God, but it was terrible to see our fellows cut up so . . . I hope I never see another battle like it. It was murder . . . This has been the bitterest battle I've been in."

Fire was coming from pillboxes disguised as houses. An attempt by the Hussars to support the attack was stopped cold when Lieutenant Bill Gerrard's tank was disabled and blocked the road. Standing in the turret hatch, Gerrard calmly used the wireless to direct artillery fire onto the German fortifications.

All through the night, 'D' Company tried, but failed, to inch forward. Soon it was running out of ammunition, and 'C' Company was detailed to resupply it. Lieutenant Colonel Boyd Somerville realized the attack was completely unravelled. Standing next to 'A' Squadron's Major Tim Ellis, he said, "This is a bad one, Tim. [Major] Harry Boates' [D] Company is trapped in a barn on the polder [or] pinned down in the drainage ditches trying to keep their weapons dry."[33]

Dawn found the company totally stalled, but 'C' Company managed to get through to it under cover of a smokescreen. Ammunition replenished, Boates led his men creeping forward. It was 'B' Company, however, that broke the deadlock when its attack on the right gained the railway station at 1014 hours. Somerville hurried 'A' Company past the station, and soon it had a platoon firm on the bank of the Eems Canal, which cleaved the town tidily in half. They reported many Germans escaping in boats across the Ems Estuary. Things loosening rapidly, 'D' Company completed its mission and rounded up three hundred prisoners at the gun position. In the early afternoon all resistance ceased, and those Germans left in Delfzijl surrendered. The Cape Bretoners had been hit hard. Two officers and eighteen other ranks were dead, precisely half from 'D' Company. Another three officers and fifty men had been wounded. They had taken 1,520 prisoners.[34]

All the harbour facilities were found wired with explosives, but none had been detonated. The port was secured intact, the explosives removed, and a good number of fishing boats and other small ships captured.

With Delfzijl taken, the pocket was reduced to Farmsum across the Eems Canal from the port town. The Irish Regiment compressed this area on May 1 and the following day took the surrender of the garrison commander, along with thirty-seven other officers and thirteen hundred other ranks. The Delfzijl Pocket was declared collapsed at 0700 hours.[35]

The only Germans remaining in Holland were those buttoned up in the west behind the Grebbe Line, and while 5th Division had fought at Delfzijl, unusual developments had taken place on that front.

26

Thank You, Canadians

THREE MILES EAST of Amersfoort, Achterveld lay within the operational zone facing the Grebbe Line, held by 1st Canadian Infantry Division's Princess Patricia's Canadian Light Infantry. When the PPCLI had established its battalion headquarters here on April 23, the village had come under its first and last German shelling.[1] While several buildings had suffered tiles torn off roofs, every window in St. Joseph's School next to the Catholic church had been blown to shards. As the PPCLI was using the building, pioneers had hastily covered the gaping holes with tar paper.[2] Due to the prevailing phony war, Achterveld often seemed much farther behind the front than it really was. Across from the church and school, a barber and tailor had re-opened their respective shops, happily serving the Canadians. Mobile baths were established, and the rifle companies rotated from the forward positions to wash up and draw clean uniforms. The auxiliary services showed films regularly in the schoolhouse.[3] "Soldiers moved about with real carelessness," one 1 Canadian Corps headquarters staffer noted, and discipline was becoming distinctly casual.

This all changed abruptly on the morning of April 27, when "a smart guard who stood in his best parade-square manner and directed traffic with regimental pride and formality" was posted next to a sign in the main intersection that read: "Danger No

Vehicles Past This Point." No sooner had the man taken his post than he was directing a convoy of three-ton trucks "carrying loads of most unoperational gear. In the shaded grounds of the church, marquees and mess tents were set up with tables, chairs and cooking utensils complete with table cloths . . . carefully arranged. Six white-washed flag poles appeared and were neatly pegged down and their guy-ropes adjusted with military precision. Near the mess tent a Canadian flag was hoisted. On right and left of the entrance between the school and the church grounds appeared the flags of Canada and Britain and deployed down the street in front of the school stood the flags of the United States, the USSR and Holland. There were no flags at the entrance on the other side of the school. The Dutch flag was nearest, but still quite aloof." The tar paper was stripped away by Canadian engineers and replaced with glass. Inside, the two separate rooms—one small, the other larger—were set up for conferences. Signallers installed a phone line and hooked it into a network that directly connected the school to Supreme Headquarters Allied Expeditionary Force in Reims.

As these preparations continued, all attempts to keep secret their purpose failed locally. Soldiers and citizens alike whispered that the school was being readied for secret negotiations with the Germans. Whenever an unauthorized soldier or civilian walked across the street towards the L-shaped schoolhouse—surrounded by a tall wire fence that in peacetime provided security for the children—provosts shooed them away. Other military police drifted quietly, but watchfully, through the clusters of citizens. When word got out that Prince Bernhard would attend, the Dutch became excited. Every house in Achterveld sprouted at least one Dutch flag and the orange pennant of the royal family. The citizens were all smiling, chattering away to each other in large gaggles, men stepping forward to shake the hands of passing Canadians and young women offering hugs, as if they were yet again being liberated. Peace was at hand, one rumour held. And it would be decided here in Achterveld, over there in their little schoolhouse.[4]

Once General Eisenhower had authorized direct negotiations with Reichskommissar Arthur Seyss-Inquart on April 23, events had developed rapidly. Two days later, staff at various Canadian brigade headquarters reported German wireless operators cutting in on their secret radio frequencies and claiming to act on behalf of senior commanders. In English, the operators requested "that food be sent to the starving Dutch and guaranteeing a fair and just distribution through the Dutch Food Ministry." First Canadian Army intelligence officers immediately issued instructions that the messages not be acknowledged, but that the compromised frequencies be kept clear and monitored for future signals. Repeatedly, between April 25 and 28, the Germans sent more signals, but they were met with only silence.[5]

Whether these messages emanated from Seyss-Inquart or someone else was never determined. They played no perceptible role in the process of arranging a meeting in Achterveld for April 28. The Allies were well aware, as Eisenhower had warned on April 23, that "the situation is so bad that something must be done to arrange for the introduction of food into Holland by free droppings and by every other possible means." Preparations were well in hand for air drops of food, 10 million rations already stockpiled in England for this purpose. Half of these rations were provided from stocks intended as emergency aid to Allied prisoners of war abandoned by their German guards. On April 16, SHAEF had ordered Bomber Command and the U.S. 8th Air Force to keep two hundred bombers readied for immediate deployment. As the school in Achterveld was being readied on April 27, SHAEF air staff directed that aerial drops, code-named Operation Manna, commence the following morning.[6]

At 1700 hours on April 27, First Canadian Army ordered 1 Canadian Corps to ensure a complete twenty-four-hour ceasefire across its front to begin at 0800 the following morning and specified that there would be no "advance westward." Subsequently, Twenty-First Army Group's chief of staff, Major General Francis "Freddie" de Guingand, phoned Lieutenant General Guy Simonds to say "that it would not be possible to instruct the Germans to cease fire for the same period . . . because our only direct means of communication would be by wireless, in clear, and it would not do to create the 'flap' which this would cause all over the world!" He assured Simonds that his staff was "endeavouring by other means, to make this arrangement as far as the enemy forces are concerned." This information reached Lieu-tenant General Charles Foulkes at 1900 hours, about the same time he was given instructions for where the Allied and German represen-tatives were to be picked up for transport to Achterveld.[7]

At 1000 hours on April 28, de Guingand and several other offi-cers descended from a plane at Kluis airfield near Nijmegen and were hurried in four First Canadian staff cars to Achterveld. Accom-panying de Guingand were Prince Bernhard; Major General Sandy Galloway, the British commander of Netherlands District; and Colo-nel J. Zenkowitsch, who represented Soviet interests. Because of the Allied reconfirmation during the Yalta Conference in February that any surrender of German forces must be unconditional, it was imperative that the Soviets consent to the terms of any agreement. Otherwise, the Soviets could accuse the western Allies of deceit and claim this as justification for breaching other agreements reached at Yalta. Before the Germans arrived, de Guingand briefed the other Canadian officers involved on how he would guide the discussions and the concessions sought. Meanwhile, 2nd Canadian Infantry Bri-gade's Brigadier Pat Bogert and his brigade major were approaching the German line at 1100 hours on the Amersfoort–Apeldoorn highway. Four Germans carrying a white flag emerged and walked to meet the Canadians. After being blindfolded, they were helped into a car and driven "by a devious route to the conference."[8]

Standing in for Seyss-Inquart was Reichrichter Dr. Ernst Schwebel and Dr. Friederich Plutzer, while Generaloberst Johannes Blaskowitz was represented by Hauptman Dr. Stoeckle and Ober-leutnant von Massow. Alighting from the car, these men were led through the door beside which no flags were flying.

Before convening the full meeting, de Guingand met just Schwebel and Plutzer. The two men offered a brisk salute and then extended their hands, an invitation de Guingand ignored. Schwebel disgusted the tall, very upper-class British officer. "A plump, sweat-ing German, who possessed the largest red nose I have ever seen, the end of which was like several ripe strawberries sewn together."[9] (De Guingand was not alone in his appreciation of Schwebel. The PPCLI war diarist felt moved to comment that battalion staff had dubbed the German senior representative "Big Nose.") After credentials had been checked and confirmation made that each man had representative authority, the doors of the room were opened and everyone else filed to their places at the tables.

This meeting with "the enemy delegates," de Guingand opened, was held "with the object of reaching an agreement with the least possible delay which would enable the Allies to introduce food into German occupied Holland, to be used for the Dutch population who were known to be starving as a result of the . . . German inability to feed them." The Allies, he said, were proposing to send supplies by air, sea, rail, and barge. He "emphasized that it was essential to get something moving at once."[10]

None of the Germans disputed their inability to feed the Dutch, but Schwebel cautioned that neither he nor the army representatives had authority to commit to any specific proposals. Only Seyss-Inquart could do that. Schwebel then proposed a second meeting on April 30 with Seyss-Inquart attending.

There followed a short adjournment while de Guingand telephoned Eisenhower's chief of staff, Lieutenant General Walter Bedell Smith, in Reims. The Germans could make no decisions, he reported, but Seyss-Inquart had agreed to a meeting on Monday if Smith were present. Agreement, de Guingand thought, might "lead to further developments toward surrender of the German forces." Smith consented.

Adjourning for lunch, the Allied representatives left the school to dine on sandwiches laid out on tables under the tented marquees. 1 Canadian Corps had been "instructed that in NO circumstances will the German representatives be included," so they remained inside and were served separately.

Once the meeting reconvened, de Guingand summoned several more Allied representatives—including Prince Bernhard—to brief the Germans on the relief plan's logistics. British Air Commodore Andrew Geddes said the most immediate, albeit least efficient, delivery means was by air, possibly delivering food to thirty drop zones close to the major cities. Drops could be carried out day and night. If the Germans agreed not to fire on the aircraft, Geddes said the only

Allied planes allowed to operate over western Holland would be dedicated to food delivery. Geddes announced that the Allies had already proceeded with air drops without awaiting German permission and asked for a "report on the success of today's drop." The Germans, expressing neither surprise nor objection to the Allied jumping of the gun, "undertook to do so."

Obviously, the massive tonnages required to relieve the situation could never depend on air drops alone—they were a stopgap measure. Major General Galloway, who had developed SHAEF's extensive relief plan, said he had a fleet of barges loaded with tons of food and ready to go. The Germans, however, had to guarantee the flotilla "freedom of movement in rivers and waterways and [Galloway] proposed that we should introduce supplies by Dordrecht to Rotterdam." Schwebel said this would likely be acceptable. Galloway stressed that Rotterdam's port was essential for allowing ships to approach by sea. Basically, the more ports the Germans opened, the more rapidly food could be delivered throughout the whole region.

As Galloway described the tonnages involved, the Russian delegate interjected that "he was anxious that the supplies should be used solely for the Dutch population and Allied PW, including any Russian displaced persons, and in no circumstances by the forces of the occupying powers." The Germans assured him that this was accepted.

Discussion turned to delivery of food by road and rail. The Canadians had large truck convoys already mustered for road shipments, but it might be necessary for the cargoes to be transferred over to German vehicles. Were trucks available, and were the Germans able to provide rolling railway stock? Trains, the Germans replied, could only be used if the Allies supplied coal. Availability of German trucks and the fuel to power them was something they would have to determine.

How would the food be distributed? Through Dutch authorities, the Germans said, and Prince Bernhard concurred. It was agreed that Dutch representatives, especially the Dutch Director of Food, Dr. S.L. Louwes, would attend the next meeting. Schwebel wanted this meeting held in No Man's Land to "spare the Reichskommissar the humiliation of the blindfold!" De Guingand refused to change the venue, arguing that by the rules of war, responsibility for feeding the Dutch rested with the Germans. Seyss-Inquart would not have to wear a blindfold. Arrangements were made for Lieutenant General Foulkes to meet with a German officer of identical rank at an agreed point in No Man's Land to decide how to move German and Dutch delegates through the lines. Schwebel pleaded that the details of both this and the meeting to come be kept secret, which de Guingand agreed to.[11]

THROUGHOUT THE MEETING, Allied representatives had believed a first aerial drop was already underway. Due to bad weather over England, however, no planes were able to take off, including one that was to have returned General Harry Crerar to his command. But Sunday morning dawned with the acceptable conditions of no cloud cover below one thousand feet and visibility of three miles in the drop zone. Between 1256 and 1430 hours, about 240 aircraft—Lancaster bombers from RAF Nos. 1 and 3 Groups guided by about a dozen Mosquito Pathfinders—arrived over designated drop zones. Three of these were airfields, one outside Leiden, another The Hague, and the third Rotterdam. The fourth drop zone was a racecourse at The Hague. A total of five hundred long tons consisting of 550,000 rations spewed out of bomb bay doors from an altitude of four hundred feet. Two aircraft reported being fired on "by desultory rifle fire, but otherwise the fire was nil." Operation Manna had begun.[12]

The deliveries continued daily through to May 8. On April 30, 502 sorties were flown and 1,074.6 long tons containing 1,070,300 rations dropped. Almost seven hundred British and American planes sortied on May 1 to deliver close to 1.6-million rations. The highest tonnage fell the following day, and the lowest delivery was 319 long tons on May 8. For the entire period, 9,866,300 British POW rations, 720,000 U.S. POW rations and 889,000 Canadian standard rations were dropped. Earlier estimates had predicted that wastage due to boxes breaking open on striking the ground or being unrecoverable would reach 14 per cent, but it proved a fraction of that figure.[13]

Pilot Officer Colin Friesen from Saskatoon flew five Manna missions, including the first one, in a RAF No. 150 Squadron Liberator. The crews had been briefed on the conditions imposed by the

Germans. They were to fly at a specified altitude along a rigidly set course and were prohibited from tipping their wings, which could be construed as sending signals to the Dutch. Friesen's squadron dropped its load over The Hague that day and again on April 30. By the second drop, he noticed that almost every barn roof had the message "Thank You, Canadians!" painted on it. Friesen was touched. Until these missions, all he had dealt in was destruction. Flying in at one thousand feet that second day, Friesen saw thousands of civilians gathered around the drop zone. They clung to treetops and stood on rooftops, a dense mat of humanity waving banners and caps. Friesen fancied he could hear their cheering. Also tracking their flight were the anti-aircraft guns, the barrels silently following the planes as they passed. Friesen flew his last mission on May 3, a drop outside Rotterdam.[14]

Despite how close so many Dutch were to the food dropped, they were not allowed to help themselves. Instead, Dutch food authorities took control of the rations. Due to a series of miscalculations and logistical difficulties in moving the rations, none of this food, so hurriedly delivered by air, reached the people in need until May 9. Brigadier L.F. Field, one of the SHAEF staffers involved in the plan, complained afterwards that the Dutch "were extremely slow in getting the supplies distributed. In fact, they proposed to wait until 14 May before beginning distribution, but were forced by [Canadian] Civil Affairs officers who arrived after the Armistice to speed up their efforts."

Part of the problem was that the rations had been originally intended for prisoner-of-war camps. Fully 10.5 million of the 11.5 million tons dropped were "packed in sets which, when prepared, made up a day's rations for 800 men. Had they been dropped in a POW camp, it would have been a simple affair to have . . . distributed them. Absorbing them in the individual civilian rations, though, proved an arduous task."[15]

Further explanations were given in a subsequent Canadian Civil Affairs report by Brigadier A.K. Reid. The distribution system involved the establishment of base supply depots staffed by Dutch Interior Forces, where the rations were to be broken down and transferred to civil distributing points for doling out to the populace. Although the concept was sound, the organization responsible for implementation "had been so disrupted by many of its members having become refugees or been forced to 'go underground' that its efficiency was proportionately impaired." There was also an acute "shortage of vehicles, which was remedied only when Canadian military vehicles were made available to assist in 'first line distribution.'" Also, "due to their weakened condition, civilians were physically incapable of manhandling supplies in bulk."[16] Another Canadian report noted that there was "hesitancy on the part of local authorities unfamiliar with the problems to take the initiative."[17]

Delivery would become more efficient and effective once 1 Canadian Corps was involved in the distribution process and also aiding the movement of supplies into western Holland by land and sea. But on April 29, there was still no German agreement to allow such deliveries.

ON MONDAY, APRIL 30, the Dutch and German delegates headed towards Achterveld in separate parties. Departing The Hague with Seyss-Inquart were Schwebel, Generalleutnant Paul Reichelt—Blaskowitz's chief of staff—and about six other functionaries. Seyss-Inquart had offered the Dutch officials cars, but fearful of being compromised, Louwes had declined. Instead, he and six other Dutchmen crammed into a car powered by a gas generator and lurched towards the Grebbe Line. They met up with the Germans at Amersfoort, then in convoy continued to Hoevelaken. Leaving the cars and surrounded by German soldiers carrying white flags, the party headed cross-country on foot, clambering in places over barbed wire and jumping water-filled ditches. Where the Amersfoort–Apeldoorn highway crossed a railway, a group of Canadians waited with white flags visible. Taking the German and Dutch delegates from the German soldiers, the Canadians guided them to jeeps for transfer to a point behind the lines, where they boarded limousines for the journey on to Achterveld.[18]

As the limousines bearing the Germans drove into the gravel lot next to the school and church, Seyss-Inquart was angered to see

Prince Bernhard casually leaning against a large Mercedes touring car with the number-plate RK-1 (Reichkommissar 1) on it. Seyss-Inquart had lost the car during the evacuation from Apeldoorn, and the local resistance had presented it to the prince. He had deliberately parked the vehicle opposite the gate through which the Germans were to pass.[19]

Lieutenant General Walter Bedell Smith, an American, had become Eisenhower's chief of staff in 1943. Nicknamed "Beetle," he had proven a capable manager and tough hatchetman when required. Seyss-Inquart was a hard man, but Smith was his match. Besides Smith, most Allied officers attending were the same present at the meeting two days earlier. Lieutenant General Charles Foulkes and his chief of staff, Brigadier George Kitching, were also present because 1 Canadian Corps would play a pivotal role in the relief effort. So as not to be overshadowed in rank, the Soviets had sent a new representative, Major General Ivan Susloparov, to replace Colonel Zenkowitch.

The Canadian guides directed the Germans towards the school entrance still absent any nearby flag. Staring straight ahead, Seyss-Inquart limped into the school. Only when the Germans were inside did the Dutch and Allied delegates enter. Kitching thought Seyss-Inquart an "unpleasant man . . . His eyes were pale blue and very cold, his blond hair was sparse, his lips were thin. He had a cruel face . . . It was obvious Seyss-Inquart could not be trusted; he alternated between a cold aloofness and an ingratiating warmth."[20] The Germans sat with their backs to the two doors leading into the conference room. Seyss-Inquart was in the middle with German representatives from the army, navy, and air force on either side. Their interpreter, the intelligence officer for 6th Fallschirmjäger Division, stood behind Seyss-Inquart. The Allied delegation was seated facing the Germans.[21]

Lieutenant General de Guingand delivered a terse précis of the first meeting. Seyss-Inquart stated he would "of course agree to our demands to feed the poor Dutch people and would make all arrangements for this. He would not ask Berlin for permission to do it because he knew it would be refused."

Once more Air Commodore Geddes and Major General Galloway described the SHAEF plan, and details were quickly agreed. Kitching thought Seyss-Inquart was anxious to "place on record his deep feeling for the plight of the Dutch people," but none of the Allied officers were convinced.[22]

"In cold, matter-of-fact language the points connected with this food distribution were discussed. At the same time, the nature of the whole proceedings became more and more obvious. Here were the Allies, forced by a set of circumstances beyond their control, to negotiate with this man, one of the worst of the war criminals. Everyone realized at this stage [that] personal hatreds and true feelings regarding this unpleasant gentleman with whom we were dealing had to be subordinated to the common good. But all were determined that the Dutch should have food, come what might, and furthermore, that supplies should reach them with the very greatest speed," recorded First Canadian Army's chief of staff, Brigadier C.C. "Church" Mann.

Broad principles settled, the conference broke into "commissions" with designated Allied, German, and Dutch representatives working out details. Mann thought it "fantastic . . . to see high-ranking German officers still in their own way masters of their own destinies, and still able to exercise command as they had been used to in the last five years, sitting alongside and discussing these problems of food distribution at the same table with the Allied officers. For six years the only proper place for German officers of this kind was either as corpses on the battle field or behind the bars of the PW cage. During these discussions they still held a semblance of power, even though it was diminishing so rapidly as to be almost non-existent."[23]

One of these subcommittee meetings was between Foulkes and Generalleutnant Hermann Plocher of 6th Fallschirmjäger Division to decide how convoys "by land and by water could pass freely from the Allied to the German side." Plocher was a "tall, bald-headed individual and, unusual in a German officer," Mann thought, "slightly grubby [and] not overburdened with wits and intelligence. During the whole of the ensuing conversation he appeared desperately anxious to avoid making any decisions which would put him out of faith with his superiors." Plocher proposed only one road be considered neutral and only for a few hours each day. "When the ludicrous side of this suggestion was pointed out to him, he agreed that the idea was not particularly clever and could not work. To fight from ten to one, and from two to four, excluding Bank Holidays, appeared even to him to verge on the childish."

The convoys had to pass unmolested, Foulkes declared, so a truce over the complete battle front stretching from the Waal River to the IJsselmeer was desirable. Plocher looked aghast, claiming such a suggestion would have to be referred to higher authority. Foulkes offered to consider a smaller area, but it had to be sufficiently large to assure security for the convoys and so demarcated that it "could not possibly be mistaken by the stupidest man." Plocher continued to try to whittle the area down to little or nothing, until finally Foulkes snapped that "he had had enough." He would talk only with a military commander who "had authority to deal with him on his terms." Either Blaskowitz must give Plocher such authority, or he must come to meet Foulkes personally and "thrash out the whole question." Plocher telephoned Blaskowitz, who agreed to either meet directly or send someone empowered to act on his behalf. Meanwhile, Blaskowitz had assured Plocher that "the truce conditions existing on the whole front would continue." Plocher seemed relieved. Mann realized the man feared being held responsible for any agreement constituting a formal ceasefire or, worse, a general surrender.[24]

Blaskowitz had a question for the Allied representatives that showed he was thinking about surrendering but worried about the consequences. Was he on any Allied war criminal list? Phone calls were made to SHAEF and assurances given that he did not appear on any lists.[25]

During the afternoon, Smith, Seyss-Inquart, Prince Bernhard, de Guingand and some others had discussed the possibility of German surrender in Holland. Clearly, the Germans had lost the war and surrender was inevitable, Smith declared. "I entirely agree," Seyss-Inquart responded, but insisted that it was up to Blaskowitz to make such a decision. Smith dismissed this argument. The Reich-kommissar was the political authority, and politicians rather than soldiers decided diplomacy. As for authority, Seyss-Inquart was free to act on his own initiative. Stubbornly, Seyss-Inquart invoked his standing in the eyes of future generations of Germans. He did not want his reputation stained by being responsible for an unconditional surrender. Smith snapped back that he would then be held responsible for further useless bloodshed.[26]

Finally, in frustration, Smith said flatly, "Well, in any case, you are going to be shot."

"That leaves me cold," Seyss-Inquart said softly.

"It will," Smith replied.[27]

At 1730 hours, the general conference reconvened, and the subcommittee reports were presented for endorsement. Continuation of air drops was agreed, and Seyss-Inquart promised to ensure dropzone security. Supply by ship could begin on May 4. The ships would be manned by merchant rather than Royal Navy personnel. They would dock in Rotterdam, and only three ships at a time would be allowed in. The road running from Wageningen on the Canadian side to Rhenen in the German-occupied zone would open at 0700 hours on May 2 for a lift of one thousand tons of supplies. Deliveries of equal size would continue each day thereafter. The Dutch would supervise the Rhenen depot. To help the Dutch with distribution from the depot, the Allies would provide two hundred lorries, of which one hundred would be delivered on May 2. Because freedom of movement on the canals could not be guaranteed without a ceasefire in place, the use of barges was shelved. Once documents confirming the agreements had been signed, the meeting broke up.[28]

As Seyss-Inquart walked outside, Prince Bernhard pointed out the Mercedes. Seyss-Inquart didn't rise to the bait. "Calm and indifferent as always, the German merely remarked that he had long wanted an excuse for a bigger one. The Germans entered their staff cars while the Dutch civilians crowded uncomfortably into another vehicle; then motors roared and the procession swung off down the street back through the German lines."[29]

AT NOON THE following day, Foulkes and Kitching arrived at a small dark-green wooden house about a mile west of Wageningen on the road running to Utrecht and just inside the Allied lines. They were joined by Generalleutnant Paul Reichelt, Blaskowitz's chief of staff. Reichelt said Blaskowitz had agreed that a ten-mile-wide corridor between the Arnhem–Utrecht railway and the Waal River at Ochten would be opened to enable "unhindered" passage of supplies into western Holland.

Foulkes countered that to facilitate moving supplies quickly to Amersfoort, Hilversum, and Utrecht, it would be preferable to extend the neutral area north from the railway to the IJsselmeer and declare a truce across the entire frontage where 1 Canadian Corps and the Germans faced each other. Any German offensive action, he warned, would present "consequent risks" to the whole plan for relief deliveries to these northern towns. Foulkes said he sought not a written truce but a "gentleman's agreement."

Reichelt said he had no authority to offer one, but he would take the proposal to Blaskowitz. They should meet again in forty-eight hours. Foulkes added that he would order cessation of "any shelling, patrolling, or other form of offensive action. Thus, the responsibility for any incident that might occur would be on the shoulders of the Germans." Reichelt said the Germans would not jeopardize the food deliveries.

Foulkes warned that the Germans would be held responsible if their forces pillaged, looted, or pilfered any supplies—stressing he was particularly concerned about the Dutch ss stationed in the area. Reichelt said he would prefer the dumps be established in No Man's Land but "was not averse to the Allied lorries entering the German main defence line and dumping behind their lines so long as the drivers did not leave their vehicles. He would also provide guards with orders to protect the dumps."[30]

Back at his headquarters, Foulkes ordered all units to stand fast while keeping the front fully manned and ready to meet any attack. There would be no fraternization with the Germans, and the troops were to be "informed that this arrangement is still secret and should not be discussed or referred to in any letters. Any breach of security may prejudice the completion of this most important task."[31]

Operation Faust, the 1 Canadian Corps food-delivery plan, had only awaited a signal from Foulkes. Lieutenant Colonel M.V. "Curly" McQueen, the bald-headed deputy director of supplies and transport for I Corps, had twelve platoons each with thirty trucks bearing ninety tons of food and medical supplies ready to roll.[32] Eight platoons were Canadian and four British. At 0730 hours on May 2, the first platoon departed Wageningen towards the depot on the German side at Rhenen. Every thirty minutes another platoon hit the road. The Germans had insisted that no trucks were to be inside their lines after 1800 hours, so a precisely timed schedule was established to ensure that the convoys met the objective of delivering one thousand tons per day.[33]

Captain Robert H. Parkinson's platoon from 1st Canadian Armoured Brigade, Royal Canadian Army Service Corps, was first to enter the German lines. Each truck had a white flag mounted on the front fender, but the drivers all had a weapon discreetly hidden in the cab and were under instructions not to get out of the truck for any reason. "We knew we were taking food to the Dutch people. It was interesting and somewhat scary as we passed German soldiers who were fully armed and probably they were as interested or frightened as we were . . . We offloaded the food at the side of the road and turned it over to some kind of Dutch authorities . . . They took charge of the food and we didn't at any time have . . . contact with the Germans."[34] The twelve platoons continued moving food into Holland even after the war ended, delivering the last thousand-ton allotment on May 10.

Until the German surrender, the Canadians feared that the unofficial truce might collapse. Foulkes kept hammering at Blaskowitz, trying to persuade him to surrender or formalize the ceasefire. He and Reichelt met again on May 3 at the house outside Wageningen. To demonstrate the futility of their situation, he produced a map of Europe on which he had marked the few remaining small areas still in German hands. "I pointed out the ridiculousness of the 25th German Army [position] in Holland [and] a few Huns hanging on in Denmark. They were rather impressed with the map, and I told them to take it away with them, and I suggested now was the time to surrender. Then . . . Reichelt made a very impassioned speech, in which he said they were ready to blow the dykes, destroy the country, and fight to the last man, rather than be prisoners and sent to Russia as slave labour.

"This annoyed me. I told him there was no intention of putting the German Army into Russia... [but] if they flooded Holland they would be war criminals... and... punished accordingly. This rather shook the Germans and they agreed to surrender, provided that I would give them an undertaking that they would not be sent to Russia.

"I pointed out that my instructions were 'unconditional surrender.'"[35]

That evening, Foulkes learned through First Canadian Army headquarters that Field Marshal Bernard Montgomery was negotiating with the German High Command the surrender of all forces in Holland, northwest Germany, and Denmark. In Germany, 3rd Canadian Infantry Division had been readying attacks on Aurich and Jever unless the garrison commanders surrendered on the morning of May 4. Crerar immediately ordered the attacks cancelled and sent instructions to his corps and divisional commanders to cease offensive action until further notice.[36]

On receiving a copy of the surrender agreement Montgomery was presenting in his negotiations, Foulkes sent instructions for Reichelt to meet him in Wageningen at 1100 hours to receive the Allied terms. Foulkes dictated the terms and ordered him to return with Blaskowitz to sign the surrender on May 5.[37]

At about 2000 hours on the evening of May 4, the BBC reported that the Germans had signed the surrender agreement and hostilities would cease at 0800 hours the following morning. Along the Grebbe Line, it was obvious the Germans had been monitoring the British radio, for immediately they fired off "all the Verey pistols they owned, along with jubilant bursts of tracer [ammunition]. Much singing and Schnapps-happy parties developed whilst our [forward] troops tried to cope with the hordes of the vanquished who came over to be made prisoners. Much explaining had to be done that such conduct 'was not on,' as the war did not end until 0800 the following morning."

At 1100 hours on May 5, Germans, Canadians, and Prince Bernhard gathered in the Hotel De Wereld in Wageningen. The entire town had suffered in the recent fighting. Trestle tables had been set up in the dining room with kitchen chairs arrayed around them. "The wallpaper was torn, and through the glassless windows and the cracks in the walls the wind blew freely. But the sun was shining."[38]

For the first time, the media attended, and the "remainder of the room was crowded with chairs for press photographers, movie camera-men, war correspondents and a variety of official onlookers."[39] The tables were brilliantly illuminated by floodlights. Blaskowitz struck the I Corps intelligence officer as looking "very tired and disconsolate" when he and Reichelt took their places behind the table.[40] Foulkes sat opposite with Kitching and Prince Bernhard on either side. A large number of staff officers and interpreters hovered close by and at times took places at the table to clarify one or another detail of the surrender document's hundreds of paragraphs. Foulkes read each condition, Blaskowitz signifying approval with either a nod or the single word, "understood." Rarely did he question a clause, and even more seldom would Foulkes write altered wording next to a condition and initial the change. One such occurrence regarded a clause requiring the Germans to safeguard United Nations personnel. What was the UN, Blaskowitz asked, and how were such people to be recognized? Foulkes eliminated the clause. "Looking old and grey," Blaskowitz "never smiled."[41]

The general terms were that the Germans would retain command of their troops and be responsible for their maintenance. All units were to remain where they were. German police would come under military command, and all personnel guarding concentration camps and other detention centres were to be arrested. Demolitions were to be immediately removed from dykes, and obstacles were to be cleared to allow barge traffic to use the canals to assist with feeding the Dutch. [42]

When the agreement was signed at 1604 hours, Reichelt was asked to produce the dispositions and strength of German forces in western Holland. He said that including all army, navy, and air force personnel they numbered 120,000. Throughout the day, Reichelt had exuded a "dignified gloom." But as the meeting broke up, one Canadian officer mentioned that the air force had been chasing Reichelt's headquarters for some time. "He burst into a wide grin and replied, 'I know, you got me out of bed twice!'"

As the German officers returned to their car, they each "gave a stiff periscope Nazi salute" before driving off.[43] The German vehicles no sooner left than they "became hopelessly entangled with a food convoy winding through the village."[44]

THE PROTRACTED NEGOTIATIONS that resulted in the surrender of Twenty-Fifth Army in western Holland were not replicated by 11 Canadian Corps in northwestern Germany. In the last days of the war, the surrender of various towns had been negotiated as the defences collapsed. On May 5, however, considerable effort was made to confirm that the German formations the Canadians had been fighting would accept the terms of the surrender. Establishing contact with the group's commander, General der Infanterie Erich von Straube, proved complicated because the German communication system was in shambles. Finally, von Straube was reached, and 8th Canadian Infantry Brigade's Brigadier Jim Roberts escorted him by jeep from Aurich to Bad Zwischenahn at 1630 hours.

While Blaskowitz had conducted himself wearily but professionally during the surrender, von Straube was much less composed. Having only recently assumed command, he demonstrated "noticeable ignorance" of his force's composition. Only after much consultation could he confirm that they numbered 4,106 officers and 88,793 other ranks. He seemed "appalled by the number of detailed instructions involved [in] the surrender terms . . . and was also shocked to learn that he was to be held responsible for internment and concentration camps." When he balked at this, Simonds directed his attention to Paragraph 3 of the surrender, which "prescribed strict and immediate execution of orders by the German command." Such clear direction seemed to accord with the man's mindset, for he "rallied magnificently" and the documents were soon signed.[45]

Throughout the meeting, von Straube had seemed puzzled by the Canadian informality. From the back of the jeep during the return trip to Aurich, von Straube tapped Roberts on the shoulder and asked his pre-war occupation. The question unsettled Roberts, opening his mind to a future beyond the war—what until now had seemed an "improbable dream." Before he could phrase a reply, von Straube asked with a hopeful expression whether he had been a professional soldier. Roberts thought for a moment, recalling the jobs he had drifted through in those days before the world went mad. "No, I wasn't a professional soldier," he said. "Very few Canadians were. In civilian life, I made ice cream."[46]

A RETURN TO civilian life was not to come quickly for Canadians wearing khaki in Europe. While combat actions ceased, implementing and administrating the immediate peace remained. There was also the need to take stock and tally losses. From the launch of Operation Plunder on March 23 to 0600 hours on May 6, Canadian Army casualties were 6,289, with 1,482 of these being fatal. Of these casualties, 365 officers and 5,165 other ranks were Canadian.[47] Excluded from this figure were the approximately 61 paratroops of 1st Canadian Parachute Battalion either killed or wounded during Operation Varsity and subsequent fighting through to the war's end.[48] How many men died during the last days of March was not recorded, but in April, 1,191 Canadian soldiers died, and during the first days of May, another 114 lost their lives.[49]

All Allied forces were engaged in the hunt for war criminals, the Canadians mostly within their sector of Germany. At times, entire communities were surrounded and methodically searched for Germans on wanted lists.[50] Seyss-Inquart, who had left the Netherlands after Hitler's death to seek instructions from Doenitz at Wilhelmshaven, was caught by Canadians. Tried at Nuremberg, he was hanged on October 16, 1946. Arrested on the basis of trumped-up Russian charges, Blaskowitz was being tried at Nuremberg when he broke free of his guards and jumped to his death from a balcony on February 5, 1948. ss police czar Hans Albin Rauter was handed over to the Dutch by the British. On March 24, 1949, he was shot by a firing squad and buried in a secret site.

With the surrender, First Canadian Army found itself in control of 213,000 Germans who had to be disarmed, processed, and, in the case of the almost 120,000 still in Holland, repatriated.[51] As Captain T.J. Allen, 1st Division's historical officer, noted, Operation Eclipse,

as this latter task was known, was without "precedent" and complicated by the fact that the Germans vastly outnumbered the
Canadians. It was also being carried out "in a country whose friendly
people and resistance forces are lusting to see the last of the Germans." To prevent reprisals against the Germans, the Canadians
prohibited the resistance from carrying arms and also stopped allowing the rounding-up of collaborators. Both restrictions were "not
altogether pleasing to the Dutch."[52] On May 25, the German return
home began. Moving mostly on foot in large formations numbering
about ten thousand, the Germans "tramped homeward at the rate of
about 15 miles each day." Their route took them across the IJsselmeer
causeway, then through northern Holland, and across the border to
a concentration area in the Emden–Wilhelmshaven peninsula that
was administered by 11 Canadian Corps.

While the Germans moved out of Holland, increasing numbers
of Canadians came in from Germany to be based there until repatriation to Canada. Throughout May, the ongoing supply of food and
other vital supplies to the Dutch continued. On May 12, "aid started
pouring into western Holland," as the transportation network
increasingly improved. Seyss-Inquart had estimated this as the date
when "acute starvation would commence." The earlier aid, however,
and the opening of the floodgates that day resulted in a better situation than expected. "Conditions in Western Holland were not as
black as we anticipated, but it is obvious that we got there just in
time," SHAEF staff reported. The actual number of people diagnosed
as suffering from starvation was 125,000. All hospitals were badly
overcrowded with people stricken with edema. Fifteen thousand
people in Amsterdam were hospitalized and 10,000 in Haarlem. In
the large cities, hospitals were unable to take in many thousands
more who were acutely ill.

On May 27, Netherlands District reported average weight loss
during the occupation at twenty to thirty-five pounds per person. In
most cities, 2 per cent of the population was considered to be suffering from "dropsy and wasting." Amsterdam and Haarlem were
harder hit, with the figure for both set at 10 per cent. However,
virtually full recovery was predicted for the population "if given an
adequate ration."[53]

Approximately twenty thousand Dutch died from starvation. Three times the number of babies died in the first five months of 1945 as in the same period in 1944, and twice as many children between one and five years old succumbed. The occupation claimed many other Dutch lives. Of the 120,000 Jews sent to the extermination camps, 104,000 perished. Air raids killed 23,000, more than 5,000 died in prisons and concentration camps, 2,800 were executed, and of the 550,000 men taken to Germany as forced labourers, 30,000 never returned. The Dutch government concluded that from a population of 8.8 million, the war claimed 237,300.

The country itself had been laid waste. Most everything in the way of factory equipment, vehicles, rail stock, shipping and barges, and livestock had been carried off to Germany. Even the ubiquitous bicycles had been halved from a pre-war number of four million.[54]

Given the state of suffering throughout Holland and the brutality of the German occupation, it was easy to see why the Dutch were so grateful to their Canadian liberators. The Dutch recognized the price Canadian soldiers had paid. First Canadian Army in Northwest Europe had suffered 44,339 casualties since the Juno Beach landings of June 6, 1944. Of these, 961 officers and 10,375 other ranks were killed.[55] Most of these men were volunteers, the largest such body to fight in the war. When the Dutch learned that these men had come to their liberation freely and at such great cost in lives, the depth of gratitude only deepened.

It was a feeling that did not lessen in the months that followed the liberation until the last Canadian soldier went home. Indeed, the bond between the Dutch and Canadians strengthened—a bond that still persists between the two countries. In the days following the Seaforth Highlanders' entry into Amsterdam, Lieutenant Colonel Budge Bell-Irving captured the Canadian side of this sentiment well. "Before this," he wrote, "few of our men could have given a clear reason why they came . . . But here in Amsterdam, in one day, all that was changed . . . Every life lost, every long day away from home, had been spent in a good and necessary endeavour."[56]

The Liberation Campaign in Memory

IN DUTCH MEMORY, the last weeks of the war remain the "sweetest of springs." Their Remembrance Day falls on May 4, followed immediately on May 5 by the less sombre Liberation Day. Over their course, people gather by the thousands or dozens—the crowd dictated by community size—at monuments, cemeteries, and other appropriate sites to both remember and celebrate the gift of freedom one country gave another. While Canadian troops did not fight alone in the campaign that freed the Netherlands from Nazi tyranny, they were the first soldiers to arrive in most of its cities, towns, villages, and hamlets. They were also the ones who remained stationed in such cities as Utrecht, Hilversum, Amersfoort, Apeldoorn, and Groningen during the long process of repatriation to Canada that was not concluded until the latter part of 1946.

During that time personal friendships developed, and various regiments established lasting bonds with communities their men were billeted in or had participated in liberating. Thousands of individual soldiers also became romantically involved with Dutch women. It is estimated that 1,886 brought a Dutch wife home, 428 of them also returning with a child. "Whatever you do, don't fall in love with any of them. They're all going back to Canada and you're staying right here in Amsterdam!" Margriet Blaisse's father had warned her as she set off to welcome the Seaforth Highlanders of Canada to Amsterdam. She married the first soldier she saw, Wilf Gildersleeve. Wilhelmina Klaverdijk, the young woman who tried to kiss all the Canadians in Rotterdam that spring day, also married one after a whirlwind courtship.

Those months following the war were heady times for young people from two countries tossed together in the aftermath of a tragic era. For the soldiers, the cruelty of war and the ever-present fear of death or dismemberment was replaced by a world at peace and the dawning realization that they were among the lucky ones, destined to survive and likely to grow old. For the Dutch, a long, repressive occupation had passed. Many teenage girls had matured into young womanhood between the Dutch defeat in May 1940 and the liberation almost precisely five years later.

Thousands of their male cohorts were still awaiting return from Germany, where they had been imprisoned or detained as forced labourers. Most other young Dutch men were generally undernourished and attempting to pick up lives derailed by war. Their country was in economic ruins and required massive reconstruction. The Canadians were noticeably stronger, healthier, and wealthier than their male Dutch counterparts. There was also about them a slight air of the exotic. Little wonder that in their wake they left behind six thousand young mothers, of whom fifteen hundred were already married. The Dutch are noted for their long memories, but they are also unerringly pragmatic. So, while not entirely forgetting the issue of abandoned young women and babies, they set aside recrimination in recognition that the Canadians had given more to the Dutch overall than they took.

IT IS OVERWHELMINGLY the sacrifice of Canadian soldiers that remains imprinted on the national consciousness. During an April to May research trip for this book, I see repeated examples of how the Dutch continue to honour Canadians both as a community and personally. One day in Amsterdam I speak with a Dutch publisher, who recalls cycling as a teenager past what turned out to be a Canadian

Commonwealth Cemetery. Turning in, she walked along the seemingly endless rows of headstones and read the names, ages, and birthplaces of all these young men. The realization that in giving their lives they had made it possible for her to enjoy freedom moved her to tears.

Bernard Diepman, the youth whose farm was used by the Stormont, Dundas and Glengarry Highlanders for an overnight stop during the fighting near Dalfsen, stands with me in front of Salvo Bridge and describes two days when the war swirled around his family. That was almost a lifetime ago, but he has carefully nurtured those memories and returned to the farms here many times to walk the ground and consider the way the small action—not really a battle—unfolded. Along with many others, Bernard immigrated to Canada. After the war, during the 1950s and early 1960s, the Dutch government actively encouraged its youth to leave in order to alleviate the nation's continuing poverty by reducing its population. But he returns to Holland regularly and is always drawn back to this place and the memories of that time.

Not far away, on the southern outskirts of Zwolle, the few farms that made up Leesten have been replaced by a new, ultramodern subdivision still under construction. There are rows of tightly packed houses on streets where lawns have yet to be planted, and the back yards face streets still awaiting the arrival of builders. Most of the residents are young couples with small children. Few grew up anywhere near Leesten or have any knowledge of the day when 9th Canadian Infantry Brigade fought a stiff, small battle that left the farms ruined, the old windmill destroyed, and some Canadian dead. Yet at the suggestion of a resident who was born in the area, the people of this new community decided that each street would bear the name of one of the regiments that fought here or of a man who fell. "There was no disagreement," a fellow standing on his doorstep explains. "It was the right thing to do."

There are other Dutch towns, such as Woensdrecht, that have more Canadian-themed street names than Leesten has, but I am struck by the fact that this initiative is coming from young people today. In Canada, people of this age, facing the responsibility of recent parenthood, are among those least likely to give much thought to remembering our nation's role in World War II and of their countrymen who fell.

Monuments commemorating Canada's role in liberating specific communities in the Netherlands are common coin. Some are modest, often a restored Sherman tank or other army relic. Many others are statues adorned with regimental crests of units that fought in the vicinity. As part of its 50th Anniversary celebration of the war's end, Groningen created Liberation Forest just outside the city. Here, thirteen thousand maple trees were initially planted. Since its inception in 1995, the number of trees has grown to about thirty thousand and more are planted during ceremonies each year. Most of the trees were purchased by local residents. They border a long path that winds through the countryside. At one end, a large stylized metal maple leaf stands in a pond. Before it is a monument that bears the crests of all the regiments involved in the city's liberation. The entire site is tidy and well maintained. A man out walking his dog tells me that each year some of the trees die during the winter, but that they are planting more than enough to replace them, and that thousands of people come from the city to attend ceremonies held here. The path through the trees is also a popular walking and cycling route.

A poem written by a local resident, John Plëst, to mark the forest's creation in 1995, is also on display. It describes the fierce battle in Groningen's streets, and closes: "Thanks to the Canadians, a tough job done/ to commemorate them we dedicate a forest yet/ Maple leaves fell for us, lest we forget."

Of course the Dutch don't forget. I visit Holten Canadian War Cemetery where 1,355 Canadians soldiers lay at rest. Lieutenant General Guy Simonds personally selected the location because the surrounding forest reminded him of Ontario. It is a warm spring day, just two days after the Remembrance Day ceremonies. Before each headstone, a single yellow daffodil has been set on the ground and methodically centred. My friend Johan van Doorn explains that each flower was laid by a schoolchild who had researched the name of the soldier to learn about him and give this simple act of remembrance more personal resonance. This is done every year.

Looking out across the wide expanse of headstones, I am reminded that their number could easily have been three to four times as many had it not been for the secret negotiations that yielded a ceasefire at the Grebbe Line, averting a pitched battle to liberate the great cities of western Holland. There is no doubt that the Germans in Fortress Holland would have otherwise made good on the threat to inundate the region. Many thousands, perhaps millions, of Dutch would have drowned or succumbed to starvation and disease. Canadian casualties resulting from an attempt to win the cities and surrounding flooded countryside would have far exceeded the number suffered during the rest of the campaign in Holland and western Germany. The success of those negotiations proves that sometimes the pen truly is mightier than the sword.

As I walk down one long row of headstones after another, pausing before each to note the name, age, unit of service, hometown, and often touching sentiment added by family, the story of a country at war is revealed. Some of these soldiers were terribly young, others were already husbands and fathers. They came from the cities and small towns of a nation just beginning a transformation from agrarianism to industrialization—a transition completed while they were away and at war. Those that survived returned to a country forever changed by the conflict. And they brought to Canada even greater change. Most buried the painful memories of the war deep within themselves and turned to building better lives for their families. They had gone overseas while the nation was still being rocked by the Great Depression. In the army, they had learned to take care of each other, for therein lay the only path that might ensure survival. At home, they helped create a country where programs existed to provide basic security for all. They had, after all, fought not just for the freedom of subjugated peoples to live a decent life, but equally for every Canadian.

AMERICAN

President, Franklin Delano Roosevelt

Supreme Headquarters, Allied Expeditionary Force (SHAEF), Gen. Dwight G. Eisenhower

SHAEF Chief of Staff, Lt. Gen. Walter Bedell Smith

Twelfth U.S. Army Group, Gen. Omar Bradley

Third Army, Gen. George S. Patton

Ninth Army, Lt. Gen. William H. Simpson

BRITISH

Prime Minister, Winston Churchill

Chief of Imperial General Staff, Gen. Sir Alexander Brooke

Twenty-First Army Group, Field Marshal Bernard Law Montgomery

Twenty-First Army Group Chief of Staff, Maj. Gen. Francis "Freddie" de Guingand

Second Army, Gen. Miles Dempsey

XXX Corps, Gen. Brian Horrocks

51st Highland Division, Maj. Gen. Thomas Rennie (KIA Mar. 24, 1945)

Netherlands District, Maj. Gen. Sandy Galloway

CANADIAN

Prime Minister, William Lyon Mackenzie King

First Army, Gen. Harry Crerar

First Army Chief of Staff, Brig. C.C. "Church" Mann

1 Corps, Lt. Gen. Charles Foulkes
11 Corps, Lt. Gen. Guy Simonds
11 Corps, Commander Corps Royal Artillery, Brig. Stanley Todd
1st Division, Maj. Gen. Harry Foster
2nd Division, Maj. Gen. Bruce Matthews
3rd Division, Maj. Gen. R.H. "Holly" Keefler
4th Division, Maj. Gen. Chris Vokes
5th Division, Maj. Gen. Bert Hoffmeister
1st Armoured Brigade, Brig. Bill Murphy
2nd Brigade, Brig. Pat Bogert
4th Armoured Brigade, Brig. Robert Moncel
4th Brigade, Brig. Fred Cabeldu
5th Armoured Brigade, Brig. Ian Cumberland
5th Brigade, Brig. W.J. "Bill" Megill
6th Brigade, Brig. Jean Allard
7th Brigade, Brig. Graeme Gibson
8th Brigade, Brig. J.A. "Jim" Roberts
9th Brigade, Brig. J.M. "Rocky" Rockingham
10th Brigade, Brig. Jim Jefferson
11th Brigade, Brig. Ian Johnston

DUTCH
Government-in-Exile:
Head of State, Queen Wilhelmina
Prime Minister, Pieter Sjoerds Gerbrandy
Commander, Dutch Armed Forces, Prince Bernhard
Member of the College van Vertrouwensmannen (committee within
the Netherlands representing Dutch government-in-exile), Jacob van
der Gaag (aka Richard)

Occupation Government:
Director of Food, Dr. S.L. Louwes
Secretary-General of the Departments of Agriculture and Fisheries,
and Commerce, Industry and Shipping, Dr. H.M. "Max" Hirschfeld

Resistance:

Commander of the Nederlandse Binnenlandse Strijdkrachten (NBS) (Dutch Forces of the Interior), Col. Henri Koot

GERMAN

Netherlands Governor, Reichkommissar Arthur Seyss-Inquart

Netherlands Höherer SS und Polizeiführer Hans Albin Rauter

Commander-in-Chief West, Generalfeldmarschall Albert Kesselring

Supreme Commander, Wehrmacht in the Netherlands, Gen. der Flieger Friedrich Christiansen to Apr. 7, then Generaloberst Johannes Blaskowitz

Army Group H, Generaloberst Johannes Blaskowitz to Apr. 7

Twenty-Fifth Army, Christiansen to Apr. 7, then Blaskowitz

Twenty-Fifth Army Chief of Staff, Generalleutnant Paul Reichelt

First Fallschirmjäger Army, Gen. der Fallschirmtruppen Alfred Schlemm until Mar. 28, then Gen. der Infanterie Günther Blumentritt

II Fallschirmjäger Corps, Gen. der Flieger Eugen Meindl

LXXXVI Corps, Gen. der Infanterie Erich von Straube

XLVII Panzer Corps, Gen. der Panzertruppen Heinrich Freiherr von Lüttwitz

6th Fallschirmjäger Division, Generalleutnant Hermann Plocher

THE CANADIAN ARMY IN THE LIBERATION CAMPAIGN

(COMBAT UNITS ONLY)

FIRST CANADIAN ARMY TROOPS
Royal Montreal Regiment
1st Armoured Personnel Carrier Regiment

1st Army Group, Royal Canadian Artillery:
11th Field Regiment
1st Medium Regiment
2nd Medium Regiment
5th Medium Regiment

2nd Army Group, Royal Canadian Artillery:
19th Field Regiment
3rd Medium Regiment
4th Medium Regiment
7th Medium Regiment
2nd Heavy Anti-Aircraft Regiment (Mobile)

Corps of Royal Canadian Engineers:
10th Field Park Company
5th Field Company
20th Field Company
23rd Field Company

I CANADIAN CORPS TROOPS
1st Armoured Car Regiment (Royal Canadian Dragoons)
7th Anti-Tank Regiment
1st Survey Regiment

1st Light Anti-Aircraft Regiment
(Lanark and Renfrew Scottish Regiment)

Corps of Royal Canadian Engineers:
9th Field Park Company
12th Field Company
13th Field Company
14th Field Company

II CANADIAN CORPS TROOPS
18th Armoured Car Regiment (12th Manitoba Dragoons)
6th Anti-Tank Regiment
2nd Survey Regiment
6th Light Anti-Aircraft Regiment

Corps of Royal Canadian Engineers:
8th Field Park Company
29th Field Company
30th Field Company
31st Field Company

1ST CANADIAN INFANTRY DIVISION
4th Reconnaissance Regiment (Princess Louise Dragoon Guards)
Saskatoon Light Infantry (MG)

The Royal Canadian Artillery:
1st Field Regiment (Royal Canadian Horse Artillery)
2nd Field Regiment
3rd Field Regiment
1st Anti-Tank Regiment
2nd Light Anti-Aircraft Regiment

Corps of Royal Canadian Engineers:
1st Field Company
3rd Field Company
4th Field Company
2nd Field Park Company

1st Canadian Infantry Brigade:
Royal Canadian Regiment (Permanent Force)
Hastings and Prince Edward Regiment
48th Highlanders of Canada Regiment

2nd Canadian Infantry Brigade:
Princess Patricia's Canadian Light Infantry Regiment
(Permanent Force)
Seaforth Highlanders of Canada Regiment
Loyal Edmonton Regiment

3rd Canadian Infantry Brigade:
Royal 22e Regiment (Permanent Force)
Carleton and York Regiment
West Nova Scotia Regiment

2ND CANADIAN INFANTRY DIVISION
8th Reconnaissance Regiment (14th Canadian Hussars)
Toronto Scottish Regiment (MG)

The Royal Canadian Artillery:
4th Field Regiment
5th Field Regiment
6th Field Regiment
2nd Anti-Tank Regiment
3rd Light Anti-Aircraft Regiment

Corps of Royal Canadian Engineers:
1st Field Park Company
2nd Field Company
7th Field Company
11th Field Company

4th Canadian Infantry Brigade:
Royal Regiment of Canada
Royal Hamilton Light Infantry
Essex Scottish Regiment

5th Canadian Infantry Brigade:
Black Watch (Royal Highland Regiment) of Canada
Le Régiment de Maisonneuve
Calgary Highlanders

6th Canadian Infantry Brigade:
Les Fusiliers Mont-Royal
Queen's Own Cameron Highlanders
South Saskatchewan Regiment

3RD CANADIAN INFANTRY DIVISION
7th Reconnaissance Regiment (17th Duke Of York's
Royal Canadian Hussars)
Cameron Highlanders of Ottawa (MG Battalion)

The Royal Canadian Artillery:
12th Field Regiment
13th Field Regiment
14th Field Regiment
3rd Anti-Tank Regiment
4th Light Anti-Aircraft Regiment

Corps of Royal Canadian Engineers:
3rd Field Park Company
6th Field Company
16th Field Company
18th Field Company

7th Canadian Infantry Brigade:
Royal Winnipeg Rifles
Regina Rifle Regiment
1st Battalion, Canadian Scottish Regiment

8th Canadian Infantry Brigade:
Queen's Own Rifles of Canada
Le Régiment de la Chaudière
North Shore (New Brunswick) Regiment

9th Canadian Infantry Brigade:
Highland Light Infantry of Canada
Stormont, Dundas and Glengarry Highlanders
North Nova Scotia Highlanders

4TH CANADIAN ARMOURED DIVISION
29th Armoured Reconnaissance Regiment
(South Alberta Regiment)
10th Canadian Independent MG Company
(New Brunswick Rangers)
Lake Superior Regiment (Motor)

Royal Canadian Artillery:
15th Field Regiment
23rd Field Regiment (Self-Propelled)
5th Anti-Tank Regiment
4th Light Anti-Aircraft Regiment

Royal Canadian Corps of Engineers:
6th Field Park Squadron
8th Field Squadron
9th Field Squadron

4th Canadian Armoured Brigade:
21st Armoured Regiment (Governor General's Foot Guards)
22nd Armoured Regiment (Canadian Grenadier Guards)
23rd Armoured Regiment (British Columbia Regiment)

10th Canadian Armoured Brigade:
Lincoln and Welland Regiment
Algonquin Regiment
Argyll and Sutherland Highlanders of Canada

5TH CANADIAN ARMOURED DIVISION
3rd Canadian Armoured Reconnaissance Regiment
(Governor General's Horse Guards)
11th Independent Machine Gun Company

(Princess Louise Fusiliers)
Westminster Regiment (Motor)

The Royal Canadian Artillery:
17th Field Regiment
8th Field Regiment (Self-Propelled)
4th Anti-Tank Regiment
5th Light Anti-Tank Regiment

Royal Canadian Corps of Engineers
1st Field Squadron
4th Field Park Squadron
10th Field Squadron

5th Canadian Armoured Brigade
2nd Canadian Armoured Regiment (Lord Strathcona's Horse)
5th Canadian Armoured Regiment
(8th Princess Louise New Brunswick Hussars)
9th Canadian Armoured Regiment
(British Columbia Dragoons)

11th Canadian Infantry Brigade
Perth Regiment
Cape Breton Highlanders
Irish Regiment of Canada

1ST CANADIAN ARMOURED BRIGADE
11th Canadian Armoured Regiment (Ontario Tanks)
12th Canadian Armoured Regiment (Three Rivers Tanks)
14th Canadian Armoured Regiment (Calgary Tanks)

2ND CANADIAN ARMOURED BRIGADE
6th Armoured Regiment (1st Hussars)
10th Armoured Regiment (Fort Garry Horse)
27th Armoured Regiment
(Sherbrooke Fusiliers Regiment)

APPENDIX C:
CANADIAN INFANTRY BATTALION
(TYPICAL ORGANIZATION)

HQ COMPANY
No. 1: Signals Platoon
No. 2: Administrative Platoon

SUPPORT COMPANY
No. 3: Mortar Platoon (3-inch)
No. 4: Bren Carrier Platoon
No. 5: Assault Pioneer Platoon
No. 6: Anti-Tank Platoon (6-pounder)

A COMPANY
No. 7 Platoon
No. 8 Platoon
No. 9 Platoon

B COMPANY
No. 10 Platoon
No. 11 Platoon
No. 12 Platoon

C COMPANY
No. 13 Platoon
No. 14 Platoon
No. 15 Platoon

D COMPANY
No. 16 Platoon
No. 17 Platoon
No. 18 Platoon

CANADIAN AND GERMAN ARMY
ORDER OF RANKS
(LOWEST TO HIGHEST)

Like most Commonwealth nations, the Canadian Army used the British ranking system. Except for the lower ranks, this system differed little from one service arm to another. The German Army system, however, tended to identify service and rank throughout most of its command chain. The translations are roughly based on the Canadian ranking system, although there is no Canadian equivalent for many German ranks and some differentiation in the responsibility each rank bestowed on its holder.

CANADIAN ARMY	GERMAN ARMY/ LUFTWAFFE
Private, infantry	Schütze
Rifleman, rifle regiments	Schütze
Private	Grenadier
Gunner (artillery equivalent of private)	Kanonier
Trooper (armoured equivalent of private)	Panzerschütze
Guardsman (guards equivalent of private)	Panzerschütze
Sapper (engineer equivalent of private)	Pionier
Signaller (signals equivalent of private)	Funker

Lance Corporal	Gefreiter
Corporal	Obergefreiter
Lance Sergeant	Unteroffizier
Sergeant	Unterfeldwebel
Company Sergeant Major	Feldwebel
Battalion Sergeant Major	Oberfeldwebel
Regimental Sergeant Major	Stabsfeldwebel
Second Lieutenant	Leutnant
Lieutenant	Oberleutnant
Captain	Hauptmann
Major	Major
Lieutenant Colonel	Oberstleutnant
Colonel	Oberst
Brigadier	Generalmajor
Major General	Generalleutnant
Lieutenant General	General der (service arm)

(No differentiation)	General der Artillerie
	General der Flieger
	General der Infanterie
	General der Kavallerie
	General der Pioniere
	General der Panzertruppen
General	Generaloberst
Field Marshal	Generalfeldmarschall
Commander-in-Chief	Oberbefehlshaber

APPENDIX E:
ARMY DECORATIONS

The decoration system that Canada used in World War II, like most other aspects of its military organization and tradition, derived from Britain. Under this class-based system, most military decorations can be awarded either to officers or to "other ranks," but not both. The Canadian army, navy, and air force also have distinct decorations. Only the Victoria Cross—the nation's highest award—can be won by personnel from any arm of the service or of any rank. The decorations and qualifying ranks are as follows.

VICTORIA CROSS (VC): Awarded for gallantry in the presence of the enemy. Instituted in 1856. Open to all ranks. The only award that can be granted for action in which the recipient was killed, other than Mentioned in Despatches—a less formal honour whereby an act of bravery was given specific credit in a formal report.

DISTINGUISHED SERVICE ORDER (DSO): Army officers of all ranks, but more commonly awarded to officers with ranks of major or higher.

MILITARY CROSS (MC): Army officers with a rank normally below major and, rarely, warrant officers.

DISTINGUISHED CONDUCT MEDAL (DCM): Army warrant officers and all lower ranks.

MILITARY MEDAL (MM): Army warrant officers and all lower ranks.

BIBLIOGRAPHY

BOOKS

Alexander, G.M., ed. *Europe, July 1944–May 1945: A Brief History of the 4th Canadian Armoured Brigade in Action*. Mitcham, UK: West Brothers, 1945.

Allard, Jean V. *The Memoirs of Jean V. Allard*. Vancouver: University of British Columbia Press, 1988.

Antal, Sandy, and Kevin R. Shackleton. *Duty nobly done: the official history of the Essex and Kent Scottish Regiment*. Windsor: Walkerville Publishing, 2006.

Ashworth, Gregory John. *War and the City*. London: Routledge, 1991.

Barnard, W.T. *The Queen's Own Rifles of Canada, 1860–1960: One Hundred Years of Canada*. Don Mills, ON: Ontario Publishing Company, 1960.

Barrett, William W. *History of 13th Canadian Field Artillery*. N.p., 1945.

Beattie, Kim. *Dileas: History of the 48th Highlanders of Canada, 1929–1956*. Toronto: 48th Highlanders of Canada, 1957.

Bell, T.J. *Into Action with the 12th Field*. Utrecht: J. van Boekhoven, 1945.

Bennett, Ralph. *Ultra in the West: The Normandy Campaign, 1944–45*. London: Hutchinson & Co., 1980.

Bercuson, David. *Battalion of Heroes: The Calgary Highlanders in World War II*. Calgary: Calgary Highlanders Regimental Funds Foundation, 1994.

Bird, Will R. *North Shore (New Brunswick) Regiment*. Fredericton: Brunswick Press, 1963.

———. *No Retreating Footsteps: The Story of the North Nova Scotia Highlanders*. Hantsport, NS: Lancelot Press, 1983.

Blackburn, George. *The Guns of Victory: A Soldier's Eye View, Belgium, Holland, and Germany, 1944–45*. Toronto: McClelland & Stewart, 1944.

Boegel, Gary C. *Boys of the Clouds: An Oral History of the 1st Canadian Parachute Battalion*. Victoria: Trafford, 2005.

Boss, William. *Up the Glens: Stormont, Dundas and Glengarry Highlanders, 1783–1994,* 2nd ed. Cornwall, ON: Old Book Store, 1995.

Bouchery, Jean. *The Canadian Soldier in North-West Europe, 1944–1945.* Translated by Alan McKay. Paris: Histoire & Collections, 2003.

Breuer, William B. *Storming Hitler's Rhine: The Allied Assault, February–March, 1945.* New York: St. Martin's Press, 1985.

Brown, Gordon, and Terry Copp. *Look to Your Front . . . Regina Rifles: A Regiment at War, 1944–45.* Waterloo, ON: Laurier Centre Military Strategic Disarmament Studies, 2001.

Brown, Kingsley, Sr., Kingsley Brown, Jr., and Brereton Greenhous. *Semper Paratus: The History of The Royal Hamilton Light Infantry (Wentworth Regiment), 1862–1977.* Hamilton: The RHLI Historical Association, 1977.

Buchanan, G.B. *The March of the Prairie Men: A Story of the South Saskatchewan Regiment.* N.p., n.d.

Cassidy, G.L. *Warpath: The Story of the Algonquin Regiment, 1939–1945.* Markham, ON: PaperJacks, 1980.

Castonguay, Jacques, and Armand Ross. *Le Régiment de la Chaudière.* Lévis, QC: n.p., 1983.

Caya, G.L. *Ne-Kan-Ne-Tah (We Lead, Others Follow).* N.p., 1999.

Cent ans d'histoire d'un regiment canadien-français: les Fusiliers Mont-Royal, 1869–1969. Montreal: Éditions Du Jour, 1971.

Churchill, Winston S. *Triumph and Tragedy.* Toronto: Thomas Allen, 1953.

Conron, Brandon. *A History of the First Hussars Regiment, 1856–1980.* N.p., 1981.

Copp, Terry. *The Brigade: The Fifth Canadian Infantry Brigade, 1939–1945.* Stoney Creek, ON: Fortress Publications, 1992.

——. *Cinderella Army: The Canadians in Northwest Europe, 1944–1945.* Toronto: University of Toronto Press, 2006.

Delaney, Douglas E. *The Soldier's General: Bert Hoffmeister at War.* Vancouver: University of British Columbia Press, 2005.

Den Hartog, Kirsten, and Tracy Kasaboski. *The Occupied Garden: Recovering the Story of a Family in the War-Torn Netherlands.* Toronto: McClelland & Stewart, 2008.

Dickson, Paul Douglas. *A Thoroughly Canadian General: A Biography of General H.D.G. Crerar.* Toronto: University of Toronto Press, 2007.

Duguid, A. Fortescue. *History of the Canadian Grenadier Guards, 1760–1964.* Montreal: Gazette Printing, 1965.

VIII CDN Recce Rgt 14 CH: Battle History of the Regt. Victoria: 8th Cdn Recce Association, 1993.

Farran, Roy. *The History of the Calgary Highlanders, 1921–54.* Calgary: Bryant Press, 1954.

I Battalion, The Essex Scottish Regiment, 1940–1945: A Brief Narrative. Aldershot, UK: Gale and Polden, 1946.

1st Battalion, The Highland Light Infantry of Canada: 1940–1945. Galt, ON: Highland Light Infantry of Canada Association, 1951.

Flatt, Samuel Alexander. *History of the 6th Field Company, Royal Canadian Engineers: 1939–1945.* New Westminster: n.p., 1946.

Foot, Michael Richard Daniell, ed. *Holland at War Against Hitler: Anglo–Dutch Relations, 1940–45*. London: Frank Cass, 1990.

Foster, Robert M., et al. *Steady the Buttons Two by Two: Governor General's Foot Guards Regimental History, 125th Anniversary: 1872–1997*. Ottawa: Governor General's Foot Guards, 1999.

Fraser, Robert L. *Black Yesterdays: The Argyll's War*. Hamilton: Argyll Foundation, 1996.

Frost, C. Sydney. *Once a Patricia: Memoirs of a Junior Officer in World War II*. Ottawa: Borealis Press, 2004.

Galloway, Strome. *"55 Axis," With the Royal Canadian Regiment, 1939–1945*. Montreal: Provincial Publishing, 1946.

Goodspeed, D.J. *Battle Royal: A History of the Royal Regiment of Canada, 1862–1962*. Toronto: Royal Regiment of Canada Association, 1962.

The Governor General's Horse Guards, 1939–1945. Toronto: Canadian Military Journal, 1945.

Graves, Donald. *South Albertas: a Canadian Regiment at war*. Toronto: Robin Brass Studio, 1998.

Harker, Douglas E. *The Dukes: The Story of the men who have served in Peace and War with the British Columbia Regiment (D.C.O.), 1883–1973*. British Columbia Regiment, 1974.

Hart, Stephen. *Montgomery and "Colossal Cracks": The 21st Army Group in Northwest Europe, 1944–1945*. Westport, CT: Greenwood Publishing Group, 2000.

Hayes, Geoffrey. *The Lincs: A History of the Lincoln and Welland Regiment at War*. Alma, ON: Maple Leaf Route, 1986.

History of 17th Field Regiment, Royal Canadian Artillery, 5th Canadian Armoured Division. Groningen: J. Niemeiser, 1946.

History of the 3rd Canadian Field Regiment, Royal Canadian Artillery: September 1939 to July 1945–World War II. Canada: n.p., 1945.

The History of the 23rd Field Regiment (S.P.) RCA. N.p., 1945.

Hornd, Bernd and Michel Wyczynski. *Paras Versus the Reich: Canada's Paratroopers at War, 1942–45*. Toronto: Dundurn, 2003.

Hornd, Bernd and Stephen Harris, eds. *Warrior Chiefs*. Toronto: Dundurn, 2001.

Horrocks, Brian, with Eversley Belfield and H. Essame. *Corps Commander*. London: Sidgwick & Jackson, 1977.

How, Douglas. *The 8th Hussars: A History of the Regiment*. Sussex, NB: Maritime Publishing, 1964.

Huizinga, Menno. *Sporen van Strijd in de Stad Groningen*. Repr. Groningen: Jemeentelijk 5 Mei Comité Groningen, 2004.

Hutchison, Paul P. *Canada's Black Watch: The First Hundred Years, 1862–1962*. Montreal: The Black Watch (RHR) of Canada, 1962.

Jackson, H.M. *The Argyll and Sutherland Highlanders of Canada (Princess Louise's), 1928–1953*. Montreal: Industrial Shops for the Deaf, 1953.

——. *The Sherbrooke Regiment (12th Armoured Regiment)*. N.p., 1958.

Johnston, Stafford. *The Fighting Perths: The Story of the First Century in the Life of a Canadian County Regiment*. Stratford, ON: Perth Regiment Veterans' Assoc., 1964.

Jones, Gwilym. *To The Green Fields Beyond: A Soldier's Story.* Burnstown, ON: General Store Publishing House, 1993.

Kaufman, David, and Michiel Horn. *A Liberation Album: Canadians in the Netherlands, 1944–45.* Toronto: McGraw-Hill Ryerson, 1980.

Kember, Arthur K. *The Six Years of 6 Canadian Field Regiment Royal Canadian Artillery: September 1939–September 1945.* Amsterdam: Town Printing, 1945.

Kerry, A.J., and W.A. McDill. *History of the Corps of Royal Canadian Engineers.* Vol. 2. Ottawa: Military Engineers Assoc. of Canada, 1966.

Kitching, George. *Mud and Green Fields: The Memoirs of Major General George Kitching.* Langley, BC: Battleline Books, 1985.

Kuppers, Alex, ed. *Perspectives.* Royal Winnipeg Rifles Association, British Columbia Branch, 2003.

Lockwood, A.M. *History of the 7th Canadian Medium Regiment, R.C.A.–From 1st September, 1939 to 8th June, 1945.* Toronto: Macmillan, 1945.

Luxton, Eric, ed. *1st Battalion, The Regina Rifles Regiment, 1939–1946.* Regina: The Regiment, 1946.

Maass, Walter B. *The Netherlands at War: 1940–1945.* Toronto: Abelard-Schuman, 1970.

Marchand, Gérard. *Le Régiment de Maisonneuve Vers la Victoire, 1944–1945.* Montréal: Les Presses Libres, 1980.

Marmbrunn, Werner. *The Dutch Under German Occupation, 1940–1945.* Stanford, CA: Stanford University Press, 1963.

Martin, Charles Cromwell. *Battle Diary: from D-Day and Normandy to the Zuider Zee.* Toronto: Dundurn, 1994.

McAvity, J.M. *Lord Strathcona's Horse (Royal Canadians): A Record of Achievement.* Toronto: Bridgens, 1947.

Mein, Stewart A.G. *Up the Johns! The Story of the Royal Regina Rifles.* North Battleford, SK: Turner-Warwick Publications, 1992.

Montgomery, Bernard Law. *The Memoirs of Field Marshal The Viscount Montgomery of Alamein, K.G.* London: Collins, 1958.

Morrison, Alex, and Ted Slaney. *The Breed of Manly Men: The History of the Cape Breton Highlanders.* Toronto: Canadian Institute of Strategic Studies, 1994.

Mowat, Farley. *The Regiment.* 2nd ed. Toronto: McClelland & Stewart, 1973.

Munro, Ross. *Gauntlet to Overlord: The Story of the Canadian Army.* Toronto: Macmillan, 1945.

Nicholson, G.W.L. *The Gunners of Canada.* Vol. 2. Toronto: McClelland & Stewart, 1972.

Oldfield, J.E. *The Westminster's War Diary: An Unofficial History of the Westminster Regiment (Motor) in World War II.* New Westminster: n.p., 1964.

Pavey, Walter G. *An Historical Account of the 7th Canadian Reconnaissance Regiment (17th Duke of York's Royal Canadian Hussars).* Gardenvale, Quebec: Harpell's Press, 1948.

Pearce, Donald. *Journal of a War: North-west Europe, 1944–45.* Toronto: Macmillan, 1965.

Phillips, Maj. Norman, and J. Nikerk. *Holland and the Canadians.* Amsterdam: Contact Publishing, 1946.

Portugal, Jean E. *We Were There: The Navy, the Army and the RCAF—a record for Canada.* Vols. 1–7. Shelburne, ON: Battered Silicon Dispatch Box, 1998.

Quayle, J.T.B. *In Action: A Personal Account of the Italian and Netherlands Campaigns of ww 11*. Abbotsford, BC: Blue Stone Publishers, 1997.

Queen-Hughes, R.W. *Whatever Men Dare: A History of the Queen's Own Cameron Highlanders of Canada, 1935–1960*. Winnipeg: Bulman Bros., 1960.

Raddall, Thomas H. *West Novas: A History of the West Nova Scotia Regiment*. N.p., 1947.

The Regimental History of the Governor General's Foot Guards. Ottawa: Mortimer, 1948.

Rogers, R.L. *History of the Lincoln and Welland Regiment*. Montreal: Industrial Shops for the Deaf, 1954.

Rollefson, M.O., ed. *Green Route Up: 4 Canadian Armoured Division*. The Hague: Mouton, 1945.

Ross, Alexander. *Slow March to a Regiment*. St. Catharines, ON: Vanwell, 1993.

Ross, Richard M. *The History of the 1st Battalion Cameron Highlanders of Ottawa (MG)*. N.p, n.d.

Roy, Reginald, *The Canadians in Normandy*. Toronto: Macmillan, 1984.

——. *Ready for the Fray: The History of the Canadian Scottish Regiment (Princess Mary's), 1920 to 1955*. Vancouver: Evergreen Press, 1958.

——. *The Seaforth Highlanders of Canada, 1919–1965*. Vancouver: Evergreen Press, 1969.

——. *Sinews of Steel: The History of the British Columbia Dragoons*. Repr. Toronto: Charters, 1965.

Royal Canadian Dragoons, 1939–1945. Montreal: The Regiment, 1946.

Ruffee, G.E.M. *The History of the 14 Field Regiment Royal Canadian Artillery, 1940–1945*. Amsterdam: Wereldbibliotheek, 1945.

Spencer, Robert A. *History of the Fifteenth Canadian Field Regiment, Royal Canadian Artillery: 1941 to 1945*. New York: Elsevier, 1945.

Stacey, C.P. *Six Years of War: The Army in Canada, Britain and the Pacific*. Vol. 1. Ottawa: Queens Printer, 1957.

——. *The Victory Campaign: The Operations in North-West Europe, 1944–1945*. Vol. 2. Ottawa: Queen's Printer, 1960.

Stafford, David. *Endgame 1945: The Missing Final Chapter of World War 11*. New York: Little, Brown and Company, 2007.

Stanley, George F.G. *In the Face of Danger: The History of the Lake Superior Regiment*. Port Arthur, ON: Lake Superior Scottish Regiment, 1960.

Stevens, G.R. *A City Goes to War*. Brampton, ON: Charters, 1964.

——. *Princess Patricia's Canadian Light Infantry: 1919–1957*. Vol. 3. Griesbach, AB: Historical Committee of the Regiment, n.d.

——. *The Royal Canadian Regiment, 1933–1966*. Vol. 2. London, ON: London Printing, 1967.

Tascona, Bruce, and Eric Wells. *Little Black Devils: A History of the Royal Winnipeg Rifles*. Winnipeg: Frye Publishing, 1983.

Tooley, Robert. *Invicta: The Carleton and York Regiment in the Second World War*. Fredericton, NB: New Ireland Press, 1989.

Vanguard: The Fort Garry Horse in the Second World War. Doetincham, Holland: Uitgevers-Maatschappij, 'C. Misset, n.d.

van der Zee, Henri. *The Hunger Winter: Occupied Holland, 1944–45*. London: Jill Norman and Hobhouse, 1982.

Veenendaal, A.J. *Railways in the Netherlands, 1834–1994*. Stanford, CA: Stanford University Press, 2001.

Whistrich, Robert S. *Who's Who in Nazi Germany*. New York: Routledge, 2001.

Whitaker, W. Denis, and Shelagh Whitaker. *Rhineland: The Battle to End the War*. Toronto: Stoddart, 1989.

Whitsed, Roy. *Canadians: A Battalion at War*. Mississauga, ON: Burlington Books, 1996.

Willes, John A. *Out of the Clouds: The History of the 1st Canadian Parachute Battalion*. Port Perry, ON: Perry Printing, 1995.

Williams, Jeffrey. *The Long Left Flank: The Hard Fought Way to the Reich, 1944–1945*. Toronto: Stoddart, 1988.

Wilmot, Chester. *The Struggle for Europe*. London: Collins, 1952.

Wood, Gordon. *The Story of the Irish Regiment of Canada, 1939–1945*. Heerenveen, Holland: Hepkema, 1945.

Worthington, Larry. *The Spur and Sprocket: The Story of the Royal Canadian Dragoons*. Kitchener: Reeve Press, 1968.

MAGAZINES, NEWSPAPERS, ARTICLES

Bond, James C. "The Fog of War: Large-Scale Smoke Screening Operations of First Canadian Army in Northwest Europe, 1944–1945." *Canadian Military History*. Vol. 8, no. 1 (Winter 1999).

Dykstra, Ralph. "The Liberation of Groningen—An Urban Battlefield." *The Army Doctrine and Training Bulletin*. Sept. 22, 2002.

Eldridge, Justin L.C. "Defense on the Rhine." *Military Intelligence Professional Bulletin*. Vol. 21, issue 1 (Jan.–Mar. 1995).

Windsor, Lee. "Too Close for the Guns!" *Canadian Military History*. Vol. 13, nos. 1 and 2 (Winter/Spring 2003).

WEBSITES

"Almost Continuous Roar." In *Heroes Remember, Glen Tomlin*. Tomlin interview, March 7, 2005. Veteran Affairs Canada, www.vac- acc.gc.ca/remembers/sub. cfm?source=collections/hrp/hrp_detail&media_id=2150 (accessed November 24, 2008).

"Almost Fatal Mistake." In *Heroes Remember, Glen Tomlin*. Tomlin interview, March 7, 2005. Veteran Affairs Canada, www.vac-acc.gc.ca/remembers/sub. cfm?source=collections/hrp/hrp_detail&media_id=2147 (accessed November 24, 2008).

Bannerman, Gordon. www.gordiebannerman.com (accessed February 24, 2009).

Bentley, Stewart. "The Dutch Resistance and the OSS, of Market-Garden and Melanie." www.cia.gov/library/center-for-the-study-of-intelligence/csi-publications/csi-studies/studies/Holland.html (accessed August 25, 2009).

"Canadian Army Overseas Honours and Awards Citation Details." Directorate of

Heritage and History, Department of National Defence. www.cmp-cpm.forces. gc.ca/dhh-dhp/gal/cao-aco/index-eng.asp (various citations and accession dates given in endnotes).

Regina Rifles Intelligence Logs and War Diaries, March–May 1945. www.reginarifles.ca (various sheets cited in endnotes, all accessed July 15, 2009). www.metsystems.np.ig.org/irish/ (accessed March 29, 2009).

UNPUBLISHED MATERIALS

"Actions at Leer and North of Groningen, Prepared by 1st BN Regina Rifles Regiment." 145.2R11011(D5). Directorate of Heritage and History, Department of National Defence.

Algonquin Regiment War Diary, April–May 1945. RG24, Library and Archives Canada.

Angle, Lt. Col. H.H. "Lt. Col. H.H. Angle Diary," RG24, vol. 20405, Library and Archives Canada.

Argyll and Sutherland Highlanders War Diary, April–May 1945. RG24, Library and Archives Canada.

"Artillery Notes on Operation Plunder." 142.4F14011(D1), Directorate of Heritage and History, Department of National Defence.

Bannerman, Lt. George. "Some Aspects of the Technique of Flame Throwing: 'WASP' and 'Lifebuoy' (Account by Lt. George Bannerman, Sask L. I. (M.G.), Tech Offr (Flame), First Canadian Army, Given to Historical Officer, 2 CDN INF DIV, 26 Nov 44), Canadian Operations in North-West Europe: June–November 1944." Extracts from War Diaries and Memoranda (Series 17), 018(D2), Directorate of Heritage and History, Department of National Defence.

Bannerman, Gordon. "Gordon Bannerman account re: Sergeant Humble." Possession of author.

"The Battle of Otterloo, Account by Capt. D. Wagner." RG24, vol. 10941, Library and Archives Canada.

Black Watch of Canada War Diary, April–May 1945. RG24, Library and Archives Canada.

Blackburn, George. *The History of the 4th Field Regiment.* N.p., 1945.

"Brief Historical Outline of the Occupation of N.W. Holland by 1 Canadian Corps." RG24, vol. 10796, Library and Archives Canada.

British Columbia Dragoons War Diary, April–May 1945. RG24, Library and Archives Canada.

Broomhall, George E. "Second World War Letter Collection of Captain George E. Broomhall." 20060029-001, Canadian War Museum.

Calgary Highlanders War Diary, March–May 1945. RG24, Library and Archives Canada.

Calgary Regiment War Diary, Mar–May 1945. RG24, Library and Archives Canada.

"Canadian Civil Affairs contribution to feeding the Dutch in Western Holland (B2 Area)." RG24, vol. 10662, Library and Archives Canada.

Cass, Samuel. "Letter to Annabel, 21 April 1945." Samuel Cass Letters, MG30, vol. 3, Personal Correspondence Samuel to Annabel Cass, April 1945, Library and Archives Canada.

Canadian Scottish Regiment War Diary, March–May 1945. RG24, Library and Archives Canada.

Cape Breton Highlanders War Diary, April–May 1945. RG24, Library and Archives Canada.

Carleton and York Regiment War Diary, April–May 1945. RG24, Library and Archives Canada.

"Comment on Operation 'Cannonshot' by Major General H.W. Foster, DSO, GOC I CDN INF DIV." RG24, vol. 10896, Library and Archives Canada.

"Diary Charlie Coy Seaforths, 23 Apr–9 July 45." RG24, vol. 20409, Library and Archives Canada.

"Draft Outline of Ops of I CDN Corps in Clearing Western Holland April 1945." RG24, vol. 10796, Library and Archives Canada.

Durnford, Roy C.H. "Diary of Major Roy Durnford, Chaplain (Padre), the Seaforth Highlanders of Canada, June 1943–June 1945." RG24, vol. 20405, Library and Archives Canada.

Dykman, Henk. "The Glens in Leesten." Possession of author.

8th Canadian Infantry Brigade War Diary, April–May 1945. RG24, Library and Archives Canada.

8th Canadian Reconnaissance Regiment (14th Canadian Hussars) War Diary, March–May 1945. RG24, Library and Archives Canada.

8th Light Anti-Aircraft Regiment War Diary, March–May 1945. RG24, Library and Archives Canada.

8th Princess Louise's (New Brunswick) Hussars War Diary, April–May 1945. RG24, Library and Archives Canada.

"The 11th Canadian Armoured Regiment (Ont. R.) Actions Kommerdijk." 141.4A11, Directorate of Heritage and History, Department of National Defence.

11th Canadian Armoured Regiment (Ontario Regiment) War Diary, April–May 1945. RG24, Library and Archives Canada.

"Extracts Polish Armoured Division History." RG24, vol. 10538, Library and Archives Canada.

"5th Canadian Armoured Division Intelligence Summary, No. 131, 25 Apr. 45." RG24, vol. 10941, Library and Archives Canada.

1st Battalion, The Black Watch (RHR) of Canada War Diary, March–May 1945. RG24, Library and Archives Canada.

"1st Battalion, The Queen's Own Rifles of Canada: Operation 'Plunder', Phase 4." 145.2Q2011(D6), Directorate of Heritage and History, Department of National Defence.

1st Canadian Armoured Brigade War Diary, April–May 1945. RG24, Library and Archives Canada.

"1 Canadian Corps Intelligence Summary." No. 271, April 17, 1945. RG24, vol. 109421, Library and Archives Canada.

———. No. 275, April 21, 1945." RG24, vol. 109421, Library and Archives Canada.

———. No. 289, May 5, 1945." RG24, vol. 109421, Library and Archives Canada.

———. No. 290, May 6, 1945." RG24, vol. 109421, Library and Archives Canada.

"1st CDN INF DIV Op Order No. 51: OP CANNONSHOT." RG24, vol. 10896, Library and Archives Canada.

"1 CDN INF DIV OPS From R. IJssel to R. Emm, 11 Apr–5 May." RG24, vol. 10896, Library and Archives Canada.

1st Canadian Parachute Battalion War Diary, March 1945. RG24, Library and Archives Canada.

1st Essex Scottish Regiment War Diary, April–May 1945. RG24, Library and Archives Canada.

5th Canadian Infantry Brigade War Diary, April–May 1945. RG24, Library and Archives Canada.

15th Field Regiment, RCA War Diary, April–May 1945. RG24, Library and Archives Canada.

"Food for the Dutch." RG24, vol. 10540, Library and Archives Canada.

Fort Garry Horse War Diary, April–May 1945. RG24, Library and Archives Canada.

"The 48th Highlanders of Canada, Report on Ops, 11 Apr–19 Apr 45." RG24, vol. 10896, Library and Archives Canada.

48th Highlanders of Canada War Diary, April–May 1945. RG24, Library and Archives Canada.

4th Canadian Armoured Brigade War Diary, March–May 1945. RG24, Library and Archives Canada.

4th Canadian Infantry Brigade War Diary, April–May 1945. WO 179/Canadian Forces/4th Infantry Brigade, UK National Archives.

"4th Canadian Light Anti Aircraft Regiment From: 18 February 1941 to 8 May 1945." Canadian War Museum. Governor General's Foot Guards War Diary, April–May 1945. RG24, Library and Archives Canada.

14th Field Regiment, RCA War Diary, March–May 1945. RG24, Library and Archives Canada.

Hartigan, Dan R. "1st Canadian Parachute Battalion Assault on the Rhine: The Ride, The Drop, and The Objectives." Calgary. Privately published, 1988.

Hastings and Prince Edward Regiment War Diary, April–May 1945. RG24, Library and Archives Canada.

Highland Light Infantry War Diary, March–May 1945. RG24, Library and Archives Canada.

"History of the 3rd Canadian Anti-tank Regiment Royal Canadian Artillery: October 1st 1940–May 8th 1945." Canada, 1945. Canadian War Museum.

Irish Regiment of Canada War Diary, April–May 1945. RG24, Library and Archives Canada.

Keith, J. Walter. "J. Walter Keith Account." Unpublished reminiscence. Possession of author.

Lake Superior Regiment (Motor) War Diary, April–May 1945. RG24, Library and Archives Canada.

Le Régiment de la Chaudière War Diary, April–May 1945. RG24, Library and Archives Canada.

Les Fusiliers Mont-Royal War Diary, March–May 1945. RG24, Library and Archives Canada.

Lincoln and Welland Regiment War Diary, March–May 1945. RG24, Library and Archives Canada.

Lord Strathcona's Horse War Diary, April–May 1945. RG24, Library and Archives Canada.

Loyal Edmonton Regiment War Diary, April–May 1945. RG24, Library and Archives Canada.

"Memorandum of Interview with Lt Col R.D. Hodgins O.C., H.L.I. of C, Given to Hist Offr HQ 3 CDN Inf Div 20 Apr 45." 145.2H2011(D4), Directorate of Heritage and History, Department of National Defence.

"Memo Summarizing Arrangements for Meeting with Representatives of the German Authorities in Holland, 27 April 1945." RG24, vol. 10658, Library and Archives Canada.

"Memorandum of Interview Given by Brig. R.W. Moncel, COMD 4 CDN ARMD BDE: The Final Punch–Operations and Activities of 4 CDN ARMD BDE, 30 Mar–5 May 45," RG24, vol. 10992, Library and Archives Canada.

"Memorandum of Interview Given by Lt. Col. G.M. Robinson: The Final Punch, Operations and Activities of 4 CDN ARMD DIV, 30 Mar–5 May 45." RG24, vol. 10935, Library and Archives Canada.

"Memorandum of Interview with Brig. J.M. Rockingham, DSO and Bar, Comd 9 CDN INF BDE and other officers, given to Hist Offr 3 CDN INF DIV 4 May 45: Operation Duck." RG24, vol. 10987, Library and Archives Canada.

"Memorandum of an interview given by Lt. Col. G.D. de S. Witherspoon, 19 May 45." 141.4A29011(1), Directorate of Heritage and History, Department of National Defence.

"Memorandum: Negotiations between Dutch Forces of the Interior and Seyss-Inquart in Amsterdam." RG24, vol. 10658, Library and Archives Canada.

Murphy, W.C. "Brigadier W.C. Murphy Diary." RG24, vol. 20405, Library and Archives Canada.

"Narrative of Operation Varsity, 24 March 1945." RG24, vol. 10825, box 228, Library and Archives Canada.

"Negotiations with Germans in W. Holland 16 Apr–7 May 45, memos, notes, etc., compiled by 1st Army." RG24, vol. 10658, Library and Archives Canada.

9th Canadian Infantry Brigade War Diary, March–May 1945. RG24, Library and Archives Canada.

North Nova Scotia Highlanders War Diary, April–May 1945. RG24, Library and Archives Canada.

North Shore (New Brunswick) Regiment War Diary, March–May 1945. RG24, Library and Archives Canada.

"Notes on Monograph 'Relief For the Netherlands,' prepared by Hist Sec G-5 Division, SHAEF." RG24, vol. 10249, Library and Archives Canada.

Ontario Regiment War Diary, April–May 1945. RG24, Library and Archives Canada.

"Operation Plunder (Capture of Wehl)." 1452.R11011(D6), Directorate of Heritage and History, Department of National Defence.

"Operation Plunder: Prepared by Q.O.R. of C." 145.2Q2011(D7), Directorate of Heritage and History, Department of National Defence.

"Operation Plunder: Prepared by R. de Chaud." 145.2R2011(D2), Directorate of Heritage and History, Department of National Defence.

"Operation Plunder: Regina RIF–Battle Narrative Emmerich." 1452R.11011(D6), Directorate of Heritage and History, Department of National Defence.

"Operation Plunder: Report prepared by Hist Offr HQ 3 CDN INF DIV 20 Apr 45." RG24, vol. 10907, box 269, Library and Archives Canada.

"Operation 'Varsity,' the Airborne Crossing of R. Rhine, detailed account of operation in which 1 Cdn Para Bn participated–Apr 45, Operation Report as of 30 March, 1945." RG24, vol. 10825, box 228, Library and Archives Canada.

"Operation Varsity–Plunder, 1 CDN BN 00 No. 1, March 1945." 1st Canadian Parachute Battalion Operation Order. Possession of author.

"The Operations of 8th New Brunswick Hussars for Period 25 Apr–5 May, covering the Regiment's activities in the area of Delfzijl." 20020045.1641, Canadian War Museum.

"Outline of Operations to Secure North-West Holland (West of line Hilversum–Utrecht), with Appendix." RG24, vol. 10535, Library and Archives Canada.

"Period 12 Apr 45–19 Apr 45, Dealing with the Breakthrough at Arnhem and the Thrust to the Zuider Zee." 20020045.1641, Canadian War Museum.

Perth Regiment War Diary, April–May 1945. RG24, Library and Archives Canada.

Princess Patricia's Canadian Light Infantry War Diary, April–May 1945. RG24, Library and Archives Canada.

Queen's Own Cameron Highlanders of Canada War Diary, March–May 1945. RG24, Library and Archives Canada.

Queen's Own Rifles of Canada War Diary, April–May 1945. RG24, Library and Archives Canada.

"RCA 3 CDN INF DIV: OP ORDER NO. 2, OP 'Duck.'" RG24, vol. 10914, Library and Archives Canada.

Régiment de Maisonneuve War Diary, April–May 1945. RG24, Library and Archives Canada.

Regina Rifles Regiment War Diary, April–May 1945. RG24, Library and Archives Canada.

"Report No. 17, The 1st Canadian Parachute Battalion in the Low Countries and in Germany: Final Operations 2 Jan–18 Feb and 24 Mar–5 May 45." Historical Section (G.S.) Army Headquarters. Directorate of Heritage and History, Department of National Defence.

"Report No. 19, 'Operation Plunder': The Canadian Participation in the Assault Across the Rhine and the Expansion of the Bridgehead by 2 Cdn Corps 23/24 Mar–1 Apr 45." Directorate of Heritage and History, Department of National Defence.

"Report No. 32, The Concluding Phase of Operations by the First CDN Army: Part I, Part II, and Part III." Directorate of Heritage and History, Department of National Defence.

"Report No. 39, Operations of 1 Cdn Corps in North-West Europe, 15 Mar–5 May 45." Directorate of Heritage and History, Department of National Defence.

"Report No. 56, The German Surrender, May 1945." Directorate of Heritage and History, Department of National Defence.

"Report No. 172, Canadian Participation in Civil Affairs/Military Government, Part IV: Belgium and the Netherlands, General Historical Survey." Historical Section, Canadian Military Headquarters. Directorate of Heritage and History, Department of National Defence.

"Report No. 181, Operation 'Goldflake,' the Move of 1 Cdn Corps from Italy to North-West Europe Feb–Mar 1945." Historical Section, Canadian Military Headquarters. Directorate of Heritage and History, Department of National Defence.

"Report on Operations of the Cape Breton Highlanders, Holland, for Period 27 March 1945 to the 8th May 1945." 145.2C5013(D2), Directorate of Heritage and History, Department of National Defence.

"Report on operations of 9 Cdn Armd Regt (BCD) for period 14–19 Apr 45." 141.4A9011(D2), Directorate of Heritage and History, Department of National Defence.

"Report on Pepperpot: Operation Plunder, 4 Cdn Lt. A.A. Regt., Various accounts, 25 Mar 45. 142.82A4013(D3), Directorate of Heritage and History, Department of National Defence.

"Reports by Gen H.D.G. Crerar, C.B., D.S.O., on Operations 1st Cdn Army to McNaughton: 7.11 Mar to 5 May 45." RG24, vol. 10636, Library and Archives Canada.

"Royal Canadian Dragoons." 141.4A1013(D4), Directorate of Heritage and History, Department of National Defence.

Royal Canadian Dragoons (1st Armoured Car Regiment) War Diary, April–May 1945. RG24, Library and Archives Canada.

"The Royal Canadian Regiment Report on Ops, 12 Apr–18 Apr 45," RG24, vol. 10896, Library and Archives Canada.

Royal Canadian Regiment War Diary, April–May 1945. RG24, Library and Archives Canada.

Royal Hamilton Light Infantry War Diary, April–May 1945. RG24, Library and Archives Canada.

Royal Regiment of Canada War Diary, April–May 1945. RG24, Library and Archives Canada.

Royal Winnipeg Rifles War Diary, March–May 1945. RG24, Library and Archives Canada.

Seaforth Highlanders of Canada War Diary, April–May 1945. RG24, Library and Archives Canada.

"S&T Maintenance 1 Cdn Corps Second Maintenance Plan, Operation 'Faust.'" RG24, vol. 10797, Library and Archives Canada.

7th Canadian Infantry Brigade War Diary, March–May 1945. RG24, Library and Archives Canada.

7th Canadian Medium Regiment War Diary, March–May 1945. RG24, Library and Archives Canada.

7th Canadian Reconnaissance Regiment (17th Duke of York's Royal Canadian Hussars) War Diary, March–May 1945. RG 24, Library and Archives Canada.

17th Field Regiment, RCA War Diary, April–May 1945. RG24, Library and Archives Canada.

6th Canadian Infantry Brigade War Diary, April–May 1945. RG24, Library and Archives Canada.

"Sitreps from Netherlands District, April 1945." RG24, vol. 10538, Library and Archives Canada.

"Some notes on negotiations with the German Higher Comd in Holland, 27 Apr to 5 May, 1945 by Hist Offr I CDN Corps (Maj. L.A. Wrinch)." RG24, vol. 10796, Library and Archives Canada.

South Alberta Regiment War Diary, April–May 1945. RG24, Library and Archives Canada.

South Saskatchewan Regiment War Diary, April–May 1945. RG24, Library and Archives Canada.

"Supreme Headquarters Allied Expeditionary Force: G-5 Division Historical Section– Relief for the Netherlands." RG24, vol. 10249, Library and Archives Canada.

Stormont, Dundas and Glengarry Highlanders War Diary, March–May 1945. RG24, Library and Archives Canada.

3rd Armoured Reconnaissance Regiment (Governor General's Horse Guards) War Diary, April–May 1945. RG24, Library and Archives Canada.

13th Canadian Field Regiment, RCA War Diary, March–May 1945. RG24, Library and Archives Canada.

10th Canadian Independent Machinegun Company (New Brunswick Rangers) War Diary, April–May 1945. WO 179/4551, UK National Archives.

10th Canadian Infantry Brigade War Diary, March–May 1945. RG24, Library and Archives Canada.

37th Field Battery, 17th Field Regiment War Diary. Possession of author.

"12th Canadian Field Regiment Op 'Plunder,'" April 28, 1945." 142.4F12011(D1), Directorate of Heritage and History, Department of National Defence.

Toronto Scottish Regiment (MG) War Diary, April–May 1945. RG24, Library and Archives Canada.

"WNSR Report on Operations in Holland, 1945." RG24, vol. 10896, Library and Archives Canada.

West Nova Scotia Regiment War Diary, April–May 1945. RG24, Library and Archives Canada.

"The Westminster Regiment (Motor) Report on Operations for Period 24 Apr–1 May 1945, Operation Canada." 145.2W1011(D1), Directorate of Heritage and History, Department of National Defence.

Westminster Regiment (Motor) War Diary, April–May 1945. RG24, Library and Archives Canada.

INTERVIEWS AND CORRESPONDENCE

Bannerman, George. Interview by author. Calgary, March 19, 2009.

Diepman, Bernard. Correspondence with author. April 3, 2009.

Dudley, Robert Woodhouse. Interview by Cameron Falconer. March 16, 1983. University of Victoria Special Collections.

Gildersleeve, Wilf and Margriet (née Blaisse). Interview by Ken MacLeod. Vancouver, 1999.

Goodman, Charles. Interview by author. Saanichton, BC, January 27, 2009.

Hoffmeister, Bert M. Interview by B. Greenhous and W. McAndrew, n.d. Directorate of Heritage and History, Department of National Defence.

——.Letter to Daniel T. Byers, March 1, 1991. Appended to: "Operation 'Canada,' The Canadian Attack on Delfzijl, April 23–May 2, 1945, Bachelor of Arts thesis, 1991, Wilfrid Laurier University.

Johns, Stuart Louis. Telephone interview by author. Windsor, ON, June 3, 2009.

MacGregor, Ernest Morgan. Interview by Rick Aylward. Victoria, July 22, 1986. University of Victoria Special Collections.

Parkinson, Robert H. Interview by Morgan Witzel. January 19, 1984. University of Victoria Special Collections.

Skinner, Wilhelmina (née Klaverdijk). Interview by Jackie Mill. Vancouver, 2003.

Spry, Dan. "Interview Spry, Oct/87." Crerar Papers. MG30, vol. 1, Library and Archives Canada.

Stone, James Riley. Interview by William S. Thackray. Victoria, May 13 and 20 and June 3, 10, and 17, 1980. University of Victoria Special Collections.

van Doorn, Johan. Personal briefing with author, Sommelsdijk, Holland. May 1, 2009; conversation with author, October 22, 2009; conversation with author, December 7, 2009; correspondence with author, December 11.

NOTES

INTRODUCTION: THE SWEETEST OF SPRINGS

1 G.R. Stevens, *Princess Patricia's Canadian Light Infantry: 1919–1957*, vol. 3 (Griesbach, AB: Historical Committee of the Regiment, n.d.), 246.

2 Princess Patricia's Canadian Light Infantry War Diary, May 1945, RG24, Library and Archives Canada, sheet 7.

3 Stevens, *Princess Patricia's Canadian Light Infantry*, 246–47.

4 Reginald H. Roy, *The Seaforth Highlanders of Canada, 1919–1965* (Vancouver: Evergreen Press, 1969), 439.

5 Diary of Major Durnford, RG24, vol. 20405, Library and Archives Canada, 139.

6 Wilf and Margriet Gildersleeve, interview by Ken MacLeod, Vancouver, 1999.

7 Wilhelmina (née Klaverdijk) Skinner, interview by Jackie Mill, Vancouver, 2003.

8 Jean E. Portugal, *We Were There: The Navy, the Army and the RCAF–A Record for Canada*, vol. 5 (Shelburne, ON: Battered Silicon Dispatch Box, 1998), 2308.

9 George G. Blackburn, *The Guns of Victory: A Soldier's Eye View, Belgium, Holland, and Germany, 1944–45* (Toronto: McClelland & Stewart, 1997), 484–85.

10 G.L. Cassidy, *Warpath: From Tilly-la-campagne to the Kusten Canal* (Markham, ON: PaperJacks , 1980), 370–71.

11 *1st Battalion, The Highland Light Infantry of Canada: 1940–1945* (Galt, ON: Highland Light Infantry of Canada Assoc., 1951), 112.

12 Highland Light Infantry War Diary, May 1945, RG24, Library and Archives Canada, 2.

13 Ibid., 8.

1: NO POSSIBILITY OF DOUBT

1 Jean E. Portugal, *We Were There: The Navy, the Army and the RCAF–A Record for Canada*, vol. 4 (Shelburne, ON: Battered Silicon Dispatch Box, 1998), 1826.

2 G.W.L. Nicholson, *The Gunners of Canada,* vol. 2 (Toronto: McClelland & Stewart, 1972), 422.

3 Ibid., 422–23.

4 Portugal, *We Were There,* vol. 5, 1827.

5 James C. Bond, "The Fog of War: Large-Scale Smoke Screening Operations of First Canadian Army in Northwest Europe, 1944–1945," *Canadian Military History,* vol. 8, no. 1 (Winter 1999), 55.

6 "12th Canadian Field Regiment Op 'Plunder,'" April 28, 1945, 142.4F12011(D1), Directorate of Heritage and History, Department of National Defence, 2.

7 T.J. Bell, *Into Action with the 12th Field* (Utrecht: J. van Boekhoven, 1945), 125.

8 "12th Canadian Field Regiment Op 'Plunder,'" 2.

9 Bell, 125.

10 Nicholson, 422.

11 A.M. Lockwood, *History of the 7th Canadian Medium Regiment, R.C.A.–From 1st September, 1939 to 8th June, 1945* (Toronto: Macmillan Company of Canada, 1945), 69–70.

12 7th Medium Regiment, RCA War Diary, March 1945, RG24, Library and Archives Canada, n.p.

13 "Report No. 19 Historical Section Army Headquarters: 'Operation 'Plunder:' The Canadian Participation in the Assault Across the Rhine and the Expansion of the Bridgehead by 2 Cdn Corps 23/24 Mar–1 Apr 45," Department of National Defence, June 26, 1948, para. 40.

14 C.P. Stacey, *The Victory Campaign: The Operations in North-West Europe, 1944–1945,* vol. 3 (Ottawa: Queen's Printer, 1960), 528.

15 Ibid.

16 Stephen Hart, *Montgomery and "Colossal Cracks": The 21st Army Group in Northwest Europe, 1944–1945* (Westport, CT: Greenwood Publishing Group, 2000), 141.

17 Stacey, *The Victory Campaign,* 524.

18 Brian Horrocks with Eversley Belfeld and H. Essame, *Corps Commander* (London: Sidgwick & Jackson, 1977), 182–83.

19 Paul Douglas Dickson, *A Thoroughly Canadian General: A Biography of General H.D.G. Crerar* (Toronto: University of Toronto Press, 2007), 390.

20 Dan Spry, "Interview Spry, Oct/87," Crerar Papers, MG30, vol. 1, Library and Archives Canada, 14–15.

21 Ibid., 4–5.

22 Dickson, 359.

23 Stacey, *The Victory Campaign,* 530–37.

24 "Report No. 17, Historical Section (G.S.) Army Headquarters, The 1st Canadian Parachute Battalion in the Low Countries and in Germany: Final Operations (2 January–18 February and 24 March–5 May 1945)," Department of National Defence, October 27, 1947, para. 28.

25 Stacey, *The Victory Campaign,* 530–37.

26 "Report No. 19," para. 40.

27 "Report No. 181 Historical Section Canadian Military Headquarters, Operation 'Goldflake,' the Move of 1 Cdn Corps from Italy to North-West Europe, February–March 1945, Appendix A," Department of National Defence, August 7, 1947.

28 Horrocks, 207.

29 Samuel Alexander Flatt, *History of the 6th Field Company, Royal Canadian Engineers: 1939–1945* (New Westminster: n.p., 1946), 104.

30 "Report No. 19," para. 14.

31 Stacey, *The Victory Campaign*, 532.

32 "Report No. 19," paras. 14–16.

33 Stacey, *The Victory Campaign*, 533.

34 Chester Wilmot, *The Struggle for Europe* (London: Collins, 1952), 681.

35 "Report No. 19," para. 45.

2: NEVER TO BE FORGOTTEN

1 W. Denis Whitaker and Shelagh Whitaker, *Rhineland: The Battle to End the War* (Toronto: Stoddart Publishing, 1989), 284–85.

2 Ralph Bennett, *Ultra in the West: The Normandy Campaign, 1944–45* (London: Hutchinson & Co., 1980), 217.

3 Robert S. Wistrich, *Who's Who in Nazi Germany* (New York: Routledge, 2001), 14.

4 Whitaker and Whitaker, 284–85.

5 Justin L.C. Eldridge, "Defense on the Rhine," vol. 21, issue 1 (Jan.–Mar. 1995), *Military Intelligence Professional Bulletin*, 38–44.

6 "Report No. 19, Historical Section Army Headquarters: Operation 'Plunder': The Canadian Participation in the Assault Across the Rhine and the Expansion of the Bridgehead by 2 Cdn Corps 23/24 Mar–1 Apr 45," Department of National Defence, June 26, 1948, paras. 30–31.

7 Bennett, 220.

8 Eldridge, 38–44.

9 "Report No. 19," para. 28.

10 Ibid., para. 32.

11 Bennett, 223.

12 Whitaker and Whitaker, 285.

13 Eldridge, 38–44.

14 William B. Breuer, *Storming Hitler's Rhine: The Allied Assault, February–March, 1945* (New York: St. Martin's Press, 1985), 203.

15 Ibid., 216.

16 William W. Barrett, *History of 13th Canadian Field Artillery* (n.p., 1945), 118.

17 13th Canadian Field Regiment War Diary, March 1945, RG24, Library and Archives Canada, 6.

18 Robert A. Spencer, *History of the 15th Field Regiment* (Amsterdam: Elsevier, 1945), 233–34.

19 7th Canadian Medium Regiment War Diary, March 1945, RG24, Library and Archives Canada, n.p.

20 Spencer, 234.

21 7th Canadian Infantry Brigade War Diary, March 1945, RG24, Library and Archives Canada, 10.

22 T.J. Bell, *Into Action with the 12th Field* (Utrecht: J. van Boekhoven, 1945), 126–27.

23 "Almost Continuous Roar," in *Heroes Remember,Glen Tomlin*, Tomlin interview, March 7, 2005, Veteran Affairs, www.vac-acc.gc.ca/remembers/sub. cfm?source=collections/hrp/hrp_detail&media_id=2150 (accessed November 24, 2008).

24 "4th Canadian Light Anti Aircraft Regiment From: 18 February 1941 to 8 May 1945," Canadian War Museum, 20.

25 "Report on Pepperpot; Operation Plunder, 4 Cdn. Lt. A.A. Regt., RCA, Various Accounts, 25 Mar. 1945," 142.82A4013(D3), Directorate of Heritage and History, Department of National Defence, n.p.

26 "4th Canadian Light Anti Aircraft Regiment," 20.

27 Ibid.

28 "Report on Pepperpot, Operation Plunder," n.p.

29 "Report No. 19," para. 49.

30 Brian Horrocks with Eversley Belfeld and H. Essame, *Corps Commander* (London: Sidgwick & Jackson, 1977), 209–10.

31 Winston S. Churchill, *Triumph and Tragedy* (Toronto: Thomas Allen, 1953), 411.

32 Stacey, *The Victory Campaign*, 535.

33 Whitaker and Whitaker, 295–97.

34 Breuer, 190.

35 Churchill, 411–12.

3: GO FOR THE GODDAMN WOODS

 1 "Report No. 19 Historical Section Army Headquarters: 'Operation 'Plunder': The Canadian Participation in the Assault Across the Rhine and the Expansion of the Bridgehead by 2 Cdn Corps 23/24 Mar–1 Apr 45," Department of National Defence, June 26, 1948, para. 50.

 2 Highland Light Infantry War Diary, March 1945, RG24, Library and Archives Canada, 9.

 3 Ibid., 9.

 4 "Operation Plunder: Report Prepared by Hist Offr HQ 3 CDN INF DIV 20 Apr 45," RG24, 10.907, 269; Library and Archives Canada, 3.

 5 "Report No. 19," paras. 60–61.

 6 Justin L.C. Eldridge, "Defense on the Rhine," *Military Intelligence Professional Bulletin*, vol. 21, issue 1 (Jan.–Mar. 1995), 38.

 7 Lee Windsor, "'Too Close for the Guns!' 9 Canadian Infantry Brigade in the Battle for the Rhine Bridgehead," *Canadian Military History*, vol. 13, nos. 1 and 2 (Winter/ Spring 2003), 9.

 8 Brian Horrocks with Eversley Belfeld and H. Essame, *Corps Commander* (London: Sidgwick & Jackson, 1977), 212.

 9 "Report No. 19," para. 61.

10 "Operation 'Varsity,' the Airborne Crossing of R. Rhine, detailed account of operation in which 1 Cdn Para Bn participated–Apr 45, Operation Report as of 30 March, 1945" RG24, vol. 10.825, box 228, Library and Archives Canada.

11 Bernd Horn and Michel Wyczynski, *Paras Versus the Reich: Canada's Paratroopers at War, 1942–45* (Toronto: Dundurn, 2003), 198–99.

12 "Report No. 17 Historical Section (G.S.) Army Headquarters: The 1st Canadian Parachute Battalion in the Low Countries and in Germany, Final Operations (2 January–18 February and 24 March–5 May 1945)," Directorate of Heritage and History, Department of National Defence, para. 37.

13 Dan R. Hatigan, 1st Canadian Parachute Battalion Assault on the Rhine: The Ride, The Drop, and The Objectives (Calgary, privately published, 1988), 2–3.

14 "Operation Varsity–Plunder, 1 CDN BN OO No. 1," March 1945, possession of author.

15 W. Denis Whitaker and Shelagh Whitaker, Rhineland: The Battle to End the War (Toronto: Stoddart Publishing, 1989), 321–23.

16 "Report No. 17," para. 38.

17 John A. Willes, Out of the Clouds: The History of the 1st Canadian Parachute Battalion (Port Perry, ON: Port Perry Printing, 1995), 137–38.

18 1st Canadian Parachute Battalion War Diary, March 1945, RG24, Library and Archives Canada, 3.

19 Gary C. Boegel, Boys of the Clouds: An Oral History of the 1st Canadian Parachute Battalion (Victoria, BC: Trafford, 2005), 278–79.

20 "Report No. 17," para. 39.

21 "Narrative of Operation Varsity, 24 March 1945," RG24, vol. 10825, box 228, Library and Archives Canada, 5.

22 "Narrative of Operation Varsity," 5.

23 Horn and Wyczynski, 199.

24 Hartigan, 4.

25 "Narrative of Operation Varsity," 5.

26 Hartigan, 4–6.

27 Winston S. Churchill, Triumph and Tragedy (Toronto: Thomas Allen, 1953), 413.

28 Ross Munro, Gauntlet to Overlord: The Story of the Canadian Army (Toronto: Macmillan, 1945), 256.

29 Hartigan, 7.

30 Ibid., 10.

31 Willes, 140.

32 Hartigan, 5.

33 Boegel, 299–300.

34 Horn and Wyczynski, 200–01.

35 Hartigan, 10.

36 "Canadian Army Overseas Honours and Awards Citation Details," Directorate of Heritage and History, Department of National Defence, www.cmp-cpm.forces. gc.ca/dhh-dhp/gal/cao-aco/details-eng.asp?firstname=James Oliver&lastname=Q uigley&rec=id740 (accessed June 26, 2009).

37 Horn and Wyczynski, 201.

38 "Canadian Army Overseas Honours and Awards Citation Details," Directorate of Heritage and History, Department of National Defence, www.cmp-cpm.forces. gc.ca/dhh-dhp/gal/cao-aco/details-eng.asp?firstname=George William&lastname =Green&rec=id4929 (accessed June 26, 2009).

39 Horn and Wycznski, 203–05.

40 "Canadian Army Overseas Honours and Awards Citation Details," Directorate of Heritage and History, Department of National Defence, www.cmp-cpm.forces. gc.ca/dhh-dhp/gal/cao-aco/details-eng.asp?firstname=George Fraser&lastname= Eadie&rec=id2051 (accessed June 26, 2009).

41 Hartigan, 11.

42 1st Canadian Parachute Battalion War Diary, March 1945, 4.

43 Ibid.

44 Willes, 141.

45 "Narrative of Operation Varsity," 7.

46 "Report No. 17, Appendix 1," 1.

47 Horn and Wycznski, 205–06.

48 Ibid.

4: RUGGED RESISTANCE

1 "Report No. 17 Historical Section (G.S.) Army Headquarters: The 1st Canadian Parachute Battalion in the Low Countries and in Germany, Final Operations (2 January–18 February and 24 March–5 May 1945)," Directorate of Heritage and History, Department of National Defence, para. 44.

2 "Report No. 19 Historical Section Army Headquarters: 'Operation 'Plunder': The Canadian Participation in the Assault Across the Rhine and the Expansion of the Bridgehead by 2 Cdn Corps 23/24 Mar–1 Apr 45," Department of National Defence, June 26, 1948, para. 61.

3 W. Denis Whitaker and Shelagh Whitaker, *Tug of War: The Canadian Victory that Opened Antwerp* (Toronto: Stoddart Publishing, 1984), 292.

4 *1st Battalion, The Highland Light Infantry of Canada: 1940–1945* (Galt, ON: Highland Light Infantry of Canada Assoc., 1951), 97.

5 "Report No. 19," para. 62.

6 "Artillery Notes on Operation Plunder," 142.4F14011(D1), Directorate of Heritage and History, Department of National Defence, 1–2.

7 Highland Light Infantry War Diary, March 1945, RG24, Library and Archives Canada, 9.

8 "Memorandum of Interview with Lt Col R.D. Hodgins O.C., H.L.I. of C, Given to Hist Offr HQ 3 CDN Inf Div 20 Apr 45," 145.2H2011(D4), Directorate of Heritage and History, Department of National Defence, 1.

9 "Canadian Army Overseas Honours and Awards Citation Details," Directorate of Heritage and History, Department of National Defence, www.cmp-cpm.forces. gc.ca/dhh-dhp/gal/cao-aco/details-eng.asp?firstname=Joseph Charles&lastname= King&rec=id2646 (accessed June 30, 2009).

10 George Bannerman, phone interview by author, Calgary, AB, 19 March 2009.

11 Lt. George Bannerman, "Some Aspects of the Technique of Flame Throwing: 'WASP' and 'Lifebuoy' (Account by Lt. George Bannerman, Sask L.I. (M.G.), Tech Offr (Flame), First Canadian Army, Given to Historical Officer, 2 CDN INF DIV, 26 Nov 44), Canadian Operations in North-West Europe: June–November 1944," extracts from War Diaries and Memoranda (Series 17), 018 (D2), Directorate of Heritage and History, Department of National Defence, 1–2.

12 "Canadian Army Overseas Honours and Awards Citation Details," Directorate of Heritage and History, Department of National Defence, www.cmp-cpm.forces. gc.ca/dhh-dhp/gal/cao-aco/details-eng.asp?firstname=Cornelius Jerome&lastnam e=Reidel&rec=id782 (accessed June 30, 2009).

13 "Canadian Army Overseas Honours and Awards Citation Details," Directorate of Heritage and History, Department of National Defence, www.cmp-cpm.forces. gc.ca/dhh-dhp/gal/cao-aco/details-eng.asp?firstname=Wilfred Francis&lastname =Bunda&rec=id4624 (accessed June 30, 2009).

14 Highland Light Infantry War Diary, March 1945, 9.

15 "Canadian Army Overseas Honours and Awards Citation Details," Directorate of Heritage and History, Department of National Defence, www.cmp-cpm.forces. gc.ca/dhh-dhp/gal/cao-aco/details-eng.asp?firstname=George Oxley&lastname= Macdonald&rec=id2820 (accessed June 30, 2009).

16 Bannerman interview.

17 "Memorandum of Interview with Lt Col R.D. Hodgins O.C.," 1.

18 "Almost Fatal Mistake," in Heroes Remember, Glen Tomlin, Tomlin interview, March 7, 2005, Veteran Affairs Canada, www.vac-acc.gc.ca/remembers/sub. cfm?source=collections/hrp/hrp_detail&media_id=2147 (accessed November 24, 2008).

19 Highland Light Infantry War Diary, March 1945, 9.

20 Ibid., 10.

21 Stormont, Dundas and Glengarry Highlanders War Diary, March 1945, RG24, Library and Archives Canada, 8.

22 Lee Windsor, "'Too Close for the Guns!' 9 Canadian Infantry Brigade in the Battle for the Rhine Bridgehead," Canadian Military History, vol. 13, nos. 1 and 2 (Winter/ Spring 2003), 11–13.

23 Jean E. Portugal, We Were There: The Navy, the Army and the RCAF—A Record for Canada, vol. 5 (Shelburne, ON: Battered Silicon Dispatch Box, 1998), 2612.

24 Stormont, Dundas and Glengarry Highlanders War Diary, March 1945, 8.

25 Donald Pearce, Journal of a War: North-west Europe, 1944–45 (Toronto: Macmillan of Canada, 1965), 164.

26 Ibid., 9.

27 Ibid.

28 Jean E. Portugal, We Were There, vol. 3 (Shelburne, ON: Battered Silicon Dispatch Box, 1998), 1264.

29 Stormont, Dundas and Glengarry Highlanders War Diary, March 1945, 9.

30 Portugal, We Were There, vol. 5, 2612–13.

31 "Canadian Army Overseas Honours and Awards Citation Details," Directorate of Heritage and History, Department of National Defence, www.cmp-cpm.forces. gc.ca/dhh-dhp/gal/cao-aco/details-eng.asp?firstname=Clifford John&lastname= Handley&rec=id4980 (accessed July 3, 2009).

32 "Canadian Army Overseas Honours and Awards Citation Details," Directorate of Heritage and History, Department of National Defence, www.cmp-cpm.forces. gc.ca/dhh-dhp/gal/cao-aco/details-eng.asp?firstname=Alvin Clifford&lastname= Dolan&rec=id5286 (accessed July 3, 2009).

33 "Canadian Army Overseas Honours and Awards Citation Details," Directorate of Heritage and History, Department of National Defence, www.cmp-cpm.forces.gc.ca/dhh-dhp/gal/cao-aco/details-eng.asp?firstname=James Allan William& lastname=Whitacre&rec=id1261 (accessed July 3, 2009).

34 "Canadian Army Overseas Honours and Awards Citation Details," Directorate of Heritage and History, Department of National Defence, www.cmp-cpm.forces. gc.ca/dhh-dhp/gal/cao-aco/details-eng.asp?firstname=John Alexander&lastname =Dure&rec=id2045 (accessed July 3, 2009).

35 William Boss, *Up the Glens: Stormont, Dundas and Glengarry Highlanders, 1783–1994,* 2nd ed. (Cornwall, ON: Old Book Store, 1995), 252.

5: THE ENEMY FOUGHT LIKE MADMEN

1 "Report No. 19 Historical Section Army Headquarters: 'Operation 'Plunder': The Canadian Participation in the Assault Across the Rhine and the Expansion of the Bridgehead by 2 Cdn Corps 23/24 Mar–1 Apr 45," Department of National Defence, June 26, 1948, para 68.

2 Lee Windsor, "'Too Close for the Guns!' 9 Canadian Infantry Brigade in the Battle for the Rhine Bridgehead," *Canadian Military History,* vol. 13, nos. 1 and 2 (Winter/ Spring 2003), 15.

3 "Report No. 19," para. 69.

4 Will R. Bird, *No Retreating Footsteps: The Story of the North Nova Scotia Highlanders* (Hantsport, NS: Lancelot Press, 1983), 342.

5 "Report No. 19," para. 69.

6 Bird, *No Retreating Footsteps,* 342–43.

7 "Report No. 19," para. 69.

8 9th Canadian Infantry Brigade War Diary, March 1945, RG24, Library and Archives Canada, 8.

9 14th Field Regiment, RCA War Diary, March 1945, RG24, Library and Archives Canada, 9.

10 Windsor, 18.

11 *History of the 3rd Canadian Anti-tank Regiment Royal Canadian Artillery: October 1st 1940–May 8th 1945* (Canada: n.p., 1945), 56.

12 Bird, *No Retreating Footsteps,* 343.

13 Windsor, 20.

14 13th Canadian Field Regiment, RCA War Diary, March 1945, RG24, Library and Archives Canada, 7.

15 Windsor, 20–22.

16 Donald Pearce, *Journal of a War: North-west Europe, 1944–45* (Toronto: Macmillan of Canada, 1965), 163–64.

17 Windsor, 21–22.

18 "Canadian Army Overseas Honours and Awards Citation Details," Directorate of Heritage and History, Department of National Defence, www.cmp-cpm.forces. gc.ca/dhh-dhp/gal/cao-aco/details-eng.asp?firstname=Daniel Isaac&lastname=Shanks&rec=id927 (accessed July 8, 2009).

19 "Canadian Army Overseas Honours and Awards Citation Details," Directorate of Heritage and History, Department of National Defence, www.cmp-cpm.forces. gc.ca/dhh-dhp/gal/cao-aco/details-eng.asp?firstname=Harry Jardine&lastname= Bishop&rec=id175 (accessed July 8, 2009).

20 Windsor, 22.

21 "Canadian Army Overseas Honours and Awards Citation Details," Directorate of Heritage and History, Department of National Defence, www.cmp-cpm.forces. gc.ca/dhh-dhp/gal/cao-aco/details-eng.asp?firstname=William&lastname=Myers &rec=id3138 (accessed July 9, 2009).

22 Windsor, 23.

23 "Canadian Army Overseas Honours and Awards Citation Details," Directorate of Heritage and History, Department of National Defence, www.cmp-cpm.forces. gc.ca/dhh-dhp/gal/cao-aco/details-eng.asp?firstname=Joseph&lastname=Prokopc huk&rec=id735 (accessed July 9, 2009).

24 Windsor, 22–23.

25 Bird, *No Retreating Footsteps*, 352.

26 Ibid., 345–46.

27 "Canadian Army Overseas Honours and Awards Citation Details," Directorate of Heritage and History, Department of National Defence, www.cmp-cpm.forces. gc.ca/dhh-dhp/gal/cao-aco/details-eng.asp?firstname=Lloyd Christian&lastname =Winhold&rec=id3973 (accessed July 9, 2009).

28 9th Canadian Infantry Brigade War Diary, 8.

29 *History of the 3rd Canadian Anti-tank Regiment*, 57.

30 "Canadian Army Overseas Honours and Awards Citation Details," Directorate of Heritage and History, Department of National Defence, www.cmp-cpm.forces. gc.ca/dhh-dhp/gal/cao-aco/details-eng.asp?firstname=John&lastname=Anderson &rec=id1388 (accessed July 13, 2009).

31 *History of the 3rd Canadian Anti-tank Regiment*, 57.

32 Highland Light Infantry War Diary, March 1945, RG24, Library and Archives Canada, 10.

33 "Canadian Army Overseas Honours and Awards Citation Details," Directorate of Heritage and History, Department of National Defence, www.cmp-cpm.forces. gc.ca/dhh-dhp/gal/cao-aco/details-eng.asp?firstname=Frederick James&lastname=Jarman&rec=id287 (accessed July 13, 2009).

34 Highland Light Infantry War Diary, 10.

35 "Canadian Army Overseas Honours and Awards Citation Details," Directorate of Heritage and History, Department of National Defence, www.cmp-cpm.forces. gc.ca/dhh-dhp/gal/cao-aco/details-eng.asp?firstname=Wilfred Francis&lastname =Bunda&rec=id4624 (accessed June 30, 2009).

36 Highland Light Infantry War Diary, 11.

6: MORE THAN BATTERED ABOUT

1 9th Canadian Infantry Brigade War Diary, March 1945, RG24, Library and Archives Canada, 8.

2 "Report No. 19 Historical Section Army Headquarters: Operation 'Plunder': The Canadian Participation in the Assault Across the Rhine and the Expansion of the Bridgehead by 2 Cdn Corps 23/24 Mar–1 Apr 45," Department of National Defence, June 26, 1948, para. 72.

3 Lee Windsor, "'Too Close for the Guns!' 9 Canadian Infantry Brigade in the Battle for the Rhine Bridgehead," *Canadian Military History*, vol. 13, nos. 1 and 2 (Winter/Spring 2003), 26.

4 North Shore (New Brunswick) Regiment War Diary, March 1945, RG24, Library and Archives Canada, 16.

5 Will R. Bird, *North Shore (New Brunswick) Regiment* (Fredericton, NB: Brunswick Press, 1963), 535.

6 North Shore (New Brunswick) Regiment War Diary, 16.

7 "Canadian Army Overseas Honours and Awards Citation Details," Directorate of Heritage and History, Department of National Defence, www.cmp-cpm.forces.gc.ca/dhh-dhp/gal/cao-aco/details-eng.asp?firstname=Reginald Alastar&lastname=Shepherd&rec=id944 (accessed July 14, 2009).

8 Bird, *North Shore (New Brunswick) Regiment*, 535.

9 "Canadian Army Overseas Honours and Awards Citation Details," Directorate of Heritage and History, Department of National Defence, www.cmp-cpm.forces.gc.ca/dhh-dhp/gal/cao-aco/details-eng.asp?firstname=Harry Lorne&lastname=Hamley&rec=id2365 (accessed July 14, 2009).

10 Bird, *North Shore (New Brunswick) Regiment*, 535–38.

11 William Boss, *Up the Glens: Stormont, Dundas and Glengarry Highlanders, 1783–1994*, 2nd ed. (Cornwall, ON: Old Book Store, 1995), 253.

12 Stormont, Dundas and Glengarry Highlanders War Diary, March 1945, RG24, Library and Archives Canada, 10–11.

13 "Report No. 19," para. 81.

14 A.J. Kerry and W.A. McDill, *History of the Corps of the Royal Canadian Engineers*, vol. 2 (Ottawa: The Military Engineers Assoc. of Canada, 1966), 385.

15 "Report No. 19," paras. 81–82.

16 Canadian Scottish Regiment War Diary, March 1945, RG24, Library and Archives Canada, 10.

17 Reginald H. Roy, *Ready for the Fray: The History of the Canadian Scottish Regiment (Princess Mary's), 1920 to 1955* (Vancouver: Evergreen Press, 1958), 395.

18 Jean E. Portugal, *We Were There: The Navy, the Army and the RCAF—A Record for Canada*, vol. 4 (Shelburne, ON: Battered Silicon Dispatch Box, 1998), 1827.

19 William W. Barrett, *History of 13th Canadian Field Artillery* (n.p., 1945), 120.

20 Roy, *Ready for the Fray*, 401.

21 4th Canadian Armoured Brigade War Diary, March 1945, RG24, Library and Archives Canada, 12.

22 Canadian Scottish Regiment War Diary, 11.

23 Roy, *Ready for the Fray*, 395.

24 Canadian Scottish Regiment War Diary, 11.

25 Ibid.

26 Roy, *Ready for the Fray*, 395–96.

27 Canadian Scottish Regiment War Diary, 12.

28 Roy, *Ready for the Fray*, 396.

29 7th Canadian Infantry Brigade War Diary, March 1945, RG24, Library and Archives Canada, 12.

30 "Regina Rifles Intelligence Log, March 1945," sheet 8, www.reginarifles.ca (accessed July 15, 2009).

31 "J. Walter Keith Account," unpublished reminiscence in possession of author, 4–8.

32 "Regina Rifles War Diary, March 1945," sheet 8, www.reginarifles.ca (accessed July 15, 2009).

33 4th Canadian Armoured Brigade War Diary, 13–14.

34 Stuart Louis Johns, telephone interview with author, 3 June, 2009.

35 "12th Canadian Field Regiment Op 'Plunder,'" 1424F.12011(D2), Directorate of Heritage and History, Department of National Defence, 2.

36 T.J. Bell, *Into Action with the 12th Field* (Utrecht: J. van Boekhoven, 1945), 128.

7: PRETTY STICKY

1 Reginald H. Roy, *Ready for the Fray: The History of the Canadian Scottish Regiment (Princess Mary's), 1920 to 1955* (Vancouver: Evergreen Press, 1958), 396–97.

2 Canadian Scottish Regiment War Diary, March 1945, RG24, Library and Archives Canada, 12.

3 Roy, *Ready for the Fray*, 397–98.

4 Canadian Scottish Regiment War Diary, 12.

5 "Operation Plunder: Regina RIF–Battle Narrative Emmerich," 1452R.11011(D6), Directorate of Heritage and History, Department of National Defence, 1.

6 Royal Winnipeg Rifles War Diary, March 1945, RG24, Library and Archives Canada, 7.

7 C.P. Stacey, *The Victory Campaign: The Operations in North-West Europe, 1944–1945*, vol. 3 (Ottawa: Queen's Printer, 1960), 539.

8 Bernard Law Montgomery, *The Memoirs of Field Marshal The Viscount Montgomery of Alamein, K.G.* (London: Collins, 1958), 331.

9 "Report No. 19 Historical Section Army Headquarters: Operation 'Plunder': The Canadian Participation in the Assault Across the Rhine and the Expansion of the Bridgehead by 2 Cdn Corps 23/24 Mar–1 Apr 45," Department of National Defence, June 26, 1948, para. 111.

10 Walter B. Maass, *The Netherlands at War: 1940–1945* (Toronto: Abelard-Schuman, 1970), 224.

11 "Reports by Gen. H.D.G. Crerar, C.B., D.S.O., on Operations 1st Cdn Army to McNaughton: 7.11 Mar to 5 May 45," vol. 10636, RG24, Library and Archives Canada, 3.

12 Stacey, *The Victory Campaign*, 541.

13 A.J. Kerry and W.A. McDill, *History of the Corps of the Royal Canadian Engineers*, vol. 2 (Ottawa: Military Engineers Assoc. of Canada, 1966), 385–86.

14 "Canadian Army Overseas Honours and Awards Citation Details," Directorate of Heritage and History, Department of National Defence, www.cmp-cpm.forces. gc.ca/dhh-dhp/gal/cao-aco/details-eng.asp?firstname=William Fernley&lastname=Brundrit&rec=id1634 (accessed July 24, 2009).

15 "Report No. 19," paras. 87–89.

16 Stacey, *The Victory Campaign*, 541.

17 "J. Walter Keith Account," unpublished reminiscence in possession of author, 8–9.

18 "Report No. 19," para. 89.

19 Eric Luxton, ed. *1st Battalion, The Regina Rifles Regiment, 1939–1946* (Regina: The Regiment, 1946), 59.

20 Royal Winnipeg Rifles War Diary, March 1945, RG24, Library and Archives Canada, 7.

21 Canadian Scottish Regiment War Diary, 13.

22 Roy, *Ready for the Fray*, 399.

23 "Canadian Army Overseas Honours and Awards Citation Details," Directorate of Heritage and History, Department of National Defence, www.cmp-cpm.forces. gc.ca/dhh-dhp/gal/cao-aco/details-eng.asp?firstname=Albin James&lastname= Kellerman&rec=id354 (accessed on July 24, 2009).

24 "Report No. 19," para. 90.

25 "J. Walter Keith account," 9–10.

26 Luxton, 59.

27 Ibid.

28 "Report No. 19," paras. 92–93.

29 "J. Walter Keith account," 10–11.

30 "Report No. 19," para. 94.

31 Canadian Scottish Regiment War Diary, 13.

32 Royal Winnipeg Rifles War Diary, 7–8.

33 "Report No. 19," para 94.

34 "J. Walter Keith Account," 11–12.

35 "Operation Plunder: Regina RIF–Battle Narrative Emmerich," 3.

36 Regina Rifles "Intelligence Log," March 1945, sheet 11, www.reginarifles.ca (accessed July 27, 2009).

37 "Report No. 19," para. 95.

38 "Operation Plunder: Regina RIF–Battle Narrative Emmerich," 3.

39 "Report No. 19," para. 96.

40 Alex Kuppers, ed., *Perspectives* (Vancouver: Royal Winnipeg Rifles Assoc., British Columbia Branch, 2003), 106.

41 Bruce Tascoma and Eric Wells, *Little Black Devils: A History of the Royal Winnipeg Rifles* (Winnipeg: Frye Publishing, 1994), 186.

42 *History of the 3rd Canadian Anti-tank Regiment Royal Canadian Artillery: October 1st 1940–May 8th 1945* (Canada: n.p., 1945), 59.

43 "J. Walter Keith Account," 6–12.

44 Ibid., 12.

45 Canadian Scottish Regiment War Diary, 14.

46 "Operation Plunder: Regina RIF–Battle Narrative Emmerich," 3–4.

47 Canadian Scottish Regiment War Diary, 12–14.

48 "Report No. 19 Historical Section Army Headquarters: 'OperationPlunder': The Canadian Participation in the Assault Across the Rhine and the Expansion of the Bridgehead by 2 Cdn Corps 23/24 Mar–1 Apr 45," Appendix B, Department of National Defence, June 26, 1948.

49 7th Canadian Infantry Brigade War Diary, March 1945, RG24, Library and Archives Canada, 15.

8: UTMOST TENACITY

1 "Operation Plunder: Prepared by Q.O.R. of C.," 145.2Q2011(D7), Directorate of Heritage and History, Department of National Defence, 2.
2 "Operation Plunder: Prepared by R. de Chaud.," 145.2R2011(D2), Directorate of Heritage and History, Department of National Defence, 1.
3 "Operation Plunder: Prepared by Q.O.R. of C.," 2–3.
4 "Operation Plunder: Prepared by R. de Chaud.," 1.
5 "Operation Plunder: Prepared by Q.O.R. of C.," 2–3.
6 "Report No. 19 Historical Section Army Headquarters: 'Operation 'Plunder': The Canadian Participation in the Assault Across the Rhine and the Expansion of the Bridgehead by 2 Cdn Corps 23/24 Mar–1 Apr 45," Appendix B, Department of National Defence, June 26, 1948.
7 "Report No. 19," para. 118.
8 A.J. Kerry and W.A. McDill, *History of the Corps of the Royal Canadian Engineers*, vol. 2 (Ottawa: Military Engineers Assoc. of Canada, 1966), 386–87.
9 7th Canadian Reconnaissance Regiment (17th Duke of York's Royal Canadian Hussars) War Diary, March 1945, RG24, Library and Archives Canada, 11.
10 Walter G. Pavey, *An Historical Account of the 7th Canadian Reconnaissance Regiment (17th Duke of York's Royal Canadian Hussars)* (Gardenvale, QC: Harpell's Press, 1948), 107.
11 Ibid., 107–08.
12 Queen's Own Cameron Highlanders of Canada War Diary, March 1945, RG24, Library and Archives Canada, 17–18.
13 "Canadian Army Overseas Honours and Awards Citation Details," Directorate of Heritage and History, Department of National Defence, www.cmp-cpm.forces. gc.ca/dhh-dhp/gal/cao-aco/details-eng.asp?firstname=John&lastname=Ruczak& rec=id846 (accessed July 29, 2009).
14 Queen's Own Cameron Highlanders of Canada War Diary, 17–18.
15 "Canadian Army Overseas Honours and Awards Citation Details," Directorate of Heritage and History, Department of National Defence, www.cmp-cpm.forces. gc.ca/dhh-dhp/gal/cao-aco/details-eng.asp?firstname=John&lastname=Ruczak& rec=id846 (accessed July 29, 2009).
16 R.W. Queens-Hughes, *Whatever Men Dare: A History of the Queen's Own Cameron Highlanders of Canada, 1935–1960* (Winnipeg: Bulman Brothers, 1960), 169.
17 Queen's Own Cameron Highlanders of Canada War Diary, 18.
18 "Report No. 19," para. 101.
19 8th Canadian Reconnaissance Regiment (14th Canadian Hussars) War Diary, RG24, Library and Archives Canada, 7.
20 "Report No. 19," para. 101.
21 Les Fusiliers Mont-Royal War Diary, March 1945, RG24, Library and Archives Canada, 9.
22 "Report No. 19," para. 102.

23 Paul P. Hutchinson, *Canada's Black Watch: The First Hundred Years, 1862–1962* (Montreal: Black Watch (RHR) of Canada, 1962), 235.

24 1st Battalion, The Black Watch (RHR) of Canada War Diary, April 1945, RG24, Library and Archives Canada, 1.

25 Ibid., 2.

26 "Canadian Army Overseas Honours and Awards Citation Details," Directorate of Heritage and History, Department of National Defence, www.cmp-cpm.forces. gc.ca/dhh-dhp/gal/cao-aco/details-eng.asp?firstname=Raymond Eaton&lastname =Stacey&rec=id1029 (accessed on July 30, 2009).

27 1st Battalion, The Black Watch (RHR) of Canada War Diary, 2–3.

28 Calgary Highlanders War Diary, April 1945, RG24, Library and Archives Canada, 1.

29 David Bercuson, *Battalion of Heroes: The Calgary Highlanders in World War II* (Calgary: Calgary Highlanders Regimental Funds Foundation, 1994), 226.

30 "Canadian Army Overseas Honours and Awards Citation Details," Directorate of Heritage and History, Department of National Defence, www.cmp-cpm.forces. gc.ca/dhh-dhp/gal/cao-aco/details-eng.asp?firstname=William John Henry&lastn ame=Sherring&rec=id947 (accessed July 31, 2009).

31 Calgary Highlanders War Diary, 1.

32 Roy Farran, *The History of the Calgary Highlanders, 1921–54* (Calgary: Bryant Press, 1954), 206–07.

33 Bercuson, *Battalion of Heroes*, 227–28.

34 Calgary Highlanders War Diary, 2.

35 Jean Bouchery, *The Canadian Soldier in North-West Europe, 1944–1945*, trans. Alan McKay (Paris: Histoire & Collections, 2003), 122.

36 Calgary Highlanders War Diary, 2.

38 Bercuson, *Battalion of Heroes*, 229.

37 "Report No. 19," Appendix B.

39 "Report No. 19," para. 150.

9: ALL TOGETHER AGAIN

1 C.P. Stacey, *The Victory Campaign: The Operations in North-West Europe, 1944–1945*, vol. 3 (Ottawa: Queen's Printer, 1960), 545.

2 "Extracts Polish Armoured Division History," vol. 10942, RG24, Library and Archives Canada, 85.

3 "Sitreps from Netherlands District, April 1945," 215A21.013(D13), vol. 10538, RG24, Library and Archives Canada, 1–38.

4 "Report No. 39 Historical Section (G.S.) Army Headquarters: Operations of 1 Cdn Corps in North-West Europe, 15 Mar–5 May 45," Department of National Defence, January 31, 1951, para. 6.

5 Reginald H. Roy, *The Seaforth Highlanders of Canada, 1919–1965* (Vancouver: Evergreen Press, 1969), 413–14.

6 1st Canadian Armoured Brigade War Diary, March 1945, RG24, Library and Archives Canada, 16.

7 Gwilym Jones, *To the Green Fields Beyond: A Soldier's Story* (Burnstown, ON: General Store Publishing House, 1993), 145.

8 "Report No. 39," para. 5.
9 Farley Mowat, *The Regiment,* 2nd ed. (Toronto: McClelland & Stewart, 1973), 297.
10 *History of the 3rd Canadian Field Regiment, Royal Canadian Artillery: September 1939 to July 1945–World War II* (Canada: n.p., 1945), 71.
11 Kim Beattie, *Dileas: History of the 48th Highlanders of Canada, 1929–1956* (Toronto: 48th Highlanders of Canada, 1957), 738.
12 C. Sydney Frost, *Once a Patricia: Memoirs of a Junior Infantry Officer in World War II* (Ottawa: Borealis Press, 2004), 423–24.
13 "Report No. 39," para. 8–12.
14 George Kitching, *Mud and Green Fields: The Memoirs of Major General George Kitching* (Langley, BC: Battleline Books, 1985), 249.
15 Sean M. Maloney, "General Charles Foulkes: A primer on how to be CDS," in *Warrior Chiefs,* Bernd Horn and Stephen Harris, eds. (Toronto: Dundurn Press, 2001), 220.
16 C.P. Stacey, *Six Years of War: The Army in Canada, Britain and the Pacific,* vol. 1 (Ottawa: Queens Printer, 1957), 253.
17 "Reports by Gen. H.D.G. Crerar, C.B., D.S.O., on Operations 1st Cdn Army to McNaughton: 7.11 Mar to 5 May 45," vol. 10636, RG24, Library and Archives Canada, 4.
18 Ibid., 4.
19 Stacey, *The Victory Campaign,* 543–45.
20 Ibid., 546.
21 "Outline of Operations to Secure North-West Holland (West of line Hilversum–Utrecht), with Appendix," RG24, vol. 10535, Library and Archives Canada, 1–5, Appendix 1–3.

10: A LION AND A TIGER

1 "Report No. 32 Historical Section (G.S.) Army Headquarters: The Concluding Phase of Operations by the First CDN Army: Part I," Department of National Defence, December 10, 1949, para. 5.
2 Ibid., paras. 4–6.
3 Ibid., para. 8.
4 South Alberta Regiment War Diary, April 1945, RG24, Library and Archives Canada, 3.
5 Donald Graves, *South Albertas: A Canadian Regiment at War* (Toronto: Robin Brass Studio, 1998), 305–06.
6 Ibid., 306.
7 Argyll and Sutherland Highlanders War Diary, April 1945, RG24, Library and Archives Canada, 2.
8 10th Canadian Infantry Brigade War Diary, April 1945, RG24, Library and Archives Canada, 1.
9 Argyll and Sutherland Highlanders War Diary, 2.
10 G.L. Cassidy, *Warpath: From Tilly-la-campagne to the Kusten Canal* (Markham, ON: PaperJacks, 1980), 335.
11 "Report No. 32, Part I," para. 51.

12 Ibid.

13 Lake Superior Regiment (Motor) War Diary, April 1945, RG24, Library and Archives Canada, 2.

14 4th Canadian Armoured Brigade War Diary, April 1945, RG24, Library and Archives Canada, 4.

15 Geoffrey Hayes, *The Lincs: A History of the Lincoln and Welland Regiment at War* (Alma, ON: Maple Leaf Route, 1986), 113.

16 R.L. Rogers, *History of the Lincoln and Welland Regiment* (Montreal: Industrial Shops for the Deaf, 1954), 252–53.

17 Lincoln and Welland Regiment War Diary, April 1945, RG24, Library and Archives Canada, 4.

18 Hayes, 113–14.

19 Lincoln and Welland Regiment War Diary, 4

20 Hayes, 114.

21 "Canadian Army Overseas Honours and Awards Citation Details," Directorate of Heritage and History, Department of National Defence, www.cmp-cpm.forces. gc.ca/dhh-dhp/gal/cao-aco/details-eng.asp?firstname=Clifford Lloyd&lastname= Challice&rec=id4522 (accessed August 18, 2009).

22 Hayes, 114.

23 "Canadian Army Overseas Honours and Awards," Challice.

24 Hayes, 114–16.

25 4th Canadian Armoured Brigade War Diary, 5.

26 Lake Superior Regiment (Motor) War Diary, 3.

27 George F.G. Stanley, *In the Face of Danger: The History of the Lake Superior Regiment* (Port Arthur, ON: Lake Superior Scottish Regiment, 1960), 283.

28 Lake Superior Regiment War Diary, 5.

29 4th Canadian Armoured Brigade War Diary, 6.

30 Ibid., 7.

31 Lake Superior Regiment War Diary, 6–7.

32 4th Canadian Armoured Brigade War Diary, 7–8.

33 "Report No. 32, Part 1," para. 66.

34 G.L. Cassidy, *Warpath: From Tilly-la-campagne to the Kusten Canal* (Markham, ON: PaperJacks, 1980), 337–38.

35 Algonquin Regiment War Diary, April 1945, RG24, Library and Archives Canada, 5.

36 Cassidy, 337–39.

11: FIERCE REARGUARD ACTIONS

1 D.J. Goodspeed, *Battle Royal: A History of the Royal Regiment of Canada* (Toronto: Royal Regiment of Canada Assoc., 1962), 551.

2 *VIII CDN Recce Rgt 14 CH: Battle History of the Regt* (Victoria: 8th Cdn Recce Association, 1993), 51–52.

3 "Canadian Army Overseas Honours and Awards Citation Details," Directorate of Heritage and History, Department of National Defence, www.cmp-cpm.forces. gc.ca/dhh-dhp/gal/cao-aco/details-eng.asp?firstname=Garnet William&lastname =Eldridge&rec=id4708 (accessed August 19, 2009).

4 Goodspeed, 551.

5 Royal Regiment of Canada War Diary, April 1945, RG24, Library and Archives Canada, 1–2.

6 Ibid., 2–3.

7 4th Canadian Infantry Brigade War Diary, April 1945, WO 179/Canadian Forces/4th Infantry Brigade, UK National Archives, 7.

8 Ibid., 8–9.

9 7th Canadian Infantry Brigade War Diary, April 1945, RG24, Library and Archives Canada, 1.

10 "Operation Plunder (Capture of Wehl)," 1452.R11011(D6), Directorate of Heritage and History, Department of National Defence, 1.

11 Ibid., 2–3.

12 Gordon Brown and Terry Copp, *Look to Your Front…Regina Rifles: A Regiment at War* (Waterloo, ON: Laurier Centre Military Strategic Disarmament Studies, 2001), 183.

13 Stewart A.G. Mein, *Up the Johns! The Story of the Royal Regina Rifles* (North Battleford, SK: Turner-Warwick Publications, 1992), 137.

14 Brown and Copp, 183.

15 H.M. Jackson, *The Sherbrooke Regiment (12th Armoured Regiment)* (Montreal: Christian Bros. Press, 1958), 168.

16 "J. Walter Keith Account," unpublished reminiscence in possession of author, 13.

17 "Operation Plunder (Capture of Wehl)," 3–4.

18 Reginald H. Roy, *Ready for the Fray: The History of the Canadian Scottish Regiment (Princess Mary's), 1920 to 1955* (Vancouver: Evergreen Press, 1958), 404–05.

19 "Operation Plunder: Prepared by Q.O.R. of C.," 145.2Q2011(D7), Directorate of Heritage and History, Department of National Defence, 2–3.

20 "Report No. 39 Historical Section (G.S.) Army Headquarters: Operations of 1 Cdn Corps in North-West Europe, 15 Mar–5 May 45," Department of National Defence, January 31, 1951, paras. 20–21.

21 Henk Dykman, "The Glens in Leesten," manuscript in possession of author, 7–8.

22 Stormont, Dundas and Glengarry Highlanders War Diary, April 1945, RG24, Library and Archives Canada, 3.

23 "Report No. 39," para. 22.

24 Dykman, 11–16.

25 Ibid., 17.

26 Ibid., 18.

27 William Boss, *Up the Glens: Stormont, Dundas and Glengarry Highlanders, 1783–1994*, 2nd ed. (Cornwall, ON: Old Book Store, 1995), 255.

28 Stormont, Dundas and Glengarry Highlanders War Diary, 4.

29 "The 11th Canadian Armoured Regiment (Ont. R.) Actions Kommerdijk," 141.4A 11, Directorate of Heritage and History, Department of National Defence, 1–2.

30 "Report No. 39 Historical Section (G.S.) Army Headquarters: Operations of 1 Cdn Corps in North-West Europe, 15 Mar–5 May 45," Department of National Defence, January 31, 1951, para. 16.

31 "11th Canadian Armoured Regiment Actions Kommerdijk," 2.

32 Ibid., 2.

33 11th Canadian Armoured Regiment War Diary (Ontario Regiment), April 1945, RG24, Library and Archives Canada, 3.

34 "Report No. 39," para. 17.

35 Irish Regiment of Canada War Diary, April 1945, RG24, Library and Archives Canada, n.p.

36 Cape Breton Highlanders War Diary, April 1945, RG24, Library and Archives Canada, 2.

37 Alex Morrison and Ted Slaney, *The Breed of Manly Men: The History of the Cape Breton Highlanders* (Toronto: Canadian Institute of Strategic Studies, 1994), 312–13.

38 Cape Breton Highlanders War Diary, 2–3.

39 Ibid., 3–4.

40 "Report on Operations of the Cape Breton Highlanders, Holland, for Period 27 March 1945 to the 8th May 1945," 145.2C5013(D2), Directorate of Heritage and History, Department of National Defence, 1.

41 Perth Regiment War Diary, April 1945, RG24, Library and Archives Canada, 2.

42 *The Governor General's Horse Guards, 1939–1945* (Toronto: Canadian Military Journal, 1945), 212.

43 3rd Armoured Reconnaissance Regiment (Governor General's Horse Guards) War Diary, April 1945, RG24, Library and Archives Canada, 2.

44 Perth Regiment War Diary, 2.

45 Cape Breton Highlanders War Diary, 5–6.

46 "Report No. 39," para. 20.

47 "Reports by Gen. H.D.G. Crerar, C.B., D.S.O., on Operations 1st Cdn Army to McNaughton: 7.11 Mar to 5 May 45," vol. 10636, RG24, Library and Archives Canada, 5–6.

12: ON THE BRINK

1 "Report No. 172 Historical Section Canadian Military Headquarters: Canadian Participation in Civil Affairs/Military Government, Part IV: Belgium and the Netherlands, General Historical Survey," Department of National Defence, endnote to para. 32.

2 Kirsten den Hartog and Tracy Kasaboski, *The Occupied Garden: Recovering the Story of a Family in the War-Torn Netherlands* (Toronto: McClelland and Stewart, 2008,) 31.

3 Personal briefing with author by Dutch historian Johan van Doorn, Sommelsdijk, Netherlands, May 1 2009.

4 David Stafford, *Endgame 1945: The Missing Final Chapter of World War II* (New York: Little, Brown and Company, 2007), 260.

5 Werner Marmbrunn, *The Dutch Under German Occupation, 1940–1945* (Stanford, CA: Stanford University Press, 1963), 29.

6 "Report No.172," paras. 30–31.

7 van Doorn briefing.

8 Den Hartog and Kasaboski, 99.

9 Dr. Harry Paape, "How Resistance Was Organized," in *Holland at War Against Hitler: Anglo–Dutch Relations, 1940–45*, ed. Michael Richard Daniell Foot (London: Frank Cass, 1990), 85–88.

10 Stewart Bentley, "The Dutch Resistance and the OSS, of Market-Garden and Melanie," www.cia.gov/library/center-for-the-study-of-intelligence/csi-publications/csi-studies/studies/Holland.html (accessed August 25, 2009), 4–5.

11 Den Hartog and Kasaboski, 175–76.

12 Maj. Norman Phillips and J. Nikerk, *Holland and the Canadians* (Amsterdam: Contact Publishing, 1946), 21.

13 "Supreme Headquarters Allied Expeditionary Force: G-5 Division Historical Section–Relief for the Netherlands," RG24, vol. 10249, Library and Archives Canada, 3.

14 "Notes on Monograph 'Relief For the Netherlands,' prepared by Hist Sec G-5 Division, SHAEF," RG24, vol. 10249, Library and Archives Canada, 1–2.

15 Phillips and Nikerk, 22.

16 Den Hartog and Kasaboski, 177.

17 A.J. Veenendaal, *Railways in the Netherlands, 1834–1994* (Stanford, CA: Stanford University Press, 2001), 172.

18 Henri van der Zee, *The Hunger Winter: Occupied Holland, 1944–45* (London: Jill Norman & Hobhouse, 1982), 29–30.

19 Ibid., 29.

20 Ibid., 31.

21 Phillips and Nikerk, 23.

22 "Supreme Headquarters Allied Expeditionary Force" 2–4.

23 van der Zee, 31.

24 "Supreme Headquarters Allied Expeditionary Force," 34.

25 Phillips and Nikerk, 23.

26 "Supreme Headquarters Allied Expeditionary Force," 12–14.

27 Ibid., 32–33.

28 C.P. Stacey, *The Victory Campaign: The Operations in North-West Europe, 1944–1945*, vol. 3 (Ottawa: Queen's Printer, 1960), 583.

29 "Supreme Headquarters Allied Expeditionary Force," 12–20.

30 Ibid., 34.

31 van Doorn briefing.

32 Walter B. Maass, *The Netherlands at War, 1940–1945* (Toronto: Abeland-Schuman, 1970), 221–22.

33 van der Zee, 231.

34 van Doorn briefing.

35 "Memorandum: Negotiations between Dutch Forces of the Interior and Seyss-Inquart in Amsterdam," RG24, vol. 10658, Library and Archives Canada, 1.

36 van der Zee, 231–32.

37 "Memorandum: Negotiations," 2.

38 Ibid., 2.

39 van der Zee, 233.

13: CRAZY YOUNG DEVILS

1 Chester Wilmot, *The Struggle for Europe* (London: Collins, 1952), 679–80.

2 7th Canadian Infantry Brigade War Diary, April 1945, RG24, Library and Archives Canada, 6.

3 "J. Walter Keith Account," unpublished reminiscence in possession of author, 14.

4 Walter G. Pavey, *An Historical Account of the 7th Canadian Reconnaissance Regiment (17th Duke of York's Royal Canadian Hussars)* (Gardenvale, QC: Harpell's Press, 1948), 109.

5 "Keith Account," 14–15.

6 "Report No. 32 Historical Section (G.S.) Army Headquarters: The Concluding Phase of Operations by the First CDN Army: Part I," Department of National Defence, December 10, 1949, paras. 85–86.

7 Ibid., para. 90.

8 Highland Light Infantry of Canada War Diary, April 1945, RG24, Library and Archives Canada, 2–3.

9 Stormont, Dundas and Glengarry Highlanders War Diary, April 1945, RG24, Library and Archives Canada, 4.

10 North Nova Scotia Highlanders War Diary, April 1945, RG24, Library and Archives Canada, 6–7.

11 Will R. Bird, *No Retreating Footsteps: The Story of the North Nova Scotia Highlanders* (Hantsport, NS: Lancelot Press, 1983), 362–64.

12 North Nova Scotia Highlanders War Diary, 7.

13 8th Canadian Infantry Brigade War Diary, April 1945, RG24, Library and Archives Canada, 2.

14 W.T. Barnard, *The Queen's Own Rifles of Canada, 1860–1960: One Hundred Years of Canada* (Don Mills, ON: Ontario Publishing Group, 1960), 257.

15 "Operation Plunder: Prepared by Q.O.R. of C.," 145.2Q2011(D7), Directorate of Heritage and History, Department of National Defence, 3.

16 "Operation Plunder: Prepared by Q.O.R. of C.," 4.

17 Queen's Own Rifles War Diary, April 1945, RG24, Library and Archives Canada, 4.

18 Barnard, 257.

19 Charles Cromwell Martin, *Battle Diary: From D-Day and Normandy to the Zuider Zee and VE* (Toronto: Dundurn Press, 1994), 140.

20 Jacques Castonguay and Armand Ross, *Le Régiment de la Chaudière* (Lévis, QC: Le Régiment de la Chaudière, 1983), 351.

21 Will R. Bird, *North Shore (New Brunswick) Regiment* (Fredericton, NB: Brunswick Press, 1963), 542–43.

22 H.M. Jackson, *The Sherbrooke Regiment (12th Armoured Regiment)* (Montreal: Christian Bros. Press, 1958), 169.

23 Ibid., 169–70.

24 "Canadian Army Overseas Honours and Awards Citation Details," Directorate of Heritage and History, Department of National Defence, www.cmp-cpm.forces.gc.ca/dhh-dhp/gal/cao-aco/details-eng.asp?firstname=Paul&lastname=Piche&rec=id3241 (accessed 9 September, 2009).

25 Castonguay and Ross, 352.

26 Bird, *North Shore (New Brunswick) Regiment*, 543–46.

27 North Shore (New Brunswick) War Diary, April 1945, RG24, Library and Archives Canada, 5

28 Bird, *North Shore (New Brunswick) Regiment,* 547–48.

29 Col. C.P. Stacey, *The Victory Campaign: The Operations in North-West Europe, 1944–1945,* vol. 3 (Ottawa: Queen's Printer, 1960), 550.

30 Bird, *North Shore (New Brunswick Regiment),* 549.

31 Stacey, *The Victory Campaign,* 550.

32 Bird, *North Shore (New Brunswick) Regiment,* 550.

33 Ibid., 542.

34 North Shore (New Brunswick) Regiment War Diary, 4.

35 Barnard, 257.

36 North Shore (New Brunswick) Regiment War Diary, 5.

37 Canadian Scottish Regiment War Diary, April 1945, RG24, Library and Archives Canada, 4–5.

38 7th Canadian Infantry Brigade War Diary, 8.

39 Royal Winnipeg Rifles War Diary, April 1945, RG24, Library and Archives Canada, 2.

40 "Report No. 32, Part I," para. 96.

41 Royal Winnipeg Rifles War Diary, 3.

14: MINOR SKIRMISHES

1 "Report No. 32 Historical Section (G.S.) Army Headquarters: The Concluding Phase of Operations by the First CDN Army: Part I," Department of National Defence, December 10, 1949, para. 97.

2 C.P. Stacey, *The Victory Campaign: The Operations in North-West Europe, 1944–1945,* vol. 3 (Ottawa: Queen's Printer, 1960), 551.

3 "Report No. 32, Part I," paras. 102–03.

4 Henri van der Zee, *The Hunger Winter: Occupied Holland, 1944–45* (London: Jill Norman & Hobhouse, 1982), 209–10.

5 Stacey, *The Victory Campaign,* 550.

6 Reginald H. Roy, *Ready for the Fray: The History of the Canadian Scottish Regiment (Princess Mary's), 1920 to 1955* (Vancouver: Evergreen Press, 1958), 406.

7 Regina Rifles, "Intelligence Log," April 1945, sheet 8, www.reginarifles.ca (accessed July 15, 2009).

8 Regina Rifles, "War Diary," April 1945, sheets 4–5, www.reginarifles.ca (accessed July 15, 2009).

9 7th Canadian Infantry War Diary, April 1945, RG24, Library and Archives Canada, 12.

10 Canadian Scottish Regiment War Diary, April 1945, RG24, Library and Archives Canada, 5.

11 Roy, *Ready for the Fray,* 407.

12 Canadian Scottish Regiment War Diary, 5.

13 Roy, *Ready for the Fray,* 407.

14 7th Canadian Infantry Brigade War Diary, 12.

15 Roy, *Ready for the Fray,* 407.

16 7th Canadian Infantry Brigade War Diary, 12.

17 Roy, *Ready for the Fray*, 407–08.
18 Canadian Scottish Regiment War Diary, 6.
19 7th Canadian Infantry Brigade War Diary, 12.
20 Canadian Scottish Regiment War Diary, 6.
21 Roy, *Ready for the Fray*, 408–09.
22 H.M. Jackson, *The Sherbrooke Regiment (12th Armoured Regiment)* (Montreal: Christian Bros. Press, 1958), 171.
23 Roy, *Ready for the Fray*, 409.
24 "Operation Plunder: Prepared by Q.O.R. of C.," 145.2Q2011(D7), Directorate of Heritage and History, Department of National Defence, 5–6.
25 Ibid., 6.
26 W.T. Barnard, *The Queen's Own Rifles of Canada, 1860–1960: One Hundred Years of Canada* (Don Mills, ON: Ontario Publishing Group, 1960), 258.
27 Ibid.
28 Stacey, *The Victory Campaign*, 552–54.
29 "Report No. 32, Part I," paras. 130–33.
30 Roy, *Ready for the Fray*, 410–11.
31 Ibid., 411.
32 Royal Winnipeg Rifles War Diary, April 1945, RG24, Library and Archives Canada, 4.
33 Roy, *Ready for the Fray*, 412.
34 T.J. Bell, *Into Action with the 12th Field* (Utrecht: J. van Boekhoven, 1945), 131–32.
35 Roy, *Ready for the Fray*, 412–13.
36 "Operation Plunder: Prepared by Q.O.R. of C.," 6.
37 Canadian Scottish Regiment War Diary, 6–7.

15: LONG WAY OUT FRONT

1 G.M. Alexander, ed., *4th Canadian Armoured Brigade: A Brief History of the 4th Canadian Armoured Brigade in Action, July 1944–May 1945* (Mitcham, UK: West Brothers, 1945), 33.
2 Lake Superior Regiment (Motor) War Diary, April 1945, RG24, Library and Archives Canada, 6–7.
3 4th Canadian Armoured Brigade War Diary, April 1945, RG24, Library and Archives Canada, 9.
4 Douglas Harker, *The Story of the British Columbia Regiment—1939–1945* (n.p., n.d.), n.p.
5 Lake Superior Regiment (Motor) War Diary, 7.
6 Argyll and Sutherland Highlanders War Diary, April 1945, RG24, Library and Archives Canada, 5.
7 "Report No. 32 Historical Section (G.S.) Army Headquarters: The Concluding Phase of Operations by the First CDN Army: Part I," Department of National Defence, December 10, 1949, para. 149.
8 Argyll and Sutherland Highlanders War Diary, 6–7.
9 "Report No. 32, Part I," paras. 150–51.
10 Ibid., paras. 152–53.

11 H.M. Jackson, *The Argyll and Sutherland Highlanders of Canada (Princess Louise's)*, *1928–1953* (Montreal: Industrial Shops for the Deaf, 1953), 199–200.

12 4th Canadian Armoured Brigade War Diary, April 1945, 12.

13 Jackson, *The Argyll and Sutherland Highlanders*, 200.

14 Argyll and Sutherland Highlanders War Diary, April 1945, 7.

15 "Report No. 32, Part I," paras. 155–57.

16 Lake Superior Regiment (Motor) War Diary, April 1945, 9.

17 Ibid., 9–10.

18 "Report No. 32, Part I," paras. 160–61.

19 Lincoln and Welland Regiment War Diary, April 1945, RG24, Library and Archives Canada, 8.

20 *The History of the 23rd Field Regiment (S.P.) RCA*, (Canada: n.p., 1945), 69–70.

21 Governor General's Foot Guards War Diary, April 1945, RG24, Library and Archives Canada, 10.

22 Lincoln and Welland Regiment War Diary, April 1945, 8.

23 R.L. Rogers, *History of the Lincoln and Welland Regiment* (Montreal: Industrial Shops for the Deaf, 1954), 256.

24 Robert M. Foster, et. al., *Steady the Buttons Two by Two: Governor General's Foot Guards Regimental History, 125th Anniversary: 1872-1997* (Ottawa: Governor General's Foot Guards, 1999), 220.

25 Governor General's Foot Guards War Diary, 10.

26 Foster, 220.

27 Governor General's Foot Guards War Diary, 10–12.

28 Rogers, 257.

29 Geoffrey Hayes, *The Lincs: A History of the Lincoln and Welland Regiment at War* (Alma, ON: Maple Leaf Route, 1986), 119.

30 Foster, 220.

31 Rogers, 257.

32 Lincoln and Welland Regiment War Diary, 10.

33 Hayes, 120.

34 George F.G. Stanley, *In the Face of Danger: The History of the Lake Superior Regiment* (Port Arthur, ON: The Lake Superior Scottish Regiment, 1960), 288.

35 "Report No. 32, Part I," para. 161.

36 *The History of the 23rd Field Regiment (S.P.) RCA*, 70.

37 23rd Field Regiment (SP) War Diary, April 1945, RG24, Library and Archives Canada, 4.

38 "Report No. 32, Part I," para. 161.

39 Lake Superior Regiment (Motor) War Diary, 13.

40 C.P. Stacey, *The Victory Campaign: The Operations in North-West Europe, 1944–1945*, vol. 3 (Ottawa: Queen's Printer, 1960), 558.

41 Algonquin Regiment War Diary, April 1945, RG24, Library and Archives Canada, 8.

42 Canadian Grenadier Guards War Diary, April 1945, RG24, Library and Archives Canada, 12.

43 G.L. Cassidy, *Warpath: From Tilly-la-campagne to the Kusten Canal* (Markham, ON: PaperJacks, 1980), 344.

44 Douglas E. Harker, *The Dukes: Story of the men who have served in peace and war with the British Columbia Regiment* (Vancouver: Mitchell Press, 1974), 288.

45 Cassidy, 344.

46 G.L. Caya, *Ne-Kan-Ne-Tah (We Lead, Others Follow)* (n.p., 1999), 66–67.

47 Cassidy, 344.

48 "Canadian Army Overseas Honours and Awards Citation Details," Directorate of Heritage and History, Department of National Defence, www.cmp-cpm.forces. gc.ca/dhh-dhp/gal/cao-aco/details-eng.asp?firstname=John Francis&lastname= Flannery&rec=id4775 (accessed on September 22, 2009).

49 Algonquin Regiment War Diary, 9.

50 Cassidy, 345.

51 Ibid., 348.

52 Alexander, 34.

16: ON TO GRONINGEN

1 "Reports by Gen. H.D.G. Crerar, C.B., D.S.O., on Operations 1st Cdn Army to McNaughton: 7.11 Mar to 5 May 45," vol. 10636, RG24, Library and Archives Canada, 6.

2 "Report No. 32 Historical Section (G.S.) Army Headquarters: The Operations of First CDN Army, 12–19 Apr. 45: Part 11," Department of National Defence, December 10, 1949, para. 231.

3 5th Canadian Infantry Brigade War Diary, April 1945, RG24, Library and Archives Canada, 6.

4 Black Watch of Canada War Diary, April 1945, RG24, Library and Archives Canada, 11.

5 "Report No. 32 Historical Section (G.S.) Army Headquarters: The Concluding Phase of Operations by the First CDN Army: Part I," Department of National Defence, December, 1949, paras. 134–44.

6 Ibid., 12.

7 5th Canadian Infantry Brigade War Diary,, 6.

8 "Report No. 32, Part I," para. 145.

9 *Royal Canadian Dragoons, 1939–1945* (Montreal: The Regiment, 1946), 156.

10 Ibid., 162.

11 8th Canadian Reconnaissance Regiment (14th Canadian Hussars) War Diary, April 1945, RG24, Library and Archives Canada, 5.

12 Calgary Highlanders War Diary, April 1945, RG24, Library and Archives Canada, 7.

13 6th Canadian Infantry Brigade War Diary, April 1945, RG24, Library and Archives Canada, 7.

14 Stacey, *The Victory Campaign*, 553.

15 8th Canadian Reconnaissance Regiment War Diary, April 1945, 5.

16 Royal Canadian Dragoons (1st Armoured Car Regiment) War Diary, April 1945, RG24, Library and Archives Canda, 5.

17 6th Canadian Infantry Brigade War Diary, April 1945, 7.

18 *Cent ans d'histoire d'un régiment canadien-français: les Fusiliers Mont-Royal, 1869-1969* (Montreal: Éditions Du Jour, 1971), 259.

19 Les Fusiliers Mont-Royal War Diary, April 1945, RG24, Library and Archives Canada, 4.

20 South Saskatchewan Regiment War Diary, April 1945, RG24, Library and Archives Canada, 17–18.

21 G.B. Buchanan, *The March of the Prairie Men: A Story of the South Saskatchewan Regiment* (Weyburn and Estevan, SK: Midwest Litho, 1957), 53.

22 *VIII CDN Recce Rgt 14 CH: Battle History of the Regt* (Victoria: 8th Cdn Recce Association, 1993), 57.

23 Kingsley Brown, Sr., Kingsley Brown, Jr., and Brereton Greenhous, *Semper Paratus: The History of the Royal Hamilton Light Infantry (Wentworth Regiment), 1962–1977* (Hamilton: RHLI Historical Assoc., 1977), 332–33.

24 Royal Hamilton Light Infantry War Diary, April 1945, RG24, Library and Archives Canada, 16–17.

25 "Letter to Annabel, 21 April 1945," Samuel Cass Letters, MG30, vol. 3, Personal Correspondence Samuel to Annabel Cass, April 1945, Library and Archives Canada.

26 *Vanguard: The Fort Garry Horse in the Second World War* (Doetinchem, Holland: Uitgevers-Maatschappij 'C. Nisset, 1945), 115.

27 Sandy Antal and Kevin R. Shackleton, *Duty nobly done: the official history of the Essex and Kent Scottish Regiment* (Windsor, ON: Walkerville Publishing, 2006), 518.

28 "Canadian Army Overseas Honours and Awards Citation Details," Directorate of Heritage and History, Department of National Defence, www.cmp-cpm.forces. gc.ca/dhh-dhp/gal/cao-aco/details-eng.asp?firstname=Leo Arhan&lastname= Nahmabin&rec=id563 (accessed on September 25, 2009).

29 1st Essex Scottish Regiment War Diary, April 1945, RG24, Library and Archives Canada, 4.

30 4th Canadian Infantry Brigade War Diary, April 1945, WO 179/Canadian Forces/4th Infantry Brigade, UK National Archives, 21.

31 "Canadian Army Overseas Honours and Awards Citation Details," Directorate of Heritage and History, Department of National Defence, www.cmp-cpm.forces. gc.ca/dhh-dhp/gal/cao-aco/details-eng.asp?firstname=Earl Richard&lastname= Thompson&rec=id3754 (accessed on September 25, 2009).

32 Antal and Shackleton, 518.

33 Canadian Army Overseas Honours and Awards Citation Details," Thompson.

34 *Vanguard: The Fort Garry Horse in the Second World War*, 115.

35 Antal and Shackleton, 518.

36 D.J. Goodspeed, *Battle Royal: A History of the Royal Regiment of Canada* (Toronto: Royal Regiment of Canada Assoc., 1962), 555–56.

37 4th Canadian Infantry Brigade War Diary, 21.

38 Antal and Shackleton, 518.

39 4th Canadian Infantry Brigade War Diary, 21–22.

40 1st Essex Scottish Regiment War Diary, 5.

41 Fort Garry Horse War Diary, April 1945, RG24, Library and Archives Canda, 9.

42 1st Essex Scottish Regiment War Diary, 5.

43 *Vanguard: The Fort Garry Horse in the Second World War*, 115.

44 4th Canadian Infantry Brigade War Diary, 24.

45 Ibid., 24.

46 "Canadian Army Overseas Honours and Awards Citation Details," Directorate of Heritage and History, Department of National Defence, www.cmp-cpm.forces. gc.ca/dhh-dhp/gal/cao-aco/details-eng.asp?firstname=Walter&lastname=Chaulk &rec=id4536 (accessed on September 28, 2009).

47 Ralph Dykstra, "The Liberation of Groningen—An Urban Battlefield" (September 22, 2002), *The Army Doctrine and Training Bulletin*, 46–47.

48 "Canadian Army Overseas Honours and Awards Citation Details," Chaulk.

49 4th Canadian Infantry Brigade War Diary, 25.

17: WAITED SO LONG

1 "Report No. 32 Historical Section (G.S.) Army Headquarters: The Operations of First CDN Army, 12–19 Apr. 45: Part 11," Department of National Defence, December 10, 1949, paras. 212–13.

2 Stormont, Dundas and Glengarry Highlanders War Diary, April 1945, RG24, Library and Archives Canada, 8.

3 William Boss, *Up the Glens: Stormont, Dundas and Glengarry Highlanders, 1783–1994*, 2nd ed. (Cornwall, ON: Old Book Store, 1995), 256.

4 "Report No. 32, Part 11," para. 213.

5 Boss, 256–57.

6 Bernard Diepman, correspondence with the author, April 3, 2009.

7 Boss, 256–57.

8 "Undated notes compiled by Bernard Diepman," possession of author.

9 Highland Light Infantry War Diary, April 1945, RG24, Library and Archives Canada, 7.

10 Bernard Diepman, recollection given to author at Salvo Bridge site in the Netherlands, May 3, 2009.

11 8th Canadian Infantry Brigade War Diary, April 1945, RG24, Library and Archives Canada, 4.

12 Le Régiment de la Chaudière War Diary, April 1945, RG24, Library and Archives Canada, 3.

13 "Canadian Army Overseas Honours and Awards Citation Details," Directorate of Heritage and History, Department of National Defence website, www.cmp-cpm. forces.gc.ca/dhh-dhp/gal/cao-aco/details-eng.asp?firstname=Leo&lastname= Major&rec=id4391 (accessed on September 29, 2009).

14 "Report No. 32, Part 11," paras. 214–16.

15 North Nova Scotia Highlanders War Diary, April 1945, RG24, Library and Archives Canada, 17.

16 9th Canadian Infantry Brigade War Diary, April 1945, RG24, Library and Archives Canada, 7.

17 "Royal Canadian Dragoons," 141.4A1013(D4), Directorate of Heritage and History, Department of National Defence, 4.

18 Larry Worthington, *The Spur and Sprocket: The Story of the Royal Canadian Dragoons* (Kitchener, ON: Reeve Press Limited, 1968), 106.

19 "Royal Canadian Dragoons," 4.

20 North Nova Scotia Highlanders War Diary, 17.

21 Royal Canadian Dragoons War Diary, April 1945, RG24, Library and Archives Canada, 10.

22 *Royal Canadian Dragoons, 1939–1945* (Montreal: The Regiment, 1946), 150.

23 Ibid., 176.

24 Queen's Own Rifles of Canada War Diary, April 1945, RG24, Library and Archives Canada, 8.

25 "Report No. 32, Part II," para. 222.

26 William W. Barrett, *History of 13th Canadian Field Artillery* (n.p., 1945), 127.

27 "Operation Plunder: Prepared by Q.O.R. of C.," 145.2Q2011(D7), Directorate of Heritage and History, Department of National Defence, 2.

28 Charles Cromwell Martin, *Battle Diary: From D-Day and Normandy to the Zuider Zee and VE* (Toronto: Dundurn Press, 1994), 141–45.

29 Queen's Own Rifles of Canada War Diary, 9.

18: PIECE OF CAKE

1 "Report No. 32 Historical Section (G.S.) Army Headquarters: The Concluding Phase of Operations by the First CDN Army: Part I," Department of National Defence, December 10, 1949, para. 189.

2 "I CDN INF DIV Op Order No. 51: OP CANNONSHOT," RG24, vol. 10896, Library and Archives Canada, 1–3.

3 C. Sydney Frost, *Once a Patricia: Memoirs of a Junior Infantry Officer in World War II* (Ottawa: Borealis Press, 2004), 435.

4 Ibid., 431.

5 Ibid., 430–33.

6 Reginald H. Roy, *The Seaforth Highlanders of Canada, 1919–1965* (Vancouver: Evergreen Press, 1969), 419.

7 "Diary Charlie Coy Seaforths, 23 Apr 44–9 July 45," RG24, vol. 20409, Library and Archives Canada, 246–47.

8 Frost, 434–35.

9 G.R. Stevens, *Princess Patricias Canadian Light Infantry: 1919–1957*, vol. 3 (Griesbach, AB: Historical Committee of the Regiment, n.d.), 236.

10 "Canadian Army Overseas Honours and Awards Citation Details," Directorate of Heritage and History, Department of National Defence website, www.cmp-cpm.forces.gc.ca/dhh-dhp/gal/cao-aco/details-eng.asp?firstname=Thomas&lastname=Hanberry&rec=id4978 (accessed October 2, 2009).

11 Frost, 436.

12 Roy, *The Seaforth Highlanders of Canada*, 420.

13 "I CDN INF DIV OPS From R. IJssel to R. Emm, 11 Apr–5 May 45," RG24, vol. 10896, Library and Archives Canada, 3.

14 "Diary Charlie Coy Seaforths," 247.

15 "I CDN INF DIV OPS From R. IJssel to R. Emm," 3.

16 Seaforth Highlanders of Canada War Diary, RG24, Library and Archives Canada, 16.

17 Stevens, *Princess Patricia's Canadian Light Infantry*, 237.

18 Frost, 438–39.

19 "I CDN INF DIV OPS From R. IJssel to R. Emm," 3.

20 48th Highlanders of Canada War Diary, April 1945, RG24, Library and Archives Canada, 7.

21 Kim Beattie, *Dileas: History of the 48th Highlanders of Canada, 1929–1956* (Toronto: 48th Highlanders of Canada, 1957), 746.

22 Ibid., 744–45.

23 Ibid., 745–47.

24 Ibid., 747–49.

25 "The 48th Highlanders of Canada, Report on Ops, 11 Apr–19 Apr 45," RG24, vol. 10896, Library and Archives Canada, 2.

26 Beattie, 750–51.

27 G.R. Stevens, *The Royal Canadian Regiment, 1933–1966*, vol. 2 (London, ON: London Printing, 1967), 189.

28 Jeffrey Williams, *The Long Left Flank: The Hard Won Way to the Reich, 1944–1945* (Toronto: Stoddart Publishing, 1988), 282.

29 Ontario Regiment War Diary, April 1945, RG24, Library and Archives Canada, 8.

30 "The 11th Canadian Armoured Regiment (Ont. R.)," 141.4A11, Directorate of Heritage and History, Department of National Defence, 1–2.

31 "Draft Outline of Ops of I CDN Corps in Clearing of Western Holland April 1945," RG24, vol. 10796, Library and Archives Canda, 5.

32 "Comment on Operation 'Cannonshot' by Major General H.W. Foster, DSO, GOC I CDN INF DIV," RG24, vol. 10896, Library and Archives Canada, 1.

33 "The Royal Canadian Regiment Report on Ops, 12 Apr–18 Apr 45," RG24, vol. 10896, Library and Archives Canada, 2.

34 Hastings and Prince Edward Regiment War Diary, April 1945, RG24, Library and Archives Canada, n.p.

35 Royal Canadian Regiment War Diary, April 1945, RG24, Library and Archives Canada, 9.

36 Hastings and Prince Edward Regiment War Diary, April 1945, n.p.

37 Brandon A. Conron, *A History of the First Hussars Regiment, 1856–1980* (n.p., 1981), 138.

38 Robert Tooley, *Invicta: The Carleton and York Regiment in the Second World War* (Fredericton, NB: New Ireland Press, 1989), 350.

39 Carleton and York Regiment War Diary, April 1945, RG24, Library and Archives Canada, 8.

40 "WNSR Report on Operations in Holland, 1945," RG24, vol. 10896, Library and Archives Canada, 4.

19: JERRY IS RUNNING

1 "Comment on Operation 'Cannonshot' by Major General H.W. Foster, DSO, GOC I CDN INF DIV," RG24, vol. 10896, Library and Archives Canada, 1.

2 Royal Canadian Regiment War Diary, April 1945, RG24, Library and Archives Canada, 9.

3 "The Royal Canadian Regiment Report on Ops, 12 Apr–18 Apr 45," RG24, vol. 10896, Library and Archives Canada, 2.

4 "1 CDN INF DIV OPS From R. IJssel to R. Emm, 11 Apr–5 May 45," RG24, vol. 10896, Library and Archives Canada, 5.

5 G.R. Stevens, *The Royal Canadian Regiment, 1933–1966*, vol. 2 (London, ON: London Printing, 1967), 190.

6 "The Royal Canadian Regiment Report on Ops," 2.

7 Strome Galloway, *"55 Axis," With the Royal Canadian Regiment, 1939–1945* (Montreal: Provincial Publishing, 1946), 201.

8 J.T.B. Quayle, *In Action: A Personal Account of the Italian and Netherlands Campaigns of WW II* (Abbotsford, BC: Blue Stone Publishers, 1997), 207–08.

9 "1 CDN INF DIV OPS From R. IJssel to R. Emm, 11 Apr–5 May 45," 5.

10 Loyal Edmonton Regiment War Diary, April 1945, RG24, Library and Archives Canada, 7–8.

11 James Riley Stone, interview by William Thackray, May 13, and 20, and June 3, 10, and 17, 1980, University of Victoria Special Collections.

12 G.R. Stevens, *A City Goes to War* (Brampton, ON: Charters, 1964), 344.

13 Reginald H. Roy, *The Seaforth Highlanders of Canada, 1919–1965* (Vancouver: Evergreen Press, 1969), 426.

14 Ibid., 426–28.

15 "Diary of Major Durnford," RG24, vol. 20405, Library and Archives Canada, 134.

16 "Diary Charlie Coy Seaforths, 23 Apr 44–9 July 45," RG24, vol. 20409, Library and Archives Canada, 249–50.

17 "1 CDN INF DIV OPS From R. IJssel to R. Emm," 6.

18 Princess Patricia's Canadian Light Infantry War Diary, April 1945, RG24, Library and Archives Canada, 16.

19 Loyal Edmonton Regiment War Diary, 8.

20 "1 CDN INF DIV OPS From R. IJssel to R. Emm," 6.

21 Stevens, *A City Goes to War*, 344.

22 Loyal Edmonton Regiment War Diary, 9.

23 C. Sydney Frost, *Once a Patricia: Memoirs of a Junior Infantry Officer in World War II* (Ottawa: Borealis Press, 2004), 442.

24 G.R. Stevens, *Princess Patricias Canadian Light Infantry: 1919–1957*, vol. 3 (Griesbach, AB: Historical Committee of the Regiment, n.d.), 240.

25 C.P. Stacey, *The Victory Campaign: The Operations in North-West Europe, 1944–1945*, vol. 3 (Ottawa: Queen's Printer, 1960), 573.

26 J.M. McAvity, *Lord Strathcona's Horse (Royal Canadians): A Record of Achievement* (Toronto: Brigdens, 1947), 208–10.

27 Lt. Col. H.H. Angle, "Lt. Col. H.H. Angle Diary," RG24, vol. 20405, Library and Archives Canada, 8.

28 Reginald H. Roy, *Sinews of Steel: The History of the British Columbia Dragoons* (Toronto: Charters, 1965), 384–85.

29 British Columbia Dragoons War Diary, April 1945, RG24, Library and Archives Canada, 14.

30 "Period 12 Apr 45–19 Apr 45, Canadian War Museum, 16.

31 Douglas How, *The 8th Hussars: A History of the Regiment* (Sussex, NB: Maritime Publishing, 1964), 322.

32 Ibid., 322–23.

33 How, 323–24.

34 J.E. Oldfield, *The Westminster's War Diary: An Unofficial History of the Westminster Regiment (Motor) in World War II* (New Westminster, BC: n.p., 1964), 189.

35 "5 Cdn Armd Div History of Ops, Advance from Arnhem to the Zuider Zee," RG24, vol. 10941, Library and Archives Canada, 2.

36 McAvity, 213–14.

37 Ibid., 215–18.

38 "Report on operations of 9 Cdn Armd Regt (BCD) for period 14–19 Apr 45," 141.4A9011 (D2), Directorate of Heritage and History, Department of National Defence, 2–3.

39 How, 328–29.

40 "Period 12 Apr 45–19 Apr 45," 16.

41 "5 Cdn Armd Div History of Ops," 2.

42 Roy, *Sinews of Steel*, 387–89.

43 "I CDN INF DIV OPS From R. IJssel to R. Emm, 11 Apr–5 May 45," 8.

44 "WNSR Report on Operations in Holland, 1945," RG24, vol. 10896, Library and Archives Canada, 8.

45 Royal Canadian Regiment War Diary, April 1945, RG24, Library and Archives Canada, 13.

46 Stacey, *The Victory Campaign*, 586.

47 Thomas H. Raddall, *West Novas: A History of the West Nova Scotia Regiment* (n.p., 1947), 291.

48 Hastings and Prince Edward Regiment War Diary, April 1945, RG24, Library and Archives Canada, 8.

49 Farley Mowat, *The Regiment*, 2nd ed. (Toronto: McClelland & Stewart, 1973), 302.

50 "Comment on Operation 'Cannonshot,'" 1.

51 Mowat, 302.

52 "Comment on Operation 'Cannonshot,'" 1.

20: A STERN ATONEMENT

 1 C.P. Stacey, *The Victory Campaign: The Operations in North-West Europe, 1944–1945*, vol. 3 (Ottawa: Queen's Printer, 1960), 558–59.

 2 Argyll and Sutherland Highlanders War Diary, April 1945, RG24, Library and Archives Canada, 10.

 3 Robert L. Fraser, *Black Yesterdays: The Argyll's War* (Hamilton, ON: Argyll Foundation, 1996), 431.

 4 Robert A. Spencer, *History of the 15th Field Regiment* (Amsterdam: Elsevier, 1945), 251.

 5 "Report No. 32 Historical Section (G.S.) Army Headquarters: The Operations of First CDN Army, 12–19 Apr. 45: Part II," Department of National Defence, December 10, 1949, para. 285.

 6 Fraser, 432.

 7 H.M. Jackson, *The Argyll and Sutherland Highlanders of Canada (Princess Louise's), 1928–1953* (Montreal: Industrial Shops for the Deaf, 1953), 264.

8 "Report No. 32, Part II," para. 285.

9 Argyll and Sutherland Highlanders War Diary, 10.

10 Fraser, 432.

11 Ibid., 432–35.

12 Ibid., 435–37.

13 Argyll and Sutherland Highlanders War Diary, 11.

14 Ibid.

15 4th Canadian Armoured Brigade War Diary, April 1945, RG24, Library and Archives Canada, 21.

16 Stacey, *The Victory Campaign*, 558.

17 8th Light Anti-Aircraft Regiment War Diary, April 1945, RG24, Library and Archives Canada, 10.

18 4th Canadian Armoured Brigade War Diary, 21.

19 Lake Superior Regiment (Motor) War Diary, April 1945, RG24, Library and Archives Canada, 19.

20 4th Canadian Armoured Brigade War Diary, 21.

21 George F.G. Stanley, *In the Face of Danger: The History of the Lake Superior Regiment* (Port Arthur, ON: The Lake Superior Scottish Regiment, 1960), 291–92.

22 Lake Superior Regiment (Motor) War Diary, 21.

23 4th Canadian Armoured Brigade War Diary, 22–23.

24 Geoffrey Hayes, *The Lincs: A History of the Lincoln and Welland Regiment at War* (Alma, ON: Maple Leaf Route, 1986), 123.

25 South Alberta Regiment War Diary, April 1945, RG24, Library and Archives Canada, 16.

26 "Memorandum of an interview given by Lt. Col. G.D. de S. Witherspoon, 19 May 45," 141.4A29011(1), Directorate of Heritage and History, Department of National Defence, 4.

27 Donald Graves, *South Albertas: A Canadian Regiment at War* (Toronto: Robin Brass Studio, 1998), 314.

28 Ibid., 314–15.

29 South Alberta Regiment War Diary, April 1945, 16.

30 "Memorandum of an interview given by Lt. Col. G.D. de S. Witherspoon" 4.

31 Ibid., 4–5.

32 Stacey, *The Victory Campaign*, 559.

33 "Report No. 32, Part II," para. 300.

34 G.L. Cassidy, *Warpath: From Tilly-la-campagne to the Kusten Canal* (Markham, ON: PaperJacks, 1980), 349.

35 15th Field Regiment, RCA War Diary, April 1945, RG24, Library and Archives Canada, 5.

36 10th Canadian Infantry Brigade War Diary, April 1945, RG24, Library and Archives Canada, 9.

37 8th Light Anti-Aircraft Regiment War Diary, 9.

38 10th Canadian Independent Machinegun Company (New Brunswick Rangers) War Diary, April 1945, WO 179/4551, UK National Archives, 29.

39 Cassidy, 349.

40 "Report No. 32, Part II," paras. 301–02.

41 Ibid., paras. 302–03.

42 Cassidy, 352.

43 10th Canadian Independent Machinegun Company (New Brunswick Rangers) War Diary, 29.

44 M.O. Rollefson, ed., *Green Route Up: 4 Canadian Armoured Division* (The Hague: Mouton, 1945), 90.

45 "Report No. 32, Part II," para. 304.

46 Cassidy, 352.

47 "Report No. 32, Part II," para. 306.

48 Jackson, *The Argyll and Sutherland Highlanders*, 208.

49 Cassidy, 352.

50 Argyll and Sutherland Highlanders War Diary, 13–14.

51 "Report No. 32, Part II," para. 306.

52 Cassidy, 352–53.

53 Jackson, *The Argyll and Sutherland Highlanders*, 208.

54 "Report No. 32, Part II," para. 306.

55 Cassidy, 353–54.

56 Algonquin Regiment War Diary, April 1945, RG24, Library and Archives Canada.

57 Cassidy, 354.

58 Jackson, *The Argyll and Sutherland Highlanders*, 209–10.

59 Hayes, 123.

60 Lincoln and Welland Regiment War Diary, 17.

61 Hayes, 123.

62 "Report No. 32, part II," paras. 310–11.

63 Ibid., para. 312.

64 Cassidy, 348–49.

21: LARGE-SCALE STREET FIGHTING

1 4th Canadian Infantry Brigade War Diary, April 1945, WO 179/Canadian Forces/4th Infantry Brigade, UK National Archives, 24.

2 Gregory John Ashworth, *War and the City* (London: Routledge, 1991), 124.

3 Ralph Dykstra, "The Liberation of Groningen—An Urban Battlefield," *The Army Doctrine and Training Bulletin* (September 22, 2002), 48.

4 Ibid., 47–48.

5 Terry Copp, *Cinderella Army: The Canadians in Northwest Europe, 1944–1945* (Toronto: University of Toronto Press, 2006), 271.

6 4th Canadian Infantry Brigade War Diary, 25.

7 Royal Hamilton Light Infantry War Diary, April 1945, RG24, Library and Archives Canada, 10.

8 George G. Blackburn, *The Guns of Victory: A Soldier's Eye View, Belgium, Holland, and Germany, 1944–45* (Toronto: McClelland & Stewart, 1997), 442.

9 D.J. Goodspeed, *Battle Royal: A History of the Royal Regiment of Canada* (Toronto: Royal Regiment of Canada Assoc., 1962), 557.

10 Blackburn, 442–43.

11 Goodspeed, 557.

12 Royal Regiment of Canada War Diary, April 1945, RG24, Library and Archives Canada, 7.

13 Blackburn, 444–45.

14 Royal Regiment of Canada War Diary, 8.

15 4th Canadian Infantry Brigade War Diary, 26–27.

16 Royal Hamilton Light Infantry War Diary, 20.

17 "Canadian Army Overseas Honours and Awards Citation Details," Directorate of Heritage and History, Department of National Defence, www.cmp-cpm.forces. gc.ca/dhh-dhp/gal/cao-aco/details-eng.asp?firstname=Wilfred John&lastname=King&rec=id377 (accessed October 15, 2009).

18 Royal Hamilton Light Infantry War Diary, 20–21.

19 4th Canadian Infantry Brigade War Diary, 27.

20 Toronto Scottish Regiment (MG) War Diary, April 1945, RG24, Library and Archives Canada, 7.

21 Sandy Antal and Kevin R. Shackleton, *Duty nobly done: the official history of the Essex and Kent Scottish Regiment* (Windsor, ON: Walkerville Publishing, 2006), 520.

22 1st Essex Scottish Regiment War Diary, April 1945, RG24, Library and Archives Canada, 6.

23 Antal and Shackleton, 521.

24 1st Essex Scottish Regiment War Diary, 6.

25 *1 Battalion, The Essex Scottish Regiment, 1949–1945: A Brief Narrative* (Aldershot, UK: Gale and Polden, 1946), 78.

26 4th Canadian Infantry Brigade War Diary, 27.

27 Antal and Shackleton, 521.

28 1st Essex Scottish War Diary, 6.

29 Antal and Shackleton, 521–22.

30 1st Essex Scottish War Diary, 6.

31 "Report No. 32 Historical Section (G.S.) Army Headquarters: The Operations of First CDN Army, 12–19 Apr. 45: Part II," Department of National Defence, December 10, 1949, para. 249.

32 Roy Farran, *The History of the Calgary Highlanders, 1921–54* (Calgary: Bryant Press, 1954), 208.

33 David Bercuson, *Battalion of Heroes: The Calgary Highlanders in World War II* (Calgary: Calgary Highlanders Regimental Funds Foundation, 1994), 233.

34 Farran, 208.

35 Calgary Highlanders War Diary, April 1945, RG24, Library and Archives Canada, 9.

36 Bercuson, 233.

37 Calgary Highlanders War Diary, 9.

38 Bercuson, 234.

39 Régiment de Maisonneuve War Diary, April 1945, RG24, Library and Archives Canada, 5.

40 Dykstra, 51.

41 Régiment de Maisonneuve War Diary, 5.

42 Gérard Marchand, *Le Régiment de Maisonneuve vers la Victoire, 1944–1945* (Montreal: Les Presses Libres, 1980), 225–26.

43 Black Watch of Canada War Diary, April 1945, RG24, Library and Archives Canada, 15.

44 Ibid., 15–16.

45 Ibid., 16.

46 Calgary Highlanders War Diary, 10.

47 Bercuson, 235.

48 Ibid., 236–37.

49 Calgary Highlanders War Diary, 10.

50 *Cent ans d'histoire d'un régiment canadien-français : les Fusiliers Mont-Royal, 1869–1969* (Montreal: Éditions Du Jour, 1971), 260.

51 Les Fusiliers Mont-Royal War Diary, April 1945, RG24, Library and Archives Canada, 4.

52 C.P. Stacey, *The Victory Campaign: The Operations in North-West Europe, 1944–1945,* vol. 3 (Ottawa: Queen's Printer, 1960), 555.

53 G.B. Buchanan, *The March of the Prairie Men: A Story of the South Saskatchewan Regiment* (Weyburn and Estevan, SK: Midwest Litho, 1957), 54.

54 Charles Goodman, interview by author, Saanichton, BC, January 27, 2009.

55 Buchanan, 54.

56 Jean V. Allard, *The Memoirs of Jean V. Allard* (Vancouver: University of British Columbia Press, 1988), 116.

57 Menno Huizinga, *Sporen van Strijd in de Stad Groningen* (Groningen: Jemeentelijk 5 Mei Comité Groningen, rep. 2004), 32–33.

58 Charles Goodman.

59 Les Fusiliers Mont-Royal War Diary, 5.

60 *Cent ans d'histoire d'un régiment canadien-français,* 260–61.

61 Queen's Own Cameron Highlanders of Canada War Diary, April 1945, RG24, Library and Archives Canada, 9.

62 Stacey, *The Victory Campaign,* 556.

63 Johan van Doorn email correspondence, December 11, 2009.

64 4th Canadian Infantry Brigade War Diary, 31–34.

22: OPERATION CLEANSER

1 Briefing with author by Dutch historian Johan van Doorn, Sommelsdijk, Netherlands, May 1, 2009.

2 Johan van Doorn, conversation with author, December 7, 2009.

3 Henri van der Zee, *The Hunger Winter: Occupied Holland, 1944–45* (London: Jill Norman & Hobhouse , 1982), 237–241.

4 C.P. Stacey, *The Victory Campaign: The Operations in North-West Europe, 1944–1945,* vol. 3 (Ottawa: Queen's Printer, 1960), 585.

5 van der Zee, 242.

6 Ibid., 245.

7 Stacey, *The Victory Campaign,* 584.

8 Ibid., 571–72.

9 George Kitching, *Mud and Green Fields: The Memoirs of Major General George Kitching* (Langley, BC: Battleline Books, 1985), 249.

10 "The Battle of Otterloo, Account by Capt. D. Wagner," RG24, vol. 10941, Library and Archives Canada, 1.

11 *The Governor General's Horse Guards, 1939–1945* (Toronto: Canadian Military Journal, 1954), 217.

12 Alexander Ross, *Slow March to a Regiment* (St. Catharines, ON: Vanwell, 1993), 211–12.

13 "1 Canadian Corps Intelligence Summary," No. 271, April 17, 1945, RG24, vol. 109421, Library and Archives Canada, 1.

14 Irish Regiment of Canada War Diary, April 1945, RG24, Library and Archives Canada, n.p.

15 "An Account of the Attack on the Otterloo area of 16/17 Apr 45 by Lieut J Hobson, the Divisional Interrogator," RG24, vol. 10941, Library and Archives Canada, 1.

16 "Gordon Bannerman account re: Sergeant Humble," possession of author.

17 Gordon Bannerman, www.gordiebannerman.com (accessed February 24, 2009).

18 17th Field Regiment, RCA War Diary, April 1945, RG24, Library and Archives Canada, 15.

19 "Canadian Army Overseas Honours and Awards Citation Details," Directorate of Heritage and History, Department of National Defence, www.cmp-cpm.forces. gc.ca/dhh-dhp/gal/cao-aco/details-eng.asp?firstname=Roland&lastname= Bouchard&rec=id213 (accessed October 20, 2009).

20 *The Governor General's Horse Guards, 1939–1945,* 217.

21 Irish Regiment of Canada War Diary, April 1945, n.p.

22 *The Governor General's Horse Guards, 1939–1945,* 218.

23 www.metsystems.np.ig.org/irish/ (accessed March 29, 2009).

24 17th Field Regiment, RCA War Diary, April 1945, 15.

25 Bannerman, www.gordiebannerman.com.

26 17th Field Regiment, RCA War Diary, April 1945, 16.

27 Bert M. Hoffmeister, interview by B. Greenhous and W. McAndrew, transcript, Directorate of Heritage and History, Department of National Defence, n.d., 119–20.

28 Bannerman, www.gordiebannerman.com.

29 *History of 17th Field Regiment, Royal Canadian Artillery, 5th Canadian Armoured Division* (Groningen: J. Niemeiser, 1946), 77–78.

30 Ross, 217–18.

31 37th Field Battery, 17th Field Regiment War Diary, possession of author, n.p.

32 *History of 17th Field Regiment, Royal Canadian Artillery, 5th Canadian Armoured Division,* 77–78.

33 Bannerman, www.gordiebannerman.com.

34 *History of 17th Field Regiment, Royal Canadian Artillery,* 82–83.

35 37th Field Battery War Diary, n.p.

36 *The Governor General's Horse Guards, 1939–1945,* 218–19.

37 Bannerman, www.gordiebannerman.com.

38 Gordon Wood, *The Story of the Irish Regiment of Canada, 1939–1945* (Heerenveen, Holland: Hepkema, 1945), 64.

39 "Canadian Army Overseas Honours and Awards Citation Details," Directorate of Heritage and History, Department of National Defence, www.cmp-cpm.forces. gc.ca/dhh-dhp/gal/cao-aco/details-eng.asp?firstname=Walter&lastname= Asseltine&rec=id62 (accessed October 21, 2009).

40 Ross, 218.

41 Bannerman, www.gordiebannerman.com.

42 *History of 17th Field Regiment, Royal Canadian Artillery, 5th Canadian Armoured Division*, 80.

43 Irish Regiment of Canada War Diary, n.p.

44 *The Governor General's Horse Guards, 1939–1945*, 219.

45 Johan van Doorn, conversation with author, October 22, 2009.

46 Stacey, *The Victory Campaign*, 579.

47 Douglas E. Delaney, *The Soldier's General: Bert Hoffmeister at War* (Vancouver: University of British Columbia Press, 2005), 214.

48 British Columbia Dragoons War Diary, April 1945, RG24, Library and Archives Canada, 18.

49 "Report on Operations of the Cape Breton Highlanders, Holland, for period 27 March 1945 to the 8th May 1945," 145.2C5013(D2), Directorate of Heritage and History, Department of National Defence, 1.

50 Reginald H. Roy, *Sinews of Steel: The History of the British Columbia Dragoons* (Toronto: Charters, 1965), 394–95.

51 Calgary Regiment War Diary, April 1945, RG24, Library and Archives Canada, 18.

52 Douglas How, *The 8th Hussars: A History of the Regiment* (Sussex, NB: Maritime Publishing, 1964), 331–32.

53 "Period 12 Apr 45–19 Apr 45, Dealing with the Breakthrough at Arnhem and the Thrust to the Zuider Zee," 20020045.1641, Canadian War Museum, 16.

54 J.E. Oldfield, *The Westminster's War Diary: An Unofficial History of the Westminster Regiment (Motor) in World War II* (New Westminster, BC: n.p., 1964), 192.

55 Lt. Col. J.M. McAvity, "2nd Canadian Armoured Regiment, Lord Strathcona's Horse (Royal Canadians): Account of Operations, 12 Apr 45–19 Apr 45," 141.4A2013(1), Directorate of Heritage and History, Department of National Defence, 3–4.

56 Lord Strathcona's Horse War Diary, April 1945, RG24, Library and Archives Canada, 5.

57 8th Princess Louise's (New Brunswick) Hussars War Diary, April 1945, RG24, Library and Archives Canada, 14.

58 Lord Strathcona's Horse War Diary, 5.

59 J.M. McAvity, *Lord Strathcona's Horse (Royal Canadians): A Record of Achievement* (Toronto: Brigdens, 1947), 231.

60 "1 Canadian Corps Intelligence Summary," No. 275, April 21, 1945, RG24, vol. 109421, Library and Archives Canada, 1.

23: SOUND TACTICAL PLANS

1 James Riley Stone, interview by William Thackray, May 13 and 20, and June, 3,10, and 17, 1980, University of Victoria Special Collections.

2 Ernest Morgan Keith MacGregor, interview by Rick Aylward, July 22, 1986, University of Victoria Special Collections.

3 Stone interview.

4 G.R. Stevens, *A City Goes to War* (Brampton, ON: Charters, 1964), 346.

5 ———. *Princess Patricia's Canadian Light Infantry: 1919–1957*, vol. 3 (Griesbach, AB: Historical Committee of the Regiment, n.d.), 241.

6 Reginald H. Roy, *The Seaforth Highlanders of Canada, 1919–1965* (Vancouver: Evergreen Press, 1969), 434–35.

7 Robert Woodhouse Dudley, interview by Cameron Falconer, March 16, 1983, University of Victoria Special Collections.

8 Thomas H. Raddall, *West Novas: A History of the West Nova Scotia Regiment* (n.p., 1947), 299–302.

9 C.P. Stacey, *The Victory Campaign: The Operations in North-West Europe, 1944–1945*, vol. 3 (Ottawa: Queen's Printer, 1960), 587–90.

10 Paul Douglas Dickson, *A Thoroughly Canadian General: A Biography of General H.D.G. Crerar* (Toronto: University of Toronto Press, 2007), 411.

11 Stacey, *The Victory Campaign*, 587–90.

12 Ibid., 590–91.

13 "Report No. 32 Historical Section (G.S.) Army Headquarters: The Concluding Phase of Operations by the First CDN Army: Part III," Department of National Defence, December 10, 1949, para. 357.

14 Ibid., paras. 363–78.

15 Regina Rifles War Diary, April 1945, RG24, Library and Archives Canada, 10–12.

16 "Report No. 32, Part III," paras. 372–73.

17 Bruce Tascoma and Eric Wells, *Little Black Devils: A History of the Royal Winnipeg Rifles* (Winnipeg: Frye Publishing, 1994), 187–88.

18 Royal Winnipeg Rifles War Diary, April 1945, RG24, Library and Archives Canada, 8–9.

19 Tascoma and Wells, 189.

20 Royal Winnipeg Rifles War Diary, 9.

21 Reginald H. Roy, *Ready for the Fray: The History of the Canadian Scottish Regiment (Princess Mary's), 1920 to 1955* (Vancouver: Evergreen Press, 1958), 417–26.

22 "Report No. 32, Part III," para. 386.

23 North Shore (New Brunswick) Regiment War Diary, April 1945, RG24, Library and Archives Canada, 11.

24 Will R. Bird, *North Shore (New Brunswick) Regiment* (Fredericton, NB: Brunswick Press, 1963), 554.

25 Queen's Own Rifles War Diary, April 1945, RG24, Library and Archives Canada, 11.

26 W.T. Barnard, *The Queen's Own Rifles of Canada, 1860–1960: One Hundred Years of Canada* (Don Mills, ON: Ontario Publishing Group, 1960), 260.

27 "Report No. 32, Part III," paras. 380–81.

28 H.M. Jackson, *The Sherbrooke Regiment (12th Armoured Regiment)* (Montreal: Christian Bros. Press, 1958), 175.

29 Bird, *North Shore (New Brunswick) Regiment*, 554–55.

30 North Shore (New Brunswick) Regiment War Diary, 12.

31 Bird, *North Shore (New Brunswick) Regiment*, 555.

32 "1st Bn The Queen's Own Rifles of Canada: Operation 'Plunder,' Phase 4," 145.2Q2011(D6), Directorate of Heritage and History, Department of National Defence, 3–4.

33 "Memorandum of Interview with Brig. J.M. Rockingham, DSO and Bar, Comd 9
    CDN INF BDE and other officers, given to Hist Offr 3 CDN INF DIV 4 May 45:
    Operation Duck," RG24, vol. 10987, Library and Archives Canada, 1.

34 "RCA 3 CDN INF DIV: OP ORDER NO. 2, OP 'Duck,'" RG24, vol. 10914, Library and
    Archives Canada, 1–2.

35 Stacey, *The Victory Campaign*, 596.

36 "Memorandum of Interview with Brig. J.M. Rockingham," 1.

37 "Report No. 32, Part III," para. 388.

38 "Memorandum of Interview with Brig. J.M. Rockingham," 2.

39 North Nova Scotia Highlanders War Diary, April 1945, RG24, Library and Archives
    Canada, 23.

40 Highland Light Infantry War Diary, April 1945, RG24, Library and Archives
    Canada, 13.

41 *1st Battalion, The Highland Light Infantry of Canada: 1940–1945*
    (Galt, ON: Highland Light Infantry of Canada Assoc., 1951), III.

42 William Boss, *Up the Glens: Stormont, Dundas and Glengarry Highlanders, 1783–
    1994*, 2nd ed. (Cornwall, ON: Old Book Store, 1995), 260-61.

43 "Memorandum of Interview with Brig. J.M. Rockingham," 2–3.

44 North Nova Scotia Highlanders War Diary, 24.

45 "Memorandum of Interview with Brig. J.M. Rockingham," 3.

46 Highland Light Infantry War Diary, 14.

47 "Memorandum of Interview with Brig. J.M. Rockingham," 3.

48 Stacey, *The Victory Campaign*, 596–97.

49 "Report No. 32, Part III," para. 412.

50 "J. Walter Keith Account," unpublished reminiscence, possession of author, 19.

51 "Actions at Leer and North of Groningen, Prepared by 1st BN Regina Rifle Regiment,"
    145.2R11011(D5), Directorate of Heritage and History, Department of National
    Defence, 13.

52 "J. Walter Keith Account," 19.

53 Stacey, *The Victory Campaign*, 597.

24: CROSSROAD AMBUSHES

1 C.P. Stacey, *The Victory Campaign: The Operations in North-West Europe, 1944–1945*,
   vol. 3 (Ottawa: Queen's Printer, 1960), 598–99.

2 R.L. Rogers, *History of the Lincoln and Welland Regiment* (Montreal: Industrial
   Shops for the Deaf, 1954), 265.

3 H.M. Jackson, *The Argyll and Sutherland Highlanders of Canada (Princess Louise's),
   1928–1953* (Montreal: Industrial Shops for the Deaf, 1953), 211–12.

4 "Canadian Army Overseas Honours and Awards Citation Details," Directorate of
   Heritage and History, Department of National Defence, www.cmp-cpm.forces.gc.
   ca/dhh-dhp/gal/cao-aco/details-eng.asp?firstname=William Garrison&
   lastname=Whiteside&rec=id3924 (accessed October 26, 2009).

5 10th Canadian Infantry Brigade War Diary, April 1945, RG24, Library and Archives
   Canada, 11.

6 G.L. Cassidy, *Warpath: From Tilly-la-campagne to the Kusten Canal* (Markham, ON:
   PaperJacks, 1980), 361–63.

7 Algonquin Regiment War Diary, April 1945, RG24, Library and Archives Canada, 18.

8 "Report No. 32 Historical Section (G.S.) Army Headquarters: The Concluding Phase of Operations by the First CDN Army: Part III," Department of National Defence, December 10, 1949, para. 438.

9 Ibid., para. 453.

10 Cassidy, 364.

11 "Report No. 32, Part III," para. 456.

12 "Memorandum of Interview Given by Lt. Col. G.M. Robinson: The Final Punch, Operations and Activities of 4 CDN ARMD DIV, 30 Mar–5 May 45," RG24, vol. 10935, Library and Archives Canada, 4.

13 "Memorandum of Interview Given by Brig. R.W. Moncel, COMD 4 CDN ARMD BDE: The Final Punch–Operations and Activities of 4 CDN ARMD BDE, 30 Mar–5 May 45," RG24, vol. 10992, Library and Archives Canada, 3.

14 Stacey, *The Victory Campaign*, 599.

15 Lake Superior Regiment (Motor) War Diary, April 1945, RG24, Library and Archives Canada, 31.

16 Stacey, *The Victory Campaign*, 599.

17 Rogers, 266.

18 A. Fortescue Duguid, *History of the Canadian Grenadier Guards, 1760–1964* (Montreal: Gazette Printing Company, 1965), 345.

19 Stuart Louis Johns, telephone interview by author, June 3, 2009.

20 Duguid, 345.

21 Johns interview.

22 Lake Superior Regiment (Motor) War Diary, 30–31.

23 Robert M. Foster, et al., *Steady the Buttons Two by Two: Governor General's Foot Guards Regimental History, 125th Anniversary: 1872-1997* (Ottawa: Governor General's Foot Guards, 1999), 221.

24 "Memorandum of Interview Given by Lt. Col. G.M. Robinson," 4–5.

25 4th Canadian Armoured Brigade War Diary, April 1945, RG24, Library and Archives Canada, 27.

26 Algonquin Regiment War Diary, 20.

27 Geoffrey Hayes, *The Lincs: A History of the Lincoln and Welland Regiment at War* (Alma, ON: Maple Leaf Route, 1986), 127.

28 Rogers, 268.

29 "Report No. 32, Part III," paras. 504–06.

30 Jackson, *The Argyll and Sutherland Highlanders*, 217.

31 Stanley, 301–02.

32 Stacey, *The Victory Campaign*, 601.

33 Roy Farran, *The History of the Calgary Highlanders, 1921–54* (Calgary: Bryant Press, 1954), 209.

34 David Bercuson, *Battalion of Heroes: The Calgary Highlanders in World War II* (Calgary: Calgary Highlanders Regimental Funds Foundation, 1994), 239.

35 Farran, 209.

36 "Report No. 32," paras. 565–66.

37 R.W. Queens-Hughes, *Whatever Men Dare: A History of the Queen's Own Cameron Highlanders of Canada, 1935–1960* (Winnipeg: Bulman Brothers, 1960), 178.

38 Charles Goodman, interview by author, Saanichton, BC, January 27, 2009.
39 Queen's Own Cameron Highlanders of Canada War Diary, April 1945, RG24, Library and Archives Canada, 15.
40 Queens-Hughes, 178–79.
41 George G. Blackburn, "The History of the 4th Field Regiment" (n.p., 1945), n.p.
42 George G. Blackburn, *The Guns of Victory: A Soldier's Eye View, Belgium, Holland, and Germany, 1944–45* (Toronto: McClelland & Stewart, 1997), 454–55.
43 Stacey, *The Victory Campaign,* 603.
44 "Report No. 32, Part III," paras. 635–37.
45 George E. Broomhall, "Second World War Letter Collection of Captain George E. Broomhall," 20060029-001, Canadian War Museum, May 2, 1945, 1.
46 "Brigadier W.C. Murphy Diary," RG24, vol. 20405, Library and Archives Canada, 41.
47 Jean V. Allard, *The Memoirs of Jean V. Allard* (Vancouver: University of British Columbia Press, 1988), 117–18.
48 "Report No. 32, Part III," para. 652.
49 Blackburn, "History of the 4th Field Regiment," n.p.
50 4th Canadian Infantry Brigade War Diary, May 1945, WO 179/Canadian Forces/4th Infantry Brigade, UK National Archives, 3–4.
51 South Saskatchewan Regiment War Diary, May 1945, Library and Archives Canada, 2–3.
52 4th Canadian Infantry Brigade War Diary, 4–5.

25: BITTEREST BATTLE

1 "Report No. 32 Historical Section (G.S.) Army Headquarters: The Concluding Phase of Operations by the First CDN Army: Part III," Department of National Defence, December 10, 1949, paras. 669–73.
2 Bert M. Hoffmeister, interview by B. Greenhous and W. McAndrew, Directorate of Heritage and History, Department of National Defence, n.d., 120.
3 Bert M. Hoffmeister, letter to Daniel T. Byers, March 1, 1991, appended to "Operation 'Canada,' The Canadian Attack on Delfzijl, April 23–May 2, 1945," Bachelor of Arts thesis, 1991, Wilfrid Laurier University, 41.
4 Hoffmeister interview.
5 Perth Regiment War Diary, April 1945, RG24, Library and Archives Canada, 13–15.
6 Ibid.
7 Irish Regiment of Canada War Diary, April 1945, RG24, Library and Archives Canada, 13.
8 Reginald H. Roy, *Sinews of Steel: The History of the British Columbia Dragoons,* (Toronto: Charters, 1965), 407–08.
9 "II CDN INF BDE: The Battle for Delfzijl, Appendix 6," 11th Canadian Infantry Brigade War Diary, April 1945, RG24, Library and Archives Canada, 1–4.
10 Perth Regiment War Diary, 15.
11 "Report No. 32, Part III," paras. 679–82.
12 J.E. Oldfield, *The Westminster's War Diary: An Unofficial History of the Westminster Regiment (Motor) in World War II* (New Westminster, BC: n.p., 1964), 197.
13 Westminster Regiment (Motor) War Diary, April 1945, RG24, Library and Archives Canada, 27.

14 Oldfield, 197–98.

15 Ibid., 198.

16 Irish Regiment of Canada War Diary, 14.

17 "5th Canadian Armoured Division Intelligence Summary, No. 131, 25 Apr. 45," RG24, vol. 10941, Library and Archives Canada, 1.

18 Perth Regiment War Diary, 16.

19 "The Operations 8th New Brunswick Hussars for Period 25 Apr–5 May, covering the Regiment's activities in the area of Delfzijl," 20020045.1641, Canadian War Museum, 2.

20 Westminster Regiment (Motor) War Diary, 28.

21 Ibid., 28–30.

22 Irish Regiment of Canada War Diary, 15–16.

23 Terry Copp, *Cinderella Army: The Canadians in Northwest Europe, 1944–1945* (Toronto: University of Toronto Press, 2006), 279.

24 Perth Regiment War Diary, 17–18.

25 Stafford Johnston, *The Fighting Perths: The Story of the First Century in the Life of a Canadian County Regiment* (Stratford, ON: Perth Regiment Veterans' Assoc., 1964), 118.

26 Perth Regiment War Diary, 19–20.

27 Cape Breton Highlanders War Diary, April 1945, RG24, Library and Archives Canada, 23–24.

28 "The Operations 8th New Brunswick Hussars," 3.

29 "The Westminster Regiment (Motor) Report on Operations for Period 24 Apr–1 May 1945, Operation Canada," 145.2W1011(D1), Directorate of Heritage and History, Department of National Defence, 5–6.

30 Oldfield, 204–05.

31 Irish Regiment of Canada War Diary, 16.

32 Cape Breton Highlanders War Diary, May 1945, RG24, Library and Archives Canada, 1.

33 Alex Morrison and Ted Slaney, *The Breed of Manly Men: The History of the Cape Breton Highlanders* (Toronto: Canadian Institute of Strategic Studies, 1994), 320–21.

34 Cape Breton Highlanders War Diary, May 1945, 1–3.

35 "Report No. 32, Part III," paras. 713–17.

26: THANK YOU, CANADIANS

1 Princess Patricia's Canadian Light Infantry War Diary, April 1945, RG24, Library and Archives Canada, 23.

2 "Some notes on Negotiations with the German Higher Comd in Holland, 27 Apr to 5 May, 1945 by Hist Offr 1 Cdn Corps (Maj. L.A. Wrinch)," RG24, vol. 10796, Library and Archives Canada, 1.

3 Princess Patricia's Canadian Light Infantry War Diary, 23.

4 "Some notes on Negotiations," 1.

5 "Brief Historical Outline of the Occupation of N.W. Holland by 1 Canadian Corps," RG24, vol. 10796, Library and Archives Canada, 1–2.

6 Lieutenant Colonel F. Carlisle, "Food for the Dutch," RG24, vol. 10540, March 1958, Library and Archives Canada, 2–3.

7 Memo Summarizing Arrangements for Meeting with Representatives of the German Authorities in Holland, 27 April 1945," RG24, vol. 10658, Library and Archives Canada, 1–2.

8 "Negotiations with Germans in W. Holland 16 Apr–7 May 45, memos, notes, etc., compiled by 1st Army," RG24, vol. 10658, Library and Archives Canada, n.p.

9 Henri van der Zee, *The Hunger Winter: Occupied Holland, 1944–45* (London: Jill Norman & Hobhouse, 1982), 259.

10 "Negotiations with Germans in W. Holland," Appendix C, 1.

11 Ibid., 2–5.

12 Carlisle, 1.

13 "Notes on Monograph 'Relief For the Netherlands,' prepared by Hist Sec G-5 Division, SHAEF," RG24, vol. 10249, Library and Archives Canada, 41–42.

14 David Kaufman and Michiel Horn, *A Liberation Album: Canadians in the Netherlands, 1944–45* (Toronto: McGraw-Hill Ryerson, 1980), 104–05.

15 "Notes on Monograph 'Relief For the Netherlands,'" 42.

16 "Canadian Civil Affairs contribution to feeding the Dutch in Western Holland (B2 Area)," RG24, vol. 10662, Library and Archives Canada, 6.

17 "Report No. 172, Canadian Military Headquarters—Canadian Participation in Civil Affairs/Military Government, Part IV: Belgium and the Netherlands, General Historical Survey," Directorate of Heritage and History, Department of National Defence, para. 82.

18 Van der Zee, 262.

19 "Some notes on Negotiations," 2.

20 George Kitching, *Mud and Green Fields: The Memoirs of Major General George Kitching* (Langley, BC: Battleline Books, 1985), 253.

21 "1 Canadian Corps Intelligence Summary," No. 290, May 6, 1945, RG24, vol. 109421, Library and Archives Canada, 2.

22 Kitching, 253.

23 "1 Canadian Corps Intelligence Summary," No. 290, 2–5.

24 Ibid., 4–5.

25 Kitching, 254.

26 Van der Zee, 264–65.

27 "Notes on Monograph 'Relief For the Netherlands,'" 43.

28 "Negotiations with Germans in W. Holland," Appendix C, 2–3.

29 "Some notes on Negotiations," 2.

30 "Negotiations with Germans in W. Holland," 1–2.

31 Ibid., 2.

32 Kitching, 256.

33 "S&T Maintenance 1 Cdn Corps Second Maintenance Plan, Operation 'Faust,'" RG24, vol. 10797, Library and Archives Canada, 1–3.

34 Robert H. Parkinson, interview by Morgan Witzel, January 19, 1984, University of Victoria Special Collections.

35 Charles Foulkes, "The Last Great Battle and the Surrender of the German Army," in Jean E. Portugal, *We Were There: The Navy, the Army and the RCAF—A Record for Canada*, vol. 7 (Shelburne, ON: Battered Silicon Dispatch Box, 1998), 3576–77.

36 C.P. Stacey, *The Victory Campaign: The Operations in North-West Europe, 1944–1945*, vol. 3 (Ottawa: Queen's Printer, 1960), 609–10.

37 Foulkes, 3577.

38 van der Zee, 282.

39 "Report No. 56 Historical Section Army Headquarters: The German Surrender, May 1945," Directorate of Heritage and History, Department of National Defence, para. 73.

40 1 Canadian Corps Intelligence Summary," No. 289, May 5, 1945, RG24, vol. 109421, Library and Archives Canada, 1.

41 Ibid., 2.

42 "Report No. 56," paras. 72–76.

43 "1 Canadian Corps Intelligence Summary," No. 289, 2.

44 "Report No. 56," para. 72.

45 Ibid., paras. 121–26.

46 Jeffrey Williams, *The Long Left Flank: The Hard Won Way to the Reich, 1944–1945* (Toronto: Stoddart Publishing, 1988), 300.

47 "Report No. 32, Part III," para. 793.

48 Stacey, *The Victory Campaign*, 606.

49 Terry Copp, *Cinderella Army: The Canadians in Northwest Europe, 1944–1945* (Toronto: University of Toronto Press, 2006), 261.

50 Charles Goodman, interview by author, Saanichton, BC, January 27, 2009.

51 "Notes on Monograph 'Relief For the Netherlands,'" 46–49.

52 "Report on Ops, 1 Cdn Inf Div for the Week Ending 12 May 45," RG24, vol. 10895, Library and Archives Canada, 1–2.

53 "Notes on Monograph 'Relief For the Netherlands,'" 46–49.

54 van der Zee, 303–10.

55 Stacey, *The Victory Campaign*, 611.

56 Reginald H. Roy, *The Seaforth Highlanders of Canada, 1919–1965* (Vancouver: Evergreen Press, 1969), 439.

INDEX OF FORMATIONS, UNITS, AND CORPS

521

MARK ZUEHLKE'S CANADIAN Battle Series, of which this is the eighth volume, is the most extensive account of the combat experiences of Canada's army in World War II. These best-selling books continue to confirm his reputation as the nation's leading writer of popular military history. In 2006, *Holding Juno: Canada's Heroic Defence of Canada's D-Day Beaches, June 7–12*, won the City of Victoria's Butler Book Prize. In combination with his 2007 *Terrible Victory*, *On To Victory* presents the most comprehensive English-language account of Holland's liberation from German occupation.

Besides this series, Zuehlke has written five other historical works, including *For Honour's Sake: The War of 1812 and the Brokering of an Uneasy Peace*, which won the 2007 Canadian Authors Association Lela Common Award for Canadian History. Also a novelist, he is the author of the popular Elias McCann crime series. The first in the series, *Hands Like Clouds*, won the Crime Writers of Canada Arthur Ellis Award for Best First Novel in 2000, and the later *Sweep Lotus* was a finalist for the 2004 Arthur Ellis Award for Best Novel.

Zuehlke lives in Victoria, British Columbia, and is currently at work on his next Canadian Battle book, which will carry the story of the Canadian involvement in the Normandy campaign forward from where *Juno Beach* and *Holding Juno* left off. He can be found on the web at www.zuehlke.ca.